'Much more than a retelling of the 1857 Uprising, Dalrymple's sumptuously sourced and beautifully composed narrative follows the downfall of the Mughal dynasty, and celebrates the perishable elegance of its culture in early 19th century Delhi' Boyd Tonkin, *Independent*

'What marks out William Dalrymple out among other contemporary historians of India is his relish for the subject. His love of the country permeates every page of this new book . . . His research has been prodigious, his enthusiasm is infectious and he is an incomparable guide. Dalrymple writes with great verve, clarity and style' Sebastian Shakespeare, *Literary Review*

'Brilliant on the repetitive cycles of history, unashamedly drawing parallels with today, combatative on the origins of religious fundamentalism, *The Last Mughal* is a passionate and angry book, fuelled equally strongly by a love of India and a hatred of misrepresentation and repression' Nicola Barr, *Guardian*

'Diligently researched and densely informative . . . Dalrymple's work laments the loss of an elegant tradition, a celebration of what was lost, the tone changing from epic to elegy and back' Aamer Hussein, *Independent*

'A skilfully written, impeccably researched history' *Observer*

'The Indian rebellion of 1857–8 and the deposition of the last Mughal Emperor were events of epochal importance. William Dalrymple tells this dramatic and tragic story with literary elegance, erudition and a wealth of new material' C.A. Bayly, Vere Harmsworth Professor of Imperial and Naval History, University of Cambridge

'William Dalrymple brilliantly evokes the tense equilibrium on the eve of the Indian Mutiny, and with pace and panache, leads us to the explosion . . . Dalrymple's towering achievement in providing almost hourly detail lies in his sources. Drawing widely on Persian and Urdu manuscripts, he narrates the chaos through memoirs, letters, official reports and a sweeping understanding of Indian and Muslim cultures. Dalrymple tells the story of the British retribution with anger and horror' Michael Binyon, *The Times*

'Dalrymple builds an urban narrative as evocative as Richard Cobb's depiction of Revolutionary Paris . . . There is so much to admire in this book – the depth of historical research, the finely evocative writing, the extraordinary rapport with the cultural world of late Mughal India. It is also in many ways a remarkably humane and egalitarian history A splendid work of empathetic scholarship . . . few reinterpretations of 1857 will be as bold, as insightful, or as challenging as this' *Times Literary Supplement*

'No previous book has delved so deeply into the history of Delhi in those days, nor painted such a vivid portrait of the late Mughal court' Mike Dash, *Sunday Telegraph*

'Excellent – Dalrymple's best book. Not only is it a fascinating biography of Zafar, it is a portrait of this crumbling city that Dalrymple clearly knows inside out, and confirms the author's position as the foremost expert on India of his generation' *Geographical*

'Mesmerising gripping and beautifully written' *Good Book Guide*

From the Indian reviews:

'Narrative history at its very best . . . a gripping story seen through the eyes of the Britons and Indians who were caught up in the maelstrom. At the same time the book provides larger insights into the nature of the uprising . . . Dalrymple's account is both evocative and sensitive' Swapan Dasgupta, *The Telegraph*

'Dalrymple is one of the greatest historical writers of our time, and this book will surely go down as his best so far' *Asian Age*

'Extremely well researched and vividly imagined, with a keen sense of drama and a perceptive grip of character. An entire period comes alive – atmospheric and immediate, elegiac, tragic and a thumping good read' *First City*

'Dalrymple narrates the story of Delhi's capture and fall with a rare humanity, a zest that is infectious, and in a prose that is handsome, sure-footed and flowing with breezy purpose' *The Hindu*

'A compelling, vivid account of the 1857 resistance . . . A powerfully vivid and tactile retelling' *Hindustan Times*

'Dalrymple brings out the poignancy and pathology of a Mughal Lear with the ease and élan of a master storyteller . . . In *The Last Mughal*, history is human drama at its elemental best' *India Today*

'Monumental . . . sympathetic and very accomplished. *The Last Mughal* will remain a book with lasting value for three reasons. Firstly, it a vivid portrait of a remarkable man who lived through a fascinating period of history. Secondly, it is the most meticulous work as yet on 1857 in Delhi. And finally it is proof once again of Dalrymple's ability to write history in the most gripping manner' Pavan K Varma, *DNA*

'History at its archival yet lucid best. Dalrymple combines meticulous research with a wonderful writing style. He captures the *zeitgeist* of both pre- and post-1857 brilliantly. More than anything else he has produced a book that is not just about the past, but that has contemporary significance as well. If only other Indian historians – both at home and abroad – emulated him, history would be both educative and evocative, both enlightening and entertaining' *Hindu* Books of the Year

'[*The Last Mughal*] shows the way history should be written: not as a catalogue of dry-as-dust kings, battles and treaties but to bring the past to the present, put life back in characters long dead and gone and make the reader feel he is living among them, sharing their joys, sorrows and apprehensions . . . Dalrymple's book rouses deep emotions. It will bring tears to the eyes of every Dilliwala' Khushwant Singh, *Outlook India*

From the US reviews:

'Deeply researched and beautifully written . . . A riveting and poignant account of the events of 1857 in Delhi' *Nation*

'An original, important contribution to the controversies of 1857' *Booklist*

'Dalrymple excels at bringing grand historical events within contemporary understanding' Tobin Harshaw, *New York Times Book Review*

'William Dalrymple's captivating book is not only great reading, it contributes very substantially to our understanding of the remarkable history of the Mughal empire in its dying days, and also to the history of Delhi, of India, of Hindu-Muslim collaboration, and of Indo-British relations in a critically important phase of imperialism and rebellion. It is rare indeed that a work of such consummate scholarship and insight could also be so accessible and such fun to read' Amartya Sen

From the Australian reviews:

'An extraordinarily detailed and highly readable portrait of the last tragic months [of Mughal Delhi]. It is also a lament for a lost Islamic civilisation at its most tolerant and pluralistic . . . Dalrymple brings the Uprising alive from Indian and British perspectives . . . A monumental work that breaks new ground in the study of one of the most important episodes in Indian history. Its lessons about the dangers of aggressive Western intrusion and interference in the East are as pertinent today as they were 150 years ago' John Zubrzycki, *The Australian*

THE LAST MUGHAL

THE FALL OF DELHI, 1857

WILLIAM DALRYMPLE

BLOOMSBURY
LONDON OXFORD NEW YORK NEW DELHI SYDNEY

To my beloved Ibby

First published in Great Britain 2006
This paperback edition published 2009

Copyright © 2006 by William Dalrymple

Maps and illustrations © Olivia Fraser 2006

The moral right of the author has been asserted

Quotation from *Jesting Pilate* by Aldous Huxley used by permission of Laura A. Huxley

Inside cover printing: The Mughal Emperor Akbar Shah II in procession with his sons
and the British Resident, Delhi, *c*.1811–19; photograph courtesy of Simon Ray, London.

Every reasonable effort has been made to trace copyright holders of material reproduced in this
book, but if any have been inadvertently overlooked the publishers would be glad to hear from
them. For legal purposes the list of illustrations on page xi and the acknowledgements on page
xxvii constitute an extension of the copyright page

Bloomsbury Publishing Plc
50 Bedford Square
London WC1B 3DP

www.bloomsbury.com

Bloomsbury Publishing, London, New Delhi, New York and Sydney

Bloomsbury is a trademark of Bloomsbury Publishing Plc

A CIP catalogue record for this book
is available from the British Library

ISBN 978 1 4088 0092 8

12

Typeset by Hewer Text UK Ltd, Edinburgh
Printed and bound in Great Britain by CPI (UK) Ltd, Croydon CR0 4YY

www.williamdalrymple.uk.com

CONTENTS

List of Illustrations   xi
Maps   xiv
Dramatis Personae   xvii
Acknowledgements   xxvii

Introduction   1
 1 A Chessboard King   27
 2 Believers and Infidels   58
 3 An Uneasy Equilibrium   85
 4 The Near Approach of the Storm   114
 5 The Sword of the Lord of Fury   143
 6 This Day of Ruin and Riot   193
 7 A Precarious Position   230
 8 Blood for Blood   257
 9 The Turn of the Tide   305
10 To Shoot Every Soul   346
11 The City of the Dead   393
12 The Last of the Great Mughals   446

Glossary   487
Notes   497
Bibliography   549
Index   561

BY THE SAME AUTHOR

Koh-i-Noor
Return of a King
Nine Lives
White Mughals
The Age of Kali
From the Holy Mountain
City of Djinns
In Xanadu

A NOTE ON THE AUTHOR

WILLIAM DALRYMPLE was born in Scotland and brought up on the shores of the Firth of Forth. He is the author of six books of history and travel, including the highly acclaimed bestseller *City of Djinns*, which won the 1994 Thomas Cook Travel Book Award and the *Sunday Times* Young British Writer of the Year Award. His previous book, *White Mughals*, garnered a range of prizes, including the prestigious Wolfson Prize for History 2003 and the Scottish Book of the Year Prize. It was also shortlisted for the PEN History Award, the Kiriyama Prize and the James Tait Black Memorial Prize. A stage version by Christopher Hampton has been co-commissioned by the National Theatre and the Tamasha Theatre Company.

A Fellow of the Royal Society of Literature of the Royal Asiatic Society, Dalrymple was awarded the 2002 Mungo Park Medal by the Royal Scottish Geographical Society for his 'outstanding contribution to travel literature' and the Sykes Medal of the Royal Society of Asian Affairs in 2005 for his contribution to the understanding of contemporary Islam. He wrote and presented three television series, *Stones of the Raj, Sufi Soul* and *Indian Journeys*, the last of which won the Grierson Award for Best Documentary Series at BAFTA in 2002. In December 2005 his article on the madrasas of Pakistan was awarded the prize for Print Article of the Year at the 2005 FPA Media Awards. In 2015, he was awarded the 2015 Ryszard Kapuscinski Award for Literary Reportage.

He is married to the artist Olivia Fraser, and they have three children. They divide their time between London, Scotland and Delhi.

LIST OF ILLUSTRATIONS

The Coronation Portrait of Bahadur Shah Zafar II, by Ghulam Ali Khan, *c.*1837. Collection of Stuart Cary Welch.

The Mughal Emperor Akbar Shah II in procession with his sons and the British Resident, Delhi, *c.*1811–19. Photograph courtesy of Simon Ray, London.

The great Friday mosque of Shahjahanabad, Jama Masjid, *c.*1840. Collection of William Dalrymple.

The Red Fort, *c.*1770. Add.Or.948, © British Library Board.

The 'Kootub House', from Sir Thomas Metcalfe's 'Dehlie Book', Add.Or.5475 82, © British Library Board.

Metcalfe House, from Sir Thomas Metcalfe's 'Dehlie Book'. Add.Or.5475 84v–85v, © British Library Board.

Bahadur Shah Zafar II as a young man, *c.*1790. Add.Or.343, © British Library Board.

The celebrated blind sitar player, Ustad Himmat Khan, from James Skinner's *Tazkirat al-umara*. Add 27255 134v, © British Library Board.

View from the Lahore Gate, from Mazhar Ali Khan's great Delhi Panorama. Add.Or.4126 3, © British Library Board.

A painter with his brushes and materials, from James Skinner's *Tazkirat al-umara*, *c.*1830. Add 27255 258v, © British Library Board.

Mirza Mughal, by August Schoefft, *c.*1850. Courtesy of the Lahore Fort.

View over the Jama Masjid, from Mazhar Ali Khan's great Delhi Panorama. Add.Or.4126 4, © British Library Board.

The Rao of Kotah's visit to Delhi, *c.*1840. Collection of Stuart Cary Welch.

Portrait of Zafar, from Sir Thomas Metcalfe's 'Dehlie Book', *c*.1845. Add.Or.5475 17, © British Library Board.

Zafar presides over his durbar, *c*.1840. © The Trustees of the Chester Beatty Library, Dublin.

Two elephants of state. V&A Images, Victoria and Albert Museum, London.

The durbar of the Nawab of Jhajjar in summer dress. Add.Or.4680, © British Library Board.

The Nawab of Jhajjar rides around his country garden on his pet tiger. Courtesy of the Cynthia Hazen Polsky Collection.

Detail of a Fraser Album page depicting Nine Horse Merchants, Delhi, *c*.1816–20. Photograph courtesy of Simon Ray, London.

A group of four soldiers, from the Fraser Album, attributed to Ghulam Ali Khan, *c*.1816–20. From the collection of Prince and Princess Sadruddin Aga Khan.

Mr Flowery Man, a celebrated Delhi ascetic, and his followers. V&A Images, Victoria and Albert Museum, London.

A group of Delhi Sufis and sadhus, yogins and ascetics gather around a fire. Courtesy of Joachim K. Bautze.

A dancing girl called Piari Jan, from the Fraser Album, by Lallji or Hulas Lal, 1815. From the collection of Prince and Princess Sadruddin Aga Khan.

An accountant working on his registers, from James Skinner's *Tazkirat al-umara*. Add 27255 96v, © British Library Board.

A troupe of dancing girls and musicians. V&A Images, Victoria and Albert Museum, London.

A Delhi opium den with recumbent addicts, from James Skinner's *Tazkirat al-umara*. Add 27255 337, © British Library Board.

Portrait of Malageer, a nautch girl, from the Fraser Album, by Lallji or Hulas Lal, 1815. From the collection of Prince and Princess Sadruddin Aga Khan.

A group of Delhi storytellers and comedians, from the Fraser Album, *c*.1820. From the collection of Prince and Princess Sadruddin Aga Khan.

Portrait of Zafar, by August Schoefft, *c*.1854. Courtesy of the Lahore Fort.

Hakim Momin Khan, Portrait of the Poet, attributed to Jivan Ram, India, c.1835. © President and Fellows of Harvard College, Harvard University Art Museums.

Zinat Mahal, as imagined by the *Illustrated London News*. P2380, © British Library Board.

The *Illustrated London News* image of Zafar. P1519, © British Library Board.

Zinat Mahal, taken by General McMohan, 1872. Add.Or.5475 17v, © British Library Board.

Mirza Ahsanullah Khan, the poet Ghalib. P1007/16, © British Library Board.

General Archdale Wilson, by John Jabez Edwin Mayall. National Portrait Gallery, London.

Brigadier General John Nicholson, by William Carpenter. National Portrait Gallery, London.

Harriet and Robert Tytler.

William Hodson of Hodson's Horse. P79(2), © British Library Board.

The Delhi Field Force advances on the Mughal capital. X271 3, © British Library Board.

Hodson's Horse, by Felice Beato. Wilson Centre for Photography.

The British attack Kashmiri Gate on 14 September. X271 16, © British Library Board.

'Easy Days': Zafar's Hall of Private Audience, the Diwan-i Khas, 1857. 1261.e.31, © British Library Board.

The Bridge of Boats, by Felice Beato, 1858. P193 1, © British Library Board.

The Kashmiri Gate, by Felice Beato, 1858. P25 14, © British Library Board.

The Flagstaff Tower, by Felice Beato, 1858. Wilson Centre for Photography.

Humayun's Tomb, by Felice Beato, 1858. P52 18, © British Library Board.

The deposed and broken Emperor, by 'Mr Shepherd the Photographer'. P797 37, © British Library Board.

Two princes: Mirza Jawan Bakht and Mirza Shah Abbas, by Felice Beato. Courtesy of Jane and Howard Ricketts Collection, London.

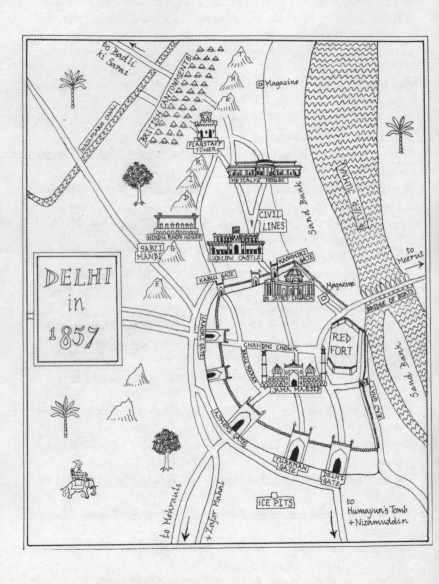

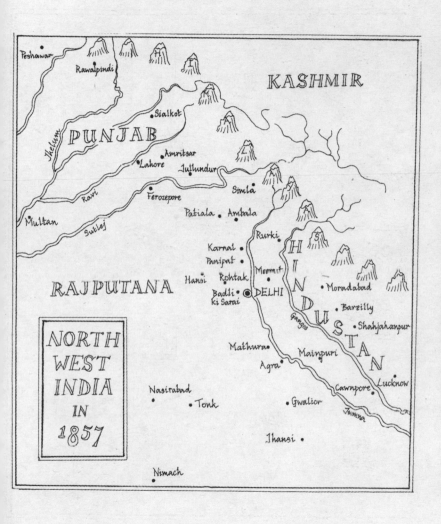

DRAMATIS PERSONAE

1. THE MUGHALS

THE MUGHAL IMPERIAL FAMILY

The Emperor Bahadur Shah Zafar II (1775–1862)

The elderly Mughal Emperor – eldest but not favourite son of the Emperor Akbar Shah II – was a calligrapher, Sufi, theologian, patron of painters of miniatures, creator of gardens and a very serious mystical poet, but by the 1850s he held little real day-to-day power beyond the still potent mystique attached to the Mughal dynasty and was in many ways 'a chessboard king'. Though he was initially horrified by the rough and desperate sepoys who barged into his palace on 11 May 1857, Zafar ultimately agreed to give his blessing to the Uprising, seeing it as the only way to save his great dynasty from extinction. It was a decision he later came to regret bitterly.

The Nawab Zinat Mahal Begum (1821–82)

Zafar's senior wife, and his only consort to come from an aristocratic background: when they married in 1840 she was nineteen while he was sixty-four. Having toppled her rival Taj Mahal Begum from the position of favourite wife and provided a son in the shape of Mirza Jawan Bakht, she worked single-mindedly to have her son – the fifteenth of Zafar's sixteen boys – declared heir apparent. Zafar was widely regarded to be completely under her influence, but during 1857 the limits of her power over him became quickly apparent.

Taj Mahal Begum

The beautiful daughter of a humble court musician, Taj presided over the celebrations that accompanied Zafar's accession to the throne in 1837 as his favourite wife and the head of his harem. Taj's fall began when Zafar married the nineteen-year-old Zinat Mahal in 1840. By 1857 she had been imprisoned for a suspected affair with Zafar's nephew, Mirza Kamran, and remained bitterly alienated from both Zafar and Zinat Mahal.

Mirza Fakhru – aka Mirza Ghulam Fakhruddin (1818–56)

When Zafar's eldest son, Mirza Dara Bakht, died from a fever in 1849, the British assumed that Zafar's next son, Mirza Fakhru, would succeed him as heir apparent. Mirza Fakhru was a talented and popular poet and historian, but under the influence of Zinat Mahal Zafar tried unsuccessfully to block his appointment as heir apparent in favour of Zinat's fifteen-year-old son, Mirza Jawan Bakht. Mirza Fakhru died in 1856, probably from cholera, but Palace gossip attributed the death to poisoning.

Mirza Mughal (1828–57)

Zafar's fifth son, by a sayyida *[descendant of the Prophet] of aristocratic birth named Sharaf ul-Mahal Sayyidani who was a senior figure in Zafar's harem. Mirza Mughal rose to prominence at court as a protégé of Zinat Mahal after the disgrace of Mirza Fakhru in 1852 and was appointed* qiladar *(fort keeper). After the death of Mirza Fakhru in 1856 he was the oldest of Zafar's surviving legitimate sons, and may at this point have made contact with the discontented sepoys in the Company's army. Certainly from 12 May onwards he became the principal rebel leader in the royal family, and worked with great industry to keep the Delhi administration running amid the chaos of the Uprising and siege.*

Mirza Khizr Sultan (1834–57)

Zafar's ninth son, the illegitimate child of a Palace concubine. Aged twenty-three in 1857, he was renowned for his physical beauty and had some capacity as a poet and marksman, but after throwing in his lot with the rebels in 1857 he did little to distinguish himself and ran away in fear from the battle of Badli Ki Serai, so causing a panic among the rebel troops. During the siege he earned himself a reputation for corruption, and is frequently criticised in the sources for making arrests and collecting taxes from the town's bankers without authority to do so.

Mirza Abu Bakr (d.1857)

Mirza Abu Bakr was the eldest son of Mirza Fakru and Zafar's oldest surviving legitimate grandson; he was also the principal badmash or ruffian in the imperial family. Within a few days of the outbreak Mirza Abu Bakr began appearing in petitions and complaints to the Emperor, accused of whoring and drunkenness, whipping his servants, beating up watchmen and casually attacking any policeman who tried to rein him in. He took nominal charge of the rebel cavalry, looting Gurgaon and various suburbs of Delhi before leading the disastrous expedition to Meerut which ended in the rebel defeat at the Hindan Bridge on 30 and 31 May.

Mirza Jawan Bakht (1841–84)
Zafar's favourite son, and the only child he had by Zinat Mahal. Though he was the fifteenth of his sixteen male offspring Zafar was determined to try to make him heir apparent. Spoilt and selfish, Mirza Jawan Bakht had few supporters other than his parents and took little interest in his studies. During the Uprising he was kept away from the rebels by his mother, who hoped that after the sepoys' defeat her son's succession would be assured.

Mirza Ilahe Bakhsh
Father-in-law of Mirza Fakhru, grandfather of Mirza Abu Bakr, and one of the leaders of the pro-British faction in the Palace, both before and after 1857. He was in close contact with William Hodson throughout the siege, and was instrumental in persuading Zafar to surrender after the fall of the city. In the weeks that followed he was responsible for identifying which of his relatives had sympathised with the rebels and, having guaranteed his own life at the cost of that of most of his family, including his own grandson, he became known as the 'Traitor of Delhi'.

THE EMPEROR'S HOUSEHOLD

Hakim Ahsanullah Khan
A highly intelligent, wily and cultured man, the Hakim was Zafar's most trusted confidant and was appointed to be both his Prime Minister and personal physician. Before 1857 the Hakim had an uneasy relationship with Zinat Mahal, but they made common cause during 1857, uniting against the rebel army and opening communication with the British. When his letters were discovered by the rebel sepoys they tried to kill him, but he was protected by Zafar. The Hakim continued to press Zafar not to commit himself to the rebel cause, and to surrender himself to the British, but when he ultimately did so the Hakim betrayed him, providing evidence against his master at his trial in return for his own pardon.

Mahbub Ali Khan (d.1857)
The Chief Eunuch of the Palace and Zinat Mahal's notoriously ruthless 'enforcer' beyond the walls of the zenana. Like his mistress he was deeply suspicious of the Uprising, and he was a leading member of the pro-British faction in the Palace after the outbreak. His death on 14 June 1857 followed a prolonged illness, but was widely rumoured to be the result of poisoning.

Mirza Asadullah Khan – 'Ghalib' (1797–1869)

The greatest lyric poet in Urdu, and from 1854 – following the death of his great rival Zauq – the Poet Laureate of Mughal Delhi. A mystical Sufi by inclination, self-consciously rakish and aristocratic by temperament, Ghalib in his writings provides some of the most sophisticated and melancholy records of the destruction of Mughal Delhi in the siege and fall of the city in 1857.

Zahir Dehlavi (1835–1911)

An attendant to Zafar at the Mughal court who had been working in the Fort since his thirteenth birthday. By 1857 he was twenty-two and had risen to the post of Darogah of the Mahi Maraatib, or Keeper of the Dynastic Fish Standard of the Mughals. A pupil of Zauq, he was a highly polished and cultured courtier and poet. His Dastan i-Ghadr, which has never been previously translated or used in any English language account of the Uprising, gives the fullest and most richly detailed surviving account of the course of the siege and Uprising from the point of view of the Palace.

THE REBEL ARMY

General Bakht Khan

A subahdar of artillery prior to 1857, Bakht Khan was a much-garlanded and battle-hardened veteran of the Afghan wars. A tall, portly and heavily built man, with huge handlebar moustache and sprouting side-burns, Bakht Khan had been elected General by the Bareilly troops and arrived in Delhi with a reputation as both an administrator and an effective military leader. When he arrived in Delhi halfway through the siege, on 2 July 1857, it initially looked as if Bakht Khan and his 3,000 men would bring a swift victory to the rebels, but the General's tactless treatment of other rebel leaders – and particularly of Mirza Mughal – quickly made him enemies, as did his 'Wahhabi' religious views. By the middle of August his failure to dent the British defences led to his demotion from rebel Commander in Chief.

General Sudhari Singh and Brigade Major Hira Singh

The leaders of the Nimach Brigade and the principal rivals of Bakht Khan. They refused to accept the latter's authority and worked to undermine his position, especially after he left their troops to their fate when ambushed by Nicholson's column at Najafgarh on 25 August.

Brigade Major Gauri Shankar Sukul

Leader of the Haryana Regiment who became the most important British mole and agent provocateur within the rebel ranks.

Maulvi Sarfaraz Ali

Bakht Khan's spiritual mentor, the 'Wahhabi' preacher Maulvi was soon known as 'the imam of the Mujahedin'. Prior to the Uprising, he had spent many years in Delhi and was well-connected to both the court and the city. He had been one of the first clerics to preach jihad against the British in the days leading up to the outbreak, and as the siege progressed and the number of jihadis increased, his influence as a rebel leader grew.

OTHER DELHIWALLAHS

Munshi Jiwan Lal

Prior to the outbreak of the Uprising, Jiwan Lal had for long been the hugely fat Mir Munshi (Chief Assistant) of Sir Thomas Metcalfe at the British Residency. Although restricted to the cellar of his house during much of the course of the siege, Jiwan Lal ran a highly effective intelligence operation from his hideaway, every day sending out 'two Brahmins and two Jats for the purpose of obtaining news of the doings of the rebels from every quarter', which he in due course passed on to William Hodson, the British chief of intelligence on the Ridge.

Mufti Sadruddin Khan – 'Azurda' (d.1868)

Mufti Sadruddin Azurda was a close friend of both Zafar and Ghalib, and played an important role as bridge between the British and Mughal elites in the early days of the British ascendancy in Delhi. For thirty years Azurda balanced his roles as chief Muslim judge (Sadr Amin) in Delhi, leading literary figure at court and prominent madrasa *teacher with a mild Anglophilia, but in 1857, alienated by the Company's encouragement of missionaries, he threw in his lot with the rebels. A natural mediator, he was responsible for reconciling the jihadis, the court and the sepoys during the crisis over cow killing which took place during the 'Id of 1 August 1857, so avoiding a potential civil war within rebel ranks.*

Muin ud-Din Husain Khan

At the outbreak of the Uprising, Muin ud-Din Husain Khan was the Thanadar, *or Head Police Officer, at Paharganj police station, a little to the south west of the walled city. Muin ud-Din was from a minor branch of the noble Loharu family; his cousins included both Ghalib and Nawab Zia ud-Din Khan. Having helped to save Theo Metcalfe's life, he joined the rebels and was elevated to the position of* Kotwal *for most of the Uprising, before being replaced by Sa'id Mubarak Shah. After the suppression of the Uprising, both former* Kotwals *survived to write excellent Urdu accounts of life in the city during the months of the siege.*

Sarvar ul-Mulk
A young Mughal nobleman, probably aged around twelve at the time of the outbreak. During the conflict, his Afghan tutor became a jihadi and his father had to defend the family house against the assaults of plundering sepoys. The family escaped from the city just after 14 September and made it safely to Hyderabad, where Sarvar ul-Mulk eventually wrote a fine description of the siege in his autobiography, My Life.

2. THE BRITISH

THE METCALFES

Sir Charles Metcalfe (1785–1846)
The first of the Metcalfes to come to Delhi, in his first spell – initially as assistant to Sir David Ochterlony from 1806 and as Resident from 1811 – Charles Metcalfe had fitted in with the tone set by his principal, building himself a house in the Mughal Shalimar Gardens and fathering three sons by a Sikh bibi *who (according to family tradition) he married 'by Indian rites'. By the time of his return to Delhi as Resident in 1826, Metcalfe had however jettisoned his* bibi *and begun to take a very different attitude to India and its Mughal rulers. 'I have renounced my former allegiance to the house of Timur,' he announced to Lord Bentinck in a letter of 1832, shortly after he had left Delhi to take up a position as Member of the Council in Calcutta.*

Sir Thomas Metcalfe (1795–1853)
Sir Thomas arrived in Delhi in 1813 as assistant to his elder brother Sir Charles Metcalfe and stayed there for his entire career, rising to become Resident in 1835. A very particular and fastidious man, much of Metcalfe's professional life was dedicated to negotiating a succession settlement that would allow the Company to expel the royal family from the Red Fort on the death of Zafar. He had some affection, but little real respect, for the man he was determined should be the last of the Timurid line. Although to Zafar's face he was always polite, in private he was less generous. '[Zafar] is mild and talented,' he wrote, 'but lamentably weak and vacillating and impressed with a very erroneous notion of his own importance.' Having negotiated a succession agreement with Mirza Fakhru that entailed the Mughals leaving the Red Fort, Metcalfe died in 1853 from a digestive disorder that his doctors believed was caused by poison, which his family believed was administered on the orders of Zinat Mahal.

Sir Theophilus Metcalfe – 'Theo' (1828–83)

In 1857 Theo Metcalfe was a junior magistrate in the Company's service, and a very different figure from his father. Where Sir Thomas was reserved and particular, Theo was sociable and expansive and also, when he wished to be, extremely charming. If the father liked solitude and disliked the business of entertaining, Theo was noisy and convivial, and enjoyed parties, riding, horses and dogs. If his father was resolutely self-disciplined and law-abiding, Theo had a tendency to cut corners and get into what his father described as 'scrapes'. At the outbreak of the Uprising on 11 May 1857, Theo was one of the only British officials within the walls successfully to make his escape, and after joining the Delhi Field Force he took the lead in the bloodthirsty work of revenge.

Sir Edward Campbell (1822–82)

Son-in-law of Sir Thomas Metcalfe and Prize Agent during the siege of Delhi. Campbell had been a protégé of Sir Charles Napier, the former Commander in Chief of the British Army in India, with whom Sir Thomas Metcalfe had had a serious disagreement. Moreover, despite his title, Campbell was more or less penniless, all of which led Sir Thomas initially to try and block Campbell's engagement to his daughter Georgina (known in the family as 'GG'). Campbell's regiment, the 60th Rifles, was one of the first to try out the new Enfield rifles; after his regiment mutinied, Campbell joined the Delhi Field Force on the Ridge and at the end of the siege was voted Prize Agent, responsible for administering the legalised looting of the captured city, a job for which his gentle and religious temperament was quite unsuited.

THE BRITISH IN DELHI

Reverend Midgeley John Jennings (d.1857)

Padre Jennings had come out to India in 1832 and, though initially posted to various quiet hill stations, had long dreamt of opening a mission in Delhi and getting stuck into some serious work as 'Missionary to the Heathen'. He finally got the job of chaplain in the Mughal capital in 1852 and moved straight into the front line, the Red Fort itself, having been invited to share the Lahore Gate lodgings of Captain Douglas, Commander of the Palace Guard. His unctuous yet tactless manner won him few friends, and he was regarded as a 'bigot' by much of the British community in Delhi. The people of Delhi disliked him even more, especially after he succeeded in converting two prominent Delhi Hindus – Master Ramchandra and Chiman Lal – in 1852. Jennings was personally responsible for convincing many of the people of Delhi that the Company intended to convert them, by force if necessary.

Robert and Harriet Tytler (Robert d.1872, Harriet d.1907)
Tytler was a veteran of the 38th Native Infantry and an officer of the old school who was close to his sepoys, concerned for their well-being and completely fluent in Hindustani. Tytler appears to have been a kind and sensitive man, a widower with two little children who had recently remarried, this time to the brisk and resilient Harriet. Harriet was half his age, and as fluent in Hindustani as her husband. Together the two Tytlers pursued their amateur artistic enthusiasms and – unexpectedly for an army couple – became pioneering photographers. At the outbreak, the couple escaped from Delhi to Amballa, where they eventually joined the Delhi Field Force. Harriet's memoirs are among the best sources on life on the Ridge during the siege of Delhi, and on the fate of the city after the fall.

Edward Vibart
In 1857 Edward Vibart of the 54th Bengal Native Infantry was a nineteen-year-old company commander in Delhi, from an Indian army family: his father was a cavalry officer in Kanpur. During the Uprising, Vibart's father was killed at the Kanpur massacre, while the son narrowly escaped from the city at the outbreak and survived to take part in the siege and recapture. His memoirs, and particularly his letters, are one of the best sources for the atrocities commited by the British during the taking of the city and during the extended reprisals that followed.

THE DELHI FIELD FORCE

General Sir Archdale Wilson (1803–74)
A small, neat, cautious gentleman of fifty-four, Archdale Wilson was one of the station commanders of Meerut at the outbreak of the Mutiny, and later led a column from the garrison which defeated Mirza Abu Bakr at the Hindan Bridge on 30 and 31 May. He rendezvoused with the Delhi Field Force at Alipore shortly before fighting the battle of Badli ki Serai on 8 June. Following the death of General Barnard and the resignation of General Reed, he took over command of British forces at the siege of Delhi from 17 July. He quickly put in place a defensive strategy, much criticised at the time but which successfully preserved British strength until reinforcements arrived shortly before the assault on 14 September. During the taking of the city Wilson's nerve finally failed him, and at one point John Nicholson threatened to shoot him if he should order a retreat.

Brigadier General John Nicholson (1821–57)

A taciturn Ulster Protestant, Nicholson was said to have personally decapitated a local robber chieftain, then kept the man's head on his desk. He had 'a commanding presence, some six feet, two inches in height, with a long black beard, dark grey eyes with black pupils which under excitement would dilate like a tiger's'. For reasons that remain unclear Nicholson inspired a religious sect, the 'Nikal Seyn', who apparently regarded him as an incarnation of Vishnu. During the Uprising Nicholson became a legend among the British in India. His mixture of piety, gravity and courage, combined with his merciless capacity for extreme brutality, were exactly the qualities needed to put heart into the British troops on the Ridge, and there were few who remained immune to the hero-worship of this great imperial psychopath. Shortly after his arrival at the siege, Nicholson led a forced march to ambush a column of sepoys at Najafgarh on 25 August. On 14 September he personally led the assault on the city, and was mortally wounded the same day.

William Hodson (1821–58)

Prior to 1857 William Hodson had been regarded by most of his colleagues as a black sheep. Hodson was the bright, university-educated son of a clergyman, and had risen rapidly to be Adjutant of the new Corps of Guides. His fall from grace was equally sudden. In 1854 Hodson was relieved of his command after an investigation declared that he had embezzled regimental funds. During the Uprising he founded an irregular cavalry regiment known as Hodson's Horse, and ran the remarkably efficient British intelligence service on the Delhi Ridge. On his own authority he negotiated the surrender of Zafar and Zinat Mahal, and on 21 September he brought them captive into Delhi. The following day he went back to bring in princes Mirza Mughal, Khizr Sultan and Abu Bakr; then, having separated them from their followers and disarmed them, he told them to strip naked and shot all three dead at point blank range. He was killed a few months later, in March 1858, at the siege of Lucknow.

OTHER BRITISH OFFICIALS

Lord Canning (1812–62)

Canning was a handsome and industrious – if somewhat reserved – Tory politician in his early forties, who had accepted the appointment of Governor General of India only because of his frustration at his consistent failure to gain a senior Cabinet berth in London. Before his departure he had had no previous interest in India, and having only arrived in there in February 1856, had yet to leave the heat and damp of

Calcutta by the time of the outbreak. However, none of this prevented him from taking a confidently dismissive attitude towards 'the farce of Mughal pretensions' and putting in place plans to depose the Mughals within a few weeks of his arrival. After the suppression of the Uprising he attempted to limit the vindictiveness of the bloody British retribution, with mixed results.

Sir John Lawrence (1811–79)

Younger brother of Sir Henry Lawrence, who in 1857 was Chief Commissioner in Avadh, Sir John was a former deputy of Sir Thomas Metcalfe in Delhi. John Lawrence had risen rapidly through the ranks of the Company's civil service thanks to his reputation for hard work and efficiency, and in 1853 he was made Chief Commissioner of the newly conquered Punjab. He forbade his officers from going up to the hills for the hot weather, and made known his disapproval of '"a cakey man", by which he meant someone who, besides presumably liking cakes, "pretended to much elegance and refinement"'. In 1857 he proved to be arguably the most capable of all the British officials in North India, disarming mutinous sepoys, raising new irregular regiments and quickly pacifying the Punjab so that the maximum number of troops could be sent to the Delhi Ridge. After the fall of the city he worked hard to minimise the scale of the retribution, and personally saved Mughal Delhi from a plan to level the entire metropolis.

ACKNOWLEDGEMENTS

This book would have been quite impossible without the scholarship and industry of my colleague Mahmood Farooqui. For four years now we have been working together on this project, and much that is most interesting within it – notably the remarkable translations from the sometimes almost indecipherable *shikastah* of the Urdu files in the Mutiny Papers – is the product of his dedication, persistence and skill. I wish him the best of luck with his next project: to publish the first scholarly edition of this extraordinarily rich and almost unused archive. Mahmood also provided at all times a wonderfully intelligent and imaginative sounding-board: one of the most enjoyable aspects of working with him on Bahadur Shah Zafar has been gradually piecing together the events and shape of this book over a Karim's kebab, a Kapashera biryani or, more usually, a simple glass of hot sweet National Archives chai.

For invaluable help with other Persian and Urdu primary sources I would like to thank Bruce Wannell, Yunus Jaffery, Azra Kidwai and Arjumand Ara; and for assistance in a million other ways, the incomparably resourceful Subramaniam Gautam. Margrit Pernau, Rudrangshu Mukherjee and Saul David were at all times sources of generous advice and encouragement as panic gradually set in over the scale of the material that I had taken on.

At the end, Professor Fran Pritchett at Columbia volunteered to give the book the most thorough edit that I think any manuscript of mine has ever received. It took me nearly two weeks to go through all her notes, improved transliterations and suggestions, so I can only imagine how much of her valuable time she gave up to produce them in the first place. Harbans Mukhia, Michael Fisher, C. M. Naim, Maya Jasanoff, Sam Miller, Sachin Mulji and my lovely parents-in-law, Simon and Jenny Fraser, were also extremely generous in carefully going through the manuscript, providing comments and pointing out errors of fact or grammar.

Vicky Bowman moved heaven and earth to get me into the Rangoon Archives, while F. S. Aijazuddin performed a similar service in Lahore. Aijaz also told me about the magnificent and previously unpublished oil painting of Zafar in the Lahore Fort, and not once but three times got it down to have it photographed for the cover of this book.

Many others have helped with advice, scholarship or friendship and I would also like to thank the following by name:

In the UK: Charles Allen, Chris Bayly, Jonathan Bond, John Falconer, Emma Flatt, Christopher Hampton, Christopher Hibbert, Amin Jaffer, Eleanor O'Keefe, Rosie Llewellyn Jones, Jerry Losty, Avril Powell, Ralph Russell, Susan Stronge, Veronica Telfer, Philippa Vaughan and Brigid Waddams. Particular thanks are due to Mehra Dalton of the wonderful Greaves Travel, who flew me back and forth from London to Delhi; and to my brothers and parents in Scotland.

In the US: Indrani Chatterjee, Niall Ferguson, Glenn Horovitz, Navina Haidar, Ruby Lal, Barbara Metcalf, Elbrun Kimmelman, Tracey Jackson, Salman Rushdie, Sylvia Shorto and Stuart Cary Welch.

In India: Seema Alavi, Pablo Bartholemew, the late Mirza Farid Beg, Rana Behal, Gurcharan Das, Sundeep Dougal, John Fritz, Narayani Gupta, Ed Luce, the late Veena Kapoor, A. R. Khaleel, Jean-Marie Lafont, Swapna Liddle, Shireen Miller, Gail Minault, Samina Mishra, Harbans Mukhia, Veena Oldenberg, Pradip Krishen, George Michell, Aslam Parvez, Arundhati Roy, Kaushik Roy, Aradhana Seth, Faith Singh, Mala Singh, Manvender Singh and Pavan Varma. Stanley, Stella and Dougal did a wonderful job keeping us all in one piece at Dr Chopra's Farm.

David Godwin fought incredibly hard (and ingeniously) to effect my move to Bloomsbury, and has been a wonderfully loyal and wise friend throughout. My different publishers have all been full of good advice – Alexandra Pringle, Nigel Newton and Trâm-Anh Doan at Bloomsbury; Sonny Mehta and Diana Tejerina at Knopf;

Thomas Abraham, Ravi Singh, David Davidar and Hemali Sodhi at Penguin India; Paolo Zaninoni at Rizzoli; and Marc Parent at Buchet Chastel. Most of all I would like to thank Michael Fishwick, who has been my wise editor and generous friend for twenty years, first at HarperCollins and now, exactly two decades on from signing me up for *In Xanadu*, at Bloomsbury.

Writing a book puts pressure on the most patient of families, and I have been especially lucky with mine: not only did they all uproot themselves from homes and schools in London and move to Delhi while I researched this book, Sam and Adam also put up with the loss of bedtime stories while I was writing; and my gentle, beautiful and sweet-natured Olivia has been almost superhumanly sensitive and forbearing with her husband as he locked himself away from family life for six months and immersed himself instead in the inner courtyards of the Mughal court.

Particularly touching has been the interest taken in the whole project by my eleven-year-old daughter, Ibby. Having appointed herself editor-in-chief, she proved a surprisingly tough critic of her father's tendency to use, as she puts it, 'too many words'. This book – somewhat shorter than it would otherwise have been – is dedicated to her, with all my love.

INTRODUCTION

At 4 p.m. on a hazy, humid winter's afternoon in Rangoon in November 1862, soon after the end of the monsoon, a shrouded corpse was escorted by a small group of British soldiers to an anonymous grave at the back of a walled prison enclosure.

This enclosure lay overlooking the muddy brown waters of the Rangoon river, a little downhill from the great gilt spire of the Shwe Dagon pagoda. Around the enclosure lay the newly constructed cantonment area of the port – an anchorage and pilgrimage town that had been seized, burned and occupied by the British only ten years earlier. The bier of the State Prisoner – as the deceased was referred to – was accompanied by two of his sons and an elderly, bearded mullah. No women were allowed to attend, and a small crowd from the bazaar who had somehow heard about the prisoner's death were kept away by armed guards. Nevertheless, one or two managed to break through the cordon to touch the shroud before it was lowered into the grave.

The ceremony was brief. The British authorities had made sure not only that the grave was already dug, but that quantities of lime were on hand to guarantee the rapid decay of both bier and body. When the shortened funeral prayers had been recited – no lamentations or panegyrics were allowed – the earth was thrown in over the lime, and the turf carefully replaced so that within a month or so no mark would remain to indicate the place of burial. A week later the British Commissioner, Captain H. N. Davies, wrote to London to report what had passed, adding:

> Have since visited the remaining State Prisoners – the very scum of the reduced Asiatic harem; found all correct. None of the family appear much affected by the death of the bed-ridden old man. His death was evidently due to pure decrepitude and paralysis in the

region of the throat. He expired at 5 o'clock on the morning of the
funeral. The death of the ex-King may be said to have had no effect
on the Mahomedan part of the populace of Rangoon, except perhaps
for a few fanatics who watch and pray for the final triumph of Islam.
A bamboo fence surrounds the grave for some considerable distance,
and by the time the fence is worn out, the grass will again have
properly covered the spot, and no vestige will remain to distinguish
where the last of the Great Moghuls rests.[1]

The State Prisoner Davies referred to was more properly known as
Bahadur Shah II, known from his pen-name as Zafar, meaning
'Victory'. Zafar was the last Mughal Emperor, and the direct
descendant of Genghis Khan and Timur, of Akbar, Jahangir and
Shah Jahan. He was born in 1775, when the British were still a
relatively modest and mainly coastal power in India, looking
inwards from three enclaves on the Indian shore. In his lifetime
he had seen his own dynasty reduced to humiliating insignificance,
while the British transformed themselves from vulnerable traders
into an aggressively expansionist military force.

Zafar came late to the throne, succeeding his father only in his
mid-sixties, when it was already impossible to reverse the political
decline of the Mughals. But despite this he succeeded in creating
around him in Delhi a court of great brilliance. Personally, he was
one of the most talented, tolerant and likeable of his dynasty: a
skilled calligrapher, a profound writer on Sufism, a discriminating
patron of painters of miniatures, an inspired creator of gardens and
an amateur architect. Most importantly he was a very serious
mystical poet, who wrote not only in Urdu and Persian but Braj
Bhasha and Punjabi, and partly through his patronage there took
place arguably the greatest literary renaissance in modern Indian
history. Himself a ghazal writer of great charm and accomplish-
ment, Zafar's provided a showcase for the talents of India's greatest
lyric poet, Ghalib, and his rival Zauq – the Mughal Poet Laureate,
and the Salieri to Ghalib's Mozart.

While the British progressively took over more and more of the
Mughal Emperor's power, removing his name from the coins, seizing
complete control even of the city of Delhi itself, and finally laying

plans to remove the Mughals altogether from the Red Fort, the court busied itself in the obsessive pursuit of the most cleverly turned ghazal, the most perfect Urdu couplet. As the political sky darkened, the court was lost in a last idyll of pleasure gardens, courtesans and *mushairas*, or poetic symposia, Sufi devotions and visits to pirs, as literary and religious ambition replaced the political variety.[2]

The most closely focused record of the Red Fort at this period is the court diary kept by a news writer for the British Resident, now in the National Archives of India, which contains a detailed day-by-day picture of Zafar's life. The Last Emperor appears as a benign old man with impeccable manners – even when treated with extreme rudeness by the British. Daily he has olive oil rubbed into his feet to soothe his aches; occasionally he rouses himself to visit a garden, go on a hunting expedition or host a *mushaira*. Evenings were spent 'enjoying the moonlight', listening to singers or eating fresh mangoes. All the while the aged emperor tries to contain the infidelities of his young concubines, one of whom becomes pregnant by the most distinguished of the court musicians.[3]

Then, on a May morning in 1857, three hundred mutinous sepoys* and cavalrymen from Meerut rode into Delhi, massacred every Christian man, woman and child they could find in the city, and declared Zafar to be their leader and emperor. Zafar was no friend of the British, who had shorn him of his patrimony, and subjected him to almost daily humiliation. Yet Zafar was not a natural insurgent either. It was with severe misgivings and little choice that he found himself made the nominal leader of an Uprising that he strongly suspected from the start was doomed: a chaotic and officerless army of unpaid peasant soldiers set against the forces of the world's greatest military power, albeit one that had just lost the great majority of the Indian recruits to its Bengal Army.

The great Mughal capital, caught in the middle of a remarkable cultural flowering, was turned overnight into a battleground. No foreign army was in a position to intervene to support the rebels, and they had limited ammunition, no money and few supplies. The chaos and anarchy that erupted in the countryside proved far more

* A sepoy is an Indian infantry private, in this case in the employ of the British East India Company. The word derives from *sipahi*, the Persian for soldier.

effective at blockading Delhi than the efforts at besieging the city attempted by the British from their perch on the Ridge. The price of food escalated and supplies rapidly dwindled. Soon both the people of Delhi and the sepoys were on the edge of starvation.

The siege of Delhi was the Raj's Stalingrad: a fight to the death between two powers, neither of whom could retreat. There were unimaginable casualties, and on both sides the combatants were driven to the limits of physical and mental endurance. Finally, on 14 September 1857, the British and their hastily assembled army of Sikh and Pathan levees assaulted and took the city, sacking and looting the Mughal capital, and massacring great swathes of the population. In one *muhalla** alone, Kucha Chelan, some 1,400 citizens of Delhi were cut down. 'The orders went out to shoot every soul,' recorded Edward Vibart, a nineteen-year-old British officer.

> It was literally murder . . . I have seen many bloody and awful sights lately but such a one as I witnessed yesterday I pray I never see again. The women were all spared but their screams, on seeing their husbands and sons butchered, were most painful . . . Heaven knows I feel no pity, but when some old grey bearded man is brought and shot before your very eyes, hard must be that man's heart I think who can look on with indifference . . .[4]

Those city dwellers who survived the killing were driven out into the countryside to fend for themselves. Delhi was left an empty ruin. Though the royal family had surrendered peacefully, most of the emperor's sixteen sons were captured, tried and hung, while three were shot in cold blood, having first freely given up their arms, then been told to strip naked: 'In 24 hours I disposed of the principal members of the house of Timur the Tartar,' Captain William Hodson wrote to his sister the following day. 'I am not cruel, but I confess I did enjoy the opportunity of ridding the earth of these wretches.'[5]

Zafar himself was put on show to visitors, displayed 'like a beast in a cage', according to one British officer.[6] Among his visitors was the *Times* correspondent, William Howard Russell, who was told

* A *muhalla* is a distinct quarter or neighbourhood of a Mughal city – i.e. a group of residential lanes usually entered through a single gate which would be locked at night.

that the prisoner was the mastermind of the most serious armed act of resistance to Western colonialism. He was a 'dim, wandering eyed, dreamy old man with a feeble hanging nether lip and toothless gums,' wrote Russell.

> Was he, indeed, one who had conceived that vast plan of restoring a great empire, who had fomented the most gigantic mutiny in the history of the world? Not a word came from his lips; in silence he sat day and night with his eyes cast on the ground, and as though utterly oblivious of the conditions in which he was placed . . . His eyes had the dull, filmy look of very old age . . . Some heard him quoting verses of his own composition, writing poetry on a wall with a burned stick.[7]

Russell was suitably sceptical of the charges being levelled against Zafar: 'He was called ungrateful for rising against his benefactors,' he wrote.

> He was no doubt a weak and cruel old man; but to talk of ingratitude on the part of one who saw that all the dominions of his ancestors had been gradually taken from him until he was left with an empty title, and more empty exchequer, and a palace full of penniless princesses, is perfectly preposterous . . .[8]

Nevertheless, the following month Zafar was put on trial in the ruins of his old palace, and sentenced to transportation. He left his beloved Delhi on a bullock cart. Separated from everything he loved, broken-hearted, the last of the Great Mughals died in exile in Rangoon on Friday, 7 November 1862, aged eighty-seven.

With Zafar's departure, there was complete collapse of the fragile court culture he had faithfully nourished and exemplified. As Ghalib noted: 'All these things lasted only so long as the king reigned.'[9] By the time of Zafar's death, much of his palace, the Red Fort, had already been torn down, along with great areas of the Mughal Delhi he loved and beautified. Meanwhile the great majority of its leading inhabitants and courtiers – poets and princes, mullahs and merchants, Sufis and scholars – had been hunted down and hanged, or else dispersed and exiled, many to the Raj's new, specially constructed gulag in the Andaman Islands. Those who were spared were left in humiliating and conspicuous poverty. As Ghalib, one of the few survivors from the old court, lamented, 'The male descendants of the deposed King – such as survived the sword – draw allowances of five rupees a month. The female descendants if old are bawds, and if young, prostitutes.'[10]

> The city has become a desert . . . By God, Delhi is no more a city, but a camp, a cantonment. No Fort, no city, no bazaars, no water-courses . . . Four things kept Delhi alive – the Fort, the daily crowds at the Jama Masjid, the weekly walk to the Yamuna Bridge, and the yearly fair of the flower-men. None of these survives, so how could Delhi survive? Yes [it is said that] there was once a city of that name in the realm of India . . .
>
> > We smashed the wine cup and the flask;
> > What is it now to us
> > If all the rain that falls from heaven
> > Should turn to rose-red wine?[11]

Although Bahadur Shah II, the last Mughal, is a central figure in this book, it is not a biography of Zafar so much as a portrait of the Delhi he personified, a narrative of the last days of the Mughal capital and its final destruction in the catastrophe of 1857. It is a story I have dedicated the last four years to researching and writing. Archives containing Zafar's letters and his court records can be found in London, Lahore and even Rangoon. Most of the material, however, still lies in Delhi, Zafar's former capital, and a city that has haunted and obsessed me for over two decades now.

I first encountered Delhi when I arrived, aged eighteen, on the foggy winter's night of 26 January 1984. The airport was surrounded by shrouded men huddled under shawls, and it was surprisingly cold. I knew nothing at all about India.

My childhood had been spent in rural Scotland, on the shores of the Firth of Forth, and of my school friends I was probably the least well travelled. My parents were convinced that they lived in the most beautiful place imaginable and rarely took us on holiday, except on an annual spring visit to a corner of the Scottish Highlands even colder and wetter than home. Perhaps for this reason Delhi had a greater and more overwhelming effect on me than it would have had on other more cosmopolitan teenagers; certainly the city hooked me from the start. I backpacked around for a few months, and hung out in Goa; but I soon found my way back to Delhi and got myself a job at a Mother Teresa's home in the far north of the city, beyond Old Delhi.

In the afternoons, while the patients were taking their siesta, I used to slip out and explore. I would take a rickshaw into the innards of the Old City and pass through the narrowing funnel of gullies and lanes, alleys and cul-de-sacs, feeling the houses close in around me. In particular what remained of Zafar's palace, the Red Fort of the Great Mughals, kept drawing me back, and I often used to slip in with a book and spend whole afternoons there, in the shade of some cool pavilion. I quickly grew to be fascinated with the Mughals who had lived there, and began reading voraciously about them. It was here that I first thought of writing a history of the Mughals, an idea that has now expanded into a quartet, a four-volume history of the Mughal dynasty which I expect may take me another two decades to complete.

Yet however often I visited it, the Red Fort always made me sad. When the British captured it in 1857, they pulled down the gorgeous harem apartments, and in their place erected a line of barracks that look as if they have been modelled on Wormwood Scrubs. Even at the time, the destruction was regarded as an act of wanton philistinism. The great Victorian architectural historian James Fergusson was certainly no whining liberal, but recorded his horror at what had happened in his *History of Indian and Eastern Architecture*: 'those who carried out this fearful piece of vandalism', he wrote, did not even think 'to make a plan of what they were destroying, or preserving any record of the most splendid palace in the world . . . The engineers perceived that by gutting the palace they could provide at no expense a wall round their barrack yard, and one that no drunken soldier could scale without detection, and for this or some other wretched motive of economy, the palace was sacrificed'. He added: 'The only modern act to be compared with this is the destruction of the summer palace in Pekin. That however was an act of red-handed war. This was a deliberate act of unnecessary Vandalism.'[12]

The barracks should of course have been torn down years ago, but the Fort's current proprietors, the Archaeological Survey of India, have lovingly continued the work of decay initiated by the British: white marble pavilions have been allowed to discolour; plasterwork has been left to collapse; the water channels have cracked and grassed over; the fountains are dry. Only the barracks look well maintained.

I have now divided my time between London and Delhi for over twenty years, and the Indian capital remains my favourite city. Above all it is the city's relationship with its past which continues to intrigue me: of the great cities of the world, only Rome, Istanbul and Cairo can even begin to rival Delhi for the sheer volume and density of historic remains. Crumbling tomb towers, old mosques or ancient colleges intrude in the most unlikely places, appearing suddenly on roundabouts or in municipal gardens, diverting the road network and obscuring the fairways of the golf course. New Delhi is not new at all; instead it is a groaning necropolis, with enough ruins to keep any historian busy through several incarnations.

I am hardly alone in being struck by this: the ruins of Delhi are something visitors have always been amazed by, perhaps especially in the eighteenth century, when the city was at the height of its decay and its mood most melancholic. For miles in every direction, half collapsed and overgrown, robbed and reoccupied, neglected by all, lay the remains of six hundred years of trans-Indian Imperium – the wrecked vestiges of a period when Delhi had been the greatest city between Constantinople and Canton. Hammams and garden palaces, thousand-pillared halls and mighty tomb towers, empty mosques and deserted Sufi shrines – there seemed to be no end to the litter of ages. 'The prospect towards Delhi, as far as the eye can reach is covered with the crumbling remains of gardens, pavilions, mosques and burying places,' wrote Lieutenant William Franklin in 1795. 'The environs of this once magnificent and celebrated city appear now nothing more than a shapeless heap of ruins . . .'[13]

The first East India Company officials who settled in these ruins at the end of the eighteenth century were a series of sympathetic and notably eccentric figures who were deeply attracted to the high courtly culture which Delhi still represented. When the formidable Lady Maria Nugent, wife of the new British Commander-in-Chief in India, visited Delhi, she was horrified by what she saw there. The British Resident and his assistants had all 'gone native', she reported in her journal.

> I shall now say a few words of Messrs. Gardner and Fraser who are still of our party. They both wear immense whiskers, and neither will eat beef or pork, being as much Hindoos as Christians, if not more; they are both of them clever and intelligent, but eccentric; and, having come to this country early, they have formed opinions and prejudices that make them almost natives.[14]

Fraser, it turned out, was a distant cousin of my wife, Olivia. It was this intriguing and unexpected period which dominated the book I wrote about Delhi fifteen years ago, entitled *City of Djinns*, and which later ignited the tinder that led to my last book, *White Mughals*, about the many British who embraced Indian culture at the end of the eighteenth century. *The Last Mughal* is therefore my third book inspired by the capital. At the centre of it lies the question of how and why the relatively easy relationship of Indian and Briton, so evident during the time of Fraser, gave way to the hatreds and racism of the high-nineteenth-century Raj. The Uprising, it is clear, was the result of that change, not its cause.

Two things in particular seem to have put paid to this easy coexistence. One was the rise of British power: in a few years the British had defeated not only the French but also all their Indian rivals; in a manner not unlike the Americans after the fall of the Berlin Wall, the changed balance of power quickly led to an attitude of undisguised imperial arrogance.

The other was the ascendancy of Evangelical Christianity, and the profound change in attitudes that this brought about. The wills written by Company servants show that the practice of marrying or cohabiting with Indian wives or *bibis* all but disappeared. Memoirs of prominent eighteenth-century British Indian worthies which mentioned their Indian wives or Anglo-Indian children were re-edited so that the consorts were removed from later editions. No longer were Indians seen as inheritors of a body of sublime and ancient wisdom as eighteenth-century luminaries such as Sir William Jones and Warren Hastings had once believed; but instead merely 'poor benighted heathen', or even 'licentious pagans', who, it was hoped, were eagerly awaiting conversion.

There is an important point here. Many historians blithely use the word 'colonialism' as if it has some kind of clearly locatable meaning, yet it is increasingly apparent that at this period there were multiple modes and very distinct phases of colonialism; there were also many very different ways of inhabiting, performing and transgressing the still fluid notion of Britishness. It was not the British per se, so much as specific groups with a specific imperial agenda – namely the Evangelicals and Utilitarians – who ushered in the most obnoxious phase of colonialism, a change which adversely affected the White Mughals as much as it did the Great Mughals.

For, by the early 1850s, many British officials were nursing plans finally to abolish the Mughal court, and to impose not just British laws and technology on India, but also Christianity. The reaction to this steady crescendo of insensitivity came in 1857 with the Great Mutiny. Of the 139,000 sepoys of the Bengal Army – the largest modern army in Asia – all but 7,796 turned against their British masters.[15] In some parts of northern India, such as Avadh, the sepoys were joined by a very large proportion of the population. Atrocities abounded on both sides.

Delhi was the principal centre of the Uprising. As mutinous troops poured into the city from all round northern India – even the rebel regiments at Kanpur intended to head straight to Delhi until diverted to attack their officers by Nana Sahib – it was clear from the outset that the British had to recapture Delhi or lose their Indian empire for ever. Equally the sepoys rallying to the throne of Bahadur Shah, whom they believed to be the legitimate ruler of Hindustan, realised that if they lost Delhi they lost everything. Every available British soldier was sent to the Delhi Ridge, and for the four hottest months of the Indian summer, the Mughal capital was bombarded by British artillery with thousands of helpless civilians caught up in the horrors.

While in the first weeks of the Uprising troops came to Delhi from all over Hindustan, thereafter the city, and especially its besiegers, remained to a great extent cut off from news of developments elsewhere. In that sense the siege of Delhi was always a war within a war, relatively independent of the momentous developments to the south and east. Until the very end of July, the British on the Delhi Ridge were still daily expecting to be relieved by General Wheeler's army at Kanpur, less than 300 miles to the south-east, quite unaware that Wheeler's army had surrendered and been slaughtered, almost to a man, more than a month earlier, on 27 June. Equally, the Delhi defenders were convinced they were about to be saved by two non-existent Persian armies, one heading down from the Khyber Pass, while the other was supposed to be making its way north-east from a seaborne landing in Bombay.

Most narratives of 1857 cut back and forth between Delhi, Lucknow, Jhansi and Kanpur in a way that suggests far more contact and flow of information than there actually was between the different centres of the Uprising. In this book I have chosen to limit references to developments elsewhere, except in cases where the Delhi participants were explicitly aware of them, thus attempting to restore the sense of intense isolation and lonely vulnerability felt by both the besiegers and the besieged engaged in the battle for control of the great Mughal capital.

Over the last four years, I and my colleagues Mahmoud Farooqi and Bruce Wannell have been working through many of the 20,000 virtually unused Persian and Urdu documents relating to Delhi in 1857, known as the Mutiny Papers, that we found on the shelves of the National Archives of India.[16] These allow 1857 in Delhi to be seen for the first time from a properly Indian perspective, and not just from the British sources through which to date it has usually been viewed.

Discovering the sheer scale of the treasures held by the National Archives was one of the highlights of the whole project. It is a

commonplace of books about 1857 that they lament the absence of
Indian sources and the corresponding need to rely on the huge
quantities of easily accessible British material – memoirs, travelo-
gues, letters, histories – which carry with them not only the British
version of events but also British attitudes and preconceptions
about the whole Uprising; in that sense little has changed since
Vincent Smith complained in 1923 'that the story has been
chronicled from one side only'.[17]

Yet all this time in the National Archives there existed as detailed
a documentation of the four months of the Uprising in Delhi as can
exist for any Indian city at any period of history – great unwieldy
mountains of chits, pleas, orders, petitions, complaints, receipts,
rolls of attendance and lists of casualties, predictions of victory and
promises of loyalty, notes from spies of dubious reliability and
letters from eloping lovers – all neatly bound in string and boxed up
in the cool, hushed, air-conditioned vaults of the Indian National
Archives.

What was even more exciting was the street-level nature of much
of the material. Although the documents were collected by the
victorious British from the Palace and the army camp, they contained huge quantities of petitions and requests from the ordinary
citizens of Delhi – potters and courtesans, sweetmeat makers and
overworked water carriers – exactly the sort of people who usually
escape the historian's net. The Mutiny Papers overflow with
glimpses of real life: the bird catchers and lime makers who have
had their charpoys stolen by sepoys; the horse trader from Haryana
looted by Gujars on the outskirts of Delhi as he walks home from
selling his wares, his pocket full of cash; the gamblers playing cards
in a recently ruined house and ogling the women next door, to the
great alarm of the family living there; the sweetmeat makers who
refuse to take their sweets up to the trenches in Qudsia Bagh until
they are paid for the last load.[18]

We meet people like Hasni the dancer, who uses a British attack
on the Idgah to escape from the serai where she is staying with her
husband and run off with her lover. Or Pandit Harichandra, who
tried to exhort the Hindus of Delhi to leave their shops and join the
fight, citing examples from the *Mahabharat*. Or Hafiz Abdurrah-

man, caught grilling beef kebabs during a ban on cow slaughter and who comes to beg the mercy of Zafar. Or Chandan, the sister of the courtesan Manglo, who rushed before the emperor as her beautiful sister was seized and raped by the cavalryman Rustam Khan: 'He has imprisoned her and beats her up and even though she shouts and screams nobody helps her . . . Should this state of anarchy and injustice continue the subjects of the Exalted One will all be destroyed.'[19]

As a source for daily events, for the motivation of the rebels, for the problems they faced, the levels of chaos in the city, and the ambiguous and equivocal response of both the Mughal elite and the Hindu trading class of the city, the Mutiny Papers contain an unrivalled quantity of unique material. Cumulatively the stories that the collection contains allow the Uprising to be seen not in terms of nationalism, imperialism, orientalism or other such abstractions, but instead as a human event of extraordinary, tragic and often capricious outcomes, and allow us to resurrect the ordinary individuals whose fate it was to be accidentally caught up in one of the great upheavals of history. Public, political and national tragedies, after all, consist of a multitude of private, domestic and individual tragedies. It is through the human stories of the successes, struggles, grief, anguish and despair of these individuals that we can best bridge the great chasm of time and understanding separating us from the remarkably different world of mid-nineteenth-century India.

As the scale and detail of the material available from the Mutiny Papers became slowly apparent, and as it became obvious that most of the material had not been accessed since it was gathered in 1857, or at least since it was catalogued when rediscovered stored in a series of trunks in Calcutta in 1921, the question that became increasingly hard to answer was why no one had properly used this wonderful mass of material before.[20] For at a time when ten thousand dissertations and whole shelves of *Subaltern Studies* have carefully and ingeniously theorised about orientalism and colonialism and the imagining of the Other (all invariably given titles with a present participle and a fashionable noun of obscure meaning – *Gendering the Colonial Paradigm*, *Constructing the Imagined Other*, *Other-*

ing the Imagined Construction, and so on) not one PhD has ever been written from the Mutiny Papers, no major study has ever systematically explored its contents.

Certainly, the *shikastah* (literally 'broken writing') script of the manuscripts is often difficult to read, written as it is in an obscure form of late Mughal scribal notation with many of the diacritical marks missing, and at times faded and ambiguous enough to defy the most persistent of researchers. Moreover many of the fragments – especially the spies' reports – are written in microscopic script on very small pieces of paper designed to be sewn into clothing or even hidden within the person of the spy. Yet the collection could not have been in a better-known or more accessible archive – the National Archives of India lies in a magnificent Lutyens-period building bang in the centre of India's capital city. Using the Mutiny Papers and properly harvesting their riches as a source for 1857 felt at times as strange and exciting – and indeed as unlikely – as going to Paris and discovering, unused on the shelves of the Bibliothèque Nationale, the entire records of the French Revolution.

No less exciting was it to discover that Delhi's two principal Urdu newspapers, the wonderfully opinionated *Dihli Urdu Akbhar* and the more staid and restrained Court Circular, the *Siraj ul-Akbhar*, had continued publication without missing an issue throughout the Uprising, and that the National Archives contained almost complete sets of both. Again only fragmentary translations of these have previously been available.[21]

Outside the National Archives, other libraries in Delhi turned out to contain equally remarkable treasures. The Delhi Commissioner's Office Archive, not far from Zafar's summer palace in Mehrauli, contained the full records of the revived British administration as the officials calmly went about their business of expelling the citizens of Delhi, rounding up and hanging any Delhiwallahs they suspected of involvement in the Uprising, and demolishing great swathes of the city. The documents allow for the first time the full scale of the viciousness and brutality of the British response to 1857 in Delhi to be properly grasped. As far as the Mughal elite were concerned, the fall of Delhi was followed by something approaching a genocide. Only the Victorian British, one feels, would keep such perfect bureaucratic records of what in many cases would today be classified as grisly war crimes.

Several fine first-person Mughal accounts of 1857 in Delhi also turned up, previously untranslated into English. Most memorable was the moving account of the destruction of an individual's entire world contained in the *Dastan i-Ghadr* of the sensitive young poet and courtier Zahir Dehlavi, written on his deathbed in Hyderabad years later, apparently from earlier notes. Unlike many other writers on 1857 he feels no compunction about recording what he believed to be the truth about what happened, and speaks equally frankly of the failings of the Mughal court, the sepoys and the British.

The longer I worked, the clearer it became that there were in fact two parallel streams of historiography, which utilised almost completely different sets of sources. The British histories, as well as a surprising number of those written in English in post-colonial India, tended to use only English-language sources, padding out the gaps, in the case of more recent work, with a thick cladding of post-Saidian theory and jargon. The Urdu histories written by contemporary Muslim scholars in India and Pakistan, on the other hand, tend to make use of an entirely separate and often very rich seam of Urdu primary sources. Moreover, in the case of Delhi there exist some wonderful works of secondary scholarship, such as Aslam Parvez's fine Urdu biography of Zafar, which remain unknown to English-speaking readers. One of the principal aims of this book is to bring the voluminous Persian and Urdu primary and secondary sources on Delhi in 1857 before an English language readership for the first time.

But it was not just Delhi which turned out to have great stashes of new material. Other almost unused repositories of documents kept turning up across South and South-East Asia. In Lahore the spectacular Punjab Archive, kept within the huge domed tomb of the Emperor Jahangir's favourite dancing girl, was the resting place not only of Anarkali herself but also of the complete pre-Mutiny records of the British Residency in Delhi, archives that historians had long assumed were destroyed in 1857.[22]

Here could be read all the correspondence between the British Resident and his superiors in Calcutta about their plans for extinguishing the Mughal court. The archives also contained much material from 1857, including sets of spies' reports and the two famous telegrams sent from Delhi on 11 May that warned the British in Lahore of what had taken place, so allowing them to disarm the sepoys of the Punjab before they themselves heard of the events in Meerut and Delhi. The tomb, then as now, is part of the Punjab Secretariat complex, from which in 1857 John Lawrence master-minded the British effort to retake Delhi. During the period I worked on the Delhi Residency archives in Anarkali's tomb, I found myself scribbling on a desk just ten feet from the marble sarcophagus said to be that of the courtesan immortalised in the great Bollywood movie *Mughal-e Azam*, and only a couple of hundred yards from the office from which John Lawrence had planned his moves to suppress the mutiny of his sepoys and restore British control of northern India.

An even bigger surprise was the remarkable National Archives in Rangoon (or Yangon, as it has been rechristened by the military government). I had gone to Rangoon mainly to visit the site of Zafar's exile and death – and perhaps at some level to seek the *barakat* (blessings) his devotees still pray for at his shrine. I thought of attempting to visit the archives only when prompted by a friend there, who knew someone who knew the director. Yet it turned out that here lay all Zafar's prison records, efficiently catalogued, scanned and digitally stored in Acrobat PDF files – something the British Library has so far failed to achieve – so that I was able to leave the archives at the end of one morning with a shelf full of research contained on a single, shining CD.

What I have found at the end of all this confirms a growing conviction of many of the more recent historians of 1857. Instead of the single coherent mutiny or patriotic national war of inde-pendence beloved of Victorian or Indian nationalist historiography, there was in reality a chain of very different uprisings and acts of resistance, whose form and fate were determined by local and regional situations, passions and grievances.

All took very different forms in different places – which goes some way to explain why, 150 years after the event, scholars are still arguing over the old chestnut of whether 1857 was a mutiny, a peasants' revolt, an urban revolution or a war of independence. The answer is that it was all of these, and many other things too: it was not one unified movement but many, with widely differing causes, motives and natures. Thanks to the fine regional studies of Eric Stokes, Rudrangshu Mukherjee and Tapti Roy, scholars have already seen how different were the situations in Muzaffarnagar and the Doab, Lucknow and Bundelkhand.[23] The form that 1857 took in Delhi was again quite distinct from the uprisings elsewhere.

For Delhi has always been quite clear about its superiority to the rest of the country. It was the seat of the Great Mughal and the place where the most chaste Urdu was spoken. It believed it had the best-looking women, the finest mangoes, the most talented poets. While many in the city initially welcomed the sepoys in their endeavour to restore the Mughal to power and to expel the hated *kafir* interlopers, nevertheless the people of Shahjahanabad* soon tired of hosting a large and undisciplined army of boorish and violent peasants from Bihar and eastern Uttar Pradesh. For the people of Avadh, the sepoys were local lads, and for them 1857 was a genuine popular uprising that touched a chord across the region.[24] In contrast, for Delhi the incoming sepoys remained strangers, with different dialects, accents and customs. The Delhi sources invariably describe them as 'Tilangas' or '*Purbias*'† – effectively, outsiders. Neither of these words is ever used of the sepoys in Avadhi sources.

The changing attitudes to the sepoys are well encapsulated in the

---

* Shahjahanabad is the walled city now known as Old Delhi, built by the fifth Mughal Emperor, Shah Jahan (1592–1666), and opened as his new capital in 1648.

† 'Tilangas' is apparently a reference to Telingana, in modern Andhra Pradesh, where the British originally recruited many of their sepoys during the Carnatic Wars of the eighteenth century. In Delhi the name seems to have stuck as an appellation for British-trained troops, although the British had long since replaced Telingana with Avadh as their principal recruitment field, so that in 1857 most sepoys would have come from modern Uttar Pradesh and parts of Bihar. 'Purbias', which in Delhi was used alternately with Tilangas, simply means Easterners. Both words carry the same connotations of foreignness, implying 'these outsiders from the East'.

shifting views of Maulvi Muhammad Baqar, the garrulous and outspoken editor of the *Dihli Urdu Akbhar*, and father of the Urdu poet and critic Muhammad Husain Azad. At the outbreak of the Uprising, in May 1857, he was one of the most enthusiastic cheerleaders of the new regime, writing in his columns of how the rebellion had been sent by God to punish the *kafirs* for their arrogant plan to wipe out the religions of India. For him the speed and thoroughness of the reverse suffered by the British were proof of miraculous divine intervention, and it was no surprise therefore that such an event should be accompanied by dreams and visions:

> One venerable man had a dream that our Prophet Mohammed, Praise Be Upon Him, said to Jesus that your followers have become an enemy of my name and wish to efface my religion. To this Lord Jesus replied that the British are not my followers, they do not follow my path, they have joined ranks with Satan's followers . . . Some people even swear that the day the troopers came here, there were camels ahead of them on which rode green-robed riders . . . These green riders instantly vanished from sight and only the troopers remained, killing whichever Englishman they found, cutting them up as if they were carrots or radishes . . .'[25]

Only two weeks later, however, in the edition of 24 May, after the unpaid sepoys had looted most of the Delhi bazaars, destroyed the library of the Delhi College, attacked the havelis of his friends and monopolised all the city's most desirable courtesans, Baqar's tone had completely changed: 'The population is greatly harassed and sick of the pillaging and plundering,' he wrote. 'Great peril confronts all the respectable and well off people of the city . . . the city is being ravaged.'[26] By August he was filling the columns of the *Dihli Urdu Akbhar* with details of the way the lazy and boorish Bihari sepoys – as he saw them – had become softened by their discovery of the luxuries and sophistication of Delhi:

> The moment they drink the water of the city and do a round of Chandni Chowk and . . . go around Jama Masjid and enjoy the sweetmeats of Ghantawala [the most famous Delhi sweet shop], they

lose all urge and determination to fight and kill the enemy, and they become shorn of all strength and resolution . . . A lot of people maintain that many sepoys go for battle without bathing after spending nights at the courtesan's quarters.* The setbacks they have suffered and the general mayhem we endure is partly the result of this unseemly practice.[27]

By this time, Baqar had already secretly changed sides and become a British informer. His intelligence reports, smuggled out of the city to the British camp on the Ridge, still survive in the archives of the Delhi Commissioner's Office.

A large proportion of the Mutiny Papers are the petitions of ordinary Delhiwallahs who have suffered at the hands of the sepoys; invariably they are addressed to Zafar, who they hope will protect them against the increasingly desperate Tilangas. Significantly, in their petitions to the court, the words the ordinary people of Delhi used to describe what was happening in 1857 were not *Ghadr* (mutiny) and still less *Jang-e Azadi* (freedom struggle or, more literally, war of freedom) so much as *fasad* (riots) and *danga* (disturbance or commotion). For the people of Delhi, the daily reality of what happened in 1857 was not so much liberation as violence, uncertainty and starvation. Indeed, reading through the Mutiny Papers there are times when it seems almost as if the siege of Delhi had become a three-cornered contest, with the sepoys and the British fighting it out, and with the people in Delhi caught in the middle, their lives wrecked by the violence of both. Clearly Zafar saw his job as protecting the people of Delhi from both *firangi* (foreigners, Franks) and Tilanga.

Yet the growing gulf between the people of Delhi and the sepoys, so very clear in the sources, has to date never been properly written up by any historian. For the imperial British, the siege of Delhi was a great moment of British heroism against the mass of ungrateful and undifferentiated natives. For the nationalist historians since Independence, 1857 was a great unified patriotic struggle waged by heroic freedom fighters against the wicked imperialists. The reality,

---

* As Muslims are supposed to wash after having sex, the complaint is as much about ritual impurity as it is about hygiene.

it turns out, was far less clear cut. Ghalib was certainly not alone in viewing the sepoys, with all the hauteur that Delhi aristocrats were capable of, simply as troublesome and ill-mannered 'blacks'.[28]

Nevertheless, for all the ambiguity of the equivocal Delhi responses to 1857, it is clear how very central Delhi was to the Uprising. For despite its diffuse and fractured nature, many of its different elements converged into a single programme: to restore the Mughal Empire.

For a century, this fact has been partially obscured by nationalist historians for whom the idea of Hindu sepoys flocking to Delhi to revive the Mughal Empire was more or less anathema. Since the time of V. D. Savarkar's book *The Indian War of Independence, 1857*, published in 1909, the March outbreak in Barrackpore has been seen as the crucial event of the Mutiny, and Mangal Pandey its central icon. This is a position which was cemented by the recent Bollywood film which, though known as *The Rising* in its English-language avatar, was called simply *Mangal Pandey* in Hindi. Yet in many ways Pandey was almost irrelevant to the outbreak which took place two months later at Meerut in May.[29]

Instead the Meerut insurgents headed straight to Delhi, drawn to the court of the Great Mughal, the one clear source of legitimacy recognised across Hindustan.[30] Even in Lucknow, which had been in rebellion against Delhi since the late eighteenth century, the sepoys rose in the name of the Emperor, and the Aradhi court, and sent an envoy to Delhi asking for Zafar to confirm the title Wazir for the young heir apparent, Birjis Qadir, who was already minting his coins in the Emperor's name. The same was true in Kanpur, where the rebels celebrated their victory as due to 'the enemy-destroying fortune of the Emperor'.[31]

If Mangal Pandey was the sepoys' inspiration, they certainly did not articulate it, nor did they rush towards Barrackpore or Calcutta. Instead it was, unequivocally, the capture of Delhi which was the great transforming masterstroke for the Uprising. The fact that Zafar gave the sepoys his tacit support instantly turned an army mutiny – one of a large number of mutinies and acts of armed resistance that had occurred under the Company – into the major political challenge to British dominance of India, and sparked off what would swiftly escalate into the most serious armed challenge to imperialism the world over during the course of the nineteenth century.

For powerless as he was in so many ways, Zafar was still the *Khalifa*, God's Regent on Earth. When Delhi people made an oath, rather than reaching for the scriptures they swore 'by the throne of the Emperor'.[32] When Emily Eden went to Delhi accompanying her brother the Governor General, Lord Auckland, even the Governor General's own entourage bowed low before the Emperor, irrespective of whether they were Hindu or Muslim: 'All our servants were in a state of profound veneration,' wrote Emily. 'The natives all look upon the King of Delhi as their rightful Lord, and so he is, I suppose.'[33]

As his coronation portrait described him, he was 'His Divine Highness, Caliph of the Age, Padshah as Glorious as Jamshed, He who is Surrounded by Hosts of Angels, Shadow of God, Refuge of Islam, Protector of the Mohammedan Religion, Offspring of the House of Timur, Greatest Emperor, Mightiest King of Kings, Emperor son of Emperor, Sultan son of Sultan'. From this point of view, it was the East India Company which was the real rebel, guilty of revolt against a feudal superior to whom it had sworn allegiance for two centuries; after all, the Company had long governed as the Mughal's tax collector in Bengal, and had until recently acknowledged itself as the vassal of the Mughal even on its own seal and coins.[34]

For this reason many ordinary people in northern India responded to Zafar's appeal, much to the astonishment of the British, who had long ceased to take him seriously, and who, having completely lost touch with Indian opinion, were amazed at how Hindustan* reacted to his call. Seeing only the powerlessness of

* Hindustan refers to the region of northern India encompassing the modern Indian states of Haryana, Delhi, Uttar Pradesh and some parts of Madhya Pradesh and Bihar, where Hindustani is spoken, and the area often referred to in modern Indian papers as the 'Cow Belt'. While the term 'India' is relatively rarely used in nineteenth-century Urdu sources, there is a strong consciousness of the existence of Hindustan as a unit, with Delhi at its political centre. This was the area that was most seriously convulsed in 1857.

Zafar, the British had ceased to recognise the charisma that the name of the Mughal still possessed for both Hindus and Muslims in northern India. Mark Thornhill, the British collector in Mathura, recorded his own surprise in his diary immediately after the rebel capture of Delhi:

> Their talk was all about the ceremonial of the palace and how it would be revived. They speculated as to who would be Grand Chamberlain, which of the chiefs of Rajpootana would guard the different gates, and who were the fifty-two Rajahs who would assemble to put the Emperor on the throne ... As I listened I realised as I never had done before the deep impression that the splendour of the ancient court had made on the popular imagination, how dear to them were the traditions and how faithfully, all unknown to us, they had preserved them. There was something weird in the Mogul Empire thus starting into a sort of phantom life after the slumber of a hundred years.[35]

For many the appeal of the Mughal Emperor was as much religious as political. As far as the Indian participants were concerned, the Uprising was overwhelmingly expressed as a war of religion, and looked upon as a defensive action against the rapid inroads missionaries and Christianity were making in India, as well as a more generalised fight for freedom from foreign domination. The Great Mutiny has usually been presented by the Marxist historians of the 1960s and 1970s primarily as a rising against British social and economic policies, as both urban revolution and a peasants' revolt sparked off by loss of land rights and employment opportunities as much as anything else. All this certainly played a part. Yet when the Indian participants of the Uprising articulate the reason for their revolt – as they do with great frequency and at some length in the Mutiny Papers – they invariably state that they were above all resisting a move by the Company to impose Christianity and Christian laws on India – something many Evangelical Englishmen were indeed contemplating.

As the sepoys told Zafar on 11 May 1857, 'we have joined hands to protect our religion and our faith'.[36] Later they stood in the Chandni Chowk, the main street of Delhi, and asked people:

'Brothers: are you with those of the faith?'[37] British men and women who had converted to Islam – and there were a surprising number of those in Delhi – were not hurt; but Indians who had converted to Christianity were cut down immediately. As late as 6 September, when calling the people of Delhi to rally against the coming assault by the British, a proclamation issued in the name of Zafar spelled out very plainly 'that this is a religious war, and is being prosecuted on account of the faith, and it behoves all Hindus and Musalman residents of the imperial city, or of the villages in the country . . . to continue true to their faith and creeds'.[38] Even if one accepts that the word 'religion' (for Muslims *din*) is often being used in the very general and non-sectarian sense of *dharma* (or duty, righteousness) – so that when the sepoys say they are rising to defend their *dharma*, they mean as much their way of life as their sectarian religious identity – it is still highly significant that the Urdu sources usually refer to the British not as *angrez* (the English) or as *goras* (whites) or even *firangis*, but instead almost always as *kafirs* (infidels) and *nasrani* (Christians).

Although the great majority of the sepoys were Hindus, in Delhi a flag of jihad was raised in the principal mosque, and many of the insurgents described themselves as mujahedin, ghazis and jihadis. Indeed, by the end of the siege, after a significant proportion of the sepoys had melted away, unpaid, hungry and dispirited, the proportion of jihadis in Delhi grew to be about a quarter of the total fighting force, and included a regiment of 'suicide ghazis' from Gwalior who had vowed never to eat again and to fight until they met death at the hands of the *kafirs*, 'for those who have come to die have no need for food'.[39]

One of the causes of unrest, according to one Delhi source, was that 'the British had closed the madrasas'.[40] These were words that had no resonance to the historians of the 1960s. Now, sadly, in the aftermath of 9/11 and 7/7, they are phrases we understand all too well, and words like jihad scream out of the dusty pages of the source manuscripts, demanding attention.

If all this has strong contemporary echoes, in other ways Delhi today feels as if it is fast moving away from its Mughal past. In modern Delhi an increasingly wealthy Punjabi middle class now lives in an aspirational bubble of shopping malls, espresso bars and multiplexes. Visiting Najafgarh, 20 kilometres beyond Indira Gandhi International Airport, and scene of one of the most important battles in the siege of Delhi, I found that no one in the town had any knowledge or family memories of the battle; but instead recruitment posters for call centres were plastered all over the last surviving Mughal ruin in the town, the Delhi Gate.

On every side, rings of new suburbs are springing up, full of back-office processing units, software companies and fancy apartment blocks, all rapidly rising on land that only two years ago was billowing winter wheat. This fast-emerging middle-class India is a country with its eyes firmly fixed on the future. Everywhere there is a profound hope that the country's growing international status will somehow compensate for a past often perceived as a long succession of invasions and defeats at the hands of foreign powers. Whatever the reason, the result is a tragic neglect of Delhi's magnificent past. Sometimes it seems as if no other great city of the world is less loved, or less cared for. Occasionally there is an outcry as the tomb of the poet Zauq is discovered to have disappeared under a municipal urinal or the haveli courtyard house of his rival Ghalib is revealed to have been turned into a coal store; but by and large the losses go unrecorded.

I find it heartbreaking: often when I revisit one of my favourite monuments it has either been overrun by some slum or container park, unsympathetically restored or reconstructed by the Archaeological Survey of India (ASI) or, more usually, simply demolished. Ninety-nine per cent of the delicate havelis or Mughal courtyard houses of Old Delhi have been destroyed, and like swathes of the city walls have disappeared into memory. According to historian Pavan Varma, the majority of the buildings he recorded in his book *Mansions at Dusk* only ten years ago no longer exist. Perhaps there is also a cultural factor here in the neglect of the past: as one conservationist told me recently: 'you must understand', he said, 'that we Hindus burn our dead'. Either way, the loss of Delhi's past is irreplaceable;

and future generations will inevitably look back at the conservation failures of the early twenty-first century with a deep sadness.

Sometimes, on winter afternoon walks, I wander to the lovely and deeply atmospheric ruins of Zafar's summer palace in Mehrauli, a short distance from my Delhi house, and as I look out from its great gateway, I wonder what Zafar would have made of all this. Looking down over the Sufi shrine that abuts his palace, I suspect he would somehow have managed to make his peace with the fast-changing cyber-India of outsourcing, call centres and software parks that are now rapidly overpowering the last remnants of his world. After all, realism and acceptance were always qualities Zafar excelled in. For all the tragedy of his life, he was able to see that the world continued to turn, and that however much the dogs might bark, the great caravan of life continued to move on. In the words of the poem commonly attributed to Zafar, and said to have been written shortly after his imprisonment:

When in silks you came and dazzled
Me with the beauty of your Spring,
You brought a flower to bloom –
Love within my being.

You lived with me, breath of my breath,
Being in my being, nor left my side;
But now the wheel of Time has turned
And you are gone – no joys abide.

You pressed your lips upon my lips,
Your heart upon my beating heart,
And I have no wish to fall in love again,
For they who sold Love's remedy
Have shut shop, and I seek in vain.

My life now gives no ray of light,
I bring no solace to heart or eye;
Out of dust to dust again,
Of no use to anyone am I.

Delhi was once a paradise,
Where Love held sway and reigned;
But its charm lies ravished now
And only ruins remain.

No tears were shed when shroudless they
Were laid in common graves;
No prayers were read for the noble dead,
Unmarked remain their graves.

The heart distressed, the wounded flesh,
The mind ablaze, the rising sigh;
The drop of blood, the broken heart,
Tears on the lashes of the eye.

But things cannot remain, O Zafar,
Thus for who can tell?
Through God's great mercy and the Prophet
All may yet be well.[41]

William Dalrymple
New Delhi, January 2006

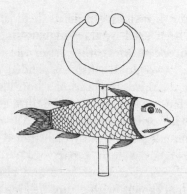

1

A CHESSBOARD KING

The marriage procession of Prince Jawan Bakht left the Lahore Gate of the Red Fort at 2 a.m. on the hot summer night of 2 April 1852.

With a salute from the cannon stationed on the ramparts, and an arc of fireworks and rockets fired aloft from the illuminated turrets of the Fort, the two gates opposite the great thoroughfare of Chandni Chowk swung open.

The first to emerge were the *chobdars* or mace-bearers. The people of Delhi have never much liked being restrained by barriers and were in the habit of breaking through the bamboo railings hung with lamps that illuminated the processional route. It was the job of the *chobdars* to clear a way through the excitable crowd, before the imperial elephants – always a little unpredictable in the presence of fireworks – appeared lumbering through the gates.

Two ministers of state on horseback began the procession proper. Shell ornaments were plaited into the horses' manes, and bells strung around their necks and fetlocks, and as they rode out, the ministers were attended by servants with punkahs (fans). Then came a troop of Mughal infantry, with polished black shields and curved swords, long lances and fluttering pennons of green and gold.

The first six of the imperial elephants followed, caparisoned with gold and saffron headcloths embroidered with the Emperor's coat of arms. From the howdahs,* officials held aloft the dynastic insignia that had been used by the Mughals since their arrival in India more than three centuries earlier: from one, the face of a rayed sun; from another, two golden fish suspended at each end of a golden bow; from the third, the head of a lion-like beast; from the fourth, a golden Hand of Fatima; from the fifth, a horse's head; and from the last, a *chatri* or imperial umbrella. All were made of gold and were raised on gilt staffs from which trailed silken streamers.

There then emerged in turn a party of red-tunicked Palace servants carrying covered trays of food and gifts for the bride's family; a squadron of camels, with drums beating and guns firing in the air; a small regiment of British sepoys led by Captain Douglas, Commandant of the Palace Guards, all in tight-fitting busbees and blue-and-saffron uniforms, and escorting two light cannon; a troop of Skinner's Horse in their yellow tunics and scarlet sashes, topped by armoured breastplates and medieval-looking helmets; a group of bullock-drawn wagons on which sat several bands of Mughal kettle drummers, *shanai* players, trumpeters and cymbal clashers; and a European brougham carriage, painted kingfisher blue, containing a party of senior princes, their gilt brocade flashing in the light of the exploding fireworks.

After each group came parties of torchbearers, holding their flames aloft, interspersed with men holding candles in glass bell jars. There were also gangs of water carriers emptying their skins on to the road in an attempt to settle the billowing summer dust kicked up by the procession.

After the brougham there came a second, smaller group of younger princes, this time riding on horseback; and among them, in the very centre, rode the groom. Mirza Jawan Bakht was only eleven years old, a young bridegroom even in a society that tended to marry its offspring early in adolescence. Immediately behind the Prince swayed the elephant on which rode the Emperor himself, sitting in his golden howdah and decked out, despite the sweltering night heat, in his state robes and jewels, and attended by his personal bearer holding a peacock fan. The rest of the court

---

* A howdah is the seat carried on an elephant's back; often in this period howdahs were covered with a canopy.

followed behind on foot, a great snaking queue stretching back through Chatta Chowk, the Fort bazaar, to the Naqqar Khana Darwaza, or the Gate of the Drum House, in the very centre of the Fort.[1]

Not long before this, the Emperor and Jawan Bakht had both sat for the Austrian artist, August Schoefft.[2] The portrait of Zafar depicts a dignified, reserved and rather beautiful old man with a fine aquiline nose and a carefully trimmed beard. Despite his height and surprisingly broad and muscular build, there is a profound gentleness and sensitivity in his large brown watery eyes with their unusually long lashes. As a teenage prince, Zafar had always appeared in his portraits as a slightly awkward and uncertain figure, plump, visibly ill at ease and thinly bearded. But as youth gave way to middle age he had grown into his looks, and in old age – unusually – looked finer than ever. Now in his mid-seventies, his cheeks were sallow, his nose more pronounced and his bearing more regal. Yet as the elderly monarch kneels, wearily fingering his beads, there remains in the expression of his dark eyes something unmistakably melancholic; in the set of his full lips there is still that air of sad, patient resignation visible in the earlier pictures. Schoefft shows Zafar a little swamped under the brocade cloth of gold which adorns him, somewhat weighed down by the huge blood-coloured rubies and the strings of vast pearls, each the size of a partridge egg, which seem to hang so heavily around his neck. It is a portrait of a man imprisoned by the trappings of his office.

By contrast, the young Jawan Bakht, the Emperor's favourite son, seems to relish all the pearls and gems, the jewelled daggers and inlaid swords with which he is bedecked with a lavishness almost equal to that of his father. His expression is different too: knowingly handsome, and oddly cocky and confident for a boy of eleven. He is as strikingly sure of himself as his father appears wearily uncertain.[3]

One person missing from both the portraits and the wedding procession was the woman who had done more than anything else to bring the marriage about. For months, Zafar's favourite wife, Zinat Mahal, had been preparing for this day. In Mughal tradition, women did not accompany the *barat* taking the groom to his marriage – not even mothers and queens; but every detail of the procession had been planned by her. For Mirza Jawan Bakht was Zinat Mahal's only son, and her one ambition, to which she held consistently throughout her life, was to see Jawan Bakht, Zafar's fifteenth son, placed on the throne at the death of his father.

The exceptionally lavish wedding she had planned was intended by her to raise the profile of the Prince, and also to consolidate her own place in the dynasty: Jawan Bakht's bride, the Nawab Shah Zamani Begum,* who was probably no more than ten years old at the time of the wedding, was Zinat's niece, and her father, Walidad Khan of Malagarh, an important ally of the Queen. While so young a couple would not be expected to consummate their marriage for a year or two, or even to live together, political considerations meant that the marriage should go ahead immediately, without having to wait for the couple to reach puberty.

As conceived by Zinat, the wedding of Mirza Jawan Bakht was of a scale unparalleled in Delhi in living memory, eclipsing the weddings of all Jawan Bakht's elder brothers. Sixty years later, the young courtier Zahir Dehlavi, whose job it was to oversee the care of the *Mahi Maraatib* or Fish Standard,† still remembered the aroma of the trays of food from the royal kitchens that had been sent out to every Palace official, and the spectacular entertainments that preceded the main celebration: 'such beauty and magnificence had never been seen before', he wrote many years later, in exile in Hyderabad. 'At least not in my lifetime. It was a celebration I shall never forget.'[4]

The festivities had begun three days before the marriage with a procession from the house of Walidad Khan to the Palace, bearing the principal wedding gifts, followed by fireworks: 'a brilliant train of elephants, camels, horses and conveyances of every denomina-

---

* Nawab originally meant a viceroy or governor, but later it was simply used as a grand title, usually for men, but occasionally – as in this case – for women. (Duke or duchess would be the nearest English equivalent, which in its original Latin form *Dux* also meant governor.)

† The *Mahi Maraatib*, a golden or pair of fish raised on a long golden standard, was the most important of the Mughal's dynastic insignia, but despite Zahir's grand-sounding official title of Daroga of the Mahi Maraatib, his daily duties appear to have been relatively humble and he was in effect the Emperor's page or ADC.

tion', according to the *Delhi Gazette*.[5] This led on to the ceremony of the mehndi, when the hands of the couple and their guests, including all the women of the Palace, were decorated with henna; the celebrations would continue for a further seven days beyond the night of the wedding ceremony.

On the evening of the great procession, at the beginning of the night vigil known as the *ratjaga*, Zafar had bestowed on Jawan Bakht a wedding veil made of strings of pearls known as a *sehra*, and simultaneous parties of escalating grandeur had been arranged for the different ranks of the Palace, each with their own musicians and troupes of dancing girls. Selected townspeople were in one courtyard, Palace children and students in another, senior officials in a third, and the princes in a fourth.[6]

Since Zafar's financial resources rarely matched his spending, let alone that of his wife, much of the initial work for the wedding had involved arranging loans from Delhi moneylenders, who knew from experience what the chances were of seeing their cash again. Since December, the British Resident's diary of court proceedings had been full of Zinat's attempts to procure the large amounts needed, something she achieved in the end with the aid of the notoriously ruthless Chief Eunuch of the Palace, Mahbub Ali Khan.[7] The Palace was repaired, spring-cleaned and superbly decorated with lamps and chandeliers.[8] Getting sufficiently magnificent fireworks was another major concern, with pyrotechnicians from across Hindustan summoned to the Palace throughout January and February to demonstrate their skills.[9]

The rockets, squibs and Roman candles were still exploding around the great red sandstone curtain walls of the Fort as the wedding procession slowly proceeded westwards down the top of Chandni Chowk, with its trees and central canal glittering in the light of the torches. It snaked onwards, past the gardens of Begum Sumru's haveli, recently taken over by the new Delhi Bank, and through the Dariba – now in the light of ten thousand candles and lanterns haloed in dust – before veering left and heading under the latticed windows of the courtesans' *kothis* (town houses) lining the Kucha Bulaqi Begum.

On the procession passed, turning again under the moonlit white marble domes of the Jama Masjid. It then looped down the Khas Bazaar, before skirting the much smaller but beautifully gilt and illuminated domes of the Suneheri Masjid, and on through the Faiz Bazaar into Daryaganj. Here lay the city's great aristocratic palaces, such as the famous *kothi* of the Nawab of Jhajjar, which, according to Bishop Heber, the Anglican Primate of Calcutta, 'far exceed in grandeur anything seen in Moscow'. Among them lay the procession's destination, the haveli of Walidad Khan.[10]

On the way, as the Palace diary puts it, 'His Majesty's officers presented their *nazrs* [ceremonial gifts] as the procession passed their several dwellings, while HM inspected the illuminations on the road.'[11] The conspicuously wealthy streets through which the procession passed were still very much a Mughal creation. In 1852, despite 150 years of decline and political reversals, Delhi was once again the largest pre-colonial city in India – a position it had recently regained from Lucknow – and as the *Dar ul-Mulk*, the seat of the Mughal, was the epitome of an elegant Mughal metropolis: 'In this beautiful city', wrote the poet Mir, 'the streets are not mere streets, they are like the album of a painter.'[12] A similar idea was conveyed by another Delhi writer of the period, who compared the waters of the canals of Delhi's gardens to the burnished border on an illuminated manuscript page: 'its waters, like mercury, a *jadval* [margin] of pure silver running over a page of stone'.[13]

At the same time as the ruling houses of Murshidabad and Lucknow were experimenting with Western fashions and Western classical architecture, Delhi remained firmly, and proudly, a centre of Mughal style. There was no question of Zafar turning up in durbar (court) dressed as a British admiral or even a vicar of the Church of England, as had been heard of in the Nawab's court in Lucknow. Nor was there much trace of Western architectural influence in the buildings erected by the later Mughal emperors: Zafar's new gateway at his summer palace, Zafar Mahal, and his delicate floating garden pavilion in Mehtab Bagh, the scented night garden of the Red Fort, were both built in the full Mughal style of Shah Jahan.

What was true of the court was true of the city: with the single exception of the Delhi Bank – formerly the great Palladian Palace of the Begum Sumru – the buildings that the marriage procession passed showed little experimentation with Western classical pediments or square Georgian windows, though such attempts at synthesis had long been common in Lucknow, and in Jaipur. In 1852, British additions within the walls of Delhi were limited to a domed church, a classical Residency building recently converted into the Delhi College, and a strongly fortified magazine, all of which stood to the north of the Fort and out of sight of the path of the procession. Moreover, there were still relatively few Europeans in Delhi – probably well under a hundred within the walls: as the poet and literary critic Azad later put it, 'those were the days when if a European was seen in Delhi, people considered him an extraordinary sample of God's handiwork, and pointed him out to each other: "Look, there goes a European!" '[14]

Others, it was true, took a less charitable view. So prevalent was the belief among Delhiwallahs that Englishmen were the product of an illicit union between apes and the women of Sri Lanka (or alternatively between 'apes and hogs') that the city's leading theologian, Shah Abdul Aziz, had to issue a fatwa expressing his opinion that such a view had no basis in the Koran or the Hadiths, and that however oddly the *firangis* might behave, they were none the less Christians and thus People of the Book.[15] As long as wine and pork were not served, it was therefore perfectly permissible to mix with them (if one should for any strange reason wish to do so) and even, on occasion, to share their food.*

Partly as a result of this lack of regular contact with Europeans, Delhi remained a profoundly self-confident place, quite at ease with its own brilliance and the superiority of its *tahzib*, its cultured and

---

* Shah Abdul Aziz also judged that it was legal in the Sharia for Muslims to take employment from Christians. On the other hand, Shah Abdul Aziz had little faith in the intellectual abilities of the British and looked down on them for their abject failure to grasp the most elementary subtleties of Muslim theology. Every race has its own particular aptitude, he wrote. 'The Hindus have a special inclination for mathematics. The Franks have a special aptitude for industry and technology. But their minds, with few exceptions, cannot grasp the finer points of logic, theology and philosophy.' Quoted in Khalid Masud, 'The World of Shah Abdul Aziz, 1746–1824', p. 304, in Jamal Malik (ed.), *Perspectives of Mutual Encounters in South Asian History, 1760–1860*, Leiden, 2000.

polished urbanity. It was a city that had yet to suffer the collapse of
self-belief that inevitably comes with the onset of open and un-
bridled colonialism. Instead, Delhi was still in many ways a bubble
of conservative Mughal traditionalism in an already fast-changing
India. When someone in Shahjahanabad wished to praise another
citizen of the city, he would still reach for the ancient yardsticks of
medieval Islamic rhetoric, cloaked in time-worn poetic tropes: the
women of Delhi were as tall and slender as cypresses; the Delhi men
as generous as Feridun, as learned as Plato, as wise as Solomon; their
physicans were as skilled as Galen. One man who was quite clear
about the virtues of his home city and its inhabitants was the young
Sayyid Ahmad Khan:* 'The water of Delhi is sweet to the taste, the
air is excellent, and there are hardly any diseases,' he wrote.

> By God's grace the inhabitants are fair and good looking, and in their
> youth uniquely attractive. Nobody from any other city can measure
> up to them . . . In particular the men of the city are interested in
> learning and in cultivating the arts, spending their days and nights
> reading and writing. If each of their traits were recounted it would
> amount to a treatise on good conduct.[16]

Rather like modern New Yorkers, Delhiwallahs of the early nineteenth century blithely took as little interest as possible in the world
beyond their own familiar and beloved streets, and had to struggle
to imagine anyone ever wishing to live anywhere else: as the poet
Zauq put it: 'Kaun jaye Zauq par Dilli ki galian chhor kar' (How
could anyone, O Zauq, forsake Delhi and its lanes?) He was
speaking in hyperbole; but behind such writing lay a real and
palpable pride in a great and civilised city whose reputation as a
centre of learning, culture and spirituality had rarely been higher,
even as its political fortunes had waned.

If there was one thing in which the town was most confident, it
was in the beauty and elegance of its language. After all, Urdu was
born in Delhi:† it was a language the poet and literary historian

---

* The future Sir Sayyid Ahmad Khan, Muslim reformer and founder of Aligarh
Muslim University.
† Albeit from Deccani parents.

Azad described as 'an orphan found wandering in the bazaars of Shahjahanabad'.[17] According to Maulvi Abd ul-Haq, 'Anyone who has not lived in Delhi could never be considered a real connoisseur of Urdu. It is as if the steps of the Jama Masjid are a school of fine language.' There was no other city like this. In Delhi poetry 'was discussed in every house', for 'the Emperor himself was a poet and a connoisseur of poetry' and 'the language of the exalted fort was the essence of refinement'.[18]

This intoxication with the elegance of Delhi's language was common to both men and women – there was a special dialect of Delhi Urdu used only in the women's quarters – and perhaps more surprisingly to all classes. Poetry in particular was an obsession not just of the elite but also, to a remarkable extent, of the ordinary people. *The Garden of Poetry*, a collection of Urdu verse published two years before Mirza Jawan Bakht's wedding, contains no fewer than 540 poets from Delhi, who range from the Emperor and fifty members of his family to a poor water seller in Chandni Chowk, a merchant in Punjabi Katra, 'Farasu', an elderly German Jewish mercenary – one of a surprising number of Europeans in Delhi who had taken to Mughal culture – a young wrestler, a courtesan and a barber.[19] At least fifty-three of these Urdu poets have clearly Hindu names.

So although Walidad Khan had laid on the best dancers in Delhi for the marriage ceremony that night, what was remembered longest and discussed most eagerly was not so much the festivities or the feasting or the fireworks so much as the marriage odes recited by the poet laureate, Zauq, and his rival Mirza Nausha, now more widely known by his pen-name, Ghalib.

To the eye of an outsider such as the newly appointed Commandant of the Palace Guards, Captain Douglas, who accompanied the procession as far as the haveli of Walidad Khan, the wedding seemed both visually stunning and a happy and harmonious occasion. Indeed, according to the account in the Palace diary the only untoward incident in the whole ceremony was on the return journey to the Fort at 10 a.m. the following morning.

Walidad Khan had just presented his guests with the bride's marriage portion – '80 trays of clothing, 2 trays of jewellery, a golden bedstead and canopy, vessels of silver, an elephant and horses with embroidered trappings and two riding camels' – and Zafar had just set out back to the Palace with the bride and bridegroom, when 'a baker threw two or three biscuits at the elephant on which Mirza Jawan Bakht was riding'. The elephant shied and the offending baker was taken off to the city jail.[20]

Nevertheless, the appearance of confidence and harmony was largely deceptive. As in so many family weddings, for all the outward show of prosperity and family unity, severe tensions lurked just beneath the surface. The very emphasis that Zafar and Zinat put on the procession was in itself significant. Certainly, the Mughals had always regarded processions as important public statements of their authority. Two hundred years earlier, the French traveller and writer François Bernier had described the magnificent ostentation of the procession which took Raushanara Begum, the daughter of Shah Jahan, on her summer outing to Kashmir in the late 1640s: 'You can conceive of nothing more imposing or grand,' he wrote in his memoirs, 'and if I had not regarded this display of magnificence with a sort of philosophical indifference, I should have been apt to be carried away by such flights of imagination as inspire most Indian poets.'[21] Since then, however, the Mughals had long since lost control of Kashmir; indeed, it had been well over a century since the Mughals had been able to process anywhere outside the environs of Delhi. As the famous doggerel went,

> The Kingdom of Shah Alam,
> Runs from Delhi to Palam.*

In the Palace itself, the greatest treasures of the Red Fort had already been removed by the Persian invader Nadir Shah in 1739. Half a

---

* Palam being less than 10 miles from the Red Fort, near the modern international airport. There is some dispute over which of the two Mughal Shah Alams the verse refers to, or indeed whether it actually refers to a pre-Mughal Shah Alam of the Sayyid dynasty.

century later, in the summer of 1788, when Zafar was a boy of thirteen, the marauder Ghulam Qadir had taken the city, personally blinded Zafar's grandfather, Shah Alam II, and made Zafar's father, the future Emperor Akbar Shah II, dance for his pleasure; he then threw vinegar in the wounds by carting off Shah Alam's fabulous library, most of which he then sold to the Nawab of Avadh, much to the Emperor's fury.[22] A blind emperor was left ruling from a ruined palace: 'only a chessboard king', as Azad put it.[23]

After the death of Shah Alam II, the authority of the Mughals had contracted further, so that Zafar did not control even as far as Palam; instead his real authority existed only within the walls of the Red Fort, as if he were an Indian pope within his own Vatican City. Even there it was in some ways circumscribed. For the British Resident,* Sir Thomas Metcalfe, kept a friendly but none the less firm eye on Zafar's daily life and frequently forbade him from exercising rights that the Emperor regarded as sacrosanct.

No nobleman from outside Delhi, for example, could enter the Red Fort without Metcalfe's permission.[24] To enforce his right to rent from his own lands, Zafar had to make an application to the British courts.[25] He could not present gems from the crown jewels even to his own family members without first informing the Resident, and was occasionally, humiliatingly, made to ask for the return of unauthorised gifts if the agent came to hear about them.[26] Zafar could not gift *khilats* (robes of honour, symbols of overlordship) on noblemen from outside the Delhi territories without Metcalfe's say-so: when on the day after Jawan Bakht's wedding Raja Gulab Singh of Kollesur paid a visit to the court, presenting a *nazr* (or offering of fealty) of 'a horse and 7 gold mohurs', in return for which Zafar gave him a *khilat*, Metcalfe promptly made the Raja return it: in the eyes of the Resident, the Raja was a British subject, and had no business publicly offering his fealty to a foreign ruler.[27]

How far Zafar felt the humiliation of this is evident in his verse, into which he learned to sublimate his feelings of profound

---

* The Resident initially acted as the Governor General's ambassador to the Mughal court, but as British power grew, and that of the Mughals diminished, he came more and more to assume the role of the Governor of Delhi and its surroundings.

frustration and imprisonment. His ghazals are full of the imagery of the caged bird, of the bulbul longing for the garden visible through the bars of his prison:

> I want to shatter the bars of my cage,
> With the flutterings of my wings.

> But like a caged bird in a painting,
> There is no possibility of being free.

> Morning breeze, tell the garden
> That Spring and Autumn for me are alike.

> How should I know,
> When one comes, and the other goes?[28]

Elsewhere, he expressed the same thought more explicitly:

> Whoever enters this gloomy palace,
> Remains a prisoner for life in European captivity.[29]

The degree of loss of control experienced by Zafar was something quite new. When the British first came to Delhi in 1803, defeating the Maratha confederacy, who were then the masters of much of Hindustan, they posed as Shah Alam's protectors and saviours:* 'Notwithstanding His Majesty's total deprivation of real power, dominion, and authority,' wrote the Governor General, Lord Wellesley, 'almost every state and every class of people in India continue to acknowledge his nominal sovereignty. The current coin of every established power is struck in the name of Shah Alam . . .'[30]

He did not add, though it was true, that this included the rupees of the East India Company itself; moreover, the Company's seal also directly acknowledged its position as the Mughal's legal vassal, and was inscribed to that end: 'Fidvi Shah Alam' (Shah Alam's devoted dependant). Wellesley wrote that he 'recoiled from the

---

* As had the Marathas before them, and indeed the Rohillas too.

thought of it being suspected in England' that he wished to 'place the East India Company, substantially or vicariously, on the throne of the Moghuls', and Lord Lake was instructed to offer his 'loyalty . . . and every demonstration of reverence, respect and attention' to the aged monarch. The new Resident also received strict instructions that he too was to use all the forms 'considered to be due to the Emperors of Hindustan'.[31]

The honeymoon did not last long. The man who began the erosion of the Mughal's status was Thomas Metcalfe's cold elder brother, Sir Charles, who preceded him as Resident. 'I have renounced my former allegiance to the house of Timur,' he announced in a letter of 1832, before persuading the Governor General unilaterally to declare an end to the old tradition of giving the Emperor the ceremonial gift or *nazr* – which represented a public confirmation of the status of the British as liegemen of the Emperor. Charles Metcalfe accepted that the British were technically still the feudal inferior of the Mughal, but was determined that given the reality of British power and Mughal weakness, this must no longer be acknowledged in public: 'We have on the whole behaved generously to the King from the first,' he wrote to the Governor General, 'and I never found him unreasonable or assuming.' But, he continued, if the Emperor refused to accept the new realities, 'I think it is our best policy in future to let him sink into insignificance instead of upholding his dignity as we have done.'[32]

The following year the Emperor's name was removed from East India Company rupees, and when Lord Auckland visited Delhi he did not even bother to pay a courtesy call on the Emperor Akbar Shah II. By 1850 his successor, Lord Dalhousie, was banning any British subject from accepting titles from the Mughal: 'covering the English with the Mughal ceremonial mantle' was dismissed as 'a solemn farce'.[33] It was a very different approach from that promised by Lord Wellesley, and amounted to an attempt by the British to try to demote their feudal lord to the status of a subject nobleman. Henceforth, more and more of the Mughal's rights and privileges were stripped away, until by 1852 Zafar was left with nothing but his palace and the lingering reputation of his dynasty.

But despite everything Zafar was still allowed his processions. Deprived of most other ways of expressing his increasingly in-

tangible sovereignty, he took full advantage of the right, and the
miniatures of Zafar's reign contain an almost touching number of
scrolls showing processions: trips to Sufi shrines, the annual exodus
to the summer palace in Mehrauli, journeys to celebrate the festival
of 'Id at the old Id Gah, and expeditions to watch the Flower-
sellers' Fair, the *Phulwalon ki Sair*, at the ancient Jog Maya temple
and the Sufi shrine of Qutb Sahib.

Seen from this point of view, the spectacular marriage procession
of Jawan Bakht was less a symbol of strength than the last desperate
fling of a terminally ill dynasty.

Understandably, the surviving official accounts of the wedding do
not dwell on the various squabbles that we know erupted in the
course of the night.

The least surprising of the spats that took place was the one
between the two great court poets, Ghalib and Zauq. Almost
everything about the two men's styles and backgrounds contained
possibilities for disagreement. Zauq wrote verse of startling simplicity; while Ghalib's verse was notoriously complex.* Zauq was
from a humble background – his father had been a common foot-
soldier; but it was he, not the self-consciously aristocratic Ghalib,
who had been made Zafar's *ustad*† in poetry, and so Poet Laureate
of Mughal Delhi.

---

* So much so that the poet Abd ur-Rahman Hudhud wrote a celebrated parody:

> The circle of the axis of heaven,
> Is not at the lip of the water
> The fingernail of the arc of the rainbow
> Does not resemble a plectrum.

Another poet agreed:

> *Kalaam-i Mir samjhey aur zubaan-i Mirja samjhey*
> *Magar inka kaha yeh khud hi samjhein ya khuda samjhey.*

> We follow the poetry of Mir, and the language of Mirja,
> But of him [Ghalib] – only he can follow his verses, or maybe God alone can.

† An *ustad* means the master of an art. In this context an *ustad* was a recognised
master-poet who accepted his own *shagirds* or pupils.

Moreover, while Zauq led a quiet and simple life, composing verse from dusk until dawn, rarely straying from the tiny courtyard where he worked, Ghalib was very proud of his reputation as a rake. Only five years before the wedding, Ghalib had been imprisoned for gambling, and subsequently wore the affair – deeply embarrassing at the time – as a badge of honour. When someone once praised the poetry of the pious Sheikh Sahbai in his presence, Ghalib shot back, 'How can Sahbai be a poet? He has never tasted wine, nor has he ever gambled; he has not been beaten with slippers by lovers, nor has he once seen the inside of a jail.'[34] Elsewhere in his letters he makes great play of his reputation as a ladies' man. To one close friend whose mistress had just died and who had written to Ghalib from the depths of misery, he replied:

> Mirza Sahib, I don't like the way you are going on. In the days of my lusty youth a man of perfect wisdom counselled me, 'Abstinence I do not approve: dissoluteness I do not forbid. Eat drink and be merry. But remember that the wise fly settles on the sugar and not on the honey.' Well I have always acted on his counsel. You cannot mourn another's death, unless you live yourself . . . Give thanks to God for your freedom, and do not grieve . . . When I think of paradise and consider how if my sins are forgiven me and I am installed in a palace with a houri, to live forever in the worthy woman's company, I am filled with dismay and fear . . . How wearisome to find her there – a greater burden than a man could bear. The same old palace, all of emerald made; the same fruit tree to cast its shade. And – God preserve her from all harm – the same old houri on my arm. Come to your sense, brother, and take another.
>
> > Take a new woman each returning spring
> > For last year's almanac is a useless thing.[35]

The squabble at the wedding was over a single verse in Ghalib's *sehra* (or wedding oration[36]) where he appeared – characteristically – to suggest that no one in the gathering could write a couplet as well as he. Most critics today would argue that it was a well-justified boast, but at the time it was taken to be a slight not just to Zauq, but also to Zafar, who was of course a considerable poet himself, and who had expressed his belief in the superiority of Zauq's talents when he appointed the latter to correct his own verses. Zafar quickly made his views apparent, presenting to Zauq a *khilat* and the honorary position of Superintendent of the Palace Gardens, while ostentatiously neglecting to provide an honour of any sort for Ghalib.[37] Zafar also encouraged Zauq to reply to Ghalib's unprovoked sally. The fine *sehra* that the Poet Laureate came up with ended with a couplet tossing the challenge back to Ghalib:

> The person who claims poetic skills,
> Recite this to him and say,
> 'Look – this is how a poet
> Weaves a real wedding veil.'

According to the account of Azad, who was admittedly a pupil and adoring partisan of Zauq's: 'Singers were in attendance and the verse was at once given to them. By evening it had spread through every street and lane of the city, and the next day it was published in the newspapers.'[38]

This particular round of the feud between the two poets went to Zauq.

One of the principal trials in Zafar's old age appears to have been the strains that existed between his different queens and concubines, and the degree to which they all seem to have been perennially conducting intrigues with younger men. These were serious tensions which formed a strong undercurrent to the wedding celebrations of 1852.

Fifteen years earlier, at the time of Zafar's accession to the throne in 1837, his chief wife had been Taj Mahal Begum, the beautiful daughter of a humble court musician, and it was she who presided over the celebrations that accompanied his accession ceremonies.[39] It was not, however, a position she was able to retain for long. Only three years later the relatively aristocratic nineteen-year-old Zinat Mahal was presented to Zafar; he was sixty-four. Within a few months she had married him, effectively toppling Taj from her position as head of the harem.

Thereafter Zinat Mahal managed to retain her position as Zafar's favourite wife until his death. This did not, however, stop the septuagenarian Zafar from contracting four further marriages in the years that followed, all to wives of relatively low status, as well as taking several new concubines: in 1853 there seem to have been at least five such women attached to the imperial bedchamber, judging by the fact that in July that year Zafar had five sets of silver feet made for their beds.[40] Zafar's harem seems in general to have been a remarkably active place, even into the Emperor's early eighties. Zafar fathered in all no fewer than sixteen sons and thirty-one daughters, his last son, Mirza Shah Abbas, being conceived as late as 1845 when the emperor was fully seventy years old.

There is no record of Zinat Mahal taking against any of the concubines – indeed, when one of them became pregnant by Tanras Khan, the court musician, Zinat intervened to spare her severe punishment.[41] But she seems to have remained permanently in a state of war with Taj Begum, and at one point even managed to have the latter imprisoned on suspicion of having an affair with one of Zafar's nephews, Mirza Kamran.[42] Taj denied the charge, but her conduct was widely believed to have been suspicious, and judging from the Palace diary she certainly seems to have spent more time at her house in the city, and to have come and gone from it at night by the back door more frequently than might have been wise for a queen concerned about maintaining proprieties.[43]

Zafar's harem was in general notoriously lax as far as discipline and security were concerned: as well as Piya Bai, who became pregnant by Tanras Khan, several other of his concubines were publicly accused of 'improprieties' at various times, and at least one other illicit pregnancy occurred: two months before Jawan Bakht's wedding, one of the sepoys stationed at the water gate on the Yamuna river frontage just below the Palace took advantage of his station to conduct an affair with another unnamed slave girl who may well have been one of Zafar's concubines, and was sentenced to 'a whipping and confinement with irons' for his pains. The girl got off relatively lightly: she was merely 'sentenced to grind grain'.[44]

Only three days after the discovery of the pregnant slave girl, other strangers were found to be defying the guard eunuchs. According to the diary entry for 1 February 1852, Zafar immediately sent for the chamberlain, telling him 'he was much displeased at the arrangements of the *zenana* [harem]; that the *chaukidars* [guards] and *chobdars* [mace-bearers] were never present and that strangers were allowed access to the *zanan-khana*; that it was represented to him by Chand Bai Concubine that Nabi Bakhsh had forcibly entered the house of Sultan Bai, although the eunuch tried to prevent his doing so . . .'. The general impression is one of complete chaos, of a once-great establishment unable to maintain basic proprieties in reduced circumstances; it is certainly a very different picture to the closely guarded and impenetrable Mughal harem of orientalist myth. Whatever his other qualities, running the domestic arrangements of the Red Fort was clearly not one of Zafar's talents, at least in his old age.

Life for the senior princes could be extremely comfortable and Zafar's own children had a fair degree of freedom to live their own lives and follow their own interests and amusements, whether these lay in scholarly and artistic directions, or in hunting, pigeon flying and quail fighting. But the options open for the junior *salatin*, or Palace-born princes and princesses, could be extremely limited. Besides the senior princes, there were over two thousand poor princes and princesses – grandchildren and great-grandchildren and great-great-grandchildren of previous monarchs – most of whom lived a life of poverty in their own walled quarter of the Palace, to the south-west of the area occupied by Zafar and his immediate family.[45] This was the darker side of the life of the Red Fort, and its greatest embarrassment; for this reason many of the *salatin* were never allowed out of the gates of the Fort, least of all on so ostentatious an occasion as the very public festivities in Daryaganj. According to one British observer:

The *salatin* quarter consists of an immense high wall so that nothing can overlook it. Within this are numerous mat huts in which these wretched objects live. When the gates were opened there was a rush

of miserable, half naked, starved beings who surrounded us. Some
men apparently nearly 80 years old were almost in a state of nature.[46]

Zafar, absorbed in his other worries, seems to have had fairly
limited patience with the sufferings and misdemeanours of his
more distant relatives. They tended to be responsible – so he
believed – for most of the thefts and disturbances that took place
within the Palace: on one occasion, when a thief was spotted darting
along the walls of the Red Fort, Zafar remarked that 'it must have
been one of the *salatin*'; on another Zafar was quoted as remarking
that 'the *salatin* were in the habit of stealing from one another' and
'of drinking and creating a disturbance'.[47] When Zafar was informed that one of the junior *salatin*, 'Mirza Mahmoud Sultan had
become insane and was in the habit of wandering around the Palace
at night', he did not hesitate to order that he should be 'confined
with chains upon his feet'.[48]

Occasionally, however, the *salatin* broke their silence and created
a more serious embarrassment for Zafar. Twice they had put
together mass petitions addressed to the British Resident claiming
that their basic rights were being abused. Ten years into Zafar's
reign, in 1847, one hundred *salatin* signed a petition complaining to
Metcalfe of oppression:

> Our conditions have approached to the extreme of humiliation and
> poverty owing to the character and conduct of the King of Delhi
> who is entirely subject to the control of his servants and bad advisers
> . . . the subordinate members are exposed to every species of
> degradation and insult by [the chief eunuch] Mahbub Ali Khan
> and the favourites of the king.'[49]

A second revolt of the *salatin* took place a year later and was timed
to coincide with the visit to Delhi of the British Lieutenant
Governor of the North West Provinces. This time a large piece
of parchment containing the seals of more than 150 *salatin* was
presented to the governor asking for protection, and claiming that
Zafar was trying to dissuade the heir apparent from meeting
Metcalfe to discuss their grievances.[50]

This second petition touched on the most sensitive of the tensions within Zafar's household. For of all the restrictions that the British had imposed on Zafar, the one that rankled most of all was the withdrawal of his right to choose his own successor. Instead the British had imposed on the Mughals the alien European notion of primogeniture.

Zafar's attempts to appoint his own choice as heir apparent first surfaced when his oldest living son, Mirza Dara Bakht, died from a fever in 1849. The British assumed that Zafar's next son, the talented and popular poet, calligrapher and historian Mirza Fakhru, should become the heir apparent in Dara's place; but Zafar, pressed by the increasingly domineering Zinat Mahal, tried instead to insist on the succession of Mirza Jawan Bakht, then barely a boy of eight years old, and the fifteenth of Zafar's many sons.[51] As Zafar explained it in a letter written to the Lieutenant Governor:

> among my other sons, no one appears to me so fit for the office as Mirza Jawan Bakht, who I am glad to say is endowed with natural good propensities. He has not as yet attained the age of maturity and has not been allowed to mix with people who are not upright. Besides, he is from my lawful wife, who is of very high family, Nawab Zinat Mahal . . . Under these circumstances therefore, he is most fit for the high office of Heir Apparent and he always remains under my Eyes, and devotes all his time to learning in different branches of education. I feel satisfied that he will never do anything contrary to my wishes.[52]

Zafar's objection to primogeniture was somewhat ironic, given that it was solely thanks to the British insisting on this principle that Zafar had himself come to the throne, much against the will of his father, Akbar Shah II. The latter had strived instead for the succession of Zafar's raffish younger brother Mirza Jahangir, and in the process developed so strong an objection to his eldest son that on 21 March 1807 he wrote a letter to the then British Resident, Archibald Seton, which closely prefigured that written by Bahadur Shah about Mirza Fakhru forty-two years later: 'My eldest son [i.e. Zafar]', wrote Akbar Shah, 'is wholly devoid of every qualification for occupying the throne.' He also accused him, without giving any evidence or details, 'of an offence against nature too delicate to admit explanation from us'.*

Zafar now acted just as his father had done to him, and continued to push for Mirza Jawan Bakht. Meanwhile his passed-over eldest son, Mirza Fakhru, began learning English, and along with his ambitiously Anglophile father-in-law, Mirza Ilahe Bakhsh, began to ingratiate himself with both Metcalfe and the senior officers of the British military stationed in Delhi. It was in the end a successful campaign. After much negotiation, Mirza Fakhru met with Met-calfe and the Lieutenant Governor in January 1852, three months before the wedding, and signed a secret understanding: the British agreed formally to recognise him as heir apparent, contrary to his father's wish; but there was a quid pro quo. After more than two centuries, Mirza Fakhru would move the court from the Red Fort to the distant suburb of Mehrauli, handing over the old fort of Shah Jahan to the British, who would use it as a barrack and a powder magazine; and when he became Emperor, Fakhru would drop the Mughal's long-standing claim of superior status to the British

---

* Seton, incidentally, thought the charge very unlikely, writing to Calcutta that the young Abu Zafar was a 'very respectable character' but not being his favourite was 'much neglected' by the King. Instead Akbar Shah lavished his attention on Mirza Jahangir, of whom, said Seton, he was 'devotedly fond'. Mirza Jahangir, irritated by Seton's support of Zafar, eventually took a potshot at the Resident from the battlements of the Red Fort, and succeeded in knocking off his hat. He was exiled to Allahabad in 1809, where he eventually died 'from an excess of Hoffman's Cherry Brandy' in 1821, aged only thirty-one. Akbar Shah's dismissive treatment of Zafar in his youth no doubt added to Zafar's perennial tendency towards paranoia and insecurity. At one point, for example, when his father sent Rajah Ram Mohan Roy to England as his envoy to try to increase his stipend, and to protest at the way the Company was consistently whittling down his status, Zafar assumed that the mission was aimed at disinheriting him and wrote angrily to both the Governor General and to Roy. The latter replied, calmly refuting Zafar's accusations, and adding a little acidly 'that those who do not comprehend their own good or evil cannot compre-hend the good or evil of others'. There are good accounts of Zafar's troubled youth and accession to the throne in Percival Spear's *Twilight of the Moghals* (Cambridge, 1951), p. 41ff; also in the first chapter of Aslam's Parvez's Urdu biography of Zafar. See also the far less comprehensive English language volume by S. M. Burke and Salim al-Din Quraishi, *Bahadur Shah: Last Mogul Emperor of India*, Lahore, 1995, pp. 43–50.

Governor General, and would henceforth meet him on terms of equality.[53]

When Zafar came to hear rumours about the terms of the agreement, he reacted with fury, believing that his son had bargained away two of the most sacred cornerstones of Mughal prestige: 'A tawny coloured dog may be mistaken for a jackal's brother,' he spat angrily – if somewhat enigmatically – to his attendants.[54] Mirza Fakhru was quickly subject to a boycott at court: 'anyone professing friendship with Mirza Fakhru was his declared enemy', announced Zafar – and Mirza Fakhru's various positions at court, his allowances, houses and estates, were all one by one given to his younger brothers, notably his ambitious and hard-working younger brother Mirza Mughal, the leading Anglophobe among the princes.[55]

As it gradually became clear, however, that nothing was going to change the British position, Zafar sank increasingly into impotent gloom, as he often did when frustrated. He announced that if his wishes were to be so blatantly ignored, he desired to abdicate and go on the haj: 'It is plain . . . that to this House nothing remains now but the bare name,' he wrote to Metcalfe.

> It is to be regretted that my wishes do not meet the sanction of government & I feel greatly distressed on this account. I therefore feel anxious that I should no more prove troublesome to the government and go on a pilgrimage to Mecca & pass the few remaining years of my life there. Because I see that I have lost this world, [but] I may not lose the other also, and I find myself unable in my old age to suffer grief.[56]

Metcalfe was at a loss how to react, and blamed what he saw as the increasingly baleful influence of Zinat Mahal: 'Hitherto when alone with HM I have always found him most plausible and rational,' Metcalfe wrote to Calcutta. 'But he has of late surrendered himself so completely to the guidance of the favourite wife, the Nawab Zinat Mahal, and her confidential advisor, the Chief Eunuch Mahbub Ali Khan, [that he] is induced to commit many unreasonable acts.'[57]

By the middle of March 1852, however, Zafar seems to have cheered up slightly, and to have pinned his hopes on one last attempt to change the Resident's mind. He abandoned his plan to go on the haj and threw himself into making arrangements for the wedding of Jawan Bakht. He seems to have believed – or to have been persuaded by Zinat Mahal – that if the wedding were made sufficiently magnificent, such would be the prestige of the bride-groom that the British might yet be forced to take Zafar's choice of successor seriously. Certainly contemporaries assumed that the magnificent wedding was Zafar's last-ditch attempt at persuading Metcalfe to recognise Jawan Bakht, and it did result in the *Delhi Gazette* openly referring to the young groom as the heir apparent.[58]

Yet in the end, the whole ruinously expensive strategy – and indeed the whole project of the marriage – was a catastrophic failure. For Metcalfe, well aware of what was going on, did not make an appearance at any point during the twelve days of the wedding celebrations, thus comprehensively snubbing the entire affair.

Sir Thomas Theophilus Metcalfe had been in Delhi nearly forty years by 1852, and knew well both the city and its ruler.

He was a slight, delicate, bookish figure with an alert, intelligent expression, a bald pate and bright blue eyes. His daughter Emily thought 'he could not be said to be handsome' but believed he did have the redeeming feature 'of beautifully small hands and feet'. Certainly he was a notably fastidious man, with feelings so refined that he could not bear to see women eat cheese. Moreover he believed that if the fair sex insisted on eating oranges or mangoes, they should at least do so in the privacy of their own bathrooms.

He would never have dreamt of dressing, as some of his pre-decessors had, in full Mughal *pagri* and *jama*. Still less would he have dreamt of imitating the example of the first British Resident at the Mughal court, Sir David Ochterlony, who every evening was said to take all thirteen of his Indian wives on a promenade around the walls of the Red Fort, each on the back of her own elephant.[59]

Instead, a widower, he lived alone, and arranged that his London tailors, Pulford of St James's, should regularly send out to Delhi a chest of sober but fashionable English clothes.

His one concession to Indian taste was to smoke a silver hookah. This he did every day after breakfast, for exactly thirty minutes. If ever one of his servants failed to perform his appointed duty, Metcalfe would call for a pair of white kid gloves. These he would pick up from their silver salver and slowly pull on over his delicate white fingers. Then, 'with solemn dignity', having lectured the servant on his failing, he 'proceeded to pinch gently but firmly the ear of the culprit, and then let him go – a reprimand that was entirely efficacious'.[60]

Sir Thomas had enjoyed an exceptionally happy marriage, but his wife Felicity died quite suddenly of an unexplained fever in September 1842, at the age of only thirty-four. In the decade that followed, with his six children all in boarding school in England, Metcalfe withdrew in his grief into himself. He became so set in his ways that by the time his children began returning to India in the early 1850s, they found that their father had became a stickler for propriety and punctuality, and greatly resented any disruption to his routine. By the early 1850s this routine was so firmly established as to be something almost set down in stone: 'He always got up at five o'clock every morning,' wrote his daughter Emily,

and having put on his dressing gown he would go to the verandah and have his *chota haziri* [small breakfast]. He used to take a walk up and down the verandah, and his different servants came at that time to receive their orders for the day. At seven o'clock he would go down to the swimming bath which he built just below the corner of the verandah, and then having dressed and had prayers in the oratory, he was ready for breakfast at eight o'clock.

Everything was ordered with the greatest punctuality, and all the household arrangements moved as if by clock work. After he had his breakfast, his hookah was brought in and placed beside his chair . . . When he had finished his smoke he went to his study to write letters until the carriage was announced. This always appeared at exactly ten o'clock under the portico, and he passed through a row of servants on his way to it – one holding his hat, another his gloves, another his handkerchief, another his gold headed cane, and another his despatch box. These having been put into the carriage, his Jamadar mounted beside the coachman and drove away, with two syces standing up behind.[61]

With no family to soften him, and a dislike for the noise of society, Metcalfe threw himself into his work, in particular negotiating a succession settlement that would allow the Company to expel the royal family from the Red Fort on the death of Zafar. He had some affection, but little real respect, for the man he was determined should be the last of the Timurid line. Although to Zafar's face he was always extremely polite, and would write to the Emperor as 'my Royal Illustrious friend . . . I beg to express the high consideration I entertain for your Majesty and subscribe myself as your Majesty's sincere friend', in private he was sometimes less generous.[62] '[Zafar] is mild and talented,' he wrote to Emily, 'but lamentably weak and vacillating and impressed with very erroneous notions of his own importance, productive of great mortification to himself and occasionally of much trouble to the local authorities.'[63]

Yet Metcalfe's attitude to Delhi and its Emperor was much more ambiguous than this might suggest. He was very proud of the resounding Persian titles given to him by Zafar, and commissioned various calligraphed versions of them which he later had bound into an album.* Moreover, almost against his better instincts, he slowly came to be fascinated with the fabulous city he presided over: 'There is something in this place to which the mind cannot be indifferent,' he wrote.

The ruins of grandeur that extend for miles on every side fill it with
serious reflection. The palaces crumbling into dust . . . the myriads

* His full titles, as he occasionally reminded his correspondents, were 'Sahib-i-Vala, Manaqube Ali Mansib, Farzand Arjmand, Paivand-e-Sultani, Muassam ud-Daula, Amin ul-Mulk Sir Thomas Metcalfe, Baron Bahadur, Firoze Jung, Sahib Kalan Bahadur of Shahjahanabad'.

of vast mausoleums, every one of which was intended to convey to futurity the deathless fame of its cold inhabitant, and all of which are now passed by, unknown and unnoticed . . . These things cannot be looked at with indifference . . .[64]

In due course, Metcalfe systematically visited all the different antiquities of the city and founded a Delhi Archaeological Society dedicated to uncovering the history behind Delhi's monuments, of which the young Sayyid Ahmad Khan was an enthusiastic and energetic member. The society had its own journal, most of whose articles Metcalfe personally commissioned from the intelligentsia of the city, and duly translated himself from Urdu into English.

Unlike most British officials – who regarded their stay in India as a temporary affair, and who waited eagerly for the moment when they could sail home with their accumulated savings to set themselves up back in Britain – Metcalfe took the decision to bring all his family possessions to India, and in Delhi built for himself not one but two large country houses, in addition to his new Residency office, known as Ludlow Castle,* which stood outside the city walls in the recently built British Civil Lines to the north of the city.

In his letters, Metcalfe sometimes envisaged himself as an English country squire. In reality, however, he seems to have had slightly more exalted ambitions, and to some extent he set up his establishment as a rival court to that of Zafar, with the Metcalfes as a parallel dynasty to the Mughals. Metcalfe House, also known as Jahan Numa ('World Showing'), his expansive and palatial Palladian bungalow on the banks of the Yamuna to the north of the city, was an indirect challenge to the Red Fort, a little downstream of it. If the Red Fort had its marble domes, its scented night gardens with their bubbling irrigation runnels and floating pavilions, then Metcalfe House had its flower beds with its English blooms, its marble columns and its swimming pool, its cypress avenues and orange groves, a library of 25,000 books, fine oil paintings and rosewood Georgian furniture. It also had a Napoleon Gallery filled with memorabilia of Bonaparte, including the Emperor's own diamond ring and a bust by Canova.

* So punningly named not for its similarity to the castle in Shropshire but after its original builder, Dr Ludlow, and its castellated Gothic battlements.

To the south of Delhi, Metcalfe established a second country house, Dilkusha (or Delighter of the Heart), in a converted octagonal Mughal tomb near Mehrauli, which became Metcalfe's answer to the nearby Mughal summer palace of Zafar Mahal; a Mughal garden – a four-part *char-bagh* – was laid out in front of the tomb house just to emphasise the parallel. Both Metcalfe's houses were surrounded by extensive estates, and were entered through colossal Georgian gateways; both were decorated with follies, and even, in the case of Dilkusha, a lighthouse, a small fort, a pigeon house, a boating pond and an ornamental ziggurat.

Like Zafar, Metcalfe was a generous patron of Delhi's artists. Between 1842 and 1844 he commissioned a whole series of images of the monuments, ruins, palaces and shrines of the city from a Delhi artist named Mazhar Ali Khan, who was also a favourite artist of Zafar's. Metcalfe had the images bound into an album, entitled *The Dehlie Book*, and wrote a long descriptive text as an accompaniment. This in due course he sent to his daughter Emily as she made her way home from an English schooling to join her father in Delhi. He also commissioned a remarkable panoramic scroll of the city, some 20 feet long. Together the two commissions remain the most complete visual picture of pre-Mutiny Delhi now extant.[65]

The commissions are also great works of art in their own right. Mazhar Ali Khan had clearly been trained in the old Mughal techniques, but working for Metcalfe, using English watercolours on English paper, and taking English architectural elevations as his models, an extraordinary fusion of English and Indian artistic impulses took place, a fusion that resulted in a new type of painting, known today as the Company School.

The brilliance and simplicity of the colours, the meticulous, almost hypnotic attention to detail, the gem-like highlights, the way the picture seems to *glow*, all these point unmistakably towards Mazhar Ali Khan's Mughal training: no English artist would have thought of using the astonishing palette of colours that still stands out like a small aesthetic firework display; the tentative washes of a memsahib's watercolour are a world away from this work. Yet the almost fanatical Mughal attention to fine detail is fused with a scientific European rationalism to produce an architectural painting that both observes and feels the qualities of a building. Thus while the picture of the tomb of Ghazi ud-Din in the Delhi College complex minutely reproduces the proportions and detail of the Mughal domes of the mosque behind it, the artist has also understood the ideal of lightness and delicacy that the architect was aiming at, and has produced an image of the building as fine and as fragile as a lace ruff: the tomb is so delicate and ethereal it could almost be blown away with a breath.

But it was not just as a patron of the arts that Sir Thomas had much in common with Zafar: in many other ways too their situations shared unexpected parallels. Politically, they both had a faint sense that they had somehow been passed over: however grandly Metcalfe might swagger through the *muhallas* of Delhi, the truth was that many of Metcalfe's juniors had long since shot past him in the Company's service: John Lawrence, for example, once one of Metcalfe's assistants, had now risen several ranks above him and was Governor of the newly conquered Punjab. More galling still, Metcalfe's elder brother Charles, who had preceded him as Resident in Delhi, had now acquired a peerage and been promoted from acting Governor General in Calcutta to actual Governor General in Canada. Thomas Metcalfe, meanwhile, remained firmly ensconced in his old position in Delhi. It was a good but hardly very senior position in the Company's civil service, despite Delhi's long history as the capital of Hindustan and the centre of the Mughal Empire. This was especially so after 1833 when the new Presidency of the North West Provinces was created, administered by a lieutenant governor based in Agra, so further reducing the authority of the Delhi Resident.*

Moreover, the family situations of Metcalfe and Zafar were in many ways surprisingly similar. If Zafar increasingly found himself at odds with his eldest son and heir, then so too did Metcalfe. For

* At the same time, the title of the Resident changed to Agent, then later to Commissioner. For ease of comprehension, however, I will use the title Resident throughout. The Resident initially acted as the Governor General's ambassador to the Mughal court; by the 1850s, however, the Agent reported to his immediate superior, the Governor of the North West Provinces in Agra, who dealt with the day-to-day matters of British–Mughal relations, and the Agent discussed only more serious matters – such as the succession – directly with the Governor General in Calcutta.

Metcalfe's son Theophilus (or Theo as he was known), a junior magistrate in the Company's service, newly returned to India after ten years' absence at school in England, was a very different figure from his father. Where Sir Thomas was reserved and particular, Theo was sociable and expansive and also, when he wished to be, extremely charming. If the father liked solitude and disliked the business of entertaining, Theo was noisy and convivial, and enjoyed parties, riding, horses and dogs. If his father was resolutely self-disciplined and law-abiding, Theo had a tendency to cut corners, and get into what his father described as 'scrapes'.[66] It was hardly surprising, therefore, that the two had a somewhat strained relationship.

For this reason, Sir Thomas was more than a little alarmed when in April 1851, exactly a year before Jawan Bakht's marriage, he received a letter from Theo announcing that he had just been posted to Delhi. 'I tell you candidly that I fear our reunion,' Sir Thomas wrote to his middle daughter Georgina, known in the family as GG.

> At my time of life, I do not wish to be put out of my way and play second fiddle in my own house. Your brother I know from experience: all must give way to his wishes. My temper is hasty too, and I keep it always under control. But I feel the result [of this]. [Moreover] I shall have to set him up with buggy and horses. I was snubbed the other day by a friend of mine who said – 'if you do not insist on his living within his salary, he is quite right to draw upon you'. This is a troubling letter [to write] – but my bile will evaporate . . .[67]

In the postscript, however, Metcalfe's tone grew more apprehensive still:

> After I wrote to you yesterday, dearest GG, the *Delhi Gazette* came in and in a paragraph of the 'Calcutta correspondents'' letter, is one allusion to an illegal act of a civil nature which, I fear has reference to your brother. If so, he has not only angered Lord Dalhousie and will be removed, but also in all probability will be prosecuted in the Supreme Court, and is likely to be [fined] cash in damages of some 10

or 12,000 rupees, which I of course, shall have to pay rather than he have to go to jail. This is a precious mess and if all I fear takes place, I cannot afford to bring out your sister [from England]. How frightening it is that Theo could not act with discretion and judgement. His extravagance is bad enough.[68]

Sir Thomas had always found his relationships with his daughters easier than those with his sons, and his correspondence with both Emily and GG was invariably warm and intimate. In 1852, however, at the same time as Zafar was struggling with the affairs taking place in his harem, Sir Thomas was busy trying to forbid the passionate love affair of the twenty-one-year-old Georgina.

Much to Metcalfe's horror, Georgina had fallen for a young Scottish army captain named Sir Edward Campbell. Campbell was a protégé and former ADC to his fellow Scot, Sir Charles Napier, the former Commander-in-Chief of the British Army in India, with whom Sir Thomas had had a serious disagreement; to make matters worse, despite his title, Campbell was more or less penniless. He and Georgina had met one morning in the house of the Company's medical officer in Delhi, Dr Grant, over a pianoforte which GG had gone to tune; and by evening they were singing parlour songs together, chaperoned by Captain Douglas, Commander of the Palace Guards.[69]

As soon as Sir Thomas found out about the affair he forbade the couple from corresponding and GG promptly went on a hunger strike. When Metcalfe took her up to the newly built hill station of Mussoorie for a change of air, she sat waiting for her lover's letters, each of which was promptly confiscated by her father on arrival. 'My beloved,' wrote the lovesick GG to Campbell from her Mussoorie bedroom after her father had retired for the night,

It is so hard to see letters come from you & to feel I may not read or see them since I know they are come! Oh! Edward! I should be so purely happy if I might write to and hear from you! One little note a week Edward would give me such intense joy. I cannot see the indelicacy and find it appears to me incomprehensible how anyone can entertain such an idea under existing circumstances. Are we not sure? Oh yes in everything now . . .[70]

Metcalfe, who was so adept at controlling the many princes of the House of Timur, found himself powerless in the face of the pain and despair of a single twenty-one-year-old girl. He returned to Delhi, leaving GG in the hills, writing helplessly from Dilkusha that

> I trust you will allow the fine climate to have fair play with you and that you will eat and recollect that you have a father who loves you and is grieved to witness your present state both of body and mind, and that whatever annoyance he may have caused you proceeded from sincere affection and a sense of duty. No father can do more.[71]

2

BELIEVERS AND INFIDELS

The Reverend Midgeley John Jennings, the chaplain of the Christian population of Delhi, was not a man to flinch from speaking his mind.

Ever since he had arrived in Delhi three months before Jawan Bakht's wedding, Jennings had been working on his plan to convert the people of Delhi to Christianity. For the Mughal capital, Jennings had concluded, was nothing less than the last earthly bastion of the Prince of Darkness himself: 'Within its walls', he wrote,

> the pride of life, the lust of the eye and all the lusts of the flesh have reigned and revelled to the full, and all the glories of the Kingdoms of this portion of the earth have passed from one wicked possessor to another. It is as though it were permitted the Evil One there at least to verify his boast that he giveth it to whom he will; but of truth, of meekness and of righteousness, the power has not been seen . . .'[1]

Jennings' plan was to rip up what he regarded as the false faiths of India, by force if necessary: 'The roots of ancient religions have here, as in all old places, struck deep and men must be able to fathom deep in order to uproot them.'[2] His method was simple: to harness the power of the rising British Empire – clearly the instrument 'of the mysterious sway of God's Providence' – towards converting the heathen.

The British Crown, argued Jennings in his prospectus for his proposed Delhi Mission, was now the proud possessor of the Koh-i-noor diamond, once the property of the Mughals, India's greatest dynasty. In gratitude, the British should now endeavour in earnest to bring about the conversion of India and so 'give in return that "pearl of great price" [the Christian faith] . . . As the course of our Empire is so marvellously taking its course from the East of India towards its West', so should the British be preparing to conquer the subcontinent for Anglicanism and the one true God.[3] There should, he believed, be no compromise with false religions.

Jennings had come out to India in 1832 and had quickly gained a reputation, in the words of his daughter, for 'striving against carelessness and neglect in religious observance'. Having initially been posted to various quiet hill stations, and forced to focus his energies on such peripheral concerns as designing suitably modest headstones for the Christian cemeteries there, he had long dreamt of opening a mission in Delhi and getting stuck into some serious work as 'Missionary to the Heathen'.[4] He finally got the job of chaplain in Delhi in 1852 and moved straight into the front line, the Red Fort itself, having been invited to share the Lahore Gate lodgings of 'the peculiarly upright' Captain Douglas and his invalid wife, whom Jennings described as 'as churchy as myself . . . a warm supporter of the mission'.[5]

The Douglases apart, however, Jennings' brash and insensitive yet silkily unctuous manner – strikingly similar to that of Obadiah Slope in the Barchester Towers – won him few friends. He was strongly disliked by the Metcalfes: Sir Thomas regarded him as 'duplicitous' and badly mannered ('He returned a book of mine through Douglas without a word or line of thanks') while Theo thought him simply 'a bigot'.[6] If Jennings was a rare subject on which Sir Thomas and Theo could wholeheartedly agree, he was also, even more remarkably, a rare point of agreement between the English-language and very British *Delhi Gazette* and the Urdu-language and wholeheartedly Mughal *Dihli Urdu Akbhar*.

While it was hardly surprising that the pious Maulvi Muhammad

Baqar, editor of the *Dihli Urdu Akhbar*, would think Jennings a 'fanatic', it was more surprising that the *Delhi Gazette* would find Jennings' missionary activities a touch over-enthusiastic.[7] Yet when Jennings went to the great Hindu festival, the Kumbh Mela, and began trying to convert the millions of pilgrims who had collected by the banks of the Ganges, loudly denouncing their 'Satanic paganism', the *Gazette* was moved to point out that Jennings and his two assistants should perhaps be a little more restrained in their approach: 'The zeal of the missionaries is greater than their discretion in selecting this Heathen pandemonium as the theatre of their exertions,' wrote a correspondent to the *Gazette*. 'They have been daily preaching to the masses, but I should say without a shadow of success, having to compete with the four great anti-Christian powers – trade, crime, pleasure and idolatry – in all their most frantic forms.' Especially angered by Jennings' appearance were the militant *naga sadhus*, 'a particularly impudent clan of mendicants who wear no garb but that of nature', who were to be found 'stalking about in the thick of the congregation, abusing or driving out any non-Hindoo interloper who crosses their presence'.[8]

Jennings was not much more popular with his own flock. According to Sir Thomas, he told one old lady who complained of the winter cold in St James's Church that 'if her heart was warmer her feet would be so also'.[9] Nor was Jennings known in Delhi as an especially engaging preacher: 'I went to evening service at the church,' wrote a British magistrate around this time. Jennings' face, he noticed, wore a

> dogged expression . . . as of one who should say 'I know this is a little burdensome but I think you must bear it . . .' [By the time he was well into his lengthy sermon] it was growing dark, and soon a candle had to be sent for. This slender, solitary light in the darkening church and the loud voice proceeding from the figure partially occupying the small disk of brightness, had a most singular effect. The sermon, which the preacher would not curtail by a syllable on account of the lateness, dwelt as far as I remember on the vicissitudes of life, and urged how unwise was the postponement of repentance

in the face of the absolute uncertainty of the future. I felt at the time a most unaccountable sinking of spirits.[10]

Whatever his personal failings, however, Jennings' views and outlook were shared by increasing numbers of the British in India. When the indomitable Indophile Fanny Parkes had visited Hindustan a decade earlier she had found that attitudes were changing and that extreme religiosity was 'gaining ground very fast in Cawnpore. Young ladies sometimes profess to believe it is highly incorrect to go to balls, plays, races, or to any party where it is possible there may be a quadrille. A number of the officers also profess these opinions, and set themselves up as New Lights'.[11]

India in the 1840s and 1850s was slowly filling with pious British Evangelicals who wanted not just to rule and administer India, but also to redeem and improve it. In Calcutta Jennings' colleague Mr Edmunds was vocal in making known his belief that the Company should use its position more forcibly to bring about the conversion of India. 'The time appears to have come', he wrote in a widely read circular letter, 'when earnest consideration should be given to the subject, whether or not all men should embrace the same system of religion. Railways, steam vessels and the electric telegraph are rapidly uniting all the nations of the earth . . . The land is being leavened and Hinduism is being everywhere undermined. Great will some day, in God's appointed time, be the fall of it.'[12]

Nor was it any longer just the missionaries who dreamt of converting India. To the north-west of Delhi, the Commissioner of Peshawar, Herbert Edwardes, firmly believed an empire had been given to Britain because of the virtues of English Protestantism: 'The Giver of Empires is indeed God,' he wrote, and He gave the Empire to Britain because 'England had made the greatest effort to preserve the Christian religion in its purest apostolic form'.[13] It followed that the more the British strove to propagate that pure faith, the more Providence would smile on their efforts at empire-building. In this spirit, the district judge of Fatehpur, Robert Tucker, had recently set up large stone columns inscribed with the Ten Commandments in Persian, Urdu, Hindi and English and used 'two or three times a week to read the Bible in Hindoostanee to large numbers of natives who were assembled in the compound to hear him'.[14]

Such Evangelical enthusiasms had even spread to the British Army in India. According to one trooper of the Dragoon Guards, 'a religious mania sprang up and reigned supreme . . . the adjutant and sergeant major having become quite sanctimonious, attending religious meetings every morning'.[15] It became a watchword in such regiments that 'no soldiers ever show themselves more invincible than those who can pray as well as fight'.[16] It was a similar case in the Company's own army, where officers like Colonel Steven Wheler, commanding officer of the 34th Native Infantry, were in the habit of reading the Bible to his sepoys as well as proselytising to 'natives of all classes . . . in the highways, cities, bazaars and villages . . . [hoping that] the Lord would make him the happy instrument of converting his neighbour to God or, in other words, of rescuing him from eternal damnation'.[17]

Similar views were also echoed by the growing band of Evangelicals among the Company's directors, the first and foremost of whom was Charles Grant. Believing that 'it is hardly possible to conceive any people more completely enchained than they [the Hindus] are by their superstitions', Grant proposed hugely to increase missionary activity so as to convert a people whom he characterised as 'universally and wholly corrupt . . . depraved as they are blind, and wretched as they are depraved'.[18] Providence, he believed, had clearly brought the British to this sink of iniquity for a higher purpose:

> Is it not necessary to conclude that our Asiatic territories were given to us, not merely that we might draw an annual profit from them, but that we might diffuse among their inhabitants, long sunk in darkness, vice and misery, the light and benign influences of Truth?[19]

The missionaries' main ally within India itself had been the bishop of Calcutta, Reginald Heber. Heber had worked hard offering encouragement to the different missionary societies and cooperating with Company officials across India to allow the missionaries to spread throughout British-controlled territory. This was something that had been explicitly banned by the Company charter as recently as 1813, and only altered after a mass petition of Parliament organised in London by the Evangelical 'Committee of the Protestant Society', which demanded the alteration of the charter to allow 'the speedy and universal promulgation' of Christianity 'throughout the regions of the East'.

Heber was the man who oversaw the process of putting this regime into place; he also wrote a series of hymns which acted as rallying cries for the aggressively self-confident new mission. His stirring verses, still sung today, are full of the imagery of Holy War and Christian militarism, as Christian Soldiers battle their way to Salvation, Fighting the Good Fight 'through peril, toil and pain': 'The Son of God goes forth to war,' begins one hymn, 'his blood red banner streams afar.' Heber's hymns are also revealing of the attitude of the missionaries towards their potential converts:

> From Greenland's icy mountains,
> From India's coral strand . . .
> They call us to deliver
> Their land from error's chain.
>
> What though the spicy breezes,
> Blow soft o'er Ceylon's isle;
> Though every prospect pleases,
> And only man is vile.
>
> In vain with lavish kindness
> The gifts of God are strewn;
> The heathen in his blindness,
> Bows down to wood and stone.

Heber's views about the vile heathen of India exactly echoed those of Padre Jennings. 'A strong attack must be made somewhere,' wrote Jennings soon after arriving in Delhi, 'and I hope we shall see it made here.'[20]

The learned Muslim *'ulama** had initially been ambiguous in their response to the arrival of the British in Hindustan at the end of the eighteenth century. While some had discussed the notion of whether Hindustan was now *Dar ul-harb*, the Abode of War, and so a legitimate focus for a Muslim jihad, most had taken the view that the British could only be an improvement on the Hindu Marathas who preceded them as the dominant power in the north, and so accepted work in the Company's employment as lawyers, munshis and teachers.[21]

There were a number of high-profile marriages between leading maulvis (Muslim clerics) and British women, most of whom converted to Islam.[22] There was also a degree of genuine intellectual interest in Christianity in learned circles in Delhi: the Mughal court was so pleased to receive an Arabic version of the New Testament in 1807, soon after the arrival of the British in Delhi, that they 'returned their thanks and requested that the supply might be continued'.[23]

Moreover, many of the Delhi *'ulama* quickly formed friendships with the notably Indophile officials who filled the British Residency in the early days of the British ascendancy: Shah Abdul Aziz, for example, had developed a great affection for Sir David Ochterlony's assistant, William Fraser, who came to him twice a week to improve his Persian and Arabic.[24] A linguist and scholar from Inverness, Fraser pruned his moustaches in the Delhi manner and fathered 'as many children as the King of Persia' from his harem of 'six or seven legitimate [Indian] wives'.[25] Shah Abdul Aziz was impressed by Fraser's sympathetic understanding of Muslim ways, and gave him advice on subjects as diverse as what shrines to visit on the road to Peshawar and the finer points of sharia law.[26]

Fraser returned the affection. Soon after his arrival in Delhi he began seeking out 'learned natives . . . [of whom] there are a few, and in poverty, but those I have met with are real treasures'.[27] Among them was the poet Ghalib, who later wrote that when

---

* In Arabic, *'ulama* means 'the ones possessing knowledge', hence the 'community of learned men'. In effect it means the Islamic clergy, the body of men with sufficient knowledge of the Koran, the Sunna and the Sharia to make decisions on matters of religion. *'Ulama* is an Arabic plural – the singular is *'alim*, a learned man.

Fraser was assassinated, he 'felt afresh the grief of a father's death'.[28] Fraser gave up eating pork and beef so that he could share his table with both Hindu and Muslim guests. He also wore Mughal clothes, and lived in a wholeheartedly Mughal style. Before long he gained a reputation for 'consorting with the grey beards of Delhi . . . almost all of them Musalmans of Mogul extraction, the wreck of the nobility of that court'.[29] As the French traveller and botanist Victor Jacquemont put it:

> [Fraser is] half-asiatick in his habits, but in other respects a Scotch Highlander, and an excellent man with great originality of thought, a metaphysician to boot . . . His mode of life has made him more familiar, perhaps, than any other European with the customs and ideas of the native inhabitants. He has, I think, a real and profound understanding of their inner life, such as is possessed by few others. Hindustani and Persian are like his two own mother tongue . . .[30]

As Fraser wrote home to his parents on 8 February 1806, in his first letter describing Delhi: 'My situation is as desirable as any one I could hold . . . I read and study with pleasure the languages. They are the chief source of my amusement, [although] Delhi affords much [other] food besides. I am also making a good collection of oriental manuscripts.'[31]

He was not alone in these Mughal enthusiasms. Fraser's superior, Sir David Ochterlony, was equally enamoured of Delhi courtly culture. With his fondness for *huqqas* and nautch girls* and Indian costumes, Ochterlony alarmed Bishop Heber, when the two met by chance in the wilds of Rajasthan, by receiving him sitting on a divan wearing Hindustani pyjamas and a turban, while being fanned by servants holding a peacock-feather punkah. To one side of Ochterlony's own tent was the red silk harem tent where Ochterlony's women slept, and on the other side the encampment of his daughters, all, according to the amazed bishop, 'hung around with red cloth and thus fenced in from the eyes of the profane . . . it was [as if] an Eastern prince [was] travelling . . .'[32]

---

* Professional dancers and courtesans.

Ochterlony was reputed to have had thirteen wives, but one of these, a former Brahmin dancing girl from Pune who converted to Islam and was referred to in his will as 'Beebee Mahruttun Moobaruck ul Nissa Begume, alias Begum Ochterlony, the mother of my younger children',[33] took precedence over any others.[34] Much younger than Ochterlony, she certainly appears to have had the upper hand in her relationship with the old general, and one observer remarked that 'making Sir David Commissioner [of Delhi was the same as] making Generallee Begum'.[35]

In such mixed households, Islamic customs and sensitivities were clearly understood and respected: in one letter, for example, it is recorded that 'Lady Ochterlony has applied for leave to make the Hadge to Mecca'.[36] Indeed, Ochterlony even considered bringing up his children as Muslims, and when his children by Mubarak Begum had grown up, he adopted a child from the family of the Nawabs of Loharu, one of the leading Delhi Muslim families.[37] Brought up by Mubarak Begum, the girl eventually married her cousin, a nephew of Ghalib.[38]

In addition to the mixed households of the British Residency, in the vicinity of Delhi there were a number of landed dynasties who also tried with varying success to bridge the gap between Islam and Christianity, between Mughal culture and that of the British. The Skinners of Hansi, the Gardners of Khasgunge and the circle around the Begum Sumru of Sardhana were all descended from eighteenth-century European mercenaries who had married into the Mughal elite of Delhi and developed a hybrid lifestyle, so forming a sort of Anglo-Mughal Islamo-Christian buffer zone between the Mughal world of the court and the world of the Company's Residency. All three dynasties nominally professed Christianity, while speaking mainly Persian and Hindustani, and living in an almost entirely Islamicised Mughal style.

This fusion of civilisations could sometimes be confusing. The American-born William Linnaeus Gardner had married a begum of Cambay, while his son James had married Mukhtar Begum, a first cousin of Zafar. Together they fathered an Anglo-Mughal dynasty, half of whose members were Muslim and half Christian; indeed, some of them, such as James Jahangir Shikoh Gardner, seem to have been both at the same time.*[39] In 1820, Gardner's begum came to Delhi to negotiate a marriage alliance between her dynasty and that of the Begum Sumru, using Sir David Ochterlony as intermediary: 'I believe James [Gardner's eldest son] is to be contracted at the next Ede,' wrote William Gardner to a cousin,

> but can say nothing certain as I am not in the secret. Eunuchs and old women are going between daily [between the two households] . . . The only thing I have interfered in was to place my veto on the whole Royal Family coming to the *shadee* [marriage] as I cannot afford it . . .[40]

Finally, just as everything seemed to be arranged, there was a death in the entourage of the Begum Sumru, who did not hesitate to declare forty days' mourning, in the Muslim manner: 'the Old Begum has thought proper to make a very expensive and tedious mourning,' reported an increasingly irritated Gardner, 'and has been feeding all Delhi besides beating herself Black and Blue, and expects Sir David as *hakim* . . . to take off her *sogh* [mourning clothes] at the end of the 40 days'. Ochterlony duly offered his assistance at the mourning rituals, but confided to one friend 'that the old Begum so mixes Christian customs with the Hindoostanee that though anxious to do that which would please the old lady, he simply did not know what was required.'[41]

The way in which the Christian converts continued doggedly to keep to their old Mughal customs was not necessarily to everyone's taste. Father Angelo de Caravaggio, the Capuchin who was sent to minister to the Begum Sumru, found it a particular struggle: 'My four years at Sardhana saw the construction of a church and a house,' he wrote to his superiors in Rome. 'Since I was unable to bring about the abandonment of Muslim customs, and seeing no chance of improvement, I took the decision to devote myself to the

* Both the Gardners and the Skinners began to give Mughal and European names to their children – thus Susan Gardner was known in the zenana as Shubbeah Begum. The Muslim branch of the Skinner family maintain the practice to this day and Frank Skinner, who controls the bicycle rickshaw rental trade in Meerut, has on the reverse of his business card his Mughal name, Sultan Mirza, written in Urdu script.

education of children . . . seeing that despite my efforts, Christianity did not affect the customs of the Muslims, I [eventually] returned to Agra with the children.'[42]

In contrast to the mild tut-tutting of Father Angelo, the intrusion of Jennings and his overtly Islamophobic mission into this overwhelmingly hybrid landscape was something quite new, and it dramatically changed the atmosphere. It undermined the hopes of those in the Mughal elite who had endeavoured to create a working relationship with the Christians, while confirming the prejudices of those who had argued all along against any attempt at accommodation with the infidel *kafirs*.

For while there had been several other missionaries passing through Delhi in the course of the early nineteenth century, preaching, debating and distributing pamphlets, none had adopted quite such a blatantly confrontational approach as Jennings. In his first report to the Society for the Propagation of the Gospel (SPG), Jennings had talked of his relish in taking on Delhi's '261 mosques and 200 temples' and had made no secret of his willingness openly to attack both Islam and the Prophet.[43] Nor did the earlier missionaries have the same degree of official patronage as Jennings, who had, among others, the Governor of the North West Provinces and the Commissioner of the Punjab on his Mission Committee. As Delhi chaplain, he also had his salary and travel arrangements paid for by the Company.

Moreover, Jennings arrived in Delhi at a time when both Muslims and Hindus were beginning to feel increasingly alarmed by the degree to which the British were beginning to use their new power to curb what had previously been regarded as legitimate religious activities, and instead to aggressively and insensitively promote Christianity. Sati, the burning of Hindu widows, had been outlawed in 1829, alarming many orthodox Hindus; another law allowing the remarriage of Hindu widows horrified many more. Since then stories had been circulating of the ways in which the British were using government orphanages to convert parentless children, a tendency that seemed to be confirmed by the legislation introduced in 1832 allowing converts to inherit ancestral property, something explicitly forbidden by the sharia. There were also claims that missionaries had been allowed a free hand to preach to the (literally) captive audience in the Company jails: not an unlikely charge, since the Superintendent of Jails for the region was also on Jennings' committee.[44]

More seriously still, in the British land settlement that had followed the conquest of Hindustan, many hundreds of temples, mosques, madrasas and Sufi shrines had had their endowments 'resumed' – effectively confiscated – on a variety of pretexts, and wherever documents proving the grantees' rights could not be produced; among the land grants resumed were the revenues bequeathed to no fewer than nine mosques in Delhi. There were other cases where the Company casually demolished revered temples and mosques to make roads – something that especially upset the influential theologian Shah Abdul Aziz.*[45] In a few cases land was taken from mosques and awarded to missionaries in order for them to build churches; on other occasions, with equally astonishing insensitivity, missionaries and the regular Christian clergy were given confiscated or ruined mosques to live in.[46]

Although the missionaries were in general notably unsuccessful in their trawl for conversions in northern India, such was the atmosphere of suspicion generated by the growing missionary phobia that even quite innocent British initiatives began to generate alarm: the construction of a hospital in Saharanpur to the north of Delhi led to a wave of anxiety that the British were going to abolish the purdah system, since veiled women had been asked to go there rather than being treated at home. By the same token, all British

---

* This was also one of the principal complaints of Begum Hazrat Mahal of Lucknow when explaining what had led her to fight the British. In her proclamation issued in the dying days of the Uprising, she mocked the British claim to allow freedom of worship: 'To eat pigs and drink wine, to bite greased cartridges and to mix pigs' fat with sweetmeats, to destroy Hindoo and Musalman temples on pretence of making roads, to build churches, to send clergy men into the streets and alleys to preach the Christian religion, to institute English schools, and pay people a monthly stipend for learning the English sciences, while the places of worship of Hindoos and Musalmans are to this day entirely neglected; with all this, how can the people believe that religion will not be interfered with?' Proclamation of Begum Hazrat Mahal; the translation of the original is in the NAI, Foreign Department, Political Consultation 17 December 1858, from J. D. Forsyth Sec. to Chief Commr Oudh, To G. J. Edmonstone, Sec. GOI, For. Dept, Dt Lucknow, 4 December 1858.

schools and colleges came to be regarded as covert organs of missionary activity.[47]

It was no accident that it was in 1852, the year of Jennings' arrival in Delhi, that the first signs emerged of an intellectual counter-attack by the Delhi *ulama*. It was in this year that the learned Maulana Rahmat Allah Kairnawi wrote a widely circulated tract, *Izalat al-awham* (The Remover of Doubts), in which he provided a very articulate defence of Islam and an attack on the scriptural inconsistencies and corruptions of the Christian Gospels, based partly on the new findings of German biblical scholars. As the Maulana explained:

> For a time the ordinary Muslims shrank from listening to the preaching [of the missionaries] and from studying their books and pamphlets, therefore none of the Indian *ulama* paid any attention to the refutation of these pamphlets. But after some time had passed there began to be a weakening in some of the people, and some of the illiterate [Muslims] were in danger of stumbling. Therefore some of us scholars of Islam turned their attention to their refutation . . .[48]

The new attitudes of the Evangelicals were only part of a more widespread and visibly growing arrogance on the part of the increasingly powerful British. Since they had finally succeeded in conquering and subduing the Sikhs in 1849, the British finally found themselves the masters of South Asia: every single one of their military rivals had now been conquered – Siraj ud-Daula of Bengal in 1757, the French in 1761, Tipu Sultan of Mysore in 1799, and the Marathas in 1803 and again, finally, in 1819.

For the first time there was a feeling that technologically, economically and politically, as well as culturally, the British had nothing to learn from India and much to teach; it did not take long for imperial arrogance to set in. This arrogance, when combined with the rise of Evangelical Christianity, slowly came to affect all aspects of relations between the British and the Indians.

The Delhi College, initially more a madrasa than a Western university, was remodelled by the Company in 1828 to provide, in addition to its oriental studies, an education in English language and literature. The object was 'to uplift' what the new college committee now saw as the 'uneducated and half-barbarous people of India'. Behind the move was Charles Trevelyan, the brother-in-law and disciple of Thomas Babingdon Macaulay, the same Macaulay whose minute famously declared that 'a single shelf of a good European library was worth the whole native literature of India and Arabia':

> the historical information which has been collected from all the books written in the Sanscrit language is less valuable than what may be found in the most paltry abridgments used at preparatory schools in England . . . The languages of Western Europe civilized Russia. I cannot doubt that they will do for the Hindoo what they have done for the Tartar.

Trevelyan now put such views into action at Delhi College, declaring that: 'Only the pure fount of English literature [can make] headway against the impenetrable barrier of habit and prejudice backed by religious feeling.'[49] Shortly afterwards, in 1837, the British abolished Persian as the language of government and replaced it with English (and occasionally the regional language as well). From now on, it was clear, the British were setting the agenda and India would be governed entirely according to their tastes, traditions and judgements.

Yet even Indians who were educated in the new English college found it did little to improve their treatment at British hands. According to Mohan Lal Kashmiri, who was a pupil in the first batch of students taught in the Delhi English College, 'the distant and contemptible manner with which we are treated by the generality of English gentlemen, wounds our hearts and compels us to forget the blessings of the British rule'. He added a word of warning: 'you may crush down the populace and keep them in awe with your arms, but until you conquer and win the hearts of the people, the peace and affection will be more an outward word of talk' than reality.[50]

To the White Mughals who had tried to bridge the two cultures, the change in tone and the sheer ever-growing rudeness of the British were deeply dispiriting. William Gardner was profoundly embedded in the tolerant and hybrid court culture of the Mughals; to him, attempts by missionaries like Jennings to force their customs and religions on an unwilling India were as horrifying as they were inexplicable. He was especially irritated by the degree to which the British seemed to have lost touch with Indian opinion. As he wrote to a cousin, over and over again the British succeeded in giving offence 'for want of knowledge of the natives . . . Injustice and Tyranny were never exceeded by any government that ever existed'.[51] His feelings were shared by Ochterlony, who in his old age was equally horrified by the way his younger colleagues treated the Emperor and his family: 'the House of Timoor far from being thought worthy to command the least consideration,' he wrote to a sympathetic William Fraser, 'is apparently sinking into the very lowest state of contempt. I fear . . . we do not gain much Popularity in the eyes of the natives by such marked degradation'.[52]

When Fanny Parkes was in Delhi, she paid a call to an old princess who was a cousin of the Gardners in the zenana of the Red Fort. At the beginning of the British ascendancy, such visits would have been routine and unremarkable. But by the late 1840s the reaction from the British community in Delhi was one of near-horror. 'I heard that I was much blamed for visiting the princess,' wrote Fanny afterwards.

Look at the poverty, the wretched poverty of these descendants of the Emperors! In former times strings of pearls and valuable jewels were placed on the necks of departing visitors. When the Princess Hyat-ool-Nissa Begum in her fallen fortunes put the necklace of freshly gathered white jasmine flowers over my head, I bowed with as much respect as if she had been the Queen of the Universe. Others may look upon these people with contempt, I cannot. Look at what they are, what they have been. One day a gentleman, speaking to me of the *extravagance* of one of the young princes, mentioned that he was always in debt, he could never live upon his allowance. The allowance of the prince was twelve rupees a month! Not more than the wages of a head servant.[53]

By the late 1830s, White Mughals like Fraser, Gardner and Ochterlony were becoming few and far between; they and their way of life were beginning to die out. The wills of Company officials show that it was at this time that the number of Indian wives or *bibis* (consorts or girlfriends) being mentioned begins to decline: from turning up in one in three wills in the period 1780–85, the practice had gone into steep decline. Between 1805 and 1810, *bibis* appear in only one in every four wills; by 1830 it is one in six; by the middle of the century they have all but disappeared.[54]

The speed of the decline of such liaisons far outstrips the speed of the arrival of the white women, whose numbers really increased dramatically only after, rather than before, 1857. This was a result of a changing pattern of Company recruitment: reforms to the Civil Service in 1856 meant that after 1857 civil servants began to come out in their mid-twenties, after undergoing competitive examinations following university, and by that time often arrived in India already married; in contrast, in the earlier period young men had to apply to join the Company before their sixteenth birthday, and thus arrived still malleable and unattached. The drift apart cannot therefore be blamed on the memsahibs, as generations of schoolchildren have been taught.

More than twenty years earlier, by the early 1830s, Englishmen who had taken on Indian wives or customs had already begun to become objects of surprise and even derision. By the mid-nineteenth century there was growing 'ridicule' of Company servants 'who allow whiskers to grow and who wear turbans &c in imitation of the Musalmans'. Pyjamas – common dress in eighteenth-century Calcutta and Madras – for the first time became something that an Englishman slept in rather than something he wore during the day. As the *Delhi Gazette* put it in an editorial of 1856:

> Instances have been known of Englishmen coming out to India early in life and becoming in the course of time so throughly Indianized, so identified with the natives (usually with the Mohammedan

natives) in habits and feelings as to lose all relish for European society, to select their associates and connections from among the Muslims, to live in every respect in Mussalman fashion, and to either openly or tacitly adopt the Mussalman creed, at any rate ceasing to manifest any interest in Christianity . . . These have frequently been men of very superior ability . . . and their familiarity with the ways of the natives may have paved the way for successes otherwise dubious or impracticable.

It is evident however that such time has gone by, and we must be careful not to be misled by their opinions, however applicable to the task of their day. It is now clear that the present practical influence of such a class, a class fast dying out, can only be to retard the progress of knowledge in India, to abet the native in his adherence to his ancient ways, to keep him tenacious to his old ideas of Oriental conservatism and hostile to all innovation . . .[55]

Comfortably settled in his rooms in the Red Fort, Padre Jennings was clear in his own mind that he represented the new broom that was needed to sweep away such morally corrupt attitudes. Before long he was joined by two junior assistants, one of whom learned Urdu and Persian with a view to targeting the Muslims, and the other Sanskrit, aiming at the Hindus. Together they quickly realised all the fears and suspicions of the Delhi elite by beginning secret Bible classes in the officially secular Delhi College.[56]

For several months, however, there was a notable absence of conversions and a growing hostility to Jennings' attempts to produce some. Then in July 1852, four months after the wedding of Jawan Bakht, Jennings pulled off a major coup. Two prominent Delhi Hindus, Dr Chaman Lal, one of Zafar's personal physicians, and his friend Master Ramchandra, a talented mathematics lecturer at the Delhi College, both announced they wished to convert. Jennings was only too anxious to oblige, and arranged to baptise them in a very public ceremony at St James's Church on Sunday, 11 July. As Jennings wrote to the SPG soon afterwards, in a report glowing with self-satisfaction,

Never was a field riper for missionary efforts than this one . . . These
men have many connections in Delhi and were high in esteem, and
their baptism consequently caused the greatest excitement throughout the city . . . The whole Hindu population assembled around the
church on Sunday evening . . .[57]

Soldiers were on hand in case of trouble, but there was no
immediate uproar, although there was, for many days afterwards,
a 'violent agitation throughout the city'.[58] Respectable families
quickly removed their children from the Delhi College where
Master Ramchandra worked. Meanwhile even the most pro-British
of the *'ulama* now began to have second thoughts about their
increasingly militant Christian masters.

One of these was Mufti Sadruddin Azurda, a close friend of both
Zafar and Ghalib, who had played an important role as bridge
between the British and the Mughal elite in the early days of the
British ascendancy in Delhi, and who had been a friend and protégé
of Sir David Ochterlony. For thirty years Azurda had balanced his
place as the chief Muslim judge (*Sadr Amin*) in Delhi and a leading
literary figure and mufti at court, with a mild Anglophilia: a natural
mediator, he had argued that employment by the Company was
entirely legitimate in Muslim law, and that any notion of jihad was
quite inappropriate since the British had allowed full religious
freedom.[59] Now, however, even Azurda began to have serious
doubts about the direction British policy was taking, and quietly
went about dissuading his students at Delhi College from paying
any attention to 'Christian propaganda'.[60] Others were more outspoken. According to one missionary: 'The Muslims would gladly
overthrow the English. They tell [us] plainly, "If you were not the
rulers, we would soon silence your preaching, not with arguments
but with the sword." '[61]

Just as militant Christians were a growing force among the British
in the early 1850s, so among Delhi's Muslims there was a parallel rise
in rigid fundamentalism that displayed the same utter certainty and

disdain for the faiths of others, as well as a similar willingness to use force against the infidel.*

If the great abolitionist William Wilberforce and the Clapham Sect had helped generate the spread of fundamentalist Evangelical attitudes in English Christianity, on the Muslim side the father of the radical Islamic Reform movement was Shah Waliullah, an eighteenth-century Delhi divine who had gone to study at Medina in the Hejaz at the same time as Ibn Abd al-Wahhab, the founder of the Arabian Wahhabis.† While there is no evidence that the two ever met, they shared an almost identical theology, and when he returned to India, Shah Waliullah quickly declared war on what he saw as the perverted and deviant interpretations of Islam practised in Delhi.[62]

Shah Waliullah and his sons – notably William Fraser's friend Shah Abdul Aziz – strongly opposed the Sufi veneration of saints, which they likened to idol worship, and were especially outspoken about the syncretic practices they believed Indian Muslims had picked up from their Hindu neighbours: making pilgrimages to Hindu holy places, consulting Hindu astrologers, piercing the noses of women for nose studs, lighting lamps on tombs, playing music in holy places, and celebrating Hindu festivals. Even the practice of eating on banana leaves was anathematised. The Shah's solution was to strip out all non-Islamic accretions and innovations, and to emphasise instead a strictly Koranic monotheism in which prayers could be directed only to God, and never through any saintly intermediary.[63]

Judging human reason to be incapable of reaching divine truth on

---

* The Hindu reformist movement led by groups such as the Arya Samaj, which would in time form a Hindu parallel to these reformist tendencies in Islam and Christianity, did not reach Delhi until two decades later, in the late 1870s. While there were many prominent Hindus in Zafar's Delhi, there was no unified Hindu leadership in the city at this time to form a coherent counterweight to the missionaries and the *ulama*. There was, however, some stirring of Hindu reformist movements in Bengal: in January 1857, General Hearsey at Barrackpore was complaining of 'some agents of the religious Hindoo party in Calcutta (I believe it is called the "Dharma Sobha") spreading rumours about the Government being intent on converting the sepoys'. See Irfan Habib, 'The Coming of 1857', *Social Scientist*, vol. 26, no. 1, January–April 1998, p.11.
† Followers of the puritanical reformed Islam first taught by Ibn Abd al-Wahhab in Medina in the eighteenth century.

its own, Shah Waliullah emphasised the importance of revealed divine revelation and urged a return to the text of the Koran and the Hadiths. In order to make those texts easily available to ordinary people, the Shah translated the Koran into Persian while his sons later translated it into Urdu and disseminated both translations through the new Delhi printing presses.[64] Like the Wahhabis, Shah Waliullah also opposed what he saw as the corrupt Muslim rulers of his day, and from his family stronghold in the Madrasa i-Rahimiyya he and his sons and grandsons encouraged Delhiwallahs to defy what he perceived as the decadence of the Mughals and not behave like 'camels with strings in their noses'.[65]

Shah Waliullah's dislike of the Mughals was as much theological as political. For generations the Mughal emperors had intermarried with Hindus – Zafar was quite typical in having a Rajput mother – and the slow seepage of Hindu ideas and customs from the harem into the rest of the Palace had led the later Mughal emperors to subscribe to a particularly tolerant and syncretic form of Sufi Islam, aligned to the liberal Chishti brotherhood, at the very opposite end of the theological spectrum from the hard-line views of Shah Waliullah; many fundamentalists regarded such liberal views as bordering on infidelity – *kufr*.[66]

In orthodox Islam, the object of creation is the worship of God – a relationship of subordination in which God is the master and the devotee is the slave. This relationship is a very straightforward one: if you worship God in the proper way you will be rewarded – on the Day of Judgement you will go to paradise – and if you do not, you will go to hell. The Sufi-minded poet-princes of the Mughal court and their circle in the Delhi *ashraf* elite completely rejected this idea. They argued instead that God should be worshipped not because he had commanded us to it, but because he was such a lovable being. As a result all traditions were tolerated: anyone was capable of expressing his or her love for God, and that ability transcended religious associations, gender or indeed one's place in the social order. This was one of the reasons why the Sufi Islam practised so enthusiastically in the court was also so popular across the city, and also why the court circle were so violently anathematised by the more Orthodox *'ulama*.

Visits to Delhi's ancient Sufi shrines – which then as now are venerated by Delhi's Hindus every bit as much as by Delhi's Muslims – are an almost weekly occurrence in the court diary of Zafar's reign, and far outnumber any mention of visits to mosques. Zafar also gave generously to the shrine keepers whenever they presented themselves at court, and paid to have flowers placed on saints' graves, something of which the school of Shah Waliullah especially disapproved.[67]

Indeed, Zafar was himself regarded as a Sufi *pir*, and used to accept pupils or *murids*.[68] The loyal *Dihli Urdu Akbhar* went so far as to call him 'one of the leading saints of the age, approved of by the divine court'.[69] Zafar even dressed the part, and in his youth, prior to his accession, made a point of living and looking like a poor scholar and dervish, in striking contrast to his three notably dressy younger brothers, Mirzas Jahangir, Salim and Babur: 'he was a man of spare figure and stature, plainly apparelled, almost approaching to meanness', reported Major Archer in 1828, when Zafar was fifty-three, and still a decade away from succeeding to the throne. 'His appearance was that of an indigent *munshi*, or teacher of languages.'[70]

Zafar's Sufism took two very distict forms. As a poet and dervish, he imbibed the highest subtleties of mystical Sufi writing. But he was also deeply susceptible to the magical and superstitious side of popular Islam. He seems to have believed, for example – as did many of his people – that his position as both Sufi master and Emperor gave him tangible spiritual powers. Thus when one of his followers was bitten by a snake, Zafar attempted to cure him by sending 'a Seal of Bezoar [a stone antidote to poison] and some water on which he had breathed', and giving it to the man to drink.[71]

The Emperor also had a great belief in charms or *ta'wiz*, especially as a palliative for his perennial complaint of piles, or to ward off evil spells.[72] During one period of illness, he gathered a group of leading Sufi *pirs* and told them that 'several Begums suspected that some party or other had cast a spell over him. He therefore requested them to take steps to remedy this so as to remove all apprehensions on this account. They replied that they would write out some charms &c for his Majesty. They were to be mixed in water which when taken [i.e. drunk] would guard him from all evil'.[73] Such *pirs*, wonder workers and Hindu astrologers were in constant attendance on the King, and on their advice he regularly sacrificed buffaloes and camels, buried eggs, and arrested supposed black magicians, as well as wearing a special ring to cure indigestion.[74] He also, on their advice, regularly donated cows to the poor, elephants to Sufi shrines and a horse to the *khadims* (clergy) of the Jama Masjid.[75]

Zafar's poetry, however, existed on a higher plain than this. Like much verse of the period, it was deeply imbued with the Sufi ideals of love, which were regarded as much the surest route to a God who was seen to be located not in the heavens, but deep within the human heart. For if the world of the heart lay at the centre of Sufism, it also formed the cornerstone of the principal literary form in late Mughal Delhi – the ghazal, which derived its name from the Arabic words 'talking to a woman about love'.[76] The love of the ghazal poet was ambiguous – it was rarely made entirely clear whether it was sacred or worldly love to which the poet referred. This ambiguity was deliberate, for just as the longing of the soul for union with God was believed to be as compelling and as all-embracing as the longing of the lover for the beloved, both loves could be carried to the point of insanity or what Sufis called *fana* – self-annihilation and immersion in the beloved.[77] In the eyes of the Sufi poets, this search for the God within liberated the seeker from the restrictions of narrowly ortho-dox Islam, encouraging the devotee to look beyond the letter of the law to its mystical essence. As Ghalib put it,

> The object of my worship lies beyond perception's reach;
> For men who see, the Ka'ba is a compass, nothing more.[78]

Look deeper, he tells the orthodox: it is you alone who cannot hear the music of His secrets. Like many of his Delhi contemporaries, Ghalib could write profoundly religious poetry, yet was sceptical about literalist readings of the Muslim scriptures. Typical were his bantering meditations on paradise, which he wrote in a letter to a friend: 'In Paradise it is true that I shall drink at dawn the pure wine mentioned in the Koran,' he wrote, but where in Paradise are the long walks with intoxicated friends in the night, or the drunken crowds shouting merrily? Where shall I find there the intoxication of Monsoon clouds? Where there is no Autumn how can Spring exist? If the beautiful houris are always there, where will be the sadness of separation and the joy of union? Where shall we find there a girl who flees away when we would kiss her?[79]

In the same spirit in Ghalib's poetry the orthodox Shaikh always represents narrow-mindedness and hypocrisy:

> The Shaikh hovers by the tavern door,
> But believe me, Ghalib,
> I am sure I saw him slip in,
> As I departed.

In his letters too Ghalib frequently contrasts the narrow legalism of the 'ulama, 'teaching the baniyas and brats, and wallowing in the problems of menstruation and post-natal bleeding', with real spirituality, for which you had to 'study the works of the mystics and take into one's heart the essential truth of God's reality and his expression in all things'.[80]

Like the rest of the court circle, Ghalib was prepared to take this insight to its natural conclusion. If God lay within and could be reached less by ritual than by love, then he was as accessible to Hindus as to Muslims. So it was that on a visit to Benares he could playfully write that he was half tempted to settle down there for good, and that he 'wished he had renounced the faith, put a sectarian mark on my forehead, tied a sacred thread around my waist and seated myself on the bank of the Ganges so that I could wash the contamination of existence away from myself and like a drop be one with the river'.[81]

This was an attitude to Hinduism that Zafar – and many of his Mughal forebears – shared. It is clear that Zafar consciously saw his role as a protector of his Hindu subjects, and a moderator of extreme Muslim demands and the chilling Puritanism of many of the 'ulama.[82] One of Zafar's verses says explicitly that Hinduism and Islam 'share the same essence', and his court lived out this syncretic philosophy, and both celebrated and embodied this composite Hindu–Muslim Indo-Islamic civilisation, at every level. The Hindu elite of Delhi went to the Sufi shrine of Nizamuddin, could quote Hafiz and were fond of Persian poetry. Their children – especially those of the administrative Khattri and Kayasth castes – studied under maulvis and attended the more liberal madrasas,* bringing offerings of food for their teachers on Hindu festivals.[83] For their part, Muslims followed the Emperor in showing honour to Hindu holy men, while many in the court, including Zafar himself, followed the old Mughal custom, borrowed from upper-caste Hindus, of drinking only Ganges water.[84] Zafar's extensive team of Hindu astrologers rarely left his side.[85]

The court diary records how Zafar would play the spring festival of Holi, spraying his courtiers, wives and concubines with different-coloured paints, initiating the celebrations by bathing in the water of seven wells.[86] The autumn Hindu festival of Dussera would be marked in the Palace by the distribution of presents and *nazrs* to Zafar's Hindu officers, and (more unexpectedly) the colouring of the horses in the Royal Stud. In the evening, the King would then watch the Ram Lila – the celebration of the Hindu god-king Ram's defeat of evil in the shape of the demon Ravana, annually celebrated in Delhi with the burning of giant effigies of the demon and his brothers.[87] Zafar even asked for a change in the route of the Ram Lila procession so that it would skirt the entire flank of the Palace, allowing it to be enjoyed in all its glory.[88] On Diwali, Zafar would weigh himself against 'seven kinds of grain, gold, coral &c and directed their distribution among the poor'.[89]

The diary is full of the daily consequences of this marked sensitivity to Hindu feelings. One evening, when Zafar was riding out across the river 'for an airing . . . a Hindoo waited on the King intimating his wish to become a Mussalman. Hakim Ahsanullah Khan [Zafar's prime minister] represented that it would not be

---

* Given the somewhat dubious and sectarian reputation of madrasas today, it is worth remembering that many of the most brilliant Hindu thinkers, including, for example, the great reformer Ram Mohan Roy (1772–1833), were the products of madrasa educations.

proper to attend to his request and HM directed that he should be
removed from the place'.[90] During the Flower-sellers' Fair, the
Phulwalon ki Sair held annually at the ancient Jog Maya temple
and the Sufi shrine of Qutb Sahib in Mehrauli, Zafar announced
that 'he would not accompany the *pankah* into the shrine as he
could not accompany it into the temple'.[91] On another occasion,
when a party of two hundred Muslims turned up at the Palace
demanding to be allowed to slaughter cows – holy to Hindus – at
'Id, Zafar told them in a 'decided and angry tone that the religion
of the Musalmen did not depend upon the sacrifice of cows'.[92]
Like Ghalib, Zafar had a deep disdain for narrow-minded
Shaikhs: one evening's entertainment at the Palace consisted of
'Kadir Bakhsh the actor personating a Maulvi [Muslim cleric] in
the presence of the King. HM was much pleased and ordered
Mahbub Alee Khan [the Chief Eunuch] to give him the usual
present'.[93]

The Delhi *'ulama* returned the disdain of the court. According to
Sir Sayyid Ahmad Khan, 'Many of the Delhi moulvies and their
followers considered the king to be little better than a heretic. They
were of the opinion that it was not right to pray in the mosques to
which he was in the habit of going and which were under his
patronage.'[94] Zafar's devotional attachment to Imam Ali was especially galling to the orthodox Sunni: the Shia festival of Muharram –
the incarnation of Islamic heresy in the eyes of the resolutely Sunni
Shah Waliullah – was celebrated with enthusiasm in the Palace, with
Zafar listening to the *marsiya* mourning poems. Partly because of
this there were persistent rumours that Zafar had actually converted
to Shiism. This led to the Emperor receiving several outraged
delegations from the Delhi *'ulama* threatening to take the ultimate
sanction of excluding his name from the Friday prayers – effectively
excommunicating him and delegitimising his rule – if the rumour
ever proved true.[95]

As the nineteenth century progressed, such rigidly orthodox
views gathered strength in Delhi, and the position of the *'ulama*
solidified, so that by the 1850s the tolerant Sufi ways of Zafar and his
court slowly came to look as old-fashioned and outdated as the
hybrid lifestyles and open-minded religious attitudes of the White

Mughals did among the now solidly Evangelical British. The stage was being set for a clash of rival fundamentalisms.

There was a strong class aspect as well to this fundamentalist opposition to the heterodoxy of Zafar's spirituality.

If Sufism and ghazal writing were the marks of court and high *sharif* culture, then patronising the Islamic reformist movement became the signature of the rising Punjabi Muslim merchant class, who though rich and literate felt themselves excluded from the elitist Sufi literary culture of the court. Shah Waliullah's theologian son Shah Abdul Aziz was a prolific giver of fatwas, or legal opinions, and it is significant how many of these concern economic matters – about the permissibility of letters of credit, or of gaining income through trade in slaves, and so on – which implies that many of those seeking his opinion were heavily involved in trade and commerce. It was certainly rich Punjabi Muslim traders who financed the radical madrasas of Delhi, especially those who called for jihad against the *kafirs* and who aimed to create an Islamic society pruned of all its non-Islamic accretions.[96]

The most outspoken of all was Sayyid Ahmad Barelvi, a notably militant alumnus of the Madrasa i-Rahimiyya, who embarked on an ill-fated jihad against the Sikhs and British on the North West Frontier in 1830. From here he wrote to the rulers of Central Asia, asking them to join hands in liberating India from British rule, the 'subversion of Islamic culture and the disruption of Islamic lifestyle by the Christians', and from the unIslamic ways of the Mughal court.[97] Though Barelvi, betrayed by the Afghans, died with his jihadis under the swords of the Sikhs in 1831, remnants of his mujahedin network survived underground along the trading route that linked Peshawar, Ambala, Delhi and Patna, the other principal centres of the jihadis.

In September 1852, five months after the wedding of Mirza Jawan Bakht, and two months after the conversion of Master Ramchandra and Dr Chaman Lal by Jennings, Metcalfe's police in Delhi came increasingly to suspect that the mujahedin network had begun to revive. Acting on a tip-off, they conducted a dawn raid on the premises of various known extremists and found evidence for what they believed was 'a Wahhabi conspiracy' in Delhi itself, seizing 'the correspondence of the Fanatic Moulvies [who were] preaching a crusade' against the British.[98] The figure at the centre of the 'conspiracy' was Shaikh Husain Bakhsh, a prominent Delhi trader from the Punjabi merchant community who was closely associated with the more radical imams of the Madrasa i-Rahimiyya circle.

It was again the *'ulama* of the same radical madrasa that had led the opposition to Jennings and his missionaries, especially when, after the baptism of Ramchandra and Chaman Lal, Padre Jennings succeeded, in May 1853, in converting an unnamed Sayyid 'of good family'.[99] If the missionaries reinforced Muslim fears, increasing opposition to British rule, driving the orthodox towards greater orthodoxy and creating a constituency for the jihadis, so the existence of 'Wahhabi conspiracies' strengthened the conviction of Jennings and his supporters that a 'strong attack' was needed to take on such deeply embedded 'Muslim fanatics'.

The histories of Islamic fundamentalism and European imperialism have very often been closely, and dangerously, intertwined. In a curious but very concrete way, the fundamentalists of both faiths have needed each other to reinforce each other's prejudices and hatreds. The venom of one provides the lifeblood of the other.

3

AN UNEASY EQUILIBRIUM

By 1852, although the British and the Mughals inhabited the same city and sometimes lived in close physical proximity to each other, the two peoples were growing farther and farther apart.

Where intermarriage – or at least cohabitation – was once very common among the small British community in Delhi, now there was virtual apartheid. There was less and less everyday contact, and still less attempt at mutual understanding. Nowhere was this more apparent than in Delhi's two leading journals; indeed, there is perhaps no better indication of the growing crevasse of misunderstanding opening up at this time between the British and Indian inhabitants of Delhi than a simple comparison of the columns of the two papers. If the *Dihli Urdu Akbhar* and the *Delhi Gazette* were in agreement about Padre Jennings' more extreme missionary activities, there were few other points on which the two saw eye to eye. Reading the newspapers' coverage of the events of 1852, there are times when it would be possible to believe that they were recording the news of two completely different cities.

The *Dihli Urdu Akbhar* officially regarded its job as being to encourage its readers to 'imbibe virtues and shun vices'.[1] Others took a different line: according to a rival Urdu newspaper, 'This is a dirty paper, full of personal gossip which attacks respectable people who do not share the religious views of the editor.'² Both apparently contradictory statements have their origin in the same tendency: the vigour with which the *Dihli Urdu Akhbar*, under its forthright Shia editor, Maulvi Muhammad Baqar, spoke out against corruption in the court, among the *'ulama*, and even in the British government.

While unwaveringly loyal to Zafar, the paper castigated the Palace administration for the corrupt way it delayed the disbursement of monthly stipends ('only those having access to the Emperor, the Mukhtar or the Royal Physician can get their salary paid') and gloated when some of the more badly behaved princes got their come-uppance – for example, when the raffish Mirza Shah Rukh was ambushed by the Delhi moneylenders as he made his way to the shrine of Qadam Sharif.[3] Wrongdoing the newspaper ascribed to the machinations of evil courtiers who were pulling the wool over the saintly Emperor's eyes.[4]

Maulvi Muhammad Baqar was a Delhi man, an alumnus of the Delhi College who had taught there for a while before leaving on account of the low salary. He had gone on to work briefly for the British, before setting up a lucrative bazaar for foreign merchants and building an *imambara*, a Shia religious hall, in which he sometimes preached.[5]

Reflecting his own interests, the concerns of the *Dihli Urdu Akhbar* centred mainly on local political and religious matters: it talked of the conversion of Master Ramchandra, described the latest miracles witnessed in the Sufi shrines, and reported on Delhi festivals, as well as the occasional fracas that occurred in them, such as Sunni–Shia riots during the Muharram of 1852. It also relayed such gossip as the punishment of yet more Palace serving girls for 'sexual vice'.[6]

Since Baqar's son, the promising young poet Muhammad Husain who wrote under the pen-name Azad, used to help his father with the paper, the *Dihli Urdu Akhbar* also took a strong interest in literary matters, reprinting the most acclaimed new ghazals recited in the *mushairas* and firmly siding with Baqar's friend – and Azad's *ustad* (guru) – Zauq in his rivalry with Ghalib: when the latter was arrested for gambling, the scandal was gleefully covered by the

Akhbar. If the paper made any reference to the world outside the walls of Delhi, it tended to be about the surrounding towns of Hindustan, and at a stretch Calcutta. Britain hardly appears in its columns – in the entire 1840s there were just seven mentions of the Company's home island, far fewer than there were about proper, civilised Muslim countries such as Egypt or Persia, where Baqar's family had originated.[7]

By contrast, the focus of the *Delhi Gazette* was that of the misty-eyed expatriate, eternally dreaming of the green hills around Cheltenham. There are a few references in its columns to the lighting of the canal in Chandni Chowk or to the ruts in the road near the *Gazette*'s Kashmiri Gate offices.[8] There are also the occasional anxious mentions of 'most daring dacoitees', reports of sad defeats suffered by the Delhi Cricket Club at the hands of a Calcutta team, and the complete results from the Delhi Derby. These included the announcement of the annual Locomotive Race 'for all bonafide wheelbarrows, to be coached by the Band boys of the regiments, one Band boy to sit in each barrow, winner to receive Rs 8'.[9]

Very special events occasionally, briefly, bring the two diverging worlds of the British and the Mughals together. But while in the early days of the British ascendancy the British and Indians had tended to come together by mutually participating in the life and festivities of the Mughal court, by the 1850s this contact now tended to take place firmly on European terms: at the Delhi horse races, when the local nobility would descend on the town from their country estates to take part in the Mogul Cup,[10] or in the Delhi Freemasons' Lodge, which admitted Indian members.[11]

One such event was the arrival of Messrs Trood and Co., who brought their travelling exhibition to Delhi. This exhibition included several microscopes, which were reported by the *Delhi Gazette* to have caused 'great consternation among native gentlemen [at] the curiosities revealed to their wondering eyes'.[12] Another such occasion was the coming of Monsieur Jordain and his Travelling Circus:

> The graceful riding and dancing of Madame Jordain called down
> repeated plaudits from the European portion of the audience, while

the natives testified their delight with involuntary wah wahs. Monsieur Jordain astonished not only the natives, but all beholders, with feats of strength, while Monsieur Oliver's novel feat on the ball, which he propelled round the circus, and up an inclined plane at the same time balancing himself on the summit . . . called forth well merited praise, as did also the performance of the obedient Pony Rajapack, who did all that he was told, and finished the evening by going to bed on a litter, and was thus carried off the ground.[13]

Yet the heart of the *Delhi Gazette*, like that of its readers, and indeed that of its restless editor, George Wagentrieber, was really elsewhere. There are frequent reports of the expansion of the British Empire – of the cannons fired to mark the end of the Second Anglo-Burmese war, the annexation of Pegu and the occupation of Rangoon; there are dispatches from the imperial front lines in the Crimea, Afghanistan and Persia. Most of all, however, the paper is full of news from home, of advertisements for comfortingly faux-English cottages in Simla and Mussoorie named Bridge View and Roseville, and for nice families in Sussex willing to take in children for an education so as to avoid their acquiring an Indian accent.[14] 'TO PARENTS AND GUARDIANS,' reads one advertisement. 'A Lady returning to England will be happy to obtain charge of a few children, and see them safe to their friends' destination on arrival.'[15] Another comes from 'a married clergyman residing on his living in a healthy part of Somersetshire, wishes to receive into his family one or two children . . . to share in the education of his own children, under his own charge. Terms from 60 guineas to 100 pounds.'[16]

This was a paper that knew exactly how to assuage the anxieties and nostalgia of impecunious exiles. But the people of Delhi, if they appear at all, are by the 1850s referred to only very occasionally, and then invariably with deep condescension, as 'natives' or 'our black bretherin'.[17] Wagentrieber's attitudes, however, were a little more complicated than these terms might indicate. For he was married to Elizabeth, the Anglo-Indian daughter of the famous James Skinner of Skinner's Horse, and a pillar of White Mughal society in Delhi.

James Skinner was the son of the Scottish mercenary Hercules Skinner, himself the son of the Provost of Montrose; his mother was a Rajputni, the daughter of a Rajput zamindar* from 'the Bojepoor country'.[18] Having fought bravely for the Marathas, Skinner eventually found himself ejected from their ranks because of his British father; later he fought for the English, only to be increasingly discriminated against by the East India Company because of his Indian blood: 'I imagined myself to be serving a people who had no prejudice against caste or colour,' he wrote in his memoirs. 'But I found myself to be mistaken.' His mixed inheritance was, he concluded, 'like a two-edged blade made to cut both ways against me'.[19] Skinner's services for the Mughal emperors led to him being given a title which his Montrose grandfather would have raised his eyebrows at: Nasir ud-Daulah Colonel James Skinner Bahadur Ghalib Jang, which the people of Delhi shortened to Sikandar Sahib, for the populace of the Mughal capital looked on him, it was said, as the reincarnation of Alexander the Great.

Skinner was a Christian who took his religion very seriously, and towards the end of his life he built St James's, the first church in Delhi,† and became a pillar of the Delhi Anglican community. This did not, however, prevent him from having a large number of *bibis* – 'there are any number of beautiful Mrs Skinners', wrote an impressed Fanny Eden,[20] fourteen according to one estimate[21] – and Skinner restored a beautiful Mughal mosque near his Delhi haveli for the Muslims among them, as well as (at least according to Delhi legend) building a temple for those who professed the Hindu faith. Fanny Eden described him as

a native colonel, very black [and] much better society than any of the white colonels we meet here, and who has done many warlike

* A zamindar was a landholder or local ruler.
† A small and little-known Armenian funerary chapel, attached to the old Armenian cemetery in Kishenganj, precedes St James's by a century or so. The chapel still remains in regular use near the Kishenganj railway station, and seems to be a last surviving fragment of the old Firangi Pura, the suburb of the European mercenaries, which was established in the late Mughal period near the later Sabzi Mandi.

wonders. He is staying here and is a very fine old man. We went on
Sunday to a large church he had built, and there is a mosque he has
also built very near it. He told me that where is God, there is religion,
but I suppose he calls himself a Musalman.[22]

Eden was wrong to make this assumption, but since Skinner lived in
an entirely Mughal style, and his English was stilted and ungram-
matical,[23] the mistake was understandable. His chief wife – who
may well have been Wagentrieber's mother-in-law – was certainly
Muslim: her name was Ashuri Khanam and she was a landowner in
her own right, while her father, a powerful Haryana zamindar
named Mirza Azim Beg, was Skinner's administrator at the barracks of Skinner's irregular cavalry regiment at Hansi.[24]

After the death of Sikandar Sahib, his different children 'of all
hues and colours' remained prominent landowners and courtiers in
Delhi, trying with increasing difficulty to bridge the widening gap
between the Mughal court and the British community, a task not
made any easier by the eccentric dress sense of some members of the
family. Even William Gardner could not help being amused by
Sikandar's brother, Robert Skinner: 'a greater dandy than ever, and
has more gold and silver chains around him than Baron Frank had
in the Magdeburg Dungeon'.[25] Some of the Skinners clearly found
being strung between two different worlds more of a strain than did
others: at one point Theo Metcalfe reported to his sister Georgina
(or GG, as everyone seems to have referred to her) that, 'Mr. J
Skinner has been intoxicated for two months and 14 days without a
lucid interval'.[26] Hence the complex undercurrents present in the
piece that Wagentrieber published in the *Gazette* bidding a firm
farewell to the era of the White Mughals, of whom his wife's own
family were so prominent a part, and whose day Wagentrieber now
clearly believed to be over. Whatever his feelings for his Skinner in-
laws, Wagentrieber clearly thought he knew where the future lay,
and which side to back.

It would not be long, however, before he would be very grateful
for his connection to this 'thoroughly Indianized' family, and for
his wife's dark skin colour, her fluency in Hindustani and her
ability to carry off a sari – all things which for Wagentrieber, and

maybe also his long-suffering wife, had up to now been a cause of mild but unmistakable embarrassment.

During the early 1850s, it sometimes seemed as if the British and the Mughals lived not only in different mental worlds, but almost in different time zones.

The British were the first up: in the cantonments to the north of the Delhi Civil Lines, the bugle sounded at 3.30 a.m., a time when the poetic *mushairas* of the Mughals were still in full flow in the Red Fort, and while in the *kothis**** of the courtesans in Chauri Bazaar the dancing and ghazal singing were drawing to a close, and the girls were progressing to the more intimate stage of their duties. As the Mughal poets and the courtesans raised their different tempos, sleepy, yawning Englishmen like Captain Robert Tytler, a fifty-year-old veteran of the 38th Native Infantry, or Lieutenant Harry Gambier, an eighteen-year-old Etonian newly arrived in India, would be sitting up in bed as their servants attempted to shave them and pull on their master's stockings.[27] A long session of drill in the cantonment parade ground lay ahead.

Two hours later, by the time the sun was beginning to rise over the Yamuna, and the poets, the courtesans and their patrons were all heading back to bed to sleep off their long nights, not only the soldiers but also the British civilians would be up and about and taking their exercise. A woman like Harriet Tytler, the brisk and no-nonsense wife of Robert, or the English community's great beauty, the lovely young Annie Forrest, to whom Harry Gambier was already writing politely admiring letters, would have been back from their morning rides round the cantonment: in order to protect a lady's complexion, it was not considered advisable to ride much after sunrise.[28]

By six, Harriet would be busy supervising her large staff of servants in her screen-darkened bungalow. The first task was preparing for the enormous breakfast without which no English-

---

* A substantial town house, often facing on to a network of courtyards.

man in Victorian India would consider starting his day: at the very
least a selection of 'crumbled chops, brain cutlets, beef rissoles,
devilled kidneys, whole spatchcocks, duck stews, Irish stews,
mutton hashes, brawns of sheep's heads and trotters, not to mention an assortment of Indian dishes such as *jhal frazie*, prawn
dopiaza, chicken *malai* and beef *Hussainee*. Added to this list were
a number of Anglo-Indian concoctions such as kidney toast Madras
style, Madras fritters, and leftover meat minced and refried with
ginger and chillies'.[29] Then of course there was the ultimate Anglo-
Indian breakfast dish of kedgeree, a perennial favourite, even
though in Delhi it was considered most inadvisable to eat fish in
high summer.*

As the cantonment memsahibs awaited the return of their menfolk from the parade ground, inside the city walls Padre Jennings
would be conducting the early morning service in the hush of St
James's Church. Soon the courts to one side of the graveyard would
come to life too: the two chief magistrates, John Ross Hutchinson
and Charles Le Bas, would already be in their offices, as would their
assiduous assistant, Arthur Galloway, and the *Sadr Amin* Mufti
Sadruddin, often known by his pen-name, Azurda. At the same
time, riding in through Kashmiri Gate, Theo Metcalfe, the other
joint magistrate, would be heading late towards his day's work,
regretting that he had not prepared his briefs as thoroughly as he
might have, and that he had not been up as early as his father, who
had already conducted half his day's business, besides taking a
swim, organising the household and reading the papers. George

---

* Overeating remained a leitmotif of British life in India right up until 1947. As late as
1926 Aldous Huxley was astonished by the sheer amount of food the imperial British
were capable of consuming: 'Five meals a day – two breakfasts, luncheon, afternoon tea
and dinner – are standard throughout India. A sixth is often added in the big towns
where there are theatres and dances to justify late supper. The Indian who eats at most
two meals a day, sometimes only one – too often none – is compelled to acknowledge
his inferiority . . . The Indians are impressed by our gastronomic prowess. Our
prestige is bound up with overeating. For the sake of the Empire the truly patriotic will
sacrifice his liver and his colon, will pave the way for future apoplexies and cancers of
the intestine. I did my best while I was in India. But at the risk of undermining our
prestige, of bringing down the whole imperial fabric in ruin around my ears, I used
from time to time unobtrusively to skip a course. The spirit is willing, but the flesh,
alas, is weak.' Aldous Huxley, *Jesting Pilate*, London, 1926, p. 108.

Wagentrieber would be up too. Having kissed his wife Elizabeth goodbye, he would now, like Theo, be heading down from the Civil Lines to the Kashmiri Gate offices of the *Delhi Gazette*, to begin his day of writing and proofreading the latest issue.

Among the people of Delhi, the poor woke long before the rich. As the sun rose, and as the British were returning from their morning rides and preparing for breakfast, up near the shrine of Qadam Sharif the first bird catchers were laying their nets and baiting them with millet, to catch the early birds out for their morning feed. Past them on the dusty road came the sellers of fruit and vegetables, some on bullock carts, most trudging on foot, streaming in from the villages of the Doab down the Alipore road, bringing their goods to the new suburb of Sabzi Mandi just outside the Kabul Gate, to the north-west of the city.

At the Raj Ghat Gate, the earlier-rising Hindu faithful – at this time of day women in their cotton saris far outnumbering the men – were streaming out to perform their *pujas* and have their morning bathe in the waters of the holy Yamuna before the crowds gathered and the dhobis appeared. Only the pandits kept them company this early in the morning: in small shrines lining the banks of the river up to Nigambodh Ghat, where according to Delhi legend the Vedas emerged from the waters, the bells were ringing now for the morning *Brahma Yagya*, celebrating the creating and re-creating of the world over and over again, morning after morning. As the differently pitched bells sounded against the Sanskrit chants, so in the dark of the inner sanctum the camphor lamps circled the images of Vishnu and the marigold-strewn black-stone Shiva lingams.

From deep inside the city – from the Masjid Kashmiri Katra in the south to Fatehpuri Masjid in the west, to the great Jama Masjid itself and on through to the elegant riverside minarets of the Zinat ul-Masajid – the last cries of the dawn *Azan* could now be heard, each call slightly out of time with the one before it, so that the successive cries of spiritual longing and assertion came to the listener on the riverbank in a series of rolling waves. In the silence that followed the end of the call to prayer, the songs of the first Delhi birds could suddenly be heard: the argumentative chuckle of the babblers, the sharp chatter of the mynahs, the alternating

clucking and squealing of the rosy parakeets, the angry exclama-
tions of the brain fever bird, and from deep inside the canopy of the
fruit trees in Zafar's gardens at Raushanara Bagh and Tis Hazari,
the woody hot-weather echo of the koel.

By now in the city itself, in the high-walled privacy of the
courtyards of the grander houses like that of the young courtier
Zahir Dehlavi in Matia Mahal, the servants were beginning to stir,
throats were being cleared, and bamboo blinds were being rolled
up to reveal water channels and fountains in the cloister gardens.
Soon bolsters and sheets were being tidied away to leave the
verandas of the courtyards free for breakfast – of mangoes or *aloo
puri* for the Hindus, or perhaps some mutton *shorba* for the
Muslims. Servants would draw water from wells, or head out
to buy fresh melons from the Sabzi Mandi; in some of the richer
houses coffee might be prepared. From the masculine side of the
house came the first gurgle of the hookah. In the zenana, children
were being dressed, *cholis, ghagras* and *angiyas* buttoned and
laced, *peshwaz* and saris wrapped. In the kitchen the daily ritual
of chopping onions, chillies and ginger would begin, and the
chickpeas and *channa dal* set to soak; elsewhere, the different
inhabitants of the zenana would begin their day praying, sewing,
embroidering, cooking or playing.

Before long the older boys would be heading off down the lanes
to arrive at the madrasas in time for the beginning of the day's
study: to work on memorising the Koran by heart, or to hear an
explication of its mysteries by the maulvi; or maybe it would be a
day for studying the arts of philosophy, theology and rhetoric. Far
from being a tedious chore, this was for many a thrilling business:
one eager pupil who came to Delhi from a small town on the Grand
Trunk Road used to go to the lectures at the Madrasa i-Rahimiyya
even in the pouring monsoon rain, carrying his books in a pot in
order to protect them from getting wet.[30] The elderly Zakaullah
remembered running at breakneck speed through the *galis* of
Shahjahanabad, such was his excitement at the new learning –
and especially the mathematics – he was being taught at the Delhi
College. Even Colonel William Sleeman, famous for his suppression of the Thugs and a leading critic of the administration of the

Indian courts, had to admit that the madrasa education given in Delhi was something quite remarkable: 'Perhaps there are few communities in the world among whom education is more generally diffused than among Muhammadans in India,' he wrote on a visit to the Mughal capital.

> He who holds an office worth twenty rupees a month commonly gives his sons an education equal to that of a prime minister. They learn, through the medium of Arabic and Persian languages, what young men in our colleges learn through those of Greek and Latin – that is grammar, rhetoric, and logic. After his seven years of study, the young Muhammadan binds his turban upon a head almost as well filled with the things which appertain to these branches of knowledge as the young man raw from Oxford – he will talk as fluently about Socrates and Aristotle, Plato and Hippocrates, Galen and Avicenna; (alias Sokrat, Aristotalis, Alflatun, Bokrat, Jalinus and Bu Ali Sena); and, what is much to his advantage in India, the languages in which he has learnt what he knows are those which he most requires through life.[31]

The reputation of Delhi madrasas was certainly sufficient to inspire the young poet Altaf Husain Hali to flee his marriage in Panipat and walk the 53 miles to Delhi, alone and penniless and sleeping rough, in an attempt to realise his dream of studying in the famous colleges there: 'Everyone wanted me to look for a job,' he wrote later, 'but my passion for learning prevailed.'[32] Delhi was after all a celebrated intellectual centre, and in the early 1850s it was at the peak of its cultural vitality. It had six famous madrasas and at least four smaller ones, nine newspapers in Urdu and Persian, five intellectual journals published out of the Delhi College, innumerable printing presses and publishers, and no fewer than 130 Yunani doctors.[33] Here many of the new wonders uncovered by Western science were being translated for the first time into Arabic and Persian, and in the many colleges and madrasas the air of intellectual openmindedness and excitement was palpable.[34]

But the biggest draw of all were the poets and intellectuals, men such as Ghalib, Zauq, Sahbai and Azurda: 'By some good fortune', wrote Hali, 'there gathered at this time in the capital, Delhi, a band of men so talented that their meetings and assemblies recalled the days of Akbar and Shah Jahan.'[35] Hali's family tracked him down eventually, but before they found him, and hauled him back to married life in the mofussil (provinces), he was able to gain admittance in the 'very spacious and beautiful' madrasa of Husain Bakhsh and to begin his studies there: 'I saw with my own eyes this last brilliant glow of learning in Delhi,' he wrote in old age, 'the thought of which now makes my heart crack with regret.'[36]

Meanwhile, on Chandni Chowk, although Mr Beresford, the manager of the Delhi Bank, had been at work since 9 a.m., it was eleven o'clock before the first shopkeepers began turning up. They opened the shutters of their booths, fed their canaries and caged parakeets, and began fending off the first of the beggars and holy mendicants who bounced coins in their bowls as they passed up the gauntlet of shops. Some of these figures were well known and even revered Delhi characters, such as the *Majzub* (holy madman) Din Ali Shah: 'He is so careless about the affairs of this world', wrote Sayyid Ahmad Khan in a sketch of Delhi's most famous citizens, 'that he remains naked most of the time, and when surrounded by a crowd is likely to break out into intemperate language. But when the desirous seekers ponder over the words, they find that behind the outward senselessness there is a clear answer to their queries.'[37] Some of the most revered mendicants were women, such as Baiji, 'a woman of exceptional talent who spent all her life under a hay thatch near the Old Idgah of Shahjahanabad. While conversing she often quoted Quranic verses . . . whatever she had said would take place exactly as she predicted'.[38]

Out on the pavements, tradesmen too humble to have their own premises were now filling their appointed places: the ear cleaner with his pick and probe, the tooth cleaner with his bundles of neem twigs, the astrologer with his cards and his parrot, the quack with his lizards and bottles of murky aphrodisiac oils, the kabutar-wallah with his fantails and fancy doves. Meanwhile, in their workshops off the main street frontage, away from the eyes of passers-by, the jewellers were preparing their emeralds and moonstones, topaz and diamonds, rubies from Burma, spinels from Badakshan and lapis from the Hindu Kush. Shoemakers took their cured leather and began curling the toes of their *juties* on the last; the sword-makers began lighting their forges; the cloth merchants pulled out their bolts of fabric; the spice merchants smoothed into shape their orange-gold mountains of turmeric.

In the largest premises of all, guarded by mace bearers, were the great Jain and Marwari moneylenders of Delhi with their family credit networks and groaning registers stuffed full of debtors' names, which included, after Mirza Jawan Bakht's wedding, Zafar himself. Down they slumped against their bolsters, dreaming of schemes for recovering the implausible sums of money they had so unwisely lent to the impecunious princes of the Red Fort – men like Lala Saligram, Bhawani Shankar and the richest of all, Lala Chunna Mal, the largest single investor in Mr Beresford's Delhi Bank, in his massive and opulent haveli in Katra Nil.[39]

Just as Chandni Chowk was waking up, 2 miles to the north, in the cantonment, the working day was already drawing to a close, and most of the soldierly duties were already completed. A bathe, a quick read of the papers and a game of billiards filled an hour or two, before the heat in the small brick bachelor bungalows became unbearable and all that remained to do until late afternoon was to sprawl around 'in loose dishabille, reading, lounging and sleeping'.[40] With little to occupy them most of the day, for many British soldiers boredom was the principal enemy they faced in India: 'My disgraceful laziness is appalling,' wrote Allen Johnson of the 5th Bengal Native Infantry in his diary around this time. 'I have hardly opened a book or written a line for the last ten days. In fact I have done absolutely nothing but lounge and saunter about, now taking up a book and gazing at it with a lack luster [*sic*] eye or kicking about restlessly in my bed. My only fixed idea have been yearnings for home and a detestation of natives and native things.'[41]

For Sir Thomas Metcalfe, a little to the south at the Residency offices of Ludlow Castle in the Civil Lines, the day's work was also nearly done: his various meetings were finished, the queries from the kotwal* and courts were answered, his letters were written, and

---

* The Indian head of the city police. A kotwal was also the chief magistrate, and in some Mughal cities the chief administrator too. A kotwal's office was called the kotwali.

the news from the Palace had been studied, summarised and forwarded to Agra and Calcutta.

Soon after 1 p.m., as Sir Thomas was heading back to Metcalfe House in his carriage, his day's work completed, things were just beginning to stir in the Red Fort. Zafar was quite capable of rising early if a hunting expedition was in store, something he enjoyed well into his late seventies;* but after a *mushaira* (poetic sympo-sium) or a *mehfil* (evening of courtly entertainment), he preferred to lie long abed. His day would begin with 'the arrival of the water women coming bearing a silver basin and silver water pots. They would spread a mat (made of either cloth or leather) and on it place the silver basin and the water pot. The female towel bearers would then come in carrying napkins to clean the Royal face and feet, and towels and handkerchiefs for cleaning the Royal nose'.[42]

Morning prayers would follow, after which Dr Chaman Lal was on hand to rub olive oil into Zafar's feet.[43] There had been calls from the *'ulama* for the doctor's dismissal after his conversion to Christianity, but Zafar had replied that the doctor's faith was his own private matter and 'there was no cause for shame in what he had done', so the doctor continued to give his daily ministrations at the Palace.[44] A light breakfast followed, eaten cross-legged on a sheet, during which the metre and rhyme pattern (*tarah*) for the evening's *mushaira* might be discussed.† Then Zafar would take a quick round of the Palace, escorted by his troupe of Abyssinian, Turkish and Tartar women guards, all of whom wore male military dress, and were armed with bows and a quiver of arrows.[45]

* One late Delhi source describes Zafar setting out hunting at 3 a.m. on a winter's morning, attended by sixty shikaris, beaters and torchbearers. According to this Urdu source, Zafar would shoot from his palanquin while the beaters drove the game towards him, or if looking for duck and waterfowl, they would drive the birds ashore. See Arsh Taimuri, *Qila-i Mua'lla ki Jhalkiyan*, ed. Dr Aslam Parvez, Urdu Academy, Delhi, 1986. The section on Zafar's hunting expeditions gives the impression of an enthusiastic and energetic sportsman, but the source was written a generation after Zafar's exile so its accuracy may be dubious.

† Zafar was known for setting his court difficult poetic tasks. Azad tells of his fondness for making his court poets practise the difficult art of *tazmin* – adding an extra line to their couplets so as to turn them into three-liners without losing the sense or the rhythm. See Muhammad Husain Azad (trans. and ed. Frances Pritchett and Shamsur Rahim Faruqi), *Ab-e Hayat: Shaping the Canon of Urdu Poetry*, New Delhi, 2001, p. 377.

Afterwards, Zafar would attend to petitions; receive visits and gifts from his gardeners, shikaris and fishermen; administer justice to any more slave girls caught in flagrante or *salatin* caught stealing; and then receive his *ustad*, Zauq, who would help correct his latest verses. Occasionally he might also receive his own pupils for composition and help correct their verses: one March, for example, the court diary records him as taking 'A Khasburdar and a female – Piram Jan – as pupils in poetical composition.'*46 Certainly writing and correcting verses took up several hours of the Emperor's day: as Azad put it simply, Zafar 'was madly in love with poetry'.†47

Meanwhile, elsewhere in his apartments within the Shah Burj tower on the river side of the Palace, Mirza Fakhru would be busy with his calligraphy, or writing his *History of the Kings and Prophets*, while his younger brothers would be beginning their schoolwork, something the Mughals took very seriously: 'All of them are kept continually at their studies and watched with great caution,' wrote one visitor. 'Few or no princes in India can vie with any of the royal persons [of Delhi] not only in acquired qualifications but also in those qualities of the mind, generally

---

* From her name, Piram Jan would appear to be a courtesan. The fact that Zafar was prepared publicly to instruct courtesans is interesting evidence of the high social status of the better courtesans in Mughal Delhi, and the degree to which many of them were renowned for their poetic talents.

† Modern Urdu critics are divided as to the merits of Zafar's poetry, but at the time contemporary descriptions of Zafar's poetic gifts often gave way to hyperbole. '*Mazmuns* [themes] of submission in his poetry are equal in rank to pride and coquetry,' wrote the critic Sabir in 1855. 'The radiance of meaning is manifest through his words.' Not just the words, but the very letters were like magical charms: 'The sequences of lines, through the reflections of *mazmuns* are lampwicks for the bed-chamber of the page. The circular letters, through the effect of meaning, are the wine marks on the flagon in the festive gathering of the pages. The colourfulness of festive meaning is the glistening of wine; in martial verses, the wetness of the ink is blood and perspiration. In mystical verses, the circular letters are seeing eyes; and in romantic verses, tear-shedding eyes. And in verses concerning the coming of Spring, the decorations between the lines are flower beds.' Just as the Emperor was the centre of the universe, the *axis mundi*, 'refuge of both worlds, for whom angels do battle, ruler of time and space, lord of crown and seal . . . at whose command, which is the twin of fate, the revolution of the sky is established', so the themes of his poetry encompassed the whole world. As Sabir put in an Urdu pun, 'from the east/opening verse [*matla*] to the West/closing verse [*maqta*] is the excursion ground of that Sun whose domes are the skies.' See Pritchett, *Nets of Awareness*, p. 11.

the gift of nature, and consequent to a good and virtuous education.'[48]

A serious princely education at this period put great stress on the study of logic, philosophy, mathematics, astronomy, law and medicine. It was also expected, as in the courts of Renaissance Europe, that any truly civilised prince should be able to compose verse, and the *Garden of Poetry*, a biographical dictionary of Urdu poets produced in 1850, mentions no fewer than fifty members of Zafar's immediate family. Several of these are women, and Bishop Heber particularly noted the emphasis Zafar put on female education in the Palace.[49]

In his youth, Zafar was himself a good example of the sort of rounded Renaissance Man that a serious Mughal education sought to produce: he was fluent in Urdu, Arabic and Persian, but had also mastered Braj Basha and Punjabi sufficiently to write verse in both.*[50] By the age of thirty-three he had already produced a volume of his collected poetry, a long verse-by-verse commentary on Sa'adi's *Gulistan* (The Rose Garden), 'a three volume dictionary of prosody', and a treatise on the Deccani language.[51] He was also, in his youth, a renowned rider, swordsman and archer, and remained a crack shot with a rifle into old age.[52] Even Sir Thomas's chilly elder brother, Sir Charles, no fan of the Mughal court, had had to admit that Zafar 'was the most respectable and accomplished of the princes'.[53]

One Mughal prince who did not show the slightest interest in studying was Mirza Jawan Bakht. He frequently skipped lessons to go off by himself on a shooting expedition, not always with happy results: on one occasion, according to the Resident's court diary, 'it was reported that Mirza Jawan Bakht had fired a pistol at a pigeon and that two of the shot had lodged in a man's leg, who was bathing in the Yamuna. HM was much displeased and sent 6 rupees to the wounded man and directed Mahbub Ali Khan to send all the guns and pistols and tulwars [swords] in the Prince's possession to HM and that the Prince was to pursue his studies'.[54]

Breakfast in the Red Fort would often coincide with the light

* Zafar composed a volume of verse in four of his five languages; only Arabic was omitted.

tiffin lunch served at 1 p.m. in the cantonment – a grilled fowl perhaps, modest in comparison to the gargantuan proportions of the Anglo-Indian breakfasts and dinners with which tiffin was flanked. Metcalfe House, however, as ever worked on its own routine, precisely set by Sir Thomas. Here dinner was served at the unusual time of 3 p.m., for Sir Thomas found this was 'conducive to his health', after which he read for a while in the Napoleon Gallery, before descending to the cool undercroft for a long solitary game of billiards, 'that was a great amusement to him and gave him the exercise he required', it also kept him occupied during the worst of the day's heat.[55]

For three hours, during seven months of the year, the Delhi afternoon heat emptied the streets, leaving them deserted: a blazing white midnight clearing the lanes and *galis*, and hushing the city into uncharacteristic silence. In the cantonments, the sweating young soldiers tossed and turned on their beds, shouting to the punkah-wallah outside to pull harder.

In the city, however, inside the cool shade of the courtyards of the high-ceilinged havelis, life would continue as normal: the *khas* screens made of fragrant grass would be soaked in scented water and then raised over the arcades of cusped arches; beautifully woven *shamianas* would be raised by ropes run through metal hoops in the projecting eves of the *baradari* pavilions. Those who had cool underground *tehkhanas* would retreat there, to continue uninterrupted the day's chores – sewing, letter writing and teaching the smaller children – and pleasures – smoking and playing cards, *pachchisi* and chess. One British traveller who was taken down to one of these subterranean catacombs was amazed at what he saw: 'So much is the temperature decreased', he wrote,

that twelve and even fourteen degrees have been discovered between the atmosphere of the Ty-Khouna, and the atmosphere of the room above ground, and seldom less than ten degrees . . . The descent to the apartment was about thirty feet, and the surprise and pleasure were equal, to find such beautiful rooms and so elegantly arranged and furnished. Coloured to resemble marble, the eye is at first deceived by the likeness; the deception is countenanced by the coolness, so different from the oppressive sensation always felt above. Long corridors lead to different apartments, embellished with coloured walls, and other decorations ... many exquisite drawings of places of celebrity in Delhi and its neighbourhood add to the appearance of this fairy palace: light is admitted from above ... a retreat of this kind in the hot months of April, May and June is a luxury scarcely to be described, when by every precaution possible to be taken, the thermometer above stairs can rarely be brought below eighty five; very often it is ninety ...'[56]

It was only towards late afternoon, around five o'clock, that things began to stir above ground and life returned to the Delhi streets. The *bhishtis* would be the first out, emptying their goatskins of water on the dust and chaff covering the roads; in their booths, the *paan* wallahs would begin preparing their betel leaves; the *kakkar-walah* or hookah man would begin roaming the dhabas; the opium shops would soon be doing good business too.* In the Sufi shrines, the pace would also quicken, as the thin stream of afternoon devotees thickened to the crowds of evening, as the rose-petal sellers in the lanes near by woke from their squatting slumbers, and the qawwals with their tablas and harmoniums struck up the qawwalis: 'Allah hoo, Allah hoo, Allah hoo ...'

In the Red Fort, for the *salatin*, this was the best time for practising archery, for quail, ram or cock fighting, and for falcon and pigeon flying.[57] In summer, some went swimming or fishing in the Yamuna just below the Palace, though this was not without its risks: one May, for example, the seventeen-year-old 'Mirza Kaus Shekoh was carried off by an alligator' only three weeks after celebrating his marriage with dancing and fireworks.[58] In the monsoon there were kites to fly (for the men) and swings to enjoy (for the women). Zafar, meanwhile, was settling down to his

---

* In northern India opium was drunk rather than smoked, and judging by the frequency with which opium shops appear in miniatures of the period, opium addiction seems to have been a major problem. Since the Company had the monopoly on the growing and trade in the substance, which by the 1850s provided an astonishing 40 per cent of their exports from India, it of course made no attempt to control the problem.

favourite early evening occupation of watching his elephants being bathed in the river below his apartments, or 'looking at the fishermen at work'.[59]

This was followed by an evening of airing among the orange trees of the Palace gardens, sometimes on foot, but usually in a palanquin.[60] For the Mughals, gardens were regarded as reflections of paradise, and a connoisseurship of plants and scents was considered a central attribute of a civilised mind. As he passed, Zafar would inspect the gardeners at work, and give orders for 'mango grafts to [be sent to] the Hyatt Bakhsh Bagh', or orange saplings and 'plaintain grafts' to be arranged in groups in the New Garden that he had personally planned, and had planted, on the riverbank below his apartments.*[61]

Occasionally, when Zafar was feeling energetic, he would descend to the riverbank and go fishing, or spend the evening flying kites on the sand near Salimgarh.[62] Sometimes he would send for Ghalib to keep him company and entertain him, though Ghalib did not much enjoy being an attentive courtier and found the whole experience fatiguing. 'My friend,' he wrote to one correspondent in December 1856, 'I swear by your head [that after a day of assiduous flattery at court] I lie down to sleep at night as exhausted as a labourer.'†[63]

Up in the cantonments, some of the more officious colonels would order an evening parade; others would save themselves the bother and head straight for the mess. Meanwhile Theo Metcalfe, released from his magistrate's court, would be out riding on the riverbank north of Metcalfe House, with his dogs running beside him, and dreaming perhaps of winning a prize (and beating off the

---

* One pair of visiting noblemen who wished to ingratiate themselves with Zafar arrived with 'carts laden with fruit, trees and flowers which they had brought from Lucknow'. They had judged their *nazr* well, and were both immediately rewarded with senior positions at court. See NAI, *Precis of Palace Intelligence*, entry for 2 August 1852.

† Part of the reason for this may have been that Zafar's kite flying often seems to have drawn an admiring crowd. When Debendrenath Tagore visited Delhi shortly before 1857 the first thing that he saw as he approached the city was a large crowd 'gathered to watch the Emperor's prowess as a kite flyer'. Cited by Narayani Gupta, *Delhi between Two Empires 1803–1931*, New Delhi, 1981, p. 13.

tough competition from the Skinners) at the annual North Indian
Coursing Club Meet, of which his father was president. The club's
annual competition for best puppy, held each winter, was an event
of such central importance to the British community that the *Delhi
Gazette* was known on occasion to give over a whole issue to it.[64]
Sir Thomas, meanwhile, was sitting on his riverside terrace, looking
forward to a quick evening meal and early bed. His terrace was his
favourite place, and this time of day found him most relaxed. 'Three
or four chairs were placed [around the terrace], and here he sat for a
couple of hours till it was time to dress for dinner in the evening. It
was the custom for his friends to come at this time to see and chat
with him . . .'

As the sun set, the churches, mosques and temples filled again:
the ringing of the bells of the evening *arti*, the final call to prayer
from the minarets, and the basso profundo of the organ chords
concluding Padre Jennings' evensong in St James's, all fusing
together with the rumble of British carriages heading out towards
the Civil Lines through the bottleneck of Kashmiri Gate – where
the bricking up of the second of the two arches was a cause of
frequent complaints in the *Delhi Gazette*.[65]

As the gloaming thickened, the lights were lit in the Red Fort by a
procession of torchbearers accompanied by tabors, trumpets and
pipes, while out in the city the streets were filling with the Delhi
College students and the madrasa boys returning in the half-light,
exhausted from a day's hard study and memorising.[66] The two streams
would rarely mingle, however. As Hali recalled many years later,

> Although the old Delhi College was then in all its glory, I'd been
> brought up in a society that believed that learning was based only on
> knowledge of Arabic and Persian . . . nobody even thought about
> English education, and if people had any opinion about it at all it was
> as a means of getting a government job, not of acquiring any kind of
> knowledge. On the contrary our religious teachers called the English
> schools barbarous.[67]

For the English, sunset was the beginning of the end of the day.
They had another vast meal to look forward to – more mulliga-

tawny, 'an overgrown turkey (the fatter the better) . . . an enormous ham, at the top of the table an enormous sirloin or round of beef; at the bottom a saddle of mutton, legs of the same, boiled and roasted down the side, together with fowls, three in a dish, geese, ducks, tongues, humps, pigeon pies . . . mutton chops and chicken cutlets', devilled bones, and stews and curries of any game the sportsmen among them had shot during the day;* but there was little to look forward to thereafter.[68] The French traveller Victor Jacquemont was particularly unimpressed by the after-dinner entertainments offered by the British society of Delhi: 'I have not seen the slightest exhibition of pleasure amongst the idlers at [Delhi] parties,' he wrote. 'None of the conditions which make a ball a pleasurable thing in Paris exist in the European community at Delhi.'[69]

It was certainly true that the British community in Delhi were an eccentric lot, even by the standards of Victorian expats. Emily Metcalfe was particularly struck by the Civil Surgeon, Dr Ross ('short and corpulent and very ugly . . . a shocking bad doctor'), whose three standard prescriptions were leeches, senna packed into dirty 'black beer bottles, and huge pills sent in a rough wooden box';[70] and Dr Alois Sprenger, the Principal of Delhi College, whose wife ('worthy but common', according to Emily) used to hide her husband's trousers to prevent his going out in the evening and leaving her alone.[71]

Certainly, the British in Delhi were always to some extent looking over their shoulder to the more Anglicised station of Meerut, which with its huge cantonment and large English community was famous for its theatre and its lavish regimental balls. But Delhi could boast almost none of that: 'There is little society here,' complained one junior Residency official, adding that after he had finished his court work he had little option but to take refuge in the company of his classical library: 'I have not quite forgot old Latin – Greek long since fled – but Livy, Tacitus or Caesar still now

---

* 'You can curry anything,' advised Mr Arnot of Greenwich in one Raj cookbook, 'old shoes should even be delicious, some old oil cloth or staircarpet not to be found fault with (though gloves if much worn are too rich).' See David Burton, *The Raj at Table*, p. 76.

and then employ an hour agreeably – and Virgil & Horace often peeped into.'[72]

Theo Metcalfe, not one to waste time on classical studies, looked for other amusements. He tried his hand at after-dinner music-making with some of the ladies of the British community: 'I have joined the Philharmonic Society,' he told his sister GG in one letter, 'and pass a pleasant enough evening – the only apparent drawback to the harmony is the presence of the Gorgons. "Hell-in-er" looked at me the other day with green eyes, just like an angry dog, but could hardly have enjoyed herself for she was not spoken to the whole evening. Miss Forrest meanwhile is currently only being worshipped by 5 Lieutenants and 3 Ensigns. Mrs Balfour [the surgeon's wife] encourages them in a very indelicate manner.'[73] Theo's sister GG also enjoyed a musical evening, though in her case piano playing was often merely an excuse to see her fiancé Edward Campbell, whose style of singing – when she was honest with herself – she admitted was a little slow for her taste, much as she adored his fine tenor.[74]

Theo also tried his hand at the Delhi Amateur Dramatics, taking parts in *Who's the Dope?* and *The Polka Mania* to raise money 'for the distressed of the Scotch Highlands and Islands', though according to the *Delhi Gazette* it was not he but 'Robin Roughhead as Jimmy [who] convulsed the house with laughter . . . the curtain fell with a hearty and well deserved applause'.[75]

None of this sort of thing was at all to the taste of Sir Thomas, who liked to be the first to bed: 'In the evening he only made a very light meal,' remembered his daughter Emily,

for it was his invariable custom to leave the dining room at eight o'clock in order to go to bed early. It used to be a great source of amusement . . . to watch his proceedings as soon as the 'retiring gun' fired and the clock struck eight. He immediately got up from the chair where he was smoking his hookah, said goodnight to every-body at the table, undid his neckcloth, threw it on the ground while he was walking to the door, unfastened his waistcoat buttons and then turned and gave a wave of his hand as he disappeared behind the curtain into his dressing room . . .[76]

For the people of Delhi, however, the best part of the day lay ahead. Chandni Chowk really came alive only after sunset, as the pavements swelled with wide-eyed boys from the mofussil or Jat farmers and Gujar herdsmen in from their villages in Haryana, ogling the gamblers locked in the stocks outside the kotwal or heading off to ask for blessings and good fortune at the city's matrix of bustling Sufi shrines. Elsewhere could be seen gentlemen visiting from Lucknow in their distinctive cut of wide-bottomed pyjamas or tall, bearded Pathan horse traders fresh in from Peshawar and Ambala, spilling out of the sarais and into Ghantawallahs, the famous sweet shop, whose *laddus* were supposed to be the best in Hindustan. The coffee houses – the *qahwa khanas* – were filling up now too, with poets reciting their verses at some tables, scholars locked in debate at others.

On the steps of the Jama Masjid, the storytellers would be beginning their recitations, which could go on for seven or eight hours with only a short break. The most popular of all the tales was the *Dastan i-Amir Hamza*, a chivalrous epic romance which collected together a great miscellany of fireside yarns, legends, religious discourses and shaggy-dog stories which over time came to gather around the story of the travels of Hamza, the uncle of the Prophet. Any factual backbone the story might once have had was swamped over the centuries with a flood of subplots and a cast of dragons, giants, sorcerers, princesses and flying carpets, as well as flying pots, the preferred mode of travel for the magicians in *Hamza*.

In its fullest form, the tale grew to contain a massive twenty thousand separate stories, and would take several weeks of all-night storytelling to complete; the printed version filled forty-six volumes. As listeners gathered around the *Dastan-go*, who was telling of the handsome, courageous and chivalrous Hamza, his beautiful Persian princess lovers and Hamza's terrible nemesis, the cruel necromancer and arch-fiend Zumurrud Shah, at the other side of the steps Jani the celebrated kebab man would now be fanning his charcoal. Delhiwallahs used to like to surprise visitors from outside by taking them to eat there without telling them of 'the pot of hot chillis' with which Jani would marinate his kebabs. Maulvi Muhammad Baqar's son, the young poet Azad, told of one stranger to

Delhi who 'hadn't eaten for a whole day. He stretched his jaws wide and fell on it [the kebab]. And instantly it was as if his brains had been blown out of his mouth by gunpowder. He leapt back with a howl. [But the Delhiwallah who brought him replied:] "we live here only for this sharp taste." '[77]

Zafar was also fond of a little chilli in his dinner, which he began to eat no earlier than 10.30 p.m., a time when most of the British were already well tucked up in their beds. Quail stew, venison, lamb kidneys on sweet nan called *shir mal, yakhni*, fish kebabs, and meat stewed with oranges were Zafar's favourite dishes, though on festive occasions the Red Fort kitchens were capable of producing astonishingly varied and prodigious quantities of Mughlai cuisine: the *Bazm i-Akhir* describes a feast consisting of twenty-five varieties of bread, twenty-five different kinds of pilaos and biryanis, thirty-five different sorts of spiced stews and curries, and fifty different puddings, as well as remarkable varieties of relishes and pickles, all eaten to the sound of singers performing ghazals, while the fragrance of musk, saffron, sandalwood and rosewater filled the air.[78]

Whatever the dish, Zafar was known to like his food heavily spiced – and he was most upset when his friend, prime minister and personal physician, Hakim Ahsanullah Khan, banned him from eating 'cayenne pepper' in August 1852, following a series of digestive disorders.[79] Another of Zafar's great pleasures, mango jam, was also forbidden by the hakim, who said that Zafar's excessive indulgence in it gave him diarrhoea. When Zafar continued to ignore his advice and then suffered from a bad stomach, the hakim 'was very annoyed and replied that if the King would act in this way he had better dismiss him at once. HM excused himself and promised greater abstinence in future'.[80]

For Ghalib, the late evening was also the time for indulging in mango-related pleasures, especially the exquisitely small, sweet *chausa* mango, a taste he shared with many other discerning Delhiwallahs, past and present. At one gathering, a group of Delhi intellectuals were discussing what qualities a good mango should have: 'In my view,' said Ghalib, 'there are only two essential points about mangoes – they should be sweet and they should be plentiful.'[81] In his old age he became worried about his declining appetite for his favourite fruit and wrote to a friend to express his anxieties. He never ate an evening meal, he told his correspondent; instead, on hot summer nights he would 'sit down to eat the mangoes when my food was fully digested, and I tell you bluntly, I would eat them until my belly was bloated and I could hardly breathe. Even now I eat them at the same time of day, but not more than ten or twelve, or if they are of the large kind, only six or seven'.*[82]

There was one other great pleasure that Ghalib reserved for the cover of darkness. 'There are seventeen bottles of good wine in the pantry,' he wrote to one friend, describing his idea of perfection. 'So I read all day and drink all night.'[83]

As Ghalib was finishing his mangoes and looking forward to his bottle of wine,† as the exhausted labourers were heading home to their villages before the *muhalla* gates were locked for the night, and as Saligram and the moneylenders began finally shutting up their shops in Chandni Chowk, so in the Fort dinner was drawing to a close. This was the signal for Zafar's hookah to be brought and the evening's entertainment to begin. This could take a number of forms: ghazals from Tanras Khan; the instrumental playing of a group of sarangi players, or the court storytellers and troupes of the Fort's dancing girls. Most celebrated of all was Himmat Khan, Zafar's famous blind sitar player: 'Nobody could come close to him in Dhrupad,' thought Sir Sayyid Ahmad Khan.

---

* There is a famous story that one day Ghalib was walking with Zafar in the Mahtab Bagh of the Red Fort at a time when the mangoes were in fruit. The mangoes were reserved for the royal family, but as they walked Ghalib kept craning his head to look with great concentration at the mangoes hanging there. 'The King asked him, "Mirza, what are you looking at so attentively?" Ghalib replied with joined hands, "My Lord and guide, some ancient poet has written:

> Upon the top of every fruit is written clear and legibly:
> This is the property of A, the son of B, the son of C

and I am looking to see whether any of these bears my name and those of my father and grandfather." The King smiled and the same day had a big basket of the finest mangoes sent to him.' Ralph Russell and Khurshid Islam, *Ghalib: Life and Letters*, New Delhi, 1994, p. 98.
† Like many writers, Ghalib was not completely averse to a wee tipple during the day too, but on these occasions tended to drink it diluted with rosewater, and sip it gradually while writing.

If [Akbar's great musician] Tansen were still alive, he would have humbly become a disciple . . . Rulers and notables from all corners pleaded with him to join their service and offered him lots of money and riches, but he refused to budge from Delhi out of that self-containment and self-contentment that is the particular preserve of Men of Art. Any singer who arrived in Shahajahanabad claiming distinction in the art would forget their *sur* and *taal* [note and beat] after hearing only one bar of his music and would accept the dust of his feet as the decoration of their eye . . . His inner pain and the joy of holy wisdom suffused the singing of this extraordinary and notably self-effacing genius.[84]

On other occasions, when Zafar felt the need for some peace, one of his great pleasures was to play chess while waiting for the new moon to come up. At other times he is described as simply sitting after dinner and 'enjoying the moonlight'.[85]

If Zafar wanted an early night – which meant one that ended around midnight – singers might be admitted to his bedchamber, where they would sing behind screens, while his masseuses worked on his head and feet, and the Abyssinian guards took their place at his door.[86] In 1852, after the disgrace of Tanras Khan, Zafar's preferred serenader was the woman referred to simply as 'Khanam the Singer'.[87] Sometimes it is clear that such singers came out from behind the bedroom screens: one of Zafar's last marriages was to a singing girl named Man Bai, who became known as Akhtar Mahal following her wedding in 1847, when Zafar was seventy-two.

On such nights, when Zafar retired relatively early, many of the princes would head out into the town as things began to wind down in the Fort. Some might have assignations in the *kothis* of the Chauri Bazaar, where lights and the movement of dancing could be seen from behind the lattices of the upper floors, and the sounds of tabla and singing could be heard from as far away as Chandni Chowk. 'The women deck themselves in finery,' noted one visitor, 'and position themselves at vantage points to attract the attention of men, either directly or through pimps. An atmosphere of lust and debauchery prevails here and the people gather at night and indulge themselves.'[88]

The beauty and coquettishness of Delhi's courtesans were famous:

people still talked of the celebrated courtesan Ad Begum of a century earlier, who would famously turn up stark naked at parties, but so cleverly painted that no one would notice: 'she decorates her legs with beautiful drawings in the style of pyjamas instead of actually wearing them; in place of the cuffs she draws flowers and petals in ink exactly as is found in the finest cloth of Rum'. Her great rival, Nur Bai, was said to be so popular that every night the elephants of the great Mughal *umrah* completely blocked the narrow lanes outside her house, yet even the most senior nobles had 'to send a large sum of money to have her admit them . . . whoever gets enamoured of her gets sucked into the whirlpool of her demands and brings ruin in on his house . . . but the pleasure of her company can only be had as long as one is in possession of riches to bestow on her'.[89]

Nevertheless, in 1852, at the height of the career of Zauq and Ghalib, the biggest draw was not the courtesans but the *mushairas* of the poets, especially those held in the courtyard of the old Delhi College just outside Ajmeri Gate, or in the house of Mufti Sadruddin Azurda.

Farhatullah Baig's *Dehli ki akhri shama* (The Last Musha'irah of Delhi) is a fictionalised but well-informed account of what purports to be one of the last great *mushairas* held in Zafar's Delhi. Around the illuminated courtyard of the haveli of Mubarak Begum, the widowed *bibi* of Sir David Ochterlony, sit several poet-princes of the royal house, as well as forty other Delhi poets, including Azurda, Momin, Zauq, Azad, Dagh, Sahbai, Shefta, Mir, a celebrated wrestler named Yal and Ghalib himself. There was also a last White Mughal, Alex Heatherly, 'one of the great poets of the Urdu language', according to one critic,[90] who was related to the Skinners and so a cousin of Elizabeth Wagentrieber.

The courtyard has been filled so as to raise it to the level of the plinth of the house. On the wooden planks were spread cotton rugs. There was a profusion of chandeliers, candelabra, wall lamps, hanging lamps and Chinese lanterns so that the house was converted into a veritable dome of light . . . From the centre of the roof were hung row upon row of jasmine garlands . . . the whole house was fragrant with musk, amber and aloes . . . Arranged in a row, at short intervals along the carpet, were the huqqas, burnished and brightly polished . . .

The seating pattern was arranged so that those assigned places on the right of the presiding poet had connections with the Lucknow court, and on the left were seated the Delhi masters and their pupils. All those who came from the fort held quails in their hand as the craze for quail and cock fighting was very strong at that time . . .[91]

The often extremely complex metre and rhyme patterns would be set well in advance; many of the participants would know each other well, and a spirit of friendly competition would be encouraged. The hookahs would be passed around, as would paan and sweets. Then the president – in this case Mirza Fakhru – would say the *Bismillah*.

At this proclamation there would be pin-drop silence. The guests from the court put away their quails in their quail pouches and disposed of them behind the bolsters. The servants removed the water pipes and in their place put down spittoons [for betel chewers], the *khasdans* with betel leaf and trays with aromatic spices in front of each guest. In the meantime the personal representative of the king arrived from the court with the king's ghazal, accompanied by several heralds . . . He sought permission to read the ghazal. Mirza Fakhru nodded his assent . . .

From this point the poets began their recitation, passing couplets backwards and forwards, half singing, half reciting, applauding and wah-wah-ing those they admired for their witty or subtle nuances, leaving those less accomplished to sink in leaden silence. The versifying would continue until dawn, when it would be the turn of Zauq and Ghalib to bring the night to its climax. But long before that, from the north, would come the distant sound of the morning bugle. Two miles away, in the British cantonments, a very different day was beginning.

In 1852, the British and Mughals found themselves in an uneasy equilibrium: at once opposed yet in balance, living lives in parallel. Despite the tension over who was to be heir apparent, and Zinat Mahal's refusal to accept the succession of Mirza Fakhru, between the Palace and the Residency a temporary truce was maintained.

This balance was, however, broken most dramatically in 1853, by a series of deaths. By the end of that year all three British officials who had signed the succession agreement with Mirza Fakhru were dead, all in suspicious circumstances. The most suspicious – a straightforward case of poisoning, according to the doctors who attended him – was the slow and lingering death of Sir Thomas Metcalfe.

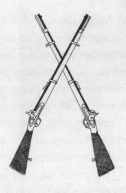

4

THE NEAR APPROACH OF THE STORM

Sir Thomas began to suspect that he had been poisoned towards the end of the summer of 1853.

He was not a man who usually suffered from ill health and by sticking to his carefully regulated schedule, by eating in moderation and by rarely going out or staying up late, he made sure he remained fit and well. Then, quite suddenly, at the beginning of the monsoon of 1853, he began to feel horribly sick. The vomiting started soon afterwards. For weeks on end he found he was unable to keep any food down. His daughter Emily was horrified by the speed with which he sank: 'He was looking thin and ill – so white,' she wrote after she saw him. 'He continually suffered from sickness – an irritating vomiting of watery stuff. The small pox marks on his face, generally very slight, became more pronounced. It was easy to see he was ill, though he suffered no pain whatever.'

The previous December the whole family had gathered to celebrate a Delhi Christmas amid the roaring wood fires of Metcalfe House. Theo was there, as more unusually was his wife Charlotte, who had chosen to stay on in Simla after her husband was posted to Delhi; it was on this trip to Metcalfe House that she became pregnant with their first child. Also in the house was Georgina, whose hunger strike had eventually had the desired effect of forcing her father to permit her to correspond with Edward Campbell; shortly afterwards she had accepted Sir Edward's proposal of marriage. To this her father had finally given his consent, to the delight of GG and the relief of all the rest of the family. Georgina's elder sister Emily was in Delhi too, down from Kangra with her new baby Annie and husband Edward, who had just been given one of the most sought-after jobs in the service, that of Commissioner of that cool and beautiful hill region: 'It was a long journey for only one month's leave,' wrote Emily.

But father decided we should go. We had all a most happy meeting there and such a joyous Christmas . . . Dear Daddy was so proud of his grandchildren and thought 'Motee' Annie [Emily's baby daughter], the most beautiful child he had ever seen and in fact, she was a most lovely babe . . . There were some other guests in the house and altogether we were a large party, and such a bright happy one. Daddy was so well and in great spirits in having so many of his children around him at once. The weather was glorious with plenty of riding and driving and picnics and dinner parties going on. But alas! It was the last Christmas . . .[2]

In the course of the celebrations, Sir Thomas had confided the details of his secret agreement with Mirza Fakhru to Emily and her husband:

The officials through whom these negotiations were being carried on were the foreign secretary, Sir Henry Elliot, the Lieutenant Governor, Mr Thomason, and the Resident at Delhi – my Daddy, Sir Thomas . . . The negotiations had been going on for more than a year and a half, until at last the Heir Apparent agreed to the terms offered . . . So far matters had gone on more favourably than my father expected, because he knew that there was a powerful clique in the palace, who were straining every nerve to prevent the Heir Apparent giving his adhesion to the proposals of Government. This clique was headed by the Queen – a clever, wicked woman . . . Her rage, therefore, when she heard that the Heir Apparent had consented to the arrangements was unbounded and she determined to take her revenge. My father knew her character well, and that she would not let any obstacle stand in the way of her ambition. My Father knew also that her revenge would not stop, and he said to us, 'The first act in the drama is played out – what will be the next?'[3]

Sir Thomas therefore strongly suspected what was happening as his digestion disintegrated in the autumn of 1853 – although, of course, he had no proof; nor was he at all surprised when he heard that Sir Henry Elliot and Mr Thomason were reporting similar symptoms. Despite his illness, however, he was determined to keep his promise to attend GG's wedding in Simla in October, particularly as the trip would also allow him to see Theo's new baby, the future heir to the family baronetcy. He made only one condition. His wife Felicity had died in Simla a decade earlier, on 26 September, and he said he was unwilling to go to the town until the anniversary had passed.

The family began collecting in Theo and Charlotte's house near the church in Simla towards the end of August. GG had been there since the beginning of the hot weather, helping look after her pregnant sister-in-law, and Emily joined them on the 31st, having ridden over from Kangra. A week later, a little prematurely, and before Theo had arrived from his work in Delhi, Charlotte gave birth to a healthy little boy. 'The infant was a fine child and all seemed full of promise for a speedy recovery,' wrote Emily.

She was kept perfectly quiet . . . when Theo arrived unexpectedly on the eighth day after the Baby's birth. It was a surprise to her – but a great pleasure and both were intensely happy over their boy. On the 9th day, she was moved to a sofa and I went out for an hour, leaving Theo sitting by her side. When I returned home, I was told she had had a shivering fit. She did not seem ill, but from that evening, she seemed to be less and less conscious of what was going on, took less interest in her baby, apparently dozing a great deal, and did not appear to be awake even while taking food.

The doctors looked graver and graver each day, and both looked as shocked as I was to hear her harping on one thing, What day is it? Your mother died on 26th September, did she not? It was the only idea that seemed to fill her thoughts and though in accordance with the doctor's orders we tried to reassure her that that date was passed, it would not do – 'No,' she said, 'your mother died on that day, and I too shall die on the 26th.'

September 22nd she was so ill that the Holy Communion was administered to her. Theo quite broke down. The next day she lay in a stupor, not turning in her bed and not taking notice of anything . . . At last the Doctor told Theo to ask if she had any particular wish to express to him or about the baby. She simply shook her head, and Theo thinking she did not understand said – 'Darling, do you not know who I am?' She looked at him with the sweetest smile and said – 'Yes, I know, you are little baby's papa.' Poor Theo! He broke down completely, and had to be taken out of the room, wild with grief.

Then began a series of convulsions which lasted through several hours, and were terrible to witness by those who loved her so dearly. At last, when she was quieter, she turned to me and said – 'Annie don't you hear them?' I said – ' What is it you hear darling?' 'Oh!' she said, 'the angels singing and the harps. I can hear them plainly.' After a little while, in the dead of the night, she turned to me and said – 'Annie, when will be September 26th?' I tried to persuade her by the doctor's orders, that the date was already passed, for they said, this idea fixed in her mind was killing her. But though dead to all else, her mind was clear on that point. After midnight the convulsions began again . . .

Just as the sun was rising and shining on her bed, she suddenly rose up in her bed and poured forth a song so wild and unearthly, not a word in it – only music – with her face in a rapturous glow that we could only look on in silence and wonder. She had not moved for days, and yet with supernatural strength, she raised herself thus suddenly. Theo rushed to support her with his arm – she took no notice of him, but when her song ceased, she fell back in her bed and never moved again. She died at 3 PM, on September 26th . . . Dearest Charlotte was buried by my mother's grave in the old cemetery in Simla, on 28th September, 1853. Her loss wrecked dear Theo's life.[4]

The news was taken down to Sir Thomas, who was camping at Kalka on the edge of the plains and at the foot of the road leading up to Simla, waiting for the anniversary of his wife's death to pass. He was now severely ill himself, pale and drawn and unable to keep down anything more than a thin soup. When the family saw him, they decided to cancel the grand church wedding that had been planned for GG and Edward Campbell, and instead to have a sombre family service in Theo's sitting room. A week later, after the bride and groom departed for their honeymoon in the hills beyond Simla, the now skeletal Sir Thomas set off back to Delhi accompanied by a greiving Theo. They made slow progress. Sir Thomas was now clearly dying. According to Emily,

> he suffered no pain, only sank from weakness caused by perpetual vomiting and retching. I followed him as quickly as possible, but on reaching Ambala – I received a message from Theo, that my loved father had died quite peaceably [in Metcalfe House] on November 3rd. The poisons which were undoubtedly used were vegetable [based and] prepared in such a way as to leave no trace behind them. But they do their work, slowly but surely – a secret well known to the famous native hakims.[5]

According to the court diary prepared every day for Sir Thomas, on the final night, a distraught and desperate Theo had sent for Hakim Ahsanullah Khan, Zafar's personal physician, to 'ascertain if possible the disease under which the Agent was suffering'. The hakim had duly driven up to Metcalfe House, but on arrival 'the surgeon in attendance however had observed there was no necessity for consulting him [the hakim] and he had therefore left'.[6] The desperate situation can easily be imagined: Sir Thomas in his death throes; Theo willing to try anything to save his father; Dr Ross refusing to allow in a man he strongly suspected could have been involved in Sir Thomas's demise.

By the end of the year, both Sir Henry Elliot and Mr Thomason were also dead, though as with Sir Thomas there was no hard evidence to show they had been poisoned, other than their suspicious symptoms.[7] As Hakim Ahsanullah Khan boasted to Harriet Tytler when asked many years later if he could poison *ad libitum*, he replied: 'I can. Show me your victim and tell me when you want him to die. In a year? Six months? One month or a day? He shall die, and what is more, your physicians will never find out the real cause of his death.'[8] True or not, the rumours of Metcalfe's poisoning, and Zinat Mahal's culpability, came to be widely believed in Company circles, and helped make its officials regard the Mughal family with an even more jaundiced eye than before.

Before he died, Sir Thomas had predicted that Mirza Fakhru would not long outlive him. It was therefore something of a surprise to everyone that he lived for nearly two and a half years longer, and that when he died in the prime of his life, on 10 July 1856, it was in fact of cholera, and not of poisoning.

If anyone in the Palace had hoped that a new Resident would reverse Sir Thomas's policy on the Mughal court, they were soon to be disappointed.

Simon Fraser was a distant kinsman of Ochterlony's old assistant William Fraser, but as different a man as could be imagined: an amiable, pious, plump and somewhat lonely old widower who was fond of singing and whose principal pleasure in life was to organise small musical evenings for his friends. A cousin of the Evangelical East India Company director Charles Grant, who had initially helped him to get a job in India, Fraser agreed on arrival to be the Patron of Padre Jennings' mission: 'Altho' I do not agree with him on many of his opinions,' wrote Fraser, 'he is a good Christian and I have a great regard for him.'[9]

Shortly afterwards Simon Fraser went as far as joining the choir of St James's Church, which was now being organised by Jennings' newly arrived daughter: a pretty, enthusiastic blonde twenty-one-year-old named Annie. Since Annie and her equally attractive friend Miss Clifford had begun to organise the singing, the number of soldiers driving in from the cantonments to attend the lengthy Sunday services at St James's had increased to a remarkable degree, and before long not only was the tenor and bass portion of the choir wonderfully consolidated, but one of the basses, Lieutenant Charlie Thomason of the Bengal Engineers, had succeeded in becoming engaged to the padre's daughter.[10]

As with Sir Thomas, Simon Fraser's wife had died young; but unlike Metcalfe, he had never been properly reunited with his children, who had been brought up in English boarding schools and then had chosen to stay on in England, barely even corresponding with their father, except occasionally to ask for money. As he chided his eldest son, 'I have literally no details of your private life. This is no doubt a very unsatisfactory state of affairs but a horror of epistolary correspondence appears to be more or less the characteristic of the members of our family.'[11] When another of his children, the Reverend Simon J. Fraser, was posted to India, Fraser went to meet him, but the two walked past each other without recognition.[12]

Fraser had spent a lifetime in the service of the Company without greatly distinguishing himself in any way. As Delhi was to be his last posting, and he had no further ambitions, he was determined to enjoy himself and make the most of the opportunities this appointment afforded. 'I am very well satisfied with my position,' he wrote to his son Simon in 1854.

> Delhi agrees with me and I am shaking off the little ailments which for some time I have suffered from . . . We have lately been making great exertions [in the choir and] got up a beautiful anthem, appropriate of course to the day. Nothing untoward occurred, and all our church going community expressed themselves highly gratified with the effort. We have one or two very fair performers at this place and I hope that throughout the hot weather I might be able to bring people together every fortnight for a little secular music, although the whole trouble always devolves upon me as master of the ceremonies. Whether the assemblies are at my own house or elsewhere, people become so apathetic that although they will take part in all that you arrange for them, still they will not take the trouble of arranging for themselves, and music cannot be properly got up without practising.[13]

Busy with his choir practice, Fraser had no intention of letting his official duties take up more of his time than they had to, and he spent an entire month in Delhi before bothering to visit the

Emperor. He even failed to turn up to the first reception arranged for him by Zafar on 1 December 1853, in the great Mughal garden of Raushanara Bagh. This left Zafar's begums, who had come to camp in the garden for the duration of the welcoming ceremonies, complaining of the 'extreme cold', while 'several concubines complained that sepoys about the Garden indulged in improper remarks'.[14]

Fraser had announced his forthcoming retirement from the service two days before news came through of the death of Mirza Fakhru, and his response to this new succession crisis bore all the marks of an old man who had had his peaceful slumbers interrupted: 'The surviving sons of the King, have no special marks of nobility, or peculiar recommendations calculated to attract the sympathy of the native population,' he wrote to the new Governor General, Lord Canning, though there is no record that Fraser had actually bothered to meet any of them before running them down to Calcutta.[15]

The day after the death of Mirza Fakhru, he explained in his letter, he had paid a rare visit to the Palace to commiserate with the Emperor. Far from the scene of mourning that might have been expected, he found instead a dry-eyed Emperor with a letter to the Governor General ready written in which he pressed yet again for the succession of Mirza Jawan Bakht; the body of Mirza Fakhru, he heard, had already been interred near the Sufi shrine of Qutb Sahib in Mehrauli. Zafar's letter argued that Jawan Bakht was suitable for the position, on the basis that his birth was legitimate and that he was, in the eyes of his adoring father at least, 'gifted with all the endowments, qualifications and virtuous habits necessary for a Prince, he having obtained a complete education under my guidance. The rest [of my sons] have no comparison with him. He [alone] merits my favour'.[16]

Fraser, however, had other ideas. He strongly urged Canning that none of the princes should be recognised as heir apparent – least of all Jawan Bakht – and argued that the death of Mirza Fakhru, following closely upon the momentous annexation of the rich and independent kingdom of Avadh five months earlier, in February 1856, provided the perfect opportunity to prepare the

Mughals for the imminent extinction of their line. This, he believed, should take place on the death of Zafar – an event which could not now be far away: 'It appears to me inexpedient to recognise any of the sons as Heir Apparent,' he concluded. 'The princes generally are not men of prominent influence or high personal character . . . little public interest is felt in the fortunes of the family and a favourable opportunity is presented, by the removal from the scene of the most respected member of the family, for the introduction of changes adapted to the altered condition of the family and the Country.'[17]

It was an idea that the new Lieutenant Governor, C. B. Thornhill, wholeheartedly supported. From his summer retreat in the hills of Nainital he wrote to Calcutta urging Canning to listen to Fraser and seize the moment, saying he would 'much regret if advantage were not taken of the favourable and easy opportunity now afforded for introducing a change which while it is obviously fitting in the actual condition of the Indian Empire, [is also] for the best interests of the Princess themselves'. He went on to explain why he believed it was in the best interests of the Mughal princes to be expelled from their homes and for them to have their privy purses – their only source of income – immediately stopped: 'The abolition of the names and forms of royal state will, it may reasonably be hoped, wean them the more readily from the habits of idle, and too often vicious and discreditable frivolities, with which their lives have hitherto been wasted.'

Lord Canning did not hesitate to take the advice offered him. After all, he had arrived in India only five months earlier, to take over from his predecessor Lord Dalhousie. Canning was a handsome, industrious if somewhat reserved Tory politician in his early forties, who had accepted the appointment of Governor General only because of his frustration at his consistent failure to gain a senior cabinet berth in London. Before his departure he had had no previous interest in India, and by July he had yet to leave the heat and damp of Calcutta. Indeed, for almost all of his first few months in India he had found himself imprisoned in the 'miserably furnished' if outwardly magnificent Government House (which, he was horrified to note, did not possess a single water closet, 'there being no fall for drainage in Calcutta', surrounded by his Himalayan piles of dispatch boxes. It was a life he described as 'little better than [that of] a galley slave'.[18]

None of this, however, prevented him from taking a confidently dismissive attitude to 'the farce of Mughal pretensions': 'Nearly all the everyday signs of authority which the native mind associates with royalty have for state reasons already been taken from the Crown of Delhie,' he wrote in a minute in response to Fraser's recommendations.

> The presents which were at one time offered to the King by the Governor General and the Commander in Chief have been discontinued; the privilege of a coinage bearing his mark is now denied to him; the Governor General's seal no longer bears a device of vassalage; and even the native chiefs have been prohibited from using one. It has been determined that these appearances of subordination and deference could not be kept up consistently with a due respect for the real and solid power of the British Government. This may also be said of the title of the King of Dehlie,* with the fiction of paramount sovereignty which attaches to it.[19]

Despite his lack of Indian experience, Canning was quite clear that now was the moment to take the dramatic and historic step of deposing the Mughal dynasty, which had ruled northern India for more than three hundred years: Babur, the first Mughal, took Delhi while Henry VIII was just beginning his rule in England. Britain's Indian Empire, wrote Canning, had never been so strong, so secure or so happy: 'The last few years have seen not only an extension but a remarkable consolidation of British power in India; its supremacy has become more uniform and unbroken even within the earlier limits of the Empire.' For this reason, 'the preservation of a titular King Paramount of Hindustan has thereby grown to be a greater anomaly than ever', and he therefore decided, in agreement with Fraser's views, that no Mughal prince would now be recognised as

---

* Even though the people of Hindustan always referred to Zafar as *Padshah*, or Emperor, the British made a point of calling him by their own less exalted name for him, the King of Delhi.

heir apparent. He concluded, 'The Upper Provinces of India are not now, as they were in 1849 or 1850, in an unsettled and uneasy condition. There is every appearance that the presence of a Royal House in Dehlie has become a matter of indifference even to the Mahometans.'[20]

Given his situation and his recent arrival in India, Canning could not have been expected to know better. But as events were shortly to show, his minute represented as comprehensive a misreading of the situation in northern India as could possibly be contained within a single passage. So removed had the British now become from their Indian subjects, and so dismissive were they of Indian opinion, that they had lost all ability to read the omens around them or to analyse their own position with any degree of accuracy. Arrogance and imperial self-confidence had diminished the desire to seek accurate information or gain any real knowledge of the state of the country.

More specifically, as far as Delhi was concerned, by extinguishing even the faintest hope of any of the princes of the royal house ever succeeding Zafar, the British created a situation where no one in the imperial family had anything to lose, and all were sufficiently disaffected to risk anything to try to save their position. It was a fatal error for which the British would shortly pay a high price.

In Delhi, one sign of the growing unrest showed itself only eight months after the death of Mirza Fakhru. Early in the morning on 18 March 1857, a flyer – 'a small dirty piece of paper, with a naked sword and shield depicted', according to Theo – was placed on the back wall of the Jama Masjid in Delhi.[21] Purporting to be a proclamation from the Shah of Iran, it announced that a British expeditionary force had just suffered a massive defeat in Persia, and that the Persian Army had crossed the Afghan border and was now marching from Herat to come and liberate Delhi from Christian rule:

God willing, the time is not far when I shall appear in the land of Hind and shall delight and make happy both the rulers and subjects of that place. Just as the English have deprived them of food and comfort, to the same measure I shall endeavour to increase their prosperity, and let it be known that I have no objections to anyone's religion . . . By the 6th March, 900 Irani soldiers, along with senior officers will have entered India and there are already five hundred soldiers present in Delhi disguised in dress and appearance . . . [In the meantime] the Muslims must refrain from helping or supporting the Christians, and it is necessary that so far as possible they should remain loyal and faithful towards their fellow Muslims.[22]

The notice was posted for three hours and a huge crowd gathered to read it, until Theo Metcalfe, who happened to be passing, rode up and ripped it down. The following day, however, the contents of the notice were reprinted in full in the court newspaper, the *Siraj ul-Akabhar*, creating a ripple of excitement across the city, although the paper also questioned – rightly – both the veracity of the proclamation and the truth of the claim of a Persian victory over the British.

Already there had been brief reports in the Urdu newspapers of mysterious chapattis (or 'fried puris', as the Delhi papers reported) being passed by nightwatchmen from village to village across Hindustan: one report in the *Nur-i Maghrebi* in February had mentioned their passing between some villages near Bulandshahr; by early March they had reached Mathura, on the main road to Agra. But they do not seem to have got any closer to Delhi than this, and even there no one seems to have understood what their significance was;* as far as the Delhi papers were concerned, it was certainly a matter given far less space than the reports of a fatwa being posted in Madras, 'calling on all believers to rise against the infidels . . . he who fell in such a war would be a martyr', and the excitable rumours that either the Russians or the Persian Army, or possibly both, were on the march and about to appear in Delhi.

---

* It is still unclear what the exact significance of the famous chapattis or puris was. Judging by the various explanations given at the time in different towns and villages, they were interpreted differently across the region. Many certainly understood them as signalling that dramatic upheavals were about to take place across Hindustan; but there is no evidence that they impinged much upon the consciousness of the people of Delhi.

Most prominent of all were reports, which began to appear from late March onwards, of unrest in the army in Bengal, especially at Berhampore and Barrackpore: according to Theo, by the spring of 1857, the people of Delhi 'were perfectly aware of the want of fidelity in the sepoy army and the subject was frequently discussed'.²³

This growing unrest in Delhi could be traced back at least to the previous winter when, on 7 February 1856, the British had unilaterally annexed the prosperous kingdom of Avadh (or Oudh, as the British called it), to the east of Delhi. The excuse for this was that its Nawab, the poet, dancer and epicure Wajd Ali Shah, was 'excessively debauched'.* The people of Delhi were used to the British bullying and plundering the Nawabs as they had done for nearly a century now; but the outright annexation of the kingdom had nevertheless caused far more alarm across northern India than the British seem to have realised or indeed anticipated, and increased awareness of the precariousness of the Mughals' own position. More importantly, it greatly unsettled the sepoys of the Company's army, most of whom were drawn from upper-caste Hindu families in rural Avadh, and who now found themselves compelled to reduce their own country to vassalage.

The venal and occasionally brutal way the annexation had been carried out caused particular distress. Even British officials were aware that what had happened was not one of the more honourable episodes in the history of the Honourable Company. One Company servant, Robert Bird, had gone so far as to produce an anonymously published book entitled *Dacoitee in Excelsis, or the Spoilation of Oude by the East India Company*.²⁴ In it Bird, an insider in all that had happened, exposed the degree to which a largely fictional dossier – eventually published as the parliamentary *Oude Blue Book* – had been assembled by interested parties within the Company to push for Avadh's annexation. The dossier had

---

* Although it hardly justified annexing Avadh, it was certainly true that Wajd Ali Shah was no blushing violet. The Royal Library at Windsor Castle contains a large folio volume entitled the *Ishq Nama* (Love History) of Wajd Ali Shah, which contains several hundred portraits of his different lovers, one to each page, and annotated with a short poem praising the qualities and amorous talents of each.

depicted a province 'given up to crime, havoc, and anarchy by the misrule of a government at once imbecile and corrupt'. This image, wrote Bird, was little more than 'a fiction of official penmanship, [an] Oriental romance' and was refuted 'by one simple and obstinate fact' – that the people of Avadh clearly 'preferred the slandered regime' of the Nawab 'to the grasping but rose-coloured government of the Company'.

Bird pointed out, in particular, 'that those who had experience of both [governments], to the number of some 50,000 employed as sepoys by the Company', felt and resented the difference in the two regimes especially strongly:

> Not only does the annexation itself appear to have been accompanied by acts of violence and spoliation wholly indefensible, but the foundation of all property seems to have been unsettled to an extent unheard of under any civilised rule. We hear on all sides of landowners dispossessed – in short of the Company dealing with the province as if it were not merely entitled to the revenues of it, but as if all the property within it had become the spoil of its bow and spear; as if, in fact, it was an uninhabited island newly discovered with which the discoverers had a right to do what they willed.[25]

Already many smaller kingdoms had been quietly – and profitably – annexed by the Company. The policy of Governor General Dalhousie (1812–60), known as the Doctrine of Lapse, had banned the age-old Hindu practice of adopted sons succeeding to their father's throne, and led to the unpopular and deeply resented annexations of Satara in 1848, Jhansi in 1853 and Nagpur in 1854; but Avadh was an acquisition on a far different scale from anything yet attempted, and was practised on 'a faithful and unresisting ally' without even the nominal justification of the absence of a recognised heir, and with only the 'fictitious charges' and 'fallacious bearings of the *Oude Blue Book*' as an excuse.[26]

After the annexation of Avadh and the death of Mirza Fakhru, the end of the Mughal line was clearly imminent.

For Zafar, now aged eighty-one, it was a particular shock. He had long made it clear that he had no wish for anything other than to preserve and hand on what little he had inherited. As early as 1843 he had attempted to write direct to Queen Victoria, asking for this bare minimum: 'From unfortunate circumstances', he wrote,

> the flower of my kingdom has faded, and the dominion of this house is placed in your hands . . . to diminish or enhance its dignity . . . I am now old, and have no ambition left for grandeur. I would devote my days entirely to religion, but I feel anxious that the name and dignity of my predecessors should be maintained, and that they may descend to my children unimpaired, according to the original engagements made by the British Government.[27]

Now, with the example of Avadh in front of him, Zafar set his sights much lower. His first action on hearing of the annexation of Avadh was to write a series of anxious begging letters to Dalhousie, saying that as the 'days of our pilgrimage on Earth are numbered . . . [and] as no reliance can be placed in one's life at the advanced age of 80 years, we have been of late engaged in reflecting on the future welfare of our family, especially of the Nawab Zinat Mahal Begum and her offspring, the Prince Mirza Jawan Bakht Bahadur, that no distress or hardships be experienced by them'. Zafar asked only for a guarantee that both would be looked after following his death. Yet Dalhousie's response was, characteristically, both dismissive and ungenerous; he got one of his secretaries to reply that 'the grants which your Majesty has made to the Begums and Prince your Majesty must be sensible cannot be upheld; they may be maintained during your Majesty's own lifetime, but cannot now be extended beyond that; for this would be contrary to former practice'.[28]

Zafar was not alone in his alarm. The demise of the Mughal and his court was something that could only cast a cloud over the whole of Delhi, much of whose prosperity and patronage derived directly or indirectly from the Red Fort. With the end of the

Mughals, many in the city would find themselves out of a job: the courtiers and Palace civil servants, the jewellers and silversmiths, the cooks and palanquin bearers, the guards and eunuchs, the musicians and the dancing girls. None of these could expect employment under British rule, whose administrators for the North West Provinces were anyway based 150 miles to the south in Agra.

It also boded extremely badly for the court poets: 'Although I am a stranger to Avadh and its affairs,' wrote Ghalib on 23 February 1856, 'the destruction of the state depresses me all the more, and I maintain that no Indian who was not devoid of all sense of justice could feel otherwise.'[29] Ghalib had received a small pension from the Nawab which he lost at the annexation in February; with the death of his pupil in poetry, Mirza Fakhru, in July, his income was further reduced: 'You must bear in mind', he wrote to a friend on 27 July 1856,

> that the death of the heir apparent has been a great blow to me. It means that my ties with the court will now last only as long as the king does. God knows who the new heir apparent will be. He who appreciated my worth has died. Who will recognise me now? I put my trust in my Creator, and resign myself to His will. And there is this immediate loss: he [Mirza Fakhru] used to give me ten rupees a month to buy fruit for my [two adopted] boys. Who will give me that now?[30]

Ghalib, like many writers before and since, suffered from the potentially combustible combination of expensive tastes, a keen sense of his own worth and insufficient financial resources to support either. Always precarious, his finances had become especially troubled after his sense of personal honour compelled him to turn down the lucrative chance to become the Persian Professor at Delhi College. Ghalib had arrived at Delhi College in his palanquin having being invited to apply for the new post. But after reaching the college gate, he refused to enter until Mr Thomason, the secretary, came and welcomed him, as he insisted his aristocratic status dictated. After a long stand-off, Mr Thomason came out personally and explained that a formal welcome was appropriate when he attended the Governor's durbar, but not in the present case, when he came as a candidate for employment. Ghalib replied, 'I contemplated taking a government appointment in the expectation that this would bring me greater honour than I now receive, not a reduction in those already accorded to me.' The secretary replied, 'I am bound by regulations.' 'Then I hope you will excuse me,' Ghalib said, and came away.[31]

In such a situation, it was an increasing irritation to Ghalib that Zafar did not value him more highly, and instead bestowed most of his favour, and the bounteous pension that went with it, on that obvious second-rater Zauq. It was something Ghalib could never understand, as he was once bold enough to point out to Zafar: 'I swear that you too must feel pride', he wrote,

> in the great kindness of fortune, that you possess a slave like Ghalib, whose song has all the power of fire. Turn your attention towards me as my skill demands, treasure me as the apple of your eye and open your heart for me to enter in . . . See my perfection, look upon my skill . . . Why talk of the poets of the Emperor Akbar's day? My presence alone bears witness that your age excels his.[32]

When Zauq died in 1854, Zafar finally appointed Ghalib as his *ustad* (guru or master, but in this case poetry teacher), with the salary that went with it, and Ghalib (at least according to Delhi tradition) was able to breathe a sigh of relief that 'the man who spoke in the language of a lodging house keeper' was no more.[33] Insufficient as Zafar's regard for Ghalib's skills may have been, the court still represented a financial lifeline Ghalib depended on. As early as 1852, when the King had been ill, Ghalib had written anxiously: 'What will happen now? And what will become of me, who sleeps in the shade of his wall?'[34] A little later he added, 'The Mughal princes gather in the Red Fort and recite their ghazals . . . This court will not last many days more. How can it be permanent? Who knows if they will meet tomorrow, and if they do whether they will meet after that? The assembly can vanish at any moment.'[35]

One reason for Ghalib's pessimism was that, unlike many in Delhi, he had always been aware of the scientific advances achieved by the West, which he had seen on display on a visit to Calcutta in 1827. When Sayyid Ahmad Khan tried to interest him in writing an introduction to an edition of the *Ain i-Akbari*, the celebrated account of the court of the Emperor Akbar, Ghalib had written back that Khan should not always be looking back to the Mughals of old, but should embrace the future: 'See the sahibs of England!' he wrote.

> They have gone far ahead of our Oriental forebears. Wind and wave they have rendered useless. They are sailing their ships under fire and steam. They are creating music without the use of the *mizrab* [plucker]. With their magic, words fly through the air like birds. Air has been set on fire . . . Cities are being lighted without oil lamps. This new law makes all other laws obsolete. Why must you pick up straws out of old time-swept barns while a treasure trove of pearls lies at your feet?[36]

Now, after the death of Mirza Fakhru and the annexation of Avadh, Ghalib thought it prudent to take immediate steps to look for other sources of income, while also teaching the English the courtly manners they so clearly lacked. To this end he forwarded a Persian ode or *qasida* to Queen Victoria via Canning. After a brief introduction praising the Queen for being 'as splendid as the stars' and flattering her Governor General 'as magnificent as Alexander, as splendid as Feridun', Ghalib quickly moved on to the main business: namely reminding the Queen of the long-established convention that sovereigns should support the poets of their dominions in return for being immortalised in verse.

As the great Begum of London was clearly not as familiar with the delicate etiquette of these matters as she should have been, Ghalib made himself a little more explicit in his covering letter. The truly great rulers of history, he reminded Queen Victoria, 'rewarded their poets and well wishers by filling their mouths with pearls, weighing them in gold, and granting them villages and recompense'. In the same way it was the duty of 'the exalted Queen to bestow upon Ghalib, the petitioner, the title of *Mihr-Khwan*, and present him with the robe of honour and a few crumbs from her bounteous table – that is, in plain English, a "pension" '.[37]

Ghalib waited eagerly for the Queen's grateful response, and her gift of a generous stipend. It never came; but this ode would soon perform the far more important function of helping to save his life.

If Ghalib found himself deeply anxious and depressed as 1856 gave way to 1857, then Theo Metcalfe was also in a very bad state.

After the sudden loss of his wife and his father, he tried to throw himself into his work and to soldier on as Joint Magistrate in Delhi. But the stress of bringing up his child on his own, and the depressing job of selling his father's library, as well as much of the other contents of Metcalfe House, all weighed down on him. He clung to his son as a last memory of his wife: 'I never can part with him,' he wrote to GG early in 1856. 'Altho' I feel the great disadvantage of leaving him many hours alone everyday, without the company of a lady, I do try to show him an affection which I never experienced when a child, the loss of which I always mourned.'[38]

As 1856 progressed, however, the stress of his mental state began to have an adverse physical effect on him, and especially on his eyes. 'You will be sorry to hear that I have been suffering greatly from pain and weakness in my left eye for months,' he finally admitted to GG in August 1856 from Meerut,

> which has necessitated the abandonment of all use of it and has compelled me to give up work for a period of three months . . . It is quite possible that even this rest may not be quite sufficient for its perfect recovery . . . I am ordered to live in a dark room so that I have no very cheering prospects before me; at present to go to Delhi to put all our father's things [in Metcalfe House] in order. If I find that my eye is stronger at the end of a month, I propose taking a trip to the hills . . . Do you know any widow who wants to take care of a single gentleman, for I am comparatively helpless and am forbidden all reading or writing.[39]

Georgina, who was summering in Kashmir, immediately offered to look after Charlie, Theo's son. Theo reluctantly, but gratefully, agreed. Soon after ripping down the flyer from the walls of the Jama Masjid, he wrote to his brother-in-law, Edward Campbell, repeating how much he needed a holiday, and that with luck, in May 1857, he would be able to join him and GG in the hills: 'I cannot account for this numbness of feeling that weighs me down and makes me helpless,' he wrote sadly to Edward. 'I think without a relief from all work, without a long and perfect holiday, I will never rise.'[40]

Edward was less sympathetic than GG to Theo's plight. Following the departure from India of his patron, Sir Charles Napier, to whom he had been ADC at headquarters in Fort William, Calcutta, Campbell's career had floundered. He and his company of the 60th Rifles were now employed in the far from prestigious or lucrative job of surveying the area around Multan on the Punjab–Sindh border, reputedly the hottest place in the entire subcontinent; it was certainly a far cry from the luxuries of Fort William. To hear how much of his meagre income was now being eaten up by Theo's baby and nanny made him furious: 'I am very much vexed with Theo,' he wrote to GG in Kashmir.

About the rent, I think there is no use asking him, and not the slightest in giving hints for he *will not* take them. I think we might just make out a little memo, showing him the actual expense we were put to by having Mrs Baxter and Charlie boarded on us, and then ask him to pay.[41]

But Campbell had other worries that were causing rather more irritation than his lack of money and his insensitive brother-in-law. For the army had just put him in charge of training the troops in the Punjab with their latest and most advanced new armament: 'I am deep in all sorts of regimental affairs,' he explained to GG,

and am taking a leading part as concerns the management of the new Enfield rifles. Our fellows don't like them as much as the old ones. I think they will, but at present do not see how. It is a disfavourable

circumstance because we cannot afford to unload and clean them as
often as we would wish. We have so little ammunition . . . and after
firing a few rounds, they get very foul and hard to load.[42]

Edward didn't trouble his wife with the technical details, but the
problem with the new Enfield guns was that, unlike their predecessors, the smooth-barrelled Brown Bess muskets, they had grooved (or
rifled) barrels. While this made them much more accurate and gave
them a longer range, it did mean they were more difficult to load, and
in order to get the ball down the barrel, quantities of grease were
needed, as well as a great deal of pushing with the ramrod. The drill
Edward had to teach his troops involved biting off the top of the
cartridge, pouring the powder into the rifle, then stuffing the ball and
the rest of the fatty cartridge down after it with the rod.[43]

This was all new technology, however, and the Company had
decided, unwisely, to have the cartridges manufactured at the
Dumdum arsenal in Calcutta, which had no previous experience
of manufacturing this type of ammunition. As a result there were
inevitably teething problems, in particular with the first few batches
of Dumdum-manufactured cartridges, which seemed to have been
coated with far too much grease. This had two results. First, as
Edward wrote to GG, it meant that the barrels quickly fouled up
with the excess fat, and needed frequent cleaning.[44] The second
problem was that the greasy coating of the cartridge was deeply
unpleasant to put in your mouth, and biting became thoroughly
repellent to any rifleman.

It was into this fertile soil that a rumour quickly took root: that
the quantities of grease used were not only unpleasant, they were
actually defiling, and made from a mixture of cow fat (offensive to
the majority of sepoys, who were high-caste and vegetarian Hindus, and who would also be extremely upset at having to touch
anything that had caused suffering to the much-revered cow) and
pig fat (an unclean animal to both Hindus and Muslims and so
offensive to just about all sepoys).

The rumours do seem to have been based on truth: initially, the
unpleasant grease had indeed been made from these defiling ingredients, as Lord Canning later admitted.[45] The ingredients of the

grease were quickly changed, and in many cases the sepoys were allowed to make up their own lubricant of beeswax and ghee, clarified butter. But the damage was done. It was not just that most of the sepoys totally refused to touch the new rifles. More dangerously still, the idea quickly gained acceptance that the mistake was far from accidental and was part of a wider Company conspiracy to break the sepoys' caste and ritual purity before embarking on a project of mass conversion.

The rumours were given some genuine credibility by the crassly tactless activities of the missionaries and their supporters among the Evangelicals of the army and administration. Had the Company chosen to recruit their sepoy armies from the lower castes this would possibly have been less important. But it had long been British policy to enlist Hindus from the ritually sensitive higher castes, and particularly those from Avadh, Bihar and the area around Benares. Encouraged to regard themselves as an elite by the British, the northern Indian peasant farmers who became sepoys had grown to become very particular about the preparation and eating of their food, and notions of caste, which in India had traditionally been relatively fluid, underwent a process of hardening, or what some scholars have called 'Sanskritisation', as the sepoys came to understand such issues as being central to their notions of self-respect.*

To make matters worse, and the situation even more combustible, the army was already on the verge of mutiny over quite separate – and more secular – issues of pay and regulations. One of the first among the senior officers to realise this was Edward

---

* In some Company regiments high-caste Hindus made up about 80 per cent of recruits, but in others this proportion had fallen slightly by 1857, which was itself a major cause of unrest. Overall, in the Bengal Native Infantry, high-caste Hindus made up around 65 per cent of the infantry at the time of the outbreak. The caste breakdown in 1842, for which detailed figures are available, was as follows: Rajputs, 27,993 (34.9 per cent); Brahmins, 24,480 (31 per cent); low-caste Hindus, 13,920 (17.3 per cent); Muslims, 12,411 (15.4 per cent); Christians, 1,076 (1.3 per cent). For more on the Company's army, and the 'Sanskritisation' of the military, see Seema Alavi's groundbreaking study, *The Sepoys and the Company: Tradition and Transition in Northern India 1770–1830*, New Delhi, 1995. See also Saul David, *The Indian Mutiny*, which is especially good on the military aspects of 1857.

Campbell's old boss, Sir Charles Napier, who had resigned as Commander-in-Chief in 1850, specifically because his growing worries that British India was in 'great peril' from the unrest among its own sepoys were comprehensively ignored by Lord Dalhousie. 'There is no justification for the cry that India is in danger,' wrote Dalhousie in answer to a written report of Napier's. 'Free from all threat of hostilities from without, and secure, through the submission of its new subjects, from insurrection within, the safety of India has never for one moment been imperilled by the partial insubordination in the ranks of its army.'[46]

Having been close to Napier, and so aware of the extent of the discontent, Edward Campbell was quick to realise the danger that this new threat posed. There were, after all, already very many good reasons for the extreme unhappiness of the sepoys. Many sons of established sepoy families in Hindustan now found themselves refused jobs in the army as the Company was busy filling its ranks with Gurkhas and Sikhs, whose fighting skills had come to impress the British during the closely fought Gurkha and Sikh wars of the early and mid nineteenth century. And for those who could get positions, there was little chance of promotion: even after years of gallant and faithful service, no Indian could rise above the ranks of subahdar (or officer, of whom there were ten to a regiment) or subahdar-major (senior officer, one per regiment); real authority remained entirely with the British.[47]

Moreover, the British officers, who once mixed with their men – and not infrequently cohabited with the men's sisters – had become increasingly distant, rude and dismissive. Gone were the days of the White Mughals, who used to join their men wrestling or dancing in the lines, and who used to send ahead to the next village on a march to have the best chess player ready and waiting. According to Sitaram Pandey, a sepoy who wrote his memoirs after 1857,

In those days the sahibs could speak our language much better than they do now, and they mixed more with us. Although officers today have to pass the language examination, and have to read books, they do not understand our language . . . the Sahibs used to give nautches [dance displays] for the regiment, and they attended all men's games.

They took us with them when they went out hunting. Now they seldom attend nautches as their Padre Sahibs have told them it is wrong. These Padre Sahibs have done, and are still doing, many things to estrange British officers from their sepoys. When I was a sepoy the captain of my company would have some men at his house all day and he talked with them . . . I have lived to see great changes in the Sahibs' attitudes towards us. I know that many officers nowadays only speak to their men when obliged to do so, and they show that the business is irksome and try to get rid of the sepoys as quickly as possible. One sahib told us he never knew what to say to us. The sahibs always knew what to say, and how to say it, when I was a young soldier.[48]

To add to their unhappiness, the relative value of the sepoys' pay had seriously declined – valuable perks such as free postage and an extra wartime allowance called *bhatta* had been slowly whittled away – yet conditions of service were now more demanding than ever: around the same time as the Company annexed Avadh, the home of many of the sepoys, it had also passed the hugely unpopular General Service Enlistment Act, which required that all sepoys should be prepared to serve abroad. Since 'Crossing the Black Water' was forbidden to orthodox high-caste Hindus, this only went further to confirm the fears of the sepoys that the Company was actively conspiring to take away their status and their religion.

In May 1855 a long article was published in the *Delhi Gazette* purporting to have been written by 'an old sepoy officer just invalided and settled in my village for the remainder of my days', but which in fact was almost certainly penned by an English officer. According to the author, none of the best potential recruits in the villages now wished to join up with 'an army which may turn into a navy at any point'. There were also, so the officer maintained, great worries that the military profession was losing its status and respectability as the Company was now actively recruiting, and promoting, men of low caste. The Company high command now came to regard such men as less troublesome and ritually over-sensitive; but for the existing troops they were 'men we cannot know and whom 1000 of the 1120 people in the village despise', as the officer put it. 'Great as is the Company's name and wealth, it is not so strong as the prejudice of caste.'[49]

One very strong candidate for the authorship of the *Delhi Gazette* piece was Captain Robert Tytler.

Tytler was a veteran of the 38th Native Infantry, and an officer of the old school who was close to his sepoys, concerned for their well-being, and completely fluent in Hindustani. Tytler appears to have been a kind and sensitive man, a widower with two little children who had recently remarried, this time to the brisk and resilient Harriet. Harriet was half his age, and as fluent in Hindustani as her husband. This she had learned as her first language from her ayah during her army childhood, following her father's regiment across the plains of India. Together the two Tytlers pursued their amateur artistic enthusiasms, and – unexpectedly for an army couple – became pioneering photographers, carefully documenting the monuments of Delhi, most of which had never been photographed before.

Several years earlier, during the Second Anglo-Burmese War, Tytler's regiment had been ordered to cross the sea to Rangoon by Dalhousie – 'a very obstinate Scotchman', according to Harriet. Tytler had been mortified by the dilemma this presented to his sepoys. In her memoirs Harriet wrote, 'They were very high caste men from Oudh and to make them go by sea to Burma would have caused a mutiny. What they should have done was to ask for volunteers . . . My husband said, "I know my men will never go if ordered, but if the Government would only ask them to volunteer, they would go to a man."'

Tytler was ignored, and the order to sail was given. The response from the sepoys was that they would go, but not by sea. As a punishment, the entire regiment was ordered by Dalhousie to march, by land, not to Rangoon but to Dacca, one of the most unhealthy postings in India; within five months all but three men in the entire regiment either were dead or had been hospitalised. In

Harriet's view, 'it was most unChristianlike to wish these poor men, who had only upheld their religious rights, to go where they were to die like dogs'.[50]

Understanding and sympathising with his sepoys' religious feelings, Tytler was therefore extremely anxious when his sepoys began to hear the rumours about the new Enfield rifle and asked him about the truth of them. By the spring of 1857 none had yet been issued to the troops stationed in the Delhi cantonments, but orders duly came that two companies from each of the regiments stationed in Delhi should be sent to Ambala, 100 miles up the Grand Trunk Road, for training with the new guns. 'Our men marched to that station,' wrote Harriet, 'and though before leaving Delhi they evinced some insubordination, still the officers hoped it would pass off as soon as they saw we had no desire to destroy their caste and turn them into Christians.'[51] The hope was quickly disappointed.

> Bulletins kept coming in from Ambala to the Brigadier stating the great dissatisfaction the men were showing to the use of the Enfield rifle and its greased cartridge, and my husband often said to me, 'if our natives were to rebel against us, India is lost.' He really became very anxious as days went on and symptoms of disaffection were showing themselves everywhere.[52]

The signs of disaffection were certainly becoming more and more apparent. On 29 March at Barrackpore in Bengal, one sepoy named Mangal Pandey called upon his fellow sepoys to rise up, and shot and wounded two officers; he was promptly tried and hanged. Soon afterwards in Ambala, so Tytler learned, the earnest requests of the British officers for the new rifles to be withdrawn were ignored by the Commander-in-Chief, General George Anson, a gambling man renowned as 'the best whist player in Europe', who had won the 1842 Derby with a horse he had bought for only £120.[53] His touch with his sepoys was, however, less sure than his feel for racehorses: 'I will never give into their beastly prejudices,' Anson said, when told that the troops were on the verge of mutiny.[54] As a result, from that evening until May, the Ambala cantonments were hit by a wave

of arson attacks; meanwhile any sepoy who bit the cartridges –
including those from the Delhi regiments – was made outcaste by
his fellows and taunted as a Christian. 'Feeling is as bad as can be,'
wrote the commander of the depot, Captain E. M. Martineau,

> and matters have gone so far that I can hardly devise any suitable
> remedy . . . I know that at the present moment an unusual agitation
> is pervading the ranks of the entire native army, but what exactly it
> will result in I am afraid to say. I can detect the near approach of the
> storm, I can hear the moaning of the hurricane, but I can't say how,
> when or where it will break forth . . . I don't think they know
> themselves what they will do, or that they have any plan of action
> except resistance of invasion of their religion, and their faith.⁵⁵

By the end of April the trouble had spread to Meerut, where the 3rd
Light Infantry also refused to fire the cartridge. The ringleaders
were arrested, and at the end of the first week of May, Tytler's
subahdar-major and close friend, Mansur Ali, travelled up from
Delhi to sit as President of the Court Martial. Before he went he
told Robert, ' "Sir if I find these men guilty, I will give them the
severest punishment in my power.'

He was true to his word. On 9 May, Mansur Ali duly sentenced no
fewer than eighty-five sepoys of the regiment to ten years' penal
servitude. That evening placards were seen in the Meerut bazaar
calling on all true Musalmans to rise up and slaughter the Christians.⁵⁶

The tenth day of May 1857 dawned suffocatingly hot and dusty in
Delhi: it was now reaching the peak of the summer heat, and 1857
had proved an even hotter and drier year than usual.

As was their habit, the Tytlers drove down from the cantonments
to the morning service at St James's, and on the way met one of their
brother officers, who had just returned from the rifle training in
Ambala. 'My husband called out, "Well Burrowes what about the
men?" His reply was, "Oh they are all right now Tytler, and are on
their way back." '

Robert, however, remained worried and alert. That evening he heard the 'tootooing of the *dak gharree* [post carriage] bugle in the [sepoy] lines, a very unusual thing for native soldiers never travel in a *dak gharree*. My husband came to the conclusion it must be Mansur Ali, our subahdar-major returning from the court martial. Presently the bearer came back to say Mansur Ali had not returned, but some men from Meerut had come to see their friends in the lines. My husband thought it was a strange thing, but never gave the matter any serious consideration.'[57]

Tytler was not the only person in Delhi to notice odd happenings connected with Meerut. On their drive to church, the Tytlers would have passed the city telegraph office, which was situated in the Civil Lines outside Kashmiri Gate. Inside, Charles Todd and his two young assistants, Brendish and Pilkington, were chatting with their friends in the Meerut telegraph office. There was great excitement and unrest in that town, they heard, due to the sentences that had just been given out. At nine o'clock both offices closed for the hottest part of the day.

When Todd returned at 4 p.m., at the end of his siesta, he found that communication with Meerut had been severed. He suspected that it was something to do with the weak link in the cable, the section that ran under the Yamuna, which, owing to 'the deterioration in the insulating material with which the cables were constructed, were a source of constant trouble'. Brendish and Pilkington were sent out to check. To their surprise they found that the cable was fine as far as the east bank of the Yamuna, and they had no problem signalling back to Todd from the far bank; the problem clearly lay somewhere towards Meerut. But by this stage it was six o'clock and too late to do anything more that day. So 'Todd made arrangements to go out himself next morning to endeavour to restore communication'. He then closed the office and went off back to his bungalow to have his dinner.[58]

As Todd was closing the office, George and Elizabeth Wagentrieber were riding past it on their way back from Jennings' evening service. That night, they had a visitor. More unusually, it was a prominent Delhi nobleman, Zia ud-Din Khan, the Nawab of Loharu, a cousin of Ghalib whose father had been a business partner and great friend of Elizabeth's father, James Skinner. According to their daughter Julia, George and Elizabeth sat huddled in earnest conversation with the Nawab on the veranda, but

> as I seldom went out to native visitors, I walked in at once and did not come out again. But when he had gone they spoke of some words of warning which he had been given about the troopers at Meerut being put in prison, that 'it was not wise policy and the Government would be sorry for it.' They thought it right to inform Sir T Metcalfe [Theo] of the Nawab's hints and my father sent him a letter that night.[59]

Theo, however, was otherwise engaged in packing for his holidays: he was due to leave on his journey to join GG and his son Charlie in Kashmir early the following morning, and he was too exhausted and depressed to act on the letter that night.

While the Nawab was visiting the Wagentriebers, another letter was given to Simon Fraser as he stepped out of the evening service at St James's. But it was a Sunday, and Fraser's mind was no doubt still on his beloved weekly performance with the choir. Whatever the reason, he put the envelope in his pocket and did not remember it until the following morning.[60]

The letter, which Fraser finally opened and read over his breakfast, was a warning that the sepoys had finally decided to rise up in Meerut, and that they intended to massacre the entire Christian population of the station on Sunday evening. Fraser was horrified and called for his buggy to take immediate action; but by then, of course, it was too late.

The Meerut sepoys had not only risen and committed a massacre, they had also ridden south-eastwards throughout the night, and at that very moment were pouring over the Bridge of Boats, and into the walled city, in search of their Emperor.

5

THE SWORD OF THE LORD OF FURY

In 1857, Monday, 11 May in the Christian calendar corresponded to the sixteenth day of Ramadan, the Muslim month of fasting and penance.

During this Islamic Lent, the usual rhythms of city life changed dramatically. The day began much earlier than usual, an hour before sunrise, when the moon was still high in the sky, with the sound of a gong ringing repeatedly in the Jama Masjid. Lamps would be lit, meals hurriedly prepared. Mendicants would earn a few paise by knocking on the doors of anyone who seemed still to be sleeping, for this would be the last chance to grab some refreshment – and for the orthodox, even a drop of water – before sunset, more than twelve hours away.[1]

It was now high summer, and the terrible, desiccating Delhi heat was at its worst. In the pre-dawn glimmer, in courtyards across Delhi, Muslim families would be sitting outside, leaning against bolsters, eating their *sahri*, the pre-fast meal of sweet *sivayan* (semolina), and for those who could muster the appetite so early in the day, kebabs too, all to be wolfed down before the sound of a cannon-shot from the Fort announced the sun's imminent appearance over the horizon. In these days of fiery winds, the early morning had the added attraction of the day's only cool breezes.

By 7 a.m. Zafar had finished his breakfast, and was saying his morning prayers in his river-front oratory, the *tasbih khana*. As he rose, leaning on a stick, he noticed that in the middle distance to his left, beyond the meandering river at the far end of the Bridge of Boats, a tall pillar of smoke was bellowing out of the Toll House, silhouetted now against the rising sun. More ominously still, the far bank of the Yamuna was cloudy with rising dust. According to the account of his young attendant, Zahir Dehlavi, Zafar shouted to Mir Fateh Ali, the Chief of his Palanquin Bearers, who was waiting outside the oratory to take him on his morning tour of the Palace. Zafar told him to send an express camel messenger to find out the cause of the fire and the rising dust; he also summoned his prime minister, Hakim Ahsanullah Khan, and Captain Douglas, the Commandant of the Palace Guards, who was responsible to the Resident for security in the Palace.[2]

By the time the hakim and the commandant appeared, the messenger had already returned. He had ridden only as far as the bastion of Salimgarh, a few thousand yards away, and from there could clearly see that Indian cavalrymen (or *sawars*) in their Company uniforms were clattering across the Bridge of Boats, swords drawn. They had already looted and burned the Toll House on the east bank of the river. They had also attacked and killed both the toll keeper and the manager of the city telegraph office, Charles Todd, who had just half an hour earlier set off in his buggy to try to find the cause of the break in the telegraph line to Meerut. Some servants of British officials whom they happened to meet on the way had also been hacked down as they passed. The messenger added that the early morning bathers were now running in panic from the river ghats and were scrambling to get into the city through the Calcutta Gate, just to the north of the Palace. On hearing this, Zafar gave immediate orders that the gates of the city and the Fort should all be closed, and that if it was not too late, the bridge should also be broken.[3]

Captain Douglas and Ahsanullah Khan were alarmed but hardly very surprised by Zafar's dramatic news. It was not just that rumours of a mutiny in the army had been circulating in the Palace for months now, and of late growing increasingly insistent and precise.[4] Twenty minutes earlier, Douglas had been summoned by the guards of the Fort's Lahore Gate, who had told him that a lone cavalryman was making a disturbance. Douglas had come straight down from the quarters immediately above the gate that he shared with Padre Jennings. Asked what he wanted, the *sawar* had coolly replied that he had mutinied at Meerut, and that he and his brothers would no longer serve the Company: the time had come, he said, to fight for their faith. But now that he had arrived in Delhi he had come to the Fort in search of a pipe and a drink of water: could Douglas go and find him one? Douglas had given orders to the guards to seize the insolent *sawar*, but before they could do so, he had ridden off laughing.[5] The hakim was just coming down the covered bazaar of the Fort to investigate the disturbance when the summons came from Zafar; both men arrived at the Emperor's oratory together.

As the three were still conferring on what action to take, a group of twenty cavalrymen trotted calmly up along the strand separating the Palace from the river: 'some had their swords drawn; others had pistols and carbines in their hands; more were coming from the direction of the bridge, accompanied by men on foot, apparently grooms, with bundles on their heads'.[6] There were also in the middle distance a crowd of 'convicts from the Meerut Jail and Gujar tribesmen* and other *badmashes* (ruffians or ne'er-do-wells) from the villages round about Delhi', who had presumably followed the

---

* The Gujars were Hindu herders and pastoralists, many of them semi-nomadic, who for centuries had roamed with their cattle and horses throughout north-west India and especially in Rajasthan. They had their own traditions and deities, and even their own oral epic of origin, about the herder-hero Dev Narayan, whose festival at Sawai Bhuj near Ajmer brought about – and still does – a great annual gathering of the different Gujar clans and their livestock. The Gujars were always treated with great suspicion by their urban neighbours who regarded them, rather as Europeans at the same period used to look on Gypsies, as thieves and criminals. Many of the watchmen or *chaukidars* in Mughal Delhi were from Gujar backgrounds, and were recruited on the basis that a former poacher made the best gamekeeper. The pacification and settlement of the Gujars and Mewaties was the great achievement of the early British administration in Delhi, and the failure of the rebels to do the same was a major cause of their defeat, as the Gujars and Mewaties effectively blockaded the town and robbed anyone entering or leaving it. The Gujars thus effectively achieved what the British were unable to bring about: a genuine siege of the city.

sepoys as they headed south.[7] They halted under the gilt dome and latticework screens of the Saman Burj, where the Mughals had for centuries attended to petitioners; then they began loudly calling for the Emperor. According to Zafar's record of the event, 'they said, we have come from Meerut after killing all the Englishmen there, because they asked us to bite bullets with our teeth that were coated with the fat of cows and pigs. This has corrupted the faith of Hindus and Muslims alike'.[8]

At this, Douglas offered to go down and talk to the men, but the Emperor forbade it, saying that he was unarmed and that the men were murderers and would surely kill him. 'I did not let him go . . . Then the Qiladar Bahadur [Douglas] went to the window and spoke to them,' saying:[9] ' "Don't come here; these are the private apartments of the ladies of the Palace; your standing opposite them is a disrespect to the king." On this they gradually, one by one, went off in the direction of the Rajghat Gate [to the south].'[10]

'After that,' according to Zafar, 'the Qiladar said, "I will go and take care of this", and took my leave.'[11]

Douglas ran off 'in a state of excitement' to make sure that all the city's many gates had followed the orders to close. But within minutes Zafar, sitting on his terrace, could see great black plumes of smoke rising to the south, from within the walls, apparently from the smartest quarter of the city – Daryaganj – where five years earlier Zafar had processed with his family to witness the wedding of Mirza Jawan Bakht.

The sepoys, Zafar could plainly see, were now inside his city.[12]

For Theo Metcalfe, 11 May meant the beginning of a six-month-long sabbatical from work in Kashmir.

He was suffering from exhaustion and depression – an intense 'numbness of feeling that weighs me down'. Moreover his left eye was now so inflamed that he had to wear an eyepatch; indeed, the people of Delhi had begun calling him 'One-eyed Metcalfe'. He was under no illusions about the critical nature of the situation in India – he had recently told a friend who was returning to England, 'you are lucky to be going home, for we shall soon be kicked out of India, or we shall fight to the death for our existence'. He badly needed a holiday, and now could not wait to get into the *dak palki* that would take him to join GG and his son Charlie in the cool green valleys of the Himlayas – his first proper break since he had arrived in India seven years earlier.[13]

He rose early, finished closing up Metcalfe House, and then around 7 a.m. set off at a leisurely place to his office at the Kutcherry Court House, just inside Kashmiri Gate, to hand over charge to his successor. There, to his surprise, he found the courts empty,

> with only the Assistant Magistrate [Arthur Galloway] present, who was waiting, not knowing what to do . . . [It was] reported that the Treasury Guard had been overheard the night before saying that the Government had been tampering with their religion, and 'what would be, would be.' The report was followed by one from the Darogah [officer] of the Yamuna Bridge, that the mutineers [from Meerut] were hastening towards the city.[14]

Theo looked out through the river-front window at the back of his office: there on the far bank, haloed in dust but still quite unmistakable, was a large body of infantry, led by a troupe of *sawars*, heading for the Bridge of Boats and making ready to cross.

Jumping back into his buggy, Theo drove straight to the fortified magazine that lay a little to the south, next to the new premises of the Delhi College, with which it shared the former site of the great Mughal haveli of Shah Jahan's son, Dara Shukoh.*[15] There he met his friend Lieutenant George Willoughby of the Bengal Artillery, who was in charge of the arsenal. Theo asked Willoughby for two guns to place at the end of the bridge so as to prevent the mutineers from crossing. But looking out over the riverside bastion at the rear of the compound, directly overlooking the bridge, the pair saw they

---

* Sylvia Shorto argues convincingly in her thesis that the gateway to the magazine – which still survives as a public urinal on a traffic island on Minto Road in Old Delhi – marks the site of the great gate of Dara Shukoh's haveli. See Sylvia Shorto, *Public Lives, Private Places, British Houses in Delhi 1803–57*, unpublished dissertation, NYU, 2004.

were already too late: several hundred mutineers were now marching in open column over the bridge, and the foremost sepoys had already taken possession of the Delhi bank of the Yamuna.[16] Leaving Willoughby to close and barricade the magazine, Theo set off at breakneck speed to see whether he might yet close the Calcutta Gate, which commanded the passage from the bridge into the city.

Here Theo was, for once, in time. Simon Fraser, the Resident, and Theo's senior colleagues, the two chief magistrates of Delhi, John Ross Hutchinson and Charles Le Bas, had already arrived at the gate and managed to get it closed before the sepoys got there. From there, Theo could hear the tramp of feet as the sepoy infantry retraced their steps, having failed to push open the gate. They were now heading south along the sandy bed of the river to try to find an alternative route into the city. The four Englishmen stood on the parapet of the gate, anxiously watching the sepoys through their binoculars; behind, a crowd of frustrated would-be bathers and increasingly restive spectators was massing between the gate and Anguri Bagh, Zafar's beloved Grape Garden, 'the riff raff of the city every moment adding fresh recruits to the already turbulent mob'.[17]

Guessing that the sepoys now planned to try to enter through either the Rajghat or Zinat ul-Masajid Gates of the city, Fraser asked Theo to head as fast as he could to the south of the Palace, to make sure that both these gates had also received, and obeyed, the orders to close. Theo jumped back into his buggy and galloped around the Palace walls; but after only a couple of thousand yards, as he neared the great Lahore Gate of the Palace, and at the crossroads with Chandni Chowk, he was met by a body of mutinous cavalry coming in the opposite direction. They were probably the same *sawars* who had earlier petitioned Zafar from below the Saman Burj. Either way, they had succeeded in entering the city, and were now hunting down any Christian they could find, 'with their swords in the air and shouting', according to the memoir of Theo's sister, Emily Metcalfe.

When they saw Sir Theophilus in his buggy, some of them rushed at him and tried to strike him and his horse, but [Theo lashed them with his riding whip and they] only succeeded in slashing the hood

... Sir Theophilus noticed that an enormous mob had already collected on the open ground in front of the palace, and that they were all dressed in white as if expecting a gala day. So he drove his buggy at full tilt amongst them, and seeing he was still pursued by the mounted mutineers, he jumped out into the middle of the mob.[18]

Here Theo threw off his dark coat and removed his trousers so that he wouldn't stand out from the rest of the crowd.[19] Pushing on in his undergarments, he

elbowed his way through the crowd, till he reached a group of mounted police standing under some trees as if in expectation of a row. As these men were under his orders as Joint Magistrate, he told them to charge the mutineers, but they would not stir. So he knocked the principal officer off his horse (Sir Theophilus was a very powerful man) and jumping onto it himself, wrenching the reins from his hands, he galloped into the heart of the city to see the Kotwal [head of the native police].

By now the whole city was in state of uproar. Shopkeepers were trying to close their shops; some of the bazaars were already being looted, and smoke was rising from the European mansions in Daryaganj; moreover, there was still no sign of any British troops from Meerut pursuing the mutineers – as Theo had assumed they would. Before long, however, Theo heard that the Indian troops stationed in the Delhi cantonments to the north had now reached Kashmiri Gate and were forming up to mount a counter-attack. Getting back on his horse, and still wearing only his 'shirt and underdraws', he headed up through the maze of gullies and back-streets in the direction of the Kashmiri Gate and the troops he hoped would save him.

As he galloped past a mosque, however, a large brick thrown from an upper window hit him squarely in the back of the neck. Theo fell from his horse, and rolled off into a ditch, still and silent.[20]

Shortly after Theo had galloped off, Simon Fraser heard shooting and the cries of the *sawars* coming from within the city.

Realising that the sepoys were now within the walls, and that he and his colleagues were trapped with their backs to a barred gate, and an increasingly angry mob – now 500 strong – just a short way down the street, Fraser came down from the parapet. He ordered his small escort of irregular cavalry – provided for him by the supposedly Anglophile Nawab of Jhajjar – to form up in line with their swords drawn, facing down the street. Hutchinson, Le Bas and Captain Douglas, who were all unarmed, stood to one side by the sentries' guardroom at the base of the gate. According to one eyewitness, a news-crier called Chunni who was in the crowd,

> This had just been done when about seven troopers and two men mounted on camels galloped up by the road along the palace from the direction of Daryaganj, and immediately on coming within pistol shot distance the whole party fired at the European gentlemen at the gate . . . The Jhajjar sawars made no resistance, but deserted Mr Fraser and fled.[21]

Hutchinson, the senior magistrate, was wounded in the right arm, just above the elbow.[22] Fraser, however, ran to the guardroom, seized a musket from the hands of a guard and shot one of the troopers dead. At the sight of the *sawar* falling, the crowd massing up the street became angry and began to head menacingly for the party. Deserted by Fraser's bodyguard, and trapped with the gate behind them, Douglas and Hutchinson jumped into the ditch of the Palace moat; the former fell badly and broke his ankle as he hit the bottom. Helped by Makhan, his mace bearer, who jumped down after him, Douglas limped along the ditch towards the Lahore Gate, supported on the other side by the wounded and bleeding Hutchinson.

Fraser, meanwhile, being too fat to jump, charged straight at the crowd with his buggy, and to his own surprise emerged unscathed on the far side. In the half-mile between him and the Palace, he was again attacked by several *sawars* who fired their pistols at him; but the shots missed, and the Resident arrived safely at the Lahore Gate of the Palace. There, the upright figure of Padre Jennings could be seen scanning the city with his telescope from the topmost chatri. His daughter Annie, and her friend Miss Clifford – Fraser's two choirmasters – were at his side.[23]

Makhan, the mace bearer, helped the two wounded men out of the ditch. According to his later testimony, Douglas 'being considerably hurt, asked to be taken into the Kuliyat Khana till he should recover a little from the shock he had received. In the meantime, the Revd Mr Jennings came down to him, and he and Mr Hutchinson conveyed him to the apartments over the gate'.[24] There Annie Jennings and Miss Clifford laid Douglas on a bed and gave him some tea, dressed his ankle and attended to Hutchinson's wound.

While Captain Douglas was being carried upstairs, Fraser had remained below, and attempted to mount a defence of the Lahore Gate. He ordered the gate to be closed and sent to Zafar for two cannon and a troop of armed guards. He also asked for two palanquins to remove Annie Jennings and her friend to the imperial zenana. But 'such was the confusion that neither the guards, nor the *palkis*, were forthcoming'.

> No heed was paid to the orders given. The will to obey was wanting; the king's household had become rebellious, refusing to obey. Fraser remained for some time awaiting the *palkis*. Seeing that no attention was likely to be paid to his orders, he turned away as if to enter Captain Douglas's house. Pressed by the crowd, he ordered them to stand off. The gateway was guarded by a company of native infantry who he now ordered to load and close the gate; but they refused. Mr Fraser then remonstrated with the men for their behaviour. They remained silent.[25]

> By this time a great crowd of men and boys had collected [and] began clapping their hands as a kind of insolent bravado at what was occurring. Mr Fraser, on seeing such marked feelings of hostility, began to return to Captain Douglas's quarters, and as he reached the foot of the stairs, Hajji, a lapidary, raised his sword to make a cut at him. Mr Fraser who had a sheathed sword in his hand, turned sharply round, and thrust at him with the sword in its sheath, saying to the havildar of the gate guard, 'What kind of behaviour is this?' Upon

which the havildar made a show of driving off the crowd; but no sooner was Mr Fraser's back turned than the havildar nodded to the lapidary, to signify to him that now he should renew his attack. The lapidary, thus encouraged, rushed upon Mr Fraser, and inflicted a deep and mortal wound on the right side of his neck. Mr Fraser at once fell, whereupon three other men who had been concealed in the outhouse adjoining, rushed out and cut him with their swords, over the head, face and chest till he was quite dead.[26]

'I was at the head of the stairs,' testified Makhan, 'and this was perpetrated at the foot of them.'

After this the crowd made a rush to the upper apartments, where the gentlemen, viz Captain Douglas, Mr Hutchinson and Mr Jennings had retired. Attacking them with swords, they at once murdered them and the two young ladies . . . [Padre Jennings being cut down just as he got as far as the door to escape down a second staircase.] On reaching the room where Captain Douglas was, I saw that he was not quite dead. Mamdoh, a bearer in the service of the King, perceiving this also, hit him with a bludgeon on the forehead, and killed him immediately. I saw the other bodies, including those of the two ladies. Mr Hutchinson was lying in one room, and the bodies of Captain Douglas, Mr Jennings and the two ladies in another on the floor, except Captain Douglas who was on the bed.

All the murders were perpetrated within a quarter of an hour of Mr Fraser's death, and it was now between 9 and 10 o'clock a.m. After the death of the gentlemen, the crowd began plundering their property. Fearing for my own life I ran off to my own house in the city, and never returned to the palace.[27]

By the time Padre Jennings was cut down, one of his two star converts had also been killed. Dr Chaman Lal had been attending to his patients at his hospital in Daryaganj when the *sawars* first charged through the Rajghat Gate. Hearing the uproar, he had gone out of the hospital to investigate, whereupon he was pointed out by the people in the street. Immediately 'one soldier pinned him down, sat on his chest, and asked what religion he was. When Dr Lal replied that he was a Christian, the sawar shot him dead at point blank range with his pistol. The cavalry then ransacked and burned the clinic'.[28]

The religious nature of the Uprising was becoming immediately apparent. British men and women who had converted to Islam were invariably spared, yet all Indian converts to Christianity – Hindu or Muslim – were sought out and hunted down. While Chaman Lal was one of the very first victims, as were Jennings and his two missionary assistants – both cut down as they ran to escape along the Chandni Chowk – an Anglo-Indian Christian named Mrs Aldwell managed to save herself because she knew the *kalima*, the Islamic profession of faith, and told her captors that she was a Muslim. The soldiers replied that if they were to kill a Muslim 'they would [themselves] be as bad as infidels; but that they were determined on killing all the Christians'.[29]

One British convert to Islam, a former Company soldier who had taken the name Abdullah Beg, remained throughout the Uprising one of the most active insurgents against British rule. On 11 May, 'on the arrival of the Mutineers, he immediately identified himself with them and became virtually a leader and advisor'; later he was seen manning the rebel artillery, assisted by another presumed convert, Sergeant-Major Gordon, 'a tall sturdy-looking man, with a naturally fair face, though extremely sun-burnt, and a fine soldier-like figure', who had been spared in the massacre of Christians at the outbreak of the Uprising at Shahja-hanpur on account of what his sepoys took to be his Muslim faith. In due course he was taken to Delhi, where he was said to have manned the guns on the northern face of the city walls.*[30]

---

* Later in the Uprising, Mr Powell, the Moradabad postmaster, and four other Englishmen who were believed to have converted to Islam (or rather that 'the Regiment had made them Mohammedan'), but who refused to fight for the rebels, were brought into Delhi with the troops who had mutinied in Shahjahanpore. They were kept under an armed guard of jihadis in the kotwal throughout the rest of the siege, but were not harmed and eventually escaped during the British assault on the city in September. See OIOC, Eur Mss B 138, *Account of Said Mobarak Shah*.

Whatever its causes, the response to the Uprising fractured along distinct class lines. From the morning of 11 May onwards, the most enthusiastic insurgents among the people of Delhi were the workmen of the lower middle class – especially the Muslim weavers and textile merchants – and the same Punjabi Muslim manufacturing and merchant class who had long supported the mujahedin movement. It was these people who immediately swelled the ranks of the initially very small number of sepoys who had arrived in the Mughal capital, creating a panic and allowing many of the poorer Delhiwallahs to set off on an orgy of looting.*

In contrast, the Delhi elite, both Hindu and Muslim, remained divided on the merits of joining the Uprising, and were from the start dubious about playing host to large numbers of desperate and violent sepoys from the east of Hindustan. According to one angry eyewitness, the nobleman Abdul Latif: 'The teachings of all religions were ignored and violated; even the poor women and children were not spared. The elite and the respected gentry of the city were appalled at the actions [of the insurgents] and were seen pleading with them. Ah! An entire world was destroyed, and as a result of these sins this city was struck down by the evil-eye.'[31] Ghalib was also quite clear that he didn't like the look of what was happening: 'Swarming through the open gates of Delhi, the intoxicated horsemen and rough foot soldiers ravished the city,' he wrote.

> Shut in my room, I listened to the noise and tumult . . . From all sides one could hear the foot soldiers running and hoof beats of the horsemen coming, wave upon wave. Looking out, there was not so much as a handful of dust which was not stained with the blood of men . . . Woe for those fair ladies of delicate form, with faces radiant as the moon and bodies gleaming like newly mined silver! A

* According to the testimony of Mohan Lal Kashmiri, who was an eyewitness: 'They [the sepoys] were soon joined by the bad character of the city, and the prisoners let loose from the jail increased the numbers of these miscreants. The residents of the Khanam Bazaar and the Nahur [where the Punjabi Muslims concentrated] were foremost of the lines of the mutineers, after this they began to pillage and slaughter the Christians and their dependants.' OIOC, Home Miscellanous, 725, pp. 389–422, *Letter Written by Munshi Mohan Lal to Brigadier Chamberlain dated November 8th 1857 at DEHLIE.*

thousand times pity those murdered children whose step was more beautiful than that of the deer and the partridge. All were sucked into the whirlpool of death, drowned in an ocean of blood.[32]

For Ghalib, the Uprising was more about the rise of the rabble of the lower classes than it was about the fall of the British. For him the most terrifying aspect of the revolution was the way his own courtly elite seemed to have lost control to a group of ill-educated ruffians of dubious ancestry: 'Noble men and great scholars have fallen from power,' he wrote,

and nameless men with neither name nor pedigree nor jewels nor gold, now have prestige and unlimited riches. One who wandered dust-stained through the streets as if blown by an idle wind, has proclaimed the wind his slave . . . In its shamelessness the rabble, sword in hand, rallied to one group after another. Throughout the day the rebels looted the city, and at night they slept in silken beds . . . The city of Delhi was emptied of its rulers and peopled instead by creatures of the Lord who accepted no lord – as if it were a garden without a gardener, and full of fruitless trees . . . The Emperor was powerless to repulse them; their forces gathered around him, and he fell under their duress, engulfed by them as the moon is engulfed by the eclipse.[33]

The young Mughal nobleman Sarvar ul-Mulk, who was then probably around twelve years old, was equally frightened by what he saw. He was being taken by a servant, Rahim Bakhsh, to visit his maternal aunt's house in Kuchah Bulaqi Begum, near the Jama Masjid, and was just crossing the Dariba on Chandni Chowk when 'we saw people running in all directions in fright'.

Rahim Bakhsh, a strong man, at once lifted me on his back and bolted. When we reached my aunt's house, the gate was being closed, but Rahim Bakhsh struck at the gate, and entered it with such force, that inside we both fell prone, and hurt ourselves badly . . . The 'Poorbyas' [sepoys from the east] one and all considered themselves to be under the orders of nobody. After their arrival, we kept our houses well guarded.[34]

Zafar's page Zahir Dehlavi was also profoundly alarmed by the outbreak. The King had summoned his attendants to him when he first saw the sepoys approaching. As the streets burned around him, Zahir buckled on his sword and knife, 'which had lain unused for years', and set out into the chaos to try to obey the Emperor's summons. Outside, Zahir could hear the sound of shooting; at some distance mobs were rampaging, alternately hunting down Christians and looting the richer shops. Steeling his nerve, he mounted his horse and set off through his deserted and shuttered *muhalla* of Matia Mahal and off towards the Jama Masjid.

When I reached the small gate I saw three or four mounted soldiers wearing *kurtas* and *dhotis* and a small scarf tied to their heads, and swords in their belt, standing under the Peepal tree against the canal wall. Hindu men were talking to them and entertaining them, some had brought them newly fried puris, some had brought sweets, some were bringing them water. I did not pay attention to them but passed on towards the fort.

Soon after I saw a mob of *badmashes* led by a big man who looked like a wrestler. He was wearing *kurta dhoti*, a cap on his head, a long bamboo *lathi* on his shoulder, and he was leading a large number of men dressed in the same way. Near the house of Ashraf Beg, the leader hit the road lantern with his bamboo stick and it broke and shattered on the road. He laughed to his friends, and said 'Hey look I have just killed another *kafir*'; then they started breaking the lock of a cloth merchant's shop. I moved quickly on on my horse.

Near the *Kotwali* had gathered a large crowd of miscreants, and all the shops on the way were being looted . . . The criminals in the city had seen that there was a great opportunity in the unrest, and quickly decided to join the rebels. Full of greed and excitement, they took the rebels to the gate of the bank, brutally killed the men, women and children [of the Beresford family] who were inside, and broke open the treasure trunks and looted the notes inside them. These rebels and rioters were the rebellious soldiers, the criminals who had been freed from the jail and the *chamars* [untouchables and sweepers], loafers, *dhobis* [laundrymen], barbers, butchers and the paper makers of the *Kaghazi Gali*, pick-pockets, wrestlers and other vagabonds. No person from a decent family was a part of this crowd of rioters, for the respectable people of the city were all locked inside their houses, and were quite unaware of what was going on in the city.

The rioters looted money to their hearts' content. They took away as much as they could carry from the bank, the *chamars*, cobblers and vagabonds taking away three bags of money each, and the residents of the *Kaghazi Gali* were able to pile their homes with the loot as they were just across the wall [from the ruins of the bank]. At least fourteen lakh rupees were looted in the space of an hour. There was rioting all around [Chandni Chowk], people were running amok, blood was flowing like a river, and the rioters were mercilessly creating hell on earth without any guilt or fear, each trying to enrich himself, and not thinking about anyone else.

When I reached the Gate of the Palace, I saw that near the moat of the Fort about fifty mounted men were lined up guarding the entrance. There was a strong breeze and torn pages from an English book were flying towards the Fort . . .[35]

Anyone who was associated with the old regime was an immediate target. Jiwan Lal, the enormously fat Head Munshi (Chief Secretary) of the British Residency, was at first anxious to do what he could for his employers, hearing how one after another of his friends among the British officials had been hunted down and killed: 'I wept to feel how utterly powerless I was,' he wrote. But he soon realised that his own position was far from secure:

I was a man of corpulent habit of body and well known, so that I could not go out without being discovered . . . Crowds of badmashes were pointing out to the soldiers the residences of the Europeans and the wealthier natives . . . Then a man reported that the badmashes were naming me as being the Mir Munshi, and as one worthy of death, and offering to point out my house. Terrified, I ordered the gates to be locked. The house had been built in the days of the [fourteenth-century] Emperor Firoz Shah [Tughluq], and was of solid stone, and as strong as a fort. The doors and windows were all closed. There were underground apartments, into which my

family all entered, and there remained concealed. I arranged all the
servants for watch and ward, both in front and behind, with orders
to admit no one . . . The city was panic struck – all houses and shops
were closed, their inmates concealed inside, praying to God for his
mercy and protection.[36]

Many were looted simply because they were rich. Some of the first
targets were Delhi's wealthy but unpopular Marwari and Jain
moneylenders, though these were in no way directly connected
with the British regime. Immediately after the sepoys entered Delhi,
the banking partners Mathura Das and Saligram became among the
first victims of the looters: 'The Tilangas assaulted the house of
Saligram with the intention of looting it but at first could not loosen
the screws,' recorded an anonymous news-writer the following
day. 'At midnight the Tilangas finally broke through the gate, along
with Muslims of the city, and [together they] looted all the goods of
the *kothi*.'[37] The partners, who had previously incurred the enmity
of the Palace by having Mirza Shah Rukh seized in an attempt to
recover their debts, were forced to come before Zafar begging for
protection: 'Your slave's house has been plundered of everything it
contained and all it possessed,' they pleaded. 'All our banking and
mercantile transactions have been utterly ruined and suspended . . .
We are now with difficulty able to procure even the daily necessities
of life.'[38]

Others less wealthy than Saligram suffered a similar fate. According to the Chief of Police, Sa'id Mubarak Shah, 'bodies of
sepoys, troopers and others went through the streets plundering
and maltreating the respectable citizens'.

In the general confusion a party of eight Ranghuirs [Muslim Rajputs]
who had been putting up at the serai assembled a body of dacoits and
gutted one whole portion of the town, loaded their camels with gold
mohurs, jewellery and other valuables and set out for their village
. . . The plundering continued the whole of that day and night.[39]

Soon so many of the richest havelis had been broken into and
looted, usually with the excuse that the inhabitants were sheltering

Christians, that Mufti Sadruddin Azurda helped form a private police force to protect himself and his circle. The men he turned to were the only Delhiwallahs with sufficient arms and military training to take on the sepoys. These were the jihadis of the underground mujahedin network, whose brotherhood, bound to fight the jihad by oaths of allegiance (or *bayat*) to a leader (or *amir*), now cast off their veil of secrecy and began to mass in Delhi, ready for the holy war they had so long dreamt of.* Before long the jihadis would become a significant force in the Delhi Uprising, operating alongside but quite independently of the rebel sepoys.

Such was the prevalence of jihadi rhetoric at the outbreak that some went so far as to term the sepoys mujahedin, even though the overwhelming majority of them were Brahmins and other high-caste Hindus. Maulvi Muhammad Baqar certainly wrote up the outbreak in his *Dihli Urdu Akbhar* as a jihad. In his view the sepoys were guided by the hand of an angry God, outraged at the attacks made on the true faith by the British. For this reason, unlike most of the educated Delhi elite, Baqar was from the beginning an enthusiastic cheerleader for the Uprising. By eight in the morning he was out on the streets, carefully noting what was happening: 'This humble writer, having heard the sound of gunshots, for the sake of Islam, came out of his house, and caring more for enjoyment and distraction of his readers than for his own life, without hesitation started moving towards the disturbance in order to inquire into the details,' he wrote.

---

* According to Jiwan Lal's diary the force was operational by 15 May. During the trial of Azurda at the end of the Uprising, the three commanders of his jihadi guard were named – 'Abd ur-Rahman Ludhianawi, his son Sayf ur-Rahman and Muhammad Munir – and the reasons for their employment were discussed in court. Later in the Uprising the jihadis did succeed in fending off an attack on Azurda's house, according to Jiwan Lal: 'The house of Moulvie Sadarud-Din Khan was attacked today by fifty soldiers; but, seeing that there were seventy jihadis ready to oppose them, they retreated, but carried off two colts from the house of Ahsanullah Khan.' Even more unequivocal is the report of Azurda's refusing a demand for money, saying that the *ghazis* he had employed would be used for his defence. See Swapna Liddle's excellent essay on Azurda in Margrit Pernau's *Delhi College*, New Delhi, 2006. For Azurda's trial see NAI, Foreign Dept, 1859, Political, 113/5. *Bayats*, or oaths of allegiance to an *amir*, are still standard practice among modern jihadi groups such as al-Qaeda, as well as among other less aggressive Muslim brotherhoods such as certain Sufi *tarikhas*.

In the Kashmiri bazaar, people were running in large numbers . . .
Several Englishmen with naked swords were running in a frenzy and
behind them ran a body of Tilangas with their guns chasing them.
Not far behind, the residents of the city, one holding a plank,
another the leg of a charpoy, someone else holding a bamboo *lathi*
were running after the Tilangas. Some of the city's populace even
tried to throw bricks at the Englishmen, shouting and screaming at
them . . .

In front of Fakhr ul-Masajid a motley group of some twenty
Tilangas were standing around and people were pointing them towards the mosque [where some of the English had taken sanctuary]. I
saw the Tilangas go inside the mosque and there they shot the people
and sent them on their journey to the hereafter. Further ahead I saw the
Church [St James's] and Collins Saheb's kothi where three hundred
Tilangas and Turk Riders [Muslim cavalrymen] were standing.*

From there, different groups were spreading out, and asking
everyone where the English are. If anybody gave any information
four or five soldiers would immediately accompany that man, and in
no time, in every lane, Christians were found lying dead. They
entered each Kothi and killed the Englishmen with their women and
children, and all the houses were plundered. All the movables from
the Church and Kutcherry, including the chairs and tables and even
the marble slabs of the floors were taken away. After a while I saw
the corpse of Nixon Saheb, the head clerk of Commissioner's office.
Some wit had even placed a biscuit in his mouth . . .

When I looked towards the Delhi College I saw that all the goods
including the portraits, pictures and instruments, chemicals and
medicines and a library of English and Persian books as well as
maps worth thousands of Rupees were all being taken as loot, and it
reached such a pass that even the flooring and the joints of the gates
were dug out. The sound of gunfire came from all sides . . .[40]

---

* The extended family of Thomas Collins, Fraser's deputy, suffered the largest
number of casualties of any British family in Delhi. According to a plaque still up
on the wall of St James's Church, no fewer than twenty-three members of the family
were 'all barbarously murdered at Delhi on or about the 11th of May 1857'. Nearby are
plaques to Padre Jennings, the Beresfords of the Delhi Bank and Dr Chaman Lal, who
is described as 'a native Christian and a Worshipper in this church'.

In his account of the events of 11 May, Muhammad Baqar remained as much the preacher as the curious journalist and war correspondent. Almost the entire front page of the 17 May edition of the paper was given over to Koranic verses concerning worldly vanity and the power of God, along with a lengthy theological exposition. For Baqar was determined not just to describe what happened, but also to interpret it – and to highlight the divine hand he believed was behind the unprecedented events:

> Some people swear that when the Turk troopers came here, there were female camels ahead of them on which rode green-robed riders and then they instantly vanished from sight. Only the troopers remained and they killed whichever Englishman they found . . .
>
> Truly the English have been afflicted with divine wrath by the true avenger. Their arrogance has brought them divine retribution for, as the Holy Koran says, 'God does not love the arrogant ones.' God has given the Christians such a bodyblow that within a short time this carnage has utterly destroyed them . . . For He has power over everything, and has overwhelmed all their schemes and ploys. It is now incumbent upon you, people of Delhi, to have faith in God and all those who should expend all their energy in protecting and being loyal to the Shadow of God on Earth, his Exalted Majesty [the Emperor Bahadur Shah Zafar]. They should always remember that they have the help and support of the Almighty himself.[41]

No less excited by the new turn of events was Baqar's twenty-seven-year-old son, Muhammad Husain, later to become famous as the poet Azad. The second edition of the paper to be published after the arrival of the sepoys in Delhi, that of 24 May, contained Azad's first-ever published poem, entitled 'A History of Instructive Reversals'. The ghazals began with a series of rhetorical questions – where now was the empire of Alexander? Where the realm of Solomon? – before moving on to the fate of the Christian empire in India, whose days were now so clearly at an end:

Yesterday the Christians were in the ascendant,
World-seizing, world-bestowing,
The possessors of skill and wisdom,
The possessors of splendour and glory
The possessors of a mighty army.

But what use was that,
Against the sword of the Lord of Fury?
All their wisdom could not save them,
Their schemes became useless,
Their knowledge and science availed them nothing –
The Tilangas of the East have killed them all.

An event such as no one has ever seen or heard of –
See how the strange revolutions of the Heavens,
Open the eyes of instruction.
See how the reality of the world,
Has been revealed.

O Azad, learn this lesson:
For all their wisdom and vision,
The Christian rulers have been erased,
Without leaving a trace in this world.[42]

Up in the cantonments to the north of the city, the morning of 11
May had started badly. At 8 a.m., when Robert Tytler returned to
his bungalow after the morning parade, he had immediately complained to his wife, now seven months pregnant, 'Harrie, my men
behaved infamously today.'[43]

He told how, when the commanding officer had read out the
sentence passed on their colleagues in Meerut, Tytler's men had
'hissed and shuffled their feet, showing by their actions their
sympathy with the sentenced sepoys'. Tytler told his wife he would
drill them to their hearts' content if they misbehaved again. 'Little
did he dream', commented Harriet in her memoirs, 'that before
evening came he would not have one man to drill.'

Although it was only an hour after sunrise, and the *khas* screens

The Coronation Portrait of Bahadur Shah Zafar II by Ghulam Ali Khan, probably painted soon after Zafar's accession to the throne in 1837. The young Mirza Mughal stands to the right. Zafar's titles are inscribed in the frieze behind him: 'His Divine Highness, Caliph of the Age, Padshah as Glorious as Jamshed, He who is Surrounded by Hosts of Angels, Shadow of God, Refuge of Islam, Protector of the Mohammedan Religion, Offspring of the House of Timur, Greatest Emperor, Mightiest King of Kings, Emperor son of Emperor, Sultan son of Sultan.'

Scroll showing a procession of the Mughal court through the streets of Delhi, c.1818. ABOVE: Zafar as Crown Prince Abu'l Zafar Siraj ud-Din (Akbar Shah II – not visible here – was still Emperor); behind him is one of his younger brothers, probably Mirza Salim.

BELOW: A party from the British Residency. The Resident with the top hat and sideburns is probably Sir Charles Metcalfe, while his assistant and younger brother Thomas (later Sir Thomas) sits behind him, also wearing a top hat.

Aerial views over Delhi.
LEFT: The great Friday mosque, Jama Masjid, *c.*1840.
BELOW: The Red Fort, *c.*1770.

The rival court of the Metcalfes.

ABOVE: The 'Kootub House', also known as Dilkusha ('Delighter of the Heart'), a converted Mughal tomb, once the resting place of the foster brother of Akbar.

BELOW: Metcalfe House, which lay to the north of the Red Fort, on the banks of the Yamuna, and was also known as Jahan Numa ('World Showing').

ABOVE [from left to far right]: Bahadur Shah Zafar as a young man, *c.*1790; the celebrated blind sitar player, Ustad Himmat Khan ('Nobody could come close to him in Dhrupad,' thought Sir Sayyid Ahmad Khan); a painter with his brushes and materials – possibly a self-portrait of Mazhar Ali Khan, *c.*1830; Mirza Mughal, *c.*1850. BELOW: *Two scenes from the panorama of Delhi commissioned by Sir Thomas Metcalfe from Mazhar Ali Khan,* c.1850.

BELOW LEFT: View from the Lahore Gate looking south over the moat and the quarters of the salatin. BELOW RIGHT: View over the Jama Masjid to the top of Chandni Chowk (right-hand side). With the exception of the fort walls and the Jama Masjid, almost all of the buildings shown in both sections were destroyed by the British in the clearances that followed the recapture of the city at the end of the uprising.

OVERLEAF: The Rao of Kotah's visit to Delhi, *c.*1840. Zafar is shown peering through a spyglass, watching the Rao arrive with all his camels and carriages from the top left-hand turret.

in the Tytlers' bungalow were fixed on the outer doors and watered, it was already fiery hot. The couple had had their baths and were just settling down to the first – melon – course of their breakfast; the tailors were out on the veranda, sewing away. Suddenly 'the door flew open and the tailor rushed in with his hands clasped and in a most excited manner said, "Sahib, sahib, the *fauj* [army] has come."' Tytler explained to his wife that 'those fellows from Meerut have come over and I suppose are kicking up a row in the city. There is nothing to be frightened about, our men will be sent to coerce them, and all will very soon be over'.[44]

Tytler was sent off with two hundred sepoys to guard the new powder magazine recently erected on the Yamuna riverbank to the north of Metcalfe House. Meanwhile Tytler's senior officer, Colonel Ripley, took his regiment down to the Kashmiri Gate, intending to begin rounding up the miscreants. Since there was clearly no time to be lost, and the job of disarming a mob of disorganised mutineers did not sound very demanding, Ripley set off straight away, leaving a young officer named Edward Vibart to bring up the two light cannons that were kept some distance away in the artillery lines.

Vibart was a nineteen-year-old company commander from an Indian army family; his father was a cavalry officer in Kanpur. It took twenty minutes for Vibart to get the guns prepared, after which he galloped as fast as he could from the cantonments down through the Civil Lines. 'We were still some distance off,' he wrote afterwards, 'when the sound of musketry was distinctly heard; and now, as the church came into view, we could plainly see, from the smoke arising around it, that our regiment was actively engaged in the locality.'

Pushing on with all speed we shortly met Captain Wallace coming out of the Kashmir Gate. He implored us for 'God's sake' to hurry on as fast as possible, as all the officers were being shot down by cavalry troopers, and their men were making no efforts to defend them. On hearing the startling news, Major Patterson desired me to halt and load. The two guns then advanced through the gate, followed by the infantry. At this moment, the body of our un- fortunate Colonel [Ripley] was carried out, literally hacked to pieces.

One arm just below the shoulder was almost severed. Such a fearful sight I never beheld. The poor man was still alive, and though scarcely able to articulate, I distinctly gathered the few words he gasped out, that we had no chance against the cavalry, as our own men had turned against us . . .

I now entered the Main Guard, and found everything in confusion. In front of the church, a few cavalry troopers in their French-grey uniforms were seen galloping back in the direction of the palace. Lt Wilson brought a gun around to bear on them, but they were out of sight before he had time to fire. As for the men of my own regiment, not a sepoy was to be seen; they had vanished . . .

At length some of us advanced beyond the inner gates, when the first thing I saw was the lifeless body of Captain Burrowes lying close by the gate of the churchyard. Other bodies were now observed scattered about the place. Five were at length found and brought in . . . Since then I have witnessed many terrible sights, but I shall never forget my feelings that day as I saw our poor fellows brought in, their faces distorted with all the agonies of a violent death, and hacked about in every conceivable way. Only a couple of hours previously we had been laughing and chatting together . . .[45]

In the eerie silence, Vibart waited 'in this state of disquietening suspense'. Occasionally stragglers reached this last British outpost in the walled city: these included three of Ripley's officers, who had escaped and hidden down a side street, and the beautiful Annie Forrest, her mother and her two younger sisters – the youngest 'a sweet girl of nine' – all of whom had been sheltered by servants while a mob looted their house. They described seeing the last defence of the Delhi Bank by their friends, the Beresfords: 'on their premises being rushed by the insurgents . . . these poor people, accompanied by a few clerks, had descended to the upper balcony of the house, where after a desperate resistance, they were all eventually overpowered. Not one of the party escaped', though Mrs Beresford had skewered no fewer than three of the *sawars* with her husband's pig-sticking spear before she was killed herself.

It was hardly surprising, therefore, according to Vibart, that 'all those ladies who had taken refuge with us remained in the utmost state of alarm', especially when the sepoys with them started muttering that now the time 'had arrived to take their revenge on people who had tried to subvert their caste and religion . . .'

'Our position here', concluded Vibart, 'can easily be imagined to have been of an exceedingly precarious nature.'[46]

By lunchtime, virtually all the British people within the city who had not reached Vibart's shaky bridgehead at the Kashmiri Gate had been killed. One of the few still alive was the British merchant James Morley.

Morley lived with his family, and that of his business partner William Clark, in the Bazaar Kashmir Katra in Daryaganj. As their area of the city was one of the first to rise up, the family had hidden in the back of their house while the servants went and kept watch at the gate in case of trouble. But the mob drifted off to loot elsewhere and for a full three hours nothing further happened. As no news had reached the family, Morley eventually decided to go out and investigate whether escape was now an option. 'I took a thick stick in my hand and walked into the street,' he wrote later.

It was altogether empty. I continued to walk down it without meeting anyone . . . There was only one old man sitting in a shop door. I stood for some time, but at some distance I could see what seemed to be a crowd of men. It was very far off, and I could only just hear the noise and shouting. As I thought they might come up to our house, I stood watching them for some time. At length I heard a great noise behind, and looking around, I saw a large crowd rushing into my gateway. They had also seen me and some men came rushing down the street towards me. I immediately ran down the street to my left. I knew that there was a small lane that led to [the rear of] my house.

I was running along when two men ran out of another lane, and calling out *mar feringee ko*,' [kill the foreigner] they rushed at me. One man had a sword in his hand and the other a lathee. I stopped suddenly, and turning quickly round, I gave the man with the sword

a blow over the head which brought him to the ground. The other
man aimed a blow at my head, but I had stooped forward, and the
lathee only grazed my shoulder. I swung my stick round and it
caught him just below the knee, which made him sit down howling
with pain.[47]

Morley saw a mob collecting behind him so ran on, eventually
hiding in a shed used for storing carts. Groups of men passed up
and down the street looking for him; from his hiding place he could
hear various passers-by discussing in which direction they thought
he had run off. For four hours he hid, then crept out, determined to
try to discover the fate of his wife and family.

At length I came to the wall of the garden below our house and I
entered through a small wicket . . . everything was as still as death.
All around were lying broken chairs, tumblers, plates, books, &c.
that had been thrown out from the house. There were some bundles
of clothes lying burning . . . At length I heard a noise, as if someone
was crying near the cow house. I went there and found it was our old
dhobi [washerman] an old man who had been in my father's service
for nearly twenty years. I called out his name and when he saw me he
burst out louder saying 'Oh! Sahib! They have killed them all – they
have killed them all.'

I felt as if I had been stunned for some time. I then got up and I
said, 'come into the house with me' . . . Everywhere things were
lying about that had been most wantonly destroyed. Tables had been
split in pieces with hatchets, cupboards had been emptied out and
everything strewn on the floor. Jams and jellies were lying in heaps,
and there was an overpowering smell from the brandy and wine that
had run out from the broken bottles.

Every minute detail is distinctly imprinted upon my mind, for
with that cowardly shrinking from a knowledge of the worst which
is common to us all, I lingered in the outer room and kept looking
around it. At length I nerved myself and stepped into the next room.
Just before, pinned to the wall was poor Clark's little son with his
head hanging down, and a black stream of blood trickling down the
wall in a large black pool which lay near his feet. And this cruel death

must have been inflicted before his mother's eyes. I closed my eyes and shuddered, but opened them again upon an even more dreadful sight. Clark and his wife lay side by side. But I will not, I could not, describe the scene. I have said she was far advanced in pregnancy.

I heard an exclamation and going into the bedroom near the hall, I saw the old dhobi wringing his hands and crying. I rushed to the door but I could not enter. I could not face that spectacle. I could not bear to think that I might see my poor wife as I had just seen poor Mrs Clark. I just sat down, and placed my hands on my knees.[48]

Muin ud-Din Husain Khan was the *thanadar* or head police officer, at Paharganj police station, a little to the south-west of the walled city.

Muin ud-Din was from a minor branch of the noble Loharu family, who had risen to eminence in Delhi after supporting the British against the Marathas at the beginning of the nineteenth century; his cousins included both Ghalib and Nawab Zia ud-Din Khan, who had gone to warn the Wagentriebers of impending trouble on the previous night.

Strongly linked to the British cause, and an old family friend of both Sir Thomas and Theo Metcalfe, he had been alarmed by the reports of the puris and chapattis passing through the villages surrounding Delhi, and the tales of British houses having gone up in flames in cantonments around northern India. Yet despite going to see Theo, and warning him that similar signals had heralded the collapse of Maratha power half a century earlier, he found that his efforts had been in vain: 'The officers of the government seemed to attach no importance to the matter,' he wrote later, 'and [they] paid no heed to what we regarded as significant warnings of the spirit of disaffection which was spreading far and wide over the country.'[49]

In the early morning of Monday the 11th, Muin ud-Din had been engaged in a criminal case at the Kutcherry courts with the chief magistrate, John Ross Hutchinson. He had been present when the

Darogah of the Yamuna Bridge had run in to warn Hutchinson of
the imminent arrival of the troops from Meerut, and had been sent
by Hutchinson to alert the city kotwal of the danger. While there he
had heard a messenger from the Rajghat Gate announcing the
arrival of the sepoys within the city. Realising the danger, he
had galloped to Hutchinson to report the news, before heading
back to his own police station through the Ajmeri Gate. He was still
busy arming and preparing his own constabulary when a lone,
dishevelled European rode up wearing only 'his shirt and underdraws'. It was Theo Metcalfe.[50]

Theo did not know how long he had been unconscious, but in the
chaos no one had noticed him lying prostrate in the ditch; moreover, his horse was still grazing not far away. He had leaped on to
the saddle and with an unsheathed sword in his hand had galloped
out of the Ajmeri Gate, one of the last Christians to make his
escape.[51]

Muin ud-Din rushed Theo inside the police *thana* before he
could be seen, and quickly dressed him in his own Hindustani
clothes. He then sent out horsemen to see whether the road to the
cantonments was open. They returned only a few minutes later,
visibly frightened, reporting that the road was already completely
occupied by a mob who were busy looting all they could.

Muin ud-Din and Theo therefore set off by small side lanes
through the outer suburbs, hoping to avoid the worst of the
trouble. But they had not got far before they realised that there
was simply going to be no safe way of getting through, and it was
agreed that it would be best for Theo to take shelter. Muin ud-Din
chose the house of a local landowner called Bhura Khan Mewati,
and advised Theo to keep himself out of sight until the worst of the
trouble had passed and the soldiers from the cantonments had
brought the situation under control.

Muin ud-Din left Theo there and returned to his police post,
where he too shed his uniform and changed into Hindustani
clothes. He then rode into the city, through the unguarded city
gates, checked on the safety of his terrified family, and then headed
off towards the Fort, determined to report for duty to the Emperor
in the absence of any British authorities.

As he rode through the closed shops of the Chauri Bazaar, he reflected how 'the suddenness of the inroad of a handful of men created such panic . . . Ignorance of the strength of the mutineers, and exaggerated reports of their numbers [had] quite paralyzed' the city elite and prevented them taking any measures to resist or even limit the anarchy. In less than two hours, the great and prosperous city had been turned into a war zone:

> The principal executive officers of the government were dead. Every man thought [only] of his own safety and that of his family and property . . . On every side the scum of the population was hurrying to and fro, laden with the plunder of European houses. Arriving at the central police station, I found it plundered even to the doors, which had been carried off.[52]

Inside, Muin ud-Din found two policemen cowering in the ruins. They told him how two *sawars* had ridden up and called out, 'Are you all here for your religion or against it?' When the kotwal had replied, 'We are all for our religion,' the convicts had been let loose by the *sawars*. Shortly after this, 'two men mounted on camels and dressed in green with red turbans rode by at a trot, calling out, "Hear, ye people, the drum of religion has sounded." Whence they had come or whither they went, my informant knew not, but the excited and terrified crowds in the streets believed they were heavenly messengers'. Then the convicts returned from the black-smith's, and having had their fetters struck off, proceeded to storm the police station and ransack its contents.[53]

The Red Fort, when he reached it, was no less chaotic. 'The place was untenanted and deserted,' wrote Muin ud-Din. Walking through the empty courts, he reached the *tasbih khana*, and persuaded the two remaining eunuchs on duty to let him see Zafar. 'I begged the king to stop this [plunder] and arrange a restoration of order. The king replied: "I am helpless; all my attendants have lost their heads or fled. I remain here alone. I have no force to obey my orders: what can I do?"'[54]

Muin ud-Din asked Zafar whether he had any orders, and the Emperor sent him off accompanied by two of his *chobdars* (mace bearers) to Daryaganj to try to rescue any Christians he could find, promising to shelter them in the Palace. 'I and the chobdars loudly proclaimed the orders of the king [that the killing should cease],' wrote Muin ud-Din,

> and our interference was so far effectual, that the lives of some dozen persons were spared. They were sent to the palace and confined in the *chhota khasa* apartments, and orders were given to feed them. Until late afternoon I laboured, going from bungalow to bungalow, hoping to find someone still living whom I might rescue. A few Christians only were found alive and taken to the palace.[55]

By four o'clock Muin ud-Din had found nineteen more survivors, and sent them over to the Emperor. But as the day progressed, and as an increasing number of ragged sepoys rode and walked into the Fort from Meerut, the chaos and tension in the Palace grew worse. When Zahir Dehlavi arrived shortly after Muin ud-Din – at about 11 a.m. – he found that on Zafar's orders Hakim Ahsanullah Khan was supervising one of the Palace tailors, who was cutting out burial shrouds for Fraser, Douglas and the Jennings family; other courtiers were gathering, ready to obey Zafar's orders that the entire Fort should participate in the funeral rites of the murdered men. At that moment, a group of cavalry *sawars* galloped menacingly and unbidden into the private courtyards of the King – the area beyond the Red Curtain (or *Lal Pardah*):

> Hakeem Ahsanullah Khan saw them and said that we should all say the *Fatiha* [prayers for the dead] as the moment of our death has arrived. We all started reciting, as the mounted men neared the Hall of Private Audience, the *Diwan e-Khas*. They got down from their horses, tethered them and walked straight inside without taking off their boots. Altogether they must have been thirty men, and they were wearing long *kurtas*, loose *paijamas* and turbans. Some had carbines, others had pistols. When they saw the long white shrouds spread out, they turned to Hakeem Ahsanullah Khan and asked him, 'What is this?' The Hakeem replied, 'This is a consequence of what you have done, and the murders you and your admirers have

perpetrated.' To this the soldiers spat, 'You are little better than infidel Christians.'* Saying this, they ripped up all shrouds which were being prepared, tearing them to pieces.

One of the sawars then put the pistol in the belly of the royal Eunuch [and chamberlain] Mahbub Ali Khan, and told him to get them supplies. Mahbub Ali Khan said 'how can I provide you with supplies when we do not have any?' Hakeem Ahsanullah Khan backed him up, saying, 'Our Majesty has admitted himself that he does not have any money: he is living almost like a beggar. Where should we get the supplies? We get enough grain for a month for the horses in the royal stable. Go ahead and take that, but how long will that last? It will be sufficient for you for one day.'

The soldiers went to the King's own garden, Mahtab Bagh, and there they tied up their horses. Soon after another group of soldiers, this time sixty in number, came asking for supplies. They were also given the same offer, then again another fifty arrived. Soon about three hundred of them had collected in the Mahtab Bagh.[56]

From the point of view of the courtiers, the arrival of the sepoys was an invasion: the last time that large numbers of soldiers had poured unbidden into the Red Fort was when Ghulam Qadir seized the Palace in 1783, blinding the then Emperor, when Zafar was only eight. Since then it had been unheard of for anyone to pass the Red Curtain on horseback, or to approach the Diwan-i-Khas without removing their shoes. When the British Resident, Francis Hawkins, had done so in 1830, during Akbar Shah's annual holiday in Mehrauli, the Emperor had complained to Calcutta about the 'offensive and disrespectful act' and demanded that steps be taken 'to wipe off the dust of grief and affliction from the polished mirror of our enlightened and resplendent mind'; Hawkins was promptly dismissed.[57] Now several hundred unwashed and dirty ex-Company sepoys had come and billeted themselves without consultation

---

* Such was the strength of the link between religion and the Uprising that throughout 1857 all Indian loyalists were routinely labelled Christians. See Rudrangshu Mukherjee, ' "Satan Let Loose upon Earth": The Kanpur Massacres in India in the Revolt of 1857', *Past and Present*, no. 128, p. 116, where he cites the Deposition of Khoda Bux, in *Depositions at Cawnpore*.

in the inner apartments of the Palace, and had stabled their horses among the fruit trees of the Emperor's favourite garden.

Towards early afternoon, around three o'clock, the situation grew yet more tense, as the sepoys gathering in the Palace began to get restive, and came to collect again around Zafar's private apartments. They had clearly expected the Emperor to shower them in gold for coming and offering service. Instead, they had received a mixed reception in the city and an openly hostile one in the Palace. Moreover, despite their having come all the way to Delhi to seek the shelter of the Emperor, Zafar had not been seen since the first party of troopers shouted up to him in the early morning. So at around 4 p.m. their leaders sent word to the King that they had come 'to fight for our religion and to pay our respects to His Majesty'.[58] When this again failed to produce the Emperor, the soldiers massed in the courtyard in front of the Diwan i-Khas and 'commenced firing their muskets, pistols and carbines in the air, making a great clamour', according to Ghulam Abbas, Zafar's vakil (attorney).

The King hearing the noise, came out, and, standing at the door of the Hall of Special Audience, told his attendants to direct the troops to discontinue the noise they were making. He told them to call the native officers forward, that they might explain the object of such proceedings. On this the noise was quelled, and the officers of the cavalry came forward, mounted as they were. They explained that they had been required to bite cartridges, the use of which deprive both Hindus and Mahomedans of their religion, as the cartridges were greased with pork and beef fat, that they accordingly had killed the Europeans at Meerut, and had come to claim his protection.

The King replied, 'I did not call for you; you have acted very wickedly.' On this about one or two hundred of the mutinous infantry, ascended the steps and came into the hall, saying that 'unless you, the King, join us, we are all dead men, and we must in that case just do what we can for ourselves.'

Zafar argued with the troopers for a while – something unheard of in a normal durbar – admonishing them for the murders they had perpetrated, so that 'the court of the palace became a scene of the wildest confusion, quarrelling and disputes'.[59] As the nobleman Abdul Latif put it,

> The king was like the king on the chessboard after the checkmate. For a long time he acted with the utmost restraint and then said: 'Why is an old soul like me being subjected to such humiliating behaviour? And what is the reason of this noise? The sun of our life has already reached its evening. These are our last days. All I wish for is retreat and seclusion.'[60]

The courtiers were furious at the behaviour of the rebels and argued with the sepoys. But they were silenced by the mob and they had to return to their places. Ahsanullah Khan told the sepoys: '"You have long been accustomed under the English rule to regular pay. The King has no treasury. How can he pay you?" The officers replied, "We will bring the revenue of the whole Empire to your treasury." '[61] For a while Zafar continued to argue with the sepoys, telling them: '"I have neither troops, magazine or treasury. I am not in a condition to join anyone." They said, "Only give us your blessing. We will provide everything else." '[62]

There was then a long pause while Zafar considered his options. For all his many good qualities, indecision was always Zafar's greatest vice. Emily Eden relates a telling anecdote from her visit to Delhi in 1838 when Zafar, then the heir apparent, 'was coaxed or threatened into waiting on' her brother, the Governor General, Lord Auckland. Unable to make up his mind whether to attend or not, Zafar had taken to his bed and sent a succession of no fewer than 'thirteen doctors to say he was too ill to come'. He dithered backwards and forwards all afternoon before 'he changed his mind yet again and came, and in the meanwhile, half our troops who were out for the durbar were fainting away from the heat'.[63] Likewise, when Zafar had had his spat with Mirza Fakhru in 1852, he oscillated week to week, one day banning his eldest son from the durbar and forbidding any of the courtiers from having contact with him, then the next he would declare his love for the Mirza and tell the members of the court that they need have no fear of befriending him or attending his monsoon parties.[64]

Yet now, at the moment of the most crucial decision Zafar would ever take, with most of the Delhi elite already instinctively lined up against the looting, mutinous sepoys, Zafar made an uncharacteristically decisive choice: he gave them his blessing. The reason is not hard to guess. With the armed, threatening and excitable sepoys surrounding him on all sides, he had little choice. Moreover, thanks to Simon Fraser and Lord Canning, he had even less to lose. For all his undoubted fear, anger and irritation with the sepoys, Zafar made the critical choice that would change both the fate of his dynasty and that of the city of Delhi, linking them both with the Uprising:

> The King then seated himself in a chair, and the soldiery, officers and all, came forward one by one, bowed their heads before him, asking him to place his hand on them. The King did so, and each withdrew . . . Picketing their horses in the courtyard, the troops took up their quarters [in the Palace and across the bridge in the old Mughal Bastille of Salimgarh] and spread their bedding in the Hall of Audience, and placed guards all about the palace.[65]

It was at this crucial moment, when the King had just publicly – if hesitantly and reluctantly – given his blessing to the mutineers, and they were settling down into quarters inside the Palace, that the entire city was shaken by a colossal explosion, a report that could be heard 20 miles away. Buildings shook; in the Palace several plaster ceilings collapsed.

Half a mile to the north of the Red Fort, Theo's friend Lieutenant Willoughby, besieged by sepoys, had just blown up the magazine, the largest arsenal of guns and ammunition in northern India; and with it the large mob of jihadis, insurgents and sepoys who were attacking it, as well as almost all of its British defenders.

Far to the north, beyond Metcalfe House, Captain Robert Tytler spent most of 11 May unaware of the fate of his fellow countrymen, or the dramatic political revolution then taking place in the Palace.

Sent with a company of 200 sepoys to guard the new powder magazine and the Yamuna ford at a large army building known as the White House, a little to the north-east of the cantonments, Tytler knew that all was not well, but remained quite ignorant of the extent of the reverses fast destroying British rule in and around Delhi.

He knew that his men had shown their sympathies for the sepoys in Meerut when the sentences had been read out on parade; he knew that the men had been 'excitable' when the news had come that the Meerut sepoys had reached Delhi 'shouting vehemently every now and then' as he prepared them to march; and he had seen that when he handed out ammunition to his men some had grabbed far more than their entitlement and he had mentally marked down the guilty men for punishment at a later date. But isolated as he was in his remote position, no precise news had reached him of what was going on, although looking downstream, he could plainly see the smoke rising from within the city, and hear the faint report of musketry and cannon.

By early afternoon, he and his colleague Captain Gardner had noticed that the sepoys were refusing to come within the shelter of the White House, and were instead forming into small groups in the heat of the sun. 'I ordered them to come in and not expose themselves thus,' he wrote later.

They said, 'we like being in the sun.' I ordered them in again. [No one moved.] I then remarked for the first time a native – from his appearance, a soldier – haranguing the men and saying that every power or Government existed its allotted time, and that it was nothing extraordinary that that of the English had come to an end, according to what had been predicted in their books. Before I could make a prisoner of him, the magazine in the city exploded, and the men of the two companies with a tremendous shout took up their arms and ran off to the city, exclaiming, 'Prithviraj ki jai!' or 'Victory to the Sovereign of the World!' Captain Gardner and myself rushed after them, and ordered those within hearing to return to their post; when orders failed, entreaties were resorted to, but proved of no avail.[66]

Tytler found himself with only eighty sepoys left, 'chiefly old soldiers that had served with me in Afghanistan', and felt 'quite at a loss how to act and what to do'. Minutes later, however, urgent orders arrived by messenger that Tytler should join his brigadier at the Flagstaff Tower in the centre of the Ridge overlooking the walled city.

The Flagstaff Tower was a scene of great confusion when Tytler finally reached it. In the course of the day, this short, isolated round tower situated on the summit of the barren Ridge had become the place of refuge for all the remaining British families from the cantonment and the Civil Lines, as well as those few who had managed to escape from the walled city. These included Tytler's wife Harriet, who was uncharacteristically flustered and weeping, feeling the weight of her advanced pregnancy: unflappable as she usually was, her steely composure had finally broken when her little four-year-old son Frank had asked her, 'Mamma, will these naughty sepoys kill my papa, and will they kill me too?' Also within the tower were the entire Wagentrieber clan, whose patriarch George had that morning had a narrow escape from the rebel sepoys at the Kashmiri Gate on his way to the now-ransacked premises of the *Delhi Gazette*.

Outside the tower stood two light field guns overseen by Brigadier Graves and the Delhi judge Charles Le Bas, the only survivor from the group of men who had closed the Calcutta Gate earlier that morning. Under their orders were a company of scowling and clearly disaffected sepoys, and the Anglo-Indian orphans from the Christian Boys' Band, whose annual wheel-barrow race had for several years been one of the highlights of the Delhi Derby, but who had now been pressed into active military service. They had been issued with muskets, and were now standing on guard behind the battlements on the top of the tower.

Crushed inside were the massed womenfolk of the station, several of whom had just been told that their husbands, sons or brothers had been killed. Equally distraught was one of the few European soldiers present, Charlie Thomason, Padre Jennings' prize tenor, who had been carried to the tower from his sickbed in the cantonments, only to be told that his fiancée, Annie Jennings, had been murdered in the Palace.

The single interior room of the tower was only 18 feet in diameter, windowless and stuffy at the best of times; at the height of the hot season it was like an oven. Worse still, for their safety, many of the women had been sent up a suffocating interior staircase, as a result of which several had fainted.[67] But more distressing even than the discomfort, the heat and the lack of water was the suspense. Over the course of the day, successive reports brought ever worse news of the British position, with reversal following reversal, death following death, and the prospects of relief from the British regiments in Meerut growing progressively more remote. According to the young Florence Wagentrieber,

> Ladies and children [as well as] servants, male and female, were all huddled together in utter confusion. Many ladies were in a miserable condition from the extreme heat and nervous excitement, little ones crying and clinging to their mothers. Here were wives made widows, sisters weeping at the report of a brother's death, and some whose husbands were still on duty in the midst of the disaffected sepoys, of whose fate they were as yet ignorant . . . There was not a tree near the tower to shelter it from the hot sun . . . the heat was unbearable and the children were stripped of every garment.[68]

Arriving into this heaving pandemonium, Tytler could see immediately that the isolated tower was quite indefensible, and that to mass the women and children in such a spot was to invite a further and much larger massacre than that which had already taken place within the walls of the city. Without hesitation, he marched straight up to Brigadier Graves and, according to the account of his wife Harriet, asked 'in a very clear and audible voice':

> 'Excuse me sir, but what are you going to do?'
> He replied: 'Stay here Tytler, and protect the women and children.'
> My husband said in a most emphatic manner, 'It's madness sir, have you any food?'
> 'No, Tytler.'
> 'Have you any water?'
> 'No, Tytler.'
> 'Then how do you propose protecting the women and children?'

'What can we do? If we put out our heads they will shoot us down.'

My husband said, 'Look here gentlemen . . . We cannot hold our post, therefore it is our duty to form a retreat.'

The officers called out, 'For God's sake, don't listen to Tytler.' My husband then said, 'Very well gentlemen, do as you like, stay here and be butchered, but I will go with my family and stand my court martial. I will not stand to see my wife and children butchered.'[69]

As Tytler was speaking, a single bullock cart appeared at the foot of the slope and slowly creaked up the incline of the Ridge from the Kashmiri Gate. Inside, under a thin covering of women's dresses stained with blood, lay the mangled and mutilated bodies of all the British officers murdered as they entered the city earlier in the morning; the sister of one of the victims, Miss Burrowes, stood perspiring inside the tower. The cart had in fact been sent up by Edward Vibart to the cantonment, and by mistake found its way to the Flagstaff Tower; but it was taken by the edgy and nervous refugees as an act of intimidation by the sepoys. Although that had not been the original intention of the sender, it certainly had that effect.

On seeing the bodies, Tytler's remaining sepoys urged their captain to flee if they were to avoid the same fate, telling him that the Meerut *sawars* were currently resting their horses in the nearby Ochterlony Gardens: 'They expect you to stay here all night, and will come and kill you at their leisure,' the sepoys told Tytler.*

* The proper name of the Ochterlony Gardens was Mubarak Bagh. It was built on land that Ochterlony purchased from his assistant William Fraser especially for his wife Mubarak Begum, a short distance to the south of Shalimar Bagh. Ochterlony's tomb was a wonderfully hybrid monument, whose central dome was apparently the model for the Delhi church, St James's, and was surmounted by a cross, though the side wings were enclosed in a forest of small minarets: it was thus the perfect architectural expression of the religious fusion Ochterlony seems to have achieved in his marriage. In the event, Ochterlony died away from Delhi and was buried in Meerut, while the empty tomb was destroyed during the fighting of 1857, in which the widowed Mubarak Begum, by then remarried to a Mughal *amir* named Vilayat Ali Khan, fought on the rebel side. It is an extraordinary and completely forgotten moment in architectural history: the last of the great Mughal garden tombs – a tradition that had already reached its finest moment in the Taj Mahal – being built not by the last of the Mughals, but by a Scottish-American general. For a picture of Ochterlony's mausoleum see Emily Bayley in M. M. Kaye (ed.), *The Golden Calm: An English Lady's Life in Moghul Delhi*, London, 1980, p. 181.

At this the nerve of the frightened crowd finally broke. 'As soon as the Brigadier and his officers heard of the fate awaiting them,' wrote Harriet Tytler, 'they realised how near their end had come, and then there was indeed a stampede. Everyone rushed to their carriage to see who could get off first.'[70]

As the day progressed, Edward Vibart's position at the main guard just inside the Kashmiri Gate of the walled city became increasingly untenable.

At one o'clock, the 200 missing sepoys of Vibart's regiment suddenly turned up again. They justified running away and leaving their officers to their fate earlier that morning by saying that they had been unarmed and taken by surprise by the mutineers, immediately as they entered Kashmiri Gate. Vibart was unsure whether this was true, and noticed 'that although the demeanour of the men was outwardly respectful, they stood about in groups talking to each other in undertones. One sepoy of my company refused to go on sentry duty when ordered to do so; he roughly disengaged himself and slunk back into the crowd. All this was very disquietening, and boded no good'.

At first, Vibart had kept up communication with both Lieutenant Willoughby at the magazine and Arthur Galloway, the Assistant Magistrate, who had refused to leave his post a short distance away in the Kutcherry building, just the other side of St James's Church. By mid-afternoon, however, Galloway had been killed by his own disaffected Kutcherry Guard, while Willoughby had blown up the magazine to prevent its contents falling into the hands of the mutineers, the 'terrific explosion shaking the foundations of the Main Guard to its centre'. By now Vibart and his companions felt insufficiently confident even to intervene to halt the looting of the church 200 yards in front of their position, 'the cushions and stools even being borne off by the rascally populace without let or hindrance'.[71]

The spirits of the defenders were momentarily lifted when Willoughby and his assistant, Lieutenant Forrest, father to the three Misses Forrest, appeared at the gate, 'begrimed with dust and powder, and the latter badly wounded in the hand from a musket ball'; some other badly singed and disabled sergeants from the magazine limped in shortly afterwards. But the signs of disaffection among the sepoys guarding the gate were now becoming unmistakable, and they began to refuse all orders. Two cannons that had been sent up to the Ridge with a guard of sepoys and two English officers returned after half an hour with the two officers mysteriously missing. When asked why they had returned, and what had happened to their officers, the men gave evasive replies. Meanwhile 'sepoys kept entering the enclosure in groups of threes and four, and we could observe our men getting very restless and uneasy', wrote Vibart.

> At this critical juncture some sepoys rushed at the gate and closed it; their next act was to discharge a volley right amongst a group of officers, and their example was rapidly followed by all the other sepoys inside the enclosure . . . I saw Captain Gordon fall from his horse . . . The horrible truth now flashed on me – we were being massacred right and left, without any means of escape. Scarcely knowing what I was doing, I made for the ramp which leads from the courtyard to the bastion above. Everyone seemed to be doing the same. Twice I was knocked over as we all rushed up the slope, the bullets whistling past us like hail, and flattening themselves against the parapet with a frightful hiss. Poor Smith and Reveley, were killed close beside me. The latter was carrying a loaded gun, and, raising himself with a dying effort, he discharged both barrels into a knot of sepoys, and the next moment expired.[72]

At the top of the slope, Vibart looked down from the castellations of the bastion. Below lay a 25-foot drop into the ditch below – 'one would have thought it madness at any other time'.[73] Several other officers made the jump, and began trying to run up the almost vertical counterscarp. Vibart was about to join them when the screams of the Misses Forrest rang out from the officers' quarters across the bastion. Their mother had just been wounded in the shoulder. Vibart ran over to where they were – 'bullets all this while whistling through the windows' – and helped them over to the parapet. The officers fastened their sword belts together, and with the help of Vibart and their father, one by one lowered the girls down.

There still remained 'one very stout old lady' who began to scream, and refused to jump. By this point, the sepoys below had a cannon trained upon them, and a shot 'crashed into the parapet a little to the right, covering us with splinters. It was madness to waste time in expostulation', wrote Vibart; 'somebody gave her a push and she tumbled headlong in the ditch beneath'.[74]

One by one, the ten survivors – five men and five women – then attempted to scale the top of the counterscarp. 'Again and again did the ladies almost reach the top, when the earth, crumbling away beneath their feet, sent them rolling back into the ditch. Despair, however, gave us superhuman energy, till at length we all succeeded in gaining the summit. We now ran down the short glacis, and plunged into some thick shrubbery that grew at the bottom.'

As darkness fell, the survivors made their way through thick scrub towards the river, and then upstream towards Metcalfe House. On the way, they saw that they were being followed.

Not waiting, however, to take a second look, we set off running hoping to reach the house before our pursuers overtook us . . . Thorny bushes tore the ladies' dresses to shreds. On we ran, the perspiration streaming down our faces, our lips parched with thirst, and not daring to look behind us.[75]

It was pitch dark by the time they reached Metcalfe House. The house was surrounded 'by a crowd of suspicious-looking individuals', but the refugees were kindly received by the staff, who were anxious to know the fate of Theo, who had not been seen since that morning. They were all taken down to the darkness of Sir Thomas's cool underground billiard room, where the three Misses Forrests promptly fell fast asleep. In due course candles, food and bottles of beer all appeared. Mrs Forrest's wound was dressed, and for three hours everyone rested.

By nine o'clock, however, the staff warned that it was only a matter of time before the sepoys appeared from the cantonments, from which direction, only a short distance away, could be heard 'the shouts of the mutineers, mingled with volleys of musketry and discharges of cannon'. Filling their pockets with food and bottles of water, the party set off again. The plan was to ford the Yamuna canal, and head off north-east cross-country, in the hope of reaching the British regiments at Meerut, 38 miles away. 'Each of us took charge of a lady,' wrote Vibart,

> and I had little Miss Forrest to my share. The poor little child kept asking all sorts of innocent questions, not being able to realise the fearful events that had occurred. In this manner we trudged on for about half an hour, when suddenly a bright streak of fire rose up behind us.

They had left only just in time. A little downstream, the eerie colours reflected in the dark waters of the Yamuna, Metcalfe House was ablaze.

By the fall of darkness, as the Muslim faithful paused to eat their *iftar*, the sunset Ramadan meal, the streets of Delhi were deserted again. Zahir Dehlavi, returning from the Fort, passed through a scene of devastation: 'When I reached the Urdu Bazar road [next to the Jama Masjid]', he wrote,

> it was completely quiet, and there was not a single bird to be heard or seen. Indeed there was a strange silence over the whole town, as if the city had turned suddenly into a wilderness. Shops were lying looted, the doors of all the houses and havelis were closed, and there was not a glimmer of light. Even the glass of the street lanterns lay broken. I went past the *Kotwali* and reached the gate of the small *Dariba* [in Chandni Chowk]. There I saw all the shops of the knife makers, sweet sellers and cloth merchants were all broken and looted, and in front of the silver merchant's shop, a Brahmin beggar lay dying. He was still groaning, and on his back were three gaping wounds from

swords. Finally I reached my house [in Matia Mahal]. It was only late
evening now but already the door was closed, locked and bolted.[76]

What remained of the British community in Delhi was now in full
flight. James Morley had spent the evening hiding in the dhobi's
hut, listening to his servants discussing the murder of his wife and
family – and his presumed death – outside. 'One man said it was
very wrong to kill the memsahib and the children, and how were
they going to get *rozgar* [employment]? But another said that we
were *kafirs*, and now the King of Delhi would provide for everyone.' With the dhobi's assistance, Morley made his escape, dressed
in the dhobi's wife's petticoat and veil. 'I had been all my life in the
country,' wrote Morley, 'but still I felt afraid lest anyone should
speak to me. I did not know if they might remark that my *chadar*
was held awkwardly and thus find me out.' But they drove safely
out of the city, past the unguarded city gates, sitting on the dhobi's
bullock cart beside a pile of dirty washing.

Despite the late hour, the road was full of excited crowds
hurrying into Delhi to loot, or else returning laden with plunder.
At one point, a gang of men surrounded them and accused the
dhobi of hiding treasures in the washing, but the old man coolly
told them to search it, and, finding nothing, they let them go. After
that the dhobi fended off further crowds by telling anyone they met
to hurry on and loot the *firangis* before it was too late. As dawn
came, they found shelter in a *dharmashala* next to a roadside
temple.[77]

Robert and Harriet Tytler, meanwhile, were heading in an
overloaded carriage up the road to Karnal. Like every other
British attempt to guide events that day, the flight from the
Flagstaff Tower had started badly and soon descended into
complete chaos. Tytler had planned a retreat that would have
taken the women and children on the road to Meerut via the ford
at Baghpat to the north-east. Almost immediately, however, the
column had become fragmented, with half of the carriages setting
off towards Baghpat while the others headed off in the wrong
direction towards the cantonments. In the panic and confusion,
Tytler lost his remaining sepoys, became separated from his wife,

and ran into a body of Gujar tribesmen who had just come in from their village to join in the looting. They made a dash at Tytler with their iron-bound lathis, and tried to unhorse him; Tytler only just made it through.

Tytler eventually caught up with Harriet and his children, who had headed off on the wrong road in a carriage accompanied by the wife of his colleague Captain Gardner. But when Mrs Gardner asked him what had happened to her husband, Tytler volunteered to go back and look for him. Gardner, it transpired, had failed to leave with the rest of the party, and was limping wounded through the burning cantonments when Tytler eventually found him. Twice more he passed through the midst of the Gujars, once on the way back to look for his friend, and one final time, with the wounded Gardner riding pillion behind him; each time the Gujars struck the men with their lathis and tried to pull them off.[78]

Catching up with the carriage a second time, Tytler jumped on to it, and the party galloped forwards, Tytler driving the horses 'at a terrific pace', conscious that the *sawar* cavalry could by now have started after them in pursuit. 'We had not gone far', wrote Harriet, 'before Gardner called out, "Tytler look back." '[79]

> We cast our eyes in the direction of the cantonments and saw that every bungalow and the lines were on fire. It was a sickening sight, knowing that all we most valued was lost to us for ever, things that no money could ever purchase – a beloved dead child's hair, manuscripts and paintings, books, clothes, furniture, a very large carriage, horses, buggy etc. Indeed we lost in money value, with my husband's uniform some £20,000, a fortune to a poor military man in those days . . . But the one absorbing thought of flying for our lives soon made us forget that which at any other time would have been an inconsolable trial.[80]

The Wagentriebers, in contrast to the fleeing Tytlers, decided to take their chances in the Delhi suburbs and to fall back on the friends of Elizabeth Wagentrieber's father, James Skinner.

After Nawab Zia ud-Din Khan had visited them the previous evening they felt confident they could rely on his friendship, so from the Flagstaff Tower they made straight for the Nawab's garden house to the north-west of the tower, a little way up the Karnal road, which the Nawab had often offered to them for weekends.

On arrival, they were warmly received by the mali (gardener). A goat was milked for Elizabeth Wagentrieber's baby, and a meal of chapattis and vegetables prepared. The carriage and horses were hidden away, all traces of the wheels were rubbed out, and the harnesses hidden in the house. George Wagentrieber went up on to the roof with his stepdaughter Julia, the young infant Florence and with the guns they had brought, while Elizabeth stayed below on a charpoy with the *chaukidar* (nightwatchman), covering her face in a chador. She told the surly-looking *chaukidar* that if he gave any hint of betraying them in any way, her husband had his guns trained on him and would make sure to shoot him first.[81]

The moon rose, and from the rooftop George could see fires burning all over Delhi and the cantonments ablaze; he could also hear the sound of repeated musket shots and the louder reports of field guns. Soon after the rattle of the last of the English carriages had passed up the Karnal road, troops of cavalry started to appear at the gate searching for Christians. 'My mother had told the chaukidar not to show any objections to people wanting to come in as that would at once make them suspicious,' remembered Julia.

She would not let the chaukidar go near the gate or trust him away from her. Twice the rebels came to the gate, and hailed the chaukidar, asking him if he had given shelter to the *Firangis*. The last one, a trooper, came to within a few yards of where she was sitting, reined in his horse, and asked to be shown all over the house. But the chaukidar obeyed the injunctions my mother had given him and told the man that some Europeans had come past but they did not stay, and drove straight up the road, and that he was welcome to go all over the house if he chose. The man's prompt reply seemed to satisfy the trooper who immediately rode off in search of those who were said to have gone past.[82]

Towards midnight, however, reports began to reach the house that someone had betrayed the Wagentriebers, and that a further troop of twenty *sawars* were on their way. There seemed no option but immediate flight. Elizabeth harnessed the horses, and drove them to the front of the house; the children were put inside and George climbed on the box. 'Before we entered upon the high road,' wrote George,

> my dear wife advised me to keep my fire arms at hand, so I took a double-barrelled gun loaded with ball, and my pistol on the box with me, leaving two rifles inside: and telling my step-daughter, who was inside the carriage with the child, to hand them [to me] the moment I fired, we commended ourselves to the protection of the Most High, and entered upon the Grand Trunk Road.[83]

The Tytlers had gone only about 15 miles from Delhi when their horse began to slow down with exhaustion. Stopping at a staging stable of the government *dak* or postal service, they were refused a replacement horse, until Tytler drew a gun on the official and took one by force.

A few miles after leaving the stables, the wheels of their over-loaded carriage all simultaneously disintegrated, leaving 'the body of the carriage a hopeless wreck. There was nothing for it but to walk'. Each of the men took a child; their two heavily pregnant wives, and Harriet's maid Marie, trudged on behind them, expecting to hear at any moment the clatter of the hoofs of the cavalry bearing down upon them.

Instead, after a few miles they heard a carriage. It belonged to a young English girl who had earlier passed them on the road heading into Delhi and who had refused to listen to their cries of warning. Now, she refused Tytler's request to take on any hitch-hikers.

> 'I will do no such thing!' was the reply to the request for a lift. 'Do you mean to break down my carriage?'
>
> 'Then I won't ask you,' said Tytler, and set to work to put Mrs Gardner, Marie and myself, with our children, inside the carriage.
>
> In this way, we went on until one of the hind wheels of the

conveyance rolled off. 'There,' said the young woman (she was only sixteen), 'I knew you would break my carriage. Now what am I to do?'[84]

This time, help came in the form of the recently widowed Mrs Nixon, whose husband the head clerk of the Commissioner's Office, Muhammad Baqar, had seen dead in the street with a biscuit in his mouth. She had made her escape on top of a mail cart, which amid all the chaos had left Delhi punctually at the appointed time as if nothing unusual was happening. The driver had ropes with which they reaffixed the wheels. The Tytlers slowly drove on for a few more miles before the springs of the carriage finally gave out completely and they abandoned their second conveyance on the road as they had done their first. They walked on 'nearly overcome with fatigue in the heat of a May night . . . our thirst was terrible, with no water to be had except greeny mire from roadside pools that had not yet dried up'.

It was nearly dawn when they commandeered their final vehicle of the day: an arms tumbrel full of broken weaponry on its way to the now-destroyed Delhi magazine. The two drivers ran away at the sight of Tytler's revolver and the party headed slowly on, arriving at Karnal at ten in the morning.

The Tytlers waited all day for their friends and colleagues to join them. But by that evening, of all the crowd that had left the Flagstaff Tower, only six Delhi refugees had so far made it through.[85]

The Wagentriebers' journey up the same road made that of the Tytlers, difficult as it was, seem like a picnic. They had left it too late, and the road was now swarming with Gujar tribesmen, intent on plundering refugees and stragglers. 'We may have proceeded a mile,' remembered George,

when my wife pointed out to me a knot of people drawn up on both sides of the road in advance of us. They were evidently up to no good, so I prepared to protect myself and my family. As we approached, they closed in across the road, and I presented my gun at them which had the effect of keeping them off, but they followed the carriage screaming and flourishing clubs and sticks in a very menacing manner.

We left them far behind, only to fall in with a second body; this time more numerous and formidable. As we approached they drew across the road in front of our horses, holding up spears, swords and lathees in a threatening manner, and loudly calling out *thammo!* [stop!] To this I replied by pointing my gun and calling out *hut jao!* [move away!] But one, more daring than the rest, stepped forward and seized the horse's head by the rein, and I seeing nothing for it, fired, the rascal falling behind the carriage. The remainder fell back, my wife whipped up the horses and dashed on, but the ruffians followed very fast, and thinking they were gaining on us I fired a rifle shot, and hit one man, the foremost, in the abdomen. He fell and the others contented themselves with howling and heaping abuse upon the heads of myself and my family for generations.[86]

When they had got a little ahead, Elizabeth stopped the carriage and got the horses' harness in order, while her husband reloaded the weapons. They had not gone far when a third set of Gujars closed in on them, and this time succeeded in clubbing one of the horses on the head. Again, Wagentrieber shot down the leading man, but not before his wife too had been struck a tremendous blow with an iron-tipped lathi. A second man ran up beside the carriage, sword in hand, and was also shot down; a third succeeded in climbing on to the hood of the carriage and was in the act of striking a potentially fatal blow when he too was shot down by George.

They had not got far ahead of the third group of Gujars before they ran straight into a large party of sepoys. They were returning from training in the Enfield rifle at Ambala, and surrounded the carriage, asking what the family were doing out on such a road at such a time, apparently ignorant of the dramatic events which had taken place. At this point the Gujars caught up, and stood glaring at the Wagentriebers from a distance. Seeing no alternative, and noticing how friendly the soldiers appeared, Elizabeth begged

the sepoys for their help, telling them that she was the daughter of
James Skinner, Sikandar Sahib, 'and so entitled to the protection of
all true soldiers'. This, it turned out, was exactly the right note to
have struck:

> 'You are indeed a great man's daughter,' they said. 'We knew Col
> Skinner, and it was our regiment which was sent to escort his
> remains from Rohtak to Delhi.'[87]

> In an instant four or five of them stepped forward and standing
> beside our carriage, levelled their muskets at our enemies, telling
> them to keep off or they would certainly fire . . .
>   After this we were not molested at close quarters, the villains
> confining their attacks to spears, lathis, and heavy stones thrown at
> us in showers from behind the parapets of bridges, which most
> providentially struck none of us. One of our mares sustained severe
> cuts and bruises, and the carriage bore marks of great ill-usage.[88]

The name of Skinner saved them yet again, when, soon after dawn,
the family drew up by a village well, and threw some water over the
horses to refresh them. A crowd soon gathered, many of whom
appeared to be far from friendly. One, however, turned out to be an
old servant of Sikandar Sahib, who had once had an estate in the
area. 'He was a respectable old man with a long white beard,'
remembered the Wagentriebers' daughter Julia. 'He seemed to
know my mother though she had no recollection of him.'

> 'You are one of Col Skinner's children,' he said, taking off his
> turban, and laying it at her feet. This mark of respect, coming at such
> a time, astonished her, especially as she saw that the man seemed to
> be of some importance by the manner of the others towards him, and
> the deferential way in which they treated him.
>   'Who are you?' she enquired.
>   'I have eaten the Colonel Sahib's salt for many years, and I will
> give my life for any of his children,' the old man replied. 'Will you
> trust yourselves to me?'[89]

In due course, the old man took the reins of the carriage and escorted them onwards. At eleven o'clock, they saw another ragged party on the road ahead of them: it was Brigadier Graves and Charles Le Bas, along with several other soldiers, all heavily armed. At 4 p.m., they reached the safety of Panipat.[90]

The morning of 12 May saw Delhi almost completely emptied of the British, who had dominated it since the British defeated the Marathas in 1803.

As Theo woke in ill-fitting Hindustani clothes, hidden in a back room in the house of a stranger; as the Tytlers in Karnal and the Wagentriebers in Panipat wolfed down their breakfasts; as James Morley, swaying on his bullock cart, pondered life without his wife and family; as Edward Vibart and his party hid in a bunch of tall grass in the fields towards Meerut, avoiding the sepoy search parties out looking for British refugees; as Ghalib peered disapprovingly through his lattices at the sepoys swaggering through his *muhalla* of Ballimaran; as Maulvi Muhammad Baqar began writing up for the *Dihli Urdu Akhbar* all the strange sights and portents that he had seen the day before; as the young Muhammad Husain Azad composed his poem on the Uprising; as Zahir Dehlavi and Hakim Ahsanullah Khan began trying to remove the sepoys from the most crucial ceremonial parts of the Palace; as all this was happening, Zafar too was anxiously trying to envisage his future.

The night before he had sheltered the forty-odd British prisoners brought in by Muin ud-Din, some of them in one of the few parts of the Palace he could still call his own: his private oratory, the *tasbih khana*. At Zinat Mahal's suggestion, he had also sent off by camel messenger a secret letter to the British Governor at Agra, telling him all that happened and asking for help. Zafar could see that the sepoys were violent and unstable; they also had no idea of manners or courtly etiquette: not the least of his objections to them was their refusal to pay him any of the proper courtesies: 'The Tilangas stood [in the Palace] with their shoes on,' wrote one news-writer, 'and His Majesty expressed his great displeasure about that.'[91]

Yet for all his hesitation and fear and anxieties, for all the chaos of a looted city and harassed courtiers, Zafar could see that the arrival of the mutineers might yet not be entirely a curse, but might in fact represent the hand of God and an opportunity he had never even dreamt of, to re-establish his great Mughal dynasty. Around midnight he sanctioned the firing of a twenty-one-gun salute to mark the beginning of this new phase in his reign. Zafar's ambivalent but increasingly engaged attitude to the revolution was noted by Mohan Lal Kashmiri, a well-connected alumnus of the Delhi College who had allied himself closely with the British cause, as a result of which he had to flee Delhi soon after the Uprising:

> I never heard from any native in Delhi or elsewhere that the King Bahadur Shah was in communication with the mutineers before the mutiny broke out. But after the miscreants had made themselves masters of the Palace and the city . . . they contrived to bring out His Majesty in a royal procession to restore confidence to the citizens. The King saw now for the first time himself surrounded with dashing and disciplined troops, ready to espouse his cause. He saw that the population who came out as spectators of his procession looked upon him not with gloomy faces. He found that the favourable turn of his affairs had been approved by a large portion of the residents. He listened to the news of [British] disasters. He perceived that regiment upon regiment had waited upon him. He received the false reports that all our European troops were engaged in Persia, and that the unsettled state of the European Politics would hardly permit reinforcements [to be sent] to India. He was informed that the mutiny had [also] taken place in Bombay and in Deccan. All these things made Bahadur Shah believe that he had been born to restore the realm of the Great Timur in the last days of his life.[92]

Zafar's increasing openness to the Uprising, though never entirely wholehearted and always ambivalent, nevertheless changed the whole nature of the rebellion. There had been many mutinies before in British India, most dramatically at Vellore in 1806; there had been even more armed acts of Indian resistance to British expansion. But never before had such a powerful combination of forces come together to challenge British supremacy.

By combining the Company's own Indian armies with the still potent mystique of the Mughals, Zafar's hesitant acceptance of the nominal leadership of the revolt in due course turned it from a simple army mutiny – albeit one supported by an incoherent eruption of murder and looting by Delhi's civilians – into the single most serious armed challenge any Western empire would face, anywhere in the world, in the entire course of the nineteenth century.

Yet for Zafar the more immediate question was whether, for all this, he had merely exchanged one set of masters for another.

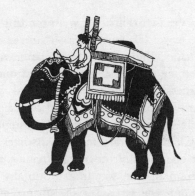

6

THIS DAY OF RUIN AND RIOT

At four o'clock on the day of the outbreak, Charles Todd's two assistant telegraph operators, Brendish and Pilkington, closed up their office and set off to flee to safety, first to the Flagstaff Tower, and then on to Meerut.

Before they did so, however, they tapped out two SOS messages in Morse code, and sent them to the Commander-in-Chief and the cantonments on the Punjab and the Frontier. Original transcriptions of both still survive in the Punjab Archives in Lahore. The first, sent some time around midday, was the fuller of the two: 'Cantonment in a state of siege,' it read.

> Mutineers from Meerut 3rd Light Cavalry number not known said to be one hundred and fifty men cut off communication with Meerut. Taken possession of the Bridge of Boats. 54th NI sent against them but would not act. Several officers killed and wounded. City in a state of considerable excitement. Troops sent down but nothing certain yet.

The second was sent just before the two operators ran off: 'We must leave office,' they tapped. 'All the bungalows are being burned down by the sepoys of Meerut. They came in this morning. We are off. Mr C Todd is dead we think. He went out this morning and has not returned.'[1]

It was a dramatic vindication of the new technology of the telegraph – something that Ghalib considered one of the miracles of the age. The messages reached Ambala, and within hours had been forwarded to Lahore, Peshawar and Simla.

Relaxing in the cool of the Himalayan summer capital, the Commander-in-Chief, General George Anson, received the message at breakfast on Tuesday morning after an express rider had carried the telegram up the winding mountain track overnight. Anson, who had not seen active service since Waterloo more than forty years earlier, did not seem to realise the seriousness of what was happening, just as he had earlier dismissed the significance of the greased cartridges.[2] The following evening one of his advisers, Colonel Keith Young, recorded in his diary that 'he appears rather to pooh-pooh the [whole] thing. We shall see'. Two days later, with the Commander-in-Chief still stuck immobile in Simla, even Anson's most loyal friends were beginning to be anxious at his response. 'The Chief is blamed,' wrote Young's wife in a letter.

> He has not been trained as a soldier and seems unable to grasp the importance of the situation. When he first received the bad news on Tuesday morning he should have started off at once. Colonel Becher, Quartermaster-General, did his utmost to persuade him not to lose any time: but he said, *no*; he would wait for the *dak* [post]. What is the use of the electric telegraph if the news it brings is not at once to be attended to?[3]

When Anson finally got as far as Ambala, four days later, on the 15th, it was discovered that logistical problems meant that his force could proceed no farther: as part of some cost-cutting exercise, the army's baggage camels had recently been sold. Now the contractors could not be found to move the three European regiments that had gathered in Ambala – already known as the Delhi Field Force – even one step on towards their destination.

There were other problems too. None of the regiments initially had any ammunition beyond the twenty rounds they kept in their pouches, since the promised supplies had failed to materialise from Simla. Moreover, the baggage of at least one regiment had been lost between the hills and Ambala, leaving the soldiers with nothing but two white jackets and a pair of trousers each.[4] Worse still, Anson had refused to heed the warnings of his staff immediately to disarm the clearly disaffected sepoy regiments stationed in Ambala, with the result that they shortly afterwards broke out into mutiny too, and took off to Delhi down the Grand Trunk Road with all their arms intact. 'Oh my dear mother,' wrote the young second lieutenant Fred Roberts.

You would not believe that Englishmen could be guilty of such imbecility as has almost invariably been displayed during this crisis . . . Perfectly ridiculous, an army going to pieces in this way . . . You would scarcely believe how paralysed everything is. We have a most dilatory undecided Commander-in-Chief.[5]

But it was not just the fault of Anson. Similar logistical problems had been behind the failure of the European regiments in Meerut to follow the mutineers to Delhi: on 12 May, two days after the Meerut outbreak, General Archdale Wilson, one of the two station commanders, wrote to his wife to admit that 'we have no power to move having no cattle only 15 elephants, and a few bullocks'.[6] Wilson's colleague General Hewitt was less effective still. As Wilson himself wrote, '[Hewitt] is a dreadful old fool and thinks of nothing but preserving his own old carcass from harm.'[7]

For ten days the troops in Ambala found themselves marooned, immobile in the terrible heat at the foot of the hills; meanwhile, cholera slowly took hold, the beginning of a plague that would eventually be responsible for nearly as many deaths as the bullets of the insurgents. 'The stench was awful,' remembered Richard Barter, a young lieutenant from the 75th Gordon Highlanders.

The dead bodies of three or four of the men who had just been carried off by the dreadful scourge were lying near rolled up in their *rezais* [quilts]. The heat was terrific, not a breath of air stirred the leaves, and there we sat among the dead and the dying, whose groans resounded through the still air under the trees.[8]

It was not until the night of 24 May – a full thirteen days after the outbreak – that Anson and his Field Force finally set off towards the Mughal capital from Ambala – only for the Commander-in-Chief himself to die of cholera on the night of the 27th, soon after arriving in Karnal. By that time, partially because of the lack of any effective response by the British, mutinies had broken out amongst sepoy regiments stationed at Nowshera in the North West Frontier; Ambala, Philour and Ferozepur in the Punjab; Nasirabad in Rajputana; and in the North West Provinces at Hansi, Hissar, Moradabad, Agra, Aligarh, Etawah, Mainpuri and as far south-east as Etah to the east of Agra.[9]

Seen on the map, the outbreaks seemed to ripple outwards in concentric circles from Delhi. The Emperor, Bahadur Shah II, and his revived Mughal Empire were now acting as a focus for all the disparate hopes and aspirations of the many disaffected individuals, groups and causes, both Muslim and Hindu, across northern India, and it was to Delhi that almost all the mutinous troops headed once they had risen against their British masters. To the surprise of the British, not all the mutinous troops rose violently; instead

> without molesting or even insulting their English officers they ...
> quietly but firmly announced that they had released themselves from
> the service of the East India Company, and were about to become
> enrolled as subjects of the King of Delhi. Then, in several instances
> even saluting their officers and showing them every mark of respect,
> they turned their faces to the great focus of the rebellion, to swell the
> number of those who were about to fight against us in the Mo-
> hammedan capital of Hindustan.[10]

For this reason, the future of both Mughal and British rule now hinged very largely on what happened at Delhi: 'The fate of all India depends on our success,' wrote Fred Roberts to his mother soon afterwards as the Delhi Field Force began rumbling slowly south along the Grand Trunk Road. 'Were a failure to be the result, God only knows what would take place.'[11]

Luckily for the British, not all their commanders had proved as slow and ineffective as Anson, Wilson and Hewitt.

In Lahore, the headquarters of the Chief Commissioner of the Punjab, the energetic Sir John Lawrence, four disaffected Indian regiments were quickly disarmed on the morning of 13 May, as twelve loaded and primed cannon manned by British artillerymen faced them across the parade ground. The night before, a regimental ball had gone ahead as planned, so as not to make the sepoys suspicious: 'The evening passed off very pleasantly,' noted one officer in his journal, 'a perfect sham of smiles over tears. Half the ladies were not present, and those that were there could barely disguise their anxiety.'[12]

Meanwhile, farther to the north-west in Peshawar, two of the most militantly Evangelical officials in India, Herbert Edwardes and John Nicholson, met to discuss strategy as soon as the telegrams from Delhi arrived there on the night of 11 May. Their solution was to form a strong Moveable Column of mainly irregular troops able to overawe and terrorise the Punjab into submission. 'It should take the field at once,' wrote Edwardes to John Lawrence on 12 May. 'This disaffection will never be talked down. It must be put down – and the sooner blood be let, the less of it will suffice.'[13] Lawrence agreed; within four days the Moveable Column had been formed in Jhelum, ready to move rapidly in any direction and crush rebellion against the Company wherever it broke out.[14]

Nicholson had some other, more bloodthirsty ideas too, which he did not convey to his superior, but communicated a little later to Edwardes when further details of the Delhi massacres had emerged. He proposed that they jointly put forward 'a Bill for the flaying alive, impalement, or burning of the murderers of the [British] women and children of Delhi . . . The idea of simply hanging the perpetrators of such atrocities is maddening . . . I will not, if I can help it, see fiends of that stamp let off with a simple hanging'. When Edwardes refused to be drawn on Nicholson's idea, Nicholson said he would propose the idea alone if Edwardes would not help him:

As regards torturing the murderers of women and children, if it be right otherwise I do not think we should refrain from it simply because it is a native custom . . . we are told in the Bible that stripes shall be meted out according to faults, and, if hanging is sufficient punishment for such wretches, it is too severe for ordinary mutineers. If I had them in my power today, I would inflict the most excruciating tortures I could think of on them with a perfectly easy conscience.[15]

John Lawrence was by no means averse in principle to strong measures. A former deputy of Sir Thomas Metcalfe in Delhi, he had risen rapidly in the ranks of the Company's civil service thanks to his reputation for hard work and efficiency. He forbade his officers from going up to the hills for the hot weather, and made known his disapproval of '"a cakey man" by which he meant someone who, besides presumably liking cakes, "pretended to much elegance and refinement" '.[16] When he heard that one of his junior officials had brought a piano to his Punjab bungalow, Lawrence spat, 'I'll smash his piano for him' and had him 'moved five times from one end of the Punjab to the other in the course of five years'.[17] As one of Lawrence's long-suffering officials remarked on hearing this story:

I had brought from Calcutta a handsome dinner-service, and I was strongly advised not to let the fact be known lest I, too, should be kicked about from one place to another till it was all smashed . . . He [Lawrence] was a rough, coarse man . . . [whose] ideal of a district officer was a hard active man in boots and breeches, who almost lived in the saddle, worked all day and nearly all night, ate and drank when and where he could, had no family ties, no wife or children to hamper him, and whose whole establishment consisted of a camp bed, an odd table and chair or so, and a small box of clothes such as could be slung on a camel.[18]

John Nicholson fitted this description perfectly. Even so, the two had a tense relationship, for Nicholson was not a man given to taking orders – and less still criticism – from anyone. One young officer described him as a commanding presence, some six feet, two inches in height, with a long black beard, dark grey eyes with black pupils which under excitement would dilate like a tiger's, [and] a colourless face over which no smile ever passed ... A stern sense of duty had made Nicholson expunge the word 'mercy' from his vocabulary ... [and] he had the reputation as the best swordsman in India.[19]

A taciturn and self-contained Ulster Protestant, it was said that while he was District Commissioner in Rawalpindi, Nicholson had personally decapitated a local robber chieftain, then kept the man's head on his desk as a memento.[20] He was, moreover, a man of few words; one typical note in the archives is a letter to Lawrence which reads, in full: 'Sir, I have the honour to inform you that I have just shot a man who came to kill me. Your Obedient Servant, John Nicholson.' For reasons that remain unclear, Nicholson inspired an entire religious sect, the *Nikal Seyn*,* who apparently regarded him as an incarnation of Vishnu. Nicholson tolerated his devotees as long as they kept quiet; but if 'they prostrated themselves or began chanting they were taken away and whipped'. The punishment never varied: 'three dozen lashes with the cat-o'-nine-tails'.[21]

Despite – or maybe partly because of – this inexplicable adoration, Nicholson loathed India with a passion ('I dislike India and its inhabitants more every day') and regarded only the Afghans as worse ('the most vicious and blood thirsty race in existence').[22] These views he had already formed before he was captured and imprisoned during the disaster of the 1842 Afghan War. By the time he was released, only to discover his younger brother's dead body, with his genitalia cut off and stuffed in his mouth, his feelings about Afghans – and indeed Indians and Muslims of any nationality – were confirmed: he felt, he said, merely 'an intense feeling of hatred'.[23] Only his wish to spread the Christian Empire of the British in this heathen wilderness kept him in the East. Indeed his survival amidst the carnage of the Afghan War left him with a near-messianic sense of destiny: if the God of Hosts had saved him when so many other Christians Soldiers had been killed, it must be for some higher purpose of Providence.

* *Nikal Seyn* in Urdu means something like 'let the army come out'.

Partly as a result of this messianic streak, Nicholson needed careful handling at the best of times, and the frank and forthright Lawrence was not necessarily the best man for the job. The previous year, after Lawrence 'insulted' Nicholson by giving him a mixed-race Anglo-Indian subordinate, Nicholson's response was to threaten to murder Lawrence, or, as he put it, 'commit justifiable homicide . . . Individuals have their rights as well as nations', as he wrote to Edwardes,

> and as an individual I have as good a *casus belli* against Lawrence, as England as a nation, had against Persia or China . . . I consider that he *humiliates* me in the eyes of the whole Punjab . . . I am sure there would be less injustice and oppression in the world, if men similarly circumstanced took their redress into their own hands, more frequently . . . As for 'praying for grace to forgive him,' I *can't* do it, it would be rank hypocrisy uttering the words while so different a feeling was in my heart.[24]

Nicholson may have been, as one observer put it, 'the very incarnation of violence', yet his near-psychopathic temperament was ideally suited to the crisis in hand. Where the Ansons and Wilsons dallied and hesitated, Nicholson immediately began marching and countermarching, disarming regiments of sepoys, putting down mutinies, then hanging their leaders – he abandoned the practice of blowing mutineers from the mouths of cannon, in the time-honoured Mughal fashion, not out of compassion, but because he believed 'that the powder so expended might be more usefully employed'.[25] His actions quickly became the source of Victorian legend, and as his own letters and dispatches are the only source for many of his actions it is difficult to tease out the truth from the myth: it was said that he never slept and knew no fear; that he stormed almost single-handed the fortress of Attock; cut up several regiments of mutinous sepoys with only a small body of Pathan irregulars; and on one occasion he actually cleaved a man in two with a single sword stroke, merely remarking afterwards 'not a bad silver, that'.[26] He took no prisoners. One officer who was part of Nicholson's Moveable Column overheard the following exchange:

'Jack, the General is here.'

'How do you know?'

'Why, look there; there's his mark!'

The 'there' the fellow-soldier was told to look at was a pair of gallows, each of which was adorned with six hanging mutineers, while close-by were several bullock-carts, all filled with sepoys who had revolted, and who were waiting for their turn . . . Few court martials were held by Nicholson.

When Sir John Lawrence wrote to him asking for 'a return of courts-martial, held upon insurgent natives, with a list of various punishments inflicted', the implacable Nicholson simply sent back the dispatch, having written on the back 'THE PUNISHMENT FOR MUTINY IS DEATH'.[27]

On the journey to Delhi, he continued to monitor security. One hot summer night in the middle of May, a group of hungry British officers attached to Nicholson's Moveable Column were sitting in a mess tent near Jalandhar waiting for their dinner. The food had been expected an hour before, but a messenger sent to the cooking tent returned with the information that it would be served a little late. Eventually the tall, craggy Nicholson strode in, and coughed to attract the attention of the company: 'I am sorry gentlemen to have kept you waiting for your dinner,' he apologised, 'but I have been hanging your cooks.'

According to Nicholson, he had discovered through his spies that the regimental cooks had just laced his brother officers' soup with aconite. He first invited the cooks to taste the soup, then, when they refused, force-fed the hot liquid to an unfortunate monkey. It writhed for a few seconds, then expired. Within minutes, as one of the officers present put it, 'our regimental cooks were ornamenting a neighbouring tree'.[28]

One other British soldier of a similar temperament also rose to prominence during this uncertain period.

Prior to 1857, William Hodson had been regarded by most of his colleagues as a black sheep. Hodson was the bright son of a clergyman, and unlike most of his army contemporaries in India, he had a university education behind him, at Trinity College, Cambridge. But according to his clergyman brother, books had a tendency to give Hodson headaches, and he was much more interested in his vocation as 'a Christian soldier'.[29]

One acquaintance described him as 'a tallish man with yellow hair, a pale, smooth face, heavy moustache, and large, restless, rather unforgiving eyes'.[30] Others talked of his impulsive, even reckless nature, and his skills as a 'perfect swordsman'. Having arrived in India in time to fight in the Sikh Wars, he had risen rapidly to be a District Commissioner in Amritsar, before heading to the North West Frontier to take up a position as Acting Deputy Commissioner of the Yusufzai tribal area, and adjutant of the new Corps of Guides. His fall from grace was equally sudden. In 1854 Hodson was relieved of his command after an investigation declared that he had misused and embezzled regimental funds, and had been guilty of corruption and falsification of the accounts, as well as gross negligence. 'My ruin is absolute and complete,' he wrote at the time.[31]

He was later acquitted of all the charges, but gossip continued to circulate about him – concerning the improper imprisonment without trial of a Yusufzai chieftain and his twelve-year-old-son, as well as the suspicious killing of a moneylender who was believed to have lent money to him.[32] It was said that he was conducting personal vendettas against 'the greater part of his Pathans and Afridis'; he was also personally unpopular with his men.[33] As a result, he continued to carry with him an extremely dubious reputation, and many agreed with the surgeon Edward Hare that he was too unscrupulous to be a good soldier and was really 'fit only to lead Italian banditti'. Shortly before the outbreak of the Uprising, on 21 March, his former patron, John Lawrence's elder brother Henry, effectively washed his hands of him, writing, 'I doubt if any man could help you just now.'[34]

At the outbreak, Hodson was still pressing for a formal, public inquiry to exonerate him of all the accusations ranged against him. But as with Nicholson's unstoppable rise in the face of the new crisis, Hodson's energy, ruthlessness and sheer brazen confidence brought him quickly to the attention of the Commander-in-Chief, and before long he had become the star of Anson's staff. Within five days of the outbreak he was appointed Assistant Quartermaster General, and was permitted to recruit his own small private army of Sikh Irregular horse 'for service in the intelligence department and as a personal escort'. A few days later, while Hodson was in Karnal scouting ahead of the main army – where he shared his lodgings with a group of Delhi refugees including Annie Jennings' fiancé, Charlie Thomason, and the entire Wagentrieber family – news came from Anson that Hodson's force was to be expanded into an entire new regiment of irregular cavalry, under his own name, Hodson's Horse.[35]

One of Hodson's first duties was to ride through the turbulent countryside to Meerut, with a small escort of Sikh cavalry, and re-establish communication with the regiments stranded there. This Hodson did with a remarkable ride, setting off at nine o'clock at night on 21 May, reaching Meerut at dawn the following day. He delivered his message to Wilson (having found the other general, Hewitt, 'in a state of helpless imbecility'), had a bath, breakfast and two hours' sleep, and then headed straight back to Karnal, having to fight his way through the last 30 miles. He reached Anson at Ambala on the 23rd, a journey of 250 miles in two days at the height of the summer heat. That night he headed back yet again to Karnal: 'as I have only had one night in bed out of five I am tolerable weary', he wrote to his wife the following evening.[36]

Like Nicholson, Hodson soon gained a reputation for dispensing with legal niceties, especially with any mutinous sepoys he captured: 'There is a tendency to treat these rebellious sepoys with a tenderness as misplaced as it would be pernicious,' he wrote to his wife on 16 May. A little later he was more explicit: 'I never let my men take prisoners,' he explained, 'but shoot them at once.'[37] He was also notorious for the pleasure he took in the kill. 'A beautiful swordsman, he never failed to kill his man,' wrote one of his officers. 'The way he used to play with the most brave and furious of these rebels was perfect. I fancy I see him now, smiling, laughing, parrying most fearful blows, as calmly as if he was brushing off flies, calling out all the time, "Why, try again now," "what's that?" "Do you call yourself a swordsman?" &c . . . If only there was a good hard scrimmage he was as happy as a king."[38]

Less dramatically, but ultimately more significantly, Hodson proved himself a ruthlessly efficient Chief of Intelligence: 'He even used to know what the rebels had for dinner,' noted one admiring officer.[39] On the march to Delhi, Hodson recruited as his principal assistant a one-eyed maulvi named Rajab Ali, who had previously worked as the Head Munshi of Sir George Clerk, the Political Agent for the Sikh States, then later with Sir Henry Lawrence across the Punjab.[40]

Rajab Ali immediately made his way into Delhi, where he set up an extensive network of spies and informants, ranging from leading Hindu bankers and Anglophile Mughal aristocrats, through former British officials, to one of Wagentrieber's former subeditors at the *Delhi Gazette*. Most remarkably of all he managed to enlist as an informant one of the most prominent sepoy commanders, Brigade Major Gauri Shankar Sukul of the Haryana Regiment, who provided a regular stream of vital strategic information, as well as acting as agent provocateur, disrupting sepoy councils by accusing several other quite innocent (and often very prominent) sepoy officers of spying and collaboration. Rajab Ali also quickly established contact with Zinat Mahal; with Zafar's prime minister, Hakim Ahsanullah Khan; and with the pro-British faction in the Palace led by Mirza Fakhru's Anglophile father-in-law, Mirza Ilahe Bakhsh.

The centre of Hodson's spy network in the city was the Residency's corpulent Mir Munshi, Jiwan Lal, who, despite being confined to the dark of his *tehkhana* (underground cool room), soon became the most important British intelligence operator within the walls. Every day he sent out 'two Brahmins and two Jats for the purpose of obtaining news of the doings of the rebels from every quarter, from the Fort, the city gates, &c, so that I might record everything for the information of my masters'.[41] According to Jiwan Lal's own diary, as early as 19 May he received instructions to stay in the city and gather intelligence from a blue-eyed European 'disguised as a faquir'.

The man wore a *kurtah* of *gairwa* [reddish] colour such as is worn
by Hindu Faquirs, called 'sadhs', had a bead of Tulsi around his
neck, and on his forehead was painted a 'Ramanandi' mark. Only his
eyes were blue . . . He also had some yellowish paint, such as of
'peori' over his face; and he told me that he had lived for a long time
at Benares, and had acquired a thorough knowledge of Sanskrit and
Urdu, so that no one could detect him in his speech . . . He sat for
two hours talking about and describing his own account, and about
the ignorance and stupidity of the rebels.

He took out from the folds of his *dhoti* – a long one, which he was
wearing like Brahmins – letters . . . with instructions that I was
desired to forward to the chiefs of Jhujjur, Bahadurgarh and Bul-
lubgarh . . . He advised me [to stay in the city] . . . furnishing such
news of the rebels as might be of use to the government. 'And,'
added he, 'our own men will be coming to you for the purpose of
carrying away the news from you.'

The great difficulty was that all persons passing by roads or
through the city gates were minutely searched by the rebels who
did not leave even trousers and shoes unsearched. If anything was
found the man was put to death. If it was discovered he was a
messenger, the sender's house was plundered, and no mercy was
shown to the sender's life. But I sent the letters . . . through my own
servants disguised as beggars, promising them very liberal rewards
for the service . . .*[42]

Thousands of notes from such spies – many of which were carried
out of the city through a network of runners masquerading as
sadhus and mendicants – still survive in the Mutiny Papers of the
National Archives of India. They range from long and detailed

* Some recent academic post-colonial writing has ridiculed the idea of Europeans
acting effectively as spies disguised as Indians, and dismissed such claims – later the
subject of much Victorian fiction – as 'fantasy' – see, for example, Gautam Chakravarty, *The Indian Mutiny and the British Imagination*, Cambridge, 2005, especially ch.
5, 'Counter-insurgency and Heroism'. Yet there seems no good reason for doubting
Jiwan Lal's own diary on this matter, as it seems otherwise to be an impeccably reliable
if somewhat sycophantic document. See *A Short Account of the Life and Family of Rai
Jiwan Lal Bahadur, Late Honorary Magistrate of Delhi with extracts from his diary
relating to the time of the Mutiny 1857 compiled by his son*, Delhi, 1902, p. 30.

analyses of the rebel positions – the gun emplacements, barracks, water supplies, regimental magazines and armouries – and the rebels' problems: from the lack of percussion caps, for example, to the squabbles and disagreements between the different sepoy regiments. They include many tiny fragments of papers designed to be sewn into shoes and clothing, and written in microscopic script, giving warning of imminent attacks and telling when and where they should be expected. They also give advice about how to improve the effectiveness of shelling, how to exploit the weak spots in the fortifications and how to damage the Bridge of Boats.[43]

Not all of the material proved either reliable or accurate; frequently the spies exaggerated the scale of the despair and disaffection within the city, and told their British paymasters what they wanted to hear – as Hodson and his fellow British intelligence officers quickly came to realise. But in the months to come, the sheer quantity of intelligence that the British received from the city, and the lack of it in the rebels' camp, did as much as anything to determine the outcome of the struggle for Delhi. As the senior city policeman, Sa'id Mubarak Shah, later put it, 'The fact was that the rebel army possessed no really trustworthy information as to the number and position of the British troops. Nor had they a single spy on whose word they could rely.'[44]

By the beginning of the first week in June, Hodson was leading the Delhi Field Force as it lumbered south along the Grand Trunk Road from Karnal towards Delhi. Its new commander, the sixty-year-old General Sir Henry Barnard, had taken the advice of Sir John Lawrence: 'Act at once, march with any body of European troops to the spot, and the danger will disappear. Give it time, it will flame through the land.'[45] At his disposal Barnard now had a modest force of around 600 cavalry and 2,400 infantry, supported by a small siege train of around fifty cannon and field guns.

Hodson and his irregular cavalry travelled ahead of the main column, scouting ahead to anticipate ambushes; on one occasion Hodson rode up as far as the Delhi Race Course, above the burned-out cantonments, before meeting any rebel sentries.[46] Nicholson, meanwhile, was busy in the Frontier, gathering Sikh and Pathan

levies of irregular horse to help replace the Hindustani troops lost
to the Mutiny.*

It would not be long before Hodson and Nicholson would
together bring the full weight of British vengefulness to the very
gates of Bahadur Shah's newly independent Mughal Delhi.

Zafar marked the afternoon of 12 May by mounting a procession.
Processing around Delhi had always been Zafar's favourite and most
effective means of ceremonially proclaiming and asserting his sovereignty; and on 12 May that sovereignty badly needed proclaiming.

As on the previous day, the streets of Delhi were empty but for
gangs of looters: 'Things were still so bad that bands of plunderers
were carrying empty sacks and were pillaging houses of any
respectable citizen they could get into,' wrote Zahir Dehlavi.

> They picked the houses of the rich and instigated rioters by saying
> that there is a memsahib hiding inside this house, or there are sahibs
> in that one. Hearing this, mobs of rioters stormed into the house, led
> by the sepoys, and before long the city rabble could be seen leaving
> the ruins with all their collected booty.[47]

Several of the leading Mughal aristocrats were manhandled, and had
their premises ransacked. These included Hamid Ali Khan, the
powerful leader of Delhi's Shia community, who was accused of
sheltering Europeans and dragged to the court, where Zafar had to
intervene to save him from execution.[48] Large areas of the city were
still burning from the fires started the day before, while the Fort
now contained so many sepoys, who placed their own guards at the
Palace gates, that, according to Maulvi Muhammad Baqar, 'the
Palace now resembles a cantonment'.[49]

---

* The Sikhs proved especially keen recruits, for although they had themselves fought
two major wars with the British, the most recent only in 1849, any dislike they may
have felt for the British was outweighed by their long hatred of the Mughals, who had
martyred two of their greatest gurus – Guru Arjan Dev in 1606 and Guru Tegh
Bahadur in 1675. There was also, of course, the lure of the celebrated wealth of Delhi.

The jewellers, moneylending *baniyas* and the famous cloth merchants in the Chota Dariba bore the brunt of the violence. So did Delhi's celebrated sweetmeat makers, whose fame had obviously reached Avadh and Bihar, as, according to the newswriter Chunni Lal, 'the infantry troops forcibly entered and plundered the shops of the confectioners in all the streets of the city'.[50] The moneylender Mahajan Narayan Das had his house looted and its entire contents removed. A jeweller named Mohan Lal was kidnapped by the sepoys and kept at gunpoint until he bought his way out of trouble by giving them 200 rupees.[51]

The courtesans were also vulnerable: several *kothis* found themselves besieged by crowds of soldiers, and at least one courtesan was abducted: the dancer Manglo, who was carried off and raped by the *sawar* Rustam Khan.[52] Sometimes the Delhiwallahs fought back: 'The infantry and cavalry made an attack on Nagar Seth street with the view to plundering it,' recorded Chunni Lal. 'But the inhabitants closed the gates and attacked the soldiery with brickbats, and drove them off.'[53] In other places too the townspeople took the law into their own hands: in Hauz Qazi, for example, there was a riot 'between some Tilangas and the residents of the Mohalla'.[54]

Occasionally the mob would find some last group of surviving Christians and drag them from their hiding place to the kotwal, where they were duly dispatched; among those killed on the morning of the 12th was the scholarly principal of Delhi College, Francis Taylor, who was discovered trying to escape in disguise, and was at once promptly beaten to death in the street. A little later, Elizabeth Wagentrieber's alcoholic cousin, Joseph Skinner, was taken from his haveli and lynched at the kotwali; Skinner's house was then comprehensively looted. Many victims remain unnamed: one typical account in the narrative of Chunni Lal records how

four European gentlemen were concealed in the house of Muhammad Ibrahim, son of Muhammad Ali, merchant. The troopers hearing this went there, and killing the Europeans, plundered the house. A European woman, dressed as a native, was going along near Ellenborough Tank, and was killed by the troopers ... Two

European gentlemen going along in the guise of natives were killed in front of the principal police station.[55]

As far as Maulvi Muhammad Baqar was concerned, there was something miraculous in the ease with which the British were being dispatched: 'Englishmen are still being discovered,' he wrote in the *Dihli Urdu Akhbar*, 'and, thanks to divine prowess, being easily overpowered: their arrogance has brought them divine retribution. The English are now suffering under the blows of the unseen power because of their enmity towards Islam and their support for efforts to destroy the Islamic faith.'[56]

Other than the targeting of Christians, there was surprisingly little patriotic or nationalistic spirit visible in the violence that rumbled on for weeks after the outbreak: the initial mutiny in the army had opened a vast Pandora's box of differences and grievances – economic, sectarian, religious and political – and now that the violence and settling of scores had begun, it would not be easy to bring them to a halt. In the meantime, many of the sepoys simply took the opportunity presented by the breakdown of law and order to enrich themselves, as did many Delhiwallahs.[57]

Judging by the petitions that poured in to the King, many of which survive among the Mutiny Papers, the worst affected were the ordinary people of Delhi who did not even have the partial protection of gates or high haveli walls. The poor proved especially vulnerable outside the city, in suburbs such as Kishenganj and Nizamuddin. There the inhabitants found themselves at the mercy not only of the incoming sepoys, but also of mobs of Gujars from the surrounding countryside. One of the largest delegations to come before Zafar and beg for protection in the first days of the Uprising arrived from the western suburb of Paharganj. The language they used to the Emperor was full of the old Mughal titles – Zafar was addressed as the Throne of the Caliphate and the Refuge of the Inhabitants of the World – but the petition that was presented demonstrated the reality of the utter helplessness of his regime:

We poor folk, residents of Jaisinghpura and Shahganj, also known as Paharganj, have come together to the Luminous Presence, because from days of old our settlement was attached to the Royal Estate, yet now the Tilangas come out from Ajmeri Gate and oppress the shopkeepers, and take goods by force without paying anything. The troops enter the houses of the poor and penniless and take anything they find – even the string beds, dishes and piles of firewood. Whenever your humble servants, or even our most respected citizens, go to the Tilangas and plead with them about the misery to which they have been reduced, they merely threaten them with their guns and swords. We have been reduced to such extremities by the depredations of the troops that we submit this petition to His Majesty that He may turn his gaze of justice and commiseration towards us. Send a Royal Order to the Tilangas that they give no more trouble, and that with the support of our gracious sovereign we may be left to live our lives in peace. May the sun of prosperity and success and all glory shine brightly, for your sake, O Lord of All![58]

Another large delegation came to the Fort from the city's provision merchants and corn chandlers, who complained that, while seizing all their stocks, the troops had paid 'not one pice and have threatened and beaten up all the merchants'.[59] The inability of the Emperor to aid any of these petitioners was made startlingly clear by the fact that special orders had to be given to protect even the traders of the Chatta Chowk, the bazaar within the walls of the Red Fort, 'and if any Telinga disobeys, his officers should immediately report him'.[60] The sepoys also looted the King's own ice factory outside Ajmeri Gate, pointlessly destroying the Fort's stocks of ice.[61] Even the *harkaras*, the royal messengers, complained that they were being attacked by the Tilingas: 'they come to our houses, make trouble and loot their contents'.[62]

The position in the countryside outside the city was even worse: when Zafar sent some riders to seek troops and support from the Raja of Alwar, Gujars attacked them on the road just outside Mehrauli; they returned naked and bruised, reporting that the Gujars had 'robbed them of their horses, clothes and money; that they had taken the King's letter and, tearing it up, had put the pieces back into their hands'.[63]

Hoping to stop the looting and bring the city back to normality, Zafar called some of the leading men of his court to the Palace and discussed what could be done. He received them sitting on a silver throne that had been in storage ever since the ceremony of receiving *nazrs* from the Governor General had been stopped in 1842; now it was brought out, given a polish and installed in the Diwan i-Khas.

With few other options open, the court decided that the Emperor should go out on elephant-back, with Mirza Jawan Bakht seated behind him, 'accompanied by a regiment of infantry, some guns, his own special armed retainers, and a band of musicians', through the deserted, looted and smoking city, in an attempt to bring peace to the streets. By the beat of the drum, the royal proclamation was read through the bazaars that 'the country had reverted to the possession of the King', that Zafar had reclaimed the supreme authority that was always his by right, that the looting must now stop and the shops must reopen for business. In addition, Prince Mirza Mughal 'went to all the principal police stations, seated on an elephant, and had a proclamation made that anyone convicted of plunder would be punished with the loss of nose and ears'.[64]

A salute of twenty-one guns was fired on Zafar's departure from the Palace, and another on his return. Yet the procession proved very different from those Zafar was used to mounting, in which the cavalcade would stop for his subjects to come forward to present symbolic offerings of fealty to the Emperor. Instead,

> from house to house the King was distracted by cries and petitions, now from servants of Europeans who had been murdered, now from shopkeepers whose shops had been plundered, now from the higher classes whose houses had been broken into – all looked to the King for immediate redress. Everywhere appeals were made to him to repress the plunder and rapine common throughout the city.[65]

That evening Zafar summoned a general durbar and 'in a Persian *rubakari* [order] beautiful with flowing language' called on all the subahdars of the different sepoy regiments to rein in the bad behaviour of their troops, saying 'that such a state of things was most unbecoming' now that the rule of the Mughals had returned, a dynasty 'at whose feet all other kings and monarchs waited on bended knee'.[66] The officers listened politely enough, but within an hour other companies of sepoys appeared complaining loudly they could get no food in the town, that the grain shops refused to open, and bluntly telling the Emperor to find something for them to eat.

> Forgetful of the lofty tone of the order, and of the high toned phraseology expressive of the King's dignity, they addressed him with such disrespectful terms as, 'I say, you King!' 'I say, you old fellow!' ('Arey, Badshah! Arey, Buddha!') 'Listen,' cried one, catching him by the hand. 'Listen to me,' said another, touching the old king's beard. Angered at their behaviour, yet unable to prevent their insolence, he found relief alone in bewailing his misfortunes and his fate before his servants . . .
>
> Throughout this eventful day he was distraught, perplexed and cowed at finding himself in a position which made him the mere puppet of those who had formerly been only too glad humbly to obey his orders, but who now, taking advantage of the spirit of insubordination which was rife in all classes of the city in this day of ruin and riot, were not ashamed to mock and humiliate him.[67]

If Zafar was in many ways an ideal monarch for the conditions imposed on him by the British before the Uprising, able from a position of virtual house arrest to act as host and part-catalyst for a major cultural renaissance, it was rapidly becoming clear that he was too old, mystical and other-worldly even to begin to fit the role of a leader in war. He was after all eighty-two years old, and lacked any of the energy, ambition and worldliness, and indeed the drive and determination, needed to ride the tiger of rebellion.

Instead his position was so weak that he was not even able to stop the sepoys from turning his Hall of Public Audience, the Diwan i-Am, into an ammunition store and dormitory for the artillery, or to prevent the rebel guards on the ramparts from peering constantly into his zenana quarters, as frequent petitions from his angry begums bear witness. Less still was he able to prevent the damage that was done to his beloved gardens. For much of May he pressed to get the cavalry to remove their horses from his garden, but all without success.[68]

The following morning, the 13th, Zafar again tried to bring some order to his city. While surveying the damage done the day before, he realised the urgent need to put out the many fires that were still burning, especially around the gutted magazine; after all, many of the houses of Delhi were built of little more than mud and thatch, and even the grander houses had wooden balconies and latticework projections.

It was Zahir Dehlavi who volunteered to go to the kotwal and attempt to gather the manpower necessary to extinguish the fires. 'I thought that if, God forbid, the remaining gunpowder catches fire, then before long the whole town will be ablaze,' Zahir wrote afterwards.

The *Kotwal* sent two or three hundred water carriers, and himself came along to help, so together we put out the fires which were burning, both in the magazine and houses around the town. It was just as well we acted when we did. Inside the magazine, on the side of the river, there were mountains of coal and gunpowder, as well as about two hundred cannons loaded and ready to fire. There was no count of the number of rifles lying scattered around, as well as innumerable pistols. Within two or three days I was told that the rabble had carried away the powder, guns and cannon, and only the cannon balls were left.

For us courtiers these were dangerous days. We Royal servants had the dagger of fate hanging over our heads at all times, and every so often I used to be surrounded by rebels who would put a pistol on my chest. One day [soon after the outbreak] twenty or twenty-five of us were sitting in the storehouse of the Fort along with Hakim Ahsanullah Khan, when the *Purbias* came and surrounded us. They pulled out their guns and said, 'You infidels! You are all closet Christians! We know you are writing letters to the English . . .' We were shocked and told them that if this was true, why didn't they just shoot us there and then – at least we would be done with the anxiety of living from day to day under such pressure. One or two of the officers among them were sensible and were able to pacify the others. They were persuaded to leave us, but we were all frightened out of our wits.

Zahir writes how every day three or four hundred more sepoys came to join the men who had collected in Delhi until gradually seven or eight thousand had collected from all over Hindustan.

They were living in luxury, drinking a lot of *bhang*,* eating the best *laddoo peras* [sweetmeats] and had stopped doing their own cooking, as for both meals they fed on delicious *puri kachoris* and sweets, and at night slept a peaceful sleep . . . They took control of Delhi and did what ever they wanted: there was no one who we could appeal to. It was like *andher nagri chaupat raj* [the proverbial city of darkness with an incompetent ruler].

The ordinary people of Delhi quickly tired of the uncertainties and were all praying God to rid them of this unexpected cataclysm and that power should be restored in the hands of rulers who would look after them. Meanwhile the rebel sepoys and the city mob were daily getting richer, looting whomever they wished. So rich did some of them become that soon they did not have enough space to keep their loot. They changed rupees for gold coins and had them tied to their belts. Meanwhile the ordinary people of Delhi were beginning to die of starvation, all the factories were closed, and people were sitting around with closed shops and no work.[69]

Against this background of lawless anarchy in the city, the Mughal court, for all its weakness, assumed a centrality and a political importance it had not had for a century.

* A traditional mildly narcotic drink in which milk and spices are mixed with marijuana.

The daily audiences, or durbars, were resumed for the first time since the Persian sack of the city in 1739, and the Emperor, Bahadur Shah II, was hailed again throughout Hindustan as Mightiest King of Kings, Emperor son of Emperor, Sultan son of Sultan. As the *Sadiq ul-Akabhar* put it, 'We humbly and greatly thank our Lord and express our gratitude to him for putting an end to the tyrannical rule of the Christians and for restoring the administration and governance of his exalted Majesty the Khalifa, the Shadow of God on Earth, the Deputy of the Divine Prophet.'[70] Yet for all this rhetoric, behind the façade the royal family reacted by splitting into competing and deeply divided factions.

The group that most enthusiastically embraced the Uprising consisted of a party of five young passed-over princes. Their future had been looking distinctly bleak until the day of the outbreak: whether or not Mirza Jawan Bakht succeeded Zafar, and whether or not the Mughals continued in the Red Fort, they all seemed destined to live out restricted lives of genteel princely poverty. For all of them the Uprising presented a unique opportunity for self-improvement. All five immediately grabbed the chance that fate had presented.

Four of these five princes were men of little obvious talent or standing at the court, and they barely appear in the Palace records prior to 1857. Mirza Khizr Sultan was Zafar's ninth son, the illegitimate child of a Palace concubine named Rahim Bakhsh Bai.[71] Aged twenty-three in 1857, he was renowned for his physical beauty – indeed, Ghalib said he was as beautiful as Yusuf, the biblical Joseph – and he had some capacity as a poet and a marksman; but his only appearances in the Palace diary had been when he had asked his father for an elephant and a house of his own in Mehrauli in 1852, and been promptly turned down. This was possibly because he was closely associated with the disgraced Mirza Fakhru; certainly his wife and Mirza Fakhru's wife appear to have been best friends.[72] His second appearance in the court diary was even less promising: in August 1852 he was publicly rebuked by Zafar in full durbar for beating his wife, at which point the prince 'fell at HM's feet and prayed forgiveness of his fault. The King struck him two or three times very angrily and then pardoned him, warning him for the future to live on good terms with his wife'.[73]

Mirza Khizr was a close friend of the second of the princes who threw their lot in with the rebels: Mirza Abu Bakr, the eldest son of Mirza Fakhru and Zafar's oldest surviving legitimate grandson. His only appearance in the records prior to 1857 was in November 1853, when he succeeded in removing one of his own fingers in a gun accident, but he quickly made up for lost time during the Uprising. Of all the royal family Mirza Abu Bakr seems most quickly to have grasped the opportunities the new dispensation presented for letting his hair down: within a few days of the outbreak he began appearing in petitions and complaints to the King, accused of whoring and drunkenness, whipping his servants, beating up watchmen and casually attacking any policeman who tried to rein him in.[74]

The third prince was even more obscure: all that is known about Mirza Bakhtawar Shah before 1857 is that he was Zafar's eleventh son, the illegitimate child of another of Zafar's concubines, Hanwa, that he was born in 1839, and that he was married to Mirza Fakhru's daughter in 1852.[75] The fourth rebel prince was another grandson of Zafar's: Mirza Abdulla, son of Zafar's eldest boy, Mirza Shah Rukh, who had died in 1847. On his father's death he and his concubine mother, Khairum Bai, had gone off on the haj to Mecca, from which they had returned in December 1853. After receiving a haj present of a fine white mare from his grandfather, Mirza Abdullah disappears from the records until the outbreak in May 1857.[76]

The fifth of the princes was, however, a man very different from the other four, and he soon established himself as the effective head of whatever civil administration existed during the months of the Uprising. Mirza Mughal was Zafar's fifth son, and his oldest surviving legitimate male child. In 1857 he was aged twenty-nine, only nine years younger than his powerful stepmother Zinat Mahal; his own mother was a sayyida (descendant of the Prophet) of aristocratic birth named Sharaf ul-Mahal Sayyidani, who was a senior figure in Zafar's harem.[77]

Unlike the four other insurgent princes, Mirza Mughal appears frequently in the court records before the Uprising and held a prominent position at court. He was the principal beneficiary of the disgrace of Mirza Fakhru: after the latter's fall in February 1852, Mirza Mughal took on the powerful offices of Palace nazir and *qiladar* [fort keeper], which effectively made him the Palace pay-master and chamberlain; he also received most of Mirza Fakhru's estates and the income that went with them.[78] He achieved this high position partly through reaching an understanding with Zinat Mahal, whose protégé he effectively became; she appears to have befriended and assisted him as a counterbalance to Mirza Fakhru: there is a telling reference in the court diary to her advising him, 'Have no fears on the subject,' when he consulted her about his problems on succeeding to Mirza Fakhru's offices.[79]

There are two pictures extant of Mirza Mughal. He is present as an earnest and serious little boy of ten, wearing full court dress, in Zafar's coronation portrait of 1838.[80] But it is the oil portrait by August Schoefft, painted some time in the early 1850s, a few years before the outbreak, which is the most revealing image.[81] It shows a handsome, dynamic and athletic-looking youth, dressed in flowing white robes that offset his dark skin, brown eyes and full black beard. If Schoefft's image of Zafar shows a benign, weary and melancholy old man, his image of Mirza Mughal is its polar opposite – an image of a restless, impatient and frustrated young man who glares out of the frame with pride, suppressed anger and even a trace of bitterness.

Although he wears as many gems as his brother Jawan Bakht and his father in their companion portraits, it is his sword and stabbing dagger which draw the eye; from the expression of Mirza Mughal's face you are left in little doubt that he would use these weapons if the need arose. He has an energy and an urge to engage with the world that are wholly absent in the gentle and other-worldly expression of his father; there is also a seriousness and gravity quite absent from the image of his vain-looking younger brother. Yet for all that, there is in his eyes just a hint of Zafar's lack of self-assurance.

Though there are no references to Mirza Mughal's whereabouts on the day that the sepoys arrived in Delhi, by the morning of the 12th he appeared in the durbar with his younger brothers, and together they 'applied for the principal commands in the army'.

Zafar dismissed the request on the advice of Zinat Mahal and Hakim Ahsanullah Khan, who argued that 'they were not of sufficient age and experience for such appointments, nor would they understand any of the duties [of soldiers]; they were much displeased in consequence'. But the following day the princes returned with 'officers of the army, to join them in their request'. Again Zafar and Hakim Ahsanullah Khan opposed the plan: 'You don't know the work,' said Zafar. 'What will you do as officers?' But the princes and the sepoys held their ground 'and accordingly, two days after [on the 15th] they were severally nominated to commands and received dresses of honour'. With the consent of the sepoys, Mirza Mughal was given the title Commander-in-Chief.[82]

It is possible that Mirza Mughal, along with his brothers Abu Bakr and Khizr Sultan, had secretly been in contact with the sepoys prior to the outbreak; certainly this was what Zinat Mahal maintained afterwards.* This would help explain the speed with which Mirza Mughal established a rapport with the sepoys, while the rest of the Palace kept a suspicious distance. Either way, from this point onwards Mirza Mughal threw himself energetically into the business of managing the army and trying to administer the town,

---

* When Zinat Mahal was imprisoned at the end of the Uprising, her jailer, Lieutenant Edward Ommaney, recorded this revealing (if blatantly self-serving) conversation in his diary for Wednesday, 30 September 1857: 'Saunders came down this morning . . . had a long conversation with the Ex-Queen, Zeenut Mehul, but only got the same information that she gave me viz. that she, her son Jumma Bakht and the old Ex-King, had had nothing to do with this rebellion, that his sons of the Harem, Meerza Moghul, Kidr Sooltan and grandson Aboo Bukur were the ones who held a prominent part in the occurrences and there was no previous intention of rebellion to her knowledge, except as regards these three men, which she did not know till afterwards and further that the old Ex-King, herself and son, were kept in a sort of confinement. They tried to prevent the commandant of the Palace, Douglas, from exposing himself and when they heard that he had been wounded, had sent food and words of consolation to him . . . She said also that she had no idea of the mutiny till the mutinous regiments arrived.' See NAM, 6301-143, Diaries of Col. E. L. Ommaney. On the other hand, it is clear that the princes were not standing by, waiting to receive the Mutineers, and making sure the Fort gates were open. While the actions of the Delhi regiments on 11 May strongly suggest a degree of collusion in advance with the Meerut mutineers, there is simply no evidence from their actions that the princes in the Fort were waiting for the outbreak, ready to take command.

which he did in collaboration with Theo Metcalfe's friend and saviour, Muin ud-Din Husain Khan, whom he made kotwal the day after his own appointment.

One of the biggest surprises contained in the Mutiny Papers is the sheer quantity of paperwork produced by Mirza Mughal and his office: the papers contain many thousands of Mirza Mughal's orders; indeed, several whole collections contain nothing else.* Collection 60 alone contains 831 orders from Mirza Mughal's secretariat.

It is striking how many of the Indian nationalist accounts of 1857 make the assumption, common among imperial British historians, that any Mughal prince must necessarily be a lazy fop, and Mirza Mughal is generally written off as an effete and useless aristocrat. Yet to judge from the documentation contained in the National Archives, Mirza Mughal was one of the most energetic and industrious of all those who espoused the cause of the Uprising in 1857. More than anyone else, it seems, Mirza Mughal realised the importance of providing some organised logistical back-up to the Uprising, and a coherent administration for Delhi. As it turned out, his administration rarely got beyond crisis management, and never succeeded in turning itself into a force able to control either the different sepoy regiments or the growing numbers of freelance jihadis collecting in Delhi; but if it failed, it was certainly not for lack of industry.

From the first week, Mirza Mughal produced an incessant stream of orders and commands: attempting to get the sepoys out of the city and into a series of coherent military camps; sending policemen or Palace guards to rescue any bazaars that were being plundered or noblemen whose houses were being attacked; promising the sepoys pay and raising the money to provide it; finding sufficient food for both the sepoys and the people of Delhi; receiving and attending to the petitions of individual sepoys; providing spades, shovels, axes and sandbags for entrenchments and defence works; imposing a strict code of conduct on the military so that, for example, there could be no house searches without a permit; negotiating to restrain

* See, for example, Collections 57, 59, 60, 61, 62 and 63.

the Gujar tribes outside the walls; establishing a mint to produce coins with Zafar's portrait upon them; and not least, attempting to rally his increasingly depressed father and control his own brothers.

Mirza Mughal was almost certainly behind a circular letter sent out in Zafar's name to all the princes and rajas of India, asking them to join the Uprising and appealing for their loyalty on the grounds that all faiths were under attack by the British. The letter refers specifically to the laws banning sati and allowing converts to inherit, and the Company's facilitation of missionary activity, and the alleged conversion of prisoners locked in British jails: 'The English are people who overthrow all religions,' it states. 'You should understand well their object of destroying the religions of Hindustan . . . It is now my firm conviction that if the English continue in Hindustan they will . . . utterly overthrow our religions. As the English are the common enemy of both [Hindus and Muslims, we] should unite in their slaughter . . . for by this alone will the lives and faiths of both be saved.'[83]

One document that probably was not, however, produced by Mirza Mughal or his chancery was a remarkable declaration known (quite erroneously) as the Manifesto of the King of Delhi or (more accurately, since it had nothing to do with Zafar) as the Azamgarh Proclamation. Unlike the circular letter, the proclamation is almost wholly secular in tone, and is aimed at a broad base of different interest groups; indeed, it is the nearest thing produced during the Uprising to a manifesto of national independence. Its opening sentence sets the tone, a cry to arms noting that 'both Hindoos and Mohammedans are being ruined under the tyranny and oppression of the infidel and treacherous English'. While noting that 'at present a war is ranging with the English on account of religion', and calling on 'pundits and fakirs' to join with Mughal armies, most of its space is given over to complaints that the English have overtaxed the landowners, monopolised 'all the posts of dignity and emolument' in the civil and armed services, and put Indian artisans out of business by flooding the market with cheap British imports.

Some historians, pleased to have found a rare document from 1857 that explicitly mentions economic and social grievances, have linked this remarkably modern document with the Red Fort, and thereby perhaps exaggerated its influence and importance. For its author was actually the rather obscure and enigmatic Mughal prince Firoz Shah, who, while probably a grandson of Zafar, fought exclusively in Avadh and Lucknow, and never once came to Delhi in the course of the Uprising. Perhaps partly because of this, the more secular issues he raises are intriguingly different, in both tone and content, from those being articulated as major grievances at the time in the Mughal capital.[84]

If most of the princes threw in their lot with the Uprising, having little to lose and much to gain, Zinat Mahal and her beloved only son, Jawan Bakht, took the opposite course – and for the same reason.

Zinat Mahal was wholly opposed to the course her husband was pursuing, and regarded it as ruinous for the chances of Jawan Bakht. It was also the first time since their marriage that Zafar had publicly gone against her advice on a major issue. According to the memoir of Hakim Ahsanullah Khan, the Queen 'remonstrated that the King paid no attention to her. [But] he [merely] replied, "Let what God wills happen."'[85]

Zinat Mahal had apparently calculated that the British would soon return and rout the sepoys, and that loyalty to them might yet result in their recognising the succession of her beloved son; either way, whatever the reasoning, it was she who encouraged Zafar to send an express camel messenger to the Governor of the North West Provinces in Agra on the night of the outbreak.[86] Later, she made sure Jawan Bakht kept his distance from the insurgents and did not become in any way implicated in their violence. When Mirza Mughal was made Commander-in-Chief, Jawan Bakht was given the nominal title of Vazir, but he was kept far away from the sepoys and did not become involved in the administration of the city.[87]

Ranged alongside Zinat Mahal and Mirza Jawan Bakht in the discreetly pro-British faction in the Palace were the head eunuch and Zinat Mahal's enforcer, Mahbub Ali Khan; Zafar's prime minister, Hakim Ahsanullah Khan; and Mirza Ilahe Bakhsh, father-in-law of the late Mirza Fakhru. In 1852, Ilahe Bakhsh had been the bitter rival of Zinat Mahal, Jawan Bakht and Mahbub Ali Khan. Now the crisis resulted in an unexpected realignment of the old court factions: Mirza Mughal, formerly Zinat's protégé, now became her rival; while Mirza Ilahe Bakhsh, formerly her enemy, became her ally.[88]

Zafar himself stood slightly apart from his wife and principal advisers. While well aware of the dangers posed by the sepoys, disgusted by their manners and profoundly alarmed and depressed by the looting of his city, he nevertheless recognised the possibility that the Uprising could yet save the House of Timur, and ensure a future for his dynasty, something he had consistently worked for since his accession in 1837. He therefore gave his blessing and public support to the Uprising, and took seriously his role as newly empowered Mughal Emperor, while doing all he could to limit the depredations of the sepoys.

The degree to which Zinat Mahal, Mahbub Ali Khan and Hakim Ahsanullah Khan were operating their own policy in regard to the Uprising, quite independent of the Emperor, and in direct opposition to Mirza Mughal and the other princes, became apparent in the most dramatic fashion five days after the outbreak, at the morning durbar on Saturday, 16 May. According to the diary of the news-writer Chunni Lal, who was present,

> The troopers and infantry soldiers, accompanied by their officers, attended and presented a letter bearing the seals of the physician Ahsanullah Khan and Nawab Mabub Ali Khan, which they said had been intercepted at the Delhi Gate of the city. They complained that the physician and the Nawab had sent this letter to the English, inviting them to come to the city immediately, and promising that provided that the English should agree to acknowledge Mirza Jawan Bakht, the son of the King by the Queen Zinat Mahal, as heir apparent, they would on their part engage to seize and make over all the soldiery now in Delhi.[89]

Both the hakim and the eunuch – who was ill and had to be brought to court prostrate in his *palki* – swore than the document was a forgery, but they were not believed. Things began to look very bad for both courtiers: 'The men of the cavalry and infantry drew their swords and surrounded the physician declaring their firm belief that he maintained an understanding with the English.'[90]

It was at this point that one of the sepoys mentioned the British prisoners that Zafar had kept in safe custody in the Palace. Their number had now grown to fifty-two after the new kotwal, Muin ud-Din, had brought in several families who were about to be killed, after having been discovered hiding in the city. The sepoys accused the hakim and the eunuch of keeping the prisoners alive so that 'when the English came he might make them over, and would have the soldiers killed' – no doubt very much what the men did indeed have in mind.[91]

The sepoys then called for the prisoners, who were being kept and fed by Zafar in a room beside the Palace kitchens, not far from the Lahore Gate. They bound them and took them to a peepul tree near the shallow tank in front of the Palace drum house, the Naqqar Khana, and began to taunt them that they were about to be slaughtered.

According to Jiwan Lal, 'the King and his courtiers stood like dumb puppets' at first, horrified by what the sepoys were contemplating. 'Then the King ordered the sepoys to separate into parties, Mahommedans and Hindus, and he appealed to each to consult their religious advisers to see if there was any authority for the slaughter of helpless men and women and children.'[92] Their murder can never be allowed,' said Zafar, adding that the Queen was also wholly opposed to any massacre.[93] Sa'id Mubarak Shah recorded that

The king wept and besought the mutineers not to take the lives of helpless women and children, saying to them 'take care – for if you commit such a deed the vengeance and angel of God will fall on us all. Why slay the innocent?' But the Mutineers refused to listen and replied 'we'll kill them, and in your palace, so that whatever the result you and we shall be considered one in this business, and you will be thought equally guilty by the English.'[94]

Both the kotwal, Muin ud-Din, and the courtier Zahir Dehlavi, who were also present, recorded that the King continued to argue with the sepoys and refused to give his consent to the murder, but was eventually silenced by Hakim Ahsanullah Khan. The hakim had been deeply shaken by the exposure of his correspondence, and warned the King that if he continued to argue both their lives would be taken.

When Zahir saw that the sepoys were preparing to go ahead with the slaughter, he begged the hakim to make a last effort to stop the massacre: 'I told him that I had seen the prisoners being taken out,' he recorded later,

> and I was afraid that they were about to kill them, and that he must do something quickly to stop them. To this I got a reply, 'What can I do?' I told him this is the time to prove our loyalty, and that if he wanted to save the King then he had to try and persuade the rebels to stop this crime and save the prisoners, otherwise the English would come and level Delhi and turn it into an empty wasteland in revenge for this spilling of innocent blood. Ahsanullah Khan replied, 'You are still a child. You do not realize that in public life a man must use his reason rather than give way to his emotions. If we try to dissuade the rebels now they will kill us before they kill the English, and then they will kill the King.'[95]

It was anyway too late. By the time Ahsanullah had finished speaking, the sepoys and the Palace mob had got to work.

> They made the prisoners sit down, and one of them fired his carbine at them. After this two of the King's personal armed retainers killed all the Europeans, men, women and children, with their swords. There were about 200 Mussalmans standing at the tank, uttering the coarsest abuse at the prisoners. The sword of one of the king's retainers broke. After the slaughter, the bodies were taken on two carts, and thrown into the river. This occurrence caused a great excitement amongst the Hindus throughout the city, who said that these Purbeas who had committed this heinous and atrocious cruelty could never be victorious against the English.[96]

For Zafar the massacre was a turning point. The sepoys were quite correct that the British would never forgive the mass killing of innocents, and Zafar's failure to prevent it proved as fatal for him and his dynasty as it was for them.

By the end of the second week of the Uprising even the formerly enthusiastic Maulvi Muhammad Baqar was beginning to have second thoughts about what was going on: 'The population is greatly harassed and sick of the pillaging and plundering,' he wrote in an editorial in the *Dihli Urdu Akhbar* on 24 May.

> Whether people of the city, or outsiders from the East, everybody is busy looting and plundering. The police stations do not have even an iota of control and authority. Colonel James Skinner's *kothi* was plundered so badly that it cannot be described. In the city and around and about, the Gujars and Jats have created havoc. The roads are blocked, and thousands of houses have been plundered and burnt. Great peril confronts all the respectable and well-off people of Delhi . . . the city is being ravaged.[97]

Baqar emphasised, however, that it wasn't just the sepoys who were looting: the city mob was equally responsible, some of whom had disguised themselves as soldiers. 'Having pillaged the guns, arms and ammunition from the magazine and from English *kothis*, people have taken to dressing up like Tilangas and committing plunder,' he wrote.

> Five men were arrested yesterday. It was eventually revealed that some were cobblers who worked in the cantonment, and that two more were *chamars* [an untouchable caste]. They were taken to the platoon they claimed to belong to, and when their lies were uncovered the Subahdar and the sepoys gave them a heavy lashing and they are now in captivity.[98]

Baqar understood that behind the anarchy there lay a fundamental problem of authority. While there was clearly a certain amount of collusion and communication between the different regiments prior to the outbreak, each regiment had mutinied individually, had come to Delhi under its own steam and, once there, looked to its own subahdars for leadership. The regiments remained self-contained: they camped separately, accepted no overall sepoy general, and strongly resisted the idea of a commander of any other regiment having authority over them. The princes remained associated with individual regiments, and Mirza Mughal's attempts to act as a co-ordinating commander-in-chief had only very limited success. Since the Mughals were never able either to pay or to properly punish errant sepoys, or indeed disobedient regiments, there was a limit to how much authority they could ever actually wield over the rebel forces, and to some extent the regiments remained a collection of disparate private armies, each under its own subahdar, who acted as a semi-independent warlord. 'The rebels are without a leader,' was how the news-writer of the Raja of Kapurthala succinctly put it.[99]

To make matters worse, by the end of the second week fights between the infantry regiments and the cavalry *sawars* were becoming increasingly common. The Meerut and Delhi sepoys remained on especially bad terms, and frequently came to blows over the division of the loot from the city.[100] As Ghalib wrote in his diary at the time, the sepoys rapidly gathering in his city were 'a thousand armies marshalled without marshals, unnumbered bands, led by no commander and yet ready for war'.[101] The Emperor was equally depressed. According to the report of a spy, after one bout of bloodshed in which the Delhi and Meerut regiments had refused to obey their commanders and had instead fought with each other, Zafar had shaken his head and said, 'The skies have fallen down upon us.'[102]

Baqar was also alarmed: 'Everyone is full of praise for the efficiency of the Kotwal of the city,' he wrote in his paper, 'but both high and low are helpless because of the lack of control over the Tilangas. Many of the poor are said to be bordering on starvation . . . moneylenders are lying low because of fear of the Tilangas. The arrangement of two things is highly imperative and urgent: first the distribution of salaries, and secondly the restraining of the Tilangas.'[103]

If the sepoys refused to obey the subahdars of other sepoy regiments, still less did they relish taking orders from the Delhi police; when the police attempted to prevent them from looting, they instantly fought back. At the Lahore Gate a policeman who tried to stop the Tilangas looting was badly beaten up: 'Below the ramparts a *barqandaz* [armed police constable] noted some sacks of loot stashed by the wall and he challenged the owner,' the local police chief afterwards reported to the new kotwal, Muin ud-Din.

The owner, a Tilanga, argued back and unsheathed a sword. There was some jostling and raised voices, until some other Tilangas came [to help their comrade] and hit the *barqandaz* until he was bleeding then they took him into their custody. The Tilangas are meant to be royal servants. If this goes on then it will be impossible to maintain order and discipline.[104]

On another occasion, a policeman tried to stop a group of sepoys from running a protection racket in Gali Qasim Jan: 'They take bribes for all the stolen goods that pass,' reported the local *thanadar* (police station chief) to the kotwal,

and if they are paid they let them be, but whoever does not give them a bribe is greatly harassed by the guards. Whenever the *barqandazes* of this police station who are posted there object, they abuse and threaten them. Recently it has got worse: they have begun arresting whomever they cannot extort money from, and now they are saying we should all withdraw from the police station and stop interfering with them.[105]

For all the weakness of Mirza Mughal's administration, Zafar realised he did possess one trump card he could play in order to try to bring some pressure on the sepoys: non-cooperation. His first glimpse of the power he wielded in this way was on 14 May, when the sepoys had disregarded his orders about moving out of his beloved Moonlight Garden, the Mehtab Bagh. Seeing this, Zafar had gone into his private apartments and, 'distracted and perplexed, shut himself up, refusing audience to all'. Before long some of the sepoys began moving out of his garden and into what was left of the cantonments to the north of the city.

Observing the effect of this, Zafar issued an edict a week later, threatening to remove himself from the city altogether, and go off into retirement in Mecca if the plundering of his people did not cease. It was the same threat he had made to Sir Thomas Metcalfe five years earlier. This time it worked. Baqar covered this development approvingly in the *Dihli Urdu Akbhar*:

> It is announced that hearing of the state of ruin and plunder being faced by the population, and the chaos and anarchy that reigns throughout the city, His Exalted Majesty has issued an edict stating that the soldiers are harassing both the population and the loyal servants of State, and making all their lives impossible: 'Earlier the *firangis* issued orders as they pleased to our dear subjects, and the population was always worried and harassed by the English soldiers. Now you Tilangas are causing even more grief and trouble with your plundering. If this continues, then these must be the Last Days. I have no love for the throne or for money, and give notice that I will proceed into retirement towards [the Sufi shrine of] Khwaja Saheb [in Mehrauli], and all the subjects of his Majesty too will accompany their ruler and go with him. Hence I plan to migrate towards the Ka'ba and the Haram Sharif of Mecca, there to spend the rest of my days in prayer, repentance and remembering the Almighty.'
>
> It is said that when this announcement was read, all present in the Durbar became tear-filled. Let us pray that God Almighty, the provider of all aid, will create a situation in which the city is brought to order. This will give relief to the people and also remove the furrows of worry and apprehension from His Majesty's brow . . .[106]

It was not to be. Instead, on 19 May, there were signs of a potentially yet more damaging division. That morning, one of the more Orthodox mullahs of Delhi, Maulvi Muhammad Sayyid, set up a standard of jihad in the Jama Masjid, in an apparent effort to turn the Uprising into an exclusively Muslim holy war. Zafar immediately ordered it to be taken down 'because such a display of fanaticism would only tend to exasperate the Hindus'.

The next day, the 20th, just as news came that the Delhi Field Force was collecting in Ambala, the maulvi turned up at the Palace to remonstrate with Zafar, claiming that the Hindus were all supporters of the English, and that a jihad against them was therefore perfectly legitimate. At the same time a delegation of Delhi Hindus also turned up at the Fort, angrily denying the maulvi's charge. Zafar declared that in his eyes Hindus and Muslims were equal and that 'such a jihad is quite impossible, and such an idea an act of extreme folly, for the majority of the *Purbia* soldiers were Hindus. Such an act would create a civil war and the results would be deplorable. The Holy War is against the English. I have forbidden it against the Hindus'.[107]

At this point in the Uprising, Zafar seems to have succeeded in silencing the jihadis. But eight weeks later, when large numbers of 'Wahhabi' mujahedin had collected in the city from all over northern India, it would prove far more difficult.

7

A PRECARIOUS POSITION

On 23 May, just as General Anson was finally setting off from Ambala, a rider in ragged Hindustani dress approached the perimeter pickets of the British camp in Karnal and demanded entry. When challenged as to his name and business, the man replied that he was Sir Theophilus Metcalfe. The guards just laughed. The Assistant Magistrate at Delhi had long been presumed dead; indeed, report had it that his head was displayed on a pole outside the Ajmeri Gate. But the stranger's remarkable claim turned out to be true: it was indeed Theo, and he had been on the run for nearly two weeks.

For the first few days after the outbreak, Theo had been sheltered on the roof of the zenana of Bhura Khan Mewati in Paharganj, and had been well looked after and fed; in the evening, he and Bhura Khan used to walk out in the direction of Delhi and watch the burning buildings and, on one night, a display of fireworks celebrating the return of Mughal power. All this time, Theo had expected to hear of the arrival of British troops from Meerut to restore British rule. But on the morning of the fourth day, 14 May, with no sign yet of their arrival, Bhura Khan told Theo that he had heard that he had been tracked to his hiding place, and that if he remained the house would be attacked and the whole family murdered. Bhura Khan begged him to move to another place, which he would provide for him. According to the memoir of Theo's sister Emily,

> In the dusk he took Theophilus to a kunker [limestone] pit, out of which material was taken for road making, in which was a small cave. He provided him with a native sword [tulwar] and a pistol, as Bhura Khan said he would be likely to be followed and attacked. The entrance to the cave was small, and Sir Theophilus felt he was equal to dealing with one man at a time. Either that night or the next, he heard footsteps and voices outside, and awaited the appearance of his assailant. There was sufficient light for him to see a man's figure in the entrance, so he sprang on him and cut him down with his tulwar.[1]

Knowing now that his hiding place had been discovered, the following morning Theo sent a message to his friend Muin ud-Din, now Zafar's kotwal, asking for assistance to travel to Jhajjar, where the Nawab was an old friend of the Metcalfe clan. Muin ud-Din had kept in discreet contact with Theo, warning him that there seemed no likelihood of a speedy resolution to the crisis, as both had previously assumed, and 'that whatever must be, would be'. Now he responded by sending 'a good horse, and some money . . . with advice how to travel . . . It was arranged that Sir Theophilus should be dressed as a native soldier, and should be called Shere Khan, by which name henceforward he passed in all our communications'.

The next day Muin ud-Din received a formal receipt of the money from Jhajjar.[2] Muin ud-Din assumed that Theo would be safe with the Nawab of Jhajjar since the two were old friends. Like Muin ud-Din's own Loharu clan, the Nawabs of Jhajjar had risen to power as a result of supporting the British, initially against the Marathas at the beginning of the nineteenth century. The Nawab and the Metcalfes also had the common bond of shared tastes: both were enthusiastic patrons of the Company School paintings of the family workshop of Ghulam and Mazhar Ali Khan. While Sir Thomas had commissioned Mazhar Ali Khan to paint the monuments of the town both in his *Dehlie Book* and in his magnificent panoramic scroll of the city, the Nawab had commissioned Ghulam Ali Khan, who was probably Mazhar's uncle, to paint a series of pictures of his court, one in light summer dress, another with the members of his durbar wrapped in winter shawls; he also commissioned a picture of himself lion hunting and another wonderful image of himself riding around his country garden on his pet tiger.[3]

Yet for all this, the Nawab did not greet Theo as expected. On arrival at the palace of the Nawab, Theo

at once demanded an audience as a friend. The Nawab sent back to ask his name, which he gave. He dismounted and was shown into a small room to await his audience. He was kept waiting some time, and then sent a message, to which the Nawab sent an answer, saying he was welcome to the shelter of his home, but that he could not see him.

During the afternoon several messages passed between them, Sir Theophilus expressing surprise that his friend should treat him in such a neglectful manner. Ultimately the Nawab sent his *sarishtadar* [secretary] with a letter in which he said he could not possibly see Sir Theophilus or keep him in the house as he would be attacked by the King of Delhi if he sheltered any Europeans, but that he would provide him with a horse and a guard of two soldiers to show him the way back to Delhi.

As the Nawab was perfectly aware that Sir Theophilus knew the way to Delhi as well as his soldiers did, it was evident that they were to be sent for no friendly purpose. However, finding that he could get nothing else, Sir Theophilus accepted the offer. The pony provided for him was not his own good pony, but a wretched *tat* which could go no pace. He made the soldiers ride in front of him, to show the way as guides, and under cover of darkness, he turned his pony off the main road, into the sandy jungle and got away as fast as he could in the direction of Hansi. His pony was soon knocked up from fatigue and he had to walk day and night, sleeping in the jungle and eating chuppatties and drinking milk given him by villagers on the road. He heard these people discussing how the Europeans (*sahib log*) had been killed and the government transferred to the King of Delhi.

The following morning, Theo had to leave the shelter of the jungle and return to the high road. He had been walking for some time, when

> he heard the sound of some horsemen riding in haste, and looking back saw two sawars in the Nawab's uniform approaching so rapidly that they would shortly overtake him. He felt convinced that he was the object of their pursuit, and the only chance of shelter was in a village that he was approaching, and which he had not intended to run the risk of entering.
>
> He had, however, no other choice, and was certain that at this hour of high noon, its inhabitants would be taking their siesta inside or in some shady nook in the streets, wrapped in their long robes, concealing their faces from the heat . . . Sir Theophilus followed this example and was fortunate enough to take his place among a group of recumbent sleepers. A few minutes later the sawars came, and demanded loudly to be informed where the Englishman was in hiding, but no answer came, since everyone was asleep. One of the sawars then pricked with his lance the man lying next Sir Theophilus, and repeated the enquiry.
>
> The sleeper, indignant at this rude awakening cursed the sawar and said that no Englishman had passed that way. The soldiers hastened on and when the sound of their galloping had died away, [Theo] crept out of the village as secretly as he had entered it, and hastening back to the jungle remained in hiding till, at a late hour, he had the satisfaction of seeing his pursuers return home, balked of their prey . . . [Several days later] he arrived more dead than alive at Hansi.[4]

In Hansi, Theo made straight for the mansion of another family friend of the Metcalfes, and here he had more luck than in Jhajjar. Alec Skinner was the oldest surviving son of Colonel James Skinner, 'Sikandar Sahib', and the eldest of Elizabeth Wagentrieber's numerous brothers. The Skinners' sprawling Georgian house at Hansi was the mansion her father had built as his principal country seat, and from where in happier days Sikandar had run both his irregular cavalry regiment and his stud.

In the event, however, Theo stayed with the Skinners only one night. The Uprising had not yet spread to Hansi, though the town was tense, and trouble was imminently expected. Instead of resting, as soon as Theo heard from Alec that General Anson was on his way to Karnal, he borrowed a horse and set off at dawn, riding without stopping until he arrived at the British camp. The following day news arrived that the troops in Hansi had broken out in mutiny a few hours after Theo had left; his host and his elderly Muslim mother had had a near-miraculous escape, fleeing through the desert to Bikaner on the back of a single racing camel.

Theo was exhausted and embittered by his ordeal; and his nerves were worn to the point of breakdown. Sir Thomas had always considered Theo unstable and something of a loose cannon; what followed was to prove him right. For Theo was disgusted by what had happened to him and what he had seen; certainly his friends and colleagues soon came to be anxious that the angry, nervy and haunted look that he had when he arrived at Karnal never left him until the end of the Uprising. In the meantime he set out to even the score, as he saw it, and to make sure that those who failed to help him, or murdered his friends or members of his household, were strung up and dealt with, inside or outside the law. As his friend Charles Saunders later put it, 'Metcalfe was so *maddened* with revenge against the Mahometans, that he seemed to have a personal animus fomented by the sight of what he had suffered, and the defection of those whom he had trusted and befriended . . .'5

The following morning Theo wrote to G. B. Thornhill, secretary to the Lieutenant Governor in Agra:

Sir,

I have the honour to inform you that I have reached Kurnul via Hansi from Delhi and although my health is not very good, I write to beg that the Lt Governor will allow me to accompany the force and the Commander in Chief to Delhi in some official capacity: and I trust what local information I possess of the Delhi town and district may be of service to Government . . . I shall be happy at all times to serve where I can be of best use, but after eight years connection with

Delhi, I naturally, in this great emergency, flatter myself that so long
a connection will ensure me employment there.

I have the honour to be, your obedient servant
T METCALFE[6]

In due course Theo's petition was granted; but as subsequent events
were to show, it would have been much better for everyone if his
request had been turned down.

Theo was not alone. All over Hindustan, troops, dacoits, tribesmen
and refugees were all on the move, and by no means all of the latter
were British. A couple of days behind Theo, for example, on the
same road, was the great Urdu literary critic Hali.

After having been tracked down by his family while he was
studying at the 'very spacious and beautiful' madrasa of Husain
Bakhsh, Hali went back with them to Panipat, which lay a little south
of Karnal, on the Grand Trunk Road. A year later, in 1856, his wife
gave birth to an infant son, and Hali realised he must now find a job.
He went alone to the administrative centre of Hissar, a few miles from
the Skinners' house at Hansi, and though he had no connections or
references, eventually found a job in the Deputy Collector's Office.
He was still working there when the Uprising broke out.

After a combination of mutinous sepoys – led by the future
British spy Brigade Major Gauri Shankar Sukul – and Mewati
tribesman rose up, murdered the collector, and marched off with
the treasury to join Zafar's army at Delhi, Hali had little choice but
to set off, 'taking his life in his hands', and return home to Panipat.
On the way he was seized by Gujars and robbed of his horse.
Walking the rest of the way, begging for food, he arrived home with
so bad a case of dysentery, and so raddled by exposure, that despite
being treated by a celebrated hakim, he was sick for more than a
year, and suffered for the rest of his life from a weak stomach, chest
and lungs.[7]

Edward Vibart's party suffered just as badly. After having fled
Metcalfe House less than an hour before it was attacked and

burned, they wandered onward trying to find a place to ford the deep Yamuna canal. To their alarm, they realised that the only way to do so was to double back and cross just below the cantonments. In the hours after darkness fell, this was the most dangerous place in Delhi: the rebel sepoys had congregated there to vent their rage on the Company by looting, destroying and burning down every British bungalow. 'With beating hearts, we crept along the canal-bank,' remembered Vibart in his memoirs,

> and gradually approached the flaming cantonments; but although the forms of numberless marauders were distinctly visible in the act of plundering the adjacent bungalows, we passed on unobserved, and, to our inexpressible relief, found the ford we were in search of without a soul in the immediate vicinity.
>
> We at once prepared to cross over, hoping to place some three or four miles between ourselves and cantonments ere morning broke. It was found not quite such an easy matter, however, to get the ladies across, as the water was considerably deeper than we anticipated, and on my going in to lead the way, I found the water breast-high.[8]

The group wandered on by the waning light of the moon through a thorny uncultivated plain. The ladies were unused to walking, and by now their feet were blistered and bleeding. More worryingly, Mr Forrest was beginning to behave oddly after his severe shock at the explosion of the magazine earlier in the day: he was beginning to lag badly behind, occasionally disappearing altogether. By dawn the refugees had gone no more than three miles from the cantonments, and were becoming increasingly aware that the only weapons they had between them were two old regimental swords and a double-barrelled fowling piece. Having made their way to some scrub jungle, they all lay down among the brushwood and, worn out with fatigue, began to drowse. 'I was just on the point of dropping off to sleep,' wrote Vibart, 'when suddenly someone shook me by the arm, exclaiming the sepoys were upon us.'

> Not one hundred yards distant, and coming in a direct line towards us, we perceived a body of some eight or ten sepoys, stragglers from

Meerut, two of whom were mounted on ponies. The imperfect light of the dawning day was just sufficient to show us they were armed, though only half were dressed in uniform. They were making for Delhi by a country track, and were bearing down straight for the spot where we lay concealed . . . We had barely time to creep under the bushes and hide ourselves as well as we could when they were upon us. We watched them in breathless anxiety, not daring to move, and scarcely to breathe.

Now they slowly pass in Indian file within a few feet of us . . . One of them stoops and picks up something from the ground, and whispers to his comrades, and then all come to a sudden halt. Alas! Our water bottle has betrayed us! In our hurry and confusion we had left it lying in the open . . . There was complete silence, broken only by the low mutterings of the sepoys . . . I involuntarily cocked my gun . . . [But] after a brief interval we saw them silently move off . . .[9]

During the following days, however, the group's luck ran out. Wandering aimlessly in the heat through a bare plain in what they hoped would be the direction of Meerut, without food or money, they watched as Forrest descended into distracted madness, hiding in bushes and refusing to follow, 'saying he felt so thoroughly worn out from all he had gone through that he would far rather be left in peace to die where he was'. Two days later, they met another equally ragged party of Delhi refugees, led by Vibart's commanding officer, Colonel Knyvett, raising the number in the party to seventeen. Shortly afterwards, however, they were all surrounded

by fierce looking men, armed with spears and bludgeons. These were none other than the dreaded Gujars themselves. Their numbers increased rapidly, and, in whichever direction we looked, we observed others, similarly armed, running towards us. At length when they had completely hemmed us in, they gave a fearful shout, and rushed upon us. We stood back to back, and made a vain attempt to beat them off; but, being [outnumbered] ten to one, we were soon overpowered. One rascal laid hold of my sword, and tried to wrench it out of my hand. In vain I resisted; a blow from behind stretched me on my back . . .

In the midst of all this melee I saw Colonel Knyvett levelling the gun he was carrying point-blank at one of the wretches . . . fortunately someone shouted out to him not to fire; so, deliberately removing the caps, he gave it up. It was as well we permitted ourselves to be disarmed for had we continued the struggle, our lives would undoubtedly have been sacrificed.

Having once got us down, they set to work stripping us of everything. Studs, rings, watches, etc. were all torn off. They did not even spare my inner vest . . . One of the ladies literally had the clothes torn off her back, whilst the others were treated with similar barbarity. At last when they had appropriated everything, leaving only our shirts and trousers, and the ladies their upper garments, the entire band retreated a short distance and commenced quarrelling over the spoil.[10]

Three further days of parched, thirsty wandering later, after Forrest had again disappeared and been found, a second Gujar war band surrounded the party, but 'finding nothing to rob us of, contented themselves with pulling off the gilt buttons on the colonel's frock-coat, which the other rascals had overlooked, and permitted us to pass on'.[11]

Help, when it finally arrived a full week after the party had fled Delhi, came from the most unlikely quarter. Franz Gottlieb Cohen, who wrote 'a camel load of poetic works' in Persian and Urdu under the pen-name 'Farasu', was one of the last of the White Mughals, an eighty-year-old relic of a very different and less polarised era.[12] The son of a German-Jewish soldier of fortune who had married a Mughal princess, Farasu was born in 1777 while his father was in the service of the enigmatic Begum Sumru of Sardhana.[13]

The Begum Sumru presided over one of the most fascinatingly hybrid courts in India. She was originally said to have been a Kashmiri dancing girl named Farzana Zeb un-Nissa, born 1751, whose rapid rise to fortune began when she became the *bibi* of a German mercenary, Walter Reinhardt, known as 'Sombre' (Indianised to 'Sumru') after his severe expression. When the Mughal Emperor gave Reinhardt a large estate in the Doab north of Delhi,

Reinhardt's begum went with him and turned the village of Sard-hana into their capital, with a ruling class drawn from both Mughal noblemen and a ragged bunch of over two hundred ne'er-do-well French and central European mercenaries, many of whom appar-ently converted to Islam.[14] Among these mercenaries was Farasu's father, John-Augustus Gottlieb Cohen.

After Sombre's death, his begum ruled in his stead, partly from Sardhana, and partly from her large Delhi palace on Chandni Chowk. She converted to Catholicism – while continuing to cover her head in the Muslim manner – and appealed directly to the Pope to send a chaplain for her court. By the time the intriguingly named Father Julius Caesar turned up in Sardhana, the begum had already begun to build the largest cathedral in northern India, in a style that promiscuously mixed baroque and Mughal motifs, with a great classical dome rising from Mughal squinches decorated with honeycombed Persian *murqana* motifs.*[15]

As the architecture of her cathedral indicated, there was nothing orthodox about the begum's Christianity. The three-day-long Christmas festivities at Sardhana were opened by high mass, while 'the following two days [were enlivened] by a nautch and a display of fireworks'. This was an opportunity for the Sardhana poets, including Farasu, to recite their Urdu verses.[16] Dussera, Diwali and Holi were celebrated with equal enthusiasm; in addition to which the begum also dabbled in witchcraft – the diary of her heir, the wonderfully named David Ochterlony Dyce Sombre, contains several references to the begum's employing women to cast spells and conduct exorcisms.[17]

Three of the begum's European mercenary officers became major Urdu poets, of whom the most distinguished was Farasu; he was even included in the list of the most prominent Indian poets

---

* Stranger still is the graveyard, now an overgrown and little-visited place hidden behind the Sardhana bus station, where the begum's European mercenaries, including Farasu and his father, are buried in miniature Palladian Taj Mahals covered with a crazy riot of hybrid ornament, where baroque putti cavort around Persian inscriptions and where latticed jali screens rise to round classical arches. At the four corners of the dome, at the base of the drum, where you would expect to find minarets or at least small minars, there stand instead four baroque amphorae.

produced by the principal of Delhi College, Alois Sprenger. According to the Persian inscription on Farasu's tomb, 'he was in the service of Her Highness for 50 years, the last 32 as *tahsildar* of Budhana'.[18]

After the British unilaterally annexed the begum's estate on her death, Farasu, now an old man, continued as *tahsildar* under the British, based in his rambling haveli in the village of Harchandpur.* It was from here that he sent out search parties as soon as news reached him that half-naked British refugees were wandering around his estates, starving and thirsty. '[When] a messenger arrived from Harchandpore, saying his master, a Mr Cohen, hearing of our miserable plight, had sent him to express his sympathy at our situation, and begging us to take shelter with him . . . we were naturally overjoyed,' wrote Vibart.

> Arriving there between seven and eight o'clock, we were cordially welcomed by the old man and his two grandsons. It appeared they owned several villages round about, for which they annually paid a certain sum to the government. The old man himself had lived here all his life – so long in fact that he had almost forgotten his own language, and had become thoroughly native in all his habits; but his two grandsons were somewhat different in this respect, and lived in a more European fashion.

---

* Deprived of the right to inherit the estate, the begum's heir, David Ochterlony Dyce Sombre, went to England to seek justice, where he was eventually elected to Parliament from Sudbury in Suffolk on the Whig Radical (Liberal) ticket, so becoming the first Asian MP. The election was subsequently declared invalid owing to the scale of the bribes Sombre had paid, while his English wife, Mary Anne Jervis, later succeeded in having him declared insane and committed to a lunatic asylum. Sombre somehow managed to escape and made his way to France, where he was certified as perfectly sane and filed a suit alleging that his wife had bribed a doctor to have him locked up so that she could seize his fortune; he also published a 591-page book, *Mr Dyce Sombre's Refutation of the Charge of Lunacy*. He continued to sue unsuccessfully in an attempt to get his fortune back, his case not helped by his increasingly eccentric and publicly immoral behaviour with a succession of prostitutes, until he eventually died, dejected and alone, on 1 July 1851. His story has some striking parallels to Wilkie Collins's *The Woman in White*; it is also said to have provided the basis of the Jules Verne novel *The Begum's Fortune*. See the excellent account in chapter eight of Michael Fisher's *Counterflows to Colonialism*, New Delhi, 2005.

We were soon refreshed with a cup of hot tea, after which clean clothes were brought, and we proceeded to divest ourselves of the soiled rags we were wearing, and enjoyed the luxury of soap and water. A room was set apart for the ladies of the party, and they too managed to procure a change of apparel, in the shape of some clean *koortas* and snowy white *chuddahs* of fine nankeen, which later they wore over their heads and draped around their shoulders in native style, and really looked so spruce and tidy in their novel costume, when they joined us at breakfast [the following morning], that we could scarcely recognise them as the forlorn creatures of yesterday . . .

As for Forrest . . . he remained shut up in old Mr Cohen's 'sanctum sanctorum,' enjoying the luxury of a punkah and smoking a fragrant hookah . . . At four o'clock pm a plentiful repast was set before us, and to our no small astonishment, several bottles of beer produced, followed, when dinner was removed, by a bottle of excellent cognac . . .[19]

Shortly afterwards, alerted by Farasu, a rescue party and an escort of cavalry arrived from Meerut. It was now eight days since the party had fled Delhi. By the following night, all seventeen refugees were safe within the shelter of the now heavily fortified and entrenched British cantonment at Meerut.

Eight days later, on the evening of 27 May, General Wilson finally gathered enough bullocks to leave Meerut in belated pursuit of the mutineers. His small force numbered only 2,000 infantry, fifty cavalry and six guns; its destination was Alipore, 8 miles north of Delhi, where it was supposed to rendezvous with the main Field Force heading south from Ambala.

Before leaving, Wilson – a small, neat, goateed gentleman of sixty – wrote confidently to his wife, who was up in the hill station of Mussoorie, that 'the mutineers . . . show no wish to come and attack us'.[20] In this, as in so many other things, General Wilson was proved quite wrong. Zafar had in fact been urging an attack on

Meerut for some time, largely with a view to getting as many sepoys as he could out of both his palace and his city. The expedition also had the added recommendation of providing a way to remove from the Red Fort Zafar's troublesome grandson, the new commander of the cavalry, Mirza Abu Bakr.

Since his promotion to lead the rebel *sawars* a fortnight earlier, Mirza Abu Bakr had become a major liability. Liberated from his former status as a minor princeling, he had begun swaggering around with his troops, committing outrages both in the city and around about. Sent out to defend the suburbs against Gujars, he had looted both the Sabzi Mandi, the area around Safdarjung's Tomb, and Gurgaon: 'the said Mirza plundered the region and set fire to it', recorded one Urdu newsletter.[21] Shortly afterwards he had led an expedition to Rohtak with Mir Nawab, 'the leader of the city rebels', where, according to one eyewitness, they

> plundered and burnt every house in the Civil Lines, looted the city, maltreated the males and outraged the women. Mir Nawab himself carried off three fair Hindoo girls loaded with costly ornaments. Mirza Abu Bukr and his army of oppressors then returned to Delhi bringing the whole of the government treasure and accompanied by the traitorous sepoy guard.[22]

Since then he and the Mir Nawab had amused themselves attacking the haveli of the leader of Delhi's Shia community, Hamid Ali Khan, 'bringing up guns against the house to blow him away on the [quite unfounded] pretext that he was in league with the English'. Zafar was outraged when a distress message from Hamid Ali Khan reached him and demanded that the assault stop immediately. But when he instructed the cavalry not to obey Abu Bakr's orders they refused, replying, 'He is our officer. Why should we not go where he tells us?'[23] Abu Bakr was briefly suspended from command of the cavalry, but the order seems to have been ignored.[24] So when Zafar heard that Mirza Abu Bakr now wished to lead an expedition against the British in Meerut, he was only too pleased to let him go, ordering him 'to go with his troops towards Meerut where there are English cannon which he must capture and deliver as soon as possible'.[25]

An expedition to Meerut had in fact been canvassed for some time by Maulvi Muhammad Baqar in the *Dihli Urdu Akbhar*, and recently his editorials had begun to complain about the unnecessary delays in the departure of the expeditionary force: 'Every day there is news that the troops are about to leave for Meerut, but it never seems to happen,' he wrote on 31 May.

> The wise have long been saying that no delay should be made in taking Meerut and Karnal, and the Christians cannot prosper when opposed by the Almighty . . . The exalted Murshidzada Mirza Abu Bakr is very keen to lead such an expedition and has in fact pleaded before his Majesty to let him take a sizeable contingent. He should be given his way as then the matter could be quickly settled.[26]

There followed one final delay when the sepoys insisted that Zafar accompany them to battle, saying:

> 'You will then see how we will fight for you.' The King replied that he was old and infirm, could with difficulty move about, and had been unable to go even as far as the 'Idgah on the great day of prayer ['Id], even though it was close outside the city walls. Nor had he or his ancestors from the time of Furuksiyar, a period of 108 years, ever seen a battle, adding, 'I know nothing of military tactics, but you do.' The officers replied that if unable to go himself he must send one of his sons.[27]

Finally, two days before Wilson left Meerut, on 25 May, 'under pressure from the King', a large force of sepoys, supported by field and horse artillery under Mirza Abu Bakr, set off from Delhi in a bid to take Meerut.[28] Neither side had any idea that an army belonging to the other was heading in its direction.

Wilson's march from Meerut proved as chaotic as Anson's had been from Simla. No camels could be found, and the rustic bullock carts

the British had commandeered proved quite unsuitable for trans-
porting an army.²⁹ 'It was a dreadful mess of confusion this first
march,' he admitted to his wife on the 28th, 'but I hope we shall do
better tonight. Our carriage is chiefly hackeries, a source of very
great trouble and inconvenience.'³⁰

Wilson did not mention it, but his march had also been remarkable for its brutal and unfocused attempts at taking revenge on any
of the local population who were unfortunate enough to come in
the way of his column: according even to the Anglophile policeman
Sa'id Mubarak Shah, who was no critic of the British, 'Reprisals
were taken as the troops advanced, and hundreds of innocent
travellers, as well as [genuine] dacoits and highway robbers were
seized and hanged.'³¹

The two rival expedionary forces finally met, to the great surprise
of both, at the new British-built steel suspension bridge over the
Hindan river, at half past four in the afternoon of 30 May. The first
short engagement ended in the British crossing the bridge and
driving back the sepoys with only light casualties; but the rebels
returned at 1 p.m. the following day for a much more fiercely fought
engagement.³² According to Muin ud-Din,

> The battle began with artillery fire. [Mirza Abu Bakr] mounted onto
> the roof of a house near the River Hindan close to the bridge across
> the river and watched the battle. From time to time he sent messages
> to his artillery to tell them of the havoc their fire was creating in the
> English ranks.
>
> Near the bridge he placed a battery with which he carried on an
> exchange of fire with the English, which became like a conversation
> of question and answer. Presently a shell burst near the battery,
> covering the gunner with dust . . . [Mirza Abu Bakr] experiencing
> for the first time the effects of a bursting shell, hastily descended
> from the roof of the house, mounted his horse, and galloped off with
> his escort of sawars far into the rear of the position, not heeding the
> cries of his troops.
>
> A general stampede then took place. When the news reached Delhi
> that the troops had been defeated, orders were issued to close the gates
> and exclude the sepoys. When these arrived they found the Yamuna

Bridge [of Boats] had been broken down.* In a hurried attempt to cross it the bridge gave way, and about two hundred were drowned.[33]

Although Wilson had won an important and symbolic victory, the artillery of the sepoys had been much more effective than anticipated and British casualties had been severe; indeed, it almost stopped Wilson's advance dead in its tracks: 'My loss has been heavy,' he wrote that evening to his wife, 'and such as I can ill afford with my small force. Another such victory would annihilate me.'[34] He himself was nearly killed twice when showers of grape twice whistled around him, but left him miraculously unhurt.[35]

Moreover, there was still no sign of General Barnard's Delhi Field Force, and the horse artillery of Major Tombs, whose rapid manoeuvres had been the key to the British victory, was now virtually out of ammunition: 'I am left with my small force to withstand the whole strength of the insurgents,' Wilson wrote anxiously on 1 June.[36] Briefly he considered retreating back to Meerut, but the following day he was unexpectedly reinforced by the Sirmoor Regiment of Gurkhas and a party of sappers who had marched down from Dehra Dun, and who were also looking for General Barnard.[37] 'I found Brigadier Wilson in rather an awkward predicament,' wrote Colonel Reid, the commander of the Sirmoor Regiment, 'and dreading another attack . . . He was rejoiced at my having joined him so soon, and was quite taken by surprise.'[38]

In the meantime, however, as Wilson hesitated, the momentum of the victory at the Hindan Bridge was lost. As Muin ud-Din noted,

The sepoys had now contended with the English on the open field. They had felt certain of success, but they had been worsted, and were filled with grave apprehension for the future . . . [But] the English did not follow up the victory; they were not to be seen, and gradually the sepoys forgot their fright.[39]

* Presumably for fear of a British pursuit.

If Barnard's force was making frustratingly slow progress to the
rendezvous with Wilson, one reason was the number of Indians it
casually slaughtered as it passed down the Grand Trunk Road: 'I
don't consider niggers in the same light as I would a white man,'
one officer wrote to his brother from the march. 'To be gracious or
merciful to these cruel brutes, these cowardly monsters, is nothing
more nor less than to be absurd in their own eyes whilst you
certainly don't advance your own cause.'[40]

The night before the Field Force met up with Wilson, a
particularly bloody incident had occurred at the village of Rhai
after 'a man of the 9th Lancers found under the bridge of a small
dried up watercourse a little [British] child's foot still in the shoe,
cut off at the ankle joint'.[41] Richard Barter, a twenty-nine-year-old
lieutenant with the 75th Gordon Highlanders, was asleep in his
tent when the foot was brought in at the height of the day's heat,
around 2 p.m.

> Immediately after there arose the hum of voices like the sound of
> some huge bee-hive disturbed, there was a rush of many feet, and in
> an incredibly short space of time every village within reach of the
> camp was in a blaze; several officers joined in the performance . . .
> nine [villagers] were hung from a large tree by the roadside after
> parade.[42]

Theo Metcalfe, it emerged later, was one of the leaders of the lynch
mobs.

For many in the Field Force, the reports of the atrocities performed
by the mutinous sepoys – already fanned by hearsay to include
non-existent mass rapes – just went to confirm their own existing
prejudices. For Robert Dunlop, a Scottish civilian who had volunteered to join an irregular cavalry unit known as the Khaki
Risalah, the slaughter of innocent women and children in Delhi and
Meerut proved to his own satisfaction what he had already long
believed about

the weak and childish but cruel and treacherous native character . . .
It is a patent fact that the proud contempt which the Anglo-Saxon
bears to the Asiatic has proved, to a great extent, the salvation of our
Indian Empire. Nearly all men come to this country fully prepared
to accord equal rights and privileges to its dusky inhabitants; but . . .
experience leads to a common conviction of their debasement.[43]

One woman on the march who stood out against such nakedly racist
attitudes was Harriet Tytler. After escaping from Delhi, she and her
husband had made their way to Ambala, where Robert, unemployed
after the disintegration of his regiment, the 38th Native Infantry,
managed to get a new appointment in charge of the Field Force's
military treasure chest. Marching now slowly back along the road
down which they had fled so desperately three weeks earlier, the
Tytlers were horrified by the wanton brutality of the British troops
they marched alongside. The same day on which the child's foot was
brought into the camp, the now heavily pregnant Harriet saw

a poor little man, a Mohammedan baker, in clean white clothes
dangling from the branch of an acacia tree. From what we could
gather, this poor man had been late for several days with his bread
for the men's breakfast, so Tommie Atkins* threatened to hang him
if it happened again and so they did. I can't understand how such a
cruel deed was allowed, for they in their turn should have been
hanged, but I suppose a single soldier could not have been spared,
even in the cause of justice. Probably most of those who committed
this deed were themselves called to account to a Higher Power
during their siege to answer for their sins.[44]

A little later Robert Tytler managed to save a camp follower from a
similar fate:

Just outside my husband's tent, we heard a piteous cry from a poor
old man of 'Duha' i Sahib Kee, Duha' i Sahib Kee' ('Mercy sirs,

---

* Victorian slang for the generic British infantryman, hence Tommies for a group of
British soldiers.

Mercy sirs') and saw some of the soldiers dragging him away, evidently to hang him. I sent my husband flying after them, telling them to save the poor old man. As soon as he got up to them he said, 'Boys what are you going to do with that poor old man?'

'Why hang him, sir, of course. He is a Pandee (a rebel).* We saw him dancing before his bullocks.'

Captain Tytler replied, 'Nonsense boys, he is no Pandee, only a bullock cart driver.'

'Oh no, we know he is a Pandee sir,' ejaculated all the men.

My husband replied again, 'I see you boys only want a little fun. Let the poor chap go and run after that dog and hang him instead.'

'I see sir, that you don't want us to hang him.'

'No indeed I don't.'

So they let him go and ran after a dog, and strung him up there and then.[45]

On Trinity Sunday, 7 June, General Wilson finally led his forces into General Barnard's newly pitched camp at Alipore, 8 miles north of Delhi. Here Theo was introduced to his new boss, Hervey Greathed, formerly the Commissioner of Meerut, who was the most senior British civilian officer with the Field Force: '[Metcalfe] says he is well enough to work,' wrote Greathed, 'and his knowledge of Delhi will prove very useful to me.' The two worked well together: 'I like Metcalfe very much,' wrote Greathed a little later. 'He is a most cheery, merry fellow, – nothing puts him out.'[46]

Here too Theo received word of his sister GG and her husband Edward Campbell: the latter had managed to escape unscathed when his troops broke out into mutiny at Sialkot, and he had since made his way to Simla, where he was reunited with the pregnant GG in Constantia, the house where they had been married in 1852.

---

* If a Tommy was the generic slang for the British soldier at this time, then a Pandee (or Pandey) was the slang for an insurgent sepoy. The name derived from Mangal Pandey, who was one of the first sepoys to rise up against the Company, shooting and wounding two of his officers from 19th Native Infantry on 29 March at Barrackpore in Bengal while shouting, 'It's for our religion. From biting these cartridges we will become infidels.' See Rudrangshu Mukherjee's brief but brilliant *Mangal Pandey: Brave Martyr or Accidental Hero?*, New Delhi, 2005.

But almost immediately Edward had been ordered to march down to join Theo in the Delhi Field Force: 'We are watching anxiously the progress of the army towards Delhi,' he wrote to his mother soon after his arrival in Simla. 'Much depends on the way it is handled . . . We are now all in God's hands.'[47]

Also in the Field Force's Alipore camp was William Hodson and his spymaster Rajab Ali, busy co-ordinating the reports now flowing in from their spies in Delhi. Hodson was deeply depressed at the slowness of the Field Force to engage with the sepoys: 'All Rohilcund is in Mutiny,' he wrote to his wife. 'In fact the district of Agra is the only one in the North West Provinces now under our control. What a terrible lesson on the evils of delay. It will be long yet, I fear, ere this business is over.' He added: 'Yet personally I have no reason to complain.'[48]

When the Field Force marched out of camp at 1 a.m. on the morning of 8 June, Hodson was in the lead, scouting ahead, and it was he who shortly afterwards brought news of the newly fortified rebel front line that had been erected just ahead of the British forces around the old Mughal caravanserai of Badli ki Serai.

Mirza Mughal had not wasted the time between the defeat at Hindan Bridge and the arrival of the Delhi Field Force at Alipore.

Teams of workmen had been pressed into service repairing the neglected walls of Delhi, while batteries of artillery had been erected at Salimgarh, on several of the bastions on the city walls, and also outside the city along the Ridge, the rocky spine of the Aravalli Hills to the north-east of the cantonments. The orders from Mirza Mughal's secretariat to the kotwal are full of urgency: 'Collect as many labourers as can be gathered for finishing the batteries. This is of the utmost urgency. Do not delay. I will not accept any excuses or laziness on the part of you or your staff.'[49] Other orders ask for camels, bullock carts, panniers to carry dirt, axes, shovels, water carriers and for yet more coolies to help in constructing entrenchments.[50]

Most impressive of all was a strong defensive position Mirza

Mughal had caused to be established at an old caravanserai on the Grand Trunk Road, blocking access to Delhi from the north. It was an ideal place for a stand. With marshland on either side, a line of artillery had been entrenched between the serai and a small hillock to the west, straddling both sides of the road and providing a small but bristling Mughal Maginot Line: any force coming from the direction of Alipore would have no option but to charge down a narrow causeway straight into the face of the massed Mughal guns.

A large infantry force commanded by Mirza Khizr Sultan, and assisted by the chief eunuch, Mahbub Ali Khan, was sent up at 6 p.m. on the 7th, and placed between and behind the batteries to await the imminent British assault, which was expected on the morning of the 8th. Before they went, Mahbub Ali Khan 'distributed tasty bread and *nuqul* [small, hard sweets, made of jaggery, cashews, almonds and sesame seeds] among the soldiers. The subahdars of the sepoys kissed the feet of the King, and so left for battle'.[51] Alerted by the sound of a bugle blowing, Zahir Dehlavi looked out from the walls of the Red Fort, and watched the troops and ammunition train leaving the city, wondering what the morning would bring.[52]

A few hours later, Mirza Mughal sent his father a note, assuring him that he need not be anxious. 'Lord and World-refuge, peace!' he wrote.

> May Your Majesty's mind be secure from any fear of our enemies: your servant has been for the last two days, together with his troops, present at the trenches. Wherever the trench-diggers are, there he is. Rest assured our enemies will come no closer – I have brought all the troops to the front line to slay the infidels. Battle is about to be joined, and with God's undiminished grace Your Majesty is about to witness the conquest of his enemies.[53]

When the British forces began to move forward at 1 a.m., Richard Barter of the 75th Gordon Highlanders found himself in the front line.

Three hours of marching later, just after 4.20 a.m., the rebel position came into view in the darkness, illuminated by a single bonfire that had been lit by the sepoy gunners. 'A jet of smoke went up from a small mound near the fire,' he wrote afterwards,

and presently a round shot from a large piece of ordnance came tearing through some trees to the right of the road. The order was now given to the 75th to wheel [to the right] ... whilst our deployment was going on another shot came from the Enemy and striking the horse of Grant, our interpreter, full in the chest, passed clean through his body and out at his tail, giving his rider a nasty fall but not hurting him otherwise. Immediately after there was a cry to my left close to where Grant's horse had been killed and I saw our first wounded man fall to the rear with his arm smashed by a shot.

They were coming in thick and fast now, and as we were directly in front of the enemy's battery and they had our range exactly, the General ordered the 75th to lie down while the other regiments were getting into position. I was not at all sorry to dismount and made myself as small as I possibly could, while the shot went shrieking over our heads with the peculiar sound which once heard is never forgotten. After a few minutes the order came, 'The 75th will advance and take that battery.' In an instant the line was up.

Soon our fellows were dropping fast . . . their shot striking the line at every discharge. I remember one in particular taking a man's head off, or rather smashing it to pieces and covering my old Colour Sergeant Walsh with blood and brains so that it was some time before he could see again.

Barter's troops soon got to within 150 yards of the sepoys' batteries, and could see their infantry drawn up in line on the low ground, firing at the advancing British.

Gaps were made in the different Companies only to be filled up the next moment, and still the line advanced . . . I saw a shrapnel shell burst exactly in the faces of one of the Companies of the right wing. It tore a wide gap and the men near it involuntarily turned away. I called out, 'Don't turn men, don't turn,' and was at once answered 'Never fear Mister Barter sir, we ain't agoing to turn.' And on they went quietly closing up the gap made by their fallen comrades.

The time had come to end all this and . . . the order was given '75th prepare to charge' and down went the long line of bayonets . . . a wild shout, or rather yell of vengeance went up from the line as it rushed to the charge. The enemy followed our movements, their bayonets were also lowered and their advance was steady as they came to meet us, but when the exultant shout arose, they could not stand it, their line wavered and undulated, many began firing with their firelocks at their hips, and at last, as we were closing on them, the whole turned and ran for dear life followed by a shout of derisive laughter from our fellows. In three minutes the 75th stood breathless but victors in the Enemy's battery, capturing the heavy guns in it, and in the large camp to the rear a number of field pieces and heaps of small arms and ammunition.[54]

This capture of the rebels' field guns proved a crucial strategic moment for the British, leaving the sepoy infantry largely unsupported for the rest of the siege.[55]

By eight o'clock in the morning it was all over. One of the first to flee on the rebel side was Mirza Khizr Sultan. He had placed himself at the forefront of the action, wearing 'a very brilliant headpiece which sparkled and glistened in the sun', but as soon as the British round-shot began falling to the Prince's right he retired on the excuse of 'bringing up magazine stores separated from the main body'.[56] Mahbub Ali Khan tried to stop him running away, but without success, and after that 'nothing could stay the sepoys as they hurried towards the city, pouring through the Kashmir, Lahore and Kabul Gates, leaving the gates open behind them'.[57] According to Sa'id Mubarak Shah, 'vast numbers of the mutineers, horse, foot and artillery were killed and still more wounded that day. Scores of dead were scattered over the battlefield, but most of the wounded either by their own exertions, or assisted by their friends, managed to reach the city'.[58]

For some of the British it proved a bittersweet victory. It was not just that they had suffered more severe casualties than they had expected, and far more than their small force could spare; it was also that among the dead the troops recognised sepoys they had known and befriended. This was particularly so for the officers of the 38th Native Infantry, which had been stationed in the Delhi cantonments until the outbreak, and which was so cut up by the British assault at Badli that it never again took to the field as one body.[59] Passing the battlefield, Robert Tytler saw his old orderly, Thakur Singh, who had begged to come in the carriage with the Tytlers when they were escaping from the Flagstaff Tower, and had been turned down as there was no room; he was lying side by side with his uncle, the regimental havildar, whom the Tytlers had known for over a decade. Harriet jotted down her complicated feelings about the dead sepoys in her memoir: 'I saw some of our fine, tall, handsome men lying somewhat swollen by the heat and stark naked,' she wrote.

> Every camp follower had robbed them of their gold and silver and jewels, and the last comers of the clothes on their bodies, leaving the poor fellows just as God made them. Such handsome, splendid specimens of high-casted Hindus. One man a hole as large as a billiard ball through his forehead, a perfect giant in death. At any other time my heart would have been full of pity and sorrow at such awful sights . . . but I could not help saying 'serves you right for killing our poor women and children who never injured you.'[60]

At eleven o'clock the front line of British troops paused briefly at Ochterlony's old garden, Mubarak Bagh, which he had bought and named for his *bibi*. Barnard, however, decided not to stop his advance, and without waiting to rest further, pressed on through the burned-out cantonments – 'costly furniture lying about in all directions and the walls of some of the bungalows besmeared with the blood of the victims' – on towards the Ridge.[61] Here he divided his force into two columns so as to be able to attack it from both sides.

On the heights, Mirza Mughal's newly erected batteries were taken with little resistance. According to Zahir Dehlavi, who was watching anxiously from the city walls, the rebels who were posted on the Ridge seeing their fellow rebels fleeing as fast as they could inside the city, left their posts and abandoned the cannons, tents and all their ammunition and fled into the city. When the English army reached the Cantonment they saw that all the entrenchments on the Ridge were completely quiet. So they went up and occupied those posts, burnt the rebel camps, and turned the abandoned cannon towards the city.[62]

The only serious resistance the British met was at the Flagstaff Tower, the scene of such confusion a month earlier. Here alone the sepoys held their ground and 'met the Europeans with a withering volley which killed many and wounded a great number'.[63] Late in the afternoon there was also a belated attempt at a counter-attack up through the Sabzi Mandi. This was driven off by the Gurkhas with the unsheathed kukhri knives.[64] By 5 p.m., the entire Ridge was in British hands.

Soon afterwards the British found that the bullock cart full of bodies from the first British casualties of the outbreak was still standing near the Flagstaff Tower; now all that remained were the victims' bare skeletons and uniforms, the regimental buttons still gleaming.[65]

Meanwhile, down in the city, there was no disguising the scale of the defeat suffered by the sepoys. Zahir Dehlavi was on his way to work at the Palace when he saw the first casualties of the battle pouring in.

About eight in the morning, I was going to the fort to attend to my duty. When I reached the gate of the Johari bazaar, I saw a large number of injured coming to the city. Each injured man was being helped by four or five *Purbias*. The road was discoloured with dripping blood, bathed in red as if it were Holi. Two mounted soldiers passed close by me. I saw that they had bullet marks on their chest like small holes, and on their backs blood was flowing like a fountain. Their guts must have been in tatters, yet in their right hand they were holding the pistols and also the reins of the horse. There was no pain or panic on their faces, they were well in command of themselves and were talking to each other. To this day I am surprised as to how it was possible for them to survive with such wounds, let alone how were they able to ride in the four miles from the battle.

A little later I saw a mounted soldier galloping fast on a horse. He too was scarred with the deep marks of bullets, and blood was flowing from the wounds like water from a tap, so that he was covered all over with gore. Behind him was another man on foot who had lost his arm. A couple of *Purbias* were with him assuring him that they would take him to the camp hospital from there, but that man was resisting this and telling them to stay away from him. By the time I reached the Fort I had encountered many such injured soldiers.[66]

Amid a rising sense of panic, only Mirza Mughal kept his head, saying that, as in a game of chess, as long as the king was next to the castle, 'he was firmly seated beyond all fear of check mate'.[67]

According to Munshi Jiwan Lal, despite the scale of the British victory, the day marked a major missed opportunity in that they did not attempt to take the city. 'The city people mounted onto the roofs of their houses,' he wrote,

and watched with great fear the distant firing . . . [They] poured volleys of abuse upon the mutineers who were seen returning to the city, accusing them of cowardice, while the troops at the city gates abused the native cavalry, which returned early in the day and took refuge in the city . . . Owing to the result of the battle, the soldiers seemed to lose all heart . . . It is much to be regretted that the English did not advance this day. Had they done so, they would have taken the city for the gates were open and the city people expressed their surprise at their holding back.[68]

Yet there was some wisdom in Barnard's decision to halt at the Ridge, and to secure the heights overlooking the city. That night the British erected their tents in the shelter of the burned-out cantonment bungalows. Having conquered the high ground, and erected their guns overlooking the north wall of the city, it did not, however, take long for them to realise the extreme precariousness of their position, even without risking it further by attempting to press on into the city streets.

In the days that followed, from their observation posts on top of the spine of the Ridge, the British could soon see regiment after mutinous regiment pouring into the city over the Bridge of Boats, and also, more alarmingly, from their own rear down the Grand Trunk Road. Every new body of mutineers arriving only emphasised that there was no prospect of relief, at least on a similar scale, for their own small force.

The next day, as shelling from the rebel batteries in the city began hitting the exposed British positions with surprising force and accuracy, and a steady succession of day and night attacks from the city began to wear away at British numbers, many started to realise that a strange reversal of roles was in the process of taking place. As the chaplain of the Field Force, the Reverend John Edward Rotton, succinctly put it:

To a civilian like myself, I freely confess it did seem to savour of rashness to dream of the capture of Delhi with little more than two battalions of infantry, a small force of European cavalry, and no great strength of artillery . . . We came to besiege Delhi, but we very soon learnt that, in reality, we were the besieged, and the mutineers the besiegers.[69]

8

BLOOD FOR BLOOD

The shelling of Delhi began on 10 June.

Initially only very slight damage was done. The British at this stage had relatively few cannon, and no large siege guns, and for most Delhiwallahs the artillery duels provided little more than entertainment. The British were hopelessly outgunned by the lines of heavy cannon massed along the bastions of the city walls and, as William Hodson himself observed on the first day of the siege, 'they are splendid artillerymen, and beat ours in accuracy of fire'.[1] So the people of Delhi poured out on to their flat roofs, while 'the King and the royal family took their seats at the top of the Palace' and the *salatin* watched from the bastions of the Red Fort.[2] 'It was hot weather at the time,' remembered Sarvar ul-Mulk, 'and every night we used to watch the glare of the cannon balls passing overhead; and we considered them pyrotechnics.'[3]

It was less entertaining, however, when one of the balls landed on your house, as happened a month later in Sarvar ul-Mulk's family haveli. 'A cannon-ball tore through the roof of the upper storey,' he wrote, 'and fell on the verandah where we were having our meal. My uncle at once ran towards it and threw pots full of water onto it.'[4]

The Palace proved an easy target for British gunners, and one British howitzer was soon fixed permanently so as to lob shells

inside Shah Jahan's red stone walls.[5] Zahir Dehlavi noticed the way
the British were singling out the beautiful white marble royal
apartments for their shelling. 'Every day there was firing from
posts all along the Ridge,' he wrote,

> and as they perfected their range, the shells used to create havoc on
> bursting. If a cannon ball fell on a several-storey building it would go
> in right through it to the floor, and if it fell on a flat surface it would
> dig deep – at least ten yards into the ground – destroying everything
> around it. Shells were worse: the old Shahjahani houses of the fort
> were completely blown apart if they received a direct hit. Later in the
> siege, on bad nights, it was like hell on earth, with ten shells fired at a
> time in the dark, and bursting one after the other.[6]

One cannonball soon damaged the great Shah Burj tower looking
out on to the Yamuna river front, while another landed near the Lal
Purdah, killing a stable boy and a public crier. A third landed on the
zenana apartments at the south of the Palace, where it crushed
Chameli, one of Zinat Mahal's maids; soon afterwards Zinat moved
out of the Fort to her private haveli in Lal Kuan, which she
considered to be less exposed – and perhaps also more independent
of the sepoys, who were now ubiquitous in the Palace. It also
allowed her to put some physical distance between herself and her
beloved only son, Mirza Jawan Bakht, on one hand, and the rebels
on the other.[7]

Soon after this, a volley of shells narrowly missed the Emperor
himself. Sa'id Mubarak Shah, who had recently been made the
kotwal in place of Muin ud-Din, was in the Palace at the time.
'About 8 o'clock one morning,' he wrote,

> before the King had come out of his apartments, thirty or forty of the
> nobles were seated round the *hauz* [ornamental tank] in the palace
> courtyard waiting for his arrival. Just as the monarch emerged from
> his private rooms, three shells fell directly in front of and behind him
> and burst, but miraculously without injury to anyone. The King
> immediately retired and all the others who had been seated there got
> up and left. That same evening the king called up the chief officers of

PREVIOUS PAGE: Portrait of Zafar, *c.*1845, from Sir Thomas Metcalfe's 'Dehlie Book'.
ABOVE: Zafar presides over his durbar, *c.*1840, flanked by his two eldest sons: Mirza Dara Bakht (*d.* 1849) and Mirza Shah Rukh (*d.* 1847).
BELOW: Two elephants of state. The right-hand elephant carries the *Mahi Maraatib* or Fish Standard, and the figure on the back of the elephant could well be Zahir Dehlavi, whose official title was the Daroga (or overseer) of the *Mahi Maraatib*.

ABOVE: The durbar of the Nawab of Jhajjar in summer dress.
BELOW: The Nawab of Jhajjar rides around his country garden on his pet tiger.

The People of Delhi.

ABOVE LEFT:
Afghan horse traders
resident in the city.

BELOW LEFT:
Soldiers of fortune
seeking employment.

ABOVE RIGHT:
Mr Flowery Man, a
celebrated Delhi ascetic,
and his followers.

BELOW RIGHT:
A night-time assembly:
a group of Delhi Sufis
and sadhus, yogins and
ascetics gather around
a fire.

The People of Delhi. ABOVE [from left to far right]: The dancing girl Piari Jan, by the artist Lallji or Hulas Lal; an accountant working on his registers; a Delhi opium den with recumbent addicts; the dancing girl Malageer.

BELOW [left to right]: A troupe of dancing girls and musicians; a group of Delhi storytellers and comedians. FOLLOWING PAGE: The great oil portrait of Zafar, *c.*1854, by the Austrian artist August Schoefft, now in the fort at Lahore.

the army and addressed them thus. 'My brothers, there is no longer any safe place for you, or the citizens of this city, or even for me to sit. The ceaseless shower of shot and shell have already prevented that for, as you see, by the very *hauz* where I was in the habit of sitting every day, the round shot and shell are now falling. You say you came here to fight and drive away the Christians. Can you not do so even so far as to stop this rain of shot and shell falling into my palace?'[8]

For Zafar it was the second upsetting event in a week: on 14 June his chamberlain, the chief eunuch, Mahbub Ali Khan, had died quite unexpectedly. He had been ill for some time, but Palace gossip put the death down to poison.[9]

Everywhere in the city, spirits were sinking. According to Sa'id Mubarak Shah, between the pillage of the rebel sepoys and the shelling of the British, the people of Delhi 'whether bad or good, well-disposed or hostile to the English, now felt that they were like rats shut in a cage, from which there was no escape'.[10]

For Ghalib the shelling was the final straw. For the last month he had endured the sight of rustic provincials lording it over his friends in the *muhallas* of his beloved city – as he put it,

> every worthless fellow, puffed up with pride, perpetrates what he will; [while] men of high rank who once in the assemblies of music and wine lit the bright lamps of pleasure and delight with the rose's fire, lie now in dark cells and burn in the flames of misery. The jewels of the city's fair-faced women . . . fill the sacks of vile, dishonoured thieves and pilferers . . . Lovers who never had to face anything more demanding than the perverse fancies of a fair-faced mistress, must suffer now the whims of these scoundrels.[11]

Worse still for such an addicted letter writer was the disruption all this caused to the mail: 'The postal system is in utter chaos,' he wrote in his account of the siege, *Dastanbuy*, 'and service has virtually stopped. It is impossible for postmen to come and go: thus letters can neither be sent or received.'[12]

Now, to increase the poet's irritation and sufferings, there was the bombardment from the Ridge: 'The heavy billows of smoke from the fire-breathing guns and lightning-striking cannons are like dark clouds hanging in the sky, and the noise is like a rain of hailstones,' he wrote.

> Cannon fire is heard all day long, as if stones were falling from the skies. In noblemen's houses there is no oil for the lamps. In total darkness they must await the flash of lightning, and so find the glass and jug with which to quench their thirst . . . In this anarchy brave men are afraid of their own shadows, and soldiers rule over dervish and king alike.[13]

For most of the people of Delhi, however, the cessation of the postal service and the intermittent shelling were the least of their worries. A month after the outbreak, life was now proving very hard for the ordinary people of the city, especially the poor. With many of the bhistis and sweepers pressed into service for building and maintaining the city defences, the sanitation of the city had fallen apart: dead camels lay rotting even in the streets of the elite quarter of Daryaganj.[14]

The presence of sepoys billeted all over the city continued to be a problem. Even when they were not looting, fear of their violence and exactions paralysed business in the city. In July, Ratan Chand, the *daroga* (officer) of the royal estates, sent a beautifully composed Persian letter to Zafar, begging him to take action to bring Chandni Chowk back to life, 'for the militia horsemen have taken quarters in the shops at the crossroads and tied up their horses there. Therefore most of the wholesalers who rent shops have fled, and those that remain are busy emptying their shops. This means that no income is available from rents, and even the shops that were repaired by the government have now gone out of business'.[15]

The rich moneylenders continued to bear the brunt. On 1 July the partners Jugal Kishor and Sheo Prasad complained that they were receiving daily visits from the cavalry, 'who come for the sake of looting, wanting to frighten us to death or imprison us. For the last three days we have been forced to go into hiding, while our employees and servants have been harassed and persecuted. Now we flee our homes in distress and confusion. All our honour and reputation has gone with the wind'.[16]

Yet even the most humble tradesmen found that the presence of sepoys billeted anywhere in their vicinity meant people were too frightened to come out and buy their goods. On 20 June the *thanadar* in charge of the Chandni Chowk police station, Hafiz Aminuddin, wrote to the kotwal that

> the person named Anandi, a woodseller, has pleaded that for the last eleven days a cavalry regiment has been quartered near Bagh Begum where his shop is located. As a result out of fear nobody comes to his shop to purchase anything and he is losing all his income. I was therefore wondering if the said shopkeeper may be allowed to move his shop from this place. Your command shall be executed.[17]

Although business was at a standstill, prices were now rising fast. This had little to do with the arrival of the British, and still less to do with any plan they might have had of encircling and besieging the city. Rather, it was caused by the Gujar and Mewati tribesmen around the city, who now effectively controlled most of Delhi's hinterland. Robbing anyone who attempted to move along the roads in and out of the capital, they kept the city in a far more effective state of blockade than anything achieved by the British to the north. Typical was the experience of the Haryanvi horse trader Mehrab Khan from Sohna. Realising that his horses would be worth a premium in war-torn Delhi, he brought three mares into town. He managed to sell two of the mares to some *sawars* stationed in Daryaganj, and was riding back home on the third horse, his takings in his pocket, when 'near Mehrauli the Gujars pounced on me and looted me'.[18]

The result of this anarchy-induced blockade was rapidly dwindling supplies in the city and fast-rising prices. 'People are beginning to suffer greatly for want of essential commodities,' wrote Maulvi

Muhammad Baqar in the first issue of the *Dihli Urdu Akbhar* to be published after the arrival of the British on the Ridge.

Even if the essentials can be found they cannot be afforded because the prices are so high. Either the shops are shut, or when they are open there are a thousand people queuing for only one hundred pomegranates. The stuff that is there is of very poor quality, but hunger is the greater master and neediness a true slave driver, so people will take what they can get and consider it a boon. As is rightly said, 'if one cannot find wheat, barley will do.'

Bitter and dirty ghee sells for two sers a rupee; flour is almost impossible to find; white wheat has become like the [mythical] Anqa bird. Even then your problems are not over: when you give it to the miller and after a thousand excuses he agrees to grind it; by the time you come back he says a Tilanga has seized it from him, and what could he do?

From the gardens inside the city, some mangoes and other produce does reach a few places, but the poor and the middle class can only lick their lips and watch as these fresh delicacies pass into the houses of the rich. The dandies of the city, and especially the ladies who are used to *paan* and tobacco suffer greatly since *paan* is now only available in one place – the bazaar outside the Jama Masjid – and there for as much as two paise a leaf, too expensive for most of us. Look at the lessons the Almighty has taught us: we used to be so fussy that we would reject the finest wheat and complain that our flour was too smelly and only good to be given to *faqirs*. Now we don't hesitate to fight for the poorest left-overs from the bazaars.[19]

Muhammad Baqar concluded by reverting to his favourite theme of loyalty to the Emperor, whom he refers to as God's representative on earth; and he obliquely criticises the sepoys for not paying him more respect:

Before long we can be sure that these *goras* [whities] will be put to eternal sleep, and we should pray for the realms of our Exalted Majesty, the Shadow of God on Earth, to increase many times. This King of ours is one of the leading saints of the era, and has been appointed by the divine court. He spent many years virtually in

British imprisonment, and though he never incited anyone to rise up, nor coveted either the throne or riches for himself, now this divine boon has come his way, brought about by the army of God. We must be sure the King does not ever again become a prisoner in the hands of anyone, and it is incumbent on both the army and the people to treat the King's decisions as akin to the approval of God and his Prophet. No one should be in awe of the British: what they achieved was done through fraud and the breaking of their contract [of loyalty to the Mughals].[20]

Others took a less metaphysical attitude to the city's food shortages. The petitions presented to Zafar at this time included a number from the royal gardeners, who complained that the Tilangas were raiding their fruit trees, despite the presence of the Palace Guards:

My Lord, our crop worth Rs 1000 consisting of bananas and grapes and plums was ready, but the Tilangas came and plundered it and whatever was left they are making away with too. The guards deployed by the government at the gate of the garden are wholly ineffective because the Tilangas do not heed them at all, and when they protest they merely snatch away their guns.[21]

Yet for all the increasing hardship, there was nevertheless a strong undercurrent of confidence about the imminent confrontation with the small British force now entrenched on the Ridge. Once the city people had got over their shock at seeing the British return, the apparent fragility and small scale of the British Field Force soon became apparent, as did the rapidly growing strength of the rebel garrison within the city walls.

All eyes were now on the attempts of the different sepoy regiments to dislodge the hated Christians from their well-fortified entrenchments; but as the first few attempts demonstrated, it was not going to be as easy as it looked.

In the two weeks after the British returned to the Ridge, the rebel forces received several thousand reinforcements – from Ambala and Jalandhar in the north, and Haryana and Nasirabad in the west. Larger than any of these was the enormous rebel army heading slowly towards Delhi from Bareilly, 200 miles to the east. Across Hindustan, of the 139,000 sepoys in the Bengal Army, all but 7,796 had now risen against the Company, and over half were now either in Delhi or on their way to it.[22] There were also reports that a large force of between three and four thousand armed civilians – Jat peasant farmers who had risen up under their leader Shah Mal Jat – had just attacked the British force left to guard the bridge to the rear of the British lines at Baghpat, so cutting off the Field Force's communications, reinforcements and supplies coming to and from Meerut.

To add to British woes, and introduce a new element to the already volatile mixture of civilians, rebels and refugees gathering within the city walls, there had also arrived at Delhi several large bodies of freelance jihadis made up of a ragtag assortment of 'Wahhabi' maulvis, militant Naqshandi *faqirs* and, most numerous of all, pious Muslim civilians – especially 'weavers, artisans and other wage earners' – who believed it was their duty to free what they regarded as the *Dar ul-Islam* from the rule of the hated *kafirs*.[23] Four hundred marched in during the first week of the siege from nearby Gurgaon, Hansi and Hissar, but much the largest contingent – well over 4,000 strong – came from the small Muslim principality of Tonk in Rajasthan, which had a history of welcoming extreme 'Wahhabi' preachers, and which had long been regarded by British intelligence officers as a hotbed of fanaticism and an underground centre of the mujahedin movement.

On arrival the jihadis set up camp both in the courtyard of the Jama Masjid and that of the riverside Zinat ul-Masajid, the most beautiful of all the Delhi mosques. It is a measure of the distrust and tension between the sepoys and the jihadis that although they often fought side by side, the sepoys seem none the less to have regularly searched individuals going in and out of both mosques, and detained several people whom they regarded as suspicious.[24] Occasionally the tension between the overwhelmingly Hindu sepoys and the militantly Muslim mujahedin erupted into full-scale street fights.[25]

The mujahedin and their firebrand maulvis calling for jihad in the city's mosques appealed to a few of Delhi's more extreme Islamists, among whom were the 'Wahhabis' of the Punjabi Muslim community.[26] Sarvar ul-Mulk's Afghan tutor, a huge bear of a man, was also one of those who went off to fight with the jihadis on the Ridge:

> This moulvi, a strongly built man, with a big head and hair falling down his shoulders, was an expert in telling beads and reciting prayers. One day he came to my father, and said that God Almighty had conferred a great boon on men these days, and it was a pity we did not avail ourselves of it; and when my father asked what the boon was, he replied, 'jihad and martyrdom.' My father tried to do his best to dissuade him, but he was in ecstasy for martyrdom, and finally with a turban on his head, a sword at his waist, and a rifle in his hand, he departed.[27]

By and large, however, the people of Delhi, already alarmed by the number of violent, unpaid and hungry sepoys gathering within their walls, remained dubious about the pleasure of hosting in addition several thousand fanatical holy warriors. This was especially so given the jihadis' far from friendly attitudes towards Delhi's Hindus – half the city's population – and the importance the Delhi elite placed on not upsetting the delicate equilibrium between Hindus and Muslims in the city: 'Their stated object was a crusade against the infidel,' wrote Sa'id Mubarak Shah, 'their real one was plunder. In this manner fully five thousand men from various quarters poured into Delhi as ghazees, the majority armed with *gundasahs* [battleaxes] and dressed in blue tunics and green turbans'.[28]

Such was the coolness of the reception given to the jihadis that it was not long before one of their maulvis came before Zafar to complain that they were being unjustly neglected. The petition addressed Zafar with a new title: 'Oh Generous and Affectionate Killer of the Degenerate Infidels,' wrote the maulvi. 'We Jihadis have displayed great valour and dedication but until now we have received no appreciation for it, nor have there even been any enquiries as to how we have fared . . . We only hope that our services will be recognised and rewarded, so we will be able to continue to participate in the battle.'[29]

A similar petition came from a man who described himself as the Principal Risaldar of the Tonk Jihadis. In his case the complaint was more serious: his jihadis had been deserted by the sepoys during an assault and left to take on the *kafir* infidels all by themselves:

> We joined in the attack yesterday, and 18 infidels were despatched to Hell by your slave's own hands, and five of his followers were killed and five wounded. Your Majesty, the rest of the army gave us no help whilst we were engaged in combat with the infidels. Had they even stood by, only to make a show of support, as was to have been expected, with the help of Providence a complete victory yesterday would have been achieved . . . I trust that now some arms, together with some trifling funds, may be bestowed on my followers, so that they might have the strength to fight and slay the infidels, and so realise their desires.

Scribbled on the back is a note by Mirza Mughal saying the imperial armoury was now empty, but to send some funds.[30] The money was clearly not enough: by the end of July parties of jihadis were coming before Zafar saying 'that they had no food and that they were starving'.[31]

The one thing that the jihadis did succeed in doing was alarming – and potentially alienating – Delhi's Hindus. Initially there had been no visible difference in the response of Delhi's Hindus and Muslims to the outbreak. During May and June, militant Hindu preachers were every bit as outspoken as their Muslim counterparts: 'in Chandni Chowk and other markets', wrote the Urdu historian Zakaullah, 'pandits were communicating commandments from the Shastras that they should fight the English *mlechhhas* [foreign barbarians]'.[32] One Brahmin in particular, Pandit Harichandra, seems to have been especially prominent and appears in several British intelligence reports: 'he tells the officers', reported one spy, that by virtue of his astrological and esoteric arts he has learned that the divine forces will support the army. He has named an auspicious day when he says there will be a terrifying fight, a new Kurukshetra [the battle at the climax of the *Mahabharat*] like the one between the Kauravas and the Pandavas of yore. He tells the sepoys that their horses' feet will be drenched in British blood and then the victory will be theirs. All the people in the army have great faith in him, so much so that the time and the place designated by the Pandit are chosen for the fighting.[33]

There are references to Hakim Ahsanullah Khan paying Brahmins – presumably on Zafar's instructions – to make daily prayers for victory 'before the [sacred] flame', and there is even one reference to a Brahmin who told Zafar that 'if he were placed in a well-protected house for three days and allowed whatever materials he required for creating oderous fumes he would contrive that the king would be victorious'. Zafar appears to have been appropriately impressed and duly gave him what he needed.[34] In all the proclamations of the Mughal court emphasis was laid again and again on Hindu–Muslim unity, on 'the fight about the cow and the pig', and for '*din* and *dharma*'. One revolutionary pamphlet called *Fath e-Islam* (The Victory of Islam), despite its title, emphasised the need for co-operation and co-existence between Hindus and Muslims and the degree to which its author believed the Mughal emperors had always looked after their Hindu subjects:

The Hindus should join the Emperor with a view to defending their religion, and should solemnly pledge themselves; the Hindus and Mahomedans, as brethren to each other, should also butcher the English, in as much as the Mahomedan Kings protected the lives and property of the Hindus with their children in the same manner as they protected those of the Mahomedans, and all the Hindus with heart and soul were obedient and loyal to the Mahomedan Kings . . . The Hindus will remain steadfast to their religion, while we also retain ours. Aid and protection will be offered by us to each other.[35]

In the same way, many of the sepoy regiments mixed Hindus and Muslims, to the extent that, as Sir Sayyid Ahmad Khan later noted, they came to consider each other as brothers.[36] Indeed, some Hindu sepoys started using Islamic language in their petitions to court, talking of the Uprising as a jihad, and describing the British as *kafirs*.*[37]

Nevertheless, as the numbers of the jihadis in the city increased and the Uprising in Delhi assumed an increasingly Islamic flavour, so the dormant underlying tensions seem to have were exacerbated, and many Hindus became increasingly anxious and disturbed. Certainly some of the jihadis were convinced 'that the entire Hindu population is with them [the British]', and that 'the money changers and Hindus were in alliance with the Christians'.[38] There is also a telling petition to Zafar from one elderly begum who clearly saw the Uprising as little more than an excuse for provincial Hindus to come and loot her haveli. 'Please send five mounted guards of the Turk variety [i.e. Muslims],' she asks Zafar, whom she addresses as 'dear relative, apple of my eye, corner of my liver', 'to protect me from evil and corruption of the Hindus. For as you know, the Hindus of the Sita Ram Bazaar are ill-disposed to us and have a deceitful headman full of trickery. God forbid that the Hindus might by trickery introduce some spy into the army, and so have my house plundered and looted.'[39]

Against this background, it is probably no coincidence that soon after the arrival of the jihadis, Maulvi Muhammad Baqar included in his columns a call for the Hindus of the city not to lose heart – which of course implied that he suspected that they were beginning to do just that. A remarkable letter aimed at his Hindu readers was included in Baqar's issue of 14 June. In it, he called for all Delhi's citizens to pull together against the common British enemy, whom he compared to Ravana, the demon king in the Hindu epic the *Ramayana*. 'O my countrymen,' he wrote,

---

* It is possible, of course, that the usage reflected the language of the probably Muslim scribe at the Palace translating their letters into Persian rather than the actual phrase used by the Hindu general.

Looking at the strategy and devious cleverness of the English, their ability to make arrangements and to order the world in the way they wish, the wide expanses of their dominions and their overflowing treasuries and revenues, you may feel disheartened and doubt that such a people could ever be overcome. But my Hindu brothers, if you look in your Holy books you will see how many magnificent dynasties have come into being in the land of Hindustan, and how they all met their end. Even Ravana and his army of demons was beaten by Raja Ramchandra [the Hindu king and deity, Lord Ram] . . . Except the Adipurush, the primaeval Deity, nothing is permanent . . .

If God brings all these magnificent kingdoms to an end after a short period, why do you not comprehend that God has sent his hidden help [to defeat] this hundred-year-old kingdom [of the British], so that this community [the Christians] who regarded the children of God with contempt, and addressed your brothers and sisters as 'black men', have now been insulted and humiliated? Realise this, and you will lose your fear and apprehension. To run away and turn your back now would be akin to denying divine help and favour . . .[40]

The jihadis may have alarmed the Hindus, but in the weeks to come their suicidal bravery often put the sepoys to shame – especially when some of the most prominent jihadis turned out to be women. According to a surprised and impressed Sa'id Mubarak Shah,

Several of these fanatics engaged in hand to hand combat, and great numbers were killed by the Europeans. Frequently two old withered Musalman women from Rampur would lead the rebels going far in advance with naked swords, bitterly taunting the sepoys when they held back, calling them cowards and shouting to them to see how women went in front where they dared not follow: 'we go without flinching among the showers of grape you flee from.' The sepoys would excuse themselves saying 'We go to fetch ammunition,' but

the women would reply 'you stop and fight, and we will get your
ammunition for you.' These women frequently did bring supplies of
cartridges to the men in the batteries, and walked fearlessly in perfect
showers of grape, but by the will of God were never hit. At length,
one of the two was taken prisoner . . . When the band of ghazees
moved off to the assault, the women invariably went in advance of
all.[41]

The reason for the repeated failure of the attacks on the Ridge, it
soon became clear, was not any lack of bravery so much as the
absence of any real strategic imagination, ingenuity or co-ordina-
tion. 'The insurrection would have died out, but for the constant
fresh infusion of mutinous troops,' wrote Hervey Greathed on 25
June. 'They get beaten in detail, and apparently fight without any
defined object.'[42] Moreover, the same problem that frustrated all
attempts to restore order in the city – the lack of a clear and
recognised figure of executive authority – also wrecked their
attempts at fighting coherently or effectively.

From the very first day of the British return to the Ridge, the rebels
had daily poured out of the Lahore Gate on the western side of the
city, and made their way up the slope of the Ridge, usually through
the western suburb of Sabzi Mandi (the vegetable market), in full
view of their British adversaries. There they mounted a series of
fearless frontal attacks on the British position, usually directing their
full fury at the key British strongpoint on the front line – the white
Palladian mansion erected in happier times by William Fraser, and
now known after its subsequent owner as Hindu Rao's House.

Yet despite the sepoys' often insane bravery, time and time again
they were driven back by the Gurkhas, who had been billeted in the
house and who had quickly and artfully fortified it. It was a strong
position, and behind their sandbags the Gurkhas were determined
to hold it: 'we heard this morning that two new regiments of
mutineers had arrived in the city', wrote Major Reid, the Gurkha
commander, on 13 June, four days into the siege.

[We were told] that they were being armed and would attack us at
4pm. Sure enough, on they came . . . I was all ready for them,

and allowed them to come within twenty paces, when I opened with grape and musketry on all sides. I charged them with a couple of companies . . . over the hill . . . My loss 3 killed and 11 wounded; 3 right arms amputated . . . They marched up the Grand Trunk Road in columns headed by the Sirdar Bahadoor of the regiment, who made himself very conspicuous, calling out to his men to keep distance, as he intended to wheel to his left. They fought most desperately. The Sirdar Bahadoor of the 60th was killed by my orderly Lall Sing. I took the Ribbon of India from his breast. The mutineers were about 5000 strong, infantry and cavalry.[43]

The courage of the sepoys invariably impressed their old officers; their tactics did not. The massed bodies of troops certainly looked magnificent when seen from the city walls – Zahir Dehlavi thought the contest was 'a strange and fascinating war which one had never heard of or seen before, for both the armies belonged to the British government, and the rebels had also been trained by the experienced English Officers, so that it was like a fight between a teacher and his student'.[44] But the sepoys' uncoordinated attacks, single regiment after single regiment, taking it in turn to attack the prepared British positions front on, day after day, rarely taxed the British despite their small numbers. Hodson was being characteristically dismissive and overconfident when he claimed, 'they do little more than annoy us, and the only great evil they cause is keeping our men out for hours in this scorching heat'.[45] Nevertheless, the sepoys' strategy did strikingly fail to make use of their overwhelming numerical advantage and reflected the fact that, owing to army regulations, none of the rebel leaders had any training in commanding units above company (100 men) level, nor had they learned how to run the larger logistical or strategic sides of a big military operation. To make matters worse, each morning the ground gained the day before had to be regained, for each night the sepoys returned to sleep in the city and in their different camps, beyond the range of British cannon, leaving the Ridge and its approaches in British hands.

At this stage in the siege, the jihadis made even less impression than the sepoys, since they rarely got close enough to the British trenches to use their axes. According to the great *Times* correspondent William Howard Russell, who saw them in action to the east of Delhi,

> The Gazees were fine fellows, grizzly-bearded elderly men for the most part, with green turbans and cummerbunds, and every one of them had a silver signet ring, [with] a long text of the Koran engraved in it. They came on with their heads down below their shields, and their *tulwars* flashing as they whirled them over their heads, shouting 'Deen! deen!' [The Faith!] and dancing like madmen. The champion as he approached shouted out to us to come on, and got within a yard of the line amid a shower of bullets. Then a young soldier stepped out of the ranks, blazed away with his Enfield between his two eyes, and followed it by a thrust of the bayonet in the face, which finished the poor champion.[46]

Initially the scale of the losses did not seem to matter to the rebels, given that new arrivals were daily pouring into the rebel camp, swelling the rebels' numbers – and filling the shoes of those mown down each morning. But as the siege dragged on from June into July, the enthusiasm of the sepoys to face either the grapeshot of the British artillery or still less the kukhris and bayonets of the Gurkhas understandably diminished. Among the Mutiny Papers, orders start to appear that indicate a slackening of rebel enthusiasm. One petition from the keepers of the shrine of Qadam Sharif complains that the sepoys were shirking their duties and hiding in the shrine; while there, they threatened the *pirzadas* (custodians of the Sufi shrine) and plundered planks, beams, rings and cots: 'they have already rendered desolate the habitations of the birdcatchers, limemakers and several others. But if we try to stop them from coming here, they show their guns to us and threaten to kill us . . .'[47]

More telling still is a desperate order from Mirza Mughal in his capacity as Commander-in-Chief, dating from as early as 23 June, begging the sepoys to finish the work they have begun. The order is addressed 'To all the Officers of the Platoons and the Sawars who have not gone to the trenches'.

Despite the fact that this war started over faith and religion, many of you have not gone to battle, and instead while your time away in gardens or shops. Others are hiding inside their quarters, protecting their lives. His Highness the Emperor has made you all swear on his salt that all the platoons would go on the attack and annihilate the Kafirs, but you no longer show the will to do so. How sad that when this confrontation is about religion and faith, and when His Highness gave you his protection, you still refrain from going for battle. Remember, the platoon that does not go to battle will have its allowances stopped from tomorrow, but those platoons and cavalry units who show courage and fortitude today, and indeed have showed it before, will receive rewards, medals and honours from the Court. Moreover His Highness the Emperor will be highly gratified.

To this same order is added a postscript:

To All the Officers of the 2nd Platoon,
  The order had been issued to you that you should go towards Teliwara and attack. But it has now been learnt that that you did not go to the front and instead are currently lounging in the gardens near there. This is completely unacceptable. You should go there immediately and destroy the *Kafirs*.[48]

The saddest aspect of the slaughter faced every day by the sepoys was that, without realising it, they had actually found the Achilles heel of the British early on in the siege. On 19 June, the sepoys broke from their normal routine to mount a far more imaginative night assault on the Ridge from three directions, stretching British resources to their limits. An hour before sunset, a major surprise attack began from the rear of the Ridge, coming not just from the Sabzi Mandi but also from Mubarak Bagh to the north-west, and Metcalfe House to the east, and led by the well-equipped rebel force from Nasirabad. The fight continued all night, allowing the British no time to recover their strength. According to the British chaplain, the Reverend John Rotton,

The enemy came out in overwhelming numbers, with artillery, cavalry and infantry . . . We often wondered that such [rear] attacks were never made by them, and made systematically and regularly: their effect must have told on us in the end, if not much sooner than we foresaw . . . We remained fighting desperately, under a very severe and unpleasant fire; the darkness of night coming on apace . . .

The result of this engagement made a very melancholy impression on most men's minds in camp; not because our success was questionable, though very dearly bought, but rather because it was at first naturally regarded as the enemy's mode of intimating to us the plan he intended to pursue in future: that his eyes were open to the advantage he might gain over us, if he only harassed us in the rear. The fact is that knowing our own weakness better than our opponent did, we were not without fears, which luckily, proved groundless.[49]

It was a measure of the rebels' critical lack of intelligence that they had no idea quite how close to victory they had come so early in the siege. Fatally for themselves, the rebels never made another attempt to mount a really concerted attack on the British rear until much later; and by then it was too late.

At the beginning of July, Theo Metcalfe's brother-in-law Edward Campbell arrived on the Ridge and was posted near Hindu Rao's House, just in time to face the full fury of a major sepoy attack. Like everyone else in the British camp, he was profoundly shaken by the precariousness of the British position. The following evening he picked up his pen and wrote to his pregnant wife GG in Simla. The last time he had been in Delhi was five years earlier, at Christmas, when he was courting her at the far end of the same Ridge, in Metcalfe House, under the disapproving eyes of Sir Thomas.

The letter began with family news: GG had written asking for more details of Theo's escape, and about how the family's two Delhi houses now looked: 'Have you been over the ruins of the old house? Is the Kootub House destroyed?'[50] In reply, Campbell explained that Theo had been sent out with Hodson's Horse almost simultaneously with his own arrival, and that they had yet to have a proper conversation: her brother was now off disarming some villages to the rear of the British position. But Theo's eyes had become swollen and painful again, Campbell told GG, and he thought his brother-in-law should take leave and go up to Simla to recover properly from the ordeal of his escape from Delhi. This would also allow him to help look after his pregnant sister. 'I cannot see the use of his being here,' added Campbell, 'except for the information he gives of the country, which they do not seem to care much [about].'[51]

Metcalfe House, he went on, was totally gutted, and its shell now formed the easternmost picket of the British position, abutting the bank of the Yamuna. So bad was the damage that Campbell thought that the looters had gone as far as 'lighting a fire in each room . . . the only roof left is on [Theo's old] Batchelor's Bungalow'. But there was better news from Dilkusha: 'We sent out some men to see the Kootub House,' he wrote, 'and they say, it is alright, it has not been looted and the servants are all there – it is very strange is it not?'

Edward knew this would mean a lot to GG, who, like the rest of the family, had been deeply upset by the loss of their much-loved family home. It also meant something to them financially, for like many other British families in Delhi they had lost almost all their assets on 11 May. Theo had been much criticised within the family in the months leading up to the outbreak for failing to get on with the auction of his father's library and artworks.[52] In the event it had made little difference: what had been auctioned had been placed in the family account at the Delhi Bank, whose books and assets had gone up in flames several hours before Metcalfe House. Now at least there was a prospect that some of their father's belongings might yet be saved intact from their other house near Mehrauli.

Having passed on that piece of good news, Campbell then went on to give GG a gloomy assessment of the current British position on the Ridge.

The Pandies came out at about 8 o'clock and kept up a vigorous attack on the advanced batteries in front of Hindoo Rao's house . . .

Our principal danger was from round shot and shell – the hottest fire
I have ever experienced.

I had to keep up a sharp fire all day to prevent the mutineers
sneaking round to our left where we were very weak. It was an
anxious time for me for I could not help feeling what a critical
position it was. Our rifle companies are now so weak – I have only 30
men fit for duty, instead of about 70. I had about 4 men wounded
<u>none</u> killed, thank God. I have much to be thankful for myself – for
the narrow shaves were many – and besides the direct fire of the
Pandies who kept trying to creep up to us, we had an incessant
shower of spent bullets passing over us and hitting the rocks on all
sides. I had one sergeant shot through the arm, one man wounded in
the hand and another in the neck . . . Morgan, my junior sub got a
touch of a spent ball in the leg – one man got a bullet through his cap,
another a bit of shell thro his haversack, and another a splinter of a
shell in his leg . . .

Just as Maulvi Muhammad Baqar had promised his readers that
divine support was clearly with the rebels, so Campbell now went
on to assure GG that God was on the side of the British: 'I trust my
God will comfort my little wife,' he wrote,

for his comfort is the only real one, the only one which will stand all
tests. You have managed so well there on your own, GG, and you
must not be over afraid of the taking of Delhi, dearest. You know, I
always told you I thought it would be a long affair, and from what I
see of the natural as well as artificial defences of the Palace, I think we
cannot take it satisfactorily, or do any good to the country until a
larger force is collected – a larger siege and a larger supply of
ammunition for our guns. I think an assault under present circumstances could not but be disastrous.

I think the hand of God has been manifestly with us . . . I trust He
will always make me do my duty bravely and honourably. I cannot
feel the pleasure that others tend to do here, in looking at the dead
mutineers. They are also all God's creatures and I feel that much of
the slaughter must be laid to our account. Pray Heaven that we may
be humbled by God's Grace.[53]

Campbell's anxieties reflected a growing realisation among the British on the Ridge. They had come to besiege, but clearly now did not have the numerical strength either to encircle or to take the town, and had no option but somehow to cling on and endure whatever the rebels threw at them until such a time as relief came. In the meantime, there were around 4,000 government troops against more than 20,000 rebels whose numbers were increasing every day. As General Wilson wrote to his wife, 'We are still remaining in the same uncertainty as to what we are to do now we are here . . . Frankly I doubt we have the means to take Delhi, and that without the merciful assistance of the Almighty, I fear the result. I trust He will not forsake the cause of His own people . . .'[54]

If there was some frustration with the current stalemate in the city, then there was much more so on the Ridge. 'We go pottering about perfectly aware that we can do nothing else,' wrote Fred Roberts. 'This hanging about Delhi is very disheartening: [it] would be nothing if we could have a good fight and have done with it, but these Pandies are innumerable and never become less.'[55]

Unlike the townspeople, the British had a fairly regular supply of food, coming down the Grand Trunk Road from Ambala in armed convoys; but in almost every other way their situation was worse than that of the Delhiwallahs below them. Quite apart from the daily attacks and the constant bombardment from the city, the troops of the Field Force had no shelter or shade except their tents, so that many of the troops 'died from apoplexy and sunstroke, their faces turning quite black in a couple of minutes – a horrible sight'.[56] There was no water, except for the Yamuna canal a mile to the rear, where the flow 'were it not for the [revolting] flavour, would have passed for pea soup'. Sewage arrangements were primitive in the extreme.

After a week or two, the smell of the bloated, blackening, rotting bodies of the sepoys piled high on the slopes leading up to the Ridge grew more and more insupportable, and the rock was too hard to allow the digging of anything but the most shallow graves. 'The day before yesterday I had the most wretched picquet,' wrote one soldier to his mother. 'There were about fifteen dead Pandies within ten yards in a state of decay, and stench was quite overpowering, inhaling it as we did for 38 hours.'[57] The small parties of British reinforcements arriving from the Punjab would always smell that they were nearing the city long before they could see it: 'Through our nasal organs, we were most painfully aware of the scenes we were about to enter upon,' wrote Colonel George Bourchier as he neared Delhi. 'From Alipore to the camp, death in every shape greeted our approach; even the trees, hacked about for the camel's food, had a most desolate appearance, throwing their naked boughs towards heaven as if invoking pity for themselves or punishment on their destroyers.'[58]

The flies were another feature of the camp which few could forget. 'They sought you out in your tent, at your meals, when occupied in the discharge of duty,' wrote Padre Rotton, the camp chaplain.

> Whatever might be the dish you selected to feed upon, as soon as it was uncovered, a legion of flies would settle upon it; and even so simple a thing as a cup of tea would be filled in a few minutes, unless you were very careful, the surface of the liquid presenting a most revolting dark appearance from the flies floating thereon, some dead, others dying.[59]

The sheer filthiness of life in the Ridge camp also horrified a young lieutenant, Charles Griffiths, who had just arrived from Ferozepur. Like Rotton, he immediately conceived a deep hatred for the flies, which seemed to be impossible to avoid. Many days, he wrote, began by being woken not by the sound of bugles or exploding shells, but with the sensation of flies crawling through your sleeping lips:

> They literally darkened the sky, descended in myriads and covering everything in our midst. Foul and loathsome they were, and we knew that they owed their existence to, and fattened upon, the putrid corpses of dead men and animals which lay rotting and unburied in every direction. The air was tainted with corruption and the heat was intense. Can it, then, be wondered that pestilence increased daily in our camp, claiming its victims from every regiment, native as well as European?[60]

Things grew worse after the monsoon broke on 27 June and overnight transformed the Ridge into what Griffiths dubbed 'a swamp and mudhole' and Hodson 'a steaming bog'. 'The camp was literally turned into a pool,' wrote Rotton in his diary, 'and became very offensive to the sense of smell.' Snakes, driven out of their holes, suddenly multiplied and were 'dreaded almost [as much as] if not more than the enemy's missiles'. Black scorpions 'like young lobsters' were regularly found crawling through the bedding.[61] At night sleep was all but impossible: if the damp heat and the smell were not enough, the boom of cannon, the baying of jackals and dogs, and what the *Delhi Gazette Extra* described as 'the gurgling moan of obstinate camels' made rest a distant hope.[62] More seriously, in this humid, stinking, stagnant quagmire, cholera also broke out again, passing through the camp with astonishing and deadly speed.[63] In such an unhealthy environment, and with only the most basic medical facilities, it was hardly surprising that almost none of the many wounded who had to go through an amputation survived to tell the tale.

The officers at least had access to a regimental mess, a courtesy that was denied to the starving Christian and Anglo-Indian refugees who made it to the camp: Padre Rotton described his horror at seeing their 'attenuated limbs, sunken and glazed eyes, drawn and pinched features, convulsive frame'.[64] The regimental mess was also denied to the heavily pregnant Harriet Tytler and her children, who were forced to live in the cart containing the army treasure chest her husband had to guard. 'We had no home outside of our cart,' she wrote. 'There we remained night and day, eating our meals in our laps.'[65] It was a dangerous and exposed position, and before long

a shell exploded quite close to the cart and a huge piece fell below the wheel, but thank God none of us were hurt . . . Captain Willock came over in the evening to see us. When a shell came over the Flagstaff Tower, whizzing as it came along until it fell within the mud walls of our sepoys' lines close to where we were, and exploded there, poor Captain Willock jumped up saying, 'My God what was that?' I replied calmly, 'Oh! It is only a shell.' He was so astounded at the indifferent way I took it that he repeated it at the mess, after which it became a byword in the camp: 'Oh! It is only a shell.' Poor fellow, he never lived long enough to discover how accustomed one can get to such sounds from hearing them night and day.

It was in her cart that Harriet gave birth to a son, at two in the morning on 21 June. It was not the joyful moment that such events usually are: 'My baby was born with dysentery,' wrote Harriet sadly (she had already seen several of her children die in India),

and [he] was not expected to live for nearly a week. When the child was out of immediate danger, the kind-hearted doctor said: 'Now, Mrs Tytler, you may think of giving him a name.' Poor child, a pauper to begin with, his advent into this troublesome world was not a promising one. There he lay, near the opening of the van, with only a small square piece of flannel thrown over him, the setting moon shining brightly on his little face and nothing but the sound of alarms, calls and shot and shell as lullabies.[66]

When the monsoon broke a week later, and water began coursing through the thatched roof of the cart, Harriet's husband Robert moved her and the baby into an empty bell of arms,* whose floor he covered for them with straw. 'I walked bare-footed with a wet sheet wrapped around my baby, and went into that bell of arms and there we remained,' she wrote.

After such an experience I quite expected the baby and myself would die, but through God's mercy we were none the worse and I was able to nurse my baby without the usual aid of a bottle of milk, there being neither bottles nor milk for love or money. We slept on the floor with only straw and a razai [quilt] under us, with no pillows to comfort us, till a poor officer who had been killed had his property sold, and my husband bought his sheets . . . [But] my baby never winked or blinked, sleeping through it all as he lay on his bed of straw. If he had laid on a feather bed in a palace he couldn't have slept more soundly.[67]

* A bell of arms was a conical, bell-shaped building used for storing weapons.

Pressed to choose an appropriate name for the child, Harriet came up with something as idiosyncratic as her circumstance: Stanley Delhi Force Tytler.

As July and the rains progressed, and the British breastworks and fortifications became over time increasingly sophisticated, more and more British began to die of cholera rather than sepoy bullets. It was part of Padre Rotton's daily duties to make regular visits to the two cholera wards of the camp hospitals. 'It required strong nerves to withstand the sickening sights of these two infirmaries,' he wrote afterwards.

> The patients constantly retching made the place very offensive. The flies alighted on your face, and crawled down your back, through the opening given by the shirt collar, and occasionally also flew into your throat when you were reading with a dying man . . . My Bible, sadly marked in consequence of this plague, recalls every time I open its soiled pages many a painful countenance which I witnessed within those walls . . . So general was this mortal sickness in these hospitals, that at last I could only hope to discharge my duty by taking up a central position, with a chair for a hassock to kneel on in prayer, and make a general supplication for all the patients, while afterwards, with Bible in hand, I read and expounded some appropriate passage of scripture . . . [68]

On 5 July, cholera claimed its second British general: having killed General Anson in Kurnal in May, it now removed his successor, General Barnard, as well. If both Anson and Barnard seemed inadequate leaders for the crisis in hand, then the third elderly commander to take the lead, General Sir Thomas Reed, was the worst of all: 'old and feeble,' thought Wilson, 'more fit for the invalid couch than assuming command'.[69] Others put it more bluntly. 'I don't see how we are ever going to get inside Delhi,' wrote the young Scottish Lieutenant Thomas Cadell from East Lothian, 'under the choice collection of muffs we have at our head.'[70]

As was predicted by Hervey Greathed the day Reed took over, the elderly general was 'too ill to do anything'.[71] A week later he was still languishing in his tent: 'we see or hear nothing of General Reed', wrote Greathed to his wife. 'I wish I could say the same of a horse he has just bought, picketed close by; it has been roaring for the last two hours.'[72] It was not long before Reed gave up the struggle completely, and opted instead for retirement in Simla. He left the Ridge on the 17th, after less than two weeks in charge, along with a caravan of sick and wounded; his last actions were to send away two units of near-mutinous cavalry who looked likely to desert, and to hand over command to General Wilson.

Wilson, though always overcautious and far from imaginative, proved himself a towering strategic genius in comparison with his three predecessors. He was under no illusions about the difficulty of the task given to him. As he wrote to his wife when he heard of his appointment, 'Oh! Ellen dear, this a fearful responsibility that has been thrown on my shoulders, and knowing as I do my own weakness and incapacity, I feel as if I should faint under the burden.'[73] Yet for all his lack of energy and confidence, Wilson was a clear military thinker and was able to see that the British had for the moment no option but to choose a defensive strategy, and preserve their position until reinforcements arrived from the Punjab.

He therefore forbade the sort of adventures that had been whittling away British numbers, such as costly and often un-disciplined counter-attacks or 'rat hunting', chasing the retreating sepoys down the hill into the gardens of the Sabzi Mandi: two of these counter-attacks had recently come near to disaster, losing 220 men on one occasion, and a further 200 only five days later. He also systematically went about improving the quality of the breastworks, defences and entrenchments, and demolishing the bridges over the Yamuna canal at the back of the British position so as to avoid any possibility of further surprise attacks from the rear.[74]

On 18 July he wrote a desperate letter to Sir John Lawrence in Lahore, outlining the seriousness of the British position, and the need, whatever the cost, for Lawrence to send reinforcements to the Ridge immediately:

Confidential:

Sir,

I have consulted with Colonel Baird-Smith, the chief engineer of the force, and we have both come to the conclusion that any attempt now to assault the city of Delhy must end in our defeat and disaster.

The force consists at present of 2200 Europeans and 1500 natives, a total of 3700 bayonets, while the insurgents are numberless, having been reinforced by the mutinous regiments from every quarter. They are in a perfect state of preparation with strong defences and well equipped . . . The insurgents have attacked our positions twenty different times, and this day, they are out again making their twenty-first attack. It is true, they have been invariably driven back, but we have lost a great many men in doing so in killed and wounded . . .

I have determined to hold out the position we now have to the last, as I consider it of the utmost importance to keep the insurgents now in Delhy from over-running the country. To enable me however to hold this position I must be strongly reinforced, and that speedily. I hear that there is no chance of relying from the forces collecting below [from Calcutta]. I therefore earnestly call upon you, to send me as quickly as you can such support as you can from the Punjab: a complete European regiment if possible, and one or two Seikh or Punjaubee regiments. I candidly tell you that unless speedily re-inforced this force will soon be so reduced by casualties and sickness that nothing will be left, but a retreat to Kurnaul. The disasters attending such an unfortunate proceeding, I cannot calculate.

May I request an immediate reply by telegraph stating what aid in reinforcements you can afford me and when I may expect them to join my camp,

Yrs etc

Archdale Wilson[75]

One reason for Wilson's extreme gloom was the arrival at the Bridge of Boats, on 1 July, of the largest rebel force the British had yet encountered. From the Ridge the columns of the Bareilly brigade could be seen stretching back as far as the eye could see, before they disappeared into the heat haze. The force consisted of no fewer than four regiments of foot – around 2,300 men, as well as 700 cavalry, 600 artillery guns, including some much-needed horse artillery, 14 elephants, 300 spare horses, a train of a thousand bullock carts and camels carrying tents, ammunition and supplies, treasure worth 400,000 rupees and, bringing up the rear, a further 'three or four thousand ghazis'.[76]

On the 2nd these troops marched in across the Bridge of Boats, welcomed at the Calcutta Gate with fruit and sweetmeats by Zinat Mahal's father, Nawab Quli Khan. As the British looked on helplessly through their binoculars, they marched in, colours flying, their sepoy bandsmen playing 'Cheers Boys Cheers!' – the very same tune to which a much smaller British force from Ferozepur had marched into the British camp that morning.[77] 'There was no open place in the city sufficient for this vast assemblage,' noted Sa'id Mubarak Shah, 'so the brigade encamped outside the Delhi Gate [south of the city] . . . This was found necessary as the crowds of sepoys already in the town were occupying all the houses and most of the shops. The entire 73rd NI had for example taken over the whole of the Ajmeri Bazaar – with six or seven sepoys [billeted] in every shop.'[78]

Just as important as the sheer scale of the Bareilly force was its leadership: two men who seemed capable of providing the direction and unity that had so far been eluding the rebels. One of these two was a subahdar of artillery, Bakht Khan, a much-garlanded and battle-hardened veteran of the Afghan wars. A tall, portly and heavily built man of Rohilla stock, with huge handlebar moustache and sprouting sideburns, Bakht Khan had been elected general by the Bareilly troops, and arrived in Delhi with a reputation both as an administrator and an effective military leader.

As chance would have it, Bakht Khan was known personally to several of the British officers on the Ridge. Colonel George Bourchier had learned Persian from him at his house in Shahja-

hanpur and wrote that he was 'very fond of English society . . .
[and] a most intelligent character'.[79] Others were less generous:
some British officers dismissed him as fat, socially ambitious and,
most damning of all to the military men on the Ridge, 'a bad
horseman'.

The other rebel leader was Bakht Khan's spiritual mentor, the
Islamist preacher Maulvi Sarfaraz Ali. The maulvi, who was now
already known as 'the imam of the Mujahedin', had spent many
years in Delhi and was well connected to both the court and the
city. He had been one of the first clerics to preach the jihad against
the British in the days leading up to the outbreak: on 1 May at
Shahjahanpur he made a speech telling his audience, '. . . Our
religion is now in danger. Having lost the sovereignty of the land,
having bowed in subjection to the impure *kafir*, shall we surrender
the inalienable privileges which we received from the Prophet, upon
whom be peace?'[80]

Yet crucially, before that, Sarfaraz Ali had taught in Delhi at
Mufti Sadruddin Azurda's madrasa, the Dar ul-Baqa, to the south
of the Jama Masjid, where thanks to his learning in algebra and
geometry he had become one of the most respected members of the
Delhi *'ulama*; indeed, before the Mutiny, he was singled out by
Sayyid Ahmad Khan for praise as one of the brightest jewels in
Delhi's intellectual crown.[81] The nature of the relationship between
Sarfaraz Ali and Bakht Khan before the outbreak is unclear, but
according to some sources it was Sarfaraz Ali who persuaded Bakht
Khan to join the rebellion; certainly by the time the army reached
Delhi, Bakht Khan was firmly under his influence. Nor was Bakht
Khan alone: the four thousand jihadis who came with the army also
looked to the maulvi for spiritual direction. If anyone could unite
the sepoys, the jihadis and the Delhi elite, here potentially were the
two men to do it.

There may have been mixed opinions about Bakht Khan up on
the Ridge, but Zafar and his advisers seem to have had no such
doubts. Within a day of their arrival, Bakht Khan and Maulvi
Sarfaraz were summoned to the Palace and given a state reception.
It was in the course of this reception that some of Bakht Khan's less
diplomatic qualities first surfaced. For like many 'Wahhabis', Bakht

Khan disdained earthly rulers, whom he regarded as unIslamic, and longed instead for a properly Islamic regime.

Bakht Khan and the maulvi arrived with 250 of their officers, all in full dress uniform, and disrespectfully rode straight past the Diwan i-Am into the private apartments without dismounting.[82] It was clear that whatever his qualities on the battlefield, and however energetic an administrator he might be, Bakht was certainly no diplomat; soon his discourteous attitude to the Emperor's court immediately began to ruffle feathers. Hakim Ahsanullah Khan was present at the audience, and was not impressed: 'Bakht Khan presented himself before the King,' he wrote,

> along with the officers of his regiment and the jihadis who were with him. But contrary to etiquette he did not make his obeisance at the *Lal Pardah* [the Red Curtain at the entrance to the King's private apartments], nor did his companions, and though many people remonstrated with him, he paid no attention. When he came near the King's chair in the Diwan-i Khas, he salaamed as though to an equal, and merely taking his sword from his side, he presented it to the King. The King was appalled by this lack of courtesy, but praised the bravery of his troops . . .
>
> [Two of Bakht Khan's officers] said, 'Your Majesty should bestow a sword and buckler on Bakht Khan, for he deserves them and such a favour is proper for such a chief.' At first the King excused himself saying that they are not ready, but being importuned called for them from the armoury, and bestowed them on Bakht Khan. But even then he offered no *nazr* to the King. [Instead] he said, 'I hear you have given the Princes jurisdiction over the army. That is not good. Give the power to me, and I will make all the proper arrangements. What do these people know of the customs of the English army?' The King answered, 'The Princes were appointed at the request of the officers of the army.' He was then dismissed.[83]

Despite his behaviour, Zafar clearly still believed that he could trust Bakht Khan, and over the following days he gave him the titles 'Farzand' [Son] and Sahib i-Alam [Lord of the World] with supreme military authority over all the rebel armies, replacing the former Commander-in-Chief, Mirza Mughal; later Zafar appointed Bakht Khan Governor General while Mirza Mughal was given the title Adjutant General, which effectively turned him from military commander into head of the administration.[84]

In return Bakht Khan made an energetic attempt to solve the many problems that had paralysed the rebels despite their overwhelming numerical superiority to the small British-led force shelling them from the Ridge. He also attempted to sort out the problems caused by the sepoys' looting of the city, and made arrangements for the payment of all the royal salaries. Stern instructions were given to the kotwal and his police to arrest all looters, and commands were issued that the sepoys should be removed from the bazaars and relocated in the new camp outside Delhi Gate. According to Munshi Jiwan Lal, the following days were a whirlwind of orders and innovation:

> The General ordered a proclamation, by beat of drum, that all shopkeepers were to keep arms, and that no one was to leave his house unarmed. Persons having no arms were to apply to the headquarters for them and were to be given them free of charge. Any soldier caught plundering was to have his arm severed from his body. All persons having [looted] ammunition were to give it over to the magazine on pain of severe punishment . . . The General inspected the Magazine, and ordered the stores and material to be properly ordered . . . An order was issued instructing the [younger] princes that they were relieved from all further duties connected with the army . . . Orders were issued for the whole of the troops to parade in the morning . . . Three spies from the English camp were executed . . . The troops were paraded from the Delhi Gate to the Ajmere Gate; the General spoke kindly to the men and comforted them . . . [but] warned [them] not to harass and plunder the people of the city.[85]

More impressive still was the new military strategy that Bakht Khan put in place. An attempt at a flanking operation – sending a force up along the Yamuna to Alipore on 3 July – was a partial failure, after it was spotted and ambushed by the British on its return from burning their supply base in the village; but it was at least an imaginative innovation. At the same time, Bakht Khan developed a new rota system so that the British would be kept continually off balance. Their spies informed the British of the new rule: that 'not a single day should pass without a skirmish, and for this purpose the army has been divided into three parts so that at least one fights every day'.[86]

The increase in the tempo of the attacks had an almost immediate effect: according to Richard Barter, thanks to the 'system organised by Bakht Khan . . . we were scarcely able to stand . . . Worn out, and knowing that there would be no hope of relief, some soldiers grew desperate and dashed at the Enemy, getting killed on purpose to be rid of such an existence as soon as possible, their idea being that as it must come sooner or later, the sooner it is over the better'.[87]

The ninth of July, exactly a week after his arrival in Delhi, was the day that Bakht Khan set for a concerted attempt to finish the British position for good.

It started brilliantly at 5 a.m., with a massive cannonade from the city followed, in pouring rain, by a rear attack by some of Bakht Khan's irregular cavalry dressed in the same white uniforms as the British irregulars. Thanks to the confusion caused by this disguise, they managed to get deep inside the British camp – the first rebel soldiers successfully to penetrate the defences – before the alarm was sounded. They cut up some of the artillery and almost succeeded in capturing the crucial British horse guns before they were driven out.

At the same time the full force of the Bareilly army poured out of the city and made for the suburb of Kishenganj with the intention of turning the right flank of the British. The British managed to drive them back; but rather than fleeing, the sepoys lured the British away from their entrenchments and continued the fight farther down the slopes, where the British had far less cover. Lieutenant Charles Griffiths was impressed by the steely discipline with which they continued retreating in perfect order, turning at intervals and file-firing their muskets, while every now and then their guns were faced about, and round-shot and grape sent among the exposed British ranks.

> The rain now descended in a steady downpour, soaking through our thin cotton clothing, and in a few minutes drenching us to the skin . . . Many of our men fell . . . It was a perfect *feu d'enfer*, and the loss on our side became so heavy that a temporary check was the result, and it was only with great trouble that the men could be urged on . . . The losses on this day exceeded that of any since the siege began. Out of our small force engaged, 221 men were killed and wounded.[88]

Elsewhere, a little to the west, Bakht Khan, supported by the jihadis, led an attack that captured the outlying British picket at the garden of Tis Hazari. It was a measure of the fragile mental state of the army – the fear, frustration and strain that the British were under – that, according to Major William Ireland, after incursion into their camp, several of the British troops

> turned their rage on a number of defenceless Indian servants, who had collected for refuge near the churchyard. Several wretches were butchered, some hiding behind tombs. One woman was shot through the breast . . . So many sanguinary fights and executions had brutalised our men, who now regarded the life of a native as of less value than that of the meanest of animals; nor had their officers endeavoured, either by precept or example, to correct them . . .
>
> Servants who behaved with astonishing fidelity were treated even by the officers with outrageous harshness. The men beat and ill-used them . . . Many were killed. The sick syces [grooms], grass cutters and dooly bearers, many of whom were wounded in our service, lay for months on the bare ground, exposed to the sun by day and the cold at night . . . The tone of conversation in the mess was wild and fierce: a general massacre of the inhabitants of Delhi, many of whom were known to wish us success, was openly proclaimed . . .[89]

The passage highlights something that is often forgotten in accounts of life on the Ridge: the fact that just over half the soldiers, and almost all the vast support staff, were not British, but Indian. It was, all in all, a very odd sort of religious war, where a Muslim emperor was pushed into rebellion against his Christian oppressors by a mutinous army of overwhelmingly Hindu sepoys, who came to him of their own free will (and initially against his) to ask for the *barakat* of a Muslim blessing and the leadership of the Mughal they regarded as their legitimate ruler.

It is even odder that one of the greatest threats to the cohesiveness and unity of the Mughal's new forces was the arrival of groups of Muslim jihadis who eventually came to make up at least half of the rebel army in Delhi; and that when the British counter-attacked against those forces they did so by raising against the Mughal a new army that consisted largely of Pathan and Punjabi Muslim irregulars. As the casualty figures on the Delhi Mutiny memorial show, no less than a third of the 'British' casualties among officers, and fully 82 per cent among other ranks, were classified as 'native'.[90] By the very end of the siege, by the time the last reinforcements reached the Ridge from the Punjab, the 'British' force was probably around four-fifths Indian. If the Uprising in Delhi started as a contest between the British and a largely Hindu sepoy army drawn mainly from Avadh, it ended as a fight between a mixed rebel force, at least half of which were civilian jihadis, taking on an army of British-paid Sikh and Muslim mercenaries from the North West Frontier and the Punjab.

Moreover, for all the rhetoric in letters from the Ridge about the 'British pluck' and 'native cowardice', this racist language came from a group whose own family backgrounds were anything but perfect Anglo-Saxon exemplars of racial 'purity'; indeed, in the cases where details are available they were in fact, perhaps to their own embarrassment, splendidly multicultural. Elizabeth Wagentrieber had of course all her Skinner cousins, many of whom – including probably her own mother – were Indian Muslims. Theo and GG Metcalfe had a number of Punjabi Sikh cousins through James Metcalfe, son of Sir Thomas's elder brother, and predecessor as Delhi Resident, Sir Charles, by the lovely Sikh *bibi* he met at the court of Ranjit Singh in Lahore and, according to family tradition, married 'by Indian rites'.[91] As a teenager the half-Punjabi James had grown up with his first cousins in England, and was currently living in London, where Theo's younger brother Charles, later to be the translator of the Mutiny Narratives of Munshi Jiwan Lal and Muin ud-Din, used to visit him and took rather a shine to his cousin's beautiful wife, 'a jolly regular girl, and such a one as I should have no hesitation to marry when my time comes', as he wrote to GG. 'In fact to say it outright I really like her exceedingly. The very moment I saw her, I said to James, Mrs J is the very image of GG.'[92]

Padre Rotton was an even more striking case. For all the padre's rhetoric about the English as God's Chosen People, the padre had a whole tribe of Anglo-Indian first cousins. These included James Rotton, who could not speak English, and the twenty-two Muslim sons of his convert cousin, Felix Rotton, by various Indian wives ('complete natives in every sense of the word'), all of whom were at that moment engaged in fighting on the rebel side in Avadh, where they took an active part in besieging the British Residency in Lucknow. According to Company documents in the India Office Library, 'Mr [Felix] Rotton seems voluntarily to have remained with the Rebels till July last [i.e. July 1857], to be the father of rebels, and to labour under the strongest presumption of disloyalty.' He did nothing to help the British, 'though the descendant of a European himself, [and] all his sons capable of bearing arms were hostile to us, and he is answerable for the sons he begot'.*[93]

Even Fred Roberts, for all his letters back home full of expletives about the 'vile natives . . . a despicable set of cowards', had a Muslim Anglo-Indian half-brother, John Roberts, also known as Chhote Saheb, who, like the padre's cousins, was at that moment engaged in the struggle against the British in Lucknow. John 'lived entirely in the style of Indians and was a devout Muslim, who was very particular about his religious observances such as *namaz* [prayers] and *roza* [fasts]'; and he had married a Lucknavi lady called Shahzadi Begum, granddaughter of Nawab Ramzan Ali Khan. John shared Fred's facility with the pen and was an Urdu poet of note under the pen-name 'Jan', though he was unable to

---

* When Felix Rotton surrendered to British forces in 1858, he claimed that he had intended to go to the Residency 'but was asleep when Indian troops entered the city'. See Rosie Llewellyn–Jones, *A Fatal Friendship: The Nawabs, the British and the City of Lucknow*, New Delhi, 1992, pp. 32–3.

read or write English. Their father, General Sir Abraham Roberts, KCB, was furious when he heard that John had sided with the rebels at the same time as his half-brother was being hailed as a hero on the Ridge, and promptly cut off his allowance. 'I hope you can get some help from the Rajah for whom you made gun carriages to go against the English,' wrote the fuming general. 'Had you gone like the others to the Resident you would have been saved, but now there is no chance of you getting anything.'[94]

As far as the rebels were concerned, the 9 July attack on the British was certainly the most successful yet. But expectations in both the Palace and the city had been too high, and there was still a strong sense of disappointment that there was as yet no great breakthrough, and that the British remained as firmly entrenched as ever on the Ridge.

This feeling of frustration deepened in the weeks that followed. The lack of intelligence reaching the city meant that no one among the rebels realised how successful Bakht Khan's tactics were proving: unaware of the fragility of the British position and the pressure Bakht Khan was putting on it, they could see only that the lines remained unchanged, and muttering against Bakht Khan soon set in. Mirza Mughal had strongly resented the manner in which he had his command taken from him, while the other sepoys disliked obeying a commander from a different regiment. Slowly, as the attacks failed to produce any clinching victory, Bakht Khan's prestige, and his grip on the sepoys, began to slip.

Towards the end of July, complaints against Bakht Khan began to be openly aired in the durbar. On the 29th one sepoy complained that 'many days had passed and the general had not led his forces to fight'. Bakht Khan was furious, but the Emperor remarked that what had been said was true.[95] A few days later, when a planned attack was called off owing to heavy rain, Zafar became angry and said, 'You will never capture the Ridge . . . All the treasure you have brought me you have expended. The Royal Treasury is empty. I hear that day by day soldiers are leaving for their homes. I have no hopes of becoming victorious.'

The following day petitions arrived from 2,000 troops in Gwalior and 6,000 jihadis in Nasirabad, saying they were ready to march on Delhi if the King gave the order. But Zafar dictated the reply: 'Say there are 60,000 men in Delhi, and they have not driven the English army from the Ridge; what can your 6,000 do?' When Bakht Khan then complained that the sepoys were no longer obeying his orders, Zafar replied, 'Tell them, then, to leave the city.'[96] A little later Zafar added that it was intolerable that the city should still be

> harassed and threatened by soldiers, who had come to the city with the avowed object of destroying the English, not their own country-men. These soldiers are always boasting that they are going out of the safety afforded by the fortifications to destroy the English, and yet are always returning to the city. It is quite clear that the English will ultimately recapture this city, and will kill me.[97]

There was little surprise, then, when, at the end of July, there was yet another change in the military command. Bakht Khan was effectively removed as Commander-in-Chief, and instead the supreme authority was given over to a Court of Administration, under the presidency of Mirza Mughal, who acted in the name of his father. The court was an odd institution: a sort of elective military junta, showing the strong influence of Western republican rather than Mughal political ideas, even to the extent of using English words for the different positions in the court. According to its remarkable twelve-point constitution, there were ten members. Six of these were chosen (*muntakhab*) from the military: two each from the infantry, cavalry and artillery. The four remaining members were from the Palace.

The court met regularly and acted as a liaison committee linking the military and civil authorities.[98] Occasionally the court intervened effectively, such as when it criticised Mirza Khizr Sultan for making arrests and collecting taxes from the town's bankers without its authority.[99] But it never acted as a unified central command, and Bakht Khan always kept his distance from it: in the records that survive among the Mutiny Papers it appears to have been very much the organ of Mirza Mughal and his military allies, from which the Bareilly brigade, still under Bakht Khan's command, remained effectively independent.

Given this, the court seems in fact to have achieved the direct opposite of what was intended for it. Rather than co-ordinating the different rebel regiments, it emphasised the existing divisions between them, polarising them even more dramatically than before into competing factions acting under their own independent warlords. Either way, the end of Bakht Khan's military system brought instant relief to the British on the Ridge. As Richard Barter noted, 'The King of Delhi in Durbar had taunted the leaders of the mutineers with their want of success; this gave rise to mutual recriminations, and refusal of some to carry out any longer the system organised by Bakht Khan. And so, when we were scarcely able to stand, the attacks ceased, as if by a dispensation of Providence, and gave our force the repose they so much needed.'[100]

The speed of Bakht Khan's fall was exacerbated by his hard-line 'Wahhabi' views. There were suggestions that he did not 'supply the wants' of high-caste Hindus, who duly applied to the King asking whether they could be transferred to the command of Mirza Mughal.[101] Later, contrary to the King's express wishes, he gathered all the *'ulama* of the city and dragooned them into signing a Fatwa of Jihad, declaring it mandatory for all Muslims to arm and fight the religious war under the command of the head of the jihadis, Maulvi Sarfaraz Ali; several maulvis, including Ghalib's friend Mufti Sadruddin Azurda, afterwards said they had been forced into signing against their will, and that they had been threatened that if they refused 'their families would be destroyed and ruined'.[102]

Embolded by this fatwa, towards the end of July the jihadis made the most serious breach in the common front that had been so successfully maintained by both Hindus and Muslims. The feast of Bakr 'Id was approaching; to the horror of the court, who had always made huge efforts never to allow the city to be divided on communal grounds, the jihadis went out of their way deliberately to offend Hindu feelings. Normally, across the Islamic world,

Muslims celebrated Bakr 'Id [or 'Id ul-Adha] by sacrificing a goat or a sheep to commemorate the sacrifice of Abraham and God's sparing of Ismail (who in the Koran is the son who is about to be offered up, not Isaac as in the Old Testament). But as Muhammad Baqar wrote,

> The Ghazees who have come from Tonk have determined to kill a cow on the open space in front of the Jama Masjid on the day of 'Id, some three days hence. They say that if the Hindus offer any opposition to this, they will kill them, and after settling accounts with the Hindus they will then attack and destroy the *Firangis*. 'For,' say they, 'we are to be martyrs for the faith and the honours of martyrdom are to be obtained just as well by killing a Hindu as by killing a *firangi*.'[103]

Shortly afterwards, on 19 July, some Hindu sepoys cut the throats of five Muslim butchers they accused of cow killing. A full-scale crisis, dividing the city down its central religious axis, looked imminent. This was something Zafar had always dreaded. Since Delhi was almost exactly half Hindu, he had always clearly understood that it would be impossible to rule without the consent and blessing of half his subjects; moreover, he had a Hindu mother, and had always followed enough Hindu customs to profoundly alarm the more orthodox *'ulama*. Now he rose to the occasion with an unusually decisive response. The same day as the butchers were killed, Zafar banned the butchery of cows, forbade the eating of beef and authorised for anyone found killing a cow the terrible punishment of being blown from a cannon. The police reacted immediately, even going so far as to arrest any kebab-wallah who was found grilling beef kebabs. One of these, Hafiz Abdurrahman, wrote to the court swearing that he was not a butcher and could not be held responsible for cow slaughter; moreover, he had taken up his current profession of kebab grilling only after his usual business had been ruined by the rioting of the sepoys. He was not, however, released.[104]

Next, Zafar issued an order that all the town's cows should be registered, with *chaukidars* and sweepers of the different *muhallas* instructed to report to the local police station all 'cow-owning

Muslim households' and for each police thana then to make out a list 'of all the cows being bred by the followers of Islam' and to send it to the Palace. This order the *thanadars* were instructed to carry out within six hours.[105] On the 30th the kotwal, Sa'id Mubarak Shah, was instructed to proclaim loudly throughout the town that cow killing was absolutely forbidden since it would cause 'unnecessary strife which will only strengthen the enemy'; anyone 'who even harbours the thought or acts in defiance of the government order will receive severe punishment'.[106]

Further orders followed, including one oddly surreal directive commanding that all the registered cows should now be given shelter in the city's central police station, the kotwali. Zafar may have been unwilling or unable to lock up the jihadis, but he could lock up the cows. This order, however, proved much more difficult to carry out. Sa'id Mubarak Shah wrote back in alarm to point out that 'if the cows of all the Muslims are called in then they would amount to something like five hundred to a thousand cows. For this purpose we need a large field or enclosure where they can be penned for a few days, but this loyal one does not know of any such place and the owners will only be suspicious and worried'. The plan was duly dropped, and instead bonds were taken from the cow owners that they would not permit the sacrifice of their cattle.[107]

Finally, Mufti Sadruddin Azurda was sent out to mediate with the mujahedin.[108] It was a clever choice of emissary, and not just because Azurda was the most respected Muslim intellectual in Delhi, 'the wisest of the wise', according to Sayyid Ahmad Khan – the one who could, thought the Delhi poet Sabir, 'kick the knowledge of Plato on the head' and bring Aristotle 'from the height of perfection to the dust of disgrace'.[109] Azurda was a natural diplomat: a product of the puritan school of Shah Waliullah who was none the less a poet and the friend of poets; a leading member of the Delhi *'ulama* who used to mediate successfully between the Mughals and the Residency. Moreover, Azurda was not only a close adviser and ally of Zafar, but also the teacher and former employer of Maulvi Sarfaraz Ali, whose career he had shaped until the latter left Delhi. There is no record of what passed between the two, but at the end of it, Maulvi Sarfaraz agreed to persuade the mujahedin to forgo the pleasure of slaughtering cows and eating beef on 'Id.

Thanks to all Zafar's precautions, 'Id passed peacefully on 1 August. The British, who were aware through their spies of the growing communal tension, and who had been eagerly hoping for a major communal riot, were disappointed. Hervey Greathed was left merely to grumble in a letter to his wife 'that it is a good satire on the Mahomedans fighting for their faith, that at this Eid, under the Mahomedan king, no one was permitted to sacrifice a cow'.[110]

For both Zafar and Maulvi Muhammad Baqar, the incident of the cows, the jihadis and the murdered butchers seems to have been a turning point.

For two and a half months now their city had been looted and terrorised by waves of incoming sepoys and jihadis. But at least it had initially looked as if, once a period of transition was over, there might be hope of a new order and the restoration of the Mughal dynasty whose emperors both men looked upon as khalifas, the only legitimate and sacred rulers of Hindustan. But by the end of July, victory over the British seemed increasingly remote. A much more likely outcome, it now seemed, was the imminent unravelling of the central stitching that held Delhi together: the peaceful co-existence of Hindu and Muslim. This seemed to both Zafar and Baqar to be too high a price to pay. In the week following the killing of the butchers, both men, quite separately, put out feelers to the British camp, hoping to reach some sort of accommodation with the troops on the Ridge.

For Zafar and Baqar, this decision had been a long time in coming. As July progressed, Zafar had become more depressed and emotionally detached from the Uprising. His loyalties had always been to his city and his dynasty, and it was becoming increasingly clear that the interests of neither were being served by this crisis; quite to the contrary, it was now much more likely that the Uprising would lead to the destruction of Delhi and the final fall of the Mughals after more than three hundred years in power. When Sarvar ul-Mulk's uncle went to the King 'in full court dress, with a turban on his head and a belt around his waist' and asked for some troops to fight the British, Zafar replied, 'I do not possess troops to give you. I am 80 years old and infirm. This fight is not mine. Mutinous troops are fighting. If you have a desire to fight, then go to the officers of these troops and settle it with them.'[111]

Unable to lean on his queen, Zinat Mahal, who had now retired to her house in the city, furious at what she saw as her husband's disastrous pro-rebel policies, and unable to fall back on the chamberlain, the eunuch Mahbub Ali Khan, Zafar's behaviour became so erratic that it seemed he was beginning to crack – he was after all eighty years old, and had shown some signs of senility even before the Uprising.

As the siege wore on, and the prospects grew bleaker, his reactions to events in the durbar became more petulant and self-centred. Sometimes indeed they were eccentric to the point of madness, like those of some Indian King Lear, such as when he appointed his father-in-law to be Nawab of Oudh, a region the Mughals had not controlled since the mid-eighteenth century.[112] Later, he tried to persuade a disaffected sepoy general to stay in Delhi by offering him the position of Subahdar of the Deccan and Gujerat, regions that had been out of Mughal hands for even longer.[113] By early August, he had retreated into writing poetry, with verses that, like his moods, swung from gloom to unrealistic optimism: 'The King is employed the whole day in composing poetical pieces,' reported the spy Gauri Shankar on 7 August. 'One verse composed by him is as follows:

> O Zafar, we are going to take London shortly,
> It is not far.'[114]

When he was not writing poetry, much of his time was spent trying to get the sepoys out of his beloved gardens, many of which he had laid out himself. This he finally achieved in June, only to find a fortnight later that '200 soldiers of the 54th NI, and a doctor with his family have located themselves there'. As he wrote in exasperation to Mirza Mughal, 'The Royal cortege frequently condescends to go in that direction, and much inconvenience is felt on such occasions. You our son are therefore directed to speak to the Officers of the Court on this matter, and to have these soldiers and the native doctor removed."[115]

At other times Zafar just seemed to wish to escape. His threat to leave Delhi and to go on haj, and there to live a life of prayer, was probably initially just a lever to try to bring unity to the Uprising, and to pressurise the sepoys to obey him and cease plundering his city. But by July it did seem to reflect a profound wish simply to escape the horror of his position; he had had enough of watching impotently as everything he had planned and worked for – the cultured and civilised oasis he had built, the survival of the dynasty he tried all his life to preserve – was torn apart and destroyed in front of his eyes.

The degree to which Zafar was trapped is revealed in one of the most pathetic documents produced at his trial: a letter to his minor feudatory, Abd ur-Rahman Khan, the Nawab of the small bazaar town of Jhajjar – the same man who had refused to shelter Theo – begging the Nawab to come and rescue him. He addressed the Nawab – a foppish aesthete who had never seen a war in his life – as the 'Tiger in Battle' and explained

> that owing to the occurrence of many unpleasant circumstances, and being unable, in consequence of our advanced age and debility of body, to attend to the affairs of government and country, we now have no desire left but to engage in such good works as are approvable to God and mankind, to spend the remainder of our life in service and worship of God.

He went on to spell out his wholly impractical plan: first to move 'with all the members of the exalted house Taimur' and 'all the property and chattels of the whole of the members of the royal family' to the Sufi shrine of Khwaja Qutb in Mehrauli and then, having gathered everything that was needed for the journey, to proceed through war-torn India to 'the Holy Tabernacles' of Mecca and Medina. So he begged the Nawab of Jhajjar, 'our slave, to come quickly to our royal presence, with those of your retainers in whom you have fullest confidence . . . to protect our divine person till our departure for the holy house of God [Mecca]. In acting thus you will secure our entire divine approval and pleasure, and your fame will likewise spread throughout mankind'. There was, however, a small logistical difficulty: 'There are no carriages whatever [procurable] here,' wrote Zafar. 'Be sure, therefore, to bring with you 400 or 500 carts, and 500 or 600 camels.'[116]

The Nawab, who was determined to sit on the fence and commit himself to neither side, made his apologies: he was very sorry, he wrote, but such was the instability of the times that he was unable to come to the assistance of the Shadow of God. It was soon after this, according to one British spy, that Zafar recited the following couplet after the sepoy officers had left him one evening:

> The skies have fallen down on us,
> I can no longer rest or sleep.
> Only my final departure is now certain,
> Whether it comes in the morning, or night.[117]

Zahir Dehlavi, who attended on Zafar as a page throughout the siege, saw him sink lower and lower as July gave way to August, until he reached a state approaching helpless despair. 'He was always in a sad and melancholy mood,' Zahir wrote long afterwards,

and at all times his eyes were full of tears. In the evenings he used to go in and sit in his oratory, the *Tasbih Khana*, by himself and would curse the rebels. We were instructed to be present by turns, and one night while I was on duty, we heard the guard asking us all to be alert, and we all put on our turbans and got ready. When the King appeared, we all stood up and greeted him. The King sat in the *Tasbih Khana* on his low throne, leaning back against a bolster. Then he addressed us saying, 'do you realize the full consequences of what is happening?' Shahzada Hamid Khan replied, 'After one hundred and fifty years your Majesty's prestige has been restored, and the lost Empire of the Mughals has returned.'

The King shook his head. 'My children,' he said, 'you do not understand. Listen: I did nothing to attract this destruction. I did not have treasures and riches, nor land nor Empire. I was always a beggar, a Sufi sitting in a corner in search of God, with a few people around me, eating my daily bread. But now the great fire that was lit in Meerut has, by the will of the Lord, blown over to Delhi, and it has set this great city alight. Now it seems I and my line are destined to be ruined. The name of the great Timurid [Mughal] Emperors is still alive, but soon that name will be completely destroyed and forgotten. These faithless people [the sepoys] who have rebelled against their masters, and have come here for shelter, will all be gone before long. When these people have been unfaithful to their own leaders what can I expect of them? They have come to ruin my house, and once they have ruined it they will flee. Then the English will cut off my head, and those of my children, and they will display them on top of the Fort. They will not spare any one of you, and if any of you are saved, then remember what I am telling you: even when you will take a morsel of bread in your mouth it will be seized and flung far off from you, and the noblemen of Hindustan will be treated like base villagers.[118]

For Zafar, making contact with the British, and exploring the possibility of coming to terms, was not difficult; in fact his wife and prime minister were already in indirect communication with the Ridge through Hodson's intelligence chief, Maulvi Rajab Ali. Baqar probably chose the same route, and was asked to collate a newsletter to be sent up to the intelligence department in the British camp. A contemporary translation, presumably made at the time on the Ridge, of what appears to be Baqar's first report survives in the archives of the Delhi Commissioner's Office and gives an indication of why such an outspokenly enthusiastic rebel had become so thoroughly disillusioned in less than three months. 'Since the Hindoo sepoys killed the five butchers for killing cows there have been great dissensions between the Hindus and Mahomedans in the rebel forces,' he wrote.

We, the respectable portion of the inhabitants are reduced to the last extremity by the violence of the sepoys, and have no hope of

escaping with our lives. The General Bakht Khan's spies dog me
wherever I go. There are sentries over the house of Mufti Sadruddin
Khan [Azurda] and all exit and entrances prohibited. Through Zinat
Mahal I suggested to the King to open the gates and invite the
English to come and seize the city, telling him that if he could
destroy the mutineers it would be of great advantage to himself and
his children. The King approved my advice and promised to do it.
But Hakim Ahsanullah Khan, on account of the difference of our
faith has prevented my counsels being carried out. The Hakim is a
Sunni, the writer of this a Shia.[19]

Neither man was to benefit from these belated attempts to make
terms. Although both General Wilson on the Ridge and Lawrence
in Lahore recommended to Calcutta that Zafar's overtures should
at least be explored, Canning was adamant that no negotiations of
any sort should take place, and that on no account should Zafar be
allowed to think that he would be permitted to keep his old title or
position once the rebellion was crushed.[120] The Mughal court was
therefore left in limbo, unable to free itself from association with an
uprising from which it felt increasingly alienated, and the defeat of
which was now increasingly likely. Meanwhile Muhammad Baqar
was kept on by Hodson as a spy, but failed to secure any sort of
guarantee that his betrayal of the cause would save his life when the
city fell.

By the end of July there were clear signs that the military balance
was now swinging irreversibly in favour of the British. Although
the troops on the Ridge were still vastly outnumbered by those in
the city, the attacks were growing fewer and less spirited every day,
while dissension was increasing among the rebel leadership. 'The
tide is beginning to turn,' wrote Greathed in a letter to his wife on
29 July, 'and the waves already beat with less force against the
rock of our defence.'[121]

In the British camp thoughts now began to turn to ideas of revenge:
the mass murder of the people of Delhi was openly and enthusias-

tically discussed, as was the levelling of the city. This vengefulness was stoked by the British press, which had just heard about the worst war crime against British civilians in the entire Uprising: the massacre of the 73 women and 124 children at the Bibigarh in Kanpur. One of the most bloodthirsty was George Wagentrieber, who, after his escape from Delhi, had made his way with his wife and family to Lahore, from where he now edited a reborn *Delhi Gazette* known as the *Delhi Gazette Extra*, which aimed at being a newsletter and cheerleader for the surviving members of the British community of Delhi. In issue after issue Wagentrieber called hysterically for the complete destruction of Delhi and the 'annihilation of the demons who have so polluted its walls and blackened the pages of history with their hellish crimes'.[122]

The storm of revolutionary atrocity and fiendish crime have swept over the British occupants of Bengal, leaving behind it a wreck of horror and desolation, only equalled by the ingratitude and crime displayed by the Hell hounds who have originated and executed thus far their diabolical scheme of raising once again the standard of the lascivious Prophet, in opposition to the new dispensation offered to mankind, in the man Christ Jesus, the son of God . . .

Hindoo and Moslem have proclaimed their caste and their religion to the world in a mass of fiendish cruelty that stands as unparalleled in the world's history. The punishment about to be inflicted will likewise be equivalent: Justice is Mercy – 'blood for blood' will be the watchword throughout the storm pending over the doomed city; the British soldier must hurry: the Avenging Angel uses you in the massacre that awaits your advance on Delhi.

Let us look a little beyond, and let us view Delhi, as Delhi must shortly be, re-occupied by the British Force, the General Commanding sitting in the Mogul's Palace, and a hempen necklace around the King's throat as a substitute for his crown, and his life sacrificed to British justice. What next? Our reply is this: Let Delhi sink into silence; still, still as the silence of the dead within its walls . . . whilst unceasing justice rolls on its course, encircling in its grasp and sacrificing at its shrine, the life of every native mixed up in this terrible storm.[123]

That massacre of the inhabitants of Delhi, commanded and justified in the eyes of Victorian Evangelicals by their reading of the Christian scriptures, drew one step nearer on 5 August, when the news arrived on the Ridge that substantial reinforcements were finally on their way. In order to manage this feat, John Lawrence had had to strip the Punjab of almost all British troops, thus taking a colossal gamble that the Punjab would remain quiet. But a siege train one mile long loaded with heavy artillery had been gathered in Ferozepur and was now on the move, lumbering down the Grand Trunk Road, while the much faster Moveable Column had reached Ambala and was just days away from relieving the Field Force.

Better still for the morale of the British troops on the Ridge, and especially for those who were looking forward to a bloody reckoning within the walls of Delhi, was the news, as the Moveable Column approached, that John Nicholson was now at its head.

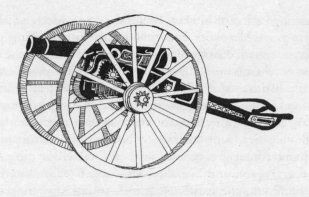

9

THE TURN OF THE TIDE

Brigadier General John Nicholson marched into the British camp on the Delhi Ridge just before breakfast on Friday, 14 August.

With him came 1,000 British troops, 600 irregular horse – all Punjabi Muslims – from Multan, and a British artillery battery; 1,600 Sikh sepoys followed soon afterwards, thus effectively doubling the size of Wilson's small army. But it was the presence of Nicholson himself, rather than the troops that accompanied him, which made the greatest impression on the beleaguered Delhi Field Force.[1] 'Nicholson is a host in himself,' wrote Hodson to his wife. 'The camp is [now] alive at the notion of something decisive taking place.' The normally restrained Charles Griffiths was even more fulsome: 'What added most to our strength was the presence amongst us of the hero John Nicholson,' he wrote.

Many stories are told of his prowess and skill . . . Spare in form, but of great stature, his whole appearance and mien stamped him as a 'king of men.' Calm and self-confident, full of resource and daring, no difficulties could daunt him. His indomitable spirit seemed at once to infuse fresh energy into the force . . . Nicholson's name was in everyone's mouth, and each soldier knew that vigorous measures would be taken to insure ultimate success.[2]

Since leaving Peshawar in May, Nicholson – previously an obscure thirty-six-year-old soldier and civil servant on the North West Frontier, unknown outside his own small circle – had in the course of a few weeks become a legend among the British in northern India. The British, after all, badly needed some heroes after the succession of blunders and insensitivities that had precipitated the outbreak, and the slow, hesitant and bungling response that had allowed it to spread with such speed. Nicholson's mixture of piety, gravity and courage, combined with his merciless capacity for extreme aggression and brutality, was exactly what was needed to put heart into the frustrated British troops sheltering behind their breastworks at the top of the Ridge.

The troops of the Field Force had been worn down by daily attacks for two months now, and were alarmed by stories slowly filtering through of further outbreaks all over Hindustan; by the bad news coming out of the siege of Lucknow and the death of the Residency's great defender, Sir Henry Lawrence; and by the massacre of the British garrison along with their women and children at Kanpur. Most of all they were depressed by the timid incompetence of the senile General Hewitt at Meerut, and that of the frail and elderly Generals Anson, Barnard and Reed, the Field Force's far from dazzling succession of commanders.

For them, Nicholson was the perfect antidote to these tired and nervous old men, and long before he arrived in Delhi stories were already circulating: about the Moveable Column's 46-mile-a-day forced marches; of how while his men rested in the shade, Nicholson would wait 'erect and immobile on his horse in the full glare of the sun', of how he never slept, and at night, when everyone else rested, would sit up writing his letters and dispatches; and of the degree to which Nicholson 'hated sepoys with a hatred that no words could describe'.

Most of all, the British camp was agog with news of Nicholson's recent victory at Trimmu Ghat, where he had, by a series of forced marches, pursued and ambushed an entire regiment of mutinous sepoys from Sialkot who were hastening to Delhi, and having caught them with their back to the River Ravi, made sure that every last sepoy was hunted down, so that 'most of the sepoys [in the end] sought for safety in the swollen [monsoon-fed] waters of the Ravi and found death, only a very few being captured, and of course shot'.[3] By August, word of the Moveable Column's bloody exploits had reached even Calcutta, where an approving Canning wrote that Nicholson, 'sweeping the country like the incarnation of vengeance, had struck terror into wavering hearts'.[4]

There were very few who remained immune to the hero worship of this great imperial psychopath, but there were exceptions. On the march the young Lieutenant Edward Ommaney was shocked by Nicholson's pointless viciousness: 'He shows himself off to be a great brute,' wrote Ommaney in his diary on 21 July. 'For instance he thrashed a cook boy, for getting in his way in the line of march (he has a regular man, very muscular, to perform this duty). The boy complained, he was brought up again, and died from the effects of the 2nd thrashing.'[5] He was equally horrified by the degree to which Nicholson had given a free hand to his troops to act with extreme violence against their helpless prisoners:

> A man of the 2nd Irregulars who showed the Sialkot Mutineers the ford, had his 2 hands cut off, a bayonet run through his body and then hung; batches of prisoners with their hands tied are taken out into jungle and the Sikhs let at them. Such cruelties must tell against us in the long run, and because these men have done the same to us . . . is no reason that we should emulate them. Kill them by all means by hanging and shooting the really guilty [but the innocent should be spared].[6]

Nicholson also made a bad impression on some of the less brutalised officers on the Ridge. Major Reid, who had borne the brunt of the sepoy attacks with his Gurkhas in Hindu Rao's House, wrote how 'I thought I had never seen a man I disliked so much at first sight. His haughty manner and peculiar sneer I could not stand. He asked several questions as to the enemy's position, and then passed silently on.'[7] Hervey Greathed was also uncertain how to respond to this stern figure, who increasingly came to be seen as the real leader of the Field Force. In the officers' mess on the night of his arrival, Nicholson sat silently throughout the meal with his huge Pathan manservant behind him, 'a cocked revolver in one hand, and

allowing none to hand a dish to his master save himself'.*[8] As
Greathed complained to his wife the following day:

> General Nicholson was at dinner. He is a fine, imposing man, who
> never speaks if he can help it, which is a great gift for a public man.
> But if we had all been as solemn and as taciturn during the last two
> months, I do not think we should have survived. Our genial, jolly
> mess dinners have kept up our spirits.[9]

Immune to any such criticism, by early the following morning
Nicholson was out and about, riding around the Ridge, studying
the defences, inspecting batteries and breastworks, and beginning to
form his plan for capturing the city. 'A stranger of very striking
appearance was remarked visiting all our pickets, and asking most
searching enquiries about their strength and history,' recalled one
soldier.

> His attire gave no clue to his rank; it evidently never cost the owner a
> thought . . . It was soon made out that this was General Nicholson,
> whose person was not yet known in camp; and it was whispered at
> the same time that he was possessed of the most brilliant military
> genius. He was a man cast in a giant mould, with massive chest and
> powerful limbs, and an expression ardent and commanding, with a
> dash of roughness; features of stern beauty, a long black beard, and a
> deep sonorous voice. There was something of immense strength,
> talent and resolution in his whole frame and manner, and a power of
> ruling men on high occasions which no one could escape noticing.[10]

The contrast with the neat, timid, goateed figure of General Wilson
could not have been more striking, and a clash between the two was
inevitable, especially given Nicholson's habitual inability to accept
orders from anyone. Wilson resented Nicholson's patronising
attitude: he was, after all, Nicholson's commanding officer; while
Nicholson was appalled by Wilson's extreme caution and constant

---

* The Pathan, whose life Nicholson was once said to have saved, also slept outside his
tent at night so that anyone entering had to step over his prostrate body. See R. G.
Wilberforce, *An Unrecorded Chapter of the Indian Mutiny*, London, 1894, pp. 28–9.

worrying. 'Wilson says he will assume the offensive on the arrival of the heavy guns,' Nicholson wrote to John Lawrence, 'but he says it in an undecided sort of way which makes me doubt if he will do so if he is not kept up to the mark . . . He is not at all equal to the crisis, and I believe he feels it himself.'

Later letters revealed the spat deepening: 'Wilson's head is going,' Nicholson told Lawrence in mid-August. 'He says so himself, and it is quite evident he speaks the truth.' Ruder still was a letter to Lawrence three weeks later: 'I have seen lots of useless generals in my day,' wrote Nicholson, 'but such an ignorant, croaking obstructive as he is I have never hitherto met with, and nothing will induce me to serve a day under his personal command after the fall of this place.'[11]

Yet even as Nicholson continued to complain, the logic of Wilson's approach – of building up the Ridge's defences and waiting until the siege train arrived – was being vindicated. For the rebel attacks had not ceased, and though they had become more infrequent, every time a new regiment of mutinous sepoys marched in over the Bridge of Boats, the troops were made to prove themselves by attacking the Ridge before they were accepted as part of the rebel army. The growing British success in dealing with such mass assaults at virtually no cost to themselves was largely due to Wilson's defensive precautions.

Several days earlier, after the Nimach sepoy regiment arrived from Rajasthan with 'several thousand men, ten field guns and three mortars', they had made a concerted attack on the Ridge. Supported by the Gwalior brigade and twelve field guns, their attack continued throughout the night, and right through until noon the following day. By lunchtime, over a thousand sepoys lay dead, but British casualties were minimal, and amounted to only forty-six wounded and killed. It was, thought Henry Daly of the Guides,* 'the most successful and scientific drubbing we have shown Pandy. His loss has been great; his ammunition has been expended by cartloads; and he has never seen our men. These are the lessons we should teach when acting on the defensive'.[12]

---

* The Corps of Guides was founded in 1846 with the intention of policing the turbulent North West Frontier with Afghanistan.

Safe within their entrenchments, the British were more aware than ever of the sheer, blind, tragic bravery of their adversaries. 'Nothing could exceed their persistent courage in fighting almost every day,' wrote Charles Griffiths, 'and though beaten on every occasion, returning over and over again to renew their combat.'[13]

The attacks from the city were not just growing more ineffective, they were also becoming more and more infrequent: as Hervey Greathed wrote to his wife on 4 August, 'scarcely a shot has been fired since the 2nd, even from the batteries, and it will be simple impertinence if they try another attack'.[14]

As the fighting grew quieter, and the confidence of the British greater, more diversions were found to occupy those with time on their hands. Some went fishing in the Yamuna canal at the back of the Ridge. Others played football, cricket and quoits, and one day there was a pony race. Greathed started going for daily rides beyond the encampment, and noted he 'could [now] ride with safety for long distances', while admitting to his wife that the stink from the 'effluvia of dead animals beyond the precincts of the camp takes away from the pleasure of such excursions'.[15]

There was also more food and more luxuries around: a vast flock of sheep had been driven down from Ferozepur, providing welcome supplies of fresh mutton, while the Anglophile rajas of the Punjab had begun sending down regular supplies of grain. A day's march to the north of Delhi, the Raja of Jheend guarded an efficiently managed British supply base at Rhai.[16] For those who could afford it, Peake & Allen of Ambala had opened a shop selling such rare exotica as tooth powder, pins, paper, chocolates and 'some good Moselle', though their brandy, at 8 rupees a bottle, was out of the reach of most pockets. More affordable was the beer offered by the Parsi merchants Jehangeer and Cowasjee, who undercut Peake & Allen to offer their 'best English bottled' for 15 rupees a dozen.[17]

There were still many deaths daily from cholera, and the stink of decaying bodies and animals on the Ridge was worse than ever; but there was widespread awareness in the trenches that the tide had

begun to turn, and spirits were much higher than a month previously. 'I must say', wrote Hervey Greathed on 6 August,

> that there is less croaking and more cheeriness here than perhaps in
> any other spot in India . . . The mutineers have been defeated in 25
> combats since we encamped on our present ground and they have
> now received all the reinforcements on which they can reckon, and
> are exhausting their supply of munitions. On the other hand our
> force will shortly be reinforced . . . and it is not likely the fall of the
> city can be delayed beyond the end of the month. The delusion that
> our Raj is at an end is losing its hold even on the minds of the most
> ignorant and turbulent. I do not anticipate much difficulty in
> restoring our authority.[18]

Others kept up their spirits by dreaming of the riches of Delhi
spread out below them, hoping to pick up 'a nice little diamond or
two' from the 'rich old niggers'.[19] 'Delhi was in 1857 one of the
largest, most beautiful and certainly the richest city in Hindostan,'
wrote Charles Griffiths. 'We knew well there was wealth untold
within its walls, and our hearts were cheered even at this time when
we thought of the prize money which would fall to our share at the
capture of the rebellious city.'[20]

The force of the monsoon was now ebbing, and the steaming
bogs of July had given way by August to lush and glossy greenery.
Some of the more aestetically sensitive British officers came to
realise what they had not before noticed: the astonishing beauty of
their position. One who did so was the articulate and intelligent
Harry Gambier. Only twenty-three years old, and not long out of
Eton, he had been in Delhi on 11 May, and had fled that night with
Colonel Knyvett. Several days later he and Knyvett had joined up
with Vibart's party, where Gambier fell head over heels in love – as
so many had done before – with the lovely Annie Forrest, whom he
had long admired from a distance.

Harry and Annie had become close through the shared ordeal of
being robbed by Gujars and wandering hungry and half naked
through the villages of the Doab, before their party was finally
rescued by Farasu. From the Ridge, Gambier now wrote cheery

and poetic letters to Annie at Meerut. He described his daily life on the Ridge, ranging from the melon-and-mango fool he had every day for breakfast, through to the military manoeuvres that he witnessed. He and Annie had both spent some time together at Delhi parties before the outbreak; now he wrote to tell her how very different the place looked under siege. 'The scene is very beautiful,' he wrote.

> Imagine yourself at the Flagstaff Tower at sunset. Behind is a glowing bank of clouds, a green undulating horizon, a white broad streak of tumble down lines, fallen pillars and blackened bungalows. Now look towards the city. The ridge is on the right and left, at your feet a level plain, exquisitely green and in places thickly planted, stretches to the City walls. The racquet court looks clean, and officers play occasionally; beyond it is the next house where Mr Curl lived – opposite them the Assembly Rooms, roofless and charred, [which provoke] very different reminiscences: of lights, music, skirts, 'bodies' and hanging head dresses, pumps, Le Bas, Lancers, and last Polkas and, as you will say it if I do not, I may as well add Miss H., with her nice angles and sulky face . . .
>
> Beyond the Assembly Rooms one can see Ludlow Castle [formerly the house of the Resident, Simon Fraser], behind it the two pukka houses in one of which latterly the Galloways lived . . . Through a telescope Pandies can be seen swarming about, sneaking up under the cover of walls and stones for a shot at our pickets, though they always miss! The city stretches out to make one's mouth water if one were an artist. The river sweeps down in a broad silver sheet spanned by a delicate line which is the still intact bridge of boats; a flash, a column of smoke, and bang comes a shot from the Water Bastion into Metcalfe's stables . . . The dome of the church is minus the cross, the Jama Masjid looks provokingly erect and towering in majesty beside it – as if Christianity lay low before the false Prophet's faith. The [guns in the] ruins of the Cashmere gate send their shot crashing into the old mosque [up on the Ridge] and the shells burst all about it. Hindu Rao's [House] receives the same little attentions from the Mori, Cabul and Lahore Gates, while the [guns on] Ajmere Gate play down Subjee Mundi.[21]

While Gambier was sensitive enough to notice and describe the beauty of the scene, he was aware that the brutality of the fighting was hardening and coarsening him, and was candid enough to write this to Annie. He described how in one engagement a force of sepoy cavalry had been beaten back, and

> a horse wandered riderless after they had retired. Two men went down the road under cover of walls & captured the horse and near him found a sawar slightly wounded, so they kicked him in the head and he died. My heart is hardened and it does not excite the pity that a similar act would in the case of a nobler enemy. It was a beautiful white arab, but a shot through the body had done its work. Doubtless it was once an officer's charger. The death-sweat dimmed his glossy coat, and the strained eye and inflated nostril and trembling limbs betrayed his agony. A bullet ended his pain, and I gave the horse the regret that I could not feel for the man.[22]

Even more changed was Edward Vibart. Harry Gambier had learned that his sister had moved from Kanpur to Lucknow just before the outbreak, and that she had therefore escaped the massacre there; Vibart was less lucky. After a period of recuperation from the ordeal of his escape from Delhi, he had discovered just before he left Meerut that both his parents, his younger brothers and two of his sisters had all been killed in the Kanpur massacre; and he suspected – wrongly as it turned out – that his sisters had been raped before being murdered.

Vibart had kept his good humour and his humanity throughout the trauma of 11 May and his subsequent flight to Meerut. But now he had lost everything he had lived for, and yearned only for revenge, to kill or be killed. Indeed, he soon convinced himself that God had spared him for this specific purpose: 'To avenge my parents – my darling mother, my little brothers and sisters – my poor father.'[23]

'I feel now that nothing could ever give me any pleasure or happiness again,' he wrote to his Uncle Gordon one of his few surviving relatives, in England.

All I think of are my poor slaughtered parents – and I go about mechanically as it were, little caring what becomes of me. Oh God! Why was I spared so mercifully, and then my parents taken from me? With an aching heart I take up each paper as it comes in and read it through – each harrowing detail of their misery at Cawnpore. Sometimes I fancy that God would never have thus afflicted them, and I think them still alive, and my beloved mother's face comes before me and I see it as she wrote me that letter as she heard of my escape, 'To my dying hour,' she wrote, 'I will bless the Almighty & remember my feelings of gratitude to him, that you my boy, my own beloved boy, have been so mercifully spared to us,' – and now I have lost that loving mother. All I have to remind me of her is that one precious letter.

My own father too – I see him as I wished him goodbye to return to Delhi, only four days before the fearful outbreak. As he held my hand, he said 'God bless you my boy,' – and now I am alive, and he is gone . . . When I think of what he may have had to suffer, with no one near him to comfort him or give him consolation, Oh I'm driven wild and I vow vengeance on these wretches, murderers and fiends . . .

I came over here [to the Ridge] – not caring for death, but only for revenge – to be able to say, if I lived, 'Yes, I was there too, I too was at Delhi and helped to revenge my parents.' Sometimes I do feel a shudder at seeing these black creatures killed, yet it is only momentary: I have seen five sepoys lying dead, and I have gone and spat on them. I saw two shot yesterday, and when they were dead they were thrown into the river – may each murderer die thus . . . Slay on and spare not ye soldiers! Remember Cawnpore![24]

News of the astonishing violence and viciousness of the British response to the Uprising elsewhere was now filtering through to Delhi. Recently there had arrived within Delhi a detachment of *sawars* fleeing the carnage of the British 'Army of Retribution' at Kanpur, who told stories of the mass murder committed by General Neill's troops after they had retaken the site of the massacre: of how every village in the path of the army was torched, and old men, women and children burned to death in their houses;

of how the Sikhs were allowed to torture, impale and burn alive the captured sepoys; how others were being made to lick clean the floor of the massacre site, and then, having been ritually outcaste by having 'pork, beef and everything which could possibly break caste' stuffed down their throats, they were sewn into pigskins and hanged. But even that was not the end: Neill ordered that, contrary to the dictates of both faiths, all Hindus were then to 'be buried, and the Mohammedans burned'.[25]

Everywhere the British convinced themselves that the atrocities committed by the sepoys against their women and children absolved them of any need to treat the rebels as human beings: 'Since they had butchered our defenceless women and children,' wrote Colonel A. R. D. Mackenzie, 'we would have been more than human, we would have been less than men, if we had not exterminated them as men kill snakes wherever they meet them.'[26] It soon became exceptional among the British to regard anyone on the opposite side of the battle lines as even belonging to the same species: 'I [simply] cannot consider these sepoys human beings,' wrote Captain J. M. Wade, 'and it is only common practice to destroy them as reptiles.'[27] George Wagentrieber helped fan such flames from his new *Delhi Gazette Extra* printing press in Lahore: 'our army is exasperated almost to madness by what they have seen of the brutality of the insurgents', he expostulated in one editorial.[28]

Moreover, as far as many of the British troops were concerned, their fury and thirst for revenge were not so much a desire as a right enshrined in the Bible. One British soldier, 'Quaker' Wallace, was in the habit of bayoneting his sepoy adversaries while chanting the 116th Psalm. As General Neill put it, 'The Word of God gives no authority to the modern tenderness for human life.'[29] Padre Rotton was in full agreement. The rebels did not realise, he wrote, that the Uprising was in fact

a battle of principles, a conflict between truth and error; and that because they had elected in favour of darkness, and eschewed the light, therefore they could not possibly succeed. Moreover, they had imbrued their hands in the innocent blood of helpless women and children, and that very blood was [now] appealing to heaven for vengeance. The appeal was unquestionably heard. The Lord could not do otherwise than be avenged on such a nation as this.[30]

Hervey Greathed was not sorry to hear of the fear spreading through Delhi at reports of the brutal British vengeance: 'The sawars who have reached the city from Cawnpore give dismal accounts of their defeat,' he wrote to his wife. 'They estimate the slaughter at 10,000 and tell terrific tales of the [kilt-wearing Scottish] Highlanders; they say they are men in petticoats, who come from Ceylon, and are Cannibals, to whom the Gurkhas are mere mice.'

He added, however, that the people and sepoys within Delhi now had many other more pressing worries, and the British now thought that rebels might flee the city altogether, so untenable had their position become in the face not of a military but rather a logistical catastrophe. 'They are badly off for money, ammunition and food,' he wrote. 'I am beginning to get letters from the princes, declaring that they have been all along fondly attached to us, and that they only want to know what they can do for us. They must find out for themselves, for I shall not answer and tell them.'[31]

As the soldiers on the Ridge found themselves with more to eat and less to worry about, their counterparts in Delhi were now every day growing closer to starvation.

The military and strategic limitation of the sepoys had been apparent for some time now, especially their failure to gather intelligence, to co-ordinate effectively with other rebel centres such as Kanpur and Lucknow, or to persuade most of the independent rajas of central India and Rajputana to come off the fence and join with the cause. In particular, the Delhi rebels failed to recognise how very easily they could have taken the British from the rear on the Ridge: 'I think Wilson has hitherto had considerable cause for anxiety,' wrote Nicholson on 28 August. 'Had the enemy had the enterprise to detach a strong force to his rear, we could not have sent more than five or six hundred men against it. But it is too late for them to try that game now, and they know it, and are at their wits' end to devise some new plan of action.'[32]

It was, however, only as the siege wore on that it became apparent that it would be the failures of the rebels' administrative and financial organisation, every bit as much as their military and strategic shortcomings, which would lead to their ultimate undoing. They had created turbulence and chaos, but could not restore order. This was particularly fatal for them in the countryside around Delhi. Their failure to establish a well-governed 'liberated area' or Mughal realm from which they could draw tax revenue, manpower and, most of all, food supplies, ultimately proved the Delhi rebels' single most disastrous failure. This was something Maulvi Muhammad Baqar recognised at the time and wrote about repeatedly in his editorials: 'What strange indifference,' he wrote, 'that we have not attempted to collect one single rupee of tax revenue.'

> God knows what design or purpose there is in this failure, and what is causing such slackness . . . Some or other Amir or nobleman should be deputed to collect tribute and revenue from the Rajahs and other notables, so that the administration and control of his exalted Majesty is established. At all places and districts where the Collectors of the *Kafirs* used to be posted, there a representative of his Exalted Majesty, as Ziladar, should be placed, along with some troops and the Islamic standard. The villages are already identified and marked, and money can be collected from there as prescribed. Everywhere a platoon or platoons should be posted. There is no doubt that without measures like this the notables and local potentates around these regions would not be able to give up the awe of the *Kafirs* which they still harbour in their hearts, and they will not give up of their deepest hope of seeing their own [Mughal] government restored.[33]

The accuracy of this observation became clearer and clearer as June gave way to July and August, and the city grew hungrier, and thirstier. The British had cut off the flow of the Yamuna canal into the city early in June, so that the only water now came from the brackish wells within the city and the river to the east, where water carriers and bathers found themselves exposed to British shellfire.[34] Despite this, many still came to take water, and even to sit and fish, exposed in the open, risking a stray shell in the hope of hooking a fresh catch.[35] The food situation was equally dire. Ever since June, petitions from starving citizens, jihadis and sepoys begging for food and sustenance had been piling into the Red Fort, and the intense hunger on the streets of the city had become a prominent theme of the spies' reports.

As early as 7 June, even the employees of the royal household were complaining that they had received no rations for a month.[36] On 12 June the deputy kotwal wrote to his assistants begging them to find some food for the new battalions from Haryana who had just marched into Delhi. At the bottom is the reply: 'It is submitted that there is nothing left in the shops, no flour, no pulses, nothing. What should we do?'[37] By 15 June, the officers of the different regiments were coming to the Fort and complaining that their troops could not attack the British on empty stomachs, and that their sepoys had begun returning, 'driven back by hunger before the battle is over'.[38]

Six weeks later, on 28 July, Kishan Dayal and Qadir Bakhsh, subahdars of the Meerut sepoys, came to court to say their men were now starving. They had left behind in Meerut all their possessions when they mutinied, 'so are now very hard pressed. Some eight–ten days have passed and we have not even received a single chick-pea. My men are dismayed at the expense of everything, and there are no money-lenders who will give them loans'.[39]

It was not just the moneylenders: the traders and shopkeepers too refused to provide credit; on 4 August, the Delhi confectioners went en masse to the kotwal, and announced that since they had not been paid for past supplies, they would no longer provide sweets without payment in cash.[40] By 14 August, the newly arrived Nimach brigade were openly threatening to desert if they were not fed. The brigade's two subahdars came before Zafar to tell him of the full desperation of their situation:

My Lord, this submission is about the Nimach force that arrived in the capital after traversing a great distance and overcoming many obstacles, with the expectation of serving your Imperial Majesty. Until now your obedient servants have themselves been paying the expenses of the horses, cavalry, artillery, cattle, elephants and camels. My Lord the cavalry and the artillery and the elephants and the camels belong to the Sarkar [British government] and until now whatever the circumstances, their allowances were always paid. But now, for four or five days, the entire force including the soldiers and the animals have been starving and there is no money left to pay even their basic expenses. All the soldiers are determined to fight, but they ask us: how can a man who has been fasting for two three days do battle?

Therefore we hope that out of your largesse and largeness of heart can you please provide for all the expenses incurred by the Royal force and honour these humble ones with a reply. Otherwise kindly inform the soldiers, for until arrangements are made for payment, no soldier is ready to do battle. Please do not construe this as disobedience, but should you not want the Nimach brigade to remain, then kindly give us a clear answer. Whatever is ordained will happen. Innumerable petitions have been sent earlier but we have yet not received any response.

With the greatest respect, and devotedly,
General Sudhari Singh and Brigade Major Hira Singh[41]

In the event, the Nimach brigade were persuaded to stay, even though no money or food was immediately available; but spies reported a growing haemorrhage of deserters from the rebel army: according to the spy Turab Ali, in the first week of August alone 750 cavalrymen and 600 jihadis went 'to their native place . . . because they could not obtain their daily bread in the city'.[42]

Throughout July and August the Court of Administration, led by Mirza Mughal, made frantic efforts to raise the money to pay for food and cover the expenses of the soldiers. At first they tried borrowing from the city's moneylenders, but succeeded in raising only 6,000 rupees, enough for just a few days' supplies. The *thanadar* of Chandni Chowk, who was given the job of extracting the money from the bankers and *baniyas* of Katra Nil, reported 'that some of these people disappear into their houses; others do not give any response, while most make one excuse or another to keep this servant at bay, and are forever on the lookout for ways of evading their dues'.[43] A month later it was the same story: 'whenever this servant goes to their houses,' reported the *thanadar*, 'they shut their doors and do not give any reply. They vanish away'. A note at the bottom in Mirza Mughal's hand, and stamped with his seal, suggested a more vigorous approach: 'Proclaim an order', suggested the Prince, 'that if these money-lenders remain hidden you will blow them from a cannon.'[44]

A message was sent to Laxmi Chand, the famously wealthy moneylender in Mathura, on the road to Agra, but although he was offered the position of *Fotadar* (Treasurer) in return for a loan of 5 lakh rupees, he said he was unable to help.*[45] In retaliation, the moneylender's Delhi agent was arrested and taken to the Bareilly troop's camp, where he was 'ill-treated'.[46]

On 7 August, in desperation, Mirza Mughal arrested all the city's leading *baniyas* and bankers and brought them to the Fort, where they were threatened with death if they did not produce their fortunes and offer them for the Uprising. Among those arrested were various former English officials, including Munshi Jiwan Lal, who was surprised by sepoys when he opened his haveli gates one evening to let in the water carriers. He was bound and taken to the Red Fort, where he was horrified by what he saw:

> I was taken upstairs before Mirza Mughal. There I saw that a great crowd of people was assembled, but in a strange irregular fashion. On one side sat Mirza Mughal reclining on his pillows . . . while in front of the Mirza was the famous Kuray Singh, the Tilanga Brigade Major, stretched at full length on his bed. There was not a semblance

---

* Before long the moneylenders of Mathura were actually raising armies to aid the British. See Eric Stokes, *The Peasant Armed: The Indian Revolt of 1857*, ed. C. A. Bayly, Oxford, 1986, p. 232. To understand why, see the excellent account of how the hated *baniyas* of Mathura were attacked, looted and tortured at the outbreak of the Uprising in Gautam Bhadra's essay 'Four Rebels of 1857' in *Subaltern Studies*, IV, ed. R. Guha, Delhi, 1985, p. 254. This helps explain why Laxmi Chand may not actually have been in a position to help the rebels, even if he felt inclined to do so. It is worth noting how much the rise of British rule in general, but especially in its infancy in Bengal, owed to the collusion of Indian moneylenders.

of court etiquette, and the King's officials were moving here and there without order. Lala Saligram, Ramji Das Gurwala and about 25 bankers were sitting there under arrest; I was also ordered to sit in the same row with them.

Money was demanded from us and we were threatened so far that guns were placed over our shoulders and fired. But in spite of this our hearts remained firm, and we made up our minds rather to die than to yield to the threats of the rebels, and so we were kept in this sad condition [all night] until 4pm [the following day].[47]

Throughout the day and night, pistols were produced and the members of the group were threatened with death. In the end, however, Munshi Jiwan Lal and the other munshis were saved by the Anglophile Mirza Ilahe Bakhsh, who took Mirza Mughal aside and warned him, 'The English will capture Delhi and you will fall into their hands. These men are the Munshis of the English and you will have recourse to their assistance. I advise you to set them free, and thus keep them under an obligation.'[48]

When threatening the bankers had failed, Mirza Mughal tried to persuade the traders in the bazaar to supply 5 lakh rupees, and also to provide food to the army on credit with the promise that 'money would be paid when the salaries were distributed'. But the traders refused to accept the court's word, even when pressured by the kotwal and threatened with imprisonment and the systematic looting of their shops.[49] By early August spies were reporting that many of the Punjabi merchants as well as 'Marwarees of Ashrafee ka Katra' had been thrown into jail until they paid up.[50] Many other moneylenders joined them there, including one of the most prominent of all, Saligram.[51] They remained in confinement until the first week of September when Zafar learned what had happened, whereupon 'Mirza Mughal was ordered not to allow such ill treatment of the King's subjects, and that it was better to take what each agreed and to realise it by gentle means'.[52]

There were also various attempts to raise 300,000 rupees from the nobles of the city, and half-hearted efforts to tax the small area to the west of Delhi – the villages of Mehrauli and Gurgaon – that were still nominally under Zafar's control; but again little money was forthcoming.⁵³ By the end of the month, Mirza Mughal's men were so desperate for money that they had begun digging for buried treasure in the Mughal Bastille of Salimgarh, opposite the Red Fort. 'People say to the Emperor that the treasures of his forebears are buried here,' recorded the spy Gauri Shankar. 'Some even mention exact spots – but nothing has emerged yet.'⁵⁴ Later, they dug up 'some small field pieces', but the promised treasure proved more elusive.⁵⁵

A similar degree of desperation fuelled the spurious rumours that the Persian Army was coming to save the rebels, that it had fought its way through Afghanistan and into India via Peshawar, and was now crossing the Indus at Attock. Another seaborne assault of Iranian troops was said to be on its way via Bombay. 'We cannot verify the news,' remarked Baqar in the *Dihli Urdu Akbhar*, 'but it is not an impossibility.'⁵⁶

For it was not just money which was running out by the middle of August: supplies of gunpowder and gun caps were also running low. This was the single most startling example of negligence on the part of the rebel administration, for at the outbreak they had inherited the largest arsenal of weapons and ammunition in northern India. For the first ten days of the Uprising, however, no guard had been placed over the munitions that had survived the explosion at the magazine, so that the townspeople, and even the Gujars from the countryside, had come and helped themselves.⁵⁷

The result was that by late July fuses for shells and percussion caps were both in short supply; gunpowder had run out, and attempts to manufacture it ran into trouble from the lack of saltpetre and sulphur in the city. Various attempts were made to send out to famous firework manufacturers across Hindustan for assistance; one of these, 'Akbar Khan, a resident of Meerut went to the Princes and offered to make a projectile of such size and power that it would destroy a whole section of men. Convinced of his ability to do so, they advanced him the sum of Rs 4000 for expenses and ordered him to commence the work at once in the Palace'; but the experiment does not seem to have been a success.⁵⁸

There was even an attempt to use the alcoholic spirits seized from English houses to manufacture explosive, and on 2 September '144 bottles of wine' were sent to the gunpowder factory, but the results were mixed at best. English observers noted that while the marks-manship of the rebel artillery remained very good throughout the siege, from July onwards it became increasingly common for the rebel shells to fail to explode.[59]

The most serious blow came on 7 August, when a stray British shell ignited one of the principal rebel gunpowder factories, located in Gali Churiwallan, incinerating the 500 people working there. The sepoys assumed there had been treachery at work, and attacked the haveli of Zafar's prime minister, Hakim Ahsanullah Khan, whom they accused of treason. The haveli was burned to the ground, saddening Ghalib: he was a close friend of the hakim, and had spent many convivial evenings in the house. In *Dastanbuy*, he saw it as yet another assault on the civilised and highly cultured Delhi he loved and had helped to create. Although the hakim's life was saved, wrote Ghalib, 'the mischief was not finished until the house was completely devastated'.

> That mansion, which in beauty and ornament, was equal to the painted palaces of China, was looted and the roofs were burned. The great beams and the inlaid panels of the ceiling were reduced to ashes. The walls were so completely blackened by smoke it seemed that, in grief, the mansion wore a black mantle.

> Do not be misled by the fortunes the skies may bestow.
> The treacherous skies entangle,
> In anguish and torment,
> Those they formerly laid in the lap of love.[60]

By mid-August, as the food shortages were beginning to bite, large numbers of hungry sepoys and jihadis had begun to drift away every day from the city, despairing of continuing the fight if there was nothing to eat.

According to one intelligence letter received by Hodson on 16 August, Zafar was too depressed, detached and possibly now too unhinged even to attempt to prevent them going; in his own eyes at least he had now removed himself from participation in the Uprising: 'Yesterday some two hundred Tilangas, fully armed, dressed and mounted, were on their way [out of the city] when some rebel forces stopped them, and reported it to the fort,' wrote an anonymous spy.

> The King called them to the court and asked them why they were going. They said, 'our wives and families would be worried about us; moreover there is nothing left to eat, that is the real reason why we are going.' So the King asked them to submit whatever arms and cavalry accoutrements they had, and then allowed them to go. He then openly declared in court, 'I do not care who goes or stays. I did not ask anybody to come here and I do not stop anyone [from leaving]. Whoever wants to stay can do so, otherwise they can go away. I have no objections. I have detained these arms so that if the English come here, I can hand it over to them. If the troops want them they can take it. I have no stake in the matter.[61]

No wonder that Maulvi Muhammad Baqar, Zafar's most loyal supporter, should write at this time that 'His Majesty's state of mind remains unwell'.[62] By the end of the month, the hunger had got worse still. On the 30th more disappointed, starving and emaciated troops came to the Palace to declare that they could not go on unless they were fed.

> My Lord, from the day we arrived here we devoted ones have prostrated ourselves at your feet. But you have not provided any upkeep for us, and whatever we brought has been expended. If you cannot provide for us then you must tell us. There is so much starvation that we have no option but to break from your Majesty and go somewhere else. Except for your Majesty, everybody else in the city of Delhi, including the civil servants, are in alliance with the English.[63]

In the city, meanwhile, the people sat behind locked doors, trying to survive as best they could. As August progressed, the impression that emerges from the petitions in the Mutiny Papers is of a wrecked, semi-derelict and starving city. Gamblers and what the

petitioners refer to as 'rogues, rascals and bad characters' sat playing
cards in the burned-out houses that had been looted by the sepoys
or received direct hits from British shells; one petition from Mir
Akbar Ali of the Faiz Bazaar complains that the gamblers used to sit
on the top of the ruins so that they could peer into his zenana
courtyard, 'ogle the women within and shout reprehensible
abuses'.[64] Most shops were shuttered and empty, unless they
had been taken over as billets for the soldiery, in which case
dispirited sepoys could be seen sitting on the steps, smoking 'bhang
and churrus [marijuana preparations]'.[65]

Law and order remained as precarious as ever. Groups of hungry
sepoys were still demanding protection money, most recently from
the shop owners of Chandni Chowk.[66] Others raided neighbouring
houses just to stave off starvation. The Gwalior Cavalry, who had
been billeted in the Delhi haveli of Franz Gottlieb Cohen – the poet
Farasu – and had up to the middle of August behaved with unusual
restraint, eventually went on the rampage in the adjacent muhalla,
stopping in at the local police station on the way back to explain,
'we do not get to eat, therefore we plunder the muhalla'.[67] Outside
the walls the situation was even worse: as early as June, Delhi's
grass-cutters were refusing to go beyond the city walls unless
accompanied by a military escort.[68]

For the poor, the moneylenders were as much an anxiety as either
the sepoys in the city or the British on the Ridge. Though the
baniyas claimed poverty to the city officials, and refused to give or
lend money to help the Uprising, they stepped up their attempts to
call in outstanding debts, and there are mountains of petitions
surviving in the Mutiny Papers from poverty-stricken Delhiwallahs
driven to distraction by their extortions. On 16 August, for example, a delegation from the area around Delhi Darwaza came to
the King complaining about Lala Jatmal and his associates, who had
come with horsemen and foot soldiers,

> threatening and extorting money even from helpless women and
> widows, and from the indigent . . . My lord, Lala Jatmal has used
> great force and coercion. He has collected money from each and
> every house . . . we poor ones are deprived of two square meals. He

should be given a stringent punishment because he adopted illegal and crooked ways. If you do this, in future others will fear to oppress or cheat anyone.[69]

With no effective police force, it was also easy to settle old scores: a petition received from the residents of Muhalla Maliwara complained that Radha and Kanhaiya, two powerful women whom they had previously prosecuted, were openly planning to take revenge: 'Now these people threaten us and say, "what harm you have caused us by filing a suit. We will now attack you because there is no government." We are all afraid for our lives. Please ask the Kotwal to investigate this matter.'[70]

The breakdown of normal life did at least provide an opportunity for lovers to run off together, and judging by the number of petitions flowing in during that month, the growing anarchy of August seems to have facilitated a bacchanal of elopement. Bala-hiyya, wife of Suraj Bali, ran off with Bhikari, 'having looted me of all my wealth which she took away by stealth', according to her surprised and hurt husband.[71] A former courtesan named Hussaini, who had married one Sheikh Islam, also took the opportunity to head off with a new man. The sheikh explained to Zafar that he was a convert from Hinduism who had fled from Meerut at the outbreak and come to seek shelter in Delhi. Not long after their arrival near the 'Id Gah, Hussaini had met Khuda Bakhsh the Shoemaker, whom the sheikh described as 'a spy and a gambler'. Perhaps missing the liveliness of her old life, and finding the company of the sheikh a little staid, Hussaini left Sheikh Islam, taking with her, said the sheikh, 'all the valuables I had brought from home'.[72]

Some of the lovers were sepoys for, as in many wars, dashing soldiers are rarely short of admirers. Certainly Pir Bakhsh the tin-beater and maker of pots and pans, who had been cohabiting not only with his own wife but also with his brother's widow Ziya, and according to the neighbours regularly beating her up, lost her in late August to a sepoy named Zamir. The sepoy apparently gave her shelter after a bad domestic fight: 'all the residents of Katra Muhalla can bear witness to Pir Bakhsh's beatings', Ziya told the court when they took evidence on the case. Pir Bakhsh denied the charge, claiming it was his wife who had beaten Ziya: 'All I did was slap her once,' he said in a statement. 'It was a fight between women.' He also said that he did not intend to marry Ziya, and it appears that Zamir was allowed to take Ziya away with him; certainly Pir Bakhsh had to sign an undertaking saying he would 'not commit any oppression on that woman and if I cause any harm I will pay a fifty rupees fine'.[73]

Others took the opportunity to satisfy their desires by abducting and raping women. The courtesans were particularly vulnerable, as they had been throughout the Uprising. The courtesan Manglo, who had been kidnapped early in May by the *sawar* Rustam Khan, was still in captivity in late July, despite his receiving two orders from the Palace to release her.

Repeated petitions about her were received at the Palace both from her brother Chandan, who seems to have worked as her pimp, and a man who described himself as 'Chhedi, a traveller from Camp Gurgaon' and who said he had been 'made homeless by the depredations of the godless Firangis' – in other words he was one of the many refugees from the countryside fleeing homeless from the acts of retribution wreaked on villages deemed to have been hostile, or to have failed to help the British as they fled Delhi on the night of 11 May. According to Chhedi, 'one gruesome incident has already taken place in this regiment when Farzand Ali, the court Dafadar [sepoy rank equivalent to a guard and petty officer], murdered a courtesan named Imamam by choking her to death. This slave fears that Rustam Khan will kill the said woman, as he threatens and beats her up all day and all night long'.[74] When yet another order to release Manglo was torn up by Rustam's risaldar (cavalry commander), a *sawar* named Faiz Khan, Chandan wrote again to the court, repeating that Rustam Khan

has imprisoned her and beats her up and even though that courtesan shouts and screams nobody helps her. In spite of repeated summons the said Risaldar has not yet obeyed the orders. Should this state of anarchy and injustice continue the subjects of the Exalted One will be destroyed. Therefore I hope that another *parwana* [written order or edict] will be issued to the said Risaldar regarding the recovery of the courtesan . . . Her statement should be registered in the office so that this poor one is compensated, and he can sing prayers for the welfare and fame of the Exalted One.[75]

It was not just the sepoys who were on the loose in the streets of the besieged city: the more delinquent princes were also at large, pursuing their pleasures as they wished. The worst offender, as ever, was Mirza Abu Bakr. One not untypical night saw him turn up at the haveli of Mirza Ghulam Ghaus, whose sisters were celebrated Delhi beauties. Mirza Abu Bakr allegedly told Ghulam Ghaus,

'I am very drunk,' and he began to say foul words. When I told my sisters to hide themselves then he (Abu Bakr) raised his sword over me, and pointed his pistol, but I succeeded in pacifying him . . . In the meantime the gates of the Muhalla had been locked to prevent any untoward incident, and as there was some delay in getting the keys, he began abusing the residents and then he fired countless volleys from double barrelled guns at the gate . . . A Grenadier from the Faiz Bazaar came up and said something, but Mirza Abu Bakr struck him thrice with a sword. By then forty soldiers from the Alexander Platoon and other Tilangas gathered and began to establish order in the Muhalla. While this was happening, I got my sisters to jump over the wall, and had them sent around to Lal Kuan for their own safety.[76]

It was just as well he did so. For before long, Mirza Abu Bakr and his companions broke into the house and looted it, even driving away with them 'a horse and a pair of oxen' they found in the inner courtyard. As they were leaving, the Prince was challenged by the deputy kotwal, who had now ridden up to investigate the disturbance, but Mirza Abu Bakr ignored his protestations and instead lunged at him with a sword, and in the mêlée managed to seize his horse too. At this point, however, Mirza Abdulla, son of Zafar's eldest boy, the late Mirza Shah Rukh, rode up and rebuked his cousin for causing such a disturbance, and managed to persuade him to leave the place and return to the Red Fort.[77]

It was hardly surprising in light of this increasingly chaotic urban breakdown that Maulvi Muhammad Baqar's *Dihli Urdu Akbhar* made for sombre reading. 'Death hovers overhead on all sides,' wrote Baqar in his editorial of 23 August. 'What is happening all around us should be seen as a result of our [bad] deeds and actions. We have taken our base selves as our God, and do not consider the words and commands of the Almighty.'

Baqar also dwelt at some length on the acts of revenge being taken by the British in Kanpur and elsewhere: 'now the *Kafir* Christians have begun to commit grave depredations, especially upon Muslims. Wherever they gain control they indiscriminately hang men, destroy entire villages, and where they cannot cause any harm to the victorious army, they take out their anger on our Emperor's subjects'.[78]

The most serious threat to any remaining hope of victory over the British continued, however, to be the disagreements between the different regiments; and these were now steadily growing worse than ever.

The leaders of the brigade from Nimach, the last large-scale addition to the rebel ranks, took against Bakht Khan's authority even more strongly than the subahdars of the Meerut and Delhi regiments, and on 23 August went as far as to accuse him – quite unjustly – of collusion with the British, 'withholding his soldiers until the British should receive reinforcements from England'.[79]

In all this, they were goaded on by the British spy and agent provocateur Gauri Shankar Sukul of the Haryana Regiment, who produced a Sikh witness who gave false evidence that he had seen Bakht Khan send notes to the Ridge. Bakht Khan swore his loyalty, but Zafar openly discussed the possibility of banning him from the Fort, while the officers of the Nimach brigade began hatching a plot to disarm the Bareilly troops by force.[80]

It was with a view to re-establishing his authority, and making one last concerted bid to oust the British, that Bakht Khan came up with an ingenious and ambitious new plan: his idea was to send out a large force by the Ajmeri Gate, which would set off as if retreating westwards. But rather than heading on towards Jaipur, the force would cross the Yamuna canal by the bridge near Najafgarh, and then double back to ambush the British from behind. It was exactly the sort of imaginative plan the rebels should have come up with two months earlier when the British were at their most vulnerable. By this stage Zafar was happy to agree to any plan that would remove the sepoys from his city. 'Go, may God protect you!' he said. 'Show your loyalty by attacking the English; destroy them and return victorious.'[81]

So it was that, in pouring rain on 24 August, Bakht Khan headed off out of the city with one of the largest forces yet gathered for a single attack: 9,000 men and thirteen guns. They struck out, over the wet roads, for the walled village of Najafgarh, hoping to cross the canal just to the south of the village.

When the sepoys reached the Yamuna canal, just to the north of Palam, it was raining harder than ever, and they found that the bridge had been destroyed on the orders of General Wilson, as part of his strategy of keeping the sepoys away from the British rear. Bakht Khan had come prepared for this, and had the bridge repaired, but the job was done badly, and the bridge broke again almost as soon as the troops began to cross it. It was twenty-four hours before the repairs were completed, and during the wait the entire force was 'exposed for a whole day and night to the inclemency of the season and thoroughly drenched with rain'. Moreover, 'the rebel troops had [now] been practically starving for three days'.[82]

On the 25th, wet, hungry and disconsolate, the rebel force moved off again, passing in narrow file along the banks of the Najafgarh swamp, which lay beyond. It was hard going, according to Sa'id Mubarak Shah: 'The troops were already greatly fatigued by the time they arrived at the swamp, or *jhil*, but had no time to rest and refresh themselves. The wheels of the gun carriages sank so continually in the swamp that the progress was very slow, and the sepoys had to wade through water which was above their knees.'[83]

When they set off from Delhi, Bakht Khan's Bareilly troops had been in the lead. But after the halt at the bridge, it was the Nimach brigade, led by Bakht Khan's rivals and enemies, General Sudhari

Singh and Brigade Major Hira Singh, who led the column, followed by a small party from the Nasirabad regiment. Only two days before, the two Nimach generals had tried to topple Bakht Khan from his command. It was not a combination that boded well for the success of the expedition.

The British watched the vast army of sepoys leave the city through their field glasses: 'They were seen from the Ridge for hours trooping out of the Lahore and Ajmir Gates,' wrote Charles Griffiths, 'and proceeding to our right rear.'[84] When the reports of Bakht Khan's departure reached General Wilson, he knew exactly whom to send to head him off: indeed, in many ways he was even more anxious to get John Nicholson out of the camp than Zafar was to lose Bakht Khan.

Nicholson set off with the Moveable Column in torrential rain at 4 a.m. the following morning, the 25th. In addition to his own men, he brought three troops of horse artillery and a mixed party of British infantry from the Field Force, including his own younger brother, Charles Nicholson, as well as Charles Griffiths and Edward Vibart. In all, Nicholson's small army amounted to 2,500 men, half of them British. In the lead, acting as guide to the back roads of Delhi, was Theo Metcalfe.

Wilson's one order had been to stick to the roads and not get lost in the monsoon bogs. Nicholson immediately ignored the advice and took a short cut that Theo recommended through flooded countryside, where the horse artillery had to be pulled out of knee-deep mud. Despite the mud and the downpour, Nicholson managed to galvanise the column to move along at his customary speed, believing as ever that surprise was all. The column quick-marched for six hours, stopped at 10 a.m. for a damp two-hour breakfast at the village of Munglaee, then resumed the march at noon, through torrents of rain.[85] Instructions were issued that the column should march in silence, 'without noise of any kind'.[86]

Just before four o'clock in the afternoon, two miles north of Najafgarh, Theo was in the lead, investigating another possible short cut, when he came across the advance scouts of the Nimach brigade, who immediately charged. The *sawars* cut at him, but as on 11 May, Theo managed to avoid their thrusts, and made it back safely to the main column.[87]

Ahead, directly in front of the British troops, on the other side of a canal, lay an old Mughal caravanserai. There the advance guard of the Nimach force were resting, guarded by nine guns, waiting for the rest of their column to catch up; well behind them, still near the Palam bridge, were Bakht Khan's Bareilly troops. Many of the sepoys were asleep; others, having piled their arms, were pitching the camp, 'and many had taken off their belts and accoutrements'.[88] The exhausted British troops had now been on the road for twelve hours, and had marched some 20 miles in pouring rain, much of it wading through thick mud, and crossing two swamps 'waist-high in the water, and carrying their ammunition pouches on their heads'; but Nicholson had no hesitation in ordering an immediate assault, so as to take the sepoys unaware.[89]

The sepoys' guns were trained on the bridge across the canal, so Nicholson got the British troops to cross the canal by a ford to one side, and quickly formed up in two lines on the other side. Nicholson rode up and down the line shouting out to the troops to reserve their fire until close to the enemy batteries, and then to charge with fixed bayonets. 'He was answered with a cheer,' wrote Charles Griffiths, 'and the line advanced across the plain, steady and unbroken as though on parade.'[90]

The enemy had opened fire, and were answered by our guns, the infantry marching with sloped guns at the quick-step till within 100 yards, when we delivered a volley. Then the war cry of the British soldiers was heard, and the two regiments came to the charge, and ran at the double towards the serai.

Lt Gabbett of my regiment was the first man to reach the entrenchment, and passing through an embrasure, received a bayonet thrust in his left breast, which stretched him on the ground . . . [dying] of an internal haemorrhage soon after. But the men followed, clearing everything before them, capturing the four guns in the serai, bayoneting the rebels, and firing at those who had taken flight at our approach.[91]

Nicholson led the charge, but one of the first to engage with the sepoys was Edward Vibart. 'We stormed their position and drove them from it . . . capturing the whole of their camp, ammunition and baggage,' he wrote to his one surviving sister the following day.

> We advanced to the charge, in the face of all their people and musketry pouring out from behind a square walled enclosure loopholed all around. With one tremendous cheer headed by our General we drove them out at the point of the bayonet – Oh I can't tell you what a maddening feeling came over me as I rushed and I thought of our beloved parents, and burned for vengeance. It was my *first battle* and God in his mercy was again pleased to preserve me, though men close to me were struck down. A bullet even hit my sword, saving the life of a man just behind me – but what pleasure is there now in describing all this? All before us is but darkness and misery. My own darling mother's face is always before me . . .[92]

Vibart was not the only person in despair that day. When Nicholson attacked, most of the sepoys were still trudging forward, strung out along the bank of the swamp, unable to move left or right, and hemmed in fore and aft by their fellow sepoys. Even at the edge of the swamp the mud was terrible, and many were wading up to their knees in the bog. 'While thus struggling in the morass, the British guns opened upon them,' wrote Sa'id Mubarak Shah.

> The grape from twelve guns now poured into the Nimach troops and the infantry and artillery became helplessly fixed in the marsh. They could neither advance nor retreat and numbers began to fall. To make matters worse they were unable to see the British guns which were dealing such destruction in their ranks, as they were hidden by trees and high standing crops. Notwithstanding the extreme difficulty of their position, the rebel artillery fired repeatedly and the sepoys also. But when men can neither advance nor retire, there is no help for them, and the brave man and the coward have nothing for it but to stop and die. On that day 470 of the Nimach brigade, horse, foot and artillery were killed by grape shot alone.[93]

Worse still for the future coherence of the rebel force was Bakht Khan's response when word reached him near the Palam bridge that the Nimach troops ahead had engaged the British. Three days earlier, the Nimach generals had accused him of treachery, and now he was in no hurry to come to their rescue. Instead, on hearing the guns, Bakht Khan halted the reserve. 'The real fact was that he and the officers of the Nimach force were not on good terms,' wrote Sa'id Mubarak Shah.

> On this account one party desired the ruin of the other. Each leader wanted his own name alone to be famous, and himself hailed as a victor. [Luckily] the Nasirabad brigade had advanced on the right and their fire proved fatal to upwards of a hundred of the British, thereby enabling the remaining portion of the Nimach men to get out of the swamp. Had it not been for this, not a man, not even an animal belonging to that brigade would have escaped alive. Their guns fell into the hands of the British, and the mutineer army fled in utter disorder, while the round shot unceasingly harassed them in their flight. At length, staggering along exhausted and totally disorganised they reached Bakht Khan's fresh troops, and retired along with them, while the Europeans took the captured guns to pieces, placed them on elephants and carried them to their camp on the Ridge.[94]

For both sides it was a crucial turning point. For the first time since Badli ki Serai two and a half months earlier, the Delhi Field Force had engaged the rebel troops in an open battle, and the scale of the defeat, and the blow to rebel morale, meant that neither side had any doubt that a full-scale assault on the city was now imminent.

A week later, on 4 September, the elephants of the 8-mile-long siege train finally trundled into the British camp, pulling with them sixty heavy howitzers and mortars, preceded by long lines of 653 'hackeries' – bullock carts full of ammunition, shrapnel shell, round-shot and grape canister, much of it newly produced in the Punjab ordnance factories, which had continued to function efficiently throughout the Uprising. Many of the siege guns were so enormous – especially the six giant 24-pounders – that it took teams of elephants to pull them.*⁹⁵ Accompanying the siege train were an escort of 400 European infantry, a large party of Sikh cavalry and 'the Belooch battalion, a most savage-looking lot of men', according to Charles Griffiths.⁹⁶

The next day Hervey Greathed went to visit all the supplies being unpacked in the Engineers Park. Here Richard Baird-Smith, an irrigation expert from the Punjab who had been conscripted as chief engineer of the Field Force, was busy making his plans: 'The supply of shot and shell seems sufficient to grind Delhi to powder,' wrote Greathed.

> I have not seen the programme of operations, but every day's work is chalked out and written down in elaborate detail. Baird Smith is not a man to forget the smallest trifle. The Engineers park is a busy scene. There are forests of gabions, and acres of fascines, all ready to be transported to the scene of action; and platform for guns and frameworks of magazines, sandbags, entrenching tools, ladders and everything requisite for the construction of batteries and for the attack.⁹⁷

The following day, the British began constructing the heavy batteries that would break down the city walls, as Punjabi sappers worked under the guidance of British military engineers. It was not work that was possible to keep secret. From the walls and bastions, the rebel artillerymen targeted the construction parties; inevitably it was the Indian coolies who suffered the brunt of their shelling, while their British masters looked on with mild, detached disdain: 'with that passive bravery so characteristic of the natives,' wrote Fred Roberts, 'as man after man was knocked over, they would stop for a moment, weep a little over a fallen friend, place his body in a row along with the rest, and then work on as before'.⁹⁸

---

* Crucially, the elephants to move the siege train had been provided by the rajas of the Punjab. Had they not provided them, the siege might have had a very different ending.

General Bakht Khan returned from Najafgarh in disgrace, and was abused at the durbar for having left the Nimach troops to be defeated without attempting to come to their aid. Even Zafar, increasingly detached from proceedings in recent weeks, regained some of his lucidity in the light of the disaster, and 'sent a messenger to General Bakht Khan, telling him he had been false to his salt in turning away from the field of battle'.[99]

For a week the army seemed on the verge of a second mutiny. There was wild talk among the sepoys of deposing Zinat Mahal – whom they rightly accused of keeping up a correspondence with the British – and replacing her as Queen with her predecessor, Taj Begum, 'unless their pay was forthcoming in fifteen days',[100] Zinat Mahal's father, Mirza Quli Khan, was also briefly arrested by a group of sepoys, apparently acting on their own initiative. Others mooted the idea of deposing Zafar in favour of Mirza Jawan Bakht, who had been almost invisible throughout the siege. One day 500 sepoys gathered outside the Diwan i-Khas and accused Mirza Abu Bakr and Mirza Khizr Sultan of embezzling funds, and that they 'had taken several lakh of rupees from people in the city and given nothing to the army'. Zafar in desperation handed over all the remaining silver in the Palace to the sepoys, telling them, 'sell it, and divide the proceeds among yourselves for pay'.[101]

Yet as the British siege batteries inched closer and, on 8 September, began pounding the city walls, the realisation that the end was now imminent galvanised the rebel forces into the state of coherence and unity that had eluded them throughout the siege. Much of the credit for this must go to Mirza Mughal, whose office began to produce a torrent of orders for the city's defence, and issued a final appeal in his father's name for the citizens to unite against the *kafirs*: 'This is a religious war,' he wrote on the 6th, ordering that the words should be proclaimed by the beat of the drum through the city. 'It is being prosecuted on account of the faith, and it behoves all Hindu and Musalman residents of the Imperial City, or of the villages out in the country to . . . continue true to their faiths and creeds, and to slay the English and their servants.'[102]

The British siege guns were now blazing away at the northern face of the city walls: by 12 September, all sixty guns were firing round after round, as fast as they could, twenty-four hours a day: 'the din and roar were defeaning', wrote Charles Griffiths. 'Day and night salvos of artillery were heard, roll following roll in endless succession.'[103] It was worse still to be on the receiving end: 'The cannons and the mortars on the Ridge were constantly at work,' wrote Zahir Dehlavi. 'God alone knows how many there were. That day all the doors and walls of the city were trembling, and fire was raining from the sky. It was as if hell had been let loose on earth.'[104]

What the British did not know was that on the other side of the walls, Mirza Mughal had begun to construct an elaborate system of barricades and street defences, including a *damdama* or mud fort in the area in front of Kashmiri Gate, realising that once the British were within the walls, their troops would be far more vulnerable than they had ever been behind their carefully built breastworks on the Ridge.[105] His plan seems to have been to encourage the British to leave their impregnable entrenchments, and lure them into the city streets, where they would lose their strategic advantage, and where cannon primed with grapeshot, as well as nests full of snipers, would be ready and waiting for them. Certainly, the British were allowed to take the ground between the Ridge and the city walls without much resistance; but once within easy range of the city walls, the rebel forces struck back with force.

Already the exposed working parties attempting to build gun platforms on the flat ground near the walls proved a more inviting target than any that had been offered to the rebels since June: 'the *kafirs* are now in range', wrote Mirza Mughal to the officers on 8 September. 'Come and give battle. We can shoot very well from the top of the walls. There should be no delay and no dereliction of duty, because the enemy is now at the gates, and everybody should courageously gird up their loins.'[106]

Moreover, for the first time the jihadis were able to get close enough to put their axes to work: Imdad Ali Khan, one of Bakht Khan's jihadis, was said to have displayed particular bravery, 'and although surrounded, managed to escape with considerable difficulty'.[107] Among those who accompanied him at this time were 'Moulvee Nawazish Ali with his 2,000 men' and a newly arrived regiment of 'suicide ghazis' from Gwalior, who had vowed never to eat again and to fight until they met death at the hands of the *kafirs*, 'for those who have come to die have no need for food'.[108]

One other rebel who distinguished himself at this time was Sergeant Gordon, the English convert to Islam who had been brought by the sepoys from Shahjahanpur. According to Sa'id Mubarak Shah, Gordon 'laid and fired the guns against the English batteries. The shot struck fair and true and so delighted the sepoys that they presented *nazrs* to the sergeant, who replied 'it is too late, I can do nothing now. If you had acted on my advice at the commencement, the British batteries could not have advanced a foot. Now that matters are hopeless you want me to stop their further progress. It is impossible, but I will die along with you.'[109]

Maulvi Sarfaraz Ali, the imam of the mujahedin, went to the court on 10 September, and said how grateful the jihadis were that at long last their 'valour and dedication' were being recognised, and that they were looking forward to participating in the coming battle with more vigour than ever.[110] According to the estimates of Hervey Greathed, owing to the number of sepoy desertions that had taken place in August, the proportion of jihadis had risen dramatically and they now numbered just under half the remaining rebel army: of the total estimated insurgent army remaining in Delhi of around 60,000 men as many as 25,000 were jihadis.*[111]

Mirza Mughal sent the town criers round the streets calling on the ordinary citizens to come and join the defence. The same call went up from the jihadis, who began touring the Delhi streets calling out, ' "Citizens, citizens, all who would be martyrs for the faith come follow us . . ." They collected in great numbers, prepared for action and took the most solemn oath that they would go

---

* Lieutenant Coghill thought the jihadis made up at least half the rebel numbers: 'The enemy had about 25 or 30,000 actual sepoys,' he wrote to his brother, 'and about 30,000 more ghazis, a race of devils and fanatics.' See NAM, 6609-139, Coghill Letters, letter From Lt Coghill to his brother, datelined Delhi, 22 September 1857. If the rebel army was changing dramatically, so was the British force, which was now probably around four-fifths made up of ethnic Indians. If the Uprising in Delhi started up as a contest between Hindustani sepoys and the British, it ended as a fight between a mixed rebel force at least half of which were Muslim civilian jihadis, taking on an army of British paid mercenaries of Sikh, Muslim Punjabi and Pathan extraction.

out and fight and if necessary die, but would never retreat.'[112] On 10 September, other orders were sent to the different subahdars to rally together for the last battle: 'His Lordship the Emperor has passed an order,' wrote Mirza Mughal,

> reminding the Hindus and Muslims that, for the sake of the cow and [against the defilement by] the pig, and abiding by religion and faith, if you want to make progress and earn merit in this life, then let us see whether you can prepare your infantry, cavalry and artillery and reach Kashmiri gate to attack our debased and unworthy opponents, the villainous *kafirs*. Let there be no delay in this. Act in accordance with his Lordship's orders. Act promptly. Now that you have fought on the grounds of religion and faith you should remain constant on that. Every officer should form sections of his platoon and cavalry and after arranging them should inform them of the order, and prepare for the attack. Should anybody, officer or sepoy, make any excuses please immediately send a report about them before His Lordship.[113]

On 11 September, the British began co-ordinating the firing of all their guns, so that the shot struck the walls simultaneously in great deafening salvoes. By midday, the city walls were finally beginning to crumble, 'sending up clouds of dust, and bringing the masonry down into the ditch'.[114] The guns on Kashmiri Gate were soon silent, and two large breaches opened in the curtain walls, one near the Kashmiri Bastion, the other near the Yamuna river front, at the Water Bastion. Yet despite their hunger, the rebels fought now with a vigour that they had never shown before, sending out squadrons of cavalry from the gates to harass the coolies, engineers and gunners; in a few days, British casualties topped the 400 mark.

'Though their batteries on the bastions had been well nigh silenced,' noticed Charles Griffiths, 'the rebels stuck well to their field guns in the open space before the walls; they sent a storm of rockets from one of the Martello Towers and fired a stream of musketry from the ramparts and advanced trenches.'[115] Several of the British batteries caught fire and were 'left a smouldering heap of sandbags, fascines and gabions'.[116] Even Edward Vibart had to admit that 'the mutineers fight with an obstinancy not to be conceived, though the bastions are a heap of ruins, yet they still return our fire and their numbers are so great that day after day they come out and attack us on all sides. They will never be driven from the walls until the bayonet is brought into play'.[117]

By Sunday, 13 September, it was clear that the assault was imminent, and most guessed it would take place the following morning.

The British troops spent the day practising escalading with siege ladders. They also voted on who among them would become prize agents, in charge of the legalised looting of the captured city: to his own surprise, Edward Campbell received the most votes. He heard of his appointment at the new front line in the old Mughal Garden of Qudsia Bagh, opposite the Kashmiri Gate, to which he had been moved from Hindu Rao's House five days earlier.

At a meeting of the senior commanders at eleven that morning, General Wilson announced that it would be Nicholson who would lead the attack, which was provisionally set for sunrise the following morning. There were to be four columns, each directed to enter the city through a different opening on the northern face of the walls, and to head to a different goal; a fifth column was to act as reserve; to his disgust, Edward Vibart found that he was assigned to this, and so would not take part in the assault. Theo Metcalfe, meanwhile, was to guide the column that aimed to enter the city through the Kashmiri Gate and capture the Jama Masjid, which would then be used as a base for assaulting the Palace.

For most, the evening was spent writing wills and last letters. 'I believe we are to escalade,' wrote one young officer to his anxious mother.

> You know what that will be – rush up a ladder, with men trying to push you down, bayonet and shoot you from above. But you must wave your sword and think it capital fun, bring your men up as fast as you can and jump down on top of men ready with fixed bayonets to receive you. All this is not very pleasant to think coolly of, but

when the moment comes excitement makes you feel as happy as possible . . . I hope it won't make me swear, though that is almost allowable for you are mad with excitement, and know not what you are saying. But I will strive against it with all my might.'[118]

Edward Campbell attended the last church service that Padre Rotton was to conduct on the Ridge, as he celebrated the Eucharist – 'a deeply solemn and impressive occasion' – and preached on the text, 'I am ready to be offered', from the letter of St Paul to Timothy. But it was the Old Testament reading, foretelling the doom of 'the bloody city' of Nineveh, 'full of lies and robbery', which really appealed to Rotton, and which he spoke about at greatest length: 'Draw thee waters for the siege, fortify thy strongholds,' he read from the Book of Nahum. 'Then shall the fire devour thee; the sword shall cut thee off; it shall eat thee up like the canker worm . . . There is a multitude of slain, and a great number of carcasses . . . They shall stumble upon their corpses.'[119]

Within the city, preparations for resisting the assault were also almost complete. Bakht Khan was busy finalising the defences in the area around the Kabul Gate that he was to command, building barricades and sandbag emplacements. That morning, he sent to his old rival Mirza Mughal, with whom he seems to have patched up a modus vivendi, asking for 200 coolies, wooden planks, baskets and gunny bags to be sent to him. Everything he asked for was promptly sent.[120] Mirza Mughal, meanwhile, was issuing a last order for the population of the town to resist the assault with every weapon they could find. He also supervised clearing the two *muhallas* nearest the breaches, and sending the inhabitants to safety in other parts of the city.[121]

In the Red Fort, Zafar made a point of continuing with his ceremonial duties as if nothing unusual was happening – in this case conferring the title of Safir ud-Dowlah on an ambassador come to offer the fealty of the Court of Lucknow. But in private he feared the worst: 'The King became greatly depressed when he heard that the guns on the city walls had been silenced,' wrote Sa'id Mubarak Shah, 'and taking up a Koran opened it to see what it would declare. The first passage his eye fell on was to the following effect: "Neither you nor your army, but those who were before." The old King remained silent, but Hakim Ahsanullah Khan tried to persuade him that it really meant that he would conquer in the strife.' Zafar suspected otherwise.[122]

Zinat Mahal, meanwhile, was at the other side of the city in her haveli in Lal Kuan, deep in last-minute negotiations with the British through Hodson's intelligence chief, Maulvi Rajab Ali. Ever since 4 August, Zafar's queen had been in regular touch with the British, putting out feelers and hoping to be able to come to terms in return for certain conditions being met. Hodson had regularly relayed developments to Sir Robert Montgomery, Lawrence's Chief of Intelligence in Lahore, reporting that Zinat Mahal 'was intriguing with British spies', was 'firmly pro-British' and had 'offered her assistance in the taking of the city' and even in 'blowing up the Bridge of Boats'.[123]

On 25 August, the day Nicholson had set off in pursuit of Bakht Khan, she had sent an emissary to Greathed, 'offering to exercise her influence with the King'; but Greathed had politely replied that while 'we wished her personally all happiness, and had no quarrel with women and children', he was not authorised to 'hold communication with anyone belonging to the Palace'.[124]

Never one to take no for an answer, Zinat Mahal now hoped she might be able to get farther by directing her communications towards Hodson. It was a shrewd move, for Hodson loved intrigue, and – though he had no authorisation – reopened communications, apparently on his own authority. On 9 September Zinat Mahal had asked for another meeting with Maulvi Rajab Ali at her haveli in Lal Kuan. By the 13th, even as her hand was weakening by the minute as the British assault drew closer and closer, she was still holding out for her old dream, the same objective for which she had worked so tirelessly for so many years. As Hodson put it in his report, Zinat Mahal demanded in return for her assistance

that her son should be pronounced heir apparent and the succession of the throne guaranteed to him, while on the part of the King that it was demanded that his position should continue undiminished, and the arrears for the five months subsequent to the outbreak in May paid up at once.

It was with considerable difficulty that I succeeded in awakening her to the real position in which the King was placed, and the utter impossibility of either the King, or any of this family, being ever restored to the throne they had forfeited. When at length she comprehended that not only the liberty, but also that the lives of the King and his son were at stake, I succeeded in enlisting Zeenut Mahal in the cause, by guaranteeing the lives of her son and father. On this condition alone would she consent to use her influence with the King.[125]

While these secret negotiations were going on in Lal Kuan, Maulvi Muhammad Baqar, meanwhile, published what he strongly suspected would be the last ever issue of the *Dihli Urdu Akbhar*. The melancholy yet resigned editorial was about repentance, and not trying to understand the mysterious ways of God: 'You should not lose heart,' he advised, 'but instead draw faith and fortify your belief in the Almighty.'

Although the *Kafirs* are advancing towards us and dig a new front almost every night, the important thing is to admire the spirit and bravery of our victorious army, and to observe that they try to assault the *Kafir* positions day and night. If the Almighty is placing this impediment in our path there must be some design in it: who knows what act of arrogance or injustice we may have unknowingly committed that has caused it? We should pray to God for forgiveness and enlightenment, and we should make it a point to refrain from committing any excesses on fellow human beings, or exploiting and injuring them in any way.

It is said that the people in the city, especially the poor, are in dire straits. It is necessary at a time like this to provide relief and succour to the toiling masses so that they pray with sincerity of heart for the final victory of the Emperor's government. Remember that when the time is ripe and when he wishes it so, the Almighty will instantly bring us victory. Who knows what kind of travail and examination he wishes to subject us to, that he delays our victory so? Only He knows the unknown. The discerning and wise ones wait for his favour.[126]

That evening, up on the Ridge, Robert Tytler made Harriet promise that if things went badly the following morning she would take the bullock cart with the children, and head off in good time to Ambala. 'He would have to remain with his treasure till a general rout took place,' wrote Harriet. 'It would have been about the worst spot in camp to remain alive, as the enemy would have made a rush to seize all the rupees they could . . . [But] if there was a reverse, I don't believe anyone could possibly have reached a place of safety. Simla would have gone, Kussowlie would have gone, and all India would have risen in arms by one consent.' Nevertheless, Robert got 'our bullocks in readiness to make a start', just in case.[127]

Most of the British retired early. 'There was not much sleep that night in our camp,' wrote Richard Barter. 'I dropped off now and then, but never for long, and when I woke I could see there was a light in more than one of the officers' tents, and talking was going on in a low tone amongst the men, the snapping of a lock or the springing of a ramrod sounding far in the still air, telling of preparation for the approaching strife.'[128]

Edward Campbell was also unable to sleep, and instead wrote what he realised might be his last letter to GG, commending himself and his family to the Almighty: 'without our God we can do nothing', he scribbled in his tent.

> My precious wife, remember that we are in His hands, who has been so merciful and forbearing to us hitherto. Put your trust in thy Lord who shall yet be our salvation. I feel more and more how important it is to seek comfort in him, who alone can give true peace . . . The alarm has just sounded so I must give up writing and get into my harness. May God watch over thee my darling wife, and keep us both and all dear to us.[129]

At midnight, the troops rose, and began to assemble in their different columns. By the light of lanterns, General Wilson's orders were read out to them. Each man was to carry 200 rounds of ammunition, and the goal of each column was outlined, as well as the route they were to take. The wounded were to be left where they fell. There was to be no plundering; all the valuables in the city would be placed in a common treasury under Edward Campbell's supervision. No prisoners were to be taken; but 'for the sake of humanity and the honour of the country', women and children were not to be hurt.

At 3 a.m., the four assault columns marched first to the Flagstaff Tower and then down in silence from the Ridge, using Zafar's fruit trees in the once lovely Mughal garden of Qudsia Bagh as cover. All this time the siege artillery and breaching batteries had been firing as rapidly as they had been for the last ten days and, according to Barter, 'the darkness before day was illuminated by constant flashes, while the air seemed alive with shells'.[130]

This went on for half an hour, until, as dawn broke over the horizon, the guns all fell suddenly silent together. For a second in the stillness the soldiers could hear 'small birds twittering among the trees' and smell the perfume of the orange blossom and Zafar's roses, both still 'apparent in spite of the sulphury smell of powder'.[131]

Then Nicholson gave the order, and after three months, the British finally advanced on the walls of Delhi.

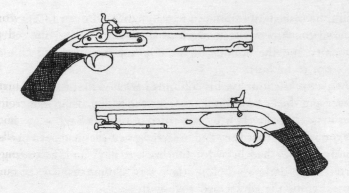

10

TO SHOOT EVERY SOUL

The assault on the city started exactly as planned. On the command, the officers leading each column gave the signal, there was a cheer, and the troops ran as fast as they could from the wooded shelter of Qudsia Bagh, through a rose garden, and out into the 50 yards of no-man's-land between the garden and the city walls. Here they were immediately met with 'a perfect hailstorm of bullets' from the ready and waiting sepoys.[1]

The first obstacle was the ditch, 20 feet deep by 25 broad. As the ladders were fetched and put into place the troops caught at the crest of the glacis, unable to get down, 'fell fast under the withering fire'. It was nearly ten minutes before the first troops had succeeded in rising out of the far side of the glacis alive; but once they had climbed to the breach, the momentum became hard to stop.[2] 'Up our men went, beautifully, like a pack of hounds,' wrote Fred Roberts to his mother. 'We gunners had done our work so well that the Breach was perfect and we gained the ramparts with comparatively slight loss.'[3]

It seemed much less smooth if, like Richard Barter, you were the first up. As he ran forward, Barter remembered seeing the heads of the defenders rising from the gap in the ramparts, 'while along the walls they swarmed thick like bees. The sun shone full upon the

white turbans and black faces, sparkling brightly on their swords
and bayonets, and our men cheered madly as they reached the
breach'.

> The enemy whose fire had slackened when ours ceased, at first
> seemed perfectly taken aback at our appearance, but recovering from
> their surprise, they now recommenced in earnest: round shot came
> screaming from the guns far to our right, while grape and shells
> whistled from those nearer, and the walls seemed a line of fire along
> our front. Bullets whistled in the air, tore up the ground about our
> feet, and men fell fast . . .
>
> Three times the ladder party was swept away, and three times
> were the ladders snatched from the dead and wounded . . . It was
> hard work getting up the breach, which was like a sloping bank of
> sea sand from the pounding of the shot. Behind it were some
> gabions, between which the enemy kept up a smart fire, so close to
> us that I could feel the flash of each discharge hot on my cheek. To
> spoil their aim, I kept firing my revolver with my right hand, while
> I scrambled up [the ladder] with my left, holding my sword under
> my arm as best I could, for we carried no scabbards. They kept
> heaving huge blocks of masonry at us, and tried to roll some
> down . . .
>
> The defenders eventually retreated back into the city, leaving
> Fitzgerald and myself standing close up to the gabions. We shook
> hands and parted, he down the right of the breach, and I along the
> parapet to the left, towards Kashmiri Gate. I never saw him again, he
> was killed by a discharge of grape inside the walls, immediately after
> I parted from him.[4]

While running along the wall-walk, Barter heard a colossal explosion and, looking up, saw the Kashmiri Gate 'blown into Delhi'.
The assault plan had called for ten sappers and a bugler to place a
large explosive charge immediately in front of the gate, and for the
troops then to rush the gap thus opened. As the assault had started a
little later than planned, and it was now broad daylight, this proved
more difficult than it sounded on paper. When the signal for the
assault was given, the defenders opened the wicket at the bottom of

the gate and began firing directly at the sappers as they tried to carry the charge into place along the damaged bridge, only one beam of which now remained.[5]

In the lead was the twenty-seven-year-old Philip Salkeld, who had been one of Edward Vibart's companions in the escape from that same gate on the evening of 11 May, and who in the days of wandering that followed had honourably donated his shoes to Annie Forrest. Now he led the explosion party's precarious charge over the remaining beam, holding the fuses that were intended to set off the powder. Four men followed carrying the explosive bag into place; seven others, including Salkeld, were supposed to nail it to the wooden door of the gate and set the fuses and slow matches than would detonate it.

As Salkeld's party neared the gate, the defenders opened fire at point blank range through the wicket and down from the loop-holes. First one of the sappers, then a second and a third and a fourth were shot down as they tried to nail the powder to the door. Within a few seconds, all the party except three were either killed or severely wounded, while Salkeld was mortally injured with two terrible wounds. But one of the three survivors, Sergeant Smith, although also badly wounded, still managed to relight the extinguished fuse and throw himself under the bridge as the charge went off, blowing the right leaf of the double gates off its hinge. One of the other survivors was the bugler, Hawthorne, who sounded the advance from the shelter of the ditch, giving the signal for the British troops to charge and take the gate.[6]

It was now a quarter to six. The troops of the third column had been lying flat, just inside Qudsia Bagh, out of range of the muskets, waiting impatiently for the bugle call. But such was the noise of musketry from the walls that Hawthorne's first two bugle calls were not audible; only the third was faintly heard. One of those waiting for the sound was the angry and violent Anglo-Irish Protestant, Lieutenant Kendal Coghill, who had been dreaming dreams of vengeance and retribution for months up on the Ridge. Now, he wrote to his father, the moment had come, and 'blood-thirsty and eager as I was for it, a species of wildness and madness came over me, knowing that the quicker the rush, the nearer the enemy, and earlier the revenge'.

> I took a firm bite of the pistol bullet in my mouth which was there to keep the mouth moist, and with a devil's yell, I rushed from under cover. The musketry poured in like rain, and men kept falling on every side of me, but I thought my life charmed and they could not touch me. The curses, moans and execrations of the wounded and dying, cursing their fate at being left outside and not being able to revenge themselves, was pitiable in the extreme and they rolled and writhed in agony.
>
> We were to have stormed the left but the fire on the right was so heavy that all the ladder party there were shot down, so we . . . rushed to the right [to take their place]. After that I felt like a drunken man. I just remember putting my sword back and seizing the ladders and throwing them down into the ditch, but the ladders were only 8 feet and the ditch we found was 20 feet deep. In the excitement we dropped below and the ladders reached the berm on the other side, and up we rushed.
>
> The brutes fought till we regularly hacked and cut our way through them with sword and bayonet. Unfortunately the first thing my sword struck was the body of a colour sergeant of mine just along side of me on the next ladder who was shot and fell on my sword. But the next moment it was shivering through a Pandy, and then another. All order and formation was over and we cut and hacked wherever we could. I never thought of drawing my pistol, but poked, thrusted and hacked, till my arms were tired.[7]

Ten minutes of desperate hand-to-hand fighting later, the gate and the main guard enclosure had fallen to the British, and the Union Jack fluttered above the archway.[8] But even fiercer resistance was met a little farther down the street at Skinner's haveli, opposite St James's Church. This had been fortified by the Nasirabad troops, who had used it as their headquarters throughout the siege. Others had taken up position firing over the low churchyard wall of St James's.[9] Both parties now let loose such a storm of grape and musketry that they managed to kill many of the front ranks of the

British before retiring – Sa'id Mubarak Shah thought maybe as many as three or four hundred British troops fell between the Kashmiri Gate and the Skinner haveli.[10] But since all three of the British columns were now concentrating their fire at the house and the churchyard, the Nasirabad sepoys had no option but to retreat, taking their guns with them.

Outside, in the open space facing St James's Church, Nicholson now gathered the troops of the three columns.[11] Realising, however, that much of his own column had already set off along the walls without him, and without wishing to pause to allow time for the rebels to regroup, Nicholson took what remained of his party and headed off westwards along the parapet. His aim was to catch up with his lost troops, and to capture the Kabul and Lahore gates as quickly as possible. There they would join up with the fourth column, under Major Reid, which was supposed to have fought its way down from Hindu Rao's House, through the suburb of Kishenganj. In this way, according to Wilson's plan, the British would gain control of the whole northern and western perimeter of the city by lunchtime.

Theo, meanwhile, set off with the second column, largely made up of Gurkhas, whom he guided through the backstreets in the direction of the Jama Masjid. The third column made its way south-east towards the Red Fort by way of the Delhi College. As the troops set off, General Wilson came in from Ludlow Castle, from the roof of which he had watched the assault, and set up his headquarters in the wreck of Skinner's gutted haveli. A canteen and field hospital were established nearby inside St James's Church.

It was at this point – just after seven in the morning – that things suddenly began to go badly wrong for the British. It had been presumed that getting within the walls was going to be the most difficult part of the assault, and this feat had now been achieved, with relatively low losses, and ahead of schedule. But it was the next stage – advancing through the streets – which was actually to prove far more costly. Once the British were known to be advancing on the Fort, it had been expected that the sepoys' nerve would fail and they would sooner or later turn and flee. Not only did this not happen, but the rebel forces now counter-attacked and fought back with such astonishing force that they very nearly succeeded in driving the British out of the city and back up to the Ridge. Bakht Khan and Mirza Mughal had made their preparations well. As Fred Roberts succinctly put it, 'from this time, we suffered severely'.[12]

Charles Griffiths was with the column that was heading southwards towards the Fort. They had just begun to advance slowly through the gardens of the wrecked and looted Delhi College when they walked straight into an ambush. Suddenly,

> from every window and door, from loopholes in the buildings, and from the tops of the houses, a storm of musketry saluted us on every side, while every now and then, when passing the corner of a street, field guns loaded with grape discharged their contents into the column. Officers and men fell fast. This only served to exasperate the remainder . . . who after some severe skirmishing, cleared the gardens and houses of the rebels, and bayoneted all who were found there.

So severe were their losses, however, that the column gave up any attempt to advance farther, and began to fortify the College as their front-line strongpoint.

Theo's column was drawn farther into the town before they found themselves cornered by the jihadis. Theo had been picking his way gingerly through the back lanes, losing men to snipers and occasional flurries of grapeshot. The streets were almost deserted, and initially they came across surprisingly little resistance. They passed nervously over Chandni Chowk, and advanced through an eerie silence as far as the north gate of the Jama Masjid.

They had just realised that they had brought no powder charges to blow open the mosque gates, when in the silence the doors slowly opened of their own accord, and the massed jihadis waiting inside emerged screaming down the steps. According to Sa'id Mubarak Shah, the jihadis 'hurled themselves upon the English who, overmatched, fell back with the loss of two guns', and around forty dead.[13] As the British retreated back into Chandni Chowk, the jihadis were supported by a field gun brought over from the Lahore Gate, which fired down the length of the bazaar and landed a shell directly 'in the midst of the English column, killing and wounding upwards of fifty of them'.[14]

The remains of Theo's force lingered for half an hour in Chandni Chowk, trying to fend off the axes and swords of the jihadis, hoping that Griffiths' column, which was now supposed to rendezvous with them, would come to their rescue. But when thirty minutes had passed, and it became clear that the other column had also run into trouble, the order was given to retreat to the Kashmiri Gate.[15]

While this was happening, up on the city walls, Nicholson's force had also found themselves in severe difficulties. During the taking of the Kashmiri Gate, the column had split up and Nicholson had lost most of his troops, as they had continued forwards along the walls without him. Richard Barter was one of these: he made his way gingerly, darting from arched recess to arched recess, along the base of the city walls. 'Into these we used to rush every time we saw the port fires being put to the guns which we ran across every now and then raking down the road. When the storm of grape had flown past, and before they could be reloaded, we used to take them with a rush and bayonet and shoot the gunners.' Every so often, Barter's party would stop to attack houses containing sepoys, surprise and kill them all, and then continue on along the foot of the walls.[16]

Others took a more careless approach to the danger. 'On we rushed [along the parapet],' wrote Lieutenant Arthur Moffat Lang in his diary, 'shouting and cheering, while the grape and musketry from each bend, and from every street leading to our left, and from rampart and housetop, knocked down men and officers'.

It was exciting to madness and I felt no feeling but to rush on: I only wondered how much longer I could go on unhit when the whole air seemed full of bullets . . . We took tower after tower, gun after gun, never stopping . . . We poured past the Kabul Gate and we went along until we nearly reached the Lahore; then a short check was given by a barricade with a gun firing grape from behind it. Brig Jones came up and called for the Engineer officer, and asked where the Kabul gate was . . . "Far behind," I said. "We shall have the Lahore presently." Alas he declared that his orders were to stop at the Kabul . . .

As long as we rushed on cheering and never stopping, all went well. But the check was sad: the men crouching behind corners, and in the archways which support the ramparts, gradually nursed a panic. One by one they tried to get back: we stopped them and staved off the flight for half an hour, but at last out they all came, and sweeping back the officers, made for the Kabul Gate.[17]

Grapeshot from the heavy guns massed on the Lahore Gate and the Burn Bastion, and manned by Bakht Khan's Bareilly troops, was now sweeping the parapet and walls, and a full-scale retreat looked imminent. It was at this point that Nicholson appeared on the street below and tried to salvage the situation. Calling the terrified troops down to ground level and rallying them, he drew his sword and, despite the musketry and grapeshot, charged straight up the narrow street with the wall to his right and houses to the left, calling for the men to follow. Halfway up the street, he realised he was alone, and turned to call to the troops to support him. As he hesitated, still waving his sword in his hand, a sepoy sniper, probably on the Burn Bastion, fired down on him. The ball entered Nicholson's chest, just below the exposed armpit. One of the other fusiliers who had belatedly come up, pointed out that he had been hit. 'Yes, yes,' replied Nicholson irritably, before sinking to the ground.[18]

He was carried back to the Kabul Gate, where two doolie bearers were instructed to take him up to the field hospital on the Ridge. In the growing chaos, however, as the British assault stumbled to a halt, and as every one of the different columns fell back in disorder, the bearers abandoned the injured general by the side of the street. Some time later, Fred Roberts happened to be passing: 'While riding through the Kashmir Gate,' he wrote, 'I observed by the side of the road a doolie without bearers, and evidently with a wounded man inside.'

I dismounted to see if I could be of any use to the occupant, when I found to my grief and consternation, that it was [the dying] John Nicholson. He told me that the bearers had put the doolie down and gone off to plunder; that he was in great pain, and wished to be taken to the hospital. He was lying on his back, no wound visible, and but for the pallor on his face, always colourless, there was no sign of the agony he must have been enduring. On my expressing a hope that he was not seriously wounded, he said: 'I am dying; there is no hope for me.' The sight of that great man lying helpless and on the point of death was almost more than I could bear. Other men had daily died around me, friends and comrades had been killed beside me, but I never felt as I felt then – to lose Nicholson seemed to me at that moment to lose everything.[19]

By noon, British spirits were sinking fast, as the exhilaration of having got inside the walls gave way to a growing realisation of the scale of the forces still ranged against them, and the strength of the rebels' determination to resist them: 'it was clear', wrote a surprised Colonel George Bourchier, 'that the enemy intended to dispute every street, foot by foot, with us'.[20]

The British now had control of just over a quarter of the city, but that quarter had cost them the largest losses they had yet suffered. No one had anticipated anything approaching the scale of the casualties that the Field Force were now taking: nearly a third of those who lined up to assault the city at dawn were dead by sunset – a loss of around 1,100 men and 60 officers, including Annie Forrest's sweetheart, Harry Gambier. Another casualty was Hervey Greathed, who had succumbed not to bullets but to cholera.

By now the field hospital on the Ridge was a scene of indescribable horror. Padre Rotton moved from bed to bed, trying to comfort the dying while 'surgeons and apothecaries [were] all busily engaged in operating. Almost every kind of amputation was performed: legs and arms, and even fingers, bloodless and shrivelled, no longer members of their respective bodies, lay carelessly on the ground'.[21] In the wards, the bodies of the wounded lay piled up, two or three to a single charpoy. Edward Vibart was there too, still smarting from being kept in the reserve and deprived of the chance to take part in the storm:

I above all others ought to have taken my place in the storming. But it was ordained by Providence that I should stop in camp and attend to the unfortunate wounded and dying men. Every minute poor fellows were brought in and I never witnessed such horrors. It made my heart ache to see those ghastly sights . . . I went to ask after our poor major who had had his leg amputated, and all I saw was his body sewn up in a blanket . . . The insurgents fought desperately. One of their batteries we were thrice repulsed from, and I believe we have not taken it yet.[22]

Spirits were no higher in the British headquarters in Skinner's House, where the full desperation of the situation was beginning to dawn on the headquarters staff. 'About 12 I got some breakfast in the church,' wrote Fred Roberts to his parents, 'through which the round shot were coming pretty fast, and such a number of woe-begone faces I think I have never seen before in my life'.

Every column had been obliged to retreat. Our best officer by ten thousand times, poor Nicholson, I had just seen put in a doolie with death on his face, and . . . no one seemed fit for anything. All of the old officers were completely at their wits end. To make matters worse, whether designedly I know not, but the shops with beer and brandy had all been left open and several of our men got drunk, others could not find their Regiments, and all were done up with the hard work we had had for the previous 5 or 6 days . . .

I dropped off to sleep, and notwithstanding all the noise, never awoke till sunset . . . [then] went around our positions. All the posts were in disorder. No rations had found their way into town. The poor devils of cook boys could not be persuaded to come in – the fire was so heavy from every corner. Europeans were drunk, and natives out plundering.[23]

Hodson was horrified by the speed with which both the discipline and the morale of the army seemed to have collapsed. 'For the first time in my life,' he wrote to his wife, 'I have lived to see English soldiers refuse repeatedly to follow their officers. The fact is that the troops are utterly demoralised by hard work and hard drink.'[24]

Worse still, General Wilson seemed to have lost all confidence in his assault, and was actively contemplating retreat. 'Wilson is fairly broken down by fatigue and anxiety,' wrote Hodson, 'he cannot [even] stand on his legs.'[25]

By mid-afternoon, still more alarming news still came in: the fourth column under Major Reid had not only failed to take the Lahore Gate, but after the Maharaja of Kashmir's troops attached to Reid's force had bolted, Reid had had to retreat back to Hindu Rao's House in the face of a determined counter-attack under Bakht Khan and his Bareilly troops, 'supported by a mass of ghazis from the Bareilly and Nimach camps'.[26] Another section of the same brigade had also launched a spirited counter-attack at sunset within the walls of the Mori Bastion 'in great numbers', and continued to probe forwards during the night.[27]

Kendal Coghill was among the troops pinned down on this north-western front between the Mori Bastion and the Kabul Gate, and found the jihadis – 'a race of devils and fanatics' – especially fearsome adversaries. Like many of his colleagues he was surprised to discover that his earlier bravado and bloodlust quickly give way to naked fear: 'the natives were defending every place inch by inch', he wrote. 'It was a tough fight, and they had numbers and field guns against our few remaining men with muskets.'

But as our orders were peremptory to take and hold it, there was no help. It was then that I found we most wanted pluck. The men and officers were fatigued to death, the excitement over for the time. Our orders being to hold each gateway to the last, at each gateway and bastion we had left a detachment, so that at the Kabul [Gate] we had only about 200 men. The enemy regularly mobbed us with about 3000 men and 2 light guns attacked our front. If we had attacked them, they would have taken us in flank and retaken the gate. So we had to lie down flat and let the guns fire over us until they came near, and then our bayonets always told. The work continued from 9 a.m. till 4 p.m. and we were being picked off from a distance without a hope of retaliation or assistance coming to us, and we did not know what was going on to the left or rear, as we were the advanced right . . .

We had nothing to eat or drink the whole day and were awfully done. My sole consolation was a soda water bottle of weak brandy and water hanging to my side, and that had now been shot through and the liquor wasted. We were under arms all night, as they attacked us all through the dark.[28]

Unnerved by the loss of Nicholson, aware that Bakht Khan's advance up to Hindu Rao's House threatened to encircle and cut off his troops from their camp, and becoming hourly 'more anxious and depressed', Wilson was now visibly cracking under the strain. He was prevented from ordering an immediate withdrawal from the city only by his officers, led by the engineer Richard Baird-Smith, the man who had planned the details of the assault and who now 'insisted that "we *must* hold on" in such a determined and uncompromising tone that it put an end to all discussion'.[29]

One of Wilson's senior officers, Neville Chamberlain, wrote to Lawrence in Lahore to express his urgent concern that Wilson's frazzled nerves were going to lose the battle for Delhi single-handedly: 'he has frequently been more like an insane man than a General commanding a victorious army,' wrote Chamberlain, 'and it is so clear that his head, as he so frequently informs everyone, is gone'.

You must take these matters in hand or otherwise nothing will be done. The General attends to no one except in fits and starts when in difficulties; his answer to all suggestions is, 'It is impossible,' and he is always raising difficulties. He told me once that it was his intention to go to the hills after the fall of Delhi, and [frankly] it is a pity that he does not carry out this intention.[30]

When news of Wilson's wish to retreat reached the dying Nicholson up in the field hospital on the Ridge, he was, characteristically, even more forthright. Despite his pain and exhaustion, he reached for his pistol: 'Thank God', roared Nicholson, 'that I still have the strength yet to shoot him, if necessary.'[31]

The following day, calmer, he got a surgeon to take down a note to Lawrence in Lahore, seconding Chamberlain's letter. 'Tell Sir John', he dictated, 'that I recommend his doing what he can to supersede Wilson, who is broken down, and is moreover aware of it himself. I consider it trifling with our National Destiny keeping a man like Wilson in command of this force.'[32]

Zahir Dehlavi had woken early on 14 September and rode as usual across town to his duties in the Red Fort. Used by now to the sound of heavy gunfire, he was quite unaware of the significance of the fighting taking place less than a mile to the north. The first sign he saw of anything unusual was when he emerged from Chandni Chowk and encountered another royal official, heading in the opposite direction, who told him there was no point going on, since the Fort gates were locked.

> It was only then that I noticed that nearly all the shops of the city were closed, and that the bazaar was unusually deserted, with only one or two men walking around. I thought that I should go and see for myself what the matter was, but when I reached the Lahore Gate [of the Fort] I saw it was barred, and that in front of the gate there were two loaded cannon. Nearby a crowd was standing around listening to a havildar give an account of the morning's fighting.
>
> At this point a regiment of mounted soldiers rode up from within, and shouted to the guards to open the gates as they wanted to get out. The Havildar instructed them to go to the city's Kabul Gate as that was where the reinforcements were gathering. Hearing this, I turned towards my house.
>
> I had not gone far when I saw the *Purbias* running out fast from the side of Bhawani Shankar's house, clearly fleeing from the fighting. The townspeople were disgusted at the sight of the cowardly Tilangas and asked them, 'after involving our city in this war, why are you now running away?' On hearing this, the *Purbias* threw down their guns and swords and said, 'we have been fighting, now why don't you give it a try?'[33]

Zahir decided it was time to head home, and warn his family; but when he got to Ballimaran, he found that the *muhalla* gate had

already been locked. He then ran back towards the gate of the Chota
Dariba on Chandni Chowk. There also the gate was locked, but the
small wicket had been left open. He squeezed through it, only to find
that the fighting had now reached the kotwali: by pure bad fortune
he had run straight into Theo's column heading for the Jama Masjid:

> A volley of shots was now directed towards me from the side of the
> Kotwali, and the shots came and hit the road and the drains just like a
> hailstorm. A unit of the English army was standing directly in front
> of the Kotwali, shooting anyone they could see. A man standing next
> to me doubled over, shot in the stomach. I pulled him to safety
> through the wicket of the gate and then ran straight home . . .
>
> On arrival I went to my room, and lay down, shocked to the
> marrow. I had just seen with my own eyes that the English army had
> entered the city, that the *Purbias* had run away, and now the English
> soldiers were going to come inside homes and start murdering. I
> thought the time to die had arrived, and that there was nothing to do
> but to pray, and wait and see what was going to happen.
>
> I did not tell my mother or the members of my family anything that I
> had seen, and instead stayed in my room praying. After about an hour
> and a half there was a loud series of reports from a cannon, which
> sounded like it was coming from just outside my house. I was surprised
> as to how a cannon had entered our lane, so I took along two or three
> servants, and went out of the house to see what was happening.[34]

When Zahir's party reached the main road they asked the passers-
by where the English Army had gone, and someone said that they
had just been chased out. Zahir then went to the Chauri Bazaar,
behind the Great Mosque, and there they saw that people were
moving around armed with swords, knives, sharpened bamboo
lathis and whatever weapons they could find.

> When I came to the side of the Jama Masjid I saw such a huge pile of
> dead bodies that for a moment it looked like a woodseller's stall.
> More dead bodies lay scattered all around the Kilhih Bazaar and the
> lanes between the mosque and the Kotwali. I asked the people in the
> streets what had happened, and they told me that a unit of the

English army had come right up to the stairs of the Jama Masjid; at
the same time some of the English soldiers had gone into the homes
of the people and started looting them.

   Then the soldiers had tried to enter the Jama Masjid, and the men
who were inside thought that if they come in they will start killing
inside the sanctuary, so it is better to go out of the mosque and
confront them. So they charged out of the mosque with their guns
. . . Many of the English troops were killed and injured . . . Eventually they retreated towards the Kashmiri Gate. There the English
made their stand and positioned their cannon.[35]

Zahir went home again, and tried to get some sleep. The following
morning, however, rumours were spreading through the city that
the English troops had gone from house to house during the night,
climbing into rooms through ladders, and barging into people's
zenanas, where they killed the women as they slept, then stole their
jewellery. It was not clear how much truth there was to the rumour
– the looting at this stage seems to have been limited to the areas that
had already fallen to the British around Kashmiri Gate – but the
feeling of triumph that had swept through the town the previous
day after the English had been driven back from the Jama Masjid
quickly began to give way, in house after house across the city, to
feelings of increasing panic.

Sarvar ul-Mulk's family had heard at breakfast on the 14th that the
British had got within the walls, and decided not to wait to be
killed: instead they consulted with a cousin, Nawab Zia ud-Daula,
and decided to take their chances and attempt to make it through to
their cousin's house in Alwar in Rajputana while it was still possible
to escape. Only Sarvar ul-Mulk's uncle was against the plan: he had
decided from his astrological calculations that the English were
definitely going to be defeated.

   My father with great regret returned [to his house near] the Delhi
Gate, so that he should escort his own people, with the necessary

things, to his elder brother's house; but he did not succeed in this, for suddenly a great hue and cry was raised in the [northern portion of the] City, and in every street and by-lane, hand-to-hand fights ensued. White soldiers, together with their Indian and Pathan allies, armed with all sorts of weapons, drunk with victory and full of the spirit of looting, made no distinction between woman and child, or young and old; and rivers of blood flowed. Then entering the zenanas, the various bodies of men began to loot and rob while the ladies – of whom Firdausi has correctly said, 'Not even the sun had penetrated to the skin of their bodies, which were so closely veiled' – unaware of the fate of their husbands, fled in all directions.

The [Delhi, or southern] gate of the city was close to our house, and my father and my maternal uncle, with the ladies and children and servants, fled through it in a great hurry and terror, and took refuge in a saint's tomb [outside the walls]. It was only when we were joined by our old servants, that we learned of the death of my uncle and Nawab Zia ud-Daula. It appeared that having armed themselves, they had left the house on foot with the ladies of the house and the children and servants, but that in the Chowk or close to it, they had encountered 'One-eyed Metcalfe' [Theo] and that in the fighting that ensued, both had been killed. It was not known what had become of the women and children.

The effect of this news on the audience was so sad it can barely be described. Our own state was little better, for we were in fear of our lives and property from both sides – on the one hand the Mutineers, and on the other, the English and their supporters; and it appeared to us that the two parties were vying with each other as to which should carry the day in pillage or robbery.[36]

Sarvar ul-Mulk's family was not alone. In all the areas that the British now precariously controlled – the north-eastern quarter of the city – all the houses were considered fair game for plunder, and no males of fighting age were considered non-combatants. A significant proportion of the inhabitants of Delhi, especially the moneylenders and those with property or businesses, having suffered four months of plunder at the hands of the sepoys, had longed for the end of the anarchy, believing that the return of the Company, for all its irritations and manifest injustices, would at least bring a return of law and order to the town. Moreover, the British were well aware of this tacit support through their many spies. None of the inhabitants of Delhi had expected a general plunder, still less a mass slaughter. But once within the walls, the British conveniently forgot all their allies and supporters. Even their most devoted spies were not safe, as Maulvi Muhammad Baqar discovered on or around 15 September when, without explanation, he was picked up and arrested.[37]

The extreme injustice of all this was something that horrified even the most sycophantic Anglophiles: 'In the city no one life's was safe,' wrote Muin ud-Din Husain Khan. 'All able-bodied men who were seen were taken for rebels and shot.' Ghalib, who had disliked the sepoys from the beginning, was now no less horrified by the barbarity of the returning British. 'The victors killed all whom they found on the streets,' he wrote in *Dastanbuy*. 'When the angry lions entered the town, they killed the helpless and weak and they burned their houses. Mass slaughter was rampant and streets were filled with horror. It may be that such atrocities always occur after conquest.'[38]

Some of the most brutal killers were those who had lost friends or members of their own family at the outbreak. Soon after the British entered the city, Charles Griffiths met John Clifford, the former collector of Gurgaon, who was the elder brother of Annie Jennings' friend and fellow choir-mistress, Miss Clifford. John had dropped his sister off to stay with the Jenningses in the Red Fort the night before the outbreak, and now blamed himself for her death, preceded – so British myth had it – by gang rape. Griffiths was no peace-loving liberal, but he was profoundly chilled by what he saw: 'My old school friend had become a changed being,' he wrote. 'All his passions were aroused to their fullest extent, and he thought of nothing but revenge.'

Armed with sword, revolver and rifle, he had been present at almost every engagement with the mutineers since leaving Meerut . . . dealing death with his rifle and giving no quarter. Caring nothing for his own life, so long as he succeeded in glutting his vengeance on the murderers of this sister, he exposed himself most recklessly . . .

> I met him in one of the streets after we had gained entrance into the city. He shook my hands, saying that he had put to death all he had come across, not excepting women and children, and from his excited manner and the appearance of his dress – which was covered with blood stains – I quite believe he told the truth . . . There were other officers of the army in camp who had lost wives and relations at Delhi who behaved in the same manner as Clifford.[39]

Over and over again, however, the British found it possible to justify such brutal war crimes with the quasi-religious reasoning that they were somehow handing out God's justice on men who were not men, but were instead more like devils. In the eyes of Victorian Evangelicals, mass murder was no longer mass murder, but instead had become divine vengeance, and the troops were thus executors of divine justice. Padre Rotton, for one, was quite explicit about the degree to which the mass murder of the inhabitants of Delhi was actually, in his view, God's own work: 'I thought of God, and what He had already done for us . . . and then I thought of man, and the precious blood which he must shed in copious and living streams, ere God, by him, could avenge atrocity and wrong without parallel in the history of nations both ancient and modern.'[40] Even Edward Campbell, a gentle figure who was by the standards of the time no fundamentalist, still wrote of the assault on Delhi as 'my Saviour's battle' and liked to think of himself performing his duty as 'a good soldier of Christ'.[41]

'Truly these were fearful times,' agreed Charles Griffiths, 'when Christian men and gallant soldiers, maddened by the foul murder of those nearest and dearest to them, steeled their hearts to pity and swore vengeance against the mutineers.'

> The same feelings to some extent pervaded the breasts of all those who were engaged in the suppression of the Mutiny. Every soldier in our ranks knew that the day of reckoning had come for the atrocities which had been committed, and with unrelenting spirit dedicated himself to the accomplishment of that purpose . . . It was a war of extermination, in which no prisoners were taken and no mercy shown – in short one of the most cruel and vindictive wars this world

has seen . . . Dead bodies lay thick in the streets and open spaces, and
numbers were killed in their houses . . . Many non-combatants lost
their lives, our men, mad and excited, making no distinction. There is
no more terrible spectacle than a city taken by storm.[42]

The attitude of many of the British to the people who fell under
their sway was well put by one soldier, who wrote from Delhi to
the *Bombay Telegraph* decrying what he called General Wilson's
'hokum' that women and children must be spared. This 'was a
mistake', he wrote, as they were 'not human beings but fiends, or, at
best, wild beasts deserving only the death of dogs'.

All the city people found within the walls when our troops entered
were bayoneted on the spot; and the number was considerable, as
you may suppose when I tell you that some forty or fifty persons
were often found hiding in one house. They were not mutineers, but
residents of the city, who trusted to our well-known mild rule for
pardon. I am glad to say that they were to be disappointed.[43]

Throughout the 15 and 16 September, the fate of Delhi hung in the
balance.

The British made no further advances, except to inch forward
from Delhi College and, on the morning of the 16th, to take the
magazine immediately to its south; they also moved slowly from
house to house from Skinner's haveli in the direction of Chandni
Chowk. As Charles Griffiths put it, 'A few houses were taken in
advance of our positions, but no further movement on any large
scale was attempted, owing to the demoralised state of the great
proportion of the European infantry.'[44]

These modest advances now brought the British within mortar
range of the Red Fort: unable to move any further owing to the
strength of the resistance, they took out their frustration by setting
up a battery in the garden of Delhi College and pouring shells down
on Shah Jahan's magnificent palace. On the western front, they

made no further advances of any sort along the city walls, and remained pinned down by Bakht Khan's troops and his artillery massed on the Burn Bastion. Frustrated, the British troops slowly dissipated themselves in drink and plunder, and soon lost all semblance of discipline. 'Our men were disorderly and unmanage-able,' wrote Major William Ireland, 'and even the sense of the danger of our position could not keep them to the ranks.'[45]

In the headquarters at Skinner's House, Wilson's officers had their hands full trying to stop their general withdrawing altogether to the Ridge, or even, in his blacker moods, to Karnal. As he wrote to his wife on the evening of the 15th, 'we are now holding what we have taken but nothing more . . . The Europeans in the column with me have got hold of lots of beer in the shops, and made themselves helpless . . . This street fighting is fearful work. We have lost very heavily, both in officers and men. I am knocked up and unequal to any exertion. Altogether our prospects are not good. I cannot write more'.[46]

At this stage the city could have gone to either side, and a really concerted rebel counter-attack, especially one that aimed to take the now virtually undefended British rear, or captured the camp on the Ridge, would have forced an immediate British retreat from the city. What could have been achieved was shown on the evening of the 15th when a modest counter-attack, supported by the fire of the rebel artillery on the bastions of Selimgarh, drove the British from their new conquests back into their old Delhi College positions.[47]

For many of the rebel leaders, as for the people of the city, the frustration at this failure to fight back more effectively grew more acute as the hours passed. There were further instances of fleeing and depressed sepoys being attacked by mobs of Delhiwallahs, 'who in return for the bad treatment to which they had been subjected deprived them of their arms, beat them with shoes and disgraced them in every possible way, crying out "Where is your boasted courage? What has become of your power, that you can no longer oppress and tyrannize over us?" '[48]

Then, in the late morning of the 16th, the people of the city spontaneously began to gather outside the Red Fort. With them were many of the jihadis, led by Maulvi Sarfaraz Ali, and 'several of the principal officers of the mutineer army', who went into the Palace and begged Zafar to lead them into battle, 'assuring him', according to Sa'id Mubarak Shah, 'that the entire army, the citizens of Delhi, and the people of the surrounding country would all follow, fight and die for him and expel the British'.[49] As more and more jihadis and city dwellers massed outside the Fort, 'some armed just with sticks, a few with swords, others with old muskets', this suddenly looked like a turning point.

Inside the Palace, the mood had been growing progressively more sombre. On the 14th Mirza Mughal had sent an urgent message to Zafar, and begged him to provide additional funds to pay the troops so that they could eat and fight properly. Zafar replied, 'send the horse harness, and the silver howdahs and chairs, to Mirza Mughal that he may sell them and pay all with the proceeds. I have nothing else left'.[50] Shells were now falling almost every minute somewhere within the Palace walls: 'The King's residence must be a very warm one,' reported Neville Chamberlain to Lahore on the evening of the 17th, 'for we are pitting shells throughout the length of the palace enclosure, from north to south.'[51] To add to the gloom, the trickle of food supplies into the city had completely stopped, and people – including the princes and *salatin* – were literally dying of starvation.

Now, with the maulvis and jihadis gathering and asking him personally to lead a counter-attack, a moment of truth had come, but Zafar did not know what to do. Since 'Id, the Emperor had oscillated incoherently between a depressed hatred of the sepoys and all they had done to his city and palace, and a tacit if unenthusiastic support of Mirza Mughal's cause. At other times he seemed to have persuaded himself that he was a neutral observer in a struggle that had nothing to do with him. Now such indecision was impossible: however ambivalent and confused he felt, he must either lead the counter-attack, as requested, or refuse to do so. 'The King, afraid for his life, hesitated,' wrote Sa'id Mubarak Shah.

But they now earnestly entreated him saying, 'Your end is now approaching – you will be captured. Why die a shameful, dishonoured death? Why not die fighting and leave an imperishable name?' The King replied that he would place himself at the head of the troops at 12 o'clock that day.

As soon as the royal intention of leading the army to battle was known, further masses of mutineers, ghazees and townsmen collected in front of the Palace, not less than seventy thousand men. Presently the royal 'tomjon' [litter] was seen slowly issuing forth from the great gates, on which the troops and citizens advanced towards the magazine but halted about two hundred yards from it, as all who went further fell by the British bullets which bounced down the street like rain.

The King's tomjon had by this time almost reached another of the gates of the Palace and he sent continually to ascertain how far his army had advanced, but they were no nearer to the magazine when Hakim Ahsanullah Khan, forcing his way to his Royal master, told him that if he went any further he would to a certainty be shot, as European riflemen were concealed in the different houses. 'Moreover', whispered the Hakim, 'if you go out with the army to fight, how can I possibly explain your conduct tomorrow to the British, what excuse can I advance for you after you have joined the mutineers in battle?'

Zafar could no longer sit on the fence. He had to make up his mind one way or another, but still he hesitated, and as he dithered and swithered, the Anglophile hakim continued playing on his fears. According to his own account, he told his master, 'God forbid that the sepoys should take your Majesty out to the front of the battle, and then run off and you be taken prisoner. Never . . . These people bring disgrace on your Majesty for nothing. You ought never to have ridden forth.'[52]

'On hearing these words,' wrote Sa'id Mubarak Shah, 'the King left the procession and re-entered the Palace on the plea of going to the evening prayer. The mass of people and troops now became confused, then alarmed, and eventually they dispersed.'[53]

If Zafar's decision to bless the Uprising on the afternoon of 11 May was a crucial turning point that transformed an army mutiny into the largest rebellion against their empire that the British would face in the course of the entire nineteenth century, so Zafar's catastrophic failure of nerve on the evening of 16 September was the decisive moment that marked the beginning of the end of that rebellion. The different Urdu sources are clear that the confidence and determination needed to resist the British, which had held up remarkably well up to that point, now began to fail the rebels in Delhi.

It was not that they had been defeated. Far from it: the British were on the point of collapse, as the morale and spirit of their troops continued to disintegrate; as late as the 18th, Wilson was still writing home that 'our men have a great dislike of street fighting . . . and get a panic and will not advance. I cannot see my way at all'.[54] But the rebels' confidence had been fatally eroded by Zafar's frightened retreat, and panic, once begun, now proceeded to pass swiftly through their ranks. The two armies had eyeballed each other for three days now, and thanks at least partly to Zafar's failure of leadership, it was the rebels who blinked first.

The people of Delhi, aware now that collapse was imminent, began to pack up and flee to safety: the British lookouts stationed on the roof of Hindu Rao's House reported that evening that 'streams of people and animals have issued from Ajmeri Gate'.[55] The trickle of sepoys leaving the city was now also becoming a flood, and Hodson saw from the 'Idgah that the Bareilly troops had begun blowing up their ammunition stores in preparation for flight. It was also reported by spies that the Bareilly and Nimach troops had sent off their baggage down the road towards Mathura, intending to follow it by forced marches as soon as the opportunity to escape from the town presented itself.[56]

'The spirit of the mutineers now completely deserted them,' wrote Sa'id Mubarak Shah,

and they contemplated the entire evacuation of the capital. Whenever the Europeans saw an opportunity, they made their way into the main streets and bazaars, and shot all who opposed them . . . Soon along the whole of the Chandni Chowk to the Palace, and even to the Lahore Gate, only scattered parties of sepoys and ghazees were to be seen – all the rest had fled.

That night, the 16th, was the last, after more than two hundred years, that a Mughal emperor spent in the Red Fort of Shahjaha-nabad.

According to the tradition preserved by the family of his favour-ite daughter, Kulsum Zamani Begum, Zafar retired to the *tasbih khana* (his oratory), praying and thinking, as outside the sound of fighting drew closer and closer to the Red Fort. Then at eleven o'clock one of the eunuchs was sent to summon Kulsum Zamani Begum:

> There were gunshots everywhere . . . The Emperor told me, 'I give you over into the hands of God. Go now with your husband. I don't want to be separated from you, but it will be safer for you now to stay away from me.' Then he prayed aloud for our safety, blessed us and handed over some jewellery and other valuables, and asked my husband Mirza Ziauddin to take us away. Our caravan left the Fort late at night. We reached the village of Korali, where we ate a simple meal of barley bread and yoghurt, but the next day, heading towards Meerut [the destination of so many of the British refugees from Delhi four months earlier], a party of Gujars attacked us and virtually stripped us naked.[57]

Some time after midnight and before dawn, in the early morning of the 17th, Zafar quietly slipped out of the Red Fort by the water gate, without telling his prime minister or even Zinat Mahal. He was alone but for a party of attendants, and brought with him only a selection of his ancestral treasures, including 'the state jewels & property with lists of the same', as well as a palanquin.[58] As dawn broke, Zafar took a boat down the Yamuna, probably to the jetty at the Old Fort, the Purana Qila, from where he made his way to the great Sufi shrine of Nizamuddin three miles south-east of Shahjahanabad.[58]

According to traditions preserved by the family of the shrine keepers, the Nizami family, Zafar then handed over his ancestral relics into their safe keeping. These included a reliquary that he had specially carried from the Red Fort. The box contained three sacred hairs from the beard of the Prophet which had passed as a sacred trust from father to son in the House of Timur since the fourteenth century, and to which Zafar had been especially attached: the Palace diary and other accounts refer to him personally bathing the hairs in rosewater.[60] Having prayed at the shine, and eaten a simple breakfast given to him by the *pirzadas*, Zafar then allegedly burst into tears, telling the head Sufi:

> I always thought these rebel soldiers would bring disaster down on our heads. I had apprehensions from the beginning; now they have come true. These soldiers have fled before the English. Brother! Though my inclinations are those of a faqir and a mystic, yet in my veins runs that great blood which would keep me fighting to the last drop in my body. My forefathers have had worse days than these and they never lost heart. But I have read the writing on the wall. I see with my own eyes the fast approaching tragedy which must end the glory of my dynasty. Now there is not a shadow of doubt left that of the great House of Timur I am the last to be seated on the throne of India. The lamp of Mughal dominion is fast burning out; it will remain but a few hours more. Since I know this, why should I cause more bloodshed? For this reason I left the Fort. The country belongs to God. He may give it to whomsoever he likes.[61]

Saying this, Zafar delivered the relics into the custody of the shrine keepers, and set off by palanquin towards his summer palace abutting the Sufi shrine of Qutb Sahib in Mehrauli, where he had agreed to meet Bakht Khan. But after he had gone some way, Mirza Ilahe Bakhsh rode up, and told him that bands of Gujars were robbing anyone who set off in that direction, just as they had earlier robbed the British.

What Ilahe Bakhsh said was quite true, but what Zafar did not know was that Ilahe Bakhsh was in the pay of Hodson, and that he had come directly on Hodson's bidding, promising his paymaster that he would do his best to betray his cousin and to prevent Zafar from fleeing far from the city. In this way, although he had consulted no higher authority as to the terms he was busy negotiating, Hodson hoped to make his name as a great imperial hero, and so cement his return to grace by bringing in the Emperor to be imprisoned and tried.[62] To the same end, Hodson had now quite separately concluded his deal with Zinat Mahal and her father, Mirza Quli Khan, who were still in Zinat Mahal's haveli in Lal Kuan. After much indecision, they had also promised to persuade Zafar to surrender, in return for the guarantee of Zinat's life, and that of the three men in her life: her father; her son Mirza Jawan Bakht; and her husband, Zafar. The guarantee that Zinat and her father negotiated very pointedly did not include any of her husband's sons by different wives.*[63]

Having been persuaded to change his mind, Zafar ordered that his palanquin be turned around and returned to Nizamuddin, where he waited for Zinat Mahal to join him.[64] Then together they made for the great mausoleum of Zafar's ancestors, which lay close by. This was the great marble-domed tomb of Humayun, the second Mughal Emperor. It was the first great monumental tomb to be built by the Mughals almost three hundred years earlier, in the mid-sixteenth century, and was still the most magnificent Mughal monument in Delhi.[65]

---

* One of the letters of guarantee that Hodson wrote to Zinat Mahal was dated 18 September and read:

> Translation of the Guarantee given by Captain Hodson to the Begum Zeenut Muhul
>
> After compliments states that the punishment of parties who have taken part in the insurrection is desirable, but that the lives of herself, her son Jawan Bukht and her father are guaranteed to them and they need not be apprehensive, but continue to occupy their premises [in Lal Kuan] as usual. That as he is to make some particular enquiries, and requests that some trustworthy man from herself may be sent to him immediately and that a guard will be furnished for the protection of her house.
>
> Dt 18th September 1857

(DCO Archive, Mutiny Papers, File no. 10, Letter no. 3, copy contained in letter from W. L. R. Hodson to C.B. Saunders, Delhi, 30 October 1857.) A later letter referred to in the correspondence, but now lost, guaranteed the life of Zafar as well.

Here Zafar sent a message, instructing that elephants should be sent to the haveli of Hakim Ahsanullah Khan, telling him to join the imperial family at the tomb.[66]

Then Zafar retired into the tomb chamber of his ancestor, to wait and to pray.

The news that Zafar had finally done what he had threatened to do for so long – to leave the Fort and make for the shrine of Khwaja Qutb – spread through the *muhallas* of the town like wildfire on the morning of the 17th.

By mid-morning great streams of people were pouring out of the Ajmeri Gate, while others – wrongly – decided they had less to fear from the British than the Gujars, and took their chances, heading out of the British-occupied Kashmiri Gate. Here many men and teenage boys were shot dead, while the women and children were allowed to proceed only after they had been systematically stripped by the guards of the money, jewellery and bundles they carried.[67]

Some of these refugees headed up the same routes – the Karnal and Meerut roads – that the fleeing British had taken four months earlier. Harriet Tytler, who herself had had to flee the town on 11 May, watched them go; almost alone among British observers, she found room in her heart to feel for them in their plight: 'What an experience it was to behold the myriads of women and children coming out of the Kashmir and Mori Gates,' she wrote.

> Women who had never seen the outside of their zenana walls or walked but a few steps across their tiny courtyards, surrounded only by their own family or their slaves, now to have to face the gaze of European soldiers as well as their own . . . I was sorry for the poor things, more especially for the poor high-casted Hindu women to whom it was agonizing pain to be jostled along with sweeperesses and other women of low birth and caste.[68]

Zahir Dehlavi's family anxiously watched the people around them leave throughout the morning of the 17th, unsure of what to do.

That evening, however, Nawab Hamid Ali Khan, the leader of Delhi's Shia community, came to beg the family to come with him and leave the city before it was too late.

'How are you sitting so coolly in your house,' he asked my father, 'when the King has left the Fort, and now all his subjects are also leaving the city? For goodness sake, leave your house and flee the city with your family this evening. Can't you see that killing and looting is going on all over Delhi? I am now going to take my wife and children, and leave this place. Please: put the women of your family with my family in the carriage.'

Nawab Hamid Ali Khan's house was next to the Kashmiri Gate, but a month earlier [after the British began shelling the area] he had rented a house next to mine [off Chandni Chowk] and was living there. My father decided to take the Nawab's advice, and though the sun was now setting, he gave the order that we should leave. In the panic, everyone left in whatever dress they were wearing. My mother was so panicky that she did not carry even a ring other than those she was wearing at the time. At least my wife had kept her wedding clothes which were worth about two thousand five hundred rupees. She also had with her a small case of jewellery. She wrapped all the things in a cotton mattress and rolled it up like a bolster, then spread the mattress in the bullock rath.

The party set off through the streets of the city in which they had lived all their lives but which was now almost unrecognisable:

In the streets there were terrible scenes: as we left we saw the agony and helplessness of the people, as well as their fear and poverty. We saw the plight of the women who had always observed pardah and had never come out like this on the streets, and who were evidently unaccustomed to walking. We heard the howling and crying of the children. It was such a heart-rending scene that only the person who has ever witnessed such a thing can really comprehend it.

We all – men, women and children – came out of the Delhi Gate, and the ground outside was like a scene from Hell. Thousands of

women in pardah with little children, along with their harassed and
worried men, were all leaving the city. Nobody was conscious of
what sort of condition they were in, or where they were heading,
they were just moving. After a lot of trouble and problems, our
group reached the *Barf Khana* [Ice House, situated under what is
now Connaught Place]. The whole place had been hired from its
owners by Nawab Hamid Ali Khan Sahab. We all spent the night
there, glad to be safe and under cover, though none of us had
anything to eat.[69]

Late that afternoon, Bakht Khan's troops had finally abandoned
their forward positions in Kishenganj which had so seriously
worried General Wilson. Now that his rear, the Ridge and the
camp, were no longer threatened, the general at long last felt capable
of pushing on with some vigour. Though the Burn Bastion still held
out, and the western half of the town continued to defy the British,
in the eastern half British troops were now making steady progress
through the streets, and by the evening of the 17th, just after Zahir
had left his house, they had taken up positions along Chandni
Chowk.

As they moved forward, the British troops paused to loot the
houses that they passed. The lucky inhabitants were expelled, the
unlucky ones killed. Either way, no house was left inhabited behind
the advance of the British troops: the conquered parts of the city
were left echoingly empty. Maulvi Muhammad Baqar's son, the
poet and critic Muhammad Husain Azad, was one of the luckier
ones, at least relatively speaking. Unlike many of the young men of
Delhi, he was not shot. He was in his house that evening with his
wife and the whole joint family when, according to his later
account,

The soldiers of the victorious army suddenly entered the house.
They flourished their rifles and shouted: 'Leave here at once!' The
world turned black before my eyes. A whole houseful of goods was
before me and I stood petrified: 'What shall I take with me?' All the
jewels and jewellery were locked in a box and were thrown into a
well. But my eye fell on the packet of [Zauq's] Ghazals [of which

Azad, Zauq's devoted pupil, was meant to be preparing the critical edition for publication following his master's death in 1854]. I thought, 'Muhammad Husain, if God is gracious, and you live, then all these material goods can be restored. But where will another ustad [master] come from, who can compose these ghazals again? While these exist Zauq lives even after his death; if these are lost his name cannot survive either.'

So I picked up the packet [of Zauq's verse] and tucked it under my arm. Abandoning a well-furnished home, with twenty-two half dead souls, I left the house – or rather the city. And the words fell from my lips, 'Hazrat Adam left paradise; and Delhi is paradise too. But if I am Adam's descendant – why shouldn't I leave my paradise just as he did?'[70]

As Azad's family limped out of Delhi, a stray bullet or a piece of shrapnel from an exploding shell struck Azad's year-old baby daughter; she slipped into a coma, and after a few days, she died.

That night, Azad's family also took shelter in the same Ice House in which Zahir was sheltering, though neither Azad's account nor that of Zahir mentions the other. Like Zahir's family, Azad's had left in a great panic, but by pooling their resources, they found they had a little flour, 'which was now as expensive as gold', and kneaded it on a piece of broken pot. A fire was built of leaves and dry twigs, and from some of the other refugees they borrowed garlic, chilli and salt to make chutney. Despite the conditions and the primitive nature of the food, Azad used to tell his children that he 'enjoyed the garlic chutney and half-cooked rotis more than any of the finest biryani, kormas or pullao' that he was to enjoy later in life.[71]

The next day bullock carts were found, and the party left for Sonepat under the care of a maulvi. But Azad did not go with them. He had already lost his home and his daughter, but he still had a father. Despite the extraordinary risk, the following day he headed back into Delhi to try to find and help Maulvi Muhammad Baqar, who was now locked up in British custody. Azad somehow managed to track down a Sikh general who was a friend of his father, and who agreed to help him. He also gave him both shelter and a cover by pretending that Azad was his groom. In this disguise, the general led Azad to the field where Baqar and the other prisoners were awaiting their trial and execution. Under these conditions, as Muhammad Baqar was led to the scaffold, father and son exchanged a long last look.

Soon afterwards, Maulvi Muhammad Baqar was hanged, and Azad, who believed that there was an arrest warrant out for him, was smuggled out of the city and began a life of wandering that would see him spend four years drifting alone and in extreme poverty through the length and breadth of India – to Madras and the Nilgiri Hills, then Lucknow, and eventually to Lahore, carrying his master's ghazals all the way.

It was only in 1861, when he managed to secure a low-level job in the postmaster general's office in Lahore, that he was able to begin rebuilding his life. It was here that he set to work preparing the edition of Zauq's work he had promised his master he would produce, and which would stand as a monument to a city, and a moment of intellectual and artistic creativity, that had now been utterly destroyed.[72]

In the middle of the following morning, 18 September, the sun was completely eclipsed for five minutes. The city darkened ominously for nearly three hours, before the light slowly returned.

The British soldiers were unnerved by the event since no one had warned them to expect it. But for the Hindus it was an event of far greater significance. Even today in India, some high-caste Hindus will not go outside during an eclipse, and for twenty-four hours either side of the moment of eclipse Hindu temples are all locked and barred. In the syncretic atmosphere of Mughal Delhi, and especially in the Mughal court where Hindus were employed as astrologers, the eclipse was an event of terrifying significance: it was the ultimate ill omen, a signal of extreme divine displeasure.*

* According to the Palace diary, after the eclipse of 2 July 1852 Zafar had attempted to counter the malignant effects by having himself weighed 'against several kinds of grain, butter, coral etc and then distributed the results among the poor.' See National Archives of India, Foreign, Foreign Dept Misc., vol. 361, *Precis of Palace Intelligence*, entry for 2 July 1852.

Although an eclipse was considered the worst possible moment to begin any journey, it was on this occasion taken as indicating that for the last lingering sepoys now was the moment to abandon the hopeless fight, and to escape the doomed city.[73]

That evening, as the heavens opened for a late monsoon downpour, the sepoys fled down the Agra road – which was already clogged with trudging Delhiwallahs heading away as fast as they could from the advancing British and their no less violent Sikh, Pathan and Gurkha allies. 'The darkness worked on their superstitious fears,' wrote Charles Griffiths, 'and hastened their flight from the city on which the wrath of the Almighty had descended.'

> That night it was reported that the rebels in great numbers were evacuating the city by the south side, and the Bareilly and Nimach brigades making off in the direction of Gwalior. Certain it was from this period that signs of waning strength appeared among the enemy, and fewer attempts at assault were made on our outposts . . .
>
> Few crossed the Bridge of Boats by day owing to it being commanded by our guns. But on the night of the 19th, when sitting in the church compound watching the shells exploding over the Palace and Selimgarh, we heard distinctly, through the intervals of firing, a distant confused hum of voices, like the murmur of a great multitude. The sound came from the direction of the river, and was caused by multitudes of human beings, who, escaping by the Bridge of Boats, to the opposite side, were deserting the city which was so soon to fall into our hands.[74]

On the afternoon of the 19th the British finally captured the Burn Bastion, having been repulsed yet again with huge losses the day before. Later that evening they captured the Delhi Bank building, and so positioned themselves for an assault on the Palace the following morning, the 20th.

The fate of the Delhi refugees of the 17th, 18th and 19th September was every bit as grim as that of their British predecessors in early

May. Passing along the same roads, in the same panic, they were attacked and robbed by the same predatory Gujar and Mewati tribes who had stripped the British earlier in the summer. Although there are few surviving contemporary first-person accounts of these Indian refugees surviving, certainly compared to the voluminous British accounts of 11 May which appeared in print within a few months of the end of the Uprising, there still survives among some old Delhi families a rich oral tradition of the misadventures that befell their great-grandparents in 1857. Some of these were collected from old people in the early twentieth century by Khwaja Hasan Nizami in a book called *Begmat ke Aansu* (Tears of the Begums), finally published in 1952.

Typical was the story of Mirza Shahzor, who fled Delhi with his pregnant wife, younger sister and mother in a pair of carts 'soon after Emperor left the court'. Like many of the Mughal refugees, they headed first for the shrine of Qutb Sahib in Mehrauli, where they spent a night. The following morning they set off again, but were attacked and looted by Gujars a few kilometres away near Chhatarpur. The tribesmen took everything they had, but spared their lives. 'The women were crying,' remembered Mirza Shahzor. 'I tried my best to console them. There was a village nearby. My mother would stumble at every step and kept lamenting the fate that was making her see such severe hardships at that age. But the village was inhabited by Muslim Mewaties, who gave us shelter in the communal *chaupal* at the centre of the village.'

The villagers took the refugees in, and fed them, but after a few days asked Mirza Shahzor to make some sort of contribution in return:

'Why do you sit all day?' they asked. 'Why don't you do something?' I said I was happy to work: 'I come from a martial family. I can fire a gun and known how to wield a sword.' But at this the villagers started laughing saying, 'here we don't need you to fire bullets, but to manage the plough and dig the earth.' There were tears in my eyes at this and seeing this the villagers took pity and said, 'alright, why don't you look after our fields, and your women can sew things and we will give you a share of the harvest.' So that was how our lives developed: I would be in the fields all day, chasing birds, and the women sewed clothes at home.[75]

For two years they lived with the villagers and suffered as they did: they learned what it was to experience real hunger; monsoon floods nearly washed them away; and with no doctor to attend her, Mirza Shahzor's wife died in childbirth. Soon after, what remained of the family was able to return to Delhi, to begin a new life on the pension of five rupees a month that the British offered the few surviving members of the imperial family.

Many others suffered a similar fate. Zafar Sultan was the favourite son of Mirza Babur, the Emperor's Anglophile younger brother, who was famous for wearing foppish British clothes and for building an English-style bungalow within the Red Fort. On 19 September, as the fall of the Palace drew nearer, he put his blind mother in a bullock cart and got a driver to take them through the Ajmeri Gate and up the road to Karnal. The first night, having successfully evaded both the British and the Gujars, they halted near a village, and fell fast asleep. The following morning they woke to discover that the driver had made off alone, taking the bullocks with him.

They found shelter in a Jat village, where they were given a meal, but before long the Jats fell on them, suspecting – correctly – that they had brought with them some priceless jewellery. When Zafar Sultan came to, he saw everything had been taken from them, they had been dumped in the jungle, and that his elderly mother, who had been struck on the head with a lathi, was now dying. 'I asked her how she was, and she said, "I am the sister-in-law of the Emperor of India and look at my fate – I am dying in the jungle, and will not even get a shroud for a burial." So saying she passed away. I somehow gathered the strength to bury her as well as I could.'

Zafar Sultan became a fakir, travelling from city to city. He went to Bombay, and thence to Mecca, where he lived for a decade on the charity of pilgrims. Eventually he returned, via Karachi, to Delhi, 'because I could not forget this city . . . Here I worked as *thelewala*, carting bricks to help build the new railway, and eventually saved up enough to buy my own brick cart'. He refused the offer of a government pension because he thought it was better 'to earn a living by hard work than to survive on a pension'.

When Khwaja Hasan Nizami came across Mirza Zafar Sultan in 1917, he was a deaf old man. His identity had been revealed when he had been taken to court after getting into a fight 'with a rich intoxicated Punjabi businessman' who had taken out his riding whip and started beating the old man after his brick cart had collided with the businessman's car. He had taken the first few blows quietly, but finally had mustered the courage to resist, and hit the businessman so hard he broke his nose. 'The rich do not think anything of the poor,' Zafar Sultan told the court. 'But sixty years ago this man's forefathers would have been my slaves. And not just them, but the whole of Hindustan used to obey my orders. I have not forgotten my lineage, so how could I tolerate such insults? Just look how that coward ran away when I hit him. It is not easy to endure a Timurid's slap.'[76]

On 20 September, the British advanced on the Red Fort from their front-line position in the ruins of the Delhi Bank. During the night of the 19th the guns lined up in front of the Palace were spiked, and at ten o'clock on the morning of the 20th an explosion party ran forward under covering fire to place the powder bags under the gates. Unlike the taking of the Kashmiri Gate, at the Palace there was virtually no resistance, and it became obvious that most of the Palace's defenders had already fled, except for a few determined jihadis who had preferred to die rather than hand over the seat of their emperor – Caliph of the Age, He who is Surrounded by Hosts of Angels – without a struggle.[77]

Edward Campbell was one of those commanding the assault, but much the fullest account was left by his deputy, a young army captain named Fred Maisey. 'After an interval of suspense, the powder bags blew up with a tremendous explosion,' he wrote to his mother and sisters in Switzerland. 'Half of the huge gate fell heavily over, then with a shout in we all went: officers, sappers, Europeans, natives, all pell mell, and with a want of order which had there been any steady resistance, would have made a terrible mess.'

I tried to get one or two officers to get their men into something like order – but away they all scampered, and all I or anyone else could do was to scamper also. There was some brisk musketry firing in the arched passage leading to the first courtyard and sundry Pandies, who were idiotic enough to fight, were slain. There was more danger from our own bullets than from theirs, so we were glad to get out of the passage and into the open.

I went to the left as that was the way towards Selimgarh, and someone said that the King was in that direction. I led the party accompanied by an Afghan sirdar, Meer Khan, who had aided our side with a body of *very* irregular horse. Such a handsome, black bearded eagle-eyed fellow, and so excited at the thought of capturing the King (whom he would most infallibly have killed). We went plunging along through several gateways and narrow streets, for you must understand that there is a complete town within the palace walls. We expected every moment to meet with a volley, but we only saw two men on our route – both of whom our Afghan friend fired on and dropped like partridges . . .

[Eventually] I caught hold of a man who peeped out of a doorway and made him come along by my side. He was not armed and appeared to be a bullock driver. I told him if he would stay near me and show us the way and give good information, I would see that he would come to no harm – but my guarantees that day were worthless. My Afghan friend was at my heels. I told him that the old fellow was my prisoner and that I had promised him that he should not be hurt. The man rubbed his head on the ground and thanked him as well as his fright would allow him. The poor wretch ran along by my side pointing out the way. We had scarcely gone ten yards when I felt a whiz and a flash, and down fell my prisoner shot through the body. That rascally Afghan had shot him, and almost set me alight in doing so. I was very angry – but the sirdar was quite independent of me, and could not understand why a promise made to a *badmash* caught in the enemy's stronghold should be binding.

After a while, Maisey and his companions heard firing from the centre of the Palace enclosure, and decided to join the centre party, as their part of the Palace seemed completely deserted.

We found the party – men, officers and horses all jumbled together, brought to a standstill by huge metal studded gates [of the Naqqar Khana Darwaza] strongly padlocked. What with bangs with heavy beams, shots from muskets, and other violent measures, the gates were forced, and then, with a rush, we went pell mell into the central square of the palace, at the far side of which is the *Diwan-i Am*, or Public Hall of Audience. The court was full of looted carriages, buggies, carts, palanquins. A gun or two was there, evidently hastily abandoned.

On we pressed to the *Diwan-i Am* which we found had been made into a sort of barrack. There were some fifteen sick or wounded men there whom the men sorely wanted to fly at. However, the officers held the men in check and we began to question the fellows. One young Musalman, evidently very ill, was close to me and I asked him where the troops were, and where was the king . . . The man begged for his life, and I told him I would protect him if he could come with me, on the condition that he disclosed where the King was. He declared the King and his wife and younger sons were in the Private Apartments which were in the next or innermost court. The rascal lied. The King had gone days before and he knew it well. However we believed him. Then a shout was raised to search the next court.

Just then up came Black Beard, and no sooner did he see the Pandies than he flew at them with his men. No one could stop him and indeed I do not think the men wished to. As to the officers, such was the crash and confusion that we scarcely knew what was going on and we were quite powerless even had we known. A few screams and groans told the tale. I left the man I had spoken to alive and in the care of some privates – for I could not stay there when all were rushing ahead – but he too was afterwards killed. I heard that out of 12 or 15 men, Meer Khan had himself killed eight. I never saw such a bloodthirsty savage.[78]

It was a measure of the secrecy with which Hodson had conducted his negotiations that no one in the storming party seemed to know that the Emperor was no longer in his palace, although Hodson was in direct communication with Mirza Ilahe Bakhsh, and knew the exact whereabouts of almost all the senior members of the imperial family. Having broken through the Lal Pardah, the British troops then poured into the inner courtyards, running down the cloister arcades searching for the royal family, who they believed still to be there.

Soon the armed heel and the ring of weapons clashed through the cloistered precincts of the *Diwan-i Khas* and within the still more exclusive chambers where never before had English feet trodden: the private rooms of the Mughal Emperors, the bowers of Nur Mahal and odalisques unnumbered, store rooms, pantries, cubbies, baths, all were ransacked by the outside barbarian without any thought at first save of discovering the King and his family. But we soon found that 'the cupboard was bare', and then the genie of plunder arose and such a scene ensued as I fancy has never yet been equalled.

A motley crowd of troops and followers ransacked every hole and corner, turning everything topsy-turvey (themselves included very often) in the search for loot. Muskets were being fired right and left to force the locks off doors. As the men got more and more scattered, the bullets flew more and more avidly, and the risk was considerable. I never saw such confusion. All sorts of loot had been brought into the palace by the mutineers and presented to the king and members of the court, and this and the palace furniture, men and women's clothing, dancing girls' frippery, vessels of food and drink, rich hangings and trappings, books and manuscripts had all been tumbled higgledy piggledy into various small rooms about, and were all retumbled and tossed over and over again by our excited soldiery.

Here you saw a group fumbling among mysterious boxes in search of jewels, there others laden with stuff of various kinds – pictures, books, guns, pistols, anything that took their fancy. Some tried the sweetmeats and sherbets, others, less lucky, took long steep draughts of what seemed some right royal drink – and alas turned out to be medicine, and found out, too late, that the old King has a passion for pharmacy, and kept large supplies close to the royal elbow.

We did not find a soul in the private apartments, and as to the plunder, the greatest part was the merest trash, and there was nothing whatever of any value. I picked up in the King's private pavilion a perfect new air cushion which Kate [Maisey's wife] now has in her *janpan* or hill litter. That was the only thing I looted at Delhi, but this little souvenir, however, I was determined to keep, and I told the Prize Agent [Edward Campbell] so. The men at last began to quieten down from sheer fatigue and were collected by the officers. A deputation was sent to report the capture of the palace to the General.[79]

That evening, as British soldiers danced jigs inside the Jama Masjid and as the Sikhs lit victory fires next to the mosque's holy *mihrab*, General Wilson and his headquarters staff moved in from St James's Church to the Fort's Diwan i-Khas, where a dinner of eggs and ham was eaten ('I wonder what the *genius loci* thought of this,' pondered Fred Maisey). The general proposed a toast to Queen Victoria: 'The Queen, God Bless Her'.[80] Later a telegram was sent by one of his officers to Lahore, proudly announcing that 'Our struggle has ended here. The widespread rebellion of mutinous Bengal army has received a complete defeat in Upper India. The days of Clive and Lake are again revived among us'.[81]

The news was also brought to Nicholson, who lay gasping and clinging on to life in his tent on the Ridge, attended by his great Pathan manservant and bodyguard. When Neville Chamberlain went to visit him to bring him the news he found him 'helpless as an infant, breathing with difficulty, and only able to jerk out his words in syllables at long intervals, and with pain'. He was, however, still well enough to fire a shot from his pistol through the side of the tent to shut up his irregular cavalry, who had gathered in vigil outside his tent.[82]

When told that the city was now in British hands, he replied, 'My desire was that Delhi should be taken before I die, and it has been granted.'[83]

He died three days later, and was buried beneath a marble plinth plundered for the purpose from Zafar's beloved Moonlight Garden, the Mehtab Bagh.

While the Palace was being stormed, and toasts to Queen Victoria proposed, elsewhere in the city some of the worst massacres of the entire Uprising were taking place. The struggle may have ended for the British, but for many of the inhabitants of Delhi the worst trials were only now beginning.

In the morning, the British had swept around the city walls, capturing the Lahore and Ajmeri gates, and the Garstin Bastion. At the same time Hodson and his irregular cavalry rode around the outside of the city walls to the large sepoy camps outside the Ajmeri and Delhi gates, so finally encircling the city. They were deserted except for some 'sick and wounded [sepoys] who could not walk', who were immediately put to the sword. Their corpses were left with the litter of the camp debris – ammunition, clothes and plunder as well as 'their drums, band instruments, bedding, cooking pots etc, and all their luxuries', which had been abandoned in their flight.[84]

Soon afterwards, the order was given to 'clear' the area around Delhi Gate. Edward Vibart was one of those who took part in the massacre that followed. 'I have seen many bloody and awful sights lately,' he wrote to his Uncle Gordon in a letter that oscillated between bloody bravado and flashes of awareness at the horrors he was committing. 'But such a one as I witnessed yesterday please God I pray I never see again.'

> The regiment was ordered to clear the houses between the Delhi and Turkman Gates, which are the two gates that we have to hold, and the orders were to shoot every soul. I think I must have seen about 30 or 40 defenceless people shot down before me. It was literally murder and I was perfectly horrified. The women were all spared,

but their screams, on seeing their husbands and sons butchered, were most terrible.

The town as you may imagine presents an awful spectacle now . . . heaps of dead bodies scattered throughout the place and every house broken into and sacked – but it is the [ordinary] townspeople who are now falling victims to our infuriated soldiery.

You can easily fancy with what feelings I visited all my old haunts yesterday, I went to all the old remembered places, and almost [succeeded in] imagining that nothing had taken place; but on looking around, the delusion was soon expelled for the marks of cannon and musketry were to be seen on all sides, telling but too well the mortal conflict that had been raging here not long before. A little further on you would come across a heap of dead bodies in the last stage of putrefaction, or some old woman in a state of starvation, and you could not help wondering how you could ever delight in bloodshed and war. And a few yards further on still some [of our] drunken soldiers would reel past, exciting your pity not unmixed with disgust. Wherever you go, you see some unfortunate man or other being dragged out of his hiding place, and barbarously put to death.

Heaven knows I feel no pity – but when some old grey bearded man is brought and shot before your very eyes – hard must be that man's heart I think who can look on with indifference. And yet it must be so for these black wretches shall atone with their blood for our murdered countrymen – my own father and mother – sister and brother all cry aloud for vengeance, and their son will avenge them. Yes! He shall be seen in the fight, and shall never shrink [from bloodshed,] for God have given him both strength and courage.[85]

Worse still was the slaughter in Kucha Chelan, where an estimated 1,400 Delhiwallahs were cut down. Here Nawab Muhammad Ali Khan had attempted to resist the plundering and had shot dead three British soldiers who had climbed over his haveli wall and entered his zenana. Their companions went back to get the rest of their regiment, and returned with a field gun with which they blew the haveli apart.

There followed the mass murder of everyone in that quarter of

Portrait of a Delhi poet, probably Hakim Momin Khan, attributed to Jivan Ram.

CLOCKWISE [from top left]: Zinat Mahal, as imagined by the *Illustrated London News*; the *Illustrated London News* image of Zafar; the only surviving photograph of Zinat Mahal, taken in captivity in Rangoon in 1872 by General McMohan; Mirza Asadullah Baig Khan, the poet Ghalib.

CLOCKWISE [from top left]: General Archdale Wilson; Brigadier General John Nicholson; Harriet and Robert Tytler; William Hodson of Hodson's Horse.

ABOVE: The Delhi Field Force advances on the Mughal capital.
BELOW: Hodson's Horse strike a pose.

ABOVE: The British attack Kashmiri Gate on 14 September.
BELOW: Easy days: the British turn Zafar's Hall of Private Audience,
the Diwan-i Khas, into an Officer's Mess, late autumn 1857.

Images of the conquered city taken by Felice Beato in 1858.
ABOVE LEFT: The Bridge of Boats. ABOVE RIGHT: The Flagstaff Tower.
BELOW LEFT: The Kashmiri Gate. BELOW RIGHT: Humayun's Tomb.

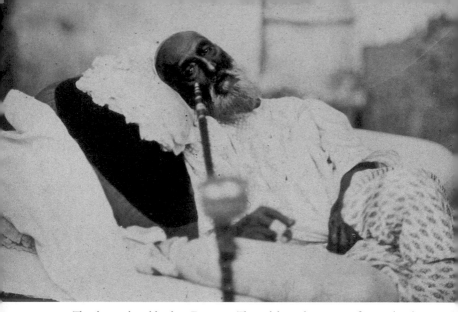

ABOVE: The deposed and broken Emperor. This celebrated image is often said to have been taken in Rangoon, but according to the diary of Zafar's jailor, Edward Ommaney, it was actually taken after the Emperor's show trial in Delhi, by 'Mr Shepherd the photographer', before Zafar was transported to Rangoon. BELOW: Zafar's two surviving younger sons, who shared his exile in Rangoon: the beloved Mirza Jawan Bakht, only son of Zinat Mahal (left), and the illegitimate Mirza Shah Abbas.

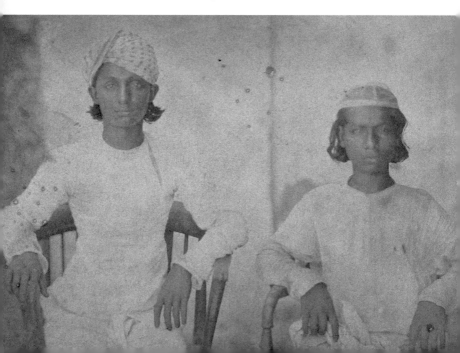

the city. After the British and their allies had tired of bayoneting the inhabitants, they marched forty survivors out to the Yamuna, lined them up below the walls of the Fort, and shot them. Among the dead were some of the most talented poets and artists in Delhi, for Kucha Chelan was famous for being the most intellectual *muhalla* in the city. 'They were well-known and well-off people, men who were the pride of Delhi,' wrote Zahir Dehlavi. 'They had had no parallels in their own day, nor will we ever see their like again.'

For example, there was Miyan Amir Panja-kash, the great calligrapher, who had no one comparable to him on this earth. Then there was one of our greatest poets, Maulvi Imam Bakhsh Sahbai and his two sons, and Mir Niyaz Ali, the celebrated story teller of Kucha Chelan. About fourteen hundred people of that Muhalla were killed. Some were arrested and taken through the Rajghat gate to the river side and there were shot. The bodies were all thrown into the river. Meanwhile many of their women were so disturbed by what they saw that they left their homes with their children and jumped into the wells. For months afterwards, all the wells of Kucha Chelan were stacked with dead bodies. My pen refuses to describe this further.[86]

One survivor was Qadir Ali, a nephew of the poet Sahbai who lived with him in Delhi, and who in his old age told the story of his escape to the Delhi historian Rashid ul-Khairi. 'Delhi was like the Place of Judgement,' he said, 'and prisoners were being shot rather than hanged.'

The soldiers readied their guns. Just then a Muslim officer came to us and said, 'Your death is imminent. There are guns in front of you and the river behind. So those among you who can swim should jump in the river and escape.' I was a good swimmer, but Mamun Sahib [Sahbai] and his son, Maulana Soz, had never learned the art. I could not bear to save my life and leave them behind, but Mamun Sahib urged me on, so I jumped in the river and swam away. I kept looking back, and after I had gone fifty or sixty yards, I heard the gunshots and saw the line of people falling dead.[87]

Zahir Dehlavi had another, more personal loss that day. His father-
in-law, who had quietly sheltered three Englishwomen throughout
the siege, felt confident that the women would guarantee his safety,
and so stayed on in the city after the rest of the family fled. But he
was gunned down by looting Englishmen regardless, alongside his
son and two servants.[88]

That night, while the officers feasted in the Diwan i-Khas, the
plundering of the city continued. One officer who was aware of
what was happening was Major William Ireland. 'The Sikh soldiers
had dreamt of carrying away jewels and treasures that would make
their families rich for ever,' he wrote. 'General Wilson had promised that the plunder of the city should, when realized, be distributed to the army . . . So guards were placed at all the gates, who
seized everything that was attempted to be passed through, [but]
the Sikhs were not so easily foiled.'

> They got bullock wagons to be driven at night to the walls, and
> dropped their booty down to their friends below. Many women,
> too, were seized and carried away by them. It was not till the spoils
> of Delhi were seen passing up the Punjab, that the news of its capture
> was fully believed in the great Musalman cities of the North West
> . . . Many of the citizens were shot, clasping their hands for mercy. It
> was known, too, that a large proportion had wished us well. Help-
> lessness ought to be respected in either sex, especially in those who
> have never done us wrong. It is as unmanly for an officer to drive his
> sword through a trembling old man, or a soldier to blow out the
> brains of a wounded boy, as to strike a woman.[89]

By the morning of the 21st, reports began to reach Zahir and his
family in the Ice House that all the pro-British loyalists at court
who had stayed behind in the city, confident of good treatment, had
nevertheless been murdered by the British. Among these was Mir
Haidar Ali, one of the leading figures in the pro-British faction at
court. Realising that anyone who had any connection with the
court was now regarded as a legitimate target, Zahir understood
that it was time that he and his brother separated from the rest of the
family, and fled to safety. 'We heard that the spies who had been

supporting the English were now continuing to work as informers, helping them to loot and kill and find people to hang, for which they received two rupees for each name . . .'

Nawab Hamid Ali Khan told my mother that he did not feel safe with my brother and me living in the Ice House. He said, 'send them away, they should go to where ever they can feel safe. These people [the British and their informers] will not leave anyone alive who has been connected with the court.' So I respectfully said to my father 'It is true: we should leave, and you will have to bear with our separation and permit my brother and me to go. We will go wherever God takes us. I am particularly concerned about my brother's safety since he has been working for the Royal Army, and the British will never spare him. If God wills to keep us alive then we will come back and find you.'

I then took a few thin pieces of silver and lined them in my shoes, between the top and the sole, and put two pieces in the fold of my pyjama string. I tied a dupatta around my waist, and took a stick in my hand. My wife, who was very shy, was weeping quietly. She had just lost her father and her brother, and now her husband was going too. As I was leaving, I whispered in her ear that she was now in the care of God: 'If I survive, I will come back for you, but if I am killed then please forgive me.' So saying, I called on the name of the Almighty and strode out towards the shrine of Khwaja Sahab [in Mehrauli].⁹⁰

Zahir had hardly gone more than half a mile when he saw a troop of cavalry coming towards them. 'On reaching us they surrounded us and said they wanted to see what we were carrying. They did not find anything but one fellow took off my turban and carried it away. I then tied the dupatta from around my waist on my head, a little later another bandit saw it, and came and took it away too.'

It was the inauspicious beginning of what would be an entirely nomadic life for the next five years, wandering the roads of northern India, hiding and avoiding British patrols. Although he returned several times to Delhi, he was never again able to make it home, and survived as best he could by trading in horses, and

travelling from court to court where his skills in calligraphy and
Urdu poetry assured him at least some food and shelter.

On the night of the 20th, General Bakht Khan stopped at
Humayun's Tomb and tried to persuade Zafar to accompany
him to Lucknow, where he intended to continue the resistance.
Again it was Hakim Ahsanullah Khan who convinced Zafar to
stay: ' "Recollect that you are the King," he said. "It is not right
for you to go. The army of the English mutinied against their
masters, fought with them, and have been utterly routed and
dispersed. What has your Highness to do with them? Be of good
courage, the English will not regard you as guilty." With such
words he restrained the King from accompanying the army in its
flight.'[91] Mirza Mughal, meanwhile, was persuaded to stay by the
devious Mirza Ilahe Bakhsh.[92]

That night, Mirza Ilahe Bakhsh came into Delhi and told Hodson
where Zafar and Mirza Mughal were sheltering, possibly at the
instigation of Zinat Mahal and Hakim Ahsanullah Khan.[93] He also
informed Hodson that Zafar had with him 'the state jewels and
property lists of the same'.[94] Hodson promptly went straight to see
Wilson and asked for permission to go and capture Zafar, arguing
that 'victory would be incomplete if the king and his male relatives
were allowed to remain at large'. Wilson at first said the enterprise
was 'too dangerous', but under pressure from Hodson and Neville
Chamberlain allowed Hodson to go if he took his own men and did
not require a large force, adding, 'don't let me be bothered with
them'; if Hodson wanted to go he could do so at his own risk, but
would have to manage the whole business himself.[95]

On the morning of the 21st, 'a royal salute at sunrise proclaimed
that Delhi was once more a dependency of the British crown'.[96] But
the captured city – the ancient capital of Hindustan, the great
Mughal metropolis – was now a desolate city of the dead, except for
parties of drunken British looters. Major William Ireland, a consistent critic of the brutality of his own colleagues throughout the
campaign, was horrified by the sight of the 'liberated' city. 'The

desolation of the great city was eloquent of the miseries of war,' he wrote. 'Save in the immediate vicinity of the houses in which soldiers were quartered, all was silent and deserted.'

There were no merchants sitting in the bazaars; no strings of camels or bullock wagons toiling through the gate; no passers-by in the thoroughfares; no men talking by the doors of the houses; no children playing in the dust; no women's voices from behind the screens. Household furniture of all kind was lying in the streets.

The spectacle was made only more melancholy by traces of recent inhabitants. The ashes were still black in the hearths, and domestic animals were roaming up and down in all directions in search of their late possessors. The houses were here and there burnt or shattered by cannon shot, and the fragments of shells scattered about, with rotten corpses now and then to be seen, half eaten by crows and jackals. The merchants had stuck to their shops to the last, and had been driven out only by the bombardment and the report of the fierce doings of our soldiers.[97]

Lieutenant Edward Ommaney of the Guides, an Urdu and Persian scholar who knew something of the history of the city, was also aghast at what he saw as the sun rose. 'The whole city is depopulated,' he wrote.

One only sees now and then, a body of sixty or so men and women going along the street to one of the gates, to leave the place; barring this, not one of the sepoys or the city people are seen. Our men may be seen in the empty houses, looting, and that is all. Of the 150,000 inhabitants, the whole nearly have left. Even when Nadir Shah conquered the city, this was not the case.*[98]

---

* This was indeed the case. Nadir Shah's legendary massacre of 1739 lasted only a few hours. According to legend it was stopped when an Indian petitioner came before him and recited a verse:

> None is left now for you to kill with your coquettish sword,
> Unless you bring them back to life and then kill them again.

Soon afterwards, William Hodson sent off Mirza Ilahe Bakhsh accompanied by his 'Chief Intelligencer', Maulvi Rajab Ali, and a small escort of Punjabi irregular cavalry; Hodson set off himself from the Fort towards Humayun's Tomb with a second body of cavalry, around fifty strong, 'after a brief interval'.[99] It was an expedition that he hoped would not only complete the restoration of his reputation in the army, but also put his name permanently in the history books.

Everything had now been arranged. The moment had come to arrest and bring back as his captive the man many of the British were now convinced lay at the heart of the whole rebellion, the spider at the centre of the web.

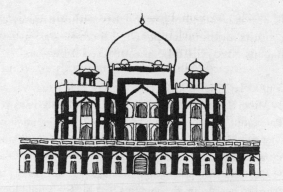

11

THE CITY OF THE DEAD

Hodson's plan for the capture of the King got off to an inauspicious start.

As Maulvi Rajab Ali and Mirza Ilahe Bakhsh approached Humayun's Tomb, they were ambushed by a party of jihadis, and four of their escort of horsemen were badly wounded. They wheeled around and fled back towards Delhi; but coming across Hodson after a short distance they were persuaded to continue with their mission, since the attack 'appeared to be the act of fanatics and not due to the King's party'.[1]

On arrival, Hodson hid in some ruins, out of sight of the gateway of the tomb, and sent in his understandably nervous negotiators, Rajab Ali and Ilahe Bakhsh. They were attended by a small armed escort of fifteen men from Hodson's Horse, led by a Sikh risaldar (cavalry commander) named Sirdar Man Singh. Hodson gave orders that the maulvi was to direct the negotiations. He was instructed to pass straight through the large and unstable rabble of refugees, *shahzadas* (princes), courtiers, hangers-on and jihadis who had taken shelter within the walls of the garden tomb. When he reached Zafar, he was 'to say to the King that if he came out quietly and gave himself up, I [Hodson] would ensure his safety, but if he ventured to leave the tomb, I had command of the entrance and would shoot him and his attendants without mercy'. For two agonising hours nothing happened. Hodson was just about to assume that his envoys had been murdered when,

> after a long delay, the Risaldar came to say that King was coming. Presently Mirza Ilahee Buksh and the Maulvee appeared escorting the King's Palanquin, closely followed by that of the Begum [accompanied by her son Mirza Jawan Bakht and her father Mirza Quli Khan] with their attendants and a host of the fugitives from the palace and city. The Palanquins stopped and a message was sent to me that the King wished to hear from my own lips that his life would be spared.
>
> I rode up to the spot, seizing the opportunity to interpose my men between the King's immediate party and the crowd pressing behind, the appearance of which was threatening. I dismounted for a moment and reassured the King and the Begum (both of whom were evidently much agitated and frightened) by the promise that his life would be spared, provided no attempt was made at a rescue.[2]

In addition to guaranteeing Zafar's life, Hodson promised the King that he would not be subject to 'dishonour (be-izzat) or any personal indignity'.[3]

> I then remounted and in sufficiently loud tone to be heard by the crowd repeated the words, adding a command to my men to shoot the first person who attempted to move. I then desired Mirza Ilahi Bakhsh and Maulvi Rajab Ali to proceed with the Palanquins as soon as they were a sufficient distance from the crowd.[4]

The journey through the no-man's-land towards Delhi seemed to Hodson to take for ever. As he told a colleague, 'the slow shuffling pace of the [palanquin] bearers, their continual changing of their shoulders, and the pressing on of the crowd,' kept the atmosphere edgy and tense. But the cavalry sawars rode close to the King's palanquin, and no attempt at a rescue was made. As the party neared the walls of the city, the crowd of stragglers slowly thinned until by the time they got to the Lahore Gate, Hodson's sawars found they were alone with their captives.[5] The guard at the gate asked who

Hodson had within the palanquin, to which he replied, 'only the King of Delhi'. They then passed down Chandni Chowk, and into the Fort, as Zafar returned to his ancestral palace no longer Emperor, but now prisoner.

Everyone stopped what they were doing to stare. One British surgeon described 'an old man with an anxious expression on his thin face' being carried through the litter of his ransacked palace. 'His countenance gave no signs of cruelty,' wrote the surgeon, 'but appeared mild.'[6] Hodson handed his prize over to Charles Saunders, the successor to Hervey Greathed as head of the civil administration of Delhi, and then went to report his coup to General Wilson.

To Hodson's surprise and disappointment, Wilson did not seem especially pleased by the news of the King's capture: 'Well I am glad you have got him,' was all he said. 'I never expected to see either of you again.'[7] According to Fred Maisey, who was also in the room at the time, the old general was actually 'in the most tremendous rage at the king being brought in alive . . . it seemed to me that the news was far from welcome, which made me doubt all along the assertion [by Hodson] that General Wilson had guaranteed the King's life'.[8] General Wilson later strongly denied that he had ever done so, and there is good reason to believe him, for both the civil and military authorities in Delhi had received strict and specific instructions from Canning in Calcutta not to offer any terms to the Mughals save that of unconditional surrender.

That afternoon, Zafar was taken to Zinat Mahal's haveli in Lal Kuan, where to add to his sufferings he was given the charmless and aggressive Kendal Coghill as a guard: 'I had the satisfaction of receiving the "King of Hindoostan" as a prisoner,' Coghill wrote to his brother the following day, 'and immediately placed him safe with a double sentry over him. It wasn't a manly thing to do, but I couldn't help calling him a pig and other appropriate epithets, and to ask him about our families. I would have shot him dead if he had only looked up, the brute, and gave the sentries orders that if he tried to stir to drop [i.e. shoot] him.'[9]

The following morning Hodson persuaded Wilson to sanction a second expedition to Humayun's Tomb.

This time the object was to pick up Mirzas Mughal, Khizr Sultan and Abu Bakr, the three princes who had commanded the Mughal forces during the Uprising, and whose presence in the tomb had now been confirmed by Mirza Ilahe Bakhsh.*[10] As before, Wilson made it a condition that he should not be bothered by the prisoners, and as no guarantees of the princes' lives had ever been discussed, Hodson interpreted his General's orders as he wished.

Hodson rode out with an escort of 100 *sawars* at eight in the morning, accompanied as before by his negotiators Maulvi Rajab Ali and Mirza Ilahe Bakhsh. Again, Hodson and his two British deputies halted outside the entrance to the tomb complex, and sent in the two Indians to negotiate. According to Lieutenant MacDowell, who left the only record of what happened, 'We sent in to say that the princes must give themselves up unconditionally, or take the consequences.'

A long half hour elapsed, when a messenger came out to say that the princes wished to know if their lives would be promised if they came out. 'Unconditional surrender' was the answer. Again we waited. It was a most anxious time. We dared not take them by force, all would have been lost, and we doubted their coming. We heard the shouts of the fanatics [jihadis] begging the princes to lead them on against us, and we had only one hundred men and were six miles from Delhi. . . . There were about three thousand Mussalman followers [in the walled tomb garden]. In a suburb close by [Nizamuddin], about three thousand more, all armed; so it was a ticklish bit of work . . .

At length imagining that sooner or later they must be taken, the princes resolved to give themselves up unconditionally, fancying, I suppose, that as we had spared the King, we would spare them. So a messenger was sent to say they were coming. We sent ten men to meet them, and by Hodson's orders, I drew the troops up across the

* In giving this piece of information, Mirza Ilahe Bakhsh was betraying his own grandson: Mirza Abu Bakr was the son of Mirza Fakhru by Ilahe Bakhsh's own daughter. He was afterwards known even by the British as 'the traitor of Delhi'.

road, ready to receive them and shoot them at once if there was any attempt at a rescue. Soon they appeared, in a small 'Rath' or Hindustanee cart, drawn by bullocks, with five troopers on each side. Behind them thronged about two or three thousand (I am not exaggerating) Mussalmans. We met them and at once Hodson and I rode up, leaving the men a little in the rear. They bowed as we came up, and Hodson, bowing, ordered the driver to move on.

Hodson told the *sawars* to hurry the princes along the road, while MacDowell and his troopers formed up between the crowd and the princes, advancing slowly towards the courtiers and attendants, forcing them back into the garden of the tomb.

Hodson and myself (I stuck to him throughout) with four men, [then] rode up the steps [and] through the arch, when he called out to the rabble to lay down their arms. There was a murmur. He reiterated the command and (God knows why, I can never understand it) they commenced doing so . . .

What we wanted was to gain time to get the princes away, for we could have done nothing had they attacked us . . . There we stayed for two hours collecting their arms, and I assure you I thought every moment they would rush on us. I said nothing, but smoked all the time to show I was unconcerned; but at last, when it was all done, and all the arms put in a cart, Hodson turned to me and said, 'We'll go now.' Very slowly we mounted, formed up the troop, and cautiously departed, followed by the crowd. As we got about a mile off, Hodson turned to me and said, 'Well, Mac, we've got them at last'; and we both gave a sigh of relief.[11]

What happened next is disputed. According to Hodson, when they finally caught up with the princes, three miles away, close to the walls of Delhi, and near an archway known ever after as the *Khuni Darwaza*, or Bloody Gate, a large and threatening crowd was closing in on the princes and looked to be on the verge of rescuing them. According to other accounts, including that of MacDowell, it was only a small crowd and was not in any way threatening. But there is no doubt as to what Hodson did next.

Stopping the cart, he ordered the three princes to get out, and
to strip naked. Then taking a Colt revolver, he shot them dead, in
cold blood and at point blank range, one after another. He then
stripped the corpses of their signet rings and turquoise *bazubands*
(armlets), which he pocketed, and seized their bejewelled swords.
The following day Hodson wrote to his sister, saying that however exhausted he was from his various exertions, 'I cannot help
being pleased with the warm congratulations I received on all
sides for my success in destroying the enemies of our race. The
whole nation will rejoice.' He added: 'I am not cruel, but I confess
I did enjoy the opportunity of ridding the earth of these
wretches.'[12]

The bodies were taken away and left out naked in front of the
kotwali, where the British troops queued up to see them. 'I saw
them there lying stark and stiff,' wrote Fred Maisey, 'and I must
say I was glad to see them, for of their guilt there never was a
doubt, and I really believe the king was, to a great extent, a puppet
in their hands.'[13] Charles Griffiths also applauded Hodson 'for
ridding the world of the miscreants', adding that 'he was upheld in
the deed by the whole Delhi army, men in every respect better
qualified to form a judgement in this particular than the senti-
mental beings at home'.

> I saw them that same afternoon; nor can it be said that I or others
> who viewed the lifeless remains felt any pity in our hearts for the
> wretches on whom had fallen a most righteous retribution for their
> crimes. The eldest [Mirza Mughal] was a strong well-knit man in the
> prime of life, the next [Khizr Sultan] somewhat younger, while the
> third [Abu Bakr] was quite a youth of not more than twenty years of
> age. Each of the Princes had two small bullet-holes over the region of
> the heart, the flesh singed by gunpowder, as the shots were fired
> close . . . The bodies remained for three days, and were then buried
> in dishonoured graves.[14]

The attitude of Maisey and Griffiths was the norm among the
British in Delhi: although there was a whole series of inquiries later
launched into Hodson's conduct, what was examined was not the

shooting of the princes, but instead his clemency in presuming to guarantee Zafar's life.*

All morning, while Hodson was busy in Humayun's Tomb, curious British soldiers had been going in parties to stare at the captive King, who sat miserably in his wife's haveli, 'like a beast in a cage', according to one officer.†[15] 'I have seen the old Pig of a king,' reported a dismissive Hugh Chichester to his father. 'He is a very old man, just like an old khitmatgar [servant]. One was always supposed to take off one's shoes on going to visit mosques, or to have an interview with the King. But these little affairs we drop now.'[16] Other officers wrote home saying how they had treated the King 'with great disrespect', forcing him to stand up and salaam to them, while one boasted that he had pulled the King's beard.[17]

Among Zafar's visitors on the night of the 22nd was the new Civil Commissioner, Charles Saunders, and his wife Matilda, who went to see the King to break the news that two of his sons and one of his grandsons had been shot dead. Charles Griffiths was part of the guard on duty. 'Sitting cross-legged on a cushion placed on a common native charpoy, in the verandah of a courtyard, was the last representative of the Great Mogul dynasty,' he wrote.

> There was nothing imposing about his appearance, save a long white beard which reached to his girdle. About middle height, and upwards of seventy years old,‡ he was dressed in white, with a conical

---

* In the end, the blame – as it was seen – was pinned on Hervey Greathed, who being dead was unable to confirm or deny Hodson's claim that he had given the authorisation to offer Zafar his life.

† This was an image than sprang readily to the pens of several visitors, not least because the same courtyard also contained Zinat Mahal's pet tiger: 'There is a Tiger here which I think had better be removed as there is no-one to feed it,' wrote Zinat's jailor on 24 September. 'It might be sold profitably to some natives. Probably if it cannot be taken away it had better be shot. There is also a magnificent Buck Antelope here.' Oriental and India Office Collections, British Library, CB Saunders Papers, Eur Mss E 186, no. 122, Ommaney to Saunders, 22 September 1857.

‡ Zafar was in fact fully eighty-two.

shaped turban of the same colour and material, while at his back two attendants stood, waving over his head large fans of peacock feathers, the emblem of sovereignty – a pitiable farce in the case of one who was already shorn of his regal attributes, a prisoner in the hands of his enemies. Not a word came from his lips; in silence he sat day and night, with his eyes cast on the ground, and as though utterly oblivious of the condition in which he was placed. On another bed, three feet away from the King, sat the officer on guard, while two stalwart European sentries, with fixed bayonets, stood on either side. The orders given were that on any attempt at a rescue, the officer was immediately to shoot the King with his own hand.[18]

When the death of the three princes was announced to Zafar, he was so shocked and depressed that he was unable to react. But according to Matilda Saunders, Zinat Mahal was thrilled when she heard the news through the purdah curtain that had been hung 'in the tiny cabin-like rooms' where she had been lodged. 'She said she rejoiced in the death of the elder sons of the King for now her son [Mirza Jawan Bakht] had a chance of succeeding to the throne. Some people might call this honest, however no throne in this world will he find, poor deluded woman, as she will soon discover.'[19]

Matilda Saunders then went and called on Taj Begum, who was being kept in a separate room from her long-time rival.

We went to see another wife once said to have been a great beauty – she is called the Taj Begum. We found her looking very sad with black muslin thrown over head and shoulders. Her mother and brother had both died of cholera since the assault, and she is now no longer the King's favourite. Zinat Mahal became very jealous of her and had her shut in prison for 3 years.

When I was leaving, the King called me back and told me he hoped to see me again, and that he hoped I would act as an ambassador between him and Charlie. I answered 'Kubbeen Nai' which means No Never! Said very emphatically. Twice I repeated it to make sure the old wretch understood me thoroughly. I spoke to the Rifle Guard outside who were guarding him while Charles was assisting Mrs Grant onto the Elephant, and said I hope you will keep the king

safely, don't let him run away. 'Oh no Ma'am,' [he replied, ']there's
no fear of that, we are a great deal too fond of him!' So I said, 'that's
right,' and walked away wishing them Good Morning.[20]

When, that same evening, a young officer, Henry Ouvry, saw the
princes' bodies lying naked at the kotwali, he wrote in his diary that
this was just the beginning of the work of retribution for which the
British had so long planned: though 'sick of blood', he wrote that he
had no doubt that 'we shall have to execute a vast number before we
are done'.[21]

Little time was lost before this self-fulfilling prophecy began to
be realised. Gallows were erected throughout the gutted city – 'they
say there is not a neighbourhood of Delhi without its own place of
execution', wrote one Delhiwallah – and the hangings began.[22] The
largest was 'right in centre of Chandni Chowk, a hideous erection
of wood that was the only new and uninjured structure' in the
entire street.[23] On a trip to take the air down the Chowk shortly
afterwards, the twenty-three-year-old Lieutenant Edward Ommaney casually noted in his diary that he saw '19 men hanged opposite
the Kotwali on one gallow, and 9 on the other'.[24]

Ommaney was disgusted to see that, as in Paris during the
Revolution, large numbers had gathered to watch the entertainment
provided by the executions. The Chowk, he noted, was 'crowded
with officers and Europeans'. 'How transient seems this life,' he
wrote in his diary that night, 'when one sees a man so quickly part
with it: a few moments and the animated body has separated from
that spirit which has gone to appear before its maker, and yet to
look at the crowd, how little they feel or seem to understand the
awful awful change taking place before their eyes.'[25] He also noted
that 'there was a very small drop as the Provost Sergeant said the
rope would not stand a long one' – the implication of this being that
a short rope meant a slow and more lingering death by throttling;
while a long drop would break the neck and bring instant death.[26]
Other observers were gleefully explicit that the short rope was a

deliberate strategy to prolong the death of the victim. According to one source, the executioners were bribed by the crowds of British soldiers who were standing around, puffing cigars, making sure that the hangmen kept their victims 'a long time dying . . . as they liked to see the criminals dance "a Pandie's hornpipe" as they termed the dying struggles of the wretches'. One provost-marshal alone put to death '400 or 500 wretches' before 'thinking of resigning his office'.[27] Some hangmen even experimented with 'artistic' methods of dispatching their victims 'in figures of eight'.[28]

It was reports of this sort of thing which began to worry Lord Canning in Calcutta. On 25 September he wrote to Queen Victoria about the

> violent rancour of a very large proportion of the English Community against every native Indian of every class. There is a rabid and indiscriminate vindictiveness abroad, even amongst many who ought to set a better example, which is impossible to contemplate without something like a feeling of shame for one's fellow countrymen. Not one man in ten seems to think that the hanging and shooting of 40 or 50,000 Mutineers beside other rebels, can be otherwise than practicable and right . . .[29]

Not all the prisoners in Delhi were hanged; many others were shot. Hugh Chichester wrote that 'There has been nothing but shooting these villains for the last three days, some 3 or 400 were shot yesterday,' noting that while some young boys that the British came across were allowed to pass freely out of the city gates, 'most of them are put to death'.[30] According to Major William Ireland, 'Offenders who were seized were handed over to a military commission to be tried. The work went on with celerity. Death was almost the only punishment, and condemnation almost the only issue of a trial. The gentlemen who had to judge offenders were in no mood for leniency.'[31] It was not just bloodlust and the urge for revenge which provided the motive for this mass slaughter: there was also money to be made. Informers were paid 2 rupees for every arrest, while the captors were allowed to keep 'all money and gold found on the persons of mutineers captured'.[32]

All this was cheered on in the *Delhi Gazette Extra* by George Wagentrieber, who returned from Lahore after the fall of the city to cover the work of retribution to which he had so long looked forward: 'Hanging is, I am happy to say, the order of the day here,' he wrote soon after his return.

> Six or eight rebels are hanged every morning and they are being brought in daily from the surrounding villages. A resident of Delhi, in peaceful times, might recognise in them the betinselled equestrians who (dis)graced the Chandnee Chowk, and sported their figures every Sunday evening. But how changed! Their features may be recognised but such a set of miserable crestfallen wretches, were never before beheld in the city of palaces.[33]

Subsequent issues of the paper kept Wagentrieber's readers up to date with the ongoing slaughter: 'Fourteen rebels were strung up opposite the Kotwalee yesterday morning,' observed an approving Wagentrieber a couple of weeks after his return, 'and some more this morning.' This was not nearly enough for Wagentrieber, who attacked Saunders in his columns for his weakness and leniency:

> We have one man in Delhi, so full of the milk of human kindness that whilst there is a universal cry for vengeance against the King of Delhi and his whole progeny for their inhuman cruelties and barbarities, his 'bowels yearn' for the innocent son and heir, and in the fullness of his compassion for the little boy of eighteen [Mirza Jawan Bakht] he endeavours to lessen the indignities the little urchin is exposed to . . . [He] never approaches the royal prisoner without the most profound reverence.

Only Metcalfe, he wrote, was going about the business of retribution and hanging with the 'appropriate energy . . . under the immediate instruction of Sir Theophilus we have won a good riddance of the *budmashes* [rascals], either by their non-appearance in the city, incarceration or – by the best of all means – the gallows'.[34]

On Sunday, 27 September, a special thanksgiving service was held by Padre Rotton in the Diwan i-Khas. Rotton preached from the text, 'What shall I render unto the Lord, for all the benefits which he has done to me?'

As far as Rotton was concerned, the service represented a thanksgiving for deliverance of Good from the hands of Evil: 'It would hardly be possible to conceive anything more impressive than this assembly,' he wrote, 'a small but victorious Christian force assembled within the Imperial Palace of the ancient Moslem capital of Hindustan, lining the four sides of that marble hall wherein the King and his advisers had not long before convened, plotting and determining evil against the British cause.'

> And now the councils of evil men had been brought to naught, and every foul purpose of theirs completely frustrated, the triumphant army – the means which God had been pleased to employ in order to bring about these gracious ends – stood devoutly in the Divine presence, ascribing unto Him praise, and saying glory and honour, power and dominion are thine.[35]

One of the few women present, Mrs Coopland, took Rotton's view of events to an even more perverse extreme: 'In this splendid hall,' she wrote, 'which once echoed to the mandates of a despotic Emperor, with sole power of life and death over millions of submissive slaves, now echoed the peaceful prayers of a Christian people.'[36]

Early the following morning, a column of troops moved off towards Agra in belated pursuit of Bakht Khan and his rebel sepoys, though by this stage only 2,600 men of the Delhi Field Force were left to carry on the fight to Agra, and hence to the last great battle of 1857, the relief of the besieged British Residency in Lucknow. Their first trial was simply crossing the deserted city: 'The march was simply awful,' wrote Richard Barter.

> Our advance guard consisting of Cavalry and Artillery had burst and squashed the dead bodies which lay swelled to an enormous size in the Chandni Chowk, and the stench was fearful. Men and officers were sick all round and I thought we would never get through the

city. It was a ride I don't care ever to take again, and the horse felt it
as much as I did, for he snorted and shook as he slid rather than
walked over the abominations with which the street was covered.[37]

Fred Roberts was equally horrified. 'The march through Delhi in the
early morning light was a gruesome proceeding. On our way to the
Lahori Gate by Chandni Chowk, not a sound was to be heard but
the falling of our own footsteps; not a living creature was to be seen.'

> Dead bodies were strewn about in all directions in every attitude that
> the death struggle had caused them to assume, in every stage of
> decomposition. In many instances the positions of the bodies were
> appallingly life-like. Some lay with their arms uplifted as if beckon-
> ing, and indeed the whole scene was weird and terrible beyond
> description . . . The atmosphere was unimaginably disgusting, laden
> as it was with the most noxious and sickening odours.[38]

Though the departing troops were heading back into conflict, and
many would lose their lives in the fierce battles that lay ahead in
Lucknow, few of the column envied the Prize Agents or the small
garrison that was left behind in the stink of this City of the Dead.

One of those who had just received the bad news that he was to stay
in Delhi was the young Lieutenant Edward Ommaney. A promising linguist, Ommaney had been part of Nicholson's Moveable
Column and had written in his diary of his horror at the latter's
brutal treatment not only of the mutineers but even of his unfortunate cook boys. Since then, however, he had himself been
scarred and brutalised by the violence he had seen and participated
in; and his diary, like Edward Vibart's letters, oscillates between
sensitive observation and moments of startling savagery.

Indeed, he was himself aware of the changes that the daily
violence were bringing about in the British army of occupation:
'How little the death of anyone affects people,' he wrote in his diary
for 1 November, after hearing about the death of John Clifford,

whose sister had been murdered with Annie Jennings and whose bloodstained appearance during the capture of the city had so shocked Charles Griffiths. '[Clifford was] so young and full of spirits when I last saw him a few days ago. I was telling some fellows [about Clifford's death] and all they said was, "Oh, I heard somebody telling so, poor fellow," and that is all. One dies, and only intimate friends mourn – and how few they are.'[39] Yet the same man was capable of writing only a few weeks later, 'coming back, we thrashed every native who did not salaam'.[40]

Two days before the departure of the columns, Ommaney had received orders from Saunders that he was to be Zafar's jailer. His first job had been to find a secure prison for the former monarch within the walls of the Red Fort. He had just found a suitable-looking house at the back of the bazaar – formerly the residence of a junior *shahzada* named Mirza Nili – when he was told that in addition to Zafar and his immediate suite, he would also be in charge of eighty-two women, forty-seven children and two eunuchs of the imperial harem. These had just been brought into the Fort from Humayun's Tomb in a procession of fourteen heavily loaded *gharries* (carts), and placed 'in strict confinement' under Ommaney's charge.[41] The following day, before he had even been able to begin thinking about how he was to feed or organise sanitary arrangements for this many people, cholera broke out among his royal prisoners, claiming the life of the first of the begums the following night.

The new quarters of Zafar and his family were both filthy and basic in the extreme: 'we entered a small, dirty, low room with white-washed walls', wrote Mrs Coopland when she took her turn to come to stare at the prisoner. 'There on a low charpoy cowered a thin, small old man, dressed in a dirty white suit of cotton, and rolled in shabby wraps and *razais* [quilts]. At our entrance he laid aside the hookah he had been smoking and he, who had formerly thought it an insult for anyone to sit in his presence, began salaaming us in the most abject manner, and saying he was "*burra kooshee*" [very glad] to see us.'[42]

'He is confined to a little room containing only one charpoy,' observed another visitor, 'and is allowed but two annas (3d) a day for his food. He is treated with great disrespect by the officers and soldiers, though Mr Saunders is civil to him.'

> The Begums and princesses of his house share his prison with him. These unfortunate ladies, to whom no guilt could be attached, were exposed to the gaze of officers and soldiers who could go into the room where they were at their pleasure. To a native woman of the very lowest class this is an unutterable shame. [Whenever any man entered] they all turned their faces to the wall.[43]

Many of Zafar's British visitors actively relished the humiliation they could now inflict on the family simply by breaking the women's purdah: 'It seemed absurd to humour thus their silly prejudices,' wrote Mrs Coopland, 'when they had spared no European in their power any indignity or insult.'[44] In addition, Zafar was forbidden access to his hakim, whom he continually asked for, as well as his dhobi and barber.[45] Even John Lawrence, who in most matters acted as a moderating influence on British excesses at this period, advised Saunders not to be too solicitous to the ex-King: 'Neither the King, nor any member of the family, deserve anything at our hands,' he wrote in December. 'In the present state of feeling it would be a great mistake for us to show him any consideration.'[46]

Whatever injustice this implied, Lawrence was quite correct in his estimation of British public opinion: when Ommaney took Mirza Jawan Bakht out for an elephant ride in Daryaganj, hoping to extract information about the origins of the Uprising from the boy by separating him from his parents, the *Lahore Chronicle* lambasted the Delhi administration for 'keeping the King in luxury' and started a campaign calling for Zafar to be hanged and his city levelled: as if it were not bad enough for 'the King [to be] spared and living in state', harrumphed the *Chronicle* in an editorial,

> [now] his youngest son is playing the prince in this city, still reeking with English blood, pounding up and down Chandni Chowk with an English officer behind him. Oh! God that an Englishman should be found base enough to accept the task, and that an English officer

should be found playing the part of a lackey to the spawn of the viper![47]

The campaign to flatten Delhi proved especially popular with the *Chronicle*'s readers: 'Having just seen your issue of the 18th instant,' wrote one reader, 'in which you most properly, as in most of your late issues, uphold the necessity for the destruction of Delhi "in toto" and no sparing of the Jumma Masjid etc for fear of offending the Moslem, I consider it a duty to my country, as it should be of all Englishmen, to assist you in the national cry of "A bloody revenge" and "Down with Delhi".'[48] The campaign also struck a chord among the British troops in Delhi. Hugh Chichester was typical. 'There are several mosques in the city most beautiful to look at,' he wrote to his father. 'But I should like to see them all destroyed. The rascally brutes desecrated our churches and graveyards and I do not think we should have any regard for their stinking religion.'[49] Charles Raikes thought the Jama Masjid should be saved, but converted into a church, 'and name each stone after a Christian martyr'.[50]

Mrs Coopland, not uncharacteristically, was even more outspoken. 'I could not but think it was a disgrace to England', she wrote in her memoirs, 'that this city, instead of being razed to the ground, should be allowed to stand, with its blood-stained walls and streets – an everlasting memorial to the insult offered to England's honour.'

Many would forget this insult; but it cannot, and ought not to be forgotten . . . If it were destroyed, being their most sacred city, and one that reminds them of their fallen grandeur, it would do more to manifest our abhorrence of their crimes, and our indignation against them, than the hanging of hundreds. Delhi ought to be raized, and on its ruins a church or monument should be erected, inscribed with a list of all the victims of the mutinies – if it be possible to gather all the names of ALL those who were massacred – and the funds for its erection should be raised by a fine levied on every native implicated in the mutinies.[51]

Amid such self-righteous hysteria, only one man dared call publicly for Zafar to be better treated. Henry Layard, the former MP for Aylesbury, came to visit Zafar and was horrified by what he saw. 'Many persons regret that the King of Delhi has not fallen in just punishment for his offence,' Layard told an audience in London. 'I saw the King of Delhi; and I will leave the meeting to judge, when it has heard me, whether he is punished.'

> I will not give any opinion as to whether the manner we are treating him is worthy of a great nation. I saw that broken-down old man – not in a room, but in a miserable hole of his palace – lying on a bedstead, with nothing to cover him but a miserable tattered coverlet. As I beheld him, so remembrance of his former greatness seemed to rise in his mind. He rose with difficulty from his couch; showed me his arms which were eaten into by disease and by flies – partly from want of water; and he said, in a lamentable voice, that he had not enough to eat. Is that the way, as Christians, we ought to treat a King? I saw his women too, all huddled up in a corner with their children; and I was told that all was allowed for their support was 16s a day! Is that not punishment enough for one that has occupied a throne?[52]

Ommaney, who firmly believed that the British had been too soft on Delhi and should have exacted a more violent retribution, was not readily inclined to ameliorate the conditions of the imprisonment. Yet to his own surprise he slowly came to be fond of Zafar, whom he thought looked 'very like Sir C Napier'. Indeed, he quickly concluded that Zafar was so old, senile and distraught that 'he was perfectly unaccountable for his actions' during the Uprising.[53] Before long the elderly King began to return his jailer's unexpected affection: by mid-October, Ommaney was recording in his diary how Zafar 'appeared as if he was going to embrace me, [but instead] put his right arm on my left shoulder and patted me'.[54]

Ommaney also grew to be increasingly intrigued by Zinat Mahal – who, he said, henpecked her ailing and senile husband; but of the sixteen harem women at his disposal, only she seemed to look after the old man.'⁵⁵ Zafar, wrote Ommaney in his diary, 'is kept greatly in order by his favourite wife, Zeenut Mehul, who if she is speaking and he puts in a word, tells him to keep quiet as she is speaking. He is always wanting trivial things, which if they do not please him, he throws away, which at times, enrages the Ex-Queen who holds the purse. His own servants and sons treat him with the greatest respect'.*⁵⁶

As for Zinat Mahal herself, he wrote in his diary that 'She talks prettily, but with difficult language for a novice.' Later he added, 'Zeenut Mehul I have never seen, [though] one day I saw her hand and arm which she showed to let me see part of her clothing at the time she wanted money. She talks nicely, but I believe she is not good looking. She strikes me as being a very clever and intriguing woman.'⁵⁷

Only one member of the family did Ommaney instantly dislike. This was Zinat Mahal's beloved son, Mirza Jawan Bakht. Spoiled and callous, Jawan Bakht soon proved himself more than willing to give evidence about any of his family's activities during the Uprising. Early on in his captivity, Jawan Bakht laughed when he saw Ommaney 'thrash' Zafar's tailor, who had entered the prison without permission. The young prince was warned by Ommaney 'that if he laughed when I punished a man, he would probably get the same'.⁵⁸ Within a short time he was offering to show Ommaney the whereabouts of his mother's buried treasure in return for 100 cheroots, which Ommaney procured from the Parsi merchants Cowasjee and Co., who had now moved from the Ridge into the Fort bazaar.⁵⁹ 'He [Jawan Bakht] is apt to get very familiar if he fancies he is encouraged,' wrote Ommaney in his diary. 'He possesses in my opinion, not the slightest spark of honor and affection, according to English ideas of those qualities.'

* Mrs Coopland gives a similar account, saying that she had 'heard that the king and queen did not live on very good terms. She said that he would still consider himself a king, and when she sent for things from the bazaar he pronounced them not good enough; and that he would not smoke tobacco when it came because he did not consider it nice enough. He complained that she had plenty of concealed money and jewels, which she would not sacrifice to his comfort; so that Mr Omanney was obliged to allow him about sixpence a day'. R. M. Coopland, *A Lady's Escape from Gwalior and Life in the Fort of Agra during the Mutinies of 1857*, London, 1859, p. 277.

He has told me of many things which implicate his father in the rebellion, he has told of the jewels and property of his mother, who declared she had none, indeed he has as much told me that his mother is a liar. After his showing his brother's treasures, he in fear and trembling went to his father and mother, telling lies as to where he had been. He has no affection for his brothers, calling them *Budmashes*. What more can be required to show the degeneracy of the once proud and powerful race of Taimoor than seeing this young descendant traitor.[60]

By the middle of November, news came through from Calcutta that the details of the military commission to try all the princes and nobles of Delhi, including the King, had all been finalised. Shortly afterwards Major J. F. Harriott arrived in Delhi as Deputy Judge Advocate General to begin work on the various trials. Ommaney was instructed to help Harriott with the translations of the documents that had been found in the Palace. These, it was assumed, would provide the evidence for the conviction of the entire Mughal family and their court.[61] It was also hoped that the trial of Zafar, now seen by many of the British as the central conspirator behind the Uprising, would act as a sort of Commission of Enquiry into the causes of the Uprising.

'Judging from Harriott's appearance and manner,' wrote Ommaney after their first meeting on 27 November, 'none of the prisoners have much chance of getting off.'[62]

However bad the conditions suffered by the royal family, they were preferable to the situation of the ordinary people of Delhi, most of whom were now dotted around the surrounding countryside, sheltering in tombs and ruins, foraging for wild fruits or begging for food as best they could. Only a very few still remained within the city walls, and most of those were starving. According to Charles Griffiths:

The *tai-khanas*, or underground rooms of houses, scattered all over the city, were found to be filled with human beings – those who, by age or infirmity, had been unable to join in the general exodus which had taken place during the last days of the siege. Hundreds of old men, women and children, were found huddled together, half-starved, in these places, the most wretched looking object I ever saw.

There was no means of feeding them in the city, where their presence would have raised a plague; so by orders of the General, they were turned out of the gates of Delhi. It was a melancholy sight seeing them troop out of the town, hundreds passing through the Lahore Gate . . . We were told that provision had been collected for their use at a place some miles distant, and it is to be hoped the poor creatures were saved from starvation; but we had our doubts on the subject, and, knowing how callous with regard to human suffering the authorities had become, I fear that many perished from want and exposure.

Within the city, even the most loyal British servants who had opted to stay in their havelis now found their life impossible. Teams of looters, official and unofficial, went from house to house, past the litter of broken furniture and the smashed contents of shops that lay scattered across the streets, seizing what they could, and forcing any inhabitants they found still sheltering in cellars to show them where they had hidden their valuables.[63] 'To all of us [soldiers], the loot of the city was to be a fitting recompense for the toils and privations we had undergone,' wrote Charles Griffiths. 'Nor did the questionable nature of the transaction weigh for one moment with us under the recognized military law – "that a city taken by assault belonged as prize to the conquerors . . ."

It would have been contrary to human nature, and utterly at variance with the predatory instinct, had the soldiers failed to take advantage of the facilities for plunder which surrounded them on every side; nor could it be expected that a man, after possessing himself of valuables, would . . . deliver up all his booty to the authorities . . . Often, when wandering through the city in search of plunder, I, in the company of others, came across officers engaged in the same quest as ourselves . . .[64]

Meanwhile the prize agents got to work. Mrs Muter described her husband setting off after breakfast

> with a troop of coolies, armed with picks, crowbars and measuring lines. A house said to contain treasure would be allotted for a day's proceedings, and the business would commence by a careful survey of the premises . . . By careful measurement of the roofs above and of the rooms below, any concealed space could be detected. Then the walls were broken through, and if there was a secret room or a built-up niche or recess it would be discovered, and some large prizes rewarded their search. On one occasion . . . he came back with thirteen wagons loaded with spoil, and among other valuables, eighty thousand rupees – in English money £8000. On another occasion, silver vessels and gold ornaments, and . . . a bag of a thousand rupees.[65]

'In a very short time,' wrote Charles Griffiths,

> the rooms of the Prize Agents were filled with treasures of every kind – jewellery and precious stones, diamonds, rubies, emeralds and pearls without number, from those as large as hen's eggs to the small species used for necklaces; gold ornaments, chains of the most beautiful workmanship, bracelets and bangles all of solid metal . . . I visited one room, the long table of which literally groaned with riches – a dazzling sight to the eye.[66]

Many spies and collaborators had written evidence that they had assisted the British, but General Wilson had ordered that 'no protection tickets should be recognised as valid unless counter-signed by him, and the consequence was that but few obtained anything like protection for their property', stated a report of the Company's Intelligence Department. 'Before two or three days had elapsed there was not a house which had not been ransacked and plundered of its contents, friends and foes of the government suffering to an equal extent.'[67] Munshi Jiwan Lal, who had been a key intelligence official throughout the siege, and only just survived successive rebel attempts to capture and execute him, had his house comprehensively looted by Sikh soldiers on 21 September.[68] A similar fate awaited even the arch-collaborator Mirza Ilahe Bakhsh, who, despite betraying his cousin, Zafar, and even his own grandson, Mirza Abu Bakr, still had his house ransacked and all his goods taken from him by the Prize Agents.[69]

The most poignant letter expressing the feelings of betrayal experienced by all pro-British loyalists was written by the former Delhi College mathematics lecturer and Christian convert, Master Ramchandra. Ramchandra had escaped from Delhi on 11 May, the same day that his fellow convert, Dr Chaman Lal, was killed on the first morning of the Uprising. Returning to Delhi after the fall of the city, he expected to be welcomed home by his fellow Christians, but instead found himself living in fear of his life just as he done during the Uprising – but while before he had been targeted on account of his faith, now he suffered merely because of his skin colour. Finally he decided to put his experiences on record in a letter to Colonel Burn, who had recently been appointed the Military Governor of Delhi. In the letter he described how he had happily worked as an assistant to the prize agents and as a translator of documents for the trials of the rebels, but even so had found his life constantly threatened. 'More than a month ago', he wrote, 'I was directed to go to Mr Murphy's house near the Church there to translate some papers from Persian into English.'

As I was passing on the road, I saw some English officers standing on Hamid Ali Khan's mosque throwing clay balls by means of a bow or *ghulail* at all native passers-by. All my explanations of being a Govt Servant and a Christian &c could not be of any use; on the contrary they were more exasperated by this; they abused me and threw their clay balls with greater force . . . [Later, going again] to the said mosque in search of some books which I was employed to collect by the Prize Agent, I was attacked again as before, though I had two Prize Agency Chuprassees [orderlies] with me and though I cried to inform the officers that I had a ticket [i.e. pass] of the Prize Agent.

After that I found to my great grief that I was not only in danger in deserted streets but in my very house also. About 12 days ago, at

about 9 o'clock at night, I and two of my friends were conversing
with each other . . . when we were suddenly confounded by the
cracking of stones against the doors and walls of my house and one
stone falling on my bed with great violence . . .

Ramchandra described how the English officers billeted opposite
his house turned out to be responsible, and that they continued to
attack him and his house at regular intervals in the days and nights
that followed. One day, returning from Edward Campbell's house
in the Fort,

I received a heavy blow on the head from an English officer passing
with another gentleman also on horseback and after inflicting this
blow with his stick the officer turned around and required me to
make a salaam.* I made many salaams instead of one and cried I was
a Christian sir, and employed by the Prize Agency, and after this he
proceeded towards the Diwan i-Khas abusing me and saying I was as
black as jet. Being much hurt and almost stunned and grieved, I
stopped a little at the place where I had received the blow, seeing
which the gentleman who struck me returned towards me galloping
and alighting from his horse inflicted many severe blows on my left
arm and back . . .

Ramchandra then described the sufferings he had undergone in the
course of the Uprising, on account of his conversion, 'but then I
was comforted in my greatest distress by reflecting that what I had
gone through was nothing compared with what the English Officers, civil and military, and the missionaries had suffered'.

Besides I thought that if the Mutineers find and kill me they will do
so on account of my having abjured the creed of my forefathers and
embraced Christianity, and that I will die a witness to the faith of the
blessed saviour, like the martyrs of old, the Apostles and early

* The officer in question may well have been Edward Ommaney, who wrote in his
diary that he 'thrashed every native who did not salaam' at exactly the time in question,
and who would have had reason to be heading into the Red Fort. National Army
Museum, 6301/143, Diaries of Col. E.L. Ommaney, vol. A, entry for 24 November.

Christians. Herein was a great comfort to me under all my trials and
dangers. But there is hardly any comfort remaining, when a native
Christian is in danger from Christian officers themselves, merely
because he was not born in England and has not a white skin. This
was not the case even among the rebels in Delhie who were
professors of false religion. A Mohomedan or Hindoo was received
as a brother among them. They hated only Christians, and those who
were known to be friendly to them.

'This my appeal', wrote the disillusioned Ramchandra, 'is not only
for native Christians, for there are very few [left] in Dehlie, but for
Hindoos and some Mohomedans also who are allowed to live in the
City, but are exposed to danger from the English soldiers, and
particularly the English officers.'[70]

Ghalib was among those very few Muslims left in the city. A
stroke of luck had protected the poet when so many of his friends
and patrons were killed or driven out. For his *muhalla*, Ballimaran, contained the hakim and several senior courtiers of the
loyalist Maharaja of Patiala, who had sent troops and supplies to
the British on the Ridge, and who now arranged for guards to
make sure that looters did not attack the street. Thanks to the
Maharaja's guards, Ghalib was one of the only citizens of Delhi to
remain unmolested in his house, and almost the only member of
the courtly elite to survive the fall of Delhi with his property,
such as it was, intact.

Even so, it was a desperate time. Ghalib wrote in *Dastanbuy* of
how he and his neighbours had shut the gate of the *muhalla* and
piled stones against it so as to barricade themselves in as all around
them 'mass arrests, assassinations and slaughter' imprisoned or
killed scores of his friends. Meanwhile, within the barricades,
Ghalib's neighbours waited nervously, hoping their meagre stocks
of food and water would last until peace returned. In his diary, the
poet scribbled down his worries as to how he could survive when
his city had been utterly destroyed around him:

There is neither merchant nor buyer; there is no seller of wheat from whom we can buy flour, nor is there a washerman to whom we can give our soiled garments; there is no barber to trim hair, or sweeper to clean our floors. It was impossible for us to leave the lane for water or to get flour. Gradually, whatever provisions we had in our houses were consumed. Although we used the water with great care, not a single drop remained in cup or jar and we were hungry and thirsty throughout the days and nights. Beyond, mass slaughter was rampant, and the streets were filled with horrors . . . We are like prisoners: nobody comes to visit us and we receive no news. We cannot leave the lane so we are unable to see what is happening with our own eyes. Then one day clouds appeared and it rained. We tied up a sheet in our courtyard and placed our jars beneath it and in this way we collected water . . . Still the two [adopted] children whom I have raised with such indulgence ask me to give them fruit, milk and sweets, and I cannot satisfy their wishes . . .[71]

Ghalib's other worry was his mentally ill brother. Unable to reach him, he heard first that his brother's house had been looted. Worse news followed: his brother had run out into the street and been shot dead by trigger-happy British soldiers. To crown this, it was impossible to get out of the city to bury him, and it was difficult even finding the water to wash the body or a proper shroud in which to lay him to rest. Finally, on 5 October, three weeks after the British entered through Kashmiri Gate, British troops climbed into the *muhalla* and hauled Ghalib off to Colonel Burn to be interrogated. Always a dapper man, Ghalib made sure he was wearing his best Turkish-style headdress for the interview.

The Colonel looked at this strange fashion and asked in broken Urdu, 'Well? You Muslim?' 'Half,' said Ghalib. 'What does that mean?' asked the Colonel. 'I drink wine,' said Ghalib, 'but I don't eat pork.' The Colonel laughed, and Ghalib then showed him the letter which he had received from the Minister for India [*sic*] in acknowledgement of the ode to Her Majesty the Queen which Ghalib has sent. The Colonel said, 'After the victory of government forces why did you not present yourself at the Ridge?' Ghalib replied, 'My rank required that I should have four palanquin bearers, but all four of them ran away and left me, so I could not come.'[72]

According to Ghalib's own account of the meeting, he also added, 'I am old and crippled and deaf, and as unfit to confer with as I am to fight. I do pray for your success, and have done all along; but I could do that from here.'[73] Colonel Burn let him go.

Almost alone of his class, Ghalib had, without leaving the city, survived the cataclysm that destroyed Delhi. But now he had to face the intense loneliness of the sole survivor – a life without anyone left with whom he could share his tastes or arts or memories. By his own estimate, there were barely a thousand Muslims left in the city; many of his best friends and rivals were dead; while the others were scattered 'in ditches and mud huts' in the surrounding countryside. Meanwhile, he kept his head low in the occupied city, 'a swimmer in this ocean of blood'. As he wrote in a verse contained in a letter to a friend in Rampur:

> Every armed British soldier
> Can do whatever he wants.
> Just going from home to market
> Makes one's heart turn to water.
> The Chowk is a slaughter ground
> And homes are prisons.
> Every grain of dust in Delhi
> Thirsts for Muslims' blood.
> Even if we were together
> We could only weep over our lives.[74]

'The light has gone out of India,' he wrote in one letter. 'The land is lampless. Lakhs have died and among the survivors hundreds are in jail.'[75] 'People go mad from great sorrow,' he wrote in another. 'Would it be surprising if I should lose my mind from this onslaught of grief?'

What grief haven't I suffered: grief in death, in separation, in loss of income, and in honour? Besides the tragic events in the Red Fort, so many of my Delhi friends have been killed ... How can I forget them? How can I ever bring them back ... relatives, friends, students, lovers. Now every one of them is gone. It is so terribly difficult to mourn for a single relative or friend. Think of me who has to mourn for so many. My God! So many of my friends and relatives have died that if now I were to die, not a single soul would be left to mourn for me.[76]

Ghalib concluded *Dastanbuy* with a similar cry of despair: 'My sorrows are incurable and my wounds will never heal,' he wrote. 'I feel as if I am already dead.'[77]

If life was difficult for those who had shown sympathies for the British, it was much more so for those who had rejoiced at their downfall, and who now starved and scavenged outside the city: 'Are the British officers not aware that many innocent and noble minded women, both young and old, with small children are roaming the forests outside Delhi?' wrote Ghalib to one correspondent, still hoping, contrary to all the evidence around him, that the British had not lost all sense of humanity. 'They have got neither meals to eat nor clothes to wear. They have got neither the place to sleep at night nor a place to take shelter from the burning rays of the sun. One can only weep over the fate of this city.'[78]

Even the implacable George Wagentrieber was shocked by what he saw of the environs of Delhi. Around the town was 'a continuous line of dead carcasses – of camels, horses, and bullocks with their skins dried into parchment over the mouldering bones and still polluting the air around'.

Every tree has either been lopped off or levelled to the ground with our shot. The Garden houses of the Nawabs and other wealthy natives of Delhi present a mass of ruins; most of them are only four walls, full of holes while in front, and indeed all around, lie bleaching remains of man and beast. Close to the road on the left, I saw the perfect skeleton of a human being, the bones all connected and

snowy-white, to all appearence uninjured with the exception of a
hole in the skull.

Approaching the once dense forest of trees in the subzee mundee [the
vegetable market] I was struck with the change six short months had
wrought. Instead of the long line of lofty peepul, mango and other trees,
the view was clear for miles, the bare trunks alone remaining of what
was an impenetrable jungle. Many of these trees, in fact most of them,
have been stripped of their foliage to feed the cattle, but there is no
mistaking the bruised, ragged appearance of those levelled by round
shot . . . Not a house here has escaped, the walls left standing are very
few, and those are well pitted with grape shot and musket balls.[79]

It was amid such ruins that the Delhiwallahs, rich and poor both,
struggled to find cover and food to eat. As Ghalib put it, 'the
inhabitants of this huge place, seven miles around, are dying daily of
starvation and want of shelter'.[80] Miserable sheds had sprung up by
the side of the road, inhabited by 'perhaps rich *baniyas*, merchants
and shopkeepers', until in November an edict was issued by the
British authorities forbidding the construction of such shanties,
which they ordered to be torn down immediately, so exposing the
refugees to the full force of the elements.[81]

Sickness soon broke out among many of the wasted refugees,
especially around Zafar's old summer palace in Mehrauli and the
shrine of Nizamuddin.[82] 'Hundreds of the feeble perished through
want and misery,' wrote Major Ireland. 'It was not till the end of
November that the Hindoo portion of the population was allowed
to return. Still no Mahomedan could get in at the gates without a
special order. A mark was set upon their houses, and they were
required to prove their loyalty before getting back again.'[83]

Sarvar ul-Mulk's aristocratic family still had their servants, but
hiding in a tomb and fearful of arrest, they found themselves living
the lives of rag pickers. 'Our two servants would go out every day,'
he wrote, 'and joining the other looters bring back various eatables
such as rice, mutton, jaggery and wheatflour, all mixed together, and
these were thrown indiscriminately into a pot which, full of water,
was kept balanced on three stones. Then whoever felt hungry would
cautiously approach this pot, satisfy himself or herself and that done

crawl away under the shelter of the wall and hide.'[84] In his old age, Sarvar ul-Mulk remembered climbing a tamarind tree so as to throw down the fruit to his friends and his terror on seeing a column of khaki-clad troops heading in his direction; he also remembered his relief when they changed course and went elsewhere.[85]

Even worse was the fate of anyone who had been associated with the court, however tangentially, for death was the usual punishment meted out to courtiers if they were caught. Zahir Dehlavi was aware of this and kept moving on as fast as he could to avoid capture. His story was not untypical. After a night in the dargah in Mehrauli he headed on towards Jhajjar with many other refugees – the same road that Theo had travelled in May – and was put up by his cousin, who was the Nawab's prime minister. Here he ate his first proper meal for many days. For a week he stayed there, recovering from his ordeal, but on the eighth night he was woken by his cousin and told that the English soldiers had arrived. They were mass-arresting Delhi refugees, and Zahir was told he had to leave immediately if he wished to save his life.[86]

From Jhajjar, he walked to Panipat, where he was reunited with the rest of his family at the house of his aunt. But again, after a few days, the English surrounded the town on all sides and started conducting house-to-house searches, looking for mutineers and Mughal nobles and courtiers. Zahir had a narrow escape, as he happened to be out of the house when the English broke in, but his uncle, brother and brother-in-law were all taken away and hanged.[87] Zahir escaped at night, in the company of Jang Baz Khan, another former attendant at the Fort; avoiding the British dragnet, they managed to cross the Ganges and make it to Bareilly. Here they finally succeeded in catching up with the fleeing rebel army, only for both boys promptly to be arrested as British spies. They were about to be taken away and shot, when Mir Fateh Ali, a Delhi nobleman who had thrown in his lot with the rebels, happened to ride past and recognised them:

> He saw me, and jumping off the horse, with his sword cut the ropes with which I and Jang Baz had been fastened, held our hands and took us to that General Sahab [Bakht Khan], and abused and scolded him. He said, 'you traitors, you ruined the house of my King, and

ruined Delhi. You destroyed his subjects and rendered them homeless and still you continue with your mischief. These are the servants
of the King, and the poor fellows are running away to save their lives
from the English, and you are treating them as informers. If I had not
come this way you would have killed these innocent men.'[88]

Narrowly escaping arrest by the British a third time in Rampur,
Zahir managed to find shelter and a position as poet and courtier in
the durbar of the Maharaja of Jaipur. From here he made his way to
Hyderabad, where, like Sarvar ul-Mulk, he eventually made a new
life in the service of the Nizam.[89]

It was here, in the first years of the twentieth century, that Zahir
finally wrote up 'in the language of Zauq, Ghalib and Momin' the
notes he had kept of his life in, and escape from, Mughal Delhi: 'My
age is past seventy now,' he wrote at the end of his manuscript. 'I
have become weak in body and mind, and my memory is beginning
to go. I am hard of hearing and can no longer see so well. My heart
has been broken by the tragedies I have witnessed.'[90]

Zahir Dehlavi never saw Delhi again. He died in 1911 and was
buried in exile in Hyderabad.

Zahir's life on the run was typical of the fate of most of the *salatin*
and courtiers of Zafar's durbar. Few avoided British search parties
for long, not least because of the generous bounty put on the heads
of everyone associated with the Red Fort.

Throughout October and November search parties were sent out
to track down the members of the royal house. The first to be brought
in were two of Zafar's younger children, Mirza Bakhtawar Shah, aged
eighteen, and Mirza Meandoo, aged seventeen. The two had commanded the Meerut troops and the regiment called the 'Alexander
Pultun' respectively. They were promptly tried by Major Harriott and
sentenced to death.

'Waterfield came down here to tell the two prisoners that they
were to be executed tomorrow,' noted Ommaney in his diary for 12
October.

I was with him. They did not appear to feel it at all, they only wished to see their women and children. I took Meerza Meandoo's two women and a child to see their husband and father for a few minutes . . . [The following day] they were taken to the ground in a bullock cart, which marched behind the artillery which led the way. On arrival at the place of execution [the sand bank in front of the Palace] the column was drawn in line and prisoners brought out of the cart and blindfolded. 12 riflemen were then ordered to within 12 paces.[91]

The Gurkhas of the firing squad deliberately fired low, however, so as to ensure a slow and painful death, and the officer in charge eventually had to finish the two off with his pistol. 'Nothing could have been more ill favoured and dirty than the wretched victims,' wrote Charles Griffiths, 'but they met their fate in silence and with the most dogged composure.'[92]

Most of Zafar's sons and grandsons met the same end, sooner or later. As Major William Ireland noted, the princes 'had every opportunity of making off. It is surprising, however, how many were caught hovering about the neighbourhood; [in the end] twenty-nine sons of the royal house were taken and put to death'.[93] So many members of the royal family met dire ends that Ghalib changed the traditional Urdu name for the Palace – the Auspicious Fort – to the Inauspicious Fort.[94]

Only two sons of Zafar are known to have succeeded in making their escape. At the same time as Mirza Bakhtawar Shah and Mirza Meandoo were arrested, two other princes – Mirza Abdulla and Mirza Qwaish – were picked up, still sheltering hopelessly in Humayun's Tomb, and kept under a Sikh guard. According to the Delhi oral tradition recorded by the Urdu writer Arsh Taimuri in the early years of the twentieth century,

The Sikh Risaldar felt pity for these young men, and asked them, 'Why are you standing here?' They replied, 'the sahib has asked us to stand here.' He glared at them and said, 'Have mercy on your lives. When he returns he will kill you; run whichever direction you can. Beware and don't stop even to take a breath.' Saying this, the Risaldar turned his back and both princes ran away in different directions. After some time, Hodson came back and saw that the prisoners had fled. He asked the Risaldar, 'Where did those men go?' 'Who?' the Risaldar asked, as if he was ignorant. Hodson said, 'The princes who were standing here.' He said, 'I don't know. What princes?'

Mirza Qwaish went straight to Nizamuddin to his brother-in-law and told him that he had escaped from the custody of Hodson. His brother said, 'Brother, run away from here.' So he got his head shaved, tied a cloth on the head and wrapped a loin-cloth around his waist; and thus changing his appearance into a fakir, managed to reach Udaipur [in Rajasthan]. There he met one of Maharaja's eunuchs who also came from Delhi. The eunuch appealed to the Maharaja that a dervish had come, and if some salary is fixed for him then he would stay and keep praying for your life and wealth. The Maharaja granted the wish and fixed for him two rupees per day. After the mutiny he lived for 32 years. He spent his entire life in Udaipur, and was popularly known as Mian Sahib.

Hodson continued his search for Mirza Qwaish and searched every nook and corner, but could not find him. The government even released a poster for his arrest and announced a huge reward. Allured by this, several people went to Udaipur, and with the help of the Kotwal of the city reached the house where Mirza Qwaish was living in disguise, but he never fell into their hands, and died a free man in Udaipur.

Mirza Abdullah meanwhile lived in the princely state of Tonk in extremely difficult conditions, roamed about as a tattered beggar in a pathetic condition and finally died in the same state.[95]

Once they were arrested there was no clear policy on what should happen to the various princes. Those who could be shown to have been in any way implicated in the Uprising were immediately hanged, but that still left large numbers of princes who were not obviously guilty of any crime other than that of belonging by birth to the Mughal dynasty. The records of the British administration in Delhi at this period, preserved intact in the Delhi Commissioner's Office archive, show the arbitrary and astonishingly chaotic nature of the British response to this problem.[96] Some of these princes were hanged, others transported to the new imperial gulag set up on the hot and impossibly humid Andaman Islands, some sent into internal exile. Most were imprisoned in Agra, Kanpur or Allahabad, where large numbers died within two years owing to the harsh conditions of their imprisonment. These included 'a cripple, a boy of 12 years of age, and a very old man'.

A review of some of these cases was held by Saunders in April 1859 on orders from John Lawrence. The Delhi Commissioner had to admit that for almost all of the imprisoned princes and *salatin* 'the enquiries I have made have not resulted in bringing blame to any of the above parties', and it was impossible in most cases 'to prove any overt act of rebellion'.

> None of the prisoners have been proved guilty of any more serious offence than that of being members of the ex-King's family. In the eyes of many this would be considered sufficient to warrant them severe punishment for it is notorious that the whole of the House of Taimur were (as might very naturally have been expected) elated with the prospect of their dynasty being once more in the ascendant and so took a very zealous and active part in the hostilities and dreadful scenes which were enacted in the palace.
>
> The retribution which has fallen upon the members of the house has however been severe, and the mortality among the prisoners whose cases have come before the commission it will be seen has been very great [annexed was a list of fifteen princes who had died in prison in the previous eighteen months]. I therefore beg to recommend that the surviving prisoners be removed to a distance from Delhi to Rangoon where they are not likely to acquire any local influence, or Benares which is a Hindu city, or Multan if it be considered necessary that they should remain under the charge of the Punjab government.[97]

It was at this point that the full chaos of the penal regime became apparent, as it strained to cope with the vast number of captives imprisoned after the Uprising. Successive prisons sent letters to Saunders denying having any of the prisoners they were on record as having received; prisoners exiled to Burma turned out to have been sent instead to the Andamans or to Karachi; and the death toll in only two years turned out to be much higher even than previously realised. One unfortunate group of *salatin* thought to be imprisoned in Agra, and then sought for in Kanpur, were eventually found to have been in Allahabad Jail, but recently had moved to Calcutta for forwarding to the Andamans; they were on the point of embarking there when they were sent instead into exile in Karachi at the other end of India. In the end, the survivors – including several who had not been arrested and were living peaceably in Delhi – were divided between a small number who were sent to Karachi, and the great majority of the male *salatin* who were exiled to Moulmein in Burma.

None was allowed to settle in Delhi, even if they could establish their complete innocence, though five of the Karachi princes later 'absconded' and were believed to have made it back to the Mughal capital incognito.[98]

It was not just the royal family which the British were intent on arresting and bringing to trial. Most of the local landowners had sat on the fence throughout the Uprising, and while attempting to placate both sides, had supported neither. Nevertheless, neutrality was taken by the British to mean guilt, and one by one, the nawabs and rajas of Zafar's court were brought in, imprisoned, tried and hanged.

Ghalib's friend Nawab Muzaffar ud-Daula was arrested in Alwar with two other leading Delhi noblemen and hanged near Gurgaon 'as the collector of the district said there was no reason to send them back to Delhi and so executed them there'.[99] The Shia leader Nawab Hamid Ali Khan, who had left Delhi with Zahir Dehalvi's family, was hunted down near Karnal. Hakim Mohammad Abdul Haq, the agent of the Raja of Ballabgarh, and Nawab Mohammad Khan, Mirza Khizr Sultan's *mukhtar*, who had commanded a wing of the rebel army at the two battles of the Hindun Bridge and at Badli ki Serai, were arrested together 'in the territory of the Nawab of Jhajjar', and after being brought back to Delhi for trial 'suffered the extreme penalty of the law' on 25 November.[100] The Farrukhnagar Nawab was brought in from his palace and turned out to be an opium addict, so that he suffered terrible withdrawal symptoms when his supply was peremptorily stopped under Ommaney's no-nonsense prison regime. He was later hanged.[101]

Theo Metcalfe went personally to arrest the Nawab of Jhajjar, who had refused him shelter on the first week of the Uprising. Ommaney was particularly impressed by the Jhajjar Nawab's bearing and bravery, describing him as 'a fine looking man, stout and rather handsome'.[102] He was also moved when news came through of his death sentence: 'the two young sons of the Jhujjur Nawab on seeing their father, the little fellows cried very much, a striking and still a painful scene . . . I felt pity for the Nawab; he was a fine looking man and bore his sentence and death very well. His servants made low salaams when he left for execution'.[103]

Ommaney was not alone in being moved by the hanging of all these noblemen. Another witness, Mrs Muter, was particularly impressed by the 'startling justice' and logic of the Jhajjar Nawab's defence in court, arguing that 'it was England who had armed and trained the ruffians who had brought the calamity on the land; and it was not fair to expect him to compel that obedience in his followers which the rulers of the country and his judges had failed in compelling among their own'.

The Prince met his fate on the gallows with a calmness, fortitude, and gentlemanly bearing that inspired my husband, who commanded the escort, with the greatest respect. More melancholy still was the death of the Rajah [of Ballabgarh], whose sympathies as a Hindoo were probably as much with the English as with the Moslem Emperor. Gentle in manner, and young and handsome in person, it was a hard fate of this noble to be placed in circumstances wherein every path was fraught with peril and to be tried when death was the award of any act hostile to our rule. There was something touching in the last words he spoke before his judges: 'I was securely seated on a goodly bough of a flourishing tree, and my own act has sawn asunder the branch on which I rested'.[104]

Theo Metcalfe soon proved himself one of the most enthusiastic bounty hunters and hangmen. His desire for revenge seems to have continually grown ever since he reached the British camp at the end of his wanderings; and by October he even went so far as to erect a gallows in Metcalfe House. There he strung up from the charred beams any Indian he took to be an offender – an explicit statement of retribution for the destruction of his family's seat and the betrayals he believed he had personally suffered. One case recorded in the *Delhi Gazetteer* concerned a village that had given up one of Theo's servants to the rebels. In retaliation, Theo is said to have summarily shot twenty-one of the leading villagers.[105]

From his new home in Zinat Mahal's magnificent Lal Kuan haveli, Theo terrorised the region around Delhi, swooping down on groups of refugees sheltering in tombs and in shrines, and hanging any men he fancied had been involved in the Uprising.[106] According to a letter published in *The Times* in January 1858, Metcalfe was 'every day trying and hanging all he can catch . . . he is held in great dread by the natives'. 'Metcalfe went on a shooting spree,' noted Zahir Dehlavi. 'Whenever he spotted a young man he would shoot him there and then with his pistol, without any reason or questioning of right and wrong.'[107]

Indeed, so frightening was Theo's reputation that he soon became a sort of Delhi bogeyman whose name alone was enough to cause terror. According to the formidable Mrs Coopland,

When I was in Delhi he was busy hunting out, trying and hanging mutineers and murderers: he had a lynx eye for detecting culprits. One day, when passing General Penny's house, amongst a guard of sawars, he detected a murderer, and instantly singled him out, tried and condemned him; he also found out poor Mr Fraser's murderer, and had him hanged. One day a native jeweller came to offer his wares to Mrs Garstin who thinking he charged too much, said 'I will send you to Metcalfe Sahib;' whereupon the man bolted in such a hurry that he left his treasures behind and never again showed his face.[108]

This was a period when daily hangings and murders were the norm rather than the exception, and were looked upon by the British with something approaching boredom. So while the details remain hazy, the fact that Theo was singled out for his readiness to shoot and hang implies that he was believed responsible for a quite exceptional number of arbitrary killings. Rumours of his excesses even began to reach Sir John Lawrence in Lahore, who quickly became concerned at the reports that 'civil officers [are] hanging at their own will and pleasure'. Before long Lawrence began to make enquiries as to whether Theo needed reining in, or even to be suspended from the service. 'If what I have heard is at all true,' wrote Lawrence to Saunders, 'it is our duty to interfere and not allow Metcalfe the power of life and death. [My informants] seemed to feel strongly that his fervor is opposed to the just deliberation required in a Special Commisioner, and that the sooner the direct power of death is taken from him the better for the interests both of the people and of our administration.'[109]

The more Lawrence heard, the more anxious he became: 'He [Theo] has good soldierly qualities,' Lawrence wrote to Saunders, 'and distinguished himself at the storm of Delhi. But he is wrong-headed and injudicious, and just now more particularly so, owing to the exasperations he feels against the Mussalmen. It is very difficult to manage him . . . Metcalfe's parents were among my oldest and best friends. Personally I would be glad to help him; but there are higher considerations than even these.'[110]

Edward Campbell's job as Prize Agent meant he was also involved in the work of vengeance, but he showed much less enthusiasm for the task than his increasingly violent and bloodthirsty brother-in-law. He wrote regularly to GG from his various excavations: 'I am digging for treasure in the city,' he scribbled on one occasion, 'and have found an old blank book, out of which I am taking a leaf to write to you, and have sent to see if I can get some ink from a Bunneah [moneylender]. I have got some little things for you from the prize, only trifles, but I think you will like them, and I will send them up the first opportunity.'[111]

Being a Prize Agent was a highly paid and potentially very lucrative post, but it was not something that appealed to Campbell:

'It is very dirty work frightening Bunneahs into disclosing where they stowed away their wealth,' he wrote to GG that week.

> You know, dearest, how I never have anything to do with torture. Wriford is the great one for extracting their wealth. I am assured I don't look cruel and severe enough – but the fact is you cannot go long on the same beat. The people hear what is going on and make their escape and unless you have one [person for every] ten houses to show you where their money is secured, you might dig for ever. But it is very sickening work,* my own wife, and I have given you enough of it.[112]

He added, 'We have found one of the old carved chairs [from Metcalfe House]. I am afraid poor Theo thinks he is entitled to these, and he will be awfully disquieted when he finds that he will have to buy them as of course [along with everything else found in Delhi], they are reckoned as prize property. This is no pleasure for me as one of the prize agents.' He then wrote something that he hoped GG would not take amiss: 'I fear Theo is not taking the part he might, but is using his knowledge of the city to his own profit, and I cannot tell you how painful it is for me.'

What he seems to have meant, as later charges would make more explicit, was that Theo was suspected of hanging prominent Delhi-wallahs if they refused to hand their fortunes over to him. There were also rumours that he was performing private looting opera-tions and accepting protection money from bankers who wished to

---

* Lieutenant A. H. Lindsay left a description of this 'very sickening work' that Edward forbore to trouble GG with: 'They caught a very nice fat sleek-looking Hindoo who they felt assured was a man of property. He refused for a long time to confess where his money was concealed, so they shut him up in a dark cellar and fired pistols over his head until he got into such a state of alarm that he told them where they could find Rs 50,000 of his own and Rs 40,000 of a friend of his, who he was determined should not get off scot free. The next day they got hold of another corpulent nigger, who however was up to the dodge of the pistols, and did not even care [about] knives being thrown, after the manner of the Chinese jugglers, so they loaded a pistol before his eyes, and sent a bullet through his turban, which he thought was getting a bit beyond a joke, so he divulged the whereabouts of his Rs 40,000.' Cited in Christopher Hibbert, *The Great Mutiny: India 1857*, London, 1978, p.321.

retain their property and were prepared to buy themselves immunity. Theo was certainly desperate enough to act in this way. He had lost everything in the outbreak – his house, his inheritance and his money, which had been invested in the Delhi Bank. Moreover, as a civilian official, he had no claims on the prize money, which was supposed only to go to the army.

This at least, Edward Campbell acknowledged, was unjust: 'I say he ought to have his share of the prize money as a military man as he was made to act like a soldier in leading one of the parties after Delhi up to the Jumma Musjid, and I hope to get this arranged. Otherwise we, as Prize Agents, must interfere with him.'

Edward concluded: 'I get so tempted to give up this Prize Agency, GG, but it may turn out a good thing and it would be wrong for me to sacrifice so much money on so short a trial . . . I hope they will bring us home [to England] soon, for we are such a small body now that it would take ever so long recruiting up to our former strength. Our killed and wounded since the 30th June [when Campbell arrived in Delhi] is around 400, nearly half the regiment.'[13]

By the end of January 1858, when all the noblemen of his durbar had been tried and hanged, it was the turn of Zafar himself to face trial.

Throughout the autumn and the early part of the winter of 1857, while the battle for Lucknow still raged in the eastern half of Hindustan, much of the effort of British administration in Delhi went into preparing for the historic trial of the man who was now clearly going to be the last of the Mughals. Translators were sent down from Lahore to help plough through the great stash of paperwork that had been retrieved from both the Palace chancellery and the rebels' camp; the legality and binding nature of the guarantee of his life that Hodson had given Zafar was examined in great detail; and the nature of the Emperor's trial, and the charges that would be brought, were discussed. In the end it was agreed that the guarantee was legally binding, although it had been given contrary to the repeated written instructions of Lord Canning; and it was settled that Zafar would be charged with 'rebellion, treason and murder' and 'not regarding his allegiance' as a British subject by a Military Commission. This would sit to hear the charges at the end of January 1858. Major Harriott, who had successfully prosecuted and hanged most of Zafar's court and family, was now to prosecute the man he made clear he regarded as 'the leading chief of the rebels'.

What was never discussed was whether the Company was legally empowered to try Zafar at all. For though the government took the position that Zafar received a pension from the Company, and was therefore the Company's pensioner and thus subject, the actual legal position was considerably more ambiguous. While the Company's 1599 charter to trade in the East derived from Parliament and the Crown, its authority to govern in India actually legally flowed from the person of the Mughal Emperor, who had officially taken on the Company as his tax collector in Bengal in the years following the battle of Plassey, on 2 August 1765.

As recently as 1832, when Zafar was fully fifty-eight years old, the Company had acknowledged itself to be the Mughal Emperor's vassal on its coins and even on its great seal, which was covered with the inscription 'Fidvi Shah Alam' (Shah Alam's devoted dependant); this was removed only under the influence of Sir Charles Metcalfe in 1833. Since then, nothing had happened to change the legal relationship of the two parties, for although the Company had unilaterally ceased to offer *nazrs* and no longer proclaimed its vassalage on its coins or seal, neither Shah Alam, nor Akbar Shah, nor Zafar himself had ever renounced their sovereignty over the Company. From this point of view, Zafar could certainly be tried as a defeated enemy king; but he had never been a subject, and so could not possibly be called a rebel guilty of treason. Instead, from a legal point of view, a good case could be made that it was the East India Company which was the real rebel, guilty of revolt against a feudal superior to whom it had sworn allegiance for nearly a century.[114]

The absurdity of the Company's charge against Zafar was wonderfully articulated by the *Times* correspondent William Howard Russell – the father of war journalism – who arrived in the ruins of Delhi around this time. Skeletons still littered the streets, and the domes and minars of the city were riddled with shell holes;

but the walls of the Red Fort still looked magnificent: 'I have seldom seen a nobler mural aspect,' wrote Russell in his Indian memoirs, 'and the great space of bright red walls put me in mind of the finest part of Windsor Castle.' Russell was also very taken with the comforts of Ludlow Castle, Simon Fraser's old residence, which Saunders, the Civil Commissioner, had recently had repaired and refurbished. 'The gharry drove up under the pillared portico,' wrote Russell. 'In a moment out came a ruddy, comely English gentleman, and before I knew where I was, I was ushered into the presence of a fair Englishwoman, who sat at a well furnished board, doing the honours of her table to a circle of guests.'

> I had not seen the face of an Englishwoman since I left Calcutta. I came in dusty – I am afraid, dirty – a hot unpleasant-looking stranger. I found myself at once back in civilized life, amid luxuries long unknown. The comfort and luxury of the house itself were a positive gratification of the senses. Large lofty rooms – soft carpets, sofas, easy chairs, books, pictures, rest and repose, within. Outside, kuskus-tatties* and punkah-wallahs. The family were at their first breakfast when we went in. I found there were two breakfasts, one at 8, the other at 3 o'clock.

Russell's ultimate destination was, however, rather less welcoming. Along 'a dark dingy back passage' of the Red Fort, he was later led to the cell of the man whom he had been told now stood accused of being the mastermind of the Uprising: 'That dim, wandering eyed, dreamy old man with a feeble hanging nether lip and toothless gums – was he, indeed, one who had conceived that vast plan of restoring a great empire, who had fomented the most gigantic mutiny in the history of the world, and who from the walls of his ancient palace had hurled defiance and shot ridicule upon the race that held every throne in India in the hollow of their palms?' asked a surprised Russell. Zafar was being sick when Russell walked in, his 'bent body nearly prostrate over a brass basin, into which he was retching violently . . .'

---

* Grass and bamboo blinds that were kept wet and fragrant during hot weather.

Crouched on his haunches [was] a diminutive, attenuated old man, dressed in an ordinary and rather dirty muslin tunic, his small lean feet bare, his head covered by a small thin cambric skull-cap . . . Not a word came from his lips; in silence he sat day and night with his eyes cast on the ground, and as though utterly oblivious of the conditions in which he was placed . . . His eyes had the dull, filmy look of very old age . . . which seems as if it were to guide us to the great darkness . . . Some heard him quoting verses of his own composition, writing poetry on a wall with a burned stick . . .[115]

Aware of his history, and stirred by the ruined magnificence of the Mughal's great palace, Russell was properly sceptical about the legality of the Company's charges against Zafar.

Here is the place from which came the haughty *ukases* [decrees] that gave to a few trembling traders the right to hold lands in India on the tenure of service and submission . . . Even in the extreme of his decrepitude, the descendant of Akbar had fenced himself round with such remnants of dignities that the Governor General of India could not approach him as an equal, and the British officers at Delhi were obliged to observe in their intercourse with him all the outward marks of respect which a sovereign had the right to demand from his servants . . .

[The King] was called ungrateful for rising against his benefactors. He was no doubt a weak and cruel old man; but to talk of ingratitude on the part of one who saw that all the dominions of his ancestors had been gradually taken from him until he was left with an empty title, and more empty exchequer, and a palace full of penniless princesses, is perfectly preposterous. Was he to be grateful to the Company for the condition he found himself?

We, it is true, have now the same right and the same charter for our dominions that the Mahomedan founders of the house of Delhi had for the sovereignty they claimed over Hindustan [i.e. the right of conquest] but we did not come into India, as they did, at the head of great armies, with the avowed intention of subjugating the country. We crept in as humble barterers, whose existence depended on the bounty and favour of the lieutenants of the kings of Delhi; and the 'generosity' we have shown was but a small acknowledgement of the favours his ancestors had conferred to our race.[116]

Russell concluded by pointing out that if the King was to be tried by a proper court of law, rather than by a Military Commission, the charges against Zafar would be almost impossible to prove: 'An English lawyer in an English court of justice might show that it would be very difficult for our Government to draw an indictment against the King of Delhi for treason, for the levying of war against us as lords paramount . . .'

Russell also wrote that he believed that Zafar could hardly be blamed for wanting to throw off his bondage. 'I could not help thinking, as I looked at the old man,' he wrote, 'that our rulers were somewhat to blame for the crimes he had committed . . .'

To my mind, the position of the King was one of the most intolerable misery long ere the revolt broke out. His palace was in reality a house of bondage; he knew that the few wretched prerogatives which were left to him, as if in mockery of the departed power they represented, would be taken away from his successors; that they would be deprived of even the right to live in their own palace, and would be exiled to some place outside the walls. We denied permission for his royal relatives to enter our service; we condemned them to a degrading existence, in poverty and debt, inside the purlieus of their palace, and then we reproached them with their laziness, meanness, and sensuality. We shut the gates of military preferment upon them – we took from them every object of honourable ambition – and then our papers and our mess rooms teemed with invective against the lazy, slothful and sensuous princes.

Better die a thousand deaths than drag on such a contemptible, degrading existence. Had the old man and his sons refrained from shedding innocent blood – had they died with harness on their backs – I for one should have felt sympathy for their fate.[117]

Zafar was still very ill on the day finally set for his trial, 27 January 1858. It dawned a cold, wet and cloudy winter's day and Edward Ommaney confided in his diary that he was glad of the fire in his bedroom.[118] 'The old man appears very much broken this morning,' Ommaney reported to Saunders. '[He is] very weak, can scarcely speak. I do not think he can go on much longer this way.'[119] Since Zafar could not walk, Ommaney had to help him out of his palanquin; he was supported on one side by Mirza Jawan Bakht, and on the other by a servant. They led him into the Diwan i-Khas, his old hall of private audience, where he was now to be tried for treason by those he had reason still to regard as his vassals.

To remind him of his subject state, Zafar was not allowed either his fly whisk or his hookah. Among the spectators already in their seats were both Charles and Matilda Saunders, and Edward Vibart, as well as George Wagentrieber, representing the *Delhi Gazette*, and Harriet Tytler, who had been given rooms in the Fort after her husband Robert moved his regimental treasure chest within its walls on the evening of its capture.[120]

The trial got off to a suitably chaotic start. Although the proceedings were to be held partly in Hindustani, none of the five judges – all army officers of relatively junior rank – proved to be fluent in that tongue. Edward Vibart wrote that the 'President alone was familiar with the Hindoostani language'.[121] Although proceedings were scheduled to begin at 11 a.m., the president of the court martial, Brigadier Showers, failed to turn up until noon, and then appeared only briefly to announce that he had been ordered to Agra to take command there. All this time, Zafar was left waiting outside 'under a strong guard of the rifles'.[122]

When proceedings finally got going later in the afternoon, under the presidency of Colonel Dawes, the charges were read out, and Zafar – now parked on a bed of cushions between Dawes and the prosecutor, Major Harriott – was asked whether he pleaded guilty or not. But it soon became clear that the old man could not understand what was going on, and there was a further 'considerable delay' before he could be persuaded to plead not guilty.

Over the days that followed, an impressive body of evidence was presented. Witnesses were called to give eyewitness accounts of the outbreak and the principal events of the Uprising, while the key passages from the manuscripts seized from the Palace chancellery, the office of Mirza Mughal, the kotwal and the army camp were read out in full. 'Each paper, as it was read, was shown to the prisoner's vakil [Zafar's lawyer, Ghulam Abbas] and identified by him,' wrote one witness, Charles Ball, 'although the King himself professed utter ignorance of the existence of such documents – denied his signature, and endeavoured, by gestures of dissent, to impress the court with the idea of his entire innocence.' Soon, however, Zafar's attention began to wander: 'The royal prisoner appeared to consider the proceedings perfectly unimportant, and merely tiresome,' wrote Ball, 'and he found relief from *ennui* by dozing . . .'

> Occasionally, however, when some particular passage was read, the dull eyes would light up, and the bowed head would be raised in marked attention for a few moments – only to relapse into a state of listless indifference . . . His son appeared more animated, and laughed and chatted with his father's attendant without appearing at all embarrassed.[123]

Before long, Mirza Jawan Bakht, who was deemed by Ommaney to be looking 'very impertinent, indecorous and disrespectful', was banned by his jailer from attending further sessions.[124] Without his beloved young son to keep him company, Zafar showed less and less interest in the proceedings. Often he was too unwell to appear at all, and the court was frequently adjourned on the grounds of the prisoner's ill health. When the court did sit, according to Ball,

> The King displayed a singular line of conduct, not at all in keeping with the serious position he occupied. Occasionally, while the evidence was progressing, he would coil himself up in his shawls, and reclining upon the cushions placed for his convenience, would appear perfectly indifferent to the proceedings around him; at other times he would suddenly rouse up, as if from a dream, and loudly deny some statement of a witness under examination; then again relapsing into a state of real or assumed insensibility, he would carelessly ask a question, or laughingly offer an explanation of some phrase used in evidence.

Upon one occasion, he affected such utter ignorance of a question before the court, in reference to his alleged intrigues with Persia, as to inquire 'whether the Persians and the Russians were the same people.' He several times declared himself perfectly innocent of everything he was charged with, and varied the weariness of his constrained attendance by amusing himself with a scarf, which he would twist and untwist around his head like a playful child.[125]

In response to the various charges, Zafar offered only a single, short but strikingly coherent written defence in Urdu, denying that he had any connection with the Uprising and maintaining that he had all along been the helpless prisoner of the sepoys. 'I had no intelligence on the subject previous to the day of the outbreak,' read Zafar's statement.

> I begged them to go away . . . I swear by God, who is my witness, that I did not give orders for the death of Mr Fraser or of any other European . . . As regards the orders given under my seal, and under my signature, the real state of the case is that from the day the soldiery came and killed the European officers and made me a prisoner, I remained in their power. All the papers they thought fit, they caused to be prepared, and bringing them to me, compelled me to fix my seal . . . Frequently they had the seal impressed on the outside of empty unaddressed envelopes. There is no knowing what papers they sent in these or to whom they sent them.
>
> They used to accuse my servants of sending letters to and keeping in league with the English . . . They even declared they would depose me and make Mirza Mughal king. It is a matter for patient and just consideration then, what power did I in any way possess? The officers of the army went even so far as to require that I should make over the Queen Zinat Mahal to them, that they might keep her a prisoner, saying she maintained friendly relations with the English . . .
>
> All that has been done was done by that rebellious army. I was in their power, what could I do? I was helpless, and constrained by my fears, I did whatever they required, otherwise they would have immediately killed me. This is universally known. I found myself in

such a predicament that I was weary of my life. In this state of things I resolved to accept poverty, and adopted the garb, coloured with red earth, of the religious mendicant, intending to go first to the shrine of Qutb Sahib, thence to Ajmer, and from Ajmer eventually to Mecca.

If I had been in league with them, how would these things have occurred? As regards the behaviour of that rebellious army, it may be stated that they never saluted me even, nor showed me any other mark of respect. They used to walk into the hall of special audience and the hall of devotion with their shoes on . . . What confidence could I place in troops who had murdered their own masters? In the same way that they murdered them, so they made me a prisoner, and tyrannised over me, keeping me on in order to make use of my name as a sanction for their acts. Seeing that these troops killed their own masters, men of high authority and power, how was I without an army, without treasure, to have resisted them . . .? God knows, and is my witness, that I have written only what is strictly true.[126]

It was just as well for the prosecution that Zafar did not attempt to mount a more serious and concerted legal defence, or choose to cross-examine any of the witnesses. For as the trial wore on, despite the density of witnesses and evidence produced, the absurdity of the principal thrust of the prosecution case became more and more apparent. Quite apart from the higher question of whether the court had the authority to try Zafar, Major Harriott, the prosecutor, chose to build a highly speculative case of such obvious flimsiness and lack of understanding of what the Uprising had been about that none of the British observers who kept accounts of the trial could be persuaded even to begin to believe his argument.

Harriott maintained that Zafar was the evil genius and linchpin behind an international Muslim conspiracy stretching from Constantinople, Mecca and Iran to the walls of the Red Fort. His intent, declared Harriott, was to subvert the British Empire and put the Mughals in its place. Contrary to all the evidence that the Uprising broke out first among the overwhelmingly Hindu sepoys, and that it was high-caste Hindu sepoys who all along formed the bulk of the fighting force; and ignoring all the evident distinctions between the sepoys, the jihadis, the Shia Muslims of Persia and the Sunni court of

Delhi, Major Harriott argued that the Mutiny was the product of the convergence of all these conspiring forces around the fanatical Islamic dynastic ambitions of Zafar: 'To Musalman intrigues and Mahommedan conspiracy we may mainly attribute the dreadful calamities of the year 1857,' argued Major Harriott. 'The Mutineers [were] in immediate connexion with the prisoner at your bar.'

> The conspiracy, from the very commencement, was not confined to the sepoys, and did not even originate with them, but had its ramifications throughout the palace and city . . . [Zafar was the] leading chief of the rebels in Delhi . . . Dead to every feeling that falls honourably on the heart of man, this shrivelled impersonation of malignity must have formed no inapt centrepiece to the group of ruffians that surrounded him . . . We see how early and how deeply the [Muslim] priesthood interested and engaged themselves in this matter, and how completely and exclusively Mahommedan in character was this conspiracy . . .
>
> [Was Zafar] the original mover, the head and front of the undertaking, or but the consenting tool . . . the forward, unscrupulous, but still pliant puppet, tutored by priestly craft for the advancement of religious bigotry? Many persons, I believe, will incline to the latter. The known restless spirit of Mahommedan fanaticism has been the first aggressor, the vindictive intolerance of that peculiar faith has been struggling for mastery, seditious conspiracy has been its means, the prisoner its active accomplice, and every possible crime the frightful result . . . The bitter zeal of Mahommedanism meets us everywhere . . . perfectly demonic in its actions . . .[127]

The Uprising in fact showed every sign of being initiated by upper-caste Hindu sepoys reacting against specifically military grievances perceived as a threat to their faith and dharma; it then spread rapidly through the country, attracting a fractured and diffuse collection of other groups alienated by aggressively insensitive and brutal British policies. Among these were the Mughal court and the many Muslim individuals who made their way to Delhi and fought as civilian jihadis united against the *kafir* enemy. Yet Harriott's bigoted and Islamophobic argument oversimplified this complex picture down to an easily comprehensible, if quite fictional, global Muslim conspiracy with an appealingly visible and captive hate figure at its centre, towards whom righteous vengeance could now be directed.

While the simplicity of this picture certainly appealed to ignorant and jingoistic newspaper readers in Britain, to anyone in Delhi the argument was clearly flawed, not least because of the demonstrable fact that the hated 'Pandies' had been at least 65 per cent upper-caste Hindu. During the hearing of 3 February, in an attempt to try to prove pre-existing links between the sepoys and Zafar, Harriott had pounced upon a reference to a dozen sepoys who had come before Zafar in 1853 asking whether they could become his *murids* or spiritual disciples. In reality this showed nothing more than the fact that Zafar was treated by some of the faithful as a holy Sufi *pir* possessed of miraculous spiritual powers; but for Harriott this was vital evidence that Zafar had been busy trying to subvert the army for at least three and a half years before the outbreak.[128]

Ommaney for one was quite clear that what the prosecution was alleging was nonsense, and that it showed a complete lack of understanding either of the complexities of Indian society or the various grievances which had led to the Uprising: 'In my opinion,' he wrote in his diary, 'the Musalman origin of the outbreak is a fallacy. The state of feeling in the company's native army is not in anyway alluded to [in Harriott's theory]. The [sepoys in the] army saw they had the power, and determined to try and conquer the country. That the Musalmen joined the army does not in anyway prove that the rebellion was of Musalman origin . . .'[129]

Indeed, as witness after witness appeared in the box it became increasingly clear that Zafar was wholly ignorant of any plans that may have existed for a co-ordinated uprising, and had all along been innocent of doing anything other than trying to protect his subjects in Delhi. 'It appeared from what I gathered', wrote one spectator at the trial, Mrs Muter, 'that he [Zafar] had condemned the [massacre carried out by] the Nana at Cawnpore; and there was abundant proof that he had striven hard to protect the citizens of Delhi from violence of the soldiery and outrages of the nobles, and the people of the country from the plunder by Gujars.'

It was clear how wretched the old man had been when eddied about in the whirlwind of the Mutiny with no energy to control, and no force of will to rule the cruel natures around. Numerous petitions from the people were translated, with the King's remarks. Much of what he said was sound and good, and his complaints were bitter of the insolence of the sepoys . . . How keenly he felt the thorns in the bed which had been prepared for him. He was a mere puppet . . .

I cannot think that in the treatment of the last of the House of Timour our country showed her usual liberality. We must keep the fact ever before us, that it was our army that set the country in a blaze – that it was our timidity that led to the catastrophe; and that we did not even have the excuse that the Mutiny was an unforeseen event.

Amid all the poverty and contempt thrown on the King, I was gratified to observe the demeanour of many of the witnesses when called to give evidence. Bowing to the ground with hands clasped before the miserable figure on the bed, addressed by them as 'Ruler of the Universe' though by the committee as *tum* (a mode of address only used to inferiors and servants), they observed to the powerless old man a degree of respect denied to the court, who had only to nod the signal for their execution.[130]

The trial dragged on for two months. Often it had to be adjourned owing to Zafar's ill health. On one occasion the Emperor was carried groaning from court. During the early stages of the trial his face had shown signs of anxiety and alarm, but as the weeks went on 'by degrees it became more vacant, and he assumed or felt indifference, remaining apparently in a state of lethargy, with his eyes closed during the greater part of the proceedings'.[131]

The court martial sat for the last time on 9 March, and at 11 a.m., in front of a crowded courtroom, Harriott made his closing speech. For two and a half hours, he again elaborated his theory of the Uprising being an international Islamic conspiracy. 'I have endeavoured to point out', he declaimed, 'how intimately the prisoner, as the head of the Mahommedan faith in India, has been connected with the organisation of that conspiracy, either as its leader or its unscrupulous accomplice . . .'

After what has been proved in regard to Mahomedan treachery, is there anyone who hears me that can believe that a deep-planned and well-concerted conspiracy had nothing to do with it . . . If we now take a retrospective view of the various circumstances which we have been able to elicit during our extended inquiries, we shall see how exclusively Mahommedan are all the prominent points that attach to it. A Mahommedan priest, with pretended visions, and assumed miraculous powers – a Mahommedan King, his dupe and his accomplice – a Mahommedan clandestine embassy to the Mahommedan powers of Persia and Turkey – Mahommedan prophecies as to the downfall of our power – Mahommedan rule as the successor to our own – the most cold blooded murders by Mahommedan assassins – a religious war for Mahommedan ascendancy – a Mahommedan press unscrupulously abetting – and Mahommedan sepoys initiating the mutiny. Hinduism, I may say, is nowhere either reflected or represented . . .'[132]

Harriott then added a concluding passage, criticising the idea that the Uprising could be in any way connected with the activity of Christian missionaries, as some were already suggesting: 'A candid undisguised endeavour to gain followers to Christ', he said, 'has never, that I am aware of, been viewed with the slightest sign of disapprobation by any portion of the natives . . . Christianity, when seen in its own pure light, has no terrors for the natives . . .'[133]

Just before 3 p.m., the judges retired to consider their verdict. A few minutes later, they returned to unanimously declare Zafar guilty 'of all and every part of the charges preferred against him'.

Normally, noted the president, such a verdict would have resulted 'in the penalty of death as a traitor and a felon'. Thanks, however, to Hodson's guarantee of his life, such a sentence was impossible. Instead, Zafar was sentenced 'to be transported for the remainder of his days, either to one of the Andaman Islands or to such other place as may be selected by the Governor General in council'.[134]

There followed a seven-month delay, while letters went back and forth between Delhi, Calcutta, Rangoon, the Andamans and even the Cape Colony, as the British tried to find a suitable place to exile Zafar. There were also anxieties that a rescue attempt might be mounted if Zafar was to be sent downcountry before fighting had completely ceased in some of the more unsettled parts of eastern Hindustan.

Finally, towards the end of September 1858, it was decided that it was now safe for Zafar to be sent away from Delhi, even though his final destination had yet to be settled. Lieutenant Ommaney was to accompany him into exile, and was to make sure that the State Prisoner (as Zafar was now referred to) should hold no communication with anyone en route.[135]

At 4 a.m. on 7 October, 332 years after Babur first conquered the city, the last Mughal Emperor left Delhi on a bullock cart. Along with him went his wives, his two remaining children,* concubines and servants – a party of thirty-one in all, who were escorted by the 9th Lancers, a squadron of horse artillery, two palanquins and three palanquin carriages. The journey had been kept secret, even from Zafar himself, and the old man knew nothing of his departure before being woken up by Ommaney at 3 a.m. one day and told to get ready.

'He was removed as quickly as possible,' wrote Matilda Saunders to her mother-in-law the following week. 'Everything was kept quite secret, though of course C[harles Saunders] knew it long before, and had been buying up conveyances for them to travel in covered carriages and palanquins &c and bullock carts and tent equipage &c.'

There was nothing wanting in the forethought and arrangements and at 3 in the morning the dear fellow [Saunders] left his bed in the fort and assisted his able co-adjuter, Mr Ommaney, in packing them up. At 4 he made them over to a guard of the Lancers and saw them

---

* In addition to Mirza Jawan Bakht, one other son was spared the British slaughter of the imperial family. This was Zafar's youngest son, Mirza Shah Abbas, the sixteenth of Zafar's boys. He was the illegitimate son of one of Zafar's concubines, Mubarak un-Nissa, and born in 1845; thus he was thirteen when he left Delhi along with Zafar and his mother.

safely over the Bridge of Boats on their way down country. The King is a blessed riddance to Dehli. His two Queens accompany him, and his two younger sons, and the wife of the elder one, besides collateral branches that had the option of staying but preferred to share the fate of the royal party.

She added: 'No one crowded to see them go; it was completely still and quiet at that early hour.'[136]

12

THE LAST OF THE GREAT MUGHALS

'The ex-King and the other prisoners stand the travelling wonderfully well,' reported Lieutenant Ommaney on 13 October. 'They are all in very good spirits. I have the prisoners comfortably settled in their tents by 8 a.m. every morning, and other than getting them up every day at 1 a.m. [for the day's march] have very little bother.'¹

Zafar had always enjoyed outings, processions and expeditions, and in his youth setting out hunting in the country around Delhi had been one of his principal forms of amusement; even in his old age, his monsoon breaks at his summer palace in Mehrauli had often been excuses for extended shooting trips in the jungle to the south. But he had never in his life travelled farther than a day or two from his capital, and his passage into exile was the longest journey he had ever taken. Now, after the intense stress of the Uprising and siege, and the humiliation of his imprisonment and trial, the journey into exile was, if not exactly a holiday, then at least a relative relief from the horrors he had undergone during the previous eighteen months.

The party travelled in convoy. A squadron of the Lancers cavalry trotted ahead as an advance guard. Then came the canopied palanquin carriage carrying Zafar and his two sons, surrounded on all four sides by groups of Lancers. Next came the closed purdah carriage of Zinat Mahal, who travelled with Mirza Jawan Bakht's young wife,

Nawab Shah Zamani Begum, and her mother, Mubarak un-Nissa. The third carriage carried the queen Taj Mahal and her attendants, including her eunuch, 'a quiet inoffensive youth' called Khwajah Balish (which meant cushion).[2] Behind trailed five 'magazine store carts with tilted tops, drawn by bullocks', containing the male and female attendants and Zafar's harem women, four in every cart, each escorted by a party of Lancers.

Other than a near-accident on the Bridge of Boats, when one of the store carts almost tipped Zafar's concubines into the Yamuna, there were no upsets and no complaints, and the family particularly approved of the arrangements Ommaney had made for their camp: a 'hill tent' shared by Zafar and his sons, and a 'soldier's tent, with kunnat [canvas zenana screening] enclosure' for the ladies.[3] The weather was perfect – the mornings and nights cool, the days bright and warm – and on arrival at Kanpur, the Mughals in the party were amazed by the sight of their first steam train 'receiving its passengers, and shortly afterwards away it went with its regular puffs and peculiar whistle', while a band played 'The Englishman' on the platform.[4] The King even confided to Ommaney that he was looking forward to seeing the sea and travelling on a ship, saying he had never been on anything larger than a riverboat before.

Only the constant evidence of recent fighting around them – the ruined and fire-blackened bungalows, and the burned-out police stations – acted as a reminder to the party of the grim cause of their journey. Very occasionally, they came across actual fighting: at one point Zafar came within sight of the rebel-held fort of Suniah, which British troops were in the process of storming, and for much of the last stage of the journey to Allahabad they passed along the edge of rebel-held territory.[5] There was also a single fatal accident: 'some of the Lancers taking their horses to water, one got into deep water, lost his seat and the horse kept him under for some seconds. His body was not recovered for three quarters of an hour'.[6]

The novelty of the journey also delighted Zafar's companions, who were said to be in high spirits: 'By all accounts the prisoners are cheerful,' reported George Wagentrieber in the *Delhi Gazette*, 'and the females may be heard talking and laughing behind their screens as if they did not much regret their departure from Delhi.'[7]

This was a striking contrast to their mood towards the end of their Delhi imprisonment when, in addition to the humiliations heaped on them by the British, the imperial family added to their miseries by feuding among themselves. According to Ommaney, prior to their departure Zinat Mahal had been squabbling loudly with Jawan Bakht after the latter had fallen in love with one of his father's harem women. He also began using the family's now scarce financial resources to bribe the guards to bring him bottles of porter: 'What an instance of the state of morals and domestic economy of Ex-Royalty,' wrote a disapproving Ommaney to Saunders. 'Mother and son at enmity, the son trying to form a connection with his father's concubine, and setting at nought the precepts of his religion, buying from, and drinking, the liquor of an infidel.'[8]

Before setting off, Zinat Mahal had also had a loud series of arguments with her old rival and enemy Taj Mahal, who had been imprisoned for three years prior to the Mutiny on the grounds that she was having an affair with Zafar's nephew, Mirza Kamran. Taj Mahal was therefore one of the very few people in Delhi whose lot had demonstrably improved because of the outbreak. But following the argument, Taj promptly announced she wanted nothing to do with either Zinat Mahal or Zafar, and moved down to the far end of the corridor from them: 'I have nothing to do with the King,' she told Ommaney. 'I have no son by him, and I don't intend to budge.' 'Very well, Mrs Taj Mahal,' replied Ommaney. 'Go you must to the ex-King's Quarters, and if you don't go of your own accord I must take you there forcibly.' Taj replied, 'You may kill me, but I'll not go.'[9] As Ommaney wrote to Saunders, 'The Ex-King's party dislike her, so altogether she'll be a great nuisance.'

For the first few weeks of the journey, the pleasures of travelling and the joy of freedom from incarceration in a squalid corridor at the back of their own palace seem to have lulled the various feuds in the royal family. But as the party neared Allahabad, the tensions again became apparent, and on arrival at the old Mughal fort there,*

* The fort of Allahabad was the place of exile to which the British had formerly exiled Zafar's younger brother, Mirza Jehangir. It was also here that a despairing Mirza Jehangir had eventually died from 'an excess of Hoffman's Cherry Brandy' in 1821.

now held by the British, half the party – led by Taj Begum, and including Zafar's concubines and Mirza Jawan Bakht's mother-in-law and sister-in-law – decided to return to Delhi rather than continue on into exile. Only fifteen out of the original party of thirty-one chose to carry on with Zafar.

While waiting to resolve this issue Canning, who also happened to be in Allahabad, met with Ommaney (though significantly, not with Zafar) and told him that he had firmly decided that Burma, rather than the Cape, should be the ex-Emperor's place of exile. He was, however, still undecided whether the deposed monarch should remain at Rangoon, or should be sent up the country to Tounghoo in the Karen hill territories, 'which offers the advantage of being isolated, and so far removed from the usual line of travellers and traffic that no stranger, least of all a native of Hindoostan, can enter it without attracting the immediate attention of the authorities'.[10]

In the meantime, Zafar had a medical check. The doctors' report decided that 'allowing for the natural decay attending his advanced age, his general physical condition is good beyond what we anticipated to find, that he is hale and vigorous for his age, and free from diseases'.

> The committee can see no objection on professional grounds to his removal by sea to Rangoon or to his future residence there or some other place in the Province of Pegu [southern Burma]. On the contrary, as compared with the Upper Provinces [of Hindustan], the climate of Pegu is mild and soft and equable throughout the year, and not liable to the considerable vicissitudes of temperature experienced in the North Western Provinces of India, and on this account possessing conditions generally considered favourable to the prolongation of life in its advanced stages.[11]

Having made his decision regarding to which country he wanted Zafar to be sent, Canning then wrote to Major Phayre, the Commissioner in Rangoon, laying down the ground rules than were to govern the future treatment of the imperial family: 'It is the desire of His Excellency the Governor-General,' Major Phayre was informed, that the prisoners should be kept in close custody, and permitted to hold no communication whatever, either verbal or written, with any person or persons, other than those who as will be precisely mentioned, will accompany them . . . Care should be taken that the prisoners should be treated with care and civility, and be exposed to no indignity, and to no other discomfort than may be necessary for their safe custody . . . Maintenance is to be liberal in every respect, but it is not expedient that any of them should receive allowances in money.

'Lt Ommaney will remain in immediate charge of the prisoners and their companions,' added Canning. 'He should be required to visit the prisoners daily and to attend to their wants, bringing to your notice, without delay, any circumstances which seem to him of any significance or importance.'[12]

The reduced party of fifteen continued on from Allahabad on 16 November. Two days later they reached Mirzapur and embarked on the steamer *Thames*. 'The state prisoners do not show any anxiety,' reported Ommaney, 'and the old man seems quite jolly, saying "It is the first time he has ever been on board a ship." '[13] They steamed slowly down the Ganges, past the magnificent ghats and temples of Benares. Shortly afterwards they passed a pair of British gunboats patrolling for rebels who might be crossing the river near the site of the battle of Buxar. Here the Mughals and the British had first come into conflict in 1764, during the reign of Zafar's grandfather Shah Alam – a battle than had begun the British territorial advance from Bengal up the country towards Delhi.[14] At Rampur they changed boats to the steamer *Koyle*, after the *Thames* developed engine trouble, and arrived at Diamond Harbour, the anchorage below Calcutta, on 4 December.*

---

* Upstream from Diamond Harbour in Calcutta lived the exiled remnants of the two other recently deposed Muslim dynasties: the household of Wajd Ali Shah, the former Nawab of Avadh, and that of the sons of Tipu Sultan of Mysore. Both families lived in some style – Wajd Ali Shah had a fine house at Garden Reach, while the Tipu sons were given the house of what is now the Tollygunge Club; but throughout 1857 they were all locked up in Fort William to prevent them becoming the focus of dissent.

Here Zafar's party were quickly transferred to the HMS *Magara*. The ship let slip its moorings, and the last Mughal Emperor steamed away from his homeland, never to return. According to an observer on the riverbank,

On the 4th December, at ten in the morning, the ex-King of Delhi was taken aboard Her Majesty's good ship of war, the *Magara*, which for a vessel of the Royal Navy presented a curious spectacle at the time, crowded as her main deck was with household furniture, live and lifeless stock in the shape of cattle, goats, rabbits, poultry, rice, peas &c &c, brought by the Royal prisoner and his attendants, for their consumption and comfort. Lt Ommaney of the 59th, who has had charge of him ever since he was taken, conducted him on this, probably the last conveyance that will ever again serve him on his peregrinations.

He had two wives* with him, so impenetrably veiled that they were led below by guides. He looked utterly broken up, and in his dotage; but not a bad type of Eastern face and manner – something King-like about his deeply furrowed countenance, and lots of robes and Cashmeres.† He was quite self-possessed, and was heard to ask some of the officers what their respective positions were on board, &c.

A son and grandson‡ are with him, and their very first care on touching the deck with their feet was to ask for cheroots – took things easy in short. The ex-King meanwhile went below, and was said to have stretched himself forthwith upon a couch of pillows and cushions, which his folk had arranged for him in a twinkling. The whole operation of transferring him and his companions was quickly effected; and then the guard of the 84th regiment returned to Calcutta, while the *Magara* steamed away down the Hooghly for its destination.

The voyage lasted five days. On 8 December, the *Magara* left the open ocean and sailed up the muddy brown waters of the swampy

* The second veiled woman was in fact Shah Zamani Begum, his daughter-in-law.
† That is, Kashmiri shawls.
‡ Actually two sons.

tidal creeks bordering the Irrawaddy Delta and into the Rangoon river. From far away, the passengers could see the great golden spire of the Shwe Dagon pagoda rising up above the thick tropical greenery of the riverbank: 'The pagoda is a magnificent object,' wrote Ommaney. 'I saw it 20 miles off directly we entered the river. There are three terraces of brickwork. From the centre of the upper one rises a heap of chaotic architecture which again throws up an elegant structure to a great height, all gilded with gold leaf.'[15]

On arrival at the port of Rangoon, according to an irritated Ommaney, 'a very large crowd of Natives and Europeans assembled to see the prisoners land and proceed to their quarters'.[16] Further annoyances followed. Food proved far more expensive in Rangoon than it was in India, as did domestic staff, whose failure to salaam like the defeated and terror-stricken Delhiwallahs angered Ommaney: the 'independence and impudence of the servants exceeds belief', he wrote to Saunders a week later. 'Their manner appears as if they thought they were conferring a favour by entering your service. I am positively struck dumb by their cool insolence.'

Most irritating of all, the Commissioner, Major Phayre, had done little to prepare for Zafar's arrival, and no proper housing was ready for their reception: 'Major Phayre does not know where the prisoners are to be permanently confined,' wrote Ommaney.

At present two little rooms, neither so large as any in the house at Delhi are set apart for them [near the Main Guard in the new cantonment area just below the Shwe Dagon] and the attendants have 4 tents pitched adjacent, and surrounded by a kanat [or *qanat*, canvas zenana screening] enclosure. The prisoners now have scarcely any comfort. The Government is bound to treat them better than this.[17]

If Rangoon was defiantly uncongenial for Ommaney, and for Zafar and his party, the town must have been above all strikingly unfamiliar: quite apart from the novelty of a hot tropical river port fringed with toddy palms and crowded with paddle steamers, rafts of teak logs and junk-like *hnaw* fishing boats with their billowing sails, there was the town's Burmese architecture with its tiers of gilded spires and finials and flying eaves. Then there were the Buddhist monasteries with their massive bells and winged gryphons; their giant Buddhas and bodhisattvas; their carved wooden struts and bamboo partitions and cane latticework; their stupas and pilgrimage sites; and everywhere, red- and yellow-robed monks with their wooden begging bowls. The silken *htamein* wraps and sequined parasols of the women, and the *pasoe* sarongs of their menfolk; the gold lacquerwork and delicate decorative pottery; the music of the street bands; the calm blue lakes that once belonged to the Burmese kings; the strange form of the *hle-yin* bullock carts with their finely woven bamboo roofs and floral side panels; the pungent Burmese cooking smells – all would have been quite new to the Mughals.

Yet for all that there was much in the abject political situation of the town which directly echoed that of the Delhi they had just left behind. In April 1852, on the very same day that Jawan Bakht was getting married to Shah Zamani Begum and processing in triumph through the streets of Mughal Delhi, an army of Company troops, including a regiment of Sikhs, had invaded Rangoon, following a show of defiance by the port's *Shwebo Wun* (Governor) against two British sea captains accused of murdering Indian members of their own crews. After British naval artillery had breached the stockades and the Burmese troops had been driven back towards Mandalay, Prize Agents had been let loose to loot the holy shrines and smash the sacred idols in search of gems.

As in Delhi, much unofficial looting had also taken place: 'the work of delving into every image in the place', reported the *Calcutta Englishman*, 'of which there are many, was perseveringly carried out, but apparently not with the knowledge of the Prize Agents, as the European Artillery sold in great numbers the silver images and the bottles of rubies that were found inside'.[18] One party of looters even tunnelled deep into the foundations of the great Shwe Dagon pagoda, determined to find the thick cladding of gems that legend said had been buried there. Now a regiment of Sikhs camped in the desecrated courts of the Shwe Dagon, just as their cousins sat lighting their cooking fires in the arcades of the Delhi Jama Masjid.

Moreover, just prior to the arrival of the prisoners, the British had begun sweeping away the ancient fishing village of Mon on the Rangoon waterfront, with its hundreds of old Buddhist landmarks and pilgrimage shrines. Gangs of impressed Burmese labourers were now in the process of clearing the debris and laying out on its ruins a new colonial town on an ordered gridiron plan.

Even as Zafar stepped ashore at Rangoon, a similar programme of mass destruction and colonial remodelling was beginning to remove many of the most familiar and beautiful landmarks of the former Mughal capital he had just left behind.

'Here it seems as if the whole city is being demolished,' wrote Ghalib about this time. 'Some of the biggest and most famous bazaars – the Khas Bazaar, the Urdu Bazaar and the Khanum ka Bazaar, each of which was practically as a small town, have all gone without a trace. You cannot even tell where they were. Householders and shopkeepers cannot point out to you where their houses and shops used to stand . . . Food is dear, and death is cheap, and grain sells so dear that you would think each grain was a fruit.'[19]

What Ghalib was describing was in fact a very reduced version of the plan, originally mooted by the *Lahore Chronicle*, to completely level Delhi as a punishment for being the centre of the defeated rebellion. The plan had many powerful supporters, both in India and London, one of whom, Lord Palmerston, wrote that Delhi should be deleted from the map, and 'every civil building connected with the Mohammedan tradition should be levelled to the ground without regard to antiquarian veneration or artistic predilections'.[20] Lord Canning had at first been quite open to the *Chronicle*'s suggestions, but was eventually, and reluctantly, persuaded not to order the levelling of the city. The man who persuaded him was John Lawrence.

Lawrence had spent several years at the beginning of his career in Delhi, serving as an assistant to Sir Thomas Metcalfe, and had grown fond of the Mughal capital. As Chief Commissioner of the

Punjab he had done as much as anyone else to facilitate the British victory in 1857, and so was in a good position to argue his colleagues out of their plans for mass destruction and legalised mass murder, both of which were currently taking place under the guise of a just retribution.

One of Lawrence's first actions when the administration of Delhi was formally transferred to the Punjab government in February 1858 was to get Theo Metcalfe sent back to England on extended leave. This he finally achieved on 2 March 1858 by direct application to Canning in Calcutta, writing that Theo had been guilty of 'wholesale slaughters'.[21] By April he was able to report that, 'I stopped the different civil officers hanging at their own will and pleasure, and appointed a commission, since when matters have greatly improved and confidence among the natives greatly increased. It was most unfortunate Metcalfe being in power at Delhi,' he added. 'He did a great deal of harm. He has however now gone home.'*[22]

In the same letter Lawrence described how he had begun pressing for a general amnesty for anyone who had not personally murdered British civilians in cold blood. It was an idea he later took up with Canning: some of the British, he argued, were acting as if they were now engaged in 'a war of extermination'. Instead he recommended a complete amnesty, as 'so long as all [mutineers] are classed under one head, all will hold together and resist to the death'. A perhaps

* Theo returned to India in 1863 after five years in England, but Lawrence, who had by then been promoted to Viceroy, blocked him from receiving any 'creditable appointment' and he was forced permanently to retire from the ICS and return to England. According to a family memoir, now in the British Library, 'Years after, Lady Bayley [Theo's sister Emily] asked Lord Lawrence [formerly Sir John] why he had been so unfriendly to her brother, and he replied because he had hanged so many people without proof of their guilt. She answered that she had asked Sir Theophilus about this, and he said he had never done so, and the only thing he could reproach himself for was the burning of Alipore, where on first going through it he had found three little white feet, a proof that Europeans had been murdered there.' Theo never returned to India after 1863, and lived on for twenty years in retirement in London, where his nephews and nieces often 'heard him telling tales of his adventures in 1857', and remembered him as 'a charming and entertaining companion', with 'a great sense of mischief'. There was little hint of the man who in 1857 was regarded as the most callous and enthusiastic hanging judge in the city. He remarried in 1876, but died only seven years later, aged only fifty-five. See Oriental and India Office Collections, British Library, Hardcastle Papers, Photo Eur 31 1 A.

unexpected supporter of Lawrence's plan turned out to to be Disraeli, who was deeply shocked by the British bloodlust that the Uprising had triggered: 'I protest against meeting atrocities with atrocities,' he told the House of Commons. 'I have seen things said, and seen written of late, which would make me suppose that . . . instead of bowing before the name of Jesus we were preparing to revive the worship of Moloch.'[23]

The idea of a general amnesty eventually became official policy, and was proclaimed in Queen Victoria's name on 1 November 1858. At the same time, in the Act for the Better Government of India, the British Crown finally assumed all governmental responsibilities held by the East India Company, and its 24,000-man military force was incorporated into the British Army. If Hindustan was to lose the Mughals, its rulers of nearly three hundred years' standing, it would at least now be ruled by a properly constituted colonial government rather than a rapacious multinational acting at least partly in the interests of its shareholders.*

Saving Delhi, and limiting the amount of house clearance carried out, took a more prolonged campaign. As late as 1863, Saunders' replacement as Commissioner for Delhi was arguing that 'the citizens of the rebellious City of Delhi, as a body, had entirely forfeited their rights' by joining the Uprising. 'It must not be forgotten', he argued, 'that the citizens of Delhi joined hand in hand with the Mutineers.'[24] Lawrence, however, used his influence to drastically scale back the planned demolitions, arguing that Delhi 'is a position of great importance and should be held by us'. He also pointed out, unfashionably at the time, that 'We have been almost as much to blame for what occurred as have the people. I have yet neither seen nor heard anything to make me believe any conspiracy existed beyond the army, and even in it one can scarcely say there was a conspiracy . . . The army had for a long time been in an unsatisfactory state.'[25]

Canning had already given orders to destroy the Delhi walls and defences, but Lawrence managed to get the orders rescinded, arguing that there was insufficient gunpowder in Delhi to blow up several

---

* What remained of the Company was finally dissolved on 1 January 1874, when the East India Stock Dividend Redemption Act came into effect.

miles of walls.²⁶ By the end of 1859, Canning had agreed to his plan only to demolish what was needed to make the Fort and city more easily defensible. By 1863, the planned demolition of the eastern half of Chandni Chowk down to the Dariba had also been stopped.²⁷ Even so, great swathes of the city – especially around the Red Fort – were still cleared away, as Ghalib recorded in a series of sad letters to his correspondents across Hindustan: 'The area between Raj Ghat [on the city's eastern edge, facing on to the Yamuna] and the Jama Masjid is without exaggeration a great mound of bricks.'

> The Raj Ghat Gate has been filled in. Only the niched battlement of the walls is apparent. The rest has been filled up with debris. For the preparation of the metalled road, a wide open ground has been made between Calcutta Gate and the Kabul Gate. Punjabi Katra, Dhobi-wara, Ramji Ganj, Sadat Khan ka Katra, the Haveli of Mubarak Begum [Ochterlony's widow], the Haveli of Sahib Ram and his garden – all have been destroyed beyond recognition.²⁸

Other letters of Ghalib mourned the destruction of some of the city's finest mosques, such as the Akbarabadi Masjid and the Masjid Kashmiri Katra; great Sufi shrines such as that of Sheikh Kalimullah Jahanabadi;* the imambara† built by Maulvi Muhammad Baqar; the *muhalla* of Bulaqi Begum; the main gate of the Dariba; and the establishment of a cleared open space 70 yards wide around the Jama Masjid.²⁹ Four of Delhi's most magnificent palaces were also completely destroyed: the havelis of the recently hanged nawabs of Jhajjar, Bahadurgarh and Farrucknagar, as well as that of the Raja of Ballabgarh.³⁰ The great caravanserai of Shah Jahan's daughter Jahanara was demolished and replaced by a new town hall. Shalimar Bagh, where Aurangzeb had been crowned, was sold off for agricultural use. Even where old Mughal structures were allowed to continue, they were often renamed: Begum Bagh, for example, became the Queen's Gardens.

---

* A modest tomb of the saint is, however, still extant in the Pigeon Sellers' Bazaar in Old Delhi.

† Shia religious hall used to hold mourning ceremonies during Muharram.

Tragically, the Red Fort was another area where Lawrence intervened too late to stop the wholesale destruction. He managed to save both the Jama Masjid and the Palace walls, arguing that they would serve the British as well as the Mughals, but 80 per cent of the rest of the Fort was levelled. Harriet Tytler, who was living in an apartment above the Diwan i-Am at this time, was horrified by the decision and decided to paint a panorama of the city before it disappeared.* It confirmed her in her disgust at the way the British had behaved in Delhi since the assault began on 14 September. 'Delhi was now truly a city of the dead,' she wrote in her memoirs. 'The death-like silence of that Delhi was appalling. All you could see were empty houses . . . The utter stillness . . . [was] indescribably sad. It seemed as if something had gone out of our lives.'[31]

The demolitions started at the Queen's Baths in November 1857, and continued through most of the Palace, destroying an area 'twice the area of the Escorial', as the horrified architectural historian

---

* The panorama appears to have been completed, but has since disappeared. The British Library does, however, possess another complete panorama of the Fort commissioned before 1857 by Sir Thomas Metcalfe, which is partially reproduced here. Some time after this, in 1862, Harriet Tytler accompanied her husband Robert, who had been appointed superintendent of the terrible British gulag in the Andaman Islands. Harriet 'hated the place from the very first day,' though she is still commemorated in the name of the highest mountain in the archipelago, Mount Harriet. Here the Tytlers attempted with little success to bring down the appalling mortality rate of the convicts which, when they arrived, stood at around seven hundred fatalities a year. Many were dying of disease within months, if not weeks, of arrival in the Andamans' humid and insalubrious jungles, and at one point only forty-five of the 10,000 convicts were pronounced 'medically fit' by the prison camp's own doctors. Others died from the frequent attacks on the prison camp by the island's aborigines, some of whom were cannibals. A large number of the transported convicts subject to this appalling regime were from Delhi: a single petition sent to the King on any subject during the Uprising was enough to earn the petitioner transportation to the Andamans for life. Among those sentenced was one of Ghalib's most brilliant and talented friends, the poet and intellectual Fazl i-Haq. Fazl had originally been a protégé of Ochterlony, and was a friend with whom Ghalib used regularly to play chess. He was accused of encouraging the Muslims of Delhi to wage jihad against the British, a charge he refused to deny in court, despite being told he would otherwise qualify for the amnesty. He died just before orders arrived for his release. Robert Tytler died a decade later in 1872. Harriet travelled to British Columbia, where she lived for some time with her daughter, but returned to India and lived in Simla, where she wrote her memoirs, before dying in 1907 at the age of seventy-nine.

James Fergusson pointed out twenty years later. 'The whole of the area between the central range of the buildings south and eastwards from the bazaar, measuring about 1000 feet each way, was occupied by the harem apartments of the palace – twice the area of any Palace in Europe.'

> According to the native plan I possess, which I see no reason for distrusting, it contained three garden courts, and some thirteen or fourteen other courts, arranged some for state, some for convenience; but what they were like we have no means of knowing. Not one vestige of them now remains . . . The whole of the harem courts of the palace were swept off the face of the earth to make way for a hideous British barrack, without those who carried out this fearful piece of vandalism, thinking it even worthwhile to make a plan of what they were destroying or preserving any record of the most splendid palace in the world.[32]

As late as March 1859 George Wagentrieber was pleased to record in the *Delhi Gazette* that 'a good deal of blowing up' was still going on in the Palace. Some of the finest buildings were the first to go, such as the Chhota Rang Mahal. Even the Fort's glorious gardens – notably Hayat Bakhsh Bagh and Mehtab Bagh – were swept away. All that was left by the end of the year was about one fifth of the original fabric – principally a few scattered, isolated marble buildings strung out along the Yamuna waterfront. These were saved owing largely to the fact than they were in use as offices and messes by the British occupation troops, but their architectural logic was completely lost once they were shorn of the courtyards of which they were originally a part.

All the gilded domes and most of the detachable marble fittings were stripped and sold off by the prize agents. As Fergusson noted,

> when we took possession of the palace, everyone seems to have looted after the most independent fashion. Among others, a Captain (afterwards Sir) John Jones [who had blown in the Lahore Gate during the capture of the fort] tore up a great part, but had the happy idea to get his loot set in marble as table tops. Two of these he

brought home and sold to the Government for £500, and were placed in the India Museum.[33]

These fragments included the rightly celebrated 'Orpheus panel' of *pietra dura* inlay which Shah Jahan had placed behind his Peacock Throne.

Meanwhile, what remained of the Mughal's Red Fort became a grey British barracks. The Naqqar Khana, where drums and trumpets had once announced the arrival of ambassadors from Isfahan and Constantinople, became the quarters of a British staff sergeant. The Diwan i-Am became a lounge for officers, the Emperor's private entrance a canteen, and the Rang Mahal an officers' mess. The Mumtaz Mahal was turned into a military prison. The magnificent Lahore Darwaza was renamed the Victoria Gate and became 'a bazaar for the benefit of the Fort's European soldiers'. Zafar's contribution to the Palace architecture – the Zafar Mahal, a delicate floating pavilion in a large red sandstone tank – became the centrepiece of a swimming pool for officers, while the surviving pavilions of Hayat Bakhsh Bagh were turned into urinals.[34]

While all this was going on, throughout 1858, Hindus were slowly being readmitted to the city, but Muslims remained almost entirely banned from within the walls. As Ghalib wrote in *Dastanbuy*,

> In the entire city of Delhi it is impossible to find one thousand Muslims; and I am one of these. Some have gone so far from the city it seems as if they were never residents of Delhi. Many very important men are living outside the city, on ridges and under thatched roofs, in ditches and mud huts. Among those people living in the wilderness are many who are anxious to return to Delhi, relatives of the imprisoned, and those living on alms.[35]

A passing traveller in 1860 was horrified by 'the old withered *Musulmanis* and gypsy-like Mughals [still] camping out at the Qutb'. Even the imperious Matilda Saunders was aware that 'numbers of people are daily dying of starvation and want of shelter'.[36]

In December 1859 the Muslims of Delhi petitioned the government to be allowed to return to their houses. They wrote to Queen Victoria praying (according to the translation commissioned by Charles Saunders)

> That they may be permitted to return to their houses in the city of Delhi. They are in the greatest distress, excluded rigorously from the town, they can obtain neither shelter nor means of subsistence. The cold weather is now at hand and they beg that they may not be exposed to its severity in their present state of destitution and misery. They trust that Her Majesty following the example of other magnanimous sovereigns, would pardon their misdeeds and permit them to reinhabit their old houses – otherwise they see nothing but beggary before them.[37]

Even when their plea was granted and they began to be given permission to return in 1860, many Muslims who could not prove their loyalty found that their houses had been confiscated. Things got so bad that even some of the British papers in India began to feel sympathy with the Delhi Muslims: 'When will agitation of European nerves subside?' asked the *Mofussilite* in June 1860. 'There is no reason for it . . .'

> The people are abject because they are starved out, banished and plundered. Thousands of Muslims are wandering houseless and homeless; the Hindus, pluming themselves on their assumed loyalty, strut about the streets giving themselves airs. Let not the public think that Delhi has not been punished. Wend through the empty grass-grown streets, mark the uprooted houses, and shot-riddled palaces.[38]

Most of the confiscated Muslim properties put up for auction by the British were bought en masse by the Hindu *khatri* (clerical caste) and Jain bankers of the city, such as Chhunna Mal and Ramji Das. These were the only Delhiwallahs who still had access to liquid cash, their main centre of Nil ka Katra having bought immunity from the depredations of the prize agents on the payment of a large sum soon after the fall of the city.[39] Hindu traders and bankers even bought up two of the city's most famous mosques: Chhunna Mal bought the Fatehpuri Masjid, while a Hindu baker bought the beautiful Zinat ul-Masajid, one of the main jihadi centres throughout the Uprising.*⁴⁰

All this exacerbated the sudden shift of power from the Muslim elite, who had dominated the city before the Uprising, to the Hindu bankers, who were its most wealthy citizens afterwards. 'The capital is in the hands of one or two men like Chhunna Mal and Mahesh Das,' wrote Edward Campbell in 1858.⁴¹ What remained of the court circle and the Mughal aristocracy were by and large left penniless. A few survived on a pittance as schoolteachers and tutors. For many, such as Maulvi Zaka'ullah, the shock of the utter devastation of their world was 'beyond all bearing', and Zaka'ullah later admitted that for a time he had succumbed to 'a melancholy that bordered on blank despair'.⁴²

'Alas my dear boy,' wrote Ghalib to a friend in January 1862. 'This is not the Delhi in which you were born, not the Delhi in which you got your schooling, not the Delhi in which you used to come to your lessons with me, not the Delhi in which I have passed fifty-one years of my life.'

> It is a camp. The only Muslims here are artisans or servants of the British authorities. All the rest are Hindus. The male descendants of the deposed King – such as survived the sword – draw allowances of five rupees a month. The female descendants, if old, are bawds; if young, are prostitutes . . .⁴³

What Ghalib did not say was that many of the Delhi begums were set on the path to prostitution by the mass rapes that followed the fall of the city. Believing that the British women in Delhi had been sexually assaulted at the outbreak – a rumour that subsequently proved quite false, as a full inquiry commissioned by Saunders later proved – British officers did little to stop their men from raping the

---

* Neither was returned to the Delhi Muslims until many years later – the Fatehpuri Masjid in 1875 and the Zinat ul-Masajid by Lord Curzon in the early years of the twentieth century. Sikh troops remained occupying the Jama Masjid until it was returned in 1862. See S. M. Ikram, *Muslim Rule in India and Pakistan*, Lahore, 1966, p. 462.

women of Delhi. At the same time as Saunders' inquiry completely exonerated the rebels of any single instance of rape, another inquiry found that perhaps as many as three hundred begums of the royal house – not including former concubines in the Palace – had been 'taken away by our troops after the fall of Delhi', and that many of those who had not been abducted were now making their livings as courtesans.[44] The fate of the women of the royal family was clearly something that deeply shocked Ghalib, and he returns to it again and again in his letters: 'Had you been here,' he told his friend Mirza Tafta, 'you would have seen the ladies of the Fort moving about the city, their faces as fair as the moon and their clothes dirty, their paijama legs torn, and their slippers falling to pieces. This is no exaggeration . . .'[45]

With the loss of the Mughal court went much of the city's reputation as a centre of culture and learning. Its libraries had been looted, its precious manuscripts lost. The madrasas were almost all closed, and their buildings were again mostly bought up – and in time demolished – by Hindu moneylenders. The most prestigious of all, the Madrasa i-Rahimiyya was auctioned off to one of the leading *baniyas*, Ramji Das, who used it as a store.[46]

By 1859 Ghalib was complaining that he could not even find a single bookseller, binder or calligrapher in this once most bookish of cities.[47] Still less were there any poets: 'Where is Mamnun? Where is Zauq? And where is Momin Khan? Two poets survive. One, Azurda – and he is silent: the other Ghalib, and he is lost in himself, in a stupor. None to write poetry, and none to judge its worth.' To make matters worse for Ghalib, much of his own verse – his life's great achievement – had been lost: he had never kept copies of his ghazals and the two private libraries in which his friends had stored his poetry had both been sacked and destroyed by the British. 'A few days ago a faqir who has a good voice and sings well discovered a ghazal of mine somewhere and got it written down,' he wrote in one letter. 'When he showed it to me, I tell you truly, tears came to my eyes.'[48]

'This whole city has become a desert,' wrote a melancholy Ghalib to a friend in 1861. 'Delhi people still pride themselves on Delhi language! What pathetic faith! My dear man, when the Urdu Bazaar is no more, where is Urdu? By God, Delhi is no more a city, but a camp, a cantonment. No Fort, no bazaars, no watercourses . . .'⁴⁹ 'Four things kept Delhi alive,' he wrote to another friend who enquired what Delhi was like these days. 'The Fort, the daily crowds at the Jama Masjid, the weekly walk to the Yamuna Bridge, and the yearly fair of the flower-men. None of these survives, so how could Delhi survive? Yes, there was once a city of that name in the realm of India.'⁵⁰

In such a situation Ghalib often wondered what the point of carrying on was when everything he had lived for was finished. 'A man cannot quench his thirst with tears,' he wrote. 'You know that when despair reaches its lowest depths, there is nothing left but to resign oneself to God's will. What lower depths can there be than this: that it is the hope of death that keeps me alive?'⁵¹ 'My soul', he wrote in June 1862, 'dwells in my body these days as restless as a bird in a cage.'⁵²

Without the Delhi College and the great madrasas, without the printing presses and the Urdu newspapers, and without the Mughal court – whose immense cultural prestige always compensated for the monetary constrictions on its actual powers of patronage – and most of all without the Emperor there to act as a focus and, to some extent, catalyst, the driving force behind Delhi's renaissance and artistic flourishing was gone. The beating heart of Indo-Islamic civilisation had been ripped out, and could not be replaced. As Ghalib wrote as he neared death: 'All these things lasted only so long as the King reigned.'⁵³

On 1 April 1859, Edward Ommaney said farewell to Zafar and his family, and set off back to India with his regiment; with him went four more of Zafar's Indian attendants who had found themselves homesick in Burma and wished to return to their families in India.

Three weeks later, Zafar was moved a short distance through the cantonment to his new quarters, half a mile below the Shwe Dagon Pagoda.⁵⁴ 'The house is situated within a few yards of the Main

Guard, & like wooden houses of the country is considerably raised off the ground,' reported Zafar's new jailer, Captain Nelson Davies. 'It is in an enclosure 100 ft square, and is surrounded by palisading 10 ft high.'

The accommodation consists of four rooms each 16 feet square, one of which is allotted for the use of the ex-King, another for Jawan Bukht and his young Begum, a third is appropriated by the Begum Zinat Mahal. To each of these rooms a bathing area is attached. Shah Abbas and his mother occupy the remaining room.

The attendants either lounge about the verandahs or put up underneath the house, which is covered by pounded brick to keep the place dry. A drain all around the house also contributes to this object. There are two bathrooms & a double necessary for the use of the servants, also a place to cook in.

The verandahs in the upper storeys of the house are surrounded with chicks battened down. Here the old and enfeebled ex-King & his sons generally sit, and as the floor of the upper storey is raised nearly to the level of the pallisading, they enjoy the benefit of the prevailing sea breeze, and also an extended and cheerful view. Watching the passers by, & gazing at the shipping, somewhat relieves the monotony of their prison life, & reconciles them in some measure to their present quarter.

Davies went on to describe the security arrangements for the guarding of the royal family: 'Two sentries mount guard by day, usually three at night.' The prisoners were visited and checked twice a day. As for the cost of feeding the Emperor and his family, it 'greatly exceeds here what it would be in India, averaging about 11 Rs a day, and as provisions are rising in price it is probable that the daily expenditure will exceed that amount. Since I have taken charge, an extra rupee is allowed to them every Sunday', continued the magnanimous Davies, 'and on the first of each month, 2 Rs extra'.

This allows them to indulge in a few articles for the toilet without the necessity of asking me for every trifle in a way they may

require. Pen, ink, paper are of course strictly forbidden. Previous
to my taking charge they had supplied themselves with many little
necessaries they required, and also their entire wearing apparel,
from their own resources, but now they state that all their funds
are expended, an assertion which may admit of some doubts. I
daily ascertain both by personal inspection & enquiry that the
food supplied them is sufficient and good. A supply of clothes has
recently been provided, but their old stock being in a very
dilapidated state, I shall presently be obliged to replenish it still
further.

The establishment kept up for the prisoners is on the lowest
possible scale, and consists of one Chupprassie whose business it
is to procure their daily supplies, & he is a sort of confidential
agent between myself and them. The man I at present have is a
Burman but speaks Hindoostanee sufficiently well to receive
orders from the prisoners regarding their bazaar requirements.
His pay is rather higher than what I could get a Hindoostanee man
for, but I thought it advisable to employ a man of a different race,
where such constant intercourse was required.

The only other servants employed are a *bheestie* [water carrier],
dhoby [washerman] & sweeper. These are necessarily Hindosta-
nee men, but they are all attached to my service & as I oblige them
all to live in my compound which is next to the prisoners, I thus
have them constantly at hand & can also keep a close supervision
over them. The public are of course not allowed to hold intercourse with the prisoners, & the servants can only gain admission
under a pass from myself which is issued daily and must be
inspected by the officer on main guard ere they gain admission.
For better security these tickets are printed and checked by a
system of numbering in addition to every signature.

Davies went on to discuss Zafar's health, which he described as
'tolerably good . . . since his removal from the former confined
quarters, his heath has considerably improved, and although much
enfeebled, yet he is not more so than might be expected from a
native of India at the advanced age of 86'.

His memory is still good, when time is allowed him to fix his ideas, but his articulation is indistinct consequent on the loss of his teeth. He certainly now does not give the impression of being capable of any extended mental energy or capacity, but on the whole he appears to bear his weight of years remarkably well. He passes his days in listless apathy, manifesting considerable indifference to all but eternal affairs. This apparently has been his normal state for a long time past, and may continue so for some time to come, until all of a sudden his career may come to a close, without taking anyone by surprise.

Davies was not able to see Zinat Mahal, who remained in pardah, but he sent in his wife to report back. She 'is described by Mrs Davies, who occasionally visits both the Begums, as a middle-aged woman'.

She enjoys very good health. I have had several conversations with her from behind the screen. She frequently enlarges on the step she took at the time of the outbreak at Delhi in writing to the late Mr Colvin, the Lt Gov of NW Provinces [at Agra], begging him to come to her assistance implying thereby that at the time the Royal Family were at the mercy of the Rebels, & she constantly avers that they were thus helpless even to protect the unfortunate European girl who sought her protection.

She also frequently alludes to the loss of her private treasure and jewels, & states that Major Hodson pledged his word and gave her a written document as security for the safety of her personal property. I am unacquainted with the exact particulars, but I consider it as well to relate the Begum's version of this circumstance. She states that her property was not disturbed until after Major Hodson's death, when she was required to give up the document he had given her as a protection. She was then dispossessed by Mr Saunders, the Commissioner at Delhi, of all her valuables to the extent of 20 lakhs (£200,000) in value, and he refused to return her the document.

I have explained to her that on her husband being convicted of Rebellion all the property of the family became escheated to the

Government, that her establishment being distinct from that of the King's, and her residing in a separate Mahal, has nothing whatever to do with it. She seemed however to think that the sequestration of her personal property is somewhat contrary to custom. However I gave her no hopes of ever being placed in a position by the possession of wealth to work the mischief her talents might render possible, were she so inclined, for she appears to be a woman of a masculine turn of mind judging from her conversations and deportment. Of the two, she most probably had more to say to the intrigues of the rebels than her imbecile husband.*

Davies then revealed the degree to which both Zafar and Zinat Mahal blamed their situation on their former confidant, personal doctor and prime minister, Hakim Ahsanullah Khan. According to several eyewitnesses, including the usually impeccably reliable Zahir Dehlavi, it was the hakim who had pressed Zafar to stop blocking the rebels' attempts to murder the European prisoners in the Fort; but while presiding over the massacre was one of the principal charges levelled against Zafar, the hakim had got off without hanging or even imprisonment in return for standing up in court and giving evidence against his former employer. 'The statement of prisoners must of course always be received with caution,' wrote Davies,

but in connection with the loss of her treasure, a certain person named Azam Oollah Khan appears to have had a hand – at least all the prisoners are very bitter against him, & assert that this individual, who was the King's hakeem and advisor, was the principal person through whose insidious counsel the destruction of the European prisoners was brought about. This is, I believe, contrary to fact,† but it is not impossible this man may have given some information regarding the secreted treasure & this incurred the enmity of the

* This was actually the opposite of the truth: Zinat Mahal always kept her distance from the rebels and remained consistently opposed to them, not least because Jawan Bakht's rivals for the succession had so enthusiastically embraced their cause.
† Davies was wrong about this. Zafar may well have succeeded in his attempt to save the prisoners if the hakim had not begged him to stop protesting.

Queen's party. However this may be, this hakeem from the account appears to have gained the confidence of the British authorities in Delhi, no doubt with good and sufficient reason, & the spleen displayed by the Begum, & her associates, only adds to confirm this opinion.

Davies then turned his attention to Shah Zamani Begum, whom he describes – presumably again second-hand through the descriptions provided by his wife – as

a young and pretty woman, probably not more than 15 years old, although she has already been the mother of two children. She appears to feel the restraint of prison life rather more than the others. This may partially be the result of a delicate state of health consequent on her accouchement, which took place shortly after her arrival here. The child, I understand from Lt Ommaney, was a male one and was still born. Both the old King and his daughter in law are particularly fond of soliciting the services of the doctor upon every trifling occasion, and the young lady is very solicitous of being allowed to go out for an airing occasionally.

As for Mirzas Jawan Bakht and Shah Abbas,

The two sons are both healthy and rather promising youths, different somewhat in bearing and manner. The elder, Jawan Bakht, exhibits an appearance and deportment of superiority. This is produced probably more from his present recognised position in the family, rather than from any decided superiority in his character and attainments, he having been born a Prince, whereas his less fortunate half-brother is but the son of a handmaiden. Both are extremely ignorant, the attainments of the elder embracing merely a slight knowledge of reading & writing in the Persian character, & when interrogated on the most ordinary topics, their want of knowledge is very apparent. Even the boundaries of their native country are wholly unknown to them.

I feel it my duty as the only medium by which their wishes can be heard, to record for the information of the Government the very laudable desire both these lads exhibit to learn. They have frequently expressed a very earnest wish to acquire a knowledge of the English language in particular, & they seem to be fully aware that by so doing they will have adopted the very last course for removing the misfortune if not disgrace attendant on their present state of ignorance, and they state they expressed a wish to the Commissioner of Delhi to be sent to England in preference to any other place. Both the parents of the lads have talked to me on the subject, & all appear anxious that a commencement should be made. The lads are possessed of sufficient intelligence to warrant a hope of speedy progress and have promised me earnestly to apply themselves if the Government permits the scheme to be undertaken. I told them I would communicate their wishes for the consideration of the Government.

In the covering letter, Davies enlarged on his hopes for the two boys, suggesting that by sending the two princes to England they could create a pair of Anglicised and Anglophile Mughal princes. Davies also added that Zafar and Zinat Mahal had both given their blessing to this plan: 'I have studiously avoided giving the lads any encouragement to expect Government will interfere on their behalf,' he wrote. 'But as the sands of their father's life are running out apace, some change in the circumstances and position of the two youths may at no very distant period become a possibility.'

In such a case it will not be denied that the cultivation of their present desire for acquiring European instruction, would afford moral and also political advantages of no slight moment. It opens out the readiness, perhaps the only method of in a measure denationalising them, and thus bringing about a result so eminently advantageous, as an assimilation of the latent, but mutual hopes . . . between the heirs and the subjects of a dynasty subjected by a foreign power.

Both the parents of the lads have talked to me on the subject, and all appear anxious that the work should at once commence . . .

Such a conclusion on their part seems to offer a favourable opportunity for completing that severance between them and their countrymen before alluded to as a desirable result, and which would be vastly facilitated by entirely removing them from the narrow world of Indian life, with all its prejudices and absurdities. And the benefit of such a change, acting on a useful mind, has always been satisfactorily exemplified in the case of Maharajah Duleep Singh;* and at present these boys are just of an age when good impressions are easily formed and natural talents cultivated, when precepts can with little difficulty be inculcated, and inherent vices uprooted, when a knowledge that morality is indispensable to real happiness might be caused to work in them for good, and the practical application of that morality might be so cultivated as to become habitual.

It cannot be overlooked that a time is at hand when these imprisoned youths will arrive at maturity, and those who are in authority over them have it in their power to give a definite direction to their future. Is there then no responsibility attached to such a position?

The first and most essential requisite therefore is to give the lads breathing room and to separate them completely from the baneful atmosphere of bigotry, superstitious ignorance and consequent degradation by which they are at present surrounded, their only companions being menials, to whom the blessings of education and morality are alike unknown – the very scum of a reduced Asiatic haram.

Davies concluded his letter by writing a little more about Zafar's attendants who had chosen to stay in exile and imprisonment with him. This quite remarkable display of loyalty cut no ice with Davies.

With regard to the attendants all I can say is that they are a low set, dirty in their habits, & much inferior to the ordinary class of domestics in an officer's household. The only exception is perhaps Ahmed Beg. He seems to be a respectable old man, & could have no motive for attending the ex-King other than fidelity. With the

* Maharaja Dalip Singh, the youngest son of the celebrated one-eyed Sikh ruler Ranjit Singh of Lahore, became ruler of the Punjab at the age of ten, before being deposed by the British after the Anglo-Sikh war of 1849. In 1854 he went to Britain, where he became a Christian and a favourite of Queen Victoria, who often invited him to stay with her at Osborne. He bought a country house at Elveden in East Anglia and the British came to regard him as a model of the 'Anglicised native gentleman', especially approving of his fondness for grouse shooting.

Begum's attendant, Abdool Rahman, the case is somewhat different. He is a low, cunning fellow, & I am not quite satisfied as to what relationship he stands in towards the Queen, whether attendant, or something more.[55]

Davies's idea that the princes could be sent to England was promptly and peremptorily turned down by his superiors in Calcutta, who forbade him in future from 'introducing into his letters and diaries the mention of trivial matters which it does not concern the Government to know'.[56] Davies was also ticked off for using 'such expressions as "the ex-King" "the ex-Royal Family" "the Begum". The Governor General in Council requests that Captain Davies may be directed to avoid these expressions in future'. He was directed to refer merely to 'the Delhi State Prisoners'.[57]

Banned from leaving their confinement in Rangoon, and now of no interest to the British government in Calcutta, the two boys now had no choice but to look to Davies for their education. They continued to visit his house 'pretty regularly', and were said to be making 'excellent progress' in English, though Davies admitted he found 'it difficult to invent anything to break the monotony of their existence . . .'

> They occasionally come over and converse with Mrs Davies and communicate their bitter woes . . . Shah Abbas gives more attention and is consequently ahead. Jawan Bakht's disposition appears more averse to Europeans than his brother who, in the absence of better opportunities, converses occasionally with the European soldiers of the guard.[58]

Other letters also hinted at Jawan Bakht's growing disaffection. 'Shah Abbas has the sense to see the necessity of rules,' wrote Davies,

> and submits to it cheerfully and generally extends his walk every morning to the gardens with a sentry. But Jawan Bakht, perhaps thinking the arrangements somewhat retrograde declines to go out at all, and has taken no exercise in the last two months. This obstinacy, if persisted in, would not be good for his health. But I have little doubt that he will be in a better mood in time.[59]

Zafar, meanwhile, sat silently watching the passing shipping from his Rangoon balcony. He was allowed no pen and paper, so his own reaction to his isolation and exile can only be guessed at. Certainly it now seems as if the famous verses attributed to him in exile, expressing his sadness and bitterness, are not the product of his own hand, though William Howard Russell explicitly described him writing verses on the walls of his prison with a burned stick, and it is not completely impossible that these could somehow have been recorded and preserved.*

By 1862, Zafar had reached the grand old age of eighty-seven. Even though he was weak and feeble, and although doctors had now been expecting his imminent demise for some two decades, he still showed no signs of succumbing to their predictions, beyond 'feeling ill with paralysis at the root of the tongue'.[60]

In late October 1862, however, at the end of the monsoon, Zafar's condition became suddenly much worse: he was unable to swallow or keep down his food, and Davies wrote in his diary that the tenure of his life was now 'very uncertain'. The old man was spoon-fed on broth, but by 3 November found it increasingly difficult to get even that down. On the 5th, Davies wrote that 'the Civil Surgeon does not think Abu Zafar can survive many days'. The following day, Davies

---

* Two celebrated ghazals long attributed to Zafar – '*Lagtaa nahii hai dil meraa*' (Nothing brings happiness to my heart) and '*Naa kissii kii aankh kaa nuur huun*' ('I bring no solace to heart or eye') – are popularly known in the subcontinent largely because of Mohammed Rafi, who sang them for the Bombay film *Lal Qila*. But before that they had already become popular in the late fifties thanks to the version sung by one Habeeb Wali Muhammad on Radio Ceylon's talent show, *Ovaltine Amateur Hour*. In the sixties, the Rafi version then became a favourite on All India Radio. Recent research by the Lahore scholar Imran Khan, and backed by several other leading scholars of Urdu literature, has, however, cast doubt on Zafar's authorship of both verses. Certainly the ghazals do not appear in any of Zafar's four published divans, nor in the periodical *Hazoor-e Wala*, where Zafar also published poems. I would like to thank Professor Fran Pritchett and Sundeep Dougal for bringing these developments to my attention, and also C. M. Naim, who, before becoming a distinguished scholar of Urdu literature, was an enthusiastic listener to *Ovaltine Amateur Hour*.

reported that the old man 'is evidently sinking from pure decrepitude and paralysis in the region of his throat'. In preparation for
the death, Davies ordered that bricks and lime be collected, and a
secluded spot at the back of Zafar's enclosure was prepared for the
burial.

After a long night's struggle, Zafar finally breathed his last at
5 a.m. on the morning of Friday, 7 November 1862. Immediately
the machinery of the Empire swung into action to make sure that
the passing of the Last Mughal would be as discreet and un-
eventful as possible. Zafar's death may have marked the end of a
great ruling dynasty 350 years old, but Davies was determined
that as few as possible would witness this sad and historic
moment. 'All things being in readiness,' wrote Davies, 'he was
buried at 4 p.m. on the same day at the rear of the Main Guard in a
brick grave, covered over with turf level with the ground.' Davies
noted how his two boys and their father's manservant attended
the burial, but the women, in accordance with Muslim custom,
did not.

'A bamboo fence surrounds the grave for some considerable
distance,' he concluded, 'and by the time the fence is worn out, the
grass will again have properly covered the spot, and no vestige will
remain to distinguish where the last of the Great Moghuls rests.'

The following day, Davies wrote his official report on the demise
of his charge. 'This event made very little impression either on the
relatives or on the Mahomedan population of this town,' Davies
noted with satisfaction. 'Probably about a couple of hundred
spectators assembled at the time of the funeral, but this event
was occasioned in a great extent by idlers coming from the
neighbouring Sudder Bazar to town to see the Races which were
going on that afternoon near the prisoners' quarters.'[61]

'The death of the ex-King may be said to have had no effect on
the Mahomedan part of the populace of Rangoon,' he added,
'except perhaps for a few fanatics who watch and pray for the
final triumph of Islam.'

News of Zafar's death reached Delhi a fortnight later on 20 November. Ghalib read the news in the *Avadh Akhbar*, the same day that it was announced that the Jama Masjid was finally going to be given back to the Muslims of Delhi. Already numbed by the news of so many other deaths and tragedies, Ghalib's reaction was resigned and muted: 'On Friday the 7th November, and the 14th Jamadu ul Awwal, Abu Zafar Siraj ud Din Bahadur Shah was freed from the bonds of the foreigner and the bonds of the flesh. "Verily we are for God, and verily to him we shall return." '[62]

Ghalib's reaction was typical. No newspaper, British or Indian, carried the news of Zafar's death in any detail. There had been so much bloodshed, and so many funerals, and to some extent Zafar had already been mourned, and then forgotten: after all, it was now five years since he had been banished from the city and sent into Burmese exile.

It was only gradually, with the distance of hindsight, that the scale of the vacuum left by the destruction and dispersal of Zafar's court became apparent. The dramatic way in which both Hindus and Muslims had rallied to the Mughal capital at the outbreak of the Uprising had demonstrated the degree to which the mystique of the dynasty was still very much alive more than a century after the Mughals had ceased to exercise any real political, economic or military power. Contrary to all expectations, the idea of the Mughal Emperor as the divinely ordained *axis mundi*, the universal sovereign, and *Padshah*, Lord of the World, still had resonance across Hindustan at this time. Even more surprisingly, and contrary to many modern assumptions, it clearly resonated as strongly for Hindus as it did for Muslims. As Mark Thornhill had written, sitting in Mathura shortly after the sepoys arrived from Meerut, listening to his office staff excitedly discuss the revival of the Mughal throne:

Their talk was all about the ceremonial of the palace and how it would be revived. They speculated as to who would be Grand Chamberlain, which of the chiefs of Rajpootana would guard the different gates, and who were the fifty-two Rajahs who would

assemble to put the Emperor on the throne . . . As I listened I
realised as I never had done before the deep impression that the
splendour of the ancient court had made on the popular imagination,
how dear to them were the traditions and how faithfully, all unknown to us, they had preserved them.[63]

The outbreak revealed the surprising degree to which the Mughal
court was still regarded across northern India not as some sort of
foreign Muslim imposition – as some, especially on the Hindu right
wing, look upon the Mughals today – but instead as the principal
source of political legitimacy, and therefore the natural centre of
resistance against British colonial rule.*

Nevertheless, if the outbreak demonstrated the power of the
Mughal name, the disastrous course of the Uprising dramatically
highlighted the shortcomings and impotence of that Old Mughal
feudal order. Zafar may have commanded the nominal loyalty and
allegiance of the sepoys and his people, but that loyalty did not
stretch to either direct obedience or submission, especially when his
treasury was shown to be empty, and the weakness of Zafar's
personal authority became apparent. The crucial failure to get even
the hinterland of Delhi to submit to Zafar's rule, or to organise a
proper logistical apparatus to feed the troops gathered within the
walls, meant that the massive – and largely Hindu – army that
collected so quickly and strikingly at Delhi soon ran out of food,
and before long was brought to the edge of starvation. For this
reason it was already well on the way to dispersing long before the
British entered the Kashmiri Gate to deliver the *coup de grâce*.

When Delhi fell in September 1857 it was not just the city and
Zafar's court which were uprooted and destroyed, but the self-
confidence and authority of the wider Mughal political and cultural
world throughout India. The scale of the devastation and defeat,

* It is true that not everyone – even among Indian Muslims – looked to the Mughals:
Tipu Sultan of Mysore, for example, made a point of seeking the blessing of the
Ottoman Caliph. Yet it is surely significant that the court of Lucknow, which had been
encouraged by the British to look to Calcutta rather than Delhi, sent an embassy to
Zafar in 1857 asking him to confirm the title Wazir for the young heir apparent, Birjis
Qadir, who was already minting his coins in the Emperor's name.

and the depths of the humiliation heaped on the vanquished Mughals, profoundly diminished not just the prestige of the old aristocratic order, but also – to at least some extent – the composite Hindu–Muslim, Indo-Islamic civilisation of which Zafar's court had been the flagship, and of whose sophisticated, tolerant and open-minded attitudes Ghalib's poems still form such a striking testament.

For the British after 1857, the Indian Muslim became an almost subhuman creature, to be classified in unembarrassedly racist imperial literature alongside such other despised and subject specimens, such as Irish Catholics or 'the Wandering Jew'. The depth to which Indian Muslims had sunk in British eyes is visible in an 1868 production called *The People of India*, which contains photographs of the different castes and tribes of South Asia ranging from Tibetans and Aboriginals (illustrated with a picture of a naked tribal) to the Doms of Bihar. The image of 'the Mahomedan' is illustrated by a picture of an Aligarh labourer who is given the following caption: 'His features are peculiarly Mahomedan . . . [and] exemplify in a strong manner the obstinacy, sensuality, ignorance and bigotry of his class. It is hardly possible, perhaps, to conceive features more essentially repulsive.'[64]

The profound contempt that the British so openly expressed for Indian Muslim and Mughal culture proved contagious, particularly to the ascendant Hindus, who quickly hardened their attitudes to all things Islamic, but also to many young Muslims, who now believed than their own ancient and much-cherished civilisation had been irretrievably discredited. Some even shared Sir Sayyid Ahmad Khan's initial conviction that Indian Muslims could never again prosper or 'receive esteem'. 'For some time,' he wrote, 'I could not even bear to contemplate the miserable state of my people. I wrestled with my grief, and believe me it made an old man of me.'[65]

Just as the amateurish Mughal-led armies had proved unable to compete with British generals and British Enfields, and just as Mirza Mughal's stumbling commissariat proved no match for the Company's bureaucracy, so in the years that followed the still-living and even thriving Mughal miniature and architectural tradition would soon come to a grinding halt in the face of Tropical

Gothic colonial architecture and other Victorian art forms. The elaborate politeness of Mughal etiquette and Indo-Islamic manners came to be regarded merely as anachronistic. The poetic world represented by Zafar's *mushairas* would find it increasingly hard to attract young Indian intellectuals seduced by the siren call of Tennyson or the Wordsworthian naturalism now taught in English-medium schools.[66] As Maulvi Muhammad Baqar's son, the poet and critic Azad, wrote: 'The important thing is that the glory of the winners' ascendant fortune gives everything of theirs – even their dress, their gait, their conversation – a radiance that makes them desirable. And people do not merely adopt them, but they are proud to adopt them.'[67]

Not all the changes, of course, were necessarily for the worse. The autocratic political structures of Mughal rule received a devastating death blow. Only ninety years separated the British victory at the gates of Delhi in 1857 from the British eviction from South Asia through the Gateway of India in 1947. But while memories of British atrocities in 1857 may have assisted in the birth of Indian nationalism, as did the growing separation and mutual suspicion of rulers and ruled that followed the Uprising, it was not the few surviving descendants of the Mughals, nor any of the old princely and feudal rulers, who were in any way responsible for India's march to independence. Instead, the Indian freedom movement was led by the new Anglicised and educated Colonial Service class who emerged from English-language schools after 1857, and who by and large used modern Western democratic structures and methods – political parties, strikes and protest marches – to gain their freedom.

Even after Independence, the arts that were cultivated by the Mughals – the miniature painting tradition, the ghazal, the delicate forms of Mughal architecture – never really regained their full vitality or artistic prestige, and remained – at least in some quarters – as discredited as the emperors who patronised them.

Today, if you visit the old Mughal city of Agra, perhaps to see the Taj Mahal, the supreme architectural achievement of Mughal rule, note how the roundabouts are full of statues of the Rani of Jhansi, Shivaji and even Subhas Chandra Bose; but not one image of any

Mughal emperor has been erected anywhere in the city since independence. Although a Bahadur Shah Zafar road still survives in Delhi, as indeed do roads named after all the other Great Mughals, for many Indians today, rightly or wrongly, the Mughals are still perceived as it suited the British to portray them in the imperial propaganda that they taught in Indian schools after 1857: as sensual, decadent, temple-destroying invaders – something that was forcefully and depressingly demonstrated by the whole episode of the demoliton of the Baburi Masjid at Ayodhya in 1992. The profoundly sophisticated, liberal and plural civilisation championed by Akbar, Dara Shukoh or the later Mughal emperors has only a limited resonance for the urban middle class in modern India. Many of these are now deeply ambivalent about the achievements of the Mughals, even if they will still happily eat a Mughal meal, or flock to the cinema to watch a Bollywood Mughal epic, or indeed head to the Red Fort to hear their Prime Minister give the annual Independence Day speech from the battlements in front of the Lahore Gate.

As for Zafar, he remained the focus of much nostalgic sympathy, especially – though not exclusively – among Indian Muslims. But romantic longing for a lost empire was not enough to protect or preserve the Mughal culture he embodied. This was especially so given his equivocal attitude to the Uprising, only partly supporting it during its ascendancy, and then completely rejecting it in defeat. There was nothing left for his supporters to cling on to, not even a coherent political idea. With his death, followed seven years later by that of Ghalib, the self-esteem and confidence of an entire civilisation also passed away, so discredited it could never hope to be revived.

The same year that Ghalib died in Delhi, 1869, there was born in Porbandar in Gujarat a boy called Mohandas Karamchand Gandhi. It would be with the political movements headed by Gandhi, rather than those represented by Zafar, or indeed by Lord Canning, that the future of India would lie.

After the death of Zafar, what survived of the Mughal royal family quickly fell apart. As Captain Davies wrote in his next report to Calcutta, the Mughals were now, like the civilisation they represented,

> A divided house . . . Begum Zeenat Mahul is a party in herself and until recently she and her son and Daughter in-law were in a deadly feud . . . Jawan Bukht and his wife form a second clique, and Shah Abbas his mother and grandmother are third. All three sections keep their premises distinct and cook and eat their meals separately and have little or no communication with each other.[68]

As the years went on, things only got worse. In 1867 the family were allowed to leave the prison enclosure and to settle elsewhere in the Rangoon cantonment.[69] But they were given such miserable allowances that by 1870, eight years after the death of Zafar, the house that Jawan Bakht shared with his mother and Nawab Shah Zamani Begum was described as 'wretched . . . a mere hovel and much overcrowded'. As a young girl of no more than ten Shah Zamani Begum had paraded gloriously through the streets of Mughal Delhi on elephant-back to marry her Mirza Jawan Bakht. Now racked with disappointment at the way her life had turned out, she became 'seriously ill . . . suffering from extreme depression', and, to the alarm of the British officials who were meant to look after her, started to go blind.[70]

Jawan Bakht and his wife were given another house, not far from the Rangoon jail, in the hope that this would improve matters. But despite his poverty, Jawan Bakht still spent more than he could afford on drink, and a government official reported to Calcutta that his pension was 'scarcely sufficient to meet the actual requirements of the family . . .'

> Whenever therefore Jawan Bakht commits the least extravagance, or falls into the slightest improvident indulgence, it is his wife and children who are the real and only sufferers. Shah Zamani Begum is the only completely innocent member of the Delhi family and yet has been the greatest sufferer of all. On more than one occasion this blind lady has been obliged to pawn her clothes and the few ornaments she has left, to procure food for herself and her children;

whilst Jawan Bakht will drown any remorse he may feel in a fit of hard drinking . . . I am really powerless to interfere; any interference would only lead him to threaten his wife and treat her very harshly.[71]

By 1872, Shah Zamani Begum was reported to be 'perfectly blind and helpless . . . The conduct of this lady has been exemplary; and her misfortunes, arising from no fault of her own, have been very great. Though Jawan Bakht's conduct has of late greatly improved, her absolute dependence on him must at times be very great and frequently very trying . . . She is an object of great pity'.[72]

Mirza Shah Abbas eventually married a girl from Rangoon – the daughter of a local Muslim merchant – and seems to have escaped some of the misery that struck down the rest of his family.* Zinat Mahal, meanwhile, lived on alone: 'in a very frugal almost penurious way . . . in a wooden house, purchased by herself, with two or three female servants . . . This widowed Begum has allowed her house to fall into great disrepair . . . She lives a quiet retired life and bears herself with some dignity . . . [though] the house she now occupies is a tumbledown, discreditable building, an eyesore to the locality in which it is situated'. In her old age, she applied to be allowed to return to India, saying she was being 'oppressed' by her son Jawan Bakht, but the application was summarily turned down.[73] Her one comfort and indulgence was opium, to which she became increasingly addicted towards the end of her life. She died in 1882, twenty years after her husband. By the time of her death, the exact place of Zafar's grave had already been forgotten and could not be located, so she was buried in a roughly similar position near a tree that was remembered to be near by. Two years later, Mirza Jawan Bakht had a severe stroke and followed her to the grave. He was aged only forty-two.

When a delegation of visitors from India came in 1903 to pay their respects at the burial place of Zafar, even the exact location of Zinat Mahal's grave had been forgotten, though some local guides pointed out the sight of the 'withered lotus tree'.[74] In 1905, however, there was a protest by the Muslims of Rangoon demanding that Zafar's grave should be marked, because, in the words of their

* His descendants still live in Rangoon today.

application, 'the Mahommedan Community of Rangoon is agitated over the resting place of the last King of the proud line of the Mughals . . . As a man or as a King, Bahadur Shah was not to be admired, but he should be remembered'. They asked to be 'allowed by the government to purchase a strip of land enclosing the grave in question, of sufficient area to permit a monument worthy of Bahadur Shah being erected over it'.[75]

The initial British response was not favourable. The application was forwarded to Calcutta, where a reply was sent straight back to the effect that 'the Viceroy concurs in your view that it would be very inappropriate for the Government to do anything to perpetuate or to pay respect to the memory of Bahadur Shah, or to erect over his remains a tomb which might become a place of pilgrimage'.[76]

Following a demonstration and a long series of newspaper articles, however, the British authorities finally agreed in 1907 to erect a 'simple engraved stone slab marked, Bahadur Shah, ex-King of Delhi. Died at Rangoon November 7th 1862 and was buried near this spot'. A railing was also allowed around the supposed site of the grave, and according to the *Rangoon Times* of 26 August 1907, in due course a meeting was held at the Victoria Hall 'to record the sense of satisfaction among the Mahommedan community for the erection of the present memorial' and 'on account of the sympathetic and beneficent interest taken by the government in the matter'.[77] A memorial stone to Zinat Mahal was added later the same year.

By 1925 the railing had become a makeshift shrine, covered with a roof of corrugated iron.[78] Eighteen years later it was in the road beside this basic mazar (shrine) that the Japanese billeted the troops of the Indian National Army during the Second World War. It was unclear whether it was deliberate or not, but one of these groups, posted directly next to the shrine in what was now Theatre Road, was the Rani of Jhansi Brigade, named after another of the leaders of the 1857 Uprising, who partly inspired their ill-fated (and, in Nehru and Gandhi's view, wrong-headed) attempt to liberate India from British rule by joining hands with the invading Japanese.[79]

Then, in 1991, on 16 February, workmen digging a drain at the back of the shrine uncovered a brick-lined grave. It was 3 feet under the ground, and about 25 feet from the shrine. The skeleton of the Last Mughal was found quite intact within.

Today the brick grave of Bahadur Shah, now located in a sort of crypt below and to one side of the old shrine, is a popular place of pilgrimage for Rangoon's Muslim population. The local Muslims regard Zafar as a powerful Sufi saint, and come to seek his *barakat* (spiritual blessing) and ask for favours, all of which would no doubt have pleased him since he enjoyed taking on *murids* (Sufi disciples) when he was alive. Zafar also receives fairly regular visits from passing politicians from South Asia, and dignitaries from India, Pakistan and Bangladesh compete to shower the grave with presents, the most generous of which is a large, though far from beautiful, carpet presented by Rajiv Gandhi.

Despite this, Zafar has few supporters in the modern history books. In some ways, it is true, his life can be seen as a study in failure: after all, he presided over the great collapse of Indo-Islamic civilisation, and his contribution to the Uprising of 1857 was hardly heroic. He is blamed by some nationalist historians for corresponding with the British during the fighting, and by others for failing to lead the rebels to victory. Yet it is difficult to see what more Zafar could have done, at least at the age of eighty-two. He was physically infirm, partially senile and had no money to pay the troops who flocked to his standard. Octogenarians can hardly lead a cavalry charge. Try as he might, he was powerless even to stop the looting of Delhi by an insurgent army that proved almost as much a threat to Zafar's subjects as it did to his enemies. Yet the Mutiny Papers bear eloquent witness to the energy he expended trying to protect his people and his city.

But while Zafar was certainly never cut out to be a heroic or revolutionary leader, he remains, like his ancestor the Emperor Akbar, an attractive symbol of Islamic civilisation at its most tolerant and pluralistic. He was himself a notable poet and calligrapher; his court contained some of the most talented artistic and literary figures in modern South Asian history; and the Delhi he presided over was undergoing one of its great periods of learning,

484 THE LAST MUGHAL

self-confidence, communal amity and prosperity. He is certainly a strikingly liberal and likeable figure when compared to the Victorian Evangelicals whose insensitivity, arrogance and blindness did much to bring the Uprising of 1857 down upon both their own heads and those of the people and court of Delhi, engulfing all of northern India in a religious war of terrible violence.

Above all, Zafar always put huge emphasis on his role as a protector of the Hindus and the moderator of Muslim demands. He never forgot the central importance of preserving the bond between his Hindu and Muslim subjects, which he always recognised was the central stitching that held his capital city together. Throughout the Uprising, his refusal to alienate his Hindu subjects by subscribing to the demands of the jihadis was probably his single most consistent policy.

There was nothing inevitable about the demise and extinction of the Mughals, as the sepoys' dramatic surge towards the court of Delhi showed. But in the years to come, as Muslim prestige and learning sank, and Hindu confidence, wealth, education and power increased, Hindus and Muslims would grow gradually apart, as British policies of divide and rule found willing collaborators among the chauvinists of both faiths. The rip in the closely woven fabric of Delhi's composite culture, opened in 1857, slowly widened into a great gash, and at Partition in 1947 finally broke in two. As the Indian Muslim elite emigrated en masse to Pakistan, the time would soon come when it would be almost impossible to imagine that Hindu sepoys could ever have rallied to the Red Fort and the standard of a Muslim emperor, joining with their Muslim brothers in an attempt to revive the Mughal Empire.

Following the crushing of the Uprising, and the uprooting and slaughter of the Delhi court, the Indian Muslims themselves also divided down two opposing paths: one, championed by the great Anglophile Sir Sayyid Ahmad Khan, looked to the West, and believed that Indian Muslims could revive their fortunes only by embracing Western learning. With this in mind, Sir Sayyid founded his Aligarh Mohamedan Anglo-Oriental College (later Aligarh Muslim University) and tried to re-create Oxbridge in the plains of Hindustan.[80]

The other approach, taken by survivors of the old Madrasa i-Rahimiyya, was to reject the West *in toto* and to attempt to return to what they regarded as pure Islamic roots. For this reason, disillusioned pupils of the school of Shah Waliullah, such as Maulana Muhammad Qasim Nanautawi – who in 1857 had briefly established an independent Islamic state north of Meerut at Shamli in the Doab – founded an influential but depressingly narrow-minded Wahhabi-like madrasa at Deoband, 100 miles north of the former Mughal capital. With their backs to the wall, they reacted against what the founders saw as the degenerate and rotten ways of the old Mughal elite. The Deoband madrasa therefore went back to Koranic basics and rigorously stripped out anything Hindu or European from the curriculum.*[81]

One hundred and forty years later, it was out of Deobandi madrasas in Pakistan and Afghanistan that the Taliban emerged to create the most retrograde Islamic regime in modern history, a regime that in turn provided the crucible from which emerged al-Qaeda, and the most radical and powerful fundamentalist Islamic counter-attack the modern West has yet encountered.

Today, West and East again face each other uneasily across a divide that many see as religious war. Jihadis again fight what they regard as a defensive action against their Christian enemies, and again innocent women, children and civilians are slaughtered. As before, Western Evangelical politicians are apt to cast their opponents and enemies in the role of 'incarnate fiends' and conflate armed resistance to invasion and occupation with 'pure evil'. Again Western countries, blind to the effect their foreign policies have on the wider world, feel aggrieved to be attacked – as they interpret it – by mindless fanatics.

Against this bleak dualism, there is much to value in Zafar's peaceful and tolerant attitude to life; and there is also much to regret in the way that the British swept away and rooted out the late Mughals' pluralistic and philosophically composite civilisation.

As we have seen in our own time, nothing threatens the liberal and moderate aspect of Islam so much as aggressive Western

---

* It was not by any means a total divide: religious education at Aligarh, for example, was in the hands of the Deobandis.

intrusion and interference in the East, just as nothing so dramatically radicalises the ordinary Muslim and feeds the power of the extremists: the histories of Islamic fundamentalism and Western imperialism have, after all, often been closely, and dangerously, intertwined. There are clear lessons here. For, in the celebrated words of Edmund Burke,[82] himself a fierce critic of Western aggression in India, those who fail to learn from history are always destined to repeat it.

GLOSSARY

Akhbars	Newspapers or, before that, Indian court newsletters
Alam	Standards used by Shi'as as focuses for their *Muharram* (qv) venerations. Usually tear-shaped (as illustrated in the text breaks of this book) or fashioned into the shape of a hand, they are stylised representations of the standards carried by Imam Hussain at the Battle of Kerbala in AD 680. Often highly ornate and beautiful objects, the best of them are among the greatest masterpieces of medieval Indian metalwork
Amir	Nobleman, leader or wealthy individual
Arrack	Indian absinthe
Arzee	Persian petition
Ashur khana	Mourning hall for use during *Muharram* (qv)
Avadh (or *Oudh*)	Region of central North India, which in the early nineteenth century was ruled by the Nawab in Lucknow, until annexed by the British in 1856. Most of the sepoys in British service were drawn from this region
Avatar	An incarnation
Azan	The Muslim call to prayer
Badmash	Rogue or ruffian
Baniya	Moneylender
Banka	Mughal gallant
Baradari	A Mughal-style open pavilion with three arches on each side (lit. 'twelve doors')
Barakat	Blessings
Barat	Marriage procession taking a groom to his marriage
Barf Khana	Ice house
Barqandaz	Armed police constable
Bayat	An oath of allegiance
Begum	Indian Muslim noblewoman. A title of rank and respect: 'Madam'
Betel	Nut used as a mild narcotic in India, and eaten as *paan* (qv)
Bhands	Buffoons, mummers or mimics
Bhang	A traditional, mildly narcotic drink in which milk and spices are mixed with marijuana

Bhatta	Extra allowance, given to the Company's sepoys in time of war
Bhisti	Water carrier
Bibi	An Indian wife or mistress
Bibi ghar	'Women's house' or *zenana* (qv)
Biryani	Rice and meat dish
Brahmin	The Hindu priestly caste and the top rung of the caste pyramid
Chamars	Untouchables often of the sweeper caste
Char bagh	A formal Mughal garden, named after its division into four (*char*) squares by a cross of runnels and fountains
Charpoy	A rustic bedstead
Chatri	A domed kiosk supported on pillars, often used as a decorative feature to top turrets and minarets (lit. 'umbrella')
Chaukidar	Guard or nightwatchman
Chobdars	Ceremonial mace bearers
Choli	Short (and at this period usually transparent) Indian bodice
Coss	Mughal measurement of distance amounting to just over three miles
Dafadar	Sepoy rank equivalent to petty officer
Daftar	Office or, in the Nizam's palace, chancellery
Damdama	Mud fort
Danga	Disturbance
Dak	Post (sometimes spelt '*dawke*' in the eighteenth and nineteenth centuries)
Dak gharee	Post carriage
Dargah	Sufi shrine
Darogah	Officer, superintendent or overseer. In the seventeenth century the *darogah* was the chief executive of the royal household, but by the nineteenth century the term was used for middle- or lower-ranking officials overseeing police stations, bridges and individual departments within the royal household
Dastan-go	Storyteller
Deorhi	Courtyard house or *haveli*
Derzi	Tailor
Dharamasala	Rest house
Dharma	Duty, righteousness and hence, faith (for Hindus)
Dhobi	Laundryman
Dhoolie (or *doolie*)	Covered litter
Dhoti	Loincloth
Din	Faith (for Muslims)
Divan	A collection of poetry by a single author

Diwan	Prime minister, or the vizier in charge of administrative finance
Dubash	Interpreter
Dupatta	Shawl or scarf, usually worn with a *salvar kemise* (lit. 'two leaves or widths'). Also known as a *chunni*
Durbar	Court
Fakir	Sufi holy man, dervish or wandering Muslim ascetic (lit. 'poor')
Fana	Mystical self-annihilation or immersion in the beloved
Farzand	Son
Fasad	Riots
Fatiha	The short opening chapter of the Koran, read at ceremonial occasions as an invocation
Fauj	Army
Firangi	Foreigner
Firman	An order of the Emperor or Sultan in a written document
Fotadar	Treasurer
Gali	Lane
Ghadr	Mutiny
Ghagra	Indian skirt
Gharri (or *gharry*)	Cart
Ghats	River front, usually reached by steps built for the benefit of bathers and washermen
Ghazal	Urdu or Persian love lyric
Ghazi	Holy warrior or jihadi
Goras	Whites
Hackery	Bullock cart
Hakim	Physician of traditional Greek/Islamic medicine
Hamam	Turkish-style steam bath
Haram	Forbidden
Harkara	Runner, messenger, and in some contexts, newswriter or spy (lit. 'all-do-er'), usually in Delhi in the employ of the Emperor
Havildar	A sepoy non-commissioned officer corresponding to a sergeant
Hindustan	Region of North India encompassing the modern Indian states of Haryana, Delhi, Uttar Pradesh and some parts of Madhya Pradesh and Bihar, where Hindustani is spoken, and the area often referred to in modern Indian papers as the 'Cow Belt'. While the term 'India' is relatively rarely used in nineteenth-century Urdu sources, there is a strong consciousness of the existence of Hindustan as a unit, with Delhi at its political centre. This was the area that was most seriously convulsed in 1857

Hle-yin	A type of Burmese bullock cart
Holi	The Hindu spring festival in which participants sprinkle red and yellow powder on one another
Howdah	The seat carried on an elephant's back. Often in this period a *howdah* was covered with a canopy
Htamien	Silken Burmese skirt-wrap for a woman
Huqqa	Waterpipe or hubble bubble
Hut Jao!	Move away!
Id	The two greatest Muslim festivals: Id ul-Fitr marks the end of Ramadan, while Id ul-Zuha commemorates the delivery of Isaac. To celebrate the latter a ram or goat is slaughtered, as on the original occasion recorded in both the Old Testament and the Koran
Iftar	The evening meal to break the Ramadan fast
Imambara	Shi'a religious hall
'Ishq	Love
Jagir	Landed estate, granted for service rendered to the State and whose revenues could be treated as income by the *jagirdar*
Jali	A latticed stone or wooden screen
Jang i-Azadi	Freedom struggle (lit. 'War of Freedom')
Jashn	Party or marriage feast
Jemadar	Junior Indian officer
Jhil	Lake, or swamp
Jihad	Holy war, or struggle, hence *jihadi*, one who wages holy war
Juties	Indian shoes
Kafir	Infidel
Kakkar-wala	Huqqa bearer
Karkhana	Workshop or factory
Khadim	Servant. In the case of a great mosque, the administrators or clergy
Khalifa	Caliph, one of the titles claimed by the Mughal Emperor, though one more usually associated with the Ottoman Emperor, who inherited the title from the Abbasids
Khansaman	In the eighteenth century the word meant butler. Today it more usually means cook
Khanum	A junior wife or concubine
Kharita	Sealed Mughal brocade bag used to send letters as an alternative to an envelope
Khidmatgar	Servant or butler
Khilat	Symbolic dress of honour, gifted by the Mughal to his vassals as a symbol of patronage
Kothi	A substantial town house, often arranged around a succession of courtyards

Kotwal	The police chief, chief magistrate or city administrator in a Mughal town
Kotwali	The office of the *Kotwal* (qv), hence central police station
Kufr	Infidelity
Kukhri	Short, sharp, curved knife worn by the Gurkhas
Kurta	Long Indian shirt
Laddu	Milk-based sweet
Lakh	One hundred thousand
Langar	Free distribution of food during a religious festival
Lathi	Truncheon or stick
Lota	Water pot
Lungi	Indian-type sarong, longer version of the *dhoti* (qv)
Madrasa	Traditional Islamic college or place of education. In this period in Delhi, many Hindus also attended *madaris* (the correct plural for *madrasas*)
Mahajan	Moneylender or banker
Mahal	Lit. 'palace', but often used to refer to sleeping apartments or the *zenana* (qv) wing of a palace or residence
Muhi Maraatib	The Mughal's dynastic ceremonial fish standard. This came in two forms, one a single golden fish on a pole (as illustrated at the beginning of Chapter 1) and the other two golden fish hanging from a bow (as illustrated in the plate section)
Majlis	Assembly, especially the gatherings during *Muharram* (qv)
Majzub	Holy madman (or *Qalandar*)
Mansabdar	A Mughal nobleman and office holder, whose rank was decided by the number of cavalry he would supply for battle – for example a *mansabdar* of 2,500 would be expected to provide 2,500 horsemen when the Nizam went to war
Marsiya	Urdu or Persian lament or dirge for the martyrdom of Hussain, the grandson of the Prophet, sung in the *ashur khana* (qv) mourning halls during the festival of *Muharram* (qv)
Masnavi	Persian or Urdu love lyric
Maula	'My Lord'
Mazmun	Theme (of a *ghazal*)
Mehfil	An evening of courtly Mughal entertainment, normally including dancing, the recitation of poetry and the singing of *ghazals* (qv)
Mihrab	The niche in a mosque pointing in the direction of Mecca
Mir	The title 'Mir' given before a name usually signifies that the holder is a *Sayyed* (qv)
Mirza	A prince or gentleman

Mohalla	A distinct quarter of a Mughal city – i.e. a group of residential lanes, usually entered through a single gate, which would be locked at night
Mohur	A gold coin of high value
Mufti	An Islamic scholar who is an interpreter or expounder of Islamic Sharia law, and who is capable of issuing a *fatwa* or legal opinion
Muharram	The great Shi'a Muslim festival commemorating the defeat and death of Imam Hussain, the Prophet's grandson. Celebrated with particular gusto in Hyderabad and Lucknow, but also in the Delhi Red Fort
Mujtahid	A cleric; one who does *ijtehad*, the interpretation of religious texts
Munshi	Indian Private Secretary or language teacher
Murid	Sufi pupil studying under a master, or *pir* (qv)
Murqana	Stalactite-type decoration over mosque or palace gateway
Mushairas	Poetic symposia where poets read their verses before an audience of connoisseurs
Musnud	The low arrangement of cushions and bolsters which forms the throne of Indian rulers at this period
Nabob	English corruption of the Hindustani *nawab* (qv), literally 'deputy', which was the title given by the Mughal emperors to their regional governors and viceroys. In England it became a term of abuse directed at returned 'old Indian hands'
Namaz	Prayers
Naqqar Khana	Ceremonial drum house
Nasrani	Christians
Nautch	An Indian dance display
Nautch girl	Professional dancer and courtesan
Nawab	The term originally referred to a viceroy or governor, but later it was simply used as a grand title, usually for men, but occasionally – as in the case of Zinat Mahal – for women. Duke or Duchess would perhaps be the nearest English equivalent, which in its original Latin form *Dux* also meant governor
Nazr	Symbolic gift given in Indian courts to a feudal superior
Nuqul	Small hard sweets made of jaggery
Paan	Mildly narcotic preparation of betel nut
Pachchisi	Indian board game
Padshah	Emperor
Pagri	Turban
Palanquin	Indian litter

Palki	Palanquin or litter
Pardah	Lit. 'a curtain', used to signify the concealment of women within the *zenana* (qv)
Parwana	Written order, or edict
Pasoe	A Burmese sarong
Peshkash	Offering or present given by a subordinate to a superior. The term was used more specifically by the Marattas as the money paid to them by 'subordinate' powers such as the Nizam
Peshwaz	Long, high-waisted gown
Phulwalon ki Sair	The Flower Sellers Fair, held in Mehrauli during the monsoon rains
Pir	Sufi master or holy man
Pirzada	Official at a Sufi shrine, often a descendant of the founding saint
Puja	Prayer (for Hindus)
Pukka	Proper, correct
Pundit	Brahmin
Punkah	Fan
Purbias	Easterners. In Delhi this word was used alternately with the term *Tilangas* (qv), to describe the rebel sepoys. Both words carry the same connotations of foreignness, implying 'these outsiders from the East'
Puri	Indian fried wholewheat flatbread
Qahwah Khana	Coffee-house – the archetypal café of Hindustan prior to the introduction of tea in the late nineteenth century
Qasida	Ode, usually a poem of praise to a patron
Qawwal	A singer of *qawwalis* (qv)
Qawwalis	Rousing hymns sung at Sufi shrines
Qila	Fort
Qiladar	Fort keeper
Qizilbash	Name given to Saffavid soldiers (and later traders) due to the tall red cap worn under their turbans (lit. 'redheads')
Rakhi	Band worn around the wrist as a sign of brotherhood, solidarity or protection
Ratjaga	Night vigil before a marriage
Razai	Quilt
Resident	The East India Company's ambassador to an Indian court. As time went on, and British power increased, Residents increasingly assumed the role of being regional governors, controlling the city and even the court administration to which they were sent

Risaldar	Indian senior officer in a cavalry regiment
Roza	Fast
Rozgar	Employment
Rubakari	An order
Sadr Amin	Chief Muslim judge
Sahri	The pre-fast meal eaten before dawn during Ramadan, the month of fasting
Salatin	Palace-born princes. In the Red Fort the *salatin* lived in their own quarter, frequently in some degree of genteel poverty
Sanyasi	Hindu ascetic
Sarpeche	Turban jewel or ornament
Sati	The practice of widow-burning, or the burned widow herself
Sawar	(sometimes anglicised to *sowar*) Cavalry trooper
Sawaree	Elephant stables, and the whole establishment and paraphernalia related to the keeping of elephants
Sayyed	(*or Sayyida*) A lineal descendant of the Prophet Mohammed. *Sayyeds* often have the title *Mir* (qv)
Sehra	A wedding veil made of a string of pearls. Also a marriage ode or oration
Sepoy	Indian infantry private, in this case in the employ of the British East India Company. The word derives from *sipahi*, the Persian for soldier
Shadi	Marriage feast or party
Shagird	A pupil in poetry apprenticed to a master or *ustad*
Shahzada	Princes
Shamiana	Indian marquee, or the screen formed around the perimeter of a tented area
Shanai	Oboe-like Hindustani instrument
Sharif	Princely or noble
Shi'a	One of the two principle divisions of Islam, dating back to a split immediately after the death of the Prophet, between those who recognised the authority of the Medinian caliphs and those who followed the Prophet's son in law Ali (*Shi'at Ali* means 'the party of Ali' in Arabic). Though most Shi'ites live in Iran, there have always been a large number in the Indian Deccan, and Hyderabad was for much of its history a centre of Shi'ite culture
Shikar	Hunting, hence *shikari*, hunter
Shikastah	An elaborate Persian and Urdu cursive script or calligraphy (lit. 'broken writing'). Popular in the late eighteenth and nineteenth centuries, *shikastah* is an elaborate and personalised form of *nasta'liq* script in which the natural pauses between letters and words are blurred by the writer joining

	up the normally empty passages of the verse or sentence, often making it very difficult to read
Shir mal	Sweet naan
Shorba	Soup
Shwebo Wun	Burmese provincial governor
Sirdar	Nobleman
Sogh	Mourning clothes
Subahdar	Indian senior officer in a sepoy regiment
Sufi	Muslim mystic
Surahis	Traditional tall, elegant North Indian water and wine cooler/flask
Taal	The beat in Hindustani music
Tahsildar	District official in charge of revenue and taxation
Tasbih	Rosary, hence *Tasbih Khana*, an oratory or prayer room
Tawaif	The cultivated and urbane dancing girls and courtesans who were such a feature of late Mughal society and culture
Ta'wiz	A charm
Tehkhana	Cool underground room or network of cool rooms
Thammo	Stop!
Thana	Police post or station, presided over by a *Thanadar*
Tilangas	This word apparently derives from Telingana, in modern Andhra Pradesh, where the British originally recruited many of their sepoys during the Carnatic Wars of the eighteenth century. In Delhi the name seems to have stuck as an appellation for British trained troops although the British had long since replaced Telingana with Avadh as their principle recruitment field, so that in 1857 most sepoys would have come from modern Uttar Pradesh and parts of Bihar. *Purbias* (qv), which in Delhi was used alternately with *Tilangas*, simply means Easterners. Both words carry the same connotations of foreignness, implying 'these outsiders from the East'
Tulwar	Indian curved sword
Ukases	Decrees
'Ulama	In Arabic, the *'ulama* means 'the ones possessing knowledge', hence the 'community of learned men'. In effect it means the Islamic clergy, the body of men with sufficient knowledge of the Koran, the Sunna and the Sharia to make decisions on matters of religion. *'Ulama* is an Arabic plural – the singular is *'alim*, a learned man
'Umbara	Covered elephant *howdah* (qv)
Umrah	Nobleman
Unani	Ionian (or Byzantine Greek) medicine, originally passed to the Islamic world through Byzantine exiles in Persia and still practised in India today

'Urs	Festival day
Ustad	The master (or teacher) of an art
Vakil	Ambassador or representative (though in modern usage the word means merely lawyer)
Vilayat	Province, homeland
Zamindar	Landholder or local ruler
Zenana	Harem, or women's quarters

NOTES

Introduction

1. National Archives of India (hereafter NAI), Foreign Department, Political, November 1862, p. 204/62.
2. Frances W. Pritchett, *Nets of Awareness: Urdu Poetry and Its Critics*, University of California Press, Berkeley and Los Angeles, 1994, p. 10.
3. NAI, Foreign, Foreign Dept, Misc., vol. 361, *Precis of Palace Intelligence*. For oil rubbing see entry for Monday, 29 March 1852; for hunting, see entry for Thursday, 13 April 1852; for visiting gardens, see Friday, 16 April 1852; for enjoying moonlight, see entry for Saturday, 10 September; for infidelities of BSZ's concubines, see entry for Saturday, 17 April; for other pregnancies among the imperial concubines, see entry for Tuesday, 30 August 1853.
4. Oriental and India Office Collections, British Library (hereafter OIOC), Vibart Papers, Eur Mss 135/19, Vibart to his Uncle Gordon, 22 September 1857.
5. Major W. S. R. Hodson, *Twelve Years of a Soldier's Life in India*, London, 1859, p. 302.
6. Sir George Campbell, *Memoirs of My Indian Career*, 1893, vol. I.
7. W. H. Russell, *My Diary in India*, London, 1860, vol I, p. 60.
8. Ibid., vol. 2, p. 51.
9. Cited in Pritchett, *Nets of Awareness*, p. 29.
10. Cited in Ralph Russell and Khurshid Islam, *Ghalib: Life and Letters*, Delhi, 1994, p. 269.
11. Ralph Russell, *The Oxford Ghalib: Life, Letters and Ghazals*, New Delhi, 2003, pp. 166, 188.
12. James Fergusson, *History of Indian and Eastern Architecture*, London, 1876, p. 594.
13. Lieutenant William Franklin in the 1795 edition of the new *Asiatick Researches*.
14. Lady Maria Nugent, *Journal of a Residence in India* 1811–15, 2 vols, John Murray, London, 1839; vol. 2, p. 9.
15. Irfan Habib, 'The Coming of 1857', *Social Scientist*, vol. 26, no. 1, January–April 1998, p. 6.
16. The collection was catalogued in 1921. See *Press List of Mutiny Papers 1857 Being a Collection of the Correspondence of the Mutineers at Delhi, Reports of Spies to English Officials and Other Miscellaneous Papers*, Imperial Records Dept, Calcutta, 1921.
17. Vincent Smith, *Oxford History of India*, Oxford, 1923, p. 731.
18. NAI, Mutiny Papers: bird catcher – collection 67, no. 50, 14 July; horse trader

– collection 67, no. 76, 27 July; gamblers – collection 62, no. 80, 3 August; confectioners – collection 61, no. 296, 4 August.

19. NAI, Mutiny Papers: Hasni the dancer – collection 62, no. 84 (no date); kebab seller – collection 103, no. 132, 10 July; Manglu the courtesan – collection 60, no. 605, 29 August.

20. It is true that several scholars – notably Aslam Parvez and Mahdi Hussain – have already drawn glancingly on some of the material in the Mutiny Papers, and Margrit Pernau has used it extensively for her forthcoming study of the Muslims of nineteenth-century Delhi, but I believe this book is the first time a properly systematic use has been made of the material for the study of Delhi in 1857.

21. Margrit Pernau is currently embarking on a project to translate and publish these riches as well as the court *Akhbarat*, which preceded the printed newspapers. Up to now scholars have used only the brief passages which are translated in Nadar Ali Khan's *A History of Urdu Journalism 1822–1857* (New Delhi, 1991).

22. The only historian of Delhi who seems to have used the Punjab Archive seems to be Sylvia Shorto, who drew on the material for her fascinating thesis, *Public Lives, Private Places, British Houses in Delhi 1803–57*; unpublished dissertation, NYU, 2004.

23. Eric Stokes, *The Peasant and the Raj – Studies in Agrarian Society and Peasant Rebellion in Colonial India*, London, 1978; Stokes, *The Peasant Armed: The Indian Revolt of 1857*, ed. C. A. Bayly, Oxford, 1986; Rudrangshu Mukherjee, *Avadh in Revolt 1857–8 – A Study of Popular Resistance*, New Delhi, 1984; Tapti Roy, *The Politics of a Popular Uprising: Bundelkhand in 1857*, Oxford, 1994.

24. See Mukherjee, *Avadh in Revolt*.

25. *Dihli Urdu Akhbar*, 17 May 1857.

26. Ibid., 24 May 1857.

27. Ibid., 23 August 1857.

28. Ghalib routinely referred to the mutineers as 'blacks' in both his public works – such as *Dastanbuy* – and his private correspondence. See, for example, Russell, *The Oxford Ghalib*, p. 167.

29. This is well argued by Rudrangshu Mukherjee in his excellent short monograph, *Mangal Pandey: Brave Martyr or Accidental Hero?*, New Delhi, 2005, p. 63.

30. Though of course there were those who resisted the Mughal claim, such as the Nawabs of Avadh and, farther away, Tipu Sultan.

31. Rudrangshu Mukherjee, '"Satan Let Loose upon Earth": The Kanpur Massacres in India in the Revolt of 1857, *Past and Present*, no. 128, pp. 110–11.

32. Akhtar Qamber, *The Last Mushaiirah of Delhi: A Translation of Farhatullah Baig's Modern Urdu Classic Dehli ki Akhri Shama*, New Delhi, 1979, p. 62.

33. Emily Eden, *Up the Country, Letters from India*, London, 1930, p. 97.

34. This important point was well argued by F. W. Buckler (1891–1960) in his righly celebrated essay 'The Political Theory of the Indian Mutiny', *Trans. of the Royal Historical Soc.*, 4 series, 5, 1922, pp. 71–100 (also reprinted in

Legitimacy and Symbols: The South Asian writings of F. W. Buckler, ed. M.
N. Pearson, Center for South and Southeast Asian Studies, University of
Michigan, Ann Arbor, MI, *c.* 1985.

35. Mark Thornhill, *Personal Adventures and Experiences of a Magistrate,
during the Rise, Progress and Suppression of the Indian Mutiny*, London,
1884, p. 7.

36. NAI, Mutiny Papers, collection 60, no. 830.

37. OIOC, Eur Mss B 138, *The City of Delhi during 1857*, translation of the
account of Said Mobarak Shah.

38. Quoted by the prosecution in the concluding speech at the trial of Zafar,
*Proceedings on the Trial of Muhammad Bahadur Shah, Titular King of
Delhi, Before a Military Commission, upon a charge of Rebellion, Treason
and Murder, held at Delhi, on the 27th Day of January 1858, and following
days*, London, 1859, p. 142.

39. OIOC, Montgomery Papers, no. 198, 7 September 1857.

40. Fazl ul-Haq, 'The Story of the War of Independence, 1857–8', *Journal Pak.
Hist. Soc.*, vol. V, pt 1, January 1957.

41. See footnote on p. 473.

1: A Chessboard King

1. National Archives of India (hereafter NAI), Foreign, Foreign Dept Misc,
vol. 361, *Precis of Palace Intelligence*, entry for Friday, 2 April 1852. Also
Delhi Gazette (OIOC microfilms), hereafter DG, issue of 31 March 1852;
Munshi Faizuddin, *Bazm i-Akhir, Yani sehr e-Delhi ke do akhiri badshahon
ka tareeq i-maashrat* (The Last Convivial Gathering – the Mode of Life of
the Last Two Kings of Delhi), Lahore, 1965, ch. 7; Zahir Dehlavi, *Dastan i-
Ghadr: An eyewitness account of the 1857 Uprising*, Lahore, 1955 pp. 17–18;
Aslam Parvez, *Bahadur Shah Zafar*, pp. 78–9. Additional details about
Mughal processions have been taken from the description given by Captain
Robert Smith in his journals, cited by Sylvia Shorto, *Public Lives, Private
Places, British Houses in Delhi 1803–57*, unpublished dissertation, NYU, 2004,
p. 136, and from the many images that survive of such processions, such as
that shown in Niall Hobhouse, *Indian Painting for the British 1780–1880*,
London, 2001, item 26, or Emily Bayley (ed. M. M. Kaye), *The Golden Calm:
An English Lady's Life in Moghul Delhi*, London, 1980, pp. 41–3, and
especially pp. 150–59. For an intriguing indication of how the Mughals lit
such night-time wedding processions, albeit two hundred years earlier, see
the images of the night-time *barats* of Shah Shuja and Dara Shukoh in Milo
Cleveland Beach and Ebba Koch, *King of the World: The Padshahnama, an
Imperial Mughal Manuscript from the Royal Library, Windsor Castle*,
London, 1997, pp. 61 and 71.

2. Schoefft was actually in Delhi in 1842 but seems to have painted all his
Mughal portraits from more recent sketches, miniatures or photographs than
those he made on his visit, as the ages of all three of his sitters – Zafar, Mirza

Jawan Bakht and Mirza Mughal – all correspond to their ages in the mid-1850s – perhaps 1854–55 – rather than ten years earlier. There are precedents for this in Schoefft's work: for example, his portrait of Ranjit Singh, who died shortly before his arrival in Lahore, and must presumably therefore have been painted from pre-existing miniatures. The pictures were exhibited for the first time in 1857. I would like to thank Jean-Marie Lafont and F. S. Aijazuddin for their help in solving this conundrum.

3. The two portraits, along with one of Mirza Mughal, hang today in the Mughal room of the Lahore Fort in Pakistan.

4. Zahir Dehlavi, *Dastan i-Ghadr*, Lahore, 1955, p. 19.

5. DG, 31 March 1852.

6. For mehndi procession see NAI, *Precis of Palace Intelligence*, entry for 31 March, and DG, 31 March 1852. For other celebrations and the *sehra*, see also Dehlavi, *Dastan i-Ghadr*, p. 19. A wedding chaplet is referred to in the entry for the wedding in the *Precis of Palace Intelligence*, Friday, 2 April 1852, and its pearls referred to in the celebratory poems of Ghalib and Zauq; see Muhammad Husain Azad (trans. and ed. Frances Pritchett and Shamsur Rahim Faruqi), *Ab-e Hayat: Shaping the Canon of Urdu Poetry*, New Delhi, 2001, pp. 410–13. From the references to strings of pearls in the poem, this chaplet would seem to be the same object that is being placed over the face of Dara Shukoh by his father Shah Jahan in Beach and Koch, *King of the World*, p. 68, item 25.

7. See, for example, the complaints against him in the Punjab Archive, Lahore (hereafter PAL), Case 1D, item 8, November 1847, where one of the princes describes himself as being 'put to extreme distress by the conduct of Mehboob, the servant of his Majesty'.

8. DG, 31 March 1852.

9. See, for example, NAI, *Precis of Palace Intelligence*, entries for 1 and 4 March.

10. Bishop Reginald Heber, *Narrative of a Journey through the Upper Provinces of India*, London, 1828; vol. 1, p. 563

11. NAI, *Precis of Palace Intelligence*, entry for Friday, 2 April 1852.

12. Mir Taqi Mir, quoted in M. Sadiq, *History of Urdu Literature*, Oxford, 1964, p. 100.

13. Muhammad Saleh Kanbu, quoted by Narayani Gupta, 'From Architecture to Archaeology: The "Monumentalising" of Delhi's History in the Nineteenth Century', in Jamal Malik (ed.), *Perspectives of Mutual Encounters in South Asian History, 1760–1860*, Leiden, 2000.

14. Azad (ed.), *Divan-e-Zauq*, p. 145, cited in in Frances W. Pritchett, *Nets of Awareness: Urdu Poetry and its Critics*, University of California Press, Berkeley and Los Angeles, 1994, p. 6.

15. Muhammad Khalid Masud, 'The World of Shah Abdul Aziz, 1746–1824', p. 304, in Jamal Malik (ed.), *Perspectives of Mutual Encounters in South Asian History, 1760–1860*, Leiden 2000. For apes and hogs, see Farhan Ahmad Nizami, *Madrasahs, Scholars and Saints: Muslim Response to the British Presence in Delhi and the Upper Doab 1803–1857*, unpublished PhD, Oxford, 1983, p. 175.

16. Sir Sayyid Ahmad Khan, *Asar us Sanadid*, Delhi, 1990, vol. 2, pp. 11–13.

17. Azad, *Ab-e Hayat*, p. 53.
18. Cited in Pritchett, *Nets of Awareness*, p. 10. The introduction to the English translation of *My Life* by Nawab Sarvar ul-Mulk remarks, 'the original autobiography is in Urdu and is written in the choice language and in a style which would only be attained by a Delhi man, and one who had intimate associations with the Red Fort, where the best and most elegant Urdu was spoken'. Sarvar ul-Mulk, *My Life, Being the Autobiography of Nawab Server ul Mulk Bahadur*, trans. from the Urdu by his son, Nawab Jiwan Yar Jung Bahadur, London, 1903.
19. Pritchett, *Nets of Awareness*, p. 10.
20. NAI, *Precis of Palace Intelligence*, entry for Friday, 2 April 1852.
21. François Bernier, *Travels in the Mogul Empire, 1656–68*, ed. Archibald Constable, trans. Irving Brock, Oxford, 1934, p. 373.
22. British Library, Warren Hastings papers, William Palmer to Warren Hastings, Add. Mss 29, 172, vol XLI, 1790, p. 184; 21st NOVEMBER 1790 AGRA: 'I applied to the Shah [Alam] in your name for permission to transcribe his copy of the Mahbharrut, and was assured that it would have been most cheerfully granted if the book had been in his possession, but his library had been totally plundered & destroyed by that villain Ghullam Khauder Khan, and he added, not without some degree of indignation, that part of the books had been purchased at Lucknow, that is by the Vizier; & upon enquiry find this to be the case, for his Excellency produced some of them to the English Gentlemen, boasting that they were the "King's".'
23. Quoted in Pritchett, *Nets of Awareness*, p. 3.
24. NAI, *Precis of Palace Intelligence*, entry for Thursday, 23 January 1851: 'A petition was received from Mirza Shoojat Shah stating that a chief had arrived from the District at Dehlee and was desirous of visiting the Palace. HM replied that without the Agent's permission no chief of a foreign territory could be allowed entrance.'
25. For example, NAI, *Precis of Palace Intelligence*, entry for 5 December 1851.
26. For example, NAI, *Precis of Palace Intelligence*, entry for 14 March 1851.
27. Ibid., entries for 3 and 8 April 1852. A *khilat* was a symbolic acceptance of the fealty offered in the *nazr*.
28. Parvez, *Bahadur Shah Zafar*, pp. 351–6. Parvez is undoubtedly right to point to the degree to which these themes dominate Zafar's verse, but it is also true that the cage, the bulbul and the garden are common tropes in eighteenth- and nineteenth-century ghazal writing. The unusual degree of pain and frustration expressed in Zafar's poetry has however also been commented on by Arsh Taimuri.
29. Naim Ahmad, *Shahr ashob*, Maktabah Jami'ah, Delhi, 1968, p. 196. Cited in Pritchett, *Nets of Awareness*, p. 5.
30. Quoted in J. K. Majumdar, *Raja Rammohun Roy and the Last Moghuls: A Selection from Official Records (1803–1859)*, Art Press, Calcutta, 1939, pp. 319–20.
31. Ibid. p. 4.
32. For Metcalfe renouncing his allegiance, see Bentinck Papers, Nottingham University, Charles Metcalfe to Lord W. Bentinck, Pw Jf 1637, Calcutta, 18 April 1832; for ceasing to give *nazrs*, see Charles Metcalfe to Lord W.

Bentinck, Pw Jf 1620, Calcutta, 18 December 1831; also, Charles Metcalfe to Lord W. Bentinck, Pw Jf 1607, Calcutta, 13 November: talking of giving *nazrs*, Metcalfe remarks: 'It is what in some degree what will be probably be done by the King of Dihlee & was done to Lord Amherst & there it is not amiss, because the superiority of the King is acknowledged and the nature of the acknowledgement cannot be mistaken.'

33. Shorto, *Public Lives*, p. 134.

34. Quoted by C. M. Naim in his forthcoming essay on Sahbai in Margrit Pernau (ed.), *Delhi College*, New Delhi, 2006.

35. This wonderful translation is by Ralph Russell. See Russell, *The Oxford Ghalib: Life, Letters and Ghazals*, New Delhi, 2003, p. 18.

36. The name of the poem is a reference to the wedding veil of pearls that the Mughals used to fix over the face of princes who were getting married. See note 6 above.

37. NAI, *Precis of Palace Intelligence*, entry for 17 April 1852.

38. Azad, *Ab-e Hayat*, pp. 410–13.

39. Ishtiaq Husain Qureshi, 'A Year in Pre Mutiny Delhi – 1837 A.C.', *Islamic Culture*, 17, pt 3, 1943, pp. 282–97.

40. For Zafar's wives, see Parvez, *Bahadur Shah Zafar*, pp. 81–5; for concubines, see NAI, *Precis of Palace Intelligence*, entry for Friday, 29 July 1853.

41. NAI, *Precis of Palace Intelligence*, entry for Saturday, 17 April 1852.

42. Delhi Commissioner's Office (hereafter DCO) Archive, Delhi, File 65A, 7 December 1858, *Report on the Character and Conduct of the Attendants of the ex royal King*, remarks: 'This lady was once a reputed beauty and attracted the admiration of the ex-king who contracted marriage with her notwithstanding that she was of low caste, a mere dommee. Their matrimonial life was not without its troubles. The Begum Zeenat Mahal, the King's favourite wife and the mother of MJB incited a great aversion to her and for two or three years before the outbreak Taj Mahal was in disgrace and imprisoned in consequence of her reputed intrigue with Mirza Kamran, a nephew of the ex-King, but as she alleges on account of Zeenat Mahal's jealousy and distaste.'

43. For example, NAI, *Precis of Palace Intelligence*, entries for 21 February 1851, 25 September 1852 and 4 October 1852.

44. NAI, *Precis of Palace Intelligence*, entries for 27 January and 6 February 1852. Other references to scandals, and accusations of impropriety, in the imperial harem can be found in the entries for 13 January 1851, 6 August 1852 and 30 August 1853.

45. Russell, *The Oxford Ghalib*, p. 274. Not all the *salatin* were poor. The court diary contains the bequests of several of them and it was not unusual for them to leave estates of up to Rs5 lakh. See, e.g., NAI, *Precis of Palace Intelligence*, entry for 29 December 1851.

46. Major George Cunningham, quoted in T. G. P. Spear, 'The Mogul Family and the Court in 19th Century Delhi', *Journal of Indian History*, vol. XX, 1941, p. 40.

47. NAI, *Precis of Palace Intelligence*, entries for 29 January 1851, 19 February 1851 and 11 April 1852.

48. Ibid., entry for Monday, 8 July 1853.
49. PAL, Case 1D, item 8, November 1847.
50. PAL, Case 94 (wrongly indexed as Case 84), Delhi, 5 February 1848.
51. Mirza Fakhru's full name was Mirza Ghulam Fakhruddin.
52. PAL, Case 1, 45, BSZ to James Thomason, 19 January 1849.
53. PAL, Case 1, pt VII, 67, letter from Sir Thomas Metcalfe (TTM) to Thornton, 24 January 1852.
54. NAI, *Precis of Palace Intelligence*, entry for 9 March 1852.
55. Ibid., entries for 14 February, 27 February and 3 March 1852.
56. PAL, Case 1, 63, 4 December 1851. Sending disgraced courtiers to Mecca was an old Mughal custom.
57. PAL, Case 1, 63, 4 December 1851, letter from TTM to Thornton.
58. For the link between the scale of the wedding and Zinat Mahal's ambitions for Jawan Bakht, see Dehlavi, *Dastan i-Ghadr*, p. 19. For MJB referred to as heir apparent, see DG (OIOC microfilms), 31 March 1852.
59. Sadly this much-repeated and thoroughly delightful story may well be apocryphal: certainly I have been unable to trace it back farther than Edward Thompson's *The Life of Charles Lord Metcalfe* (Faber, London, 1937, p. 101), where it is described as 'local tradition . . . this sounds like folklore'. It may well have been inspired by the famous miniature of Ochterlony in the India Office Library. In his will, OIOC L/AG/34/29/37, Ochterlony mentions only one *bibi*, 'Mahruttun, entitled Moobaruck ul-Nissa Begum and often called Begum Ochterlony', who was the mother of his two daughters, although his son Roderick Peregrine Ochterlony was clearly born of a different *bibi*. Nevertheless, it is quite possible that the story could be true: I frequently found Old Delhi traditions about such matters confirmed by research, and several Company servants of the period kept harems of this size. Judging by Bishop Heber's description of him, Ochterlony was clearly Indianised enough to have done so.
60. Emily Bayley quoted in Kaye, *The Golden Calm*, pp. 124–8.
61. Ibid., pp. 125–6.
62. For example, PAL, Case 1, item 45, January 1849, letter from TTM to BSZ, dated 27 May 1849.
63. Emily Bayley quoted in Kaye, *The Golden Calm*, p. 35.
64. Ibid., Sir Thomas Metcalfe's reflection on Humayun's Tomb.
65. Both are now in OIOC.
66. See, for example, South Asian Studies Library, Cambridge, Campbell Metcalfe Papers, Box VIII, From TTM to Daughters, datelined Camp Sudder Sarai, 27th (no month, no year).
67. South Asian Studies Library, Cambridge, Campbell Metcalfe Papers, Box VIII, From TTM to Georgina, datelined Kootub, 22nd (no month, no year given but clearly April 1851).
68. The nature of this illegal act is sadly not specified here, but there is reference elsewhere in TTM's correspondence to Theo wrongly imprisoning an influential moneylender, which may be the misdemeanour referred to here.
69. South Asian Studies Library, Cambridge, Campbell Metcalfe Papers, Box 1, GG to EC, Saturday, 23 October 1852.

70. Ibid.
71. South Asian Studies Library, Cambridge, Campbell Metcalfe Papers, Box VIII, TTM to GG datelined Kootub, 15th (no month, no year given but clearly October 1852).

2 : Believers and Infidels

1. Bodleian Library of Commonwealth & African Studies at Rhodes House Missionary Collections, Oxford, Jennings Papers, *Proposed Mission at Delhi*.
2. Jennings Papers, *Copies of Letters by the Revd Midgeley Jennings, Chaplain of Delhi 1851–57*, JMJ to Hawkins, 4 May 1852.
3. Jennings Papers, *Proposed Mission at Delhi*.
4. Bodleian Library of Commonwealth & African Studies at Rhodes House Missionary Collections, Oxford, *A Memoir of my Father – the Revd M.J. Jennings, M.A.*, p. 24.
5. Ibid., pp. 13, pp. 21. For Douglas, see also SPG (Society for the Propagation of the Gospels) Annual Report for 1857, pxciii.
6. South Asian Studies Library, Cambridge, Campbell Metcalfe Papers, Box VIII, TTM to his children, Letter from Camp before Hissar, 7 February (no year); TTM to his daughters, Delhi, 6 April (no year); Theo to Lady Campbell in Ferozepur, undated but probably 1854.
7. *Dihli Urdu Akhbar*, 12 July 1857.
8. *Delhi Gazette*, 8 April 1855.
9. Campbell Metcalfe Papers, Box VIII, TTM to his daughters, Delhi, 6 April (no year).
10. Derrick Hughes, *The Mutiny Chaplains*, Salisbury, 1991, p. 28.
11. Fanny Parkes, *Wanderings of a Pilgrim in Search of the Picturesque*, London, 1850, reprinted London, 1992, as *Begums, Thugs and White Mughals*, ed. William Dalrymple, p. xvi.
12. Hughes, *The Mutiny Chaplains*, p. 20.
13. Quoted by Charles Allen, *Soldier Sahibs: The Men Who Made the North-West Frontier*, London, 2000, p. 340.
14. Quoted in Christopher Hibbert, *The Great Mutiny: India 1857*, London, 1978, p. 52.
15. Ibid., p. 52.
16. Olive Anderson, 'The Growth of Christian Militarism in Mid Victorian Britain', *English Historical Review*, vol. 86, 1971, pp. 46–72. For quote see p. 52.
17. Hibbert, *The Great Mutiny*, pp. 51–2. Also Saul David, *The Indian Mutiny 1857*, London, 2002, pp. 72–3.
18. P. J. Marshall (ed.), *The British Discovery of Hinduism*, Cambridge, 1970, p. 42.
19. Quoted by A. N. Wilson, *The Victorians*, London, 2002, p. 202, and Niall Ferguson, *Empire: How Britain Made the Modern World*, London, 2003, pp. 136, 137.

20. Jennings Papers, *Copies of Letters by the Revd Midgeley Jennings, Chaplain of Delhi 1851–57*, JMJ to Hawkins, 22 November 1855.
21. Farhan Ahmad Nizami, *Madrasahs, Scholars and Saints: Muslim Response to the British Presence in Delhi and the Upper Doab 1803–1857*, unpublished PhD, Oxford, 1983, pp. 166–92.
22. Farhan Nizami discusses the case of Maulawi Abdul Ali and Muhammad Ismail Londoni, both of whom married British women. See Farhan Nizami., 'Islamization and Social Adjustment: the Muslim Religious Elite in British North India 1803–57', in *Ninth European Conference on Modern South Asian Studies*, 9–12 July 1986, South Asian Institute of Heidelberg University, p. 5.
23. Nizami, *Madrasahs, Scholars and Saints*, p. 196.
24. Averil Ann Powell, *Muslims and Missionaries in Pre Mutiny India*, Curzon Press, London, 1993, pp. 52–3.
25. Victor Jacquemont, *Letters from India (1829–32)*, 2 vols, trans. Catherine Phillips, Macmillan, London, 1936, p. 354.
26. Khalid Masud, *The World of Shah Abdul Aziz, 1746–1824*, p. 304, in Jamal Malik (ed.), *Perspectives of Mutual Encounters in South Asian History, 1760–1860*, Leiden, 2000. The ultimate source for Shah Abdul Aziz's relationship with Fraser is the *Malfazat* of Aziz where the information is given in the context of showing how the British were overcome with Aziz's learning and miraculous powers.
27. Fraser Papers, vol. 29 (private collection, Inverness, as listed by the National Register of Archives, Scotland). Letter from WF to his father, 8 February 1806.
28. Ralph Russell and Khurshid Islam, *Ghalib: Life and Letters*, OUP, Delhi, 1994, p. 53.
29. Jacquemont, *Letters from India*, VJ to his father, Delhi, 10 January 1831, pp. 344–5.
30. Ibid., pp. 150–1, 354.
31. Fraser Papers, vol. 29, letter from WF to his father, 8 February 1806.
32. Reginald Heber, *A Narrative of a Journey through the Upper Provinces of India from Calcutta to Bombay, 1824–1825*, 3 vols, London, 1827, vol. 2, pp. 362, 392.
33. Bengal Wills 1825, OIOC, L/AG/34/29/37, pp. 185–205.
34. For Mubarak Begum's background see the Mubarak Bagh papers in the archives of the Delhi Commisoner's Office: DCO F5/1861. Here it is recorded that 'Mubarik ul Nissa was originally a girl of Brahmin parentage, who was brought from Poona in the Deckan by one Mosst. Chumpa, and presented or sold by the said Chumpa to Genl. Ochterlony when 12 years of age. Mosst. Mubarik ul Nissa from that time resided in Genl. Ochterlony's house, and Mosst. Chumpa resided with her there, being known by the name of Banbahi'.
35. National Army Museum, London, Gardner Papers, Letter 90, 16 August 1821.
36. Gardner Papers, Letter 16, p. 42.
37. For Ochterlony wondering whether to bring up his children as Muslims, see Sutherland Papers, Oriental and India Office Collections, British Library (hereafter OIOC), Eur Mss. D. 547, pp. 133–4. The letter is written to Major

Hugh Sutherland, a Scottish mercenary commanding a regiment of Mahratta's troops, who, like Ochterlony, had married a Muslim begum – and who had opted to bring up his children as Muslims. Ochterlony writes that he doesn't know what to do with his two daughters by Mubarak Begum, and asks for advice. If they are brought up as Christians, he fears they will suffer from the racism of the British: 'My children dear Major,' writes Ochterlony, 'are uncommonly fair, but if educated in the European manner they will in spite of complexion labour under all the disadvantages of being known as the NATURAL DAUGHTERS OF OCHTERLONY BY A NATIVE WOMAN – In that one sentence is compressed all that ill nature inaction and illiberality can convey of which you must have seen numerous instances during your Residence in this country.' Yet for all this, Ochterlony says he still hesitates to bring them up as Muslims, with a view to them marrying into the Mughal aristocracy, as 'I own I could not bear that my child should be one of a numerous haram even were I certain that no other Disadvantages attended this mode of disposal & were I proof against the observations of the world who tho' unjust to the children, would not fail to comment on the Conduct of a father who educated his offspring in Tenets of the Prophet'. The letter ends rather movingly, 'In short my dear M[ajor] I have spent all the time since we were parted in revolving this matter in my mind but I have not yet been able to come to a positive Decision.' The letter is undated but is probably c. 1801–02, and it must immediately pre-date the Anglo-Mahratta war of 1803.

38. Private family papers in the haveli of the late Mirza Farid Beg, Old Delhi.

39. Ram Babu Saksena, *European & Indo-European Poets of Urdu & Persian*, Lucknow, 1941, pp. 100–17.

40. Gardner Papers, NAM 6305–56, Letter 14, Delhi, 6 June 1820.

41. Ibid., Letter 16, p. 41.

42. Nicholas Shreeve, *The Indian Heir*, Bookwright, Arundel, 2001, p. 7.

43. Missionary Collections, *A Memoir of my Father – the Revd M.J. Jennings, M.A.*, typescript mss by 'Miss Jennings, Chenolton, Wimbourne, Dorset'.

44. Hibbert, *The Great Mutiny*, p. 52. The Superintendent of Jails in Agra was C. Thornlute.

45. For Shah Abdul Aziz, see Nizami, *Madrasahs*, p. 157.

46. Ibid., pp. 43–54. Nizami provides evidence that nearly 2 million acres of *ma'afi* land was confiscated by the British between 1828 and 1840. For missionaries living in mosques see Jacquemont, *Letters from India*, VJ to his father, Panipat, 17 March 1830, p. 80.

47. See the proclamation of Begum Hazrat Mahal; the translation of the original is in the NAI, Foreign Department, Political Consultation 17 December 1858, from J. D. Forstythe Sec. to Chief Commr Oudh, to G. J. Edmonstone, Sec. GOI, For. Dept, Dt Lucknow, 4 December 1858.

48. Nizami, *Madrasahs*, pp. 203–4; Powell, *Muslims and Missionaries*, ch. 7, esp. pp. 193–6, 202 and 222.

49. Delhi Committee to the General Committee of Public Instruction, in J. F. Hilliker, 'Charles Edward Trevelyan as an Educational Reformer', *Canadian Journal of History*, 9, 1974, pp. 275–91. Also Michael H. Fisher, 'An Initial

Student of Delhi English College: Mohan Lal Kashmiri (1812–77)', in Margrit Pernau, *Delhi College*, New Delhi, 2006.

50. OIOC, Home Miscellaneous 725, pp. 389–422, *Letter Written by Munshi Mohun Lal to Brigadier Chamberlain dated November 8th 1857 at Dehlie*.

51. Gardner Papers, Letter 100, Babel, 27 September 1821.

52. Fraser Papers, Bundle 350, letter from DO to WF, Delhi, 31 July 1820.

53. Parkes, *Begums*, p. 313.

54. Christopher Hawes, *Poor Relations: The Making of the Eurasian Community in British India 1773–1833*, London, 1996, pp. 4–5.

55. *Delhi Gazette*, 5 January 1856.

56. Jennings Papers, *Copies of Letters by the Revd Midgeley Jennings, Chaplain of Delhi 1851–57*, JMJ to Hawkins, 26 December 1856. Also in the same archive, Calcutta Letters Received, vol. 3 (CLR 14), JMJ to Hawkins, Hissar, 17 March 1854: 'Nor have we been disappointed of our hope of forming a class from the Government College. I have seven boys who read the Bible in English and Bacon's essays on alternate evenings. These lads are with one exception Hindoo. The Musalmans are too bigoted to allow their boys to read English. They have read some of the Christian books in the Govt College library and seem well disposed towards Christianity. They propose some of the most obvious infidels to our own Holy Religion, but apparently without attaching much weight to them: they generally admit the force of my answers. I am very favourably impressed by the intelligence of these young men. I foresee that in their station they will be valuable allies to us.'

57. Jennings Papers, *Copies of Letters by the Revd Midgeley Jennings, Chaplain of Delhi 1851–57*, JMJ to Hawkins, 15 July 1852.

58. *General Report on Public Instruction* 1852–3, quoted in Powell, *Muslims and Missionaries*.

59. See the essay on Azurda by Swapna Liddle Sahbai in Pernau, *Delhi College*.

60. Nizami, *Madrasahs*, p. 173.

61. Leupolt, *Recollections*, p. 33, cited in Nizami, *Madrasahs*, p. 207.

62. Aziz Ahmed, *Studies in Islamic Culture in the Indian Environment*, Oxford, 1964, pp. 201, 210.

63. Nizami, *Islamization and Social Adjustment*, p. 11.

64. Barbara Daly Metcalf, *Islamic Revival in British India, 1860–1900*, Princeton, NJ, 1982, p. 48.

65. Nizami, *Madrasahs*, pp. 144–5.

66. Shah Waliullah was in fact a Sufi himself, but of the hard-line Naqshbandiya *silsilah* (lit. chain – line of sheiks leading a Sufi Brotherhood) which opposed most of the devotional practices of the Chishtias, such as the veneration of saints and the playing of devotional music or qawwalis at Sufi shrines. Just to add to the complexity, it seems Shah Abdul Aziz was actually rather fond of music.

67. NAI, Foreign, Foreign Dept Misc., *Precis of Palace Intelligence*, entry for 17 April 1852.

68. Percival Spear, *The Twilight of the Moghuls*, Cambridge, 1951 p. 74. Also Aslam Parvez, *Bahadur Shah Zafar*, p. 242.

69. *Dihli Urdu Akhbar*, 14 June 1857.

70. Major Archer, *Tours in Upper India*, London, 1833, vol. 1, p. 113.

71. NAI, *Precis of Palace Intelligence*, entry for Sunday, 1 August 1852.

72. Parvez, *Bahadur Shah Zafar*, p. 242.

73. NAI, *Precis of Palace Intelligence*, entry for Tuesday, 16 August 1853.

74. Ibid., entries for 12 January 1851, 29 July 1853 and 1 August 1853.

75. Ibid., entries for 24 April 1851, 4 September 1852, 23 August 1853 and 31 December 1853.

76. Harbans Mukhia, 'Celebration of Failure as Dissent in Urdu Ghazal', *Modern Asian Studies*, vol. 33, no. 4, 1999, pp. 861–81.

77. Ibid., p. 879.

78. Ralph Russell , *Hidden in the Lute: An Anthology of Two Centuries of Urdu Literature*, New Delhi, 1995, p. 150.

79. Ralph Russell (ed.), *Ghalib: The Poet and His Age*, London, 1975, p. 81.

80. Ralph Russell, *The Oxford Ghalib: Life, Letters and Ghazals*, New Delhi, 2003, p. 202.

81. Pavan K. Varma, *Ghalib: The Man, the Times*, New Delhi, 1989, p. 51.

82. This is well argued in Nizami, *Madrasahs*, p. 163.

83. C. F. Andrews, *Zakaullah of Delhi*, Cambridge, 1929, pp. 13–18; David Lelyveld, *Aligarh's First Generation: Muslim Solidarity in British India*, Princeton, NJ, 1978, p. 51. See also Yoginder Sikand, *Bastions of the Believers: Madrasas and Islamic Education in India*, New Delhi, 2005.

84. Parvez, *Bahadur Shah Zafar*, p. 50.

85. NAI, *Precis of Palace Intelligence*. For astrologers, see, for example, entry for Tuesday, 23 August 1853 when BSZ gives a cow to the poor on the advice of his astrologers.

86. NAI, *Precis of Palace Intelligence*, entry for Saturday, 6 March 1852.

87. Ibid., entries for 9, 11, 17, 18 October 1853. On the 18th 'HM sat himself on the silver chair in the DIK and inspected the Royal Stud which had been coloured for the Dusserah festival. The darogah of the King's falconry placed a hawk on HM's hand and the hunters let loose some birds over HM's head. The King bestowed on them the usual khilluts and accepted the nuzzers presented by his Hindu officers – in all Rs 43.'

88. Narayani Gupta, *Delhi between Two Empires 1803–1931*, New Delhi, 1981, p. 10.

89. NAI, *Precis of Palace Intelligence*, entry for Tuesday, 1 November 1853.

90. Ibid., entry for Friday, 28 October 1853.

91. Farhatullah Baig, *Phulwalon ki Sair*. I would like to thank Azra Kidwai for bringing this text to my attention and providing me with her translation of it.

92. NAI, *Precis of Palace Intelligence*, entry for 20 September 1852.

93. Ibid., entry for 21 September 1852.

94. Sir Sayyid Ahmad Khan, *The Causes of the Indian Revolt*, reprint edition introduced by Francis Robinson, Karachi, 2000, p. 9.

95. Zafar personally helped carry the *taziyas* in procession; he also sent donations and *alam* standards to Shia *imambaras* across India. For Zafar attending *marsiyas*, see NAI, *Precis of Palace Intelligence*, entry for Wednesday, 5 October 1853. For sending of offering to *imambaras* elsewhere, see entry for Friday, 7 October 1853: 'HM sent for Mirza Noorooddeen and having

fastened up in a case several standards of silver and copper, entrusted them to him with orders for his immediate departure for Lucknow by dak to place the said standards as offerings from HM at the shrine of Shah Abbas.' There is a long description of Muharram celebrations in the Red Fort in Munshi Faizuddin, *Bazm i-Akhir, Yani sehr e-Delhi ke do akhiri badshahon ka tareeq i-maashrat* (The Last Convivial Gathering – the Mode of Life of the Last Two Kings of Delhi), Lahore, 1965, ch. 7. Zafar asked Ghalib to defend him from this charge. For irate '*ulama* see Ralph Russell, *Ghalib – Life and Letters*, Oxford, 1964, p. 99.

96. See the brilliant essay by Margrit Pernau on class and the radicals, 'Multiple Identities and Communities: Re-contextualizing Religion', in Jamal Malik and Helmut Reifeld, *Religious Pluralism in South Asia and Europe*, New Delhi, 2005, pp. 147–69, especially pp. 160–1. Pernau estimates that a full 10 per cent of Shah Abdul Aziz's fatwas concern economic matters. The British authorities also noted that it was not the *ashraf* but 'the lower orders of the Mahommedans and particularly among the Punjabies' who subscribed to radical Islam. 'Hoosain Buksh' is, however, described as 'the great Punjabee merchant of this city . . . generally considered favourable to the Wahabee sect'. PAL Case 70, no. 152, From: A. A. Roberts Esq., Magistrate Dehlee To: T. Metcalfe, Agent Lieut Governor of the government of NWP Dehlee Dated: Dehlee, 1st Sept 1852 Subject: Fanatics.

97. Nizami, *Madrasahs*, pp. 224–9; Nizami, *Islamization and Social Adjustment*, p. 7; Metcalf, *Islamic Revival in British India*, p. 62.

98. PAL, Case 70, no. 152.

99. Missionary Collections, '*A Memoir of my Father – the Revd M.J. Jennings, M.A.*,' p. 20.

3: An Uneasy Equilibrium

1. *Dihli Urdu Akhbar* (hereafter DUA), 7 August 1853. See also Margit Pernau, 'The *Dihli Urdu Akhbar*: Between Persian Akhbarat and English Newspapers', *Annual of Urdu Studies*, 2003, vol. 18, p. 121.

2. *Subae Shamalio Maghribi ke Akhbara aur Matbuat*, p. 101., cited in Aslam Parvez, *Bahadur Shah Zafar*, p. 316.

3. Pernau, '*Dihli Urdu Akhbar*', p. 126; DUA, 10 May 1840.

4. DUA, 12 May 1841.

5. Frances W. Pritchett, *Nets of Awareness: Urdu Poetry and Its Critics*, University of California Press, Berkeley and Los Angeles, 1994, p. 19.

6. Pernau, '*Dihli Urdu Akhbar*', p. 128; Nadir Ali Khan, *A History of Urdu Journalism*, Delhi 1991, pp. 72–86. Also DUA, 22 and 29 August 1852; for Ramchandra's conversion see DUA, 25 July 1852; for 'sexual vice', 2 May 1841; for the arrest of Ghalib, 15 August 1841.

7. Pernau, '*Dihli Urdu Akhbar*', pp. 123–6.

8. *Delhi Gazette* (hereafter DG), 19 March 1842 (Moti Masjid) and 2 March 1853 (canal).

9. DG, 19 February 1853 (locomotive race); 12 January 1855 (cricket); 27 January 1855 (Hansi dacoitee).

10. Nicholas Shreeve (ed.), *From Nawab to Nabob: The Diary of David Ochterlony Dyce Sombre*, Bookwright, Arundel, 2000, pp. 71 and 75, entries for 5, 6 and 23 December 1834.

11. See Michael Fisher's essay on Mohan Lal Kashmiri in Margrit Pernau's forthcoming volume on Delhi College, New Delhi, 2006.

12. DG, 10 February 1847.

13. Ibid., 19 January 1853.

14. Ibid., 8 January 1855.

15. Ibid., 9 January 1855.

16. Ibid., 8 January 1855.

17. Ibid., 12 February 1843. See also Pernau, '*Dihli Urdu Akbhar*', p. 118.

18. James Baillie Fraser, *Military Memoirs of James Skinner*, 2 vols, Smith, Elder & Co., London, 1851, p. 105.

19. Ibid., pp. 159, 162.

20. Fanny Eden, *Journals*, reprinted as *Tigers, Durbars and Kings*, John Murray, London, 1988, p. 135.

21. Ram Babu Saksena, *European & Indo-European Poets of Urdu & Persian*, Newul Kishore, Lucknow, 1941, pp. 96–7.

22. *Tigers*, p. 135.

23. In a letter to Lord Bentinck in the Nottingham University Library, Pw Jf 2047/1–2, Hansee 12 October 1835, Skinner writes as if he is thinking in Urdu and translating it as best he can into English: 'Regarding my narrative,' he writes, 'if your Lordship thinks it is worth your Lordship's trouble, I am proude to lay it at your feet; do my Lord what you like. I am only sorry that my abilities in the English language was not sufficient as to have given you a better account than what it contains. So my gracious and kind benefactor, consider me as a piece of clay in a potters hand, and you may make me what you like.'

24. Seema Alavi, *The Sepoys and the Company*, OUP, New Delhi, 1995, pp. 254–5. In a letter to Lord Bentinck in the Nottingham University Library, Pw Jf 2047/1–2, Hansee 12 October 1835, Skinner refers to a 'wife' in the singular who sends her best to the Governor General and Lady Bentinck.

25. National Army Museum, London, Gardner Papers, Letter 16, p. 41.

26. South Asian Studies Library, Cambridge, Campbell Metcalfe Papers, Box VIII, Theo to Lady Campbell in Ferozepur, undated but probably 1854.

27. Christopher Hibbert, *The Great Mutiny: India 1857*, London, 1978, p. 34.

28. For Gambier, see National Army Musuem 6211/67, Letters of Lieutenant Charles Henry (Harry) F. Gambier, 38th Native Infantry. For Harriet, see Harriet Tytler, *An Englishwoman in India: The Memoirs of Harriet Tytler 1828–1858*, ed. Anthony Sattin, Oxford, 1986.

29. David Burton, *The Raj at Table: A Culinary History of the British in India*, London, 1993, p. 83.

30. Cited in Farhan Ahmad Nizami, *Madrasahs, Scholars and Saints: Muslim Response to the British Presence in Delhi and the Upper Doab 1803–1857*, unpublished PhD, Oxford, 1983, p. 18.

31. Major General Sir W. H. Sleeman, *Rambles and Recollections of an Indian Official*, Oxford, 1915, pp. 523-4.
32. Hali, *Kulliyat-e Nasir*, vol. 1, p. 344, cited in Pritchett, *Nets of Awareness*, p. 14.
33. Margrit Pernau, 'Middle Class and Secularisation: The Muslims of Delhi in the 19th Century', in Intiz Ahmad, Helmut Reifeld (ed.), *Middle Class Values in India and Western Europe*, New Delhi, 2003, pp. 21-42.
34. Nizami, *Madrasahs*, p. 170, on the surprising openness of the *'ulama* at this period to taking on and absorbing the new innovations and discoveries of Western science.
35. Cited in Ralph Russell, *The Oxford Ghalib: Life, Letters and Ghazals*, New Delhi, 2003, p. 40.
36. Cited in Pritchett, *Nets of Awareness*, p. 14.
37. Sir Sayyid Ahmad Khan, *Asar us-Sanadid*, Delhi, 1990, vol. 2, p. 45.
38. Ibid., vol. 2, p. 45.
39. Narayani Gupta, *Delhi between Two Empires 1803-1931*, New Delhi, 1981, p. 4; Pavan K. Verma, *Mansions at Dusk: The Havelis of Old Delhi*, New Delhi, 1992, pp. 55-63.
40. Charles John Griffiths, *The Siege of Delhi*, London, 1910, p. 4.
41. Johnson diaries, OIOC, Mss Eur A101, entry for 18 July 1850.
42. Munshi Faizuddin, *Bazm i-Akhir, Yani sehr e Delhi ke do akhiri badshahon ka tareeq i-maashrat* (The Last Convivial Gathering – the Mode of Life of the Last Two Kings of Delhi), Lahore, 1965.
43. National Archives of India (hereafter NAI) Foreign, Foreign Dept Misc., *Precis of Palace Intelligence*, entry for Sunday, 4 April 1852.
44. Percival Spear, *The Twilight of the Moghuls*, Cambridge, 1951, p. 74.
45. Faizuddin, *Bazm i-Akhir*.
46. NAI, *Precis of Palace Intelligence*, entry for 13 March 1851.
47. Muhammad Husain Azad (trans. and ed. Frances Pritchett and Shamsur Rahim Faruqi), *Ab-e Hayat: Shaping the Canon of Urdu Poetry*, New Delhi, 2001, p. 343.
48. Antoine Polier, *Shah Alam II and his Court*, Calcutta, 1947, p. 72. For Mirza Fakhru's calligraphy, see the impressive specimens in the OIOC: 3577 and especially 2972/42, a calligraphic lion. See also NAI, *Precis of Palace Intelligence*, entry for 21 February 1851. For Mirza Fakhru's *History*, see NAI, *Precis of Palace Intelligence*, entry for 10 January 1851. For Mirza Fakhru living in the Shah Burj, see NAI, *Precis of Palace Intelligence*, entry for 23 September 1852.
49. Reginald Heber, *A Narrative of a Journey through the Upper Provinces of India from Calcutta to Bombay, 1824-1825*, 3 vols, London, 1827, vol. 1, pp. 568-9.
50. Pritchett, *Nets of Awareness*, p. 4. For his more earthy verse in Punjabi and Braj Basha he used a different pen-name; rather than Zafar ('Victorious') he chose to write under Shuaq Rang ('Passionate').
51. S. M. Burke and Salim al-Din Quraishi, *Bahadur Shah: Last Mogul Emperor of India*, Lahore, 1995, pp. 218-19.
52. Arsh Taimuri, *Qila-i Mua'lla ki Jhalkiyan*, ed. Aslam Parvez, Urdu Academy, Delhi, 1986. See sections on gunmanship and archery.
53. Spear, *Twilight*, p. 73.

54. NAI, *Precis of Palace Intelligence*, entry for Tuesday, 13 January 1852.

55. Emily Bayley, quoted in M. M. Kaye (ed.), *The Golden Calm: An English Lady's Life in Moghul Delhi*, London, 1980, p. 128.

56. Major Archer, *Tours in Upper India*, London, 1833, vol. 1, pp. 108–9.

57. NAI, *Precis of Palace Intelligence*, e.g. entries for Monday, 28 July 1852, Sunday, 1 August 1852, Tuesday, 18 October 1853 and Wednesday, 21 December 1853. Akhtar Qamber, *The Last Mushai'rah of Delhi: A Translation of Farhatullah Baig's Modern Urdu Classic Dehli ki Akhri Shama*, New Delhi, 1979, p. 68.

58. NAI, *Precis of Palace Intelligence*, entry for 12 May 1851; for his marriage, see entry for 23 April.

59. Ibid., entry for Monday, 5 September 1853.

60. Ibid., entry for Tuesday, 26 July 1853.

61. Ibid., entries for 16 January 1852 and 22 September 1853.

62. For fishing, see Ibid., entry for 2 February 1852.

63. Russell, *The Oxford Ghalib*, p. 99.

64. DG, 10 April 1855.

65. E.g. DG, 15 March 1855.

66. Faizuddin, *Bazm i-Akhir*.

67. Quoted in Pritchett, *Nets of Awareness*, p. 14.

68. Burton, *The Raj at Table*, p. 18.

69. Fraser Papers, Inverness, Bundle 366, VJ to Wm Fraser, p. 62, undated but probably February 1831.

70. Emily Bayley, quoted in M. M. Kaye (ed.), *The Golden Calm*, pp. 105, 161.

71. Ibid., p. 213.

72. Fraser Papers, vol. 33, p. 279, Alec Fraser to his mother, Delhi, 3 August 1811.

73. Campbell Metcalfe Papers, Box VIII, Theo to Lady Campbell in Ferozepur, undated but probably 1854.

74. Ibid., Box 1, GG to EC, Saturday, 23 October 1852.

75. DG, 24 March 1857.

76. Emily Bayley, quoted in M. M. Kaye (ed.), *The Golden Calm*, p. 127.

77. Azad, *Ab-e Hayat*, p. 385. Although the story is actually told by a dog, it does seem to reflect the culinary practice of a well-known Delhi figure.

78. Faizuddin, *Bazm i-Akhir*, goes into lengthy detail on all this, and is one of the most startlingly detailed sources for the doings of the Red Fort kitchens. Some of the dishes mentioned can still be sampled at Karims Hotel next to the Jama Masjid, which was founded by cooks from the former royal kitchens after 1857.

79. NAI, *Precis of Palace Intelligence*, entry for Wednesday, 10 August 1852. For kebabs and stew and oranges, see Taimuri, *Qila-i mualla ki Jhalkiyan*.

80. NAI, *Precis of Palace Intelligence*, entry for 26 September 1853.

81. Russell, *The Oxford Ghalib*, p. 50.

82. Ibid., p. 183.

83. Ibid., p. 190.

84. Khan, *Asar us Sanadid*, vol.2, p. 230.

85. NAI, *Precis of Palace Intelligence*, entries for 10 September 1853 and 4 October 1853.

86. Faizuddin, *Bazm i-Akhir*.
87. NAI, *Precis of Palace Intelligence*, entry for Tuesday, 9 August 1852.
88. Dargah Quli Khan, *The Muraqqa' e-Dehli*, trans. Chander Shekhar, New Delhi, 1989, p. 50.
89. For Ad Begum, ibid., p. 107; for Nur Bai, ibid., p. 110. Both these courtesans were at the height of their fame in 1739, at the time of the invasion of Nadir Shah.
90. Saksena, *European & Indo-European Poets*, pp. 73–4.
91. Qamber, *The Last Mushai'rah of Delhi*, p. 60.

4: The Near Approach of the Storm

1. Oriental and India Office Collections, British Library (hereafter OIOC), Photo Eur 31 1B, Hardcastle Papers, pp. 247–62.
2. Ibid.
3. Ibid.
4. Ibid.
5. Ibid.
6. National Archives of India (hereafter NAI) Foreign, Foreign Dept, *Precis of Palace Intelligence*, entry for Thursday, 3 November 1853.
7. James Thomason, the Lieutenant Governor of the North West Provinces, died in Bareilly on 29 September, while Sir Henry Elliot, the Foreign Secretary, died at the Cape, on his way back to England, on 20 December.
8. Harriet Tytler, *An Englishwoman in India: The Memoirs of Harriet Tytler 1828–1858*, ed. Anthony Sattin, Oxford, 1986, p. 143.
9. OIOC, Fraser Collection, Eur Mss E258, Bundle 8, SF to SJGF, 25 March 1857.
10. For Annie's choir, see Bodleian Library of Commonwealth & African Studies at Rhodes House, Oxford, Missionary Collections, *A Memoir of my Father – the Revd M.J. Jennings, M.A.*, pp. 13, 38. For Annie's engagement, see Tytler, *An Englishwoman in India*. For Fraser joining the choir, see Fraser Collection, Mss Eur E258, Bundle 8, SF to SJGF, Delhi, 25 March 1857.
11. Fraser Collection, Mss Eur E258, Bundle 8, SF to SJGF, 21 April (?) 1854.
12. Ibid., SF to SJGF, Mynpoorie, 14 August (no year but possibly 1843).
13. Ibid., SF to SJGF, 21 April 1854, 25 March 1857.
14. NAI, *Precis of Palace Intelligence*. Fraser's arrival in Delhi is reported in the entry for Friday, 24 November 1853; a reception at Raushanara Bagh is planned for 1 December, but the Agent does not turn up, although he does pay a sightseeing visit to the Red Fort in the company of some friends when BSZ is away on Thursday the 8th. He waits for another couple of weeks before bothering to come and introduce himself on Thursday, 22 December 1853. BSZ prepares for his reception by organising a frantic bout of spring-cleaning and repairs.
15. NAI, Foreign Consultations, Item 180–193, 29 August 1856, From S Fraser Esq

Agent Lt Gov NWP, Dehlie Dated Dehlie 14th July 1856. For Fraser's retirement see the *Delhi Gazette* (DG), 12 July 1856.

16. NAI, Foreign Consultations, Item 180-193, 29 August 1856, 'Translation of a Shooqua from His Majesty the King of Dehlie to Simon Fraser Esquire Agent of Honble the Lt Gov,' dated 12 July 1856. This of course was exactly the humiliating treatment suffered by Zafar himself at the hands of his father Akbar Shah.

17. Ibid., pp. 319ff.

18. Michael Maclagan, *'Clemency' Canning*, London, 1962, pp. 38–44. See also Christopher Hibbert, *The Great Mutiny: India 1857*, London, 1978, pp. 25–7. Saul David, *The Indian Mutiny*, London, 2002, pp. 14–15.

19. NAI, Foreign Consultations, Item 180-193, 29 August 1856, Minute by Canning, the Governor General, 12 August 1856.

20. Ibid.

21. *Proceedings on the Trial of Muhammad Bahadur Shah, Titular King of Delhi, before a Military Commission, upon a charge of Rebellion, Treason and Murder, held at Delhi, on the 27th Day of January 1858, and following days*, London, 1859 (hereafter Trial), p. 80.

22. NAI, *Siraj ul-Akbhar*, 19 March 1857.

23. See Salim al-Din Quraishi, *Cry for Freedom: Proclamations of Muslim Revolutonaries of 1857*, Lahore, 1997, for reports in the Delhi press of the different manifestations of unrest in early 1857. The puris were reported in the *Nur-i Maghrebi* in the issue of 25 February 1857, while news of the mutiny in the Bengal Army appeared in the same paper's issue of 20 April 1857. See also the evidence of Metcalfe, Trial, pp. 80–81.

24. Anon. (probably Robert Bird), *Dacoitee in Excelsis, or the Spoilation of Oude by the East India Company*, London, 1857.

25. Ibid., iv–v, pp. 202–4.

26. Ibid., vi.

27. Quoted in S. M. Burke and Salim al-Din Quraishi, *Bahadur Shah: Last Mogul Emperor of India*, Lahore, 1995, p. 78.

28. Punjab Archives, Lahore, Case 1, 71, dated 24 February 1856.

29. Ralph Russell, *The Oxford Ghalib: Life, Letters and Ghazals*, New Delhi, 2003, p. 135.

30. Ibid., p. 113.

31. Hali, *Yadgar-e-Ghalib*, pp. 28–9, cited in Ralph Russell and Khurshid Islam, *Ghalib: Life and Letters*, Oxford, 1969, p. 63.

32. Ibid., pp. 73–4.

33. Russell, *The Oxford Ghalib*, p. 89.

34. Ibid., p. 112

35. Ibid., p. 112, and Gopi Chand Narang, 'Ghalib and the Rebellion of 1857', in Narang, *Urdu Language and Literature: Critical Perspectives*, New Delhi, 1991, p. 16, note 45.

36. Pavan K. Verma, *Ghalib: The Man, the Times*, New Delhi, 1989, p. 61.

37. Ghalib, *Dastanbuy* p. 48, cited in Pritchett, *Nets of Awareness: Urdu Poetry and Its Critics*, University of California Press, Berkeley and Los Angeles, 1994, p. 9; also Varma, *Ghalib*, pp. 142–3.

38. South Asian Studies Library, Cambridge, Campbell Metcalfe Papers, Box 8 (no date but clearly 1856).

39. Ibid., Box 8, Theo to GG, 12 August 1856.

40. Ibid., Box 8, Theo to EC (undated but April 1857).

41. Ibid., Box 6, EC to GG, datelined Camp Near Mooltan, 27 November 1856.

42. Ibid., Box 6, EC to GG (undated but probably late 1856/early 1857).

43. The best and fullest description of that old Indian historical chestnut, the greased cartridges, can be found in Chapter 6 of David, *The Indian Mutiny*. There is also a very good chapter in Rudrangshu Mukherjee's brief but brilliant *Mangal Pandey: Brave Martyr or Accidental Hero?*, New Delhi, 2005.

44. The fouling and clogging of the Enfields is also recorded by Richard Barter, *The Siege of Delhi*, London, 1984, p. 6.

45. Mukherjee, *Mangal Pandey*, p. 35. According to a letter of 7 February 1857, Canning stated that the fears regarding the grease 'were well founded'.

46. J. W. Kaye, *A History of the Sepoy, War in India 1857–8*, London 1877, vol 1, pp. 316–18.

47. Irfan Habib, 'The Coming of 1857', *Social Scientist*, vol. 26, no. 1, January–April 1998, p. 6.

48. Sitaram Pandey, *From Sepoy to Subedar*, London, 1873, pp. 24–5. Some scholars have questioned the authenticity of this book; it may have been written by a Briton under a pseudonym or as the ghostwriter of a sepoy. My personal suspicion is that it is the latter, for the tone reads true to my ears, and it is difficult to believe it is an outright forgery, especially when compared with the sepoy's letter from the DG, 8 May 1855 (see note below), which is clearly a fake.

49. DG, 8 May 1855. The article is full of British assumptions, usages and stereotypes about Indians and cannot actually have been written by a sepoy as it purported to be.

50. Tytler, *An Englishwoman in India*, p. 81.

51. Ibid., pp. 110–11.

52. Ibid., p. 111.

53. Hibbert, *The Great Mutiny*, p. 72.

54. K. C. Yadav, *The Revolt of 1857 in Haryana*, New Delhi, 1977, p. 41.

55. OIOC, Home Misc. 725, *Kaye Mutiny Papers*, Item 35.

56. H. H. Greathed, *Letters Written during the Siege of Delhi*, London, 1858, p.xiv.

57. Tytler, *An Englishwoman in India*, p. 114.

58. 'How the Electric Telegraph Saved India', reprinted in Col. Edward Vibart, *The Sepoy Mutiny as Seen by a Subaltern from Delhi to Lucknow*, London, 1858, pp. 253–7.

59. Julia Haldane, *The Story of Our Escape from Delhi in 1857*, Agra, 1888, p. 2.

60. Tytler, *An Englishwoman in India*, p. 114; see also Charles Theophilus Metcalfe, *Two Native Narratives of the Mutiny in Delhi*, London, 1898, 'Narrative of Mainodin', p. 42.

5: The Sword of the Lord of Fury

1. Zahir Dehlavi, *Dastan i-Ghadr: An eyewitness account of the 1857 Uprising*, Lahore, 1955, p. 38.

2. Ibid., p. 44. For the King's stick, see *Proceedings on the Trial of Muhammad Bahadur Shah, Titular King of Delhi, before a Military Commission, upon a charge of Rebellion, Treason and Murder, held at Delhi, on the 27th Day of January 1858, and following days*, London, 1859 (hereafter Trial), p. 26, Evidence of Ghulam Abbas. There are several accounts of the King's movements that morning which mutually contradict each other, especially as to when Zafar became aware of the sepoys' presence, and at what point Douglas and the hakim appeared. I have gone with Zahir Dehlavi's version of events as it is the most detailed and seems particularly credible and well informed, even though the account was written – or reached its final form – many years after the events it describes.

3. Dehlavi, *Dastan i-Ghadr*, p. 44. On the death of the toll keeper and the servants, see *The City of Delhi during 1857*, translation of the account of Said Mobarak Shah, Oriental and India Office Collections, British Library (hereafter OIOC), Eur Mss, B 138.

4. Trial, Evidence of Jat Mall, p. 72. According to Jat Mall's evidence at Zafar's trial: 'I heard a few days before the outbreak from some sepoys of the gate of the palace, that it had been arranged in case greased cartridges were pressed upon them, that the Meerut troops were to come here, where they were to be joined by the Delhi troops, and it was said that this compact had been arranged through some native officers, who went over on court martial duty to Meerut.' If this is right, then Tytler's subahdar-major and close friend, Mansur Ali, may actually have been one of the mutineers.

5. Trial, p. 78, Evidence of Makhan, mace bearer of Captain Douglas, and p. 88, evidence of Hakim Ahsanullah Khan.

6. Ibid., pp. 26–7, Evidence of Ghulam Abbas.

7. OIOC Eur Mss B 138, *Account of Said Mobarak Shah*.

8. National Archives of India (hereafter NAI), Mutiny Papers, Collection 56, no. 7, Defence of the King.

9. Ibid.

10. Trial, pp. 26–7, Evidence of Ghulam Abbas.

11. NAI, Mutiny Papers, Collection 56, no. 7, Defence of the King.

12. Ibid.

13. South Asian Studies Library, Cambridge, Campbell Metcalfe Papers, Box 8, Theo to EC (undated but ?April 1857). Also, from the same box, typescript mss by Emily Bayley, *Account of the escape of Sir Theophilus Metcalfe from Delhi after the Outbreak of the Mutiny*. Also OIOC, Eur Mss D610, Theophilus Metcalfe file. For his prophecy, see Wilkinson, Johnson and Osborn, *The Memoirs of the Gemini Generals*, London, 1896, p. 30.

14. Charles Theophilus Metcalfe, *Two Native Narratives of the Mutiny in Delhi*, London, 1898, 'Narrative of Mainodin', p. 44.

15. For the building of the magazine on the site of Dara Shukoh's palace, see Sylvia Shorto, *Public Lives, Private Places, British Houses in Delhi 1803–57*,

unpublished dissertation, NYU, 2004, p. 112. The Delhi College moved from the Ghaziuddin Medresse to the old British Residency building in the early 1850s after the Residency moved outside the walls to Ludlow Castle in the Civil Lines.

16. Edward Vibart, *The Sepoy Mutiny as Seen by a Subaltern from Delhi to Lucknow*, London, 1858, pp. 40–41.

17. Bayley, *Account of the escape*. For the mob, see Metcalfe, *Two Native Narratives*, 'Narrative of Mainodin', p. 240.

18. Bayley, *Account of the escape*.

19. Metcalfe, *Two Native Narratives*, 'Narrative of Mainodin', p. 45.

20. Bayley, *Account of the escape*. Emily says the brick was thrown from the Jama Masjid, but as this is in the opposite direction to the route Theo must have taken from the Kotwali in Chandni Chowk to the Kashmiri Gate, it must be an error.

21. Trial, Evidence of Chunni, News-writer for the Public, p. 84.

22. Ibid., Evidence of Jat Mall, News-writer to the Lt Gov. of Agra, p. 73.

23. Ibid., Evidence of Makhan, Mace bearer of Captain Douglas, p. 78. For Jennings with his glass, see ibid., Diary of Chunni Lal, News-writer, p. 102, and NAI, Mutiny Papers, Collection 39. For the problem of Fraser's girth, see Dehlavi, *Dastan i-Ghadr*, p. 58.

24. Trial, Evidence of Makhan, Mace bearer of Captain Douglas, p. 79.

25. Metcalfe, *Two Native Narratives*, 'Narrative of Mainodin', pp. 80–81.

26. Trial, Evidence of Jat Mall, News-writer to the Lt Gov. of Agra, p. 73.

27. Ibid., Evidence of Makhan, Mace bearer of Captain Douglas, p. 79.

28. Dehlavi, *Dastan i-Ghadr*, p. 57. See also OIOC, Eur Mss, B 138, *Account of Said Mobarak Shah*; Metcalfe, *Two Native Narratives*, 'Narrative of Munshi Jiwan Lal', pp. 80–81.

29. Trial, Evidence of Mrs Aldwell, p. 92.

30. For Abdullah Beg, see Metcalfe, *Two Native Narratives*, 'Narrative of Mainodin', pp. 60–61; also OIOC, Eur Mss B 138, *Account of Said Mobarak Shah*. For Gordon, see General Sir Hugh Gough, *Old Memories*, London, 1897, pp. 108–9 Also National Army Musuem, 6309–26, Lt Gen. F.C. Maisey, *The Capture of the Delhi Palace*. Gordon gave himself up to the British at the fall of Delhi but was never brought to trial. According to General Fred Maisey, who was in charge of prosecutions, Gordon had converted to save his life, and there was 'no proof' that he was guilty of firing on the British. At the end of his letter home Maisey writes, 'so I got the poor fellow off trial. He was, however, not released and the matter has been reported to the Commander in Chief. What the final result will be I do not know'.

31. Abdul Latif, *1857 Ka Tarikhi Roznamacha*, ed. K. A. Nizami, Naqwatul Musannifin, Delhi, 1958, entry for 11 May.

32. Mirza Asadullah Khan Ghalib, *Dastanbuy*, trans. Khwaja Ahmad Faruqi, Delhi, 1970, pp. 30–33. *Dastanbuy* purports to be Ghalib's diary of the Uprising. Although it was clearly rewritten after the British victory and was written partially with a view to proving his loyalty to the victorious British, there can be little real doubt that it reflects the aristocratic Ghalib's genuine dislike of the sepoy rabble. Frances Pritchett argues this case very

well in *Nets of Awareness: Urdu Poetry and Its Critics*, University of California Press, Berkeley and Los Angeles, 1990, p. 19, as does Ralph Russell in *The Oxford Ghalib: Life, Letters and Ghazals*, New Delhi, 2003, p. 12.

33. Ghalib, *Dastanbuy*, pp. 30–33. Where Faruqi's translation seems clumsy I have used instead the more colloquial version of Ralph Russell in *The Oxford Ghalib*, p. 118–19.

34. Sarvar ul-Mulk, *My Life, Being the Autobiography of Nawab Sarvar ul-Mulk Bahadur*, trans. from the Urdu by his son, Nawab Jawan Yar Jung Bahadur, London, 1903, p. 16.

35. Zahir Dehlavi, *Dastan i-Ghadr*, pp. 28–9

36. Metcalfe *Two Native Narratives*, 'Narrative of Munshi Jiwan Lal', p. 77. I have added some material from an alternative rendering and slightly different selection of material of the same original Urdu text published as *A Short Account of the Life and Family of Rai Jiwan Lal Bahadur, Late Honorary Magistrate of Delhi with extracts from his diary relating to the time of the Mutiny 1857 compiled by his son*, Delhi, 1902.

37. Account of an anonymous news-writer, NAI, Mutiny Papers, Collection 39.

38. Trial, *Petition of Mathura Das and Saligram*, p. 43.

39. OIOC, Eur Mss B 138, *Account of Said Mobarak Shah*.

40. *Dehli Urdu Akbhar* (hereafter DUA), 17 May 1857.

41. Ibid., 17 May 1857. The final paragraph is from the DUA of 31 May 1857.

42. This translation is my own colloquial reworking of the more literal translation given by Frances Pritchett in *Nets of Awareness*, p. 24.

43. Harriet Tytler, *An Englishwoman in India: The Memoirs of Harriet Tytler 1828–1858*, ed. Anthony Sattin, Oxford, 1986, p. 115.

44. Ibid., p. 116.

45. Vibart, *The Sepoy Mutiny*, pp. 14–19.

46. Ibid., p. 18.

47. N. A. Chick, *Annals of the Indian Rebellion 1857–8*, Calcutta, 1859 (reprinted London, 1972), pp. 86–7.

48. Ibid., p. 89.

49. Metcalfe, *Two Native Narratives*, 'Narrative of Mainodin', p. 41.

50. Ibid., pp. 47–8.

51. NAI, Mutiny Papers, Collection 39.

52. Metcalfe, *Two Native Narratives*, 'Narrative of Mainodin', pp. 47–8.

53. According to the account by a news-writer contained in the NAI, Mutiny Papers, Collection 39: 'The city's Muslims along with some Hindus accompanied the rebels attacked all the twelve thanas of the city and the Kotwali Chabutra and destroyed them. Sharful Haq the city Kotwal disappeared while the deputy Kotwal Baldeo Singh ran away after being injured.'

54. Metcalfe, *Two Native Narratives*, 'Narrative of Mainodin', p. 49.

55. Ibid. pp. 50–51.

56. Dehlavi, *Dastan i-Ghadr*, pp. 30–31.

57. NAI, Foreign Department, Political Proceedings, 8 January 1830, part 2, Consultation No. 42, pp. 332–5, from HM the King of Delhi, received 1 January 1830.

58. Hakim Ahsanullah Khan, 'Memoirs', trans. Dr S. Muinul Haq, *Journal of the Pakistan Historical Society*, Karachi, vol. 6, pt 1, 1958, pp. 1–33.

59. Metcalfe, *Two Native Narratives*, 'Narrative of Munshi Jiwan Lal', p. 83.
60. Latif, *1857*, entry for 11 May.
61. Metcalfe, *Two Native Narratives*, 'Narrative of Munshi Jiwan Lal', p. 83.
62. Khan, 'Memoirs', p. 4.
63. Emily Eden, *Up the Country: Letters from India*, London, 1930, p. 100.
64. NAI, foreign, Foreign Dept and Misc., *Precis of Palace Intelligence*, see, for example, entries for Tuesday, 9 March 1852, and Sunday, 1 August 1852.
65. Trial, Evidence of Ghulam Abbas, pp. 26-7. Another shorter account of the same crucial scene, apparently written on or immediately after 11 May, is contained in the NAI, Mutiny Papers, Collection 39, where an anonymous news-writer recorded that: 'Later the cavalry division and two platoons of Tilangas from the Meerutt camp and three platoons from Delhi appeared before his majesty and asked him to lead them saying we will ensure your sway over the whole country. The King assured them of his benediction and asked them to set up camp at Salimgarh.'
66. Chick, *Annals*, pp. 45-8.
67. Ibid., pp. 81-2.
68. Miss Wagentrieber, *The Story of Our Escape from Delhi in May 1857, from personal narrations by the late George Wagentrieber and Miss Haldane*, Delhi, 1894.
69. Tytler, *An Englishwoman in India*, p. 124.
70. Ibid., p. 125.
71. Vibart, *The Sepoy Mutiny*, p. 28.
72. Ibid., pp. 46-8.
73. OIOC, Vibart Papers, Eur Mss F135/19, letter datelined Meerut, 9 June.
74. Vibart, *The Sepoy Mutiny*, p. 53.
75. Ibid., p. 56.
76. Dehlavi, *Dastan i-Ghadr*, p. 81.
77. Chick, *Annals*, p. 90.
78. Tytler, *An Englishwoman in India*, pp. 129-30.
79. Ibid., p. 131.
80. Ibid., p. 131.
81. Four accounts survive of the Wagentriebers' movements that night. The earliest, and most reliable, is that of George, printed initially in the *Delhi Gazette Extra*, published out of Lahore a month later, and reprinted in Chick's *Annals*, pp. 78-86. Both the Misses Wagentrieber also produced accounts, which while more detailed seem in some parts to be less reliable: see Miss Wagentrieber, *The Story of Our Escape*, and Julia Haldane, *The Story of Our Escape from Delhi in 1857*, Agra, 1888. I also have a photocopy of a typescript of another unpublished mss of Miss Wagentrieber's adventures which is still in the possession of the Skinner family in their summer house at Sikandar Hall, Mussoorie.
82. Miss Wagentrieber, *The Story of Our Escape*, pp. 13-14.
83. Chick, *Annals*, p. 82.
84. Tytler, *An Englishwoman in India*, p. 133.
85. Ibid., pp. 134-7.
86. Chick, *Annals*, pp. 82-4.

87. Haldane, *The Story of Our Escape*, p. 20.
88. Chick, *Annals*, p. 83.
89. Haldane, *The Story of Our Escape*, pp. 24–5.
90. Ibid., p. 40.
91. NAI, Mutiny Papers, Collection 39.
92. OIOC, Home Miscellanous 725, pp. 389–422, *Letter Written by Munshi Mohun Lal to Brigadier Chamberlain dated November 8th 1857 at DEHLIE.*

6: This Day of Ruin and Riot

1. Punjab Archives, Lahore (hereafter PAL). On open display.
2. K. C. Yadav, *The Revolt of 1857 in Haryana*, New Delhi, 1977, p. 41.
3. Sir Henry W. Norman and Mrs Keith Young, *Delhi 1857*, London, 1902, pp. 11, 19.
4. Richard Barter, *The Siege of Delhi*, London, 1984, p. 3.
5. Fred Roberts, *Letters Written during the Indian Mutiny*, London, 1924, p. 8. Fred Roberts later grew up to be the celebrated Lord Roberts of Kandahar.
6. National Army Museum (hereafter NAM), Wilson Letters, AW to his wife, Meerut, 12 May 1857.
7. Ibid., AW to his wife, Camp Ghazee Oo Deen Nuggur, 3 June.
8. Barter, *The Siege of Delhi*, p. 9.
9. For the significance of this, see the excellent passage in Rudrangshu Mukherjee, *Avadh in Revolt 1857–8 – A Study of Popular Resistance*, New Delhi, 1984, pp. 65–6.
10. Charles John Griffiths, *The Siege of Delhi*, London, 1910, p. 23.
11. Roberts, *Letters*, p. 38.
12. Quoted by Saul David, *The Indian Mutiny 1857*, London, 2002, p.xxii.
13. J. W. Kaye, *A History of the Sepoy War in India 1857–8*, London, 1877, vol. II, p. 342.
14. Major W. S. R. Hodson, *Twelve Years of a Soldier's Life in India*, London, 1859, p. 186.
15. Charles Allen, *Soldier Sahibs: The Men Who Made the North-West Frontier*, London, 2000, p. 280. Allen's wonderful book contains much the best account yet written of Nicholson.
16. David Gilmour, *The Ruling Caste: Imperial Lives in the Victorian Raj*, London, 2005, p. 162.
17. John Beames, *Memoirs of a Bengal Civilian*, London, 1961, p. 103.
18. Ibid., p. 102.
19. Ensign Wilberforce, of the 52nd Light Infantry, quoted in James Hewitt, *Eyewitnesses to the Indian Mutiny*, Reading, 1972, p. 33.
20. Allen, *Soldier Sahibs*, p. 217.
21. Though the story of the *Nikal Seyn* cult sounds suspiciously like Victorian myth, it is attested by too many contemporary accounts to be a complete invention. See, for example, the eyewitness account of Ensign Wilberforce given in Hewitt, *Eyewitnesses*, p. 34, or Griffiths, *The Siege of Delhi*, p. 119.

22. Allen, *Soldier Sahibs*, pp. 55, 62.

23. Captain Lionel J. Trotter, *The Life of John Nicholson, Soldier and Administrator*, London, 1898, p. 195.

24. Oriental and India Office Collections, British Library (hereafter OIOC), Eur Mss E211, Edwardes Collection, letter from Nicholson to Edwardes, datelined Peshawar, 23 April 1857.

25. R. G. Wilberforce, *An Unrecorded Chapter of the Indian Mutiny*, London, 1894, p. 43.

26. Allen, *Soldier Sahibs*, p. 293.

27. Wilberforce, *An Unrecorded Chapter*, pp. 40–41.

28. Ibid., p. 91.

29. Hodson, *Twelve Years*, p. xiv. According to his brother, 'though he lived among the heathen, he never forgot he was a Christian and an Englishman'.

30. Christopher Hibbert, *The Great Mutiny: India 1857*, London, 1978, p. 289.

31. Allen, *Soldier Sahibs*, pp. 236–7.

32. Hewitt, *Eyewitnesses*, p. 38. There is a good account of his life in David, *Indian Mutiny*, pp. 149–51.

33. Allen, *Soldier Sahibs*, p. 236.

34. NAM, 6404 74 179, letter from Henry Lawrence to Hodson, Lucknow, 21 March 1857. For the Hare quote, see Hibbert, *The Great Mutiny*, p. 289.

35. Hodson, *Twelve Years*, pp. 185–7; David, *Indian Mutiny*, p. 151; Allen, *Soldier Sahibs*, pp. 261–2.

36. Hodson, *Twelve Years*, pp. 188–9.

37. Ibid., p. 184; Allen, *Soldier Sahibs*, p. 335.

38. Hodson, *Twelve Years*, p. 319.

39. Ibid., p. 319.

40. H. H., Greathed, *Letters Written during the Siege of Delhi*, London, 1858, pp. 28–9; Hodson, *Twelve Years*, p. 191.

41. *A Short Account of the Life and Family of Rai Jiwan Lal Bahadur, Late Honorary Magistrate of Delhi with extracts from his diary relating to the time of the Mutiny 1857 compiled by his son*, Delhi, 1902, p. 27.

42. Ibid., pp. 29–32.

43. National Archives of India (hereafter NAI), Mutiny Papers. See, for example, Collections 15, 16, 51, 61, 67 and 71. An excellent digest of the more important of these reports can be found in OIOC in the papers of the NW Provinces' intelligence chief, Sir Robert Montgomery, Montgomery Papers, Mss Eur D 1019. Kedarnath's journal has been published as Appendix No. 2, *Memoirs of Hakim Ahsanullah Khan*, ed. S. Muinul Haq, Pakistan Historial Society, Karachi, 1958. For runners disguised as religious mendicants passing messages, see *A Short Account*, p. 29.

44. OIOC, Eur Mss B 138, *Account of Said Mobarak Shah*.

45. Quoted in Allen, *Soldier Sahibs*, p. 270.

46. Hodson, *Twelve Years*, p. 196. Also Greathed, *Letters*, p. 25.

47. Zahir Dehlavi, *Dastan i-Ghadr: An eyewitness account of the 1857 Uprising*, Lahore, 1955, pp. 82–3.

48. Salim Qureshi and Ashur Kazmi (trans. and ed.) *1857 ke Ghaddaron ke Khutut*, Delhi, 2001, p. 112.

49. *Dihli Urdu Akhbar* (hereafter DUA), 17 May 1857.
50. Abdul Latif, *1857 Ka Tarikhi Roznamacha*, ed. K. A. Nizami, Naqwatul Musannifin, Delhi, 1958, p. 123. For the confectioners see *Proceedings on the Trial of Muhammad Bahadur Shah, Titular King of Delhi, before a Military Comission, upon a charge of Rebellion, Treason and Murder, held at Delhi, on the 27th Day of January 1858, and following days, London, 1859* (hereafter Trial), Narrative of Chunni Lal, news-writer, p. 103. See also Kedarnath's journal, entry for 16 May. DUA, 17 May.
51. NAI, Mutiny Papers, Collection 111a, no. 10, May 1857.
52. Ibid., Collection 60, no. 605; also Collection 62, no. 71.
53. Trial, Narrative of Chunni Lal, news-writer, p. 103.
54. NAI, Mutiny Papers, Collection 110, no. 270.
55. Trial, Narrative of Chunni Lal, news-writer, p. 103.
56. DUA, 31 May 1857.
57. Abdul Latif, *Roznamacha*, p. 123. Ayesha Jalal argues this case very well in her *Self and Sovereignty*, New Delhi, 2001, pp. 34–5.
58. NAI, Mutiny Papers, Collection 146, no. 3, May 1857.
59. Ibid., Collection 125, no. 12, May 1857.
60. Ibid., Collection 60, no. 72, 11 June 1857.
61. Ibid., Collection 67, no. 14, undated.
62. Ibid., Collection 128, no. 43, 13 June 1857.
63. Trial, Narrative of Chunni Lal, news-writer, pp. 105–6; also Eric Stokes, *The Peasant Armed: The Indian Revolt of 1857*, ed. C. A. Bayly, Oxford, 1986, p. 126.
64. Trial, Evidence of Mukund Lala, secretary, and Chunni Lal, news-writer, pp. 86–7.
65. Charles Theophilus Metcalfe, *Two Native Narratives of The Mutiny in Delhi*, 'Narrative of Munshi Jiwan Lal', p. 87.
66. Ibid., p. 87.
67. Ibid., p. 87.
68. For the garden, see NAI, Mutiny Papers, Collection 60, no. 290, 10 July 1857; for the sepoys peering into the zenana, see ibid., Collection 100, no. 6, 22 May 1857.
69. Dehlavi, *Dastan i-Ghadr*, pp. 82–3, 88.
70. *Sadiq ul-Akabhar*, 10 August 1857.
71. PAL, Case 1, 45, letter from Sir Thomas Metcalfe, Delhi, to C. Allen, Sec. to Govt of NWP, Agra, dated 11 January 1849.
72. For Ghalib's remark, see Ralph Russell, *The Oxford Ghalib: Life, Letters and Ghazals*, New Delhi, 2003, p. 90. For MKS's application for the house in Mehrauli, see NAI, Foreign, Foreign Dept Misc., *Precis of Palace Intelligence*, entry for Sunday, 8 August 1852; for his wife's friendship with the wife of Mirza Fakhru, see entry for Sunday, 1 August 1852.
73. For wife-beating, see NAI, *Precis of Palace Intelligence*, entry for Friday, 27 August 1852.
74. For gun accident see ibid., entry for Monday, 7 November 1853, which records how, 'loading his gun, it went off, and shattered one of his fingers which had been attended to by Subassistant surgeon Chimun Lal'. For

complaints against MAB, see, for example, NAI, Mutiny Papers, Collection 71, nos 95 and 96; also Kedarnath's journal, entry for 6 July 1857.

75. NAI, *Precis of Palace Intelligence*, entry for 28 September 1852, and PAL, Case 1, 45, letter from Sir Thomas Metcalfe, Delhi to C. Allen, Sec. to Govt of NWP, Agra, dated 11 January 1849.

76. NAI, *Precis of Palace Intelligence*, entry for Sunday, 1 January 1854.

77. PAL, Case 1, 45, letter from Sir Thomas Metcalfe, Delhi, to C. Allen, Sec. to Govt of NWP, Agra, dated 11 January 1849.

78. NAI, *Precis of Palace Intelligence*, entries for 14 and 27 February 1852.

79. Ibid., entry for 20 February 1852.

80. For the coronation portrait see Stuart Cary Welch, *Room for Wonder: Indian Painting during the British Period 1760–1880*, New York, 1978, pp. 118–19.

81. See Chapter 1, note 2.

82. Trial, Evidence of Hakim Ahsanullah Khan, p. 89; also, Narrative of Chunni Lal, news-writer, p. 103; *Memoirs of Hakim Ahsanullah Khan*, pp. 6–7.

83. The letter was first printed in English in N. A. Chick, *Annals of the Indian Rebellion 1857–8*, Calcutta, 1859 (reprinted London 1972), pp. 101–3. It has recently been reprinted in Salim al-Din Quraishi, *Cry for Freedom: Proclamations of Muslim Revolutionaries of 1857*, Lahore, 1997. The language is much more aggressive and intolerant than anything written by Zafar, and must presumably be the work of Mirza Mughal.

84. The entire text was published in English for the first time in the *Delhi Gazette* of 29 September 1857. It can be read in full in Quraishi, *Cry for Freedom*, or S. A. Rizvi, and M. L. Bhargava (eds), *Freedom Struggle in Uttar Pradesh*, Lucknow, 1957, vol. 1, pp. 453–6. Rudrangshu Mukherjee, *Avadh in Revolt 1857–8 – A Study of Popular Resistance*, New Delhi, 1984, has argued convincingly that the document has no connection with Delhi. See also Rudrangshu Mukherjee, 'The Azamgarh Proclamation and some questions on the Revolt of 1857 in the North Western Provinces', in *Essays in Honour of S.C. Sarkar*, Delhi, 1976.

85. *Memoirs of Hakim Ahsanullah Khan*, p. 8.

86. Ibid., p. 5.

87. Ibid., p. 8.

88. On 11 May Mirza Ilahe Bakhsh had initially 'had the whole of his property in the Fort confiscated and his person was sought by his enemy Khwaja Mehboob [Ali Khan]'. He survived the outbreak, however, and played a prominent role in the pro-British faction within the court throughout the Uprising – as a list of his services drawn up by Hodson in December 1857 makes clear. In contrast Mahbub Ali Khan was poisoned soon after the outbreak; by whom is not clear. Delhi Commissioner's Office Archive, Mutiny Papers, File no. 1, *Services performed by Mirza Elahee Bahksh for WLR Hodson*, 1 December 1857.

89. Trial, Narrative of Chunni Lal, news-writer, pp. 105–6.

90. Ibid., p. 106.

91. Ibid., p. 106.

92. Metcalfe, *Two Native Narratives*, 'Narrative of Munshi Jiwan Lal', p. 94.

93. *Memoirs of Hakim Ahsanullah Khan*, p. 10.

94. OIOC, Eur Mss B 138, *Account of Said Mobarak Shah*.
95. Dehlavi, *Dastan i-Ghadr*, p. 84.
96. Trial, Narrative of Chunni Lal, news-writer, p. 106.
97. DUA, 24 May 1857.
98. Ibid.
99. Stokes, *The Peasant Armed*, p. 70.
100. See, for example, the entry for 24 June in Kedarnath's journal; also DUA, 17 May 1857.
101. Russell, *The Oxford Ghalib*, p. 118.
102. NAI, Mutiny Papers, Collection 19, no. 10.
103. DUA, 31 May 1857.
104. NAI, Mutiny Papers, Collection 103, no. 24.
105. Ibid., Collection 110, no. 293.
106. DUA, 24 May 1857.
107. Metcalfe, *Two Native Narratives*, 'Narrative of Munshi Jiwan Lal', p. 98. There is another account of the same incident in Trial, Narrative of Chunni Lal, News-writer, p. 108.

7: A Precarious Position

1. Oriental and India Office Collections, British Library (hereafter OIOC), Photo Eur 31 1B, Hardcastle Papers, pp. 287ff. Also South Asian Studies Library, Cambridge, Campbell Metcalfe Papers, Box 8, typescript mss by Emily Bayley, *Account of the escape of Sir Theophilus Metcalfe from Delhi after the Outbreak of the Mutiny*.
2. Charles Theophilus Metcalfe, *Two Native Narratives of the Mutiny in Delhi*, London, 1898, 'Narrative of Mainodin', p. 57.
3. *The Dehlie Book* and Metcalfe's panoramic scroll are both now in the OIOC of the British Library, as are the two images of the Nawab of Jhajjar's durbar; the Nawab of Jhajjar's hunting image is in the V&A; while the image of Nawab Jhajjar riding his tiger is part of the private collection of Cynthia Polski in New York. See Andrew Topsfield (ed.), *In the Realm of Gods and Kings: Arts of India*, New York, 2004, Catalogue no. 108, *Nawab 'Abd al-Rahman Khan of Jhajjar rides a tiger in his palace garden*, pp. 254–5.
4. OIOC, Photo Eur 31 1B, Hardcastle Papers, pp. 287ff.
5. OIOC, Saunders Correspondence, Eur Mss E 185, no. 24 Agra, 12 December 1857, to J. Lawrence.
6. OIOC, Metcalfe Papers, Eur Mss D 610.
7. Frances W. Pritchett, *Nets of Awareness: Urdu Poetry and Its Critics*, Berkeley and Los Angeles, 1994, pp. 15, 26–7.
8. Edward Vibart, *The Sepoy Mutiny as Seen by a Subaltern from Delhi to Lucknow*, London, 1858, pp. 63–4.
9. Ibid., pp. 65–70.
10. Ibid., pp. 90–92.

11. Ibid., p. 93.
12. See John Lall, *Begam Samru: Fading Portrait in a Gilded Frame*, Roli Books, Delhi, 1997, pp. 126–7.
13. Ram Babu Saksena, *European & Indo-European Poets of Urdu & Persian*, Lucknow, 1941, p. 288.
14. See Linda York Leach, *Mughal and Other Paintings from the Chester Beatty Library*, Scorpion Cavendish, London, 1995, vol. II, p. 794. Two Europeans shown in the painting 7.121 are referred to by their Muslim names Khwajah Ismail Khan and Salu Khan.
15. There is a photograph and good discussion of the Sardhana monuments in Gauvin Alexander Bailey, 'Architectural Relics of the Catholic Missionary Era in Mughal India', in Rosemary Crill, Susan Stronge and Andrew Topsfield (eds), *Arts of Mughal India: Studies in Honour of Robert Skelton*, Mapin, Ahmedabad, 2004, pp. 146–50.
16. For Sardhana and the Begum *Samru* see Lall, *Begam Samru*, especially pp. 126–7 for the Christmas festivities. See also: Michael Fisher, 'Becoming and Making Family in Hindustan', in Indrani Chatterjee, *Unfamiliar Relations*, Permanent Black, New Delhi, 2004; Nicholas Shreeve, *Dark Legacy*, Bookwright, Arundel, 1996, Nicholas Shreeve (ed.), *From Nawab to Nabob: The Diary of David Ochterlony Dyce Sombre*, Bookwright, Arundel, 2000. For the Sardhana poets see Saksena, *European & Indo-European Poets*.
17. David Dyce Ochterlony Sombre's diaries: see, for example, entries for Diwali (Thursday, 30 October 1833, p. 66), Holi (Easter Sunday, 29 March 1834, p. 21), Dussera (Thursday, 1 October 1835), witchcraft (3 January 1835, p. 78) and exorcism (Tuesday, 2 September 1834).
18. Saksena, *European & Indo-European Poets*, p. 288.
19. Vibart, *The Sepoy Mutiny*, pp. 106–11.
20. National Army Museum (hereafter NAM), Wilson Letters, AW to his wife, Meerut, 25 May 1857.
21. National Archives of India (hereafter NAI), Mutiny Papers, Collection 39, entry for 14 May 1857.
22. OIOC, Eur Mss B 138, *Account of Said Mobarak Shah*.
23. *Memoirs of Hakim Ahsanullah Khan*, ed. S. Muinul Haq, Pakistan Historical Society, Karachi, 1958, p. 14.
24. NAI, Mutiny Papers, Collection 39, entry for 15 May 1857.
25. Ibid., Collection 8, no. 1, entry for 20 May 1857.
26. *Dihli Urdu Akhbar*, 31 May 1857.
27. OIOC, Eur Mss B 138, *Account of Said Mobarak Shah*.
28. Metcalfe, *Two Native Narratives*, 'Narrative of Mainodin', p. 61.
29. NAM, Wilson Letters, AW to his wife, Meerut, 26 May 1857.
30. Ibid., AW to his wife, Mehoodeenpore, 28 May 1857.
31. OIOC, Eur Mss B 138, *Account of Said Mobarak Shah*.
32. NAM, Wilson Letters, AW to his wife, Camp Ghazee Deen Nuggur, 30 May 1857.
33. Metcalfe, *Two Native Narratives*, 'Narrative of Mainodin', pp. 61–2.
34. NAM, Wilson Letters, AW to his wife, Camp Ghazee Deen Nuggur, 1 June 1857.

35. Ibid.
36. Ibid.
37. Ibid., AW to his wife, Camp Ghazee Deen Nuggur, 2 June 1857.
38. Major Charles Reid, *Defence of the Main Piquet at Hindoo Rao's House as recorded by Major Reid Commanding the Sirmoor Battalion*, London, 1957, p. 12.
39. Metcalfe, *Two Native Narratives*, 'Narrative of Mainodin', p. 62.
40. Quoted by Christopher Hibbert, *The Great Mutiny: India 1857*, London, 1978, p. 124.
41. Richard Barter, *The Siege of Delhi*, London, 1984, p. 9.
42. Ibid., p. 9.
43. Robert H. W. Dunlop, *Service and Adventure with the Khakee Ressalah*, London, 1858, pp. 156-7.
44. Harriet Tytler, *An Englishwoman in India: The Memoirs of Harriet Tytler 1828-1858*, ed. Anthony Sattin, Oxford, 1986, p. 144.
45. Ibid., p. 146.
46. H. H., Greathed, *Letters Written during the Siege of Delhi*, London, 1858, pp. 24, 27, 128.
47. Campbell Metcalfe Papers, Box 10, EC to his mother, datelined Constantia, Simla.
48. Major W. S. R. Hodson, *Twelve Years of a Soldier's Life in India*, London, 1859, p. 198.
49. NAI, Mutiny Papers, Collection 126, no. 18, entry for 1 June 1857.
50. Ibid., Collection 126, nos 14 and 17, entries for 28 and 31 May 1857.
51. Abdul Latif, *1857 Ka Tarikhi Roznamacha*, ed. K. A. Nizami, Naqwatul Musannifin, Delhi, 1958, entry for 9 June 1857.
52. Zahir Dehlavi, *Dastan i-Ghadr: An eyewitness account of the 1857 Uprising*, Lahore, 1955, p. 89.
53. NAI, Mutiny Papers, Collection 152, no. 43, entry for 7 June 1857.
54. Barter, *The Siege of Delhi*, pp. 12-17.
55. Eric Stokes, *The Peasant Armed: The Indian Revolt of 1857*, ed. C. A. Bayly, Oxford, 1986, p. 75.
56. OIOC, Eur Mss B 138, *Account of Said Mobarak Shah*.
57. Metcalfe, *Two Native Narratives*, 'Narrative of Mainodin', p. 63.
58. OIOC, Eur Mss B 138, *Account of Said Mobarak Shah*.
59. Stokes, *The Peasant Armed*, p. 75.
60. Tytler, *An Englishwoman in India*, pp. 130, 145.
61. *Delhi Gazette Extra*, issue of 20 June 1857, datelined Lahore.
62. Dehlavi, *Dastan i-Ghadr*, p. 95.
63. OIOC, Eur Mss B 138, *Account of Said Mobarak Shah*.
64. Reid, *Defence*, p. 14.
65. Vibart, *The Sepoy Mutiny*, pp. 30-31.
66. Dehlavi, *Dastan i-Ghadr*, p. 92.
67. Metcalfe, *Two Native Narratives*, 'Narrative of Munshi Jiwan Lal', p. 118.
68. Ibid., pp. 117-18.
69. John Edward Rotton, *The Chaplain's Narrative of the Siege of Delhi*, London, 1858, pp. 61-2.

8: Blood for Blood

1. Major W. S. R. Hodson, *Twelve Years of a Soldier's Life in India*, London, 1859, p. 201.
2. For the King watching, see Richard Barter, *The Siege of Delhi*, London, 1984, p. 32; for city walls and rooftops, see H. H., Greathed, *Letters Written during the Siege of Delhi*, London, 1858, p. 141.
3. Sarvar ul-Mulk, *My Life, Being the Autobiography of Nawab Server ul-Mulk Bahadur*, trans. from the Urdu by his son, Nawab Jiwan Yar Jung Bahadur, London, 1903, p. 16:
4. Ibid., p. 16.
5. Greathed, *Letters*, p. 45.
6. Zahir Dehlavi, *Dastan i-Ghadr: An eyewitness account of the 1857 Uprising*, Lahore, 1955, p. 95.
7. National Archives of India (hereafter NAI), Mutiny Papers. Collection 60, no. 253; for the stable boy, see Abdul Latif, *1857 Ka Tarikhi Roznamacha*, ed. K. A. Nizami, Naqwatul Musannifin, Delhi, 1958; for Zinat moving to her house, see NAI, Mutiny Papers, Collection 15, no. 19.
8. Oriental and India Office Collections, British Library (herafter OIOC), Eur Mss B 138, *Account of Said Mobarak Shah*.
9. *Memoirs of Hakim Ahsanullah Khan*, Appendix no. 2, ed. S. Moinul Haq, Pakistan Historical Society. Karachi, 1958, entry for 14 June 1857.
10. OIOC, Eur Mss B 138, *Account of Said Mobarak Shah*.
11. Ralph Russell, *The Oxford Ghalib: Life, Letters, and Ghazals*, New Delhi, 2003, p. 119.
12. Mirza Asadullah Khan Ghalib, *Dastanbuy*, trans. Khwaja Ahmad Faruqi, Delhi, 1970, pp. 33–4.
13. Ibid., p. 34.
14. NAI, Mutiny Papers, Collection 111b, no. 14, entry for 3 July 1857.
15. Ibid. Collection 146, nos 13 and 14, 16 July 1857.
16. Ibid. Collection 146, nos 9 and 10, 1 July 1857.
17. Ibid. Collection 61, no. 76, 20 June 1857.
18. Ibid., Collection 67, no. 76, 27 July 1857. The previous item in the collection, no. 75, is Mehrab Khan's friend Rafiullah, who says he came into town with the *ghazis* from Faridabad, sold his horse at the same time as Mehrab Khan sold his, was also robbed by the Gujars and was arrested along with his friend.
19. *Dihli Urdu Akhbar* (hereafter DUA), 14 June 1857.
20. *Ibid*.
21. See, for example, NAI, Mutiny Papers, Collection 67, no. 12, 24 June 1857.
22. Irfan Habib, 'The Coming of 1857', *Social Scientist*, Vol. 26, no. 1, January–April 1998, p. 8.
23. Ibid., p. 12.
24. See, for example, NAI, Mutiny Papers, Collection 67, no. 77, 27 July 1857 for Zinat ul-Masajid; and Collection 15, File 1 for Jama Masjid.
25. See, for example, ibid., Collection 73, no. 171.
26. See the report of the spy Gauri Shankar Sukul in ibid., Collection 18, no. 1, entry for 6 July 1857.

27. Sarvar ul-Mulk, *My Life*, pp. 16–17.

28. OIOC, Eur Mss B 138, *Account of Said Mobarak Shah*

29. NAI, Mutiny Papers, Collection 65, no. 36, Petition of Maulvi Sarfaraz Ali, 10 September 1857.

30. *Proceedings on the Trial of Muhammad Bahadur Shah, Titular King of Delhi, before a Military Commission, upon a charge of Rebellion, Treason and Murder, held at Delhi, on the 27th Day of January 1858, and following days, London, 1859* (hereafter Trial), p. 57, *Petition of Ghulam Mu'in ud-Din Khan, Principal Risaldar* (no date, but final note is dated 2 August, so petition must be ?late July).

31. Charles Theophilus Metcalfe, *Two Native Narratives of the Mutiny in Delhi*, London, 1898, 'Narrative of Munshi Jiwan Lal', p. 172.

32. Zakaullah, *Tarikh-I Uruj-e Saltanat-e Englishya*, New Delhi, 1904, p. 676.

33. NAI, Mutiny Papers, Collection 15, no. 19, undated.

34. *Memoirs of Hakim Ahsanullah Khan*, p. 31. For Zafar paying Brahmins to pray for victory, see NAI, Mutiny Papers, Collection 102, no. 113, undated.

35. Cited in Rudrangshu Mukherjee, *Avadh in Revolt 1857–8 – A Study of Popular Resistance*, New Delhi, 1984, p. 153.

36. See Habib, 'The Coming of 1857', p. 8.

37. NAI, Mutiny Papers, Collection 57, no. 483, Petition of Generals Sudhari and Hira Singh to Mirza Mughal, 12 September 1857.

38. Allamah Fazl-I Haqq Khairabadi, 'The Story of the War of Independence, 1857–8', *Journal of the Pakistan Historical Society*, pt 1, January 1957, pp. 33, 36. Some scholars have questioned the authenticity of this document, and believe it may contain significant later interpolations.

39. NAI, Mutiny Papers, Collection 100, no. 179 (undated).

40. DUA, 14 June 1857.

41. OIOC, Eur Mss B 138, *Account of Said Mobarak Shah*.

42. Greathed, *Letters*, p. 71.

43. Major Charles Reid, *Defence of the Main Piquet at Hindoo Rao's House as recorded by Major Reid Commanding the Sirmoor Battalion*, London, 1957, p. 17, entry for 13 June 1857.

44. Dehlavi, *Dastan i-Ghadr*, p. 96.

45. Hodson, *Twelve Years*, p. 214.

46. W. H. Russell, *My Diary in India*, London, 1860, vol. 2, p. 14.

47. NAI, Mutiny Papers, Collection 67, no. 50, entry for 14 July 1857.

48. Ibid., Collection 60, nos 213–14, 23 June 1857.

49. John Edward Rotton, *The Chaplain's Narrative of the Siege of Delhi*, London, 1858, pp. 91–2.

50. South Asian Studies Library, Cambridge, Campbell Metcalfe Papers, Box 4, GG to EC (undated but ?late June 1857).

51. Ibid., Box 6, EC to GG (undated but clearly 20 June 1857).

52. Ibid., Box 8, which contains a long exchange of letters between Theo and his sister and brother-in-law about the long-delayed auction of the contents of Metcalfe House, some of which was finally sold off at the end of 1856 and invested in the Delhi Bank.

53. Ibid., Box 6, EC to GG (undated but ?20 June 1857). I have added the

touching final paragraph from a subsequent letter, Box 6, EC to GG, datelined Camp before Delhie, Main Picquet, Hindu Raos, 13 July 1857.

54. National Army Museum (hereafter NAM), Wilson Letters, AW to his wife, Camp Delhi cantonments, 10 and 11 June 1857.

55. Fred Roberts, *Letters Written during the Indian Mutiny*, London, 1924, p. 29.

56. Charles John Griffiths, *The Siege of Delhi*, London, 1910, p. 81.

57. Ewart letter, cited in Hibbert, *The Great Mutiny: India 1857*, London, 1978, p. 288.

58. Colonel George Bourchier, CB, *Eight Months Campaign against the Bengal Sepoy Army during the Mutiny of 1857*, London, 1858, p. 35.

59. Rotton, *The Chaplain's Narrative*, p. 154.

60. Griffiths, *The Siege of Delhi*, pp. 69–70.

61. Quoted, without reference, in Hibbert, *The Great Mutiny*, 1857, p. 287.

62. *Delhi Gazette Extra*, 8 July 1857.

63. Rotton, *The Chaplain's Narrative*, pp. 106–7.

64. Ibid., pp. 81–2.

65. Harriet Tytler, *An Englishwoman in India: The Memoirs of Harriet Tytler 1828–1858*, ed. Anthony Sattin, Oxford, 1986, p. 145.

66. Ibid., p. 147.

67. Ibid., pp. 148, 151.

68. Rotton, *The Chaplain's Narrative*, p. 136.

69. NAM, Wilson Letters, AW to his wife, Camp Delhi cantonments, 6 and 13 July 1857.

70. Cadell mss, quoted in Hibbert, *The Great Mutiny*, p. 281.

71. Greathed, *Letters*, p. 33.

72. Ibid., p. 45.

73. NAM, Wilson Letters, AW to his wife, Camp Delhi cantonments, 17 July 1857.

74. Eric Stokes, *The Peasant Armed: The Indian Revolt of 1857*, ed. C. A. Bayly, Oxford, 1986, p. 80.

75. OIOC, John Lawrence Papers, Mss Eur F 90, Folio 19b, copy of a letter from Brigadier Gen. A. Wilson to Sir John Lawrence, Camp before Delhy, 18 July 1857.

76. Durgodas Bandyopadhyay, *Amar Jivan-Charit*, cited in Rajat Kanta Ray, *The Felt Community: Commonality and Mentality before the Emergence of Indian Nationalism*, New Delhi, 2003, p. 441.

77. Griffiths, *The Siege of Delhi*, p. 63. For fruit and sweetmeats, see Richard Barter, *The Siege of Delhi*, London, 1984, p. 32.

78. OIOC, Eur Mss B 138, *Account of Said Mobarak Shah*.

79. Bouchier, *Eight Months*, p. 44n.

80. Quoted in Farhan Ahmad Nizami, *Madrasahs, Scholars and Saints: Muslim Response to the British Presence in Delhi and the Upper Doab 1803–1857*, unpublished PhD, Oxford, 1983, pp. 212, 217.

81. See Swapna Liddle's excellent essay on Azurda in Margrit Pernau (ed.) *Delhi College*, New Delhi, 2006. Sir Sayyid Ahmad Khan mentions Maulvi Sarfaraz Ali in his list of Delhi's leading citizens and talks of him as 'a very able scholar. He teaches the traditional and rational sciences and Geometry and

Algebra with great skill. He studied Hadis and Tafsir under Maulvi Sa-druddin Khan [Azurda] and now serves as a teacher on behalf of the esteemed one at Dar ul-Baqa Madrasa'. Sir Sayyid Ahmad Khan, *Asar us Sanadid*, Delhi, 1990, vol. 2.

82. OIOC, Eur Mss B 138, *Account of Said Mobarak Shah*.

83. *Memoirs of Hakim Ahsanullah Khan*, p. 18.

84. Metcalfe, *Two Native Narratives*, 'Narrative of Munshi Jiwan Lal', pp. 134, 167.

85. Ibid. pp. 135–7, 141–3, 169.

86. NAI, Mutiny Papers, Collection 15, no. 19 (no date, but early July 1857).

87. Barter, *The Siege of Delhi*, p. 36.

88. Griffiths, *The Siege of Delhi*, pp. 90–91.

89. William W. Ireland, *A History of the Siege of Delhi by an Officer who Served There*, Edinburgh, 1861, pp. 159–61.

90. Niall Fergusson, *Empire: How Britain Made the Modern World*, London, 2003, pp. 149–50.

91. See Edward Thompson, *The Life of Charles Lord Metcalfe*, London, 1937, p. 101.

92. Campbell Metcalfe Papers, Box 8, CM in Clapham Common to GG, 30 July 1853.

93. For the Lucknow Rottons, see Rosie Llewellyn–Jones, *A Fatal Friendship: The Nawabs, the British and the City of Lucknow*, New Delhi, 1992, p. 32.

94. Ram Babu Saksena, *European & Indo-European Poets of Urdu & Persian*, Lucknow, 1941, pp. 128–33.

95. Metcalfe, *Two Native Narratives*, 'Narrative of Munshi Jiwan Lal', p. 171.

96. Ibid., pp. 177, 179.

97. Ibid., p. 180.

98. Habib, 'The Coming of 1857', p. 13; see also, in the same volume, Iqbal Husain, 'The Rebel Admininstration of Delhi', p. 30. Also Stokes, *The Peasant Armed*, p. 89. The original constitution of the court is illustrated in Surendranath Sen's *1857*, New Delhi, 1957, opposite p. 80.

99. NAI, Mutiny Papers, Collection 63, no. 36, entry for 13 August 1857.

100. Barter, *The Siege of Delhi*, p. 36.

101. Metcalfe, *Two Native Narratives*, 'Narrative of Munshi Jiwan Lal', p. 142.

102. Trial, Supplement: Evidence of Hakim Ahsanullah Khan, p. 169; see also *Memoirs of Hakim Ahsanullah Khan*, p. 22.

103. Delhi Commissioner's Office (hereafter DCO) Archive, New Delhi, Mutiny Papers, File no. 5028, July 1857, Translation of a letter from Munshee Mahomed Bakar, 28 July, editor of the *Delhi Oordoo Akhbar*.

104. NAI, Mutiny Papers, Collection 103, no. 132, entry for 14 July 1857.

105. Ibid., Collection 45, entry for 26 July 1857.

106. Ibid., Collection 111c, no. 64, entry for 30 July 1857.

107. Ibid., Collection 111c, no. 44, entry for 29 July 1857.

108. Ibid., Collection 111c, no. 64, entry for 30 July 1857.

109. See Margrit Pernau's brilliant essay, 'Multiple Identities and Communities: Re-contextualizing Religion', in Jamal Malik and Helmut Reifeld, *Religious Pluralism in South Asia and Europe*, New Delhi, 2005, p. 167.

110. Greathed, *Letters*, p. 166.
111. Sarvar ul-Mulk, *My Life*, p. 16.
112. *Siraj ul-Akbhar*, 27 July 1857.
113. OIOC, Montgomery Papers, Eur Mss D 1019, no. 236, Montgomery to the Secr. to the Chief Commissioner of the Punjab, 17 August 1857.
114. DCO Archives, New Delhi, Mutiny Papers, File 63, 7 August 1857.
115. For the return of the soldiers to Zafar's garden, see Trial, p. 17.
116. Ibid. pp. 25–26.
117. NAI, Mutiny Papers, Collection 19, no. 10, entry for 19 July 1857, letter from the spy Gauri Shankar.
118. Dehlavi, *Dastan i-Ghadr*, pp. 98–9.
119. DCO Archive, New Delhi, Mutiny Papers, File no. 5028, July 1857, Translation of a letter from Munshee Mahomed Bakar
120. Ibid., Box 4, File 17; also File 3, letters from Sec. to Gov. Gen. to H. H. Greathed, *passim*.
121. Greathed, *Letters*, pp. 153–4.
122. *Delhi Gazette Extra*, 22 July 1857.
123. Ibid.

9: The Turn of the Tide

1. John Edward Rotton, *The Chaplain's Narrative of the Siege of Delhi*, London, 1858, pp. 190–91.
2. Charles John Griffiths, *The Siege of Delhi*, London, 1910, pp. 119–20.
3. R. G. Wilberforce, *An Unrecorded Chapter of the Indian Mutiny*, London, 1894, p. 75.
4. Cited by Charles Allen, *Soldier Sahibs: The Men Who Made the North-West Frontier*, London, 2000, p. 293.
5. National Army Museum (hereafter NAM), 6301/143, Diaries of Col. E. L. Ommaney, vol. A, pt 6, entry for 21 July 1857, Umritsur.
6. Ibid.
7. Major Charles Reid, *Defence of the Main Piquet at Hindoo Rao's House as recorded by Major Reid Commanding the Sirmoor Battalion*, London, 1957, p. 44.
8. Wilberforce, *An Unrecorded Chapter*, pp. 28–9.
9. H. H. Greathed, *Letters Written during the Siege of Delhi*, London, 1858, p. 179.
10. Cited by Allen, *Soldier Sahibs*, p. 304.
11. Lionel J. Trotter, *The Life of John Nicholson, Soldier and Administrator*, London, 1898, pp. 275, 277, 281.
12. Cited by Eric Stokes, *The Peasant Armed: The Indian Revolt of 1857*, ed. C. A. Bayly, Oxford, 1986, pp. 81–2.
13. Griffiths, *The Siege of Delhi*, p. 108.
14. Greathed, *Letters*, p. 169.
15. Ibid., p. 171.

16. Robert H. W. Dunlop, *Service and Adventure with the Khakee Ressalah*, London, 1858, pp. 64–5, 69.

17. Sir Henry W. Norman and Mrs Keith Young, *Delhi 1857*, London, 1902, p. 217.

18. Greathed, *Letters*, p. 174, 6 August to his wife; Oriental and India Office Collections, British Library (hereafter OIOC), Fraser Collection, Eur Mss E 258, Bundles 11 and 12, from the same to Mr Pidcock, 5 August 1857, Camp before Delhi. For details of Peake & Allen's shop, see Christopher Hibbert, *The Great Mutiny*, London, 1978, p. 289.

19. OIOC, Eur Mss C 190, A. C. Warner to Dick, 31 May 1857, cited in Narayani Gupta, *Delhi between Empires*, New Delhi, 1991, p. 21.

20. Griffiths, *The Siege of Delhi*, p. 64.

21. NAM, 6211/67, Letters of Lieutenant Charles Henry (Harry) F. Gambier, 38th Native Infantry, HG to Annie Forrest, Camp Delhi, 20 August 1857.

22. Ibid., HG to Annie Forrest, Camp Delhi, 1 September 1857.

23. OIOC, Vibart Papers, Eur Mss F 135/19, Camp before Delhi, 12 September 1857.

24. Ibid., Camp before Delhi, 27 August 1857 to Uncle Gordon.

25. For Neill's treatment of Kanpur, see Hibbert, *The Great Mutiny*, pp. 209–11, and Andrew Ward, *Our Bones Are Scattered*, London, 1996, pp. 454–7, 477. For Sikhs grilling their captives, see Lt Vivien Dering Majendie, *Up Among the Pandies or A Year's Service in India*, London, 1859, pp. 186–7.

26. Col. A. R. D. Mackenzie, *Mutiny Memoirs – being personal reminiscences of the Great Sepoy Revolt of 1857*, Allahabad, 1891, pp. 107–8.

27. Cited by Hibbert, *The Great Mutiny*, p. 354.

28. *Delhi Gazette Extra*, 20 June 1857.

29. Cited by Hibbert, *The Great Mutiny*, pp. 201, 340.

30. Rotton, *The Chaplain's Narrative*, p. 123.

31. Greathed, *Letters*, pp. 161, 205–6.

32. Cited by Allen, *Soldier Sahibs*, p. 305.

33. *Dihli Urdu Akbhar*, 23 August 1857.

34. *Delhi Gazette Extra*, 21 June and 8 July 1857.

35. National Archives of India (hereafter NAI), Mutiny Papers, Collection 61, no. 426; 21 August 1857 refers to a search for fishing rods in the city.

36. Abdul Latif, *1857 Ka Tarikhi Roznamacha*, ed. K. A. Nizami, Naqwatul Musannifin, Delhi, 1958, entry for 7 June 1857.

37. NAI, Mutiny Papers, Collection 128, no. 39, 12 June 1857.

38. *Memoirs of Hakim Ahsanullah Khan*, ed. S. Moinul Haq, Pakistan Historial Society, Karachi, 1958, p. 16.

39. NAI, Mutiny Papers, Collection 57, no. 185/186, 28 July 1857.

40. Ibid., Collection 61, no. 296, 4 August 1857.

41. Ibid., Collection 57, no. 328, 14 August 1857.

42. Delhi Commissioner's Office (hereafter DCO) Archive, Mutiny Papers, File no. 3, letter from the spy Turab Ali, 5 August 1857.

43. NAI, Mutiny Papers, Collection 61, no. 547 (undated but probably late July/early August 1857).

44. Ibid., Collection 61, no. 396, 17 August 1857.

45. *Memoirs of Hakim Ahsanullah Khan*, p. 21.

46. Ibid., pp. 28–9.

47. *A Short Account of the Life and Family of Rai Jiwan Lal Bahadur, Late Honorary Magistrate of Delhi with extracts from his diary relating to the time of the Mutiny 1857 compiled by his son*, Delhi, 1902, pp. 43–4.

48. Ibid. p. 45.

49. NAI, Mutiny Papers, Collection 20, no. 14 (undated but late August 1857); also *Memoirs of Hakim Ahsanullah Khan*, p. 29.

50. DCO Archive, Mutiny Papers, File no. 3, letter from the spy Turab Ali, 5 August 1857.

51. Charles Theophilus Metcalfe, *Two Native Narratives of the Mutiny in Delhi*, London, 1898, 'Narrative of Munshi Jiwan Lal', pp. 199–200.

52. *Memoirs of Hakim Ahsanullah Khan*, pp. 28–9.

53. For the nobles, see Metcalfe, *Two Native Narratives*, 'Narrative of Munshi Jiwan Lal', p. 197; for tax collecting in Gurgaon, see NAI, Mutiny Papers, Collection 20, no. 14 (undated but late August 1857); also *Memoirs of Hakim Ahsanullah Khan*, p. 29.

54. NAI, Mutiny Papers, Collection 20, no. 14 (undated but late August 1857).

55. Metcalfe, *Two Native Narratives*, 'Narrative of Munshi Jiwan Lal', p. 206.

56. *Dihli Urdu Akhbar*, 23 August 1857.

57. OIOC, Eur Mss, B 138, *Account of Said Mobarak Shah*.

58. Ibid.

59. For the lack of sulphur, see NAI, Mutiny Papers, Collection 15, no. 11, 21 August. For the use of captured English spirits in gunpowder manufacture, see Collection 60, nos 627–638. For problems in gunpowder manufacture see also DCO Archive, New Delhi, Mutiny Papers, File no. 5028, July 1857, Translation of a letter from Munshee Mahomed Bakar, 28 July, editor of the *Delhi Oordoo Akhbar*. For absence of percussion caps see Greathed, *Letters*, p. 45, and for failing shells see p. 67. For Gujars looting gunpowder in the early days of the Uprising see *Dihli Urdu Akhbar*, 31 May 1857.

60. Mirza Asadullah Khan Ghalib, *Dastanbuy*, trans. Khwaja Ahmad Faruqi, Delhi, 1970, p. 37.

61. NAI, Mutiny Papers, Collection 15, nos 5 and 6, 16 August 1857.

62. *Dihli Urdu Akhbar*, 23 August 1857.

63. NAI, Mutiny Papers, Collection 70, no. 243, 30 August 1857.

64. Ibid., Collection 62, no. 80, entry for 3 August 1857.

65. OIOC, Montgomery Papers, Eur Mss D1019, no. 174, Delhee News, 2 July 1857.

66. NAI, Mutiny Papers, Collection 62, no. 167, 5 September 1857.

67. Ibid., Collection 67, no. 143 (undated but late August 1857).

68. Ibid., Collection 62, no. 54, 24 June 1857.

69. Ibid., Collection 63, no. 42, 16 August 1857.

70. Ibid., Collection 62, no. 165 (undated).

71. Ibid., Collection 62, no. 84, 4 August 1857.

72. Ibid., Collection 62, no. 71, 22 July 1857.

73. Ibid., Collection 60, no. 687, 7 September 1857, and no. 688, 11 September 1857.

74. Ibid., Collection 62, no. 71, entry for 22 July 1857.

75. Ibid., Collection 60, no. 605, entry for 29 August 1857.
76. Ibid., Collection 71, no. 96, entry for 5 July 1857.
77. Ibid., Collection 71, no. 95, entry for 5 July 1857, a second witness statement of the same incident. There is also an account of this incident in *Memoirs of Hakim Ahsanullah Khan*, p. 21.
78. *Dihli Urdu Akhbar*, 23 August 1857.
79. Metcalfe, *Two Native Narratives*, 'Narrative of Munshi Jiwan Lal', pp. 204–5.
80. Ibid. p. 204. See also Stokes, *The Peasant Armed*, p. 85.
81. Metcalfe, *Two Native Narratives*, 'Narrative of Munshi Jiwan Lal', p. 206.
82. OIOC, Eur Mss B 138, *Account of Said Mobarak Shah*.
83. Ibid.
84. Griffiths, *The Siege of Delhi*, p. 123.
85. Greathed, *Letters*, pp. 225–6.
86. Richard Barter, *The Siege of Delhi*, London, 1984, p. 44.
87. Greathed, *Letters*, p. 227.
88. Metcalfe, *Two Native Narratives*, 'Narrative of Munshi Jiwan Lal', pp. 207–8.
89. Griffiths, *The Siege of Delhi*, p. 124.
90. Ibid., p. 125.
91. Ibid., pp. 125–6.
92. OIOC, Vibart Papers, Eur Mss F 135/19, Camp before Delhi, 27 August 1857.
93. OIOC, Eur Mss B 138, *Account of Said Mobarak Shah*.
94. Ibid.
95. Colonel George Bourchier, CB, *Eight Months Campaign against the Bengal Sepoy Army during the Mutiny of 1857*, London, 1858, p. 47.
96. Griffiths, *The Siege of Delhi*, p. 135.
97. Greathed, *Letters*, p. 251.
98. Lord Roberts of Kandahar, *Forty One Years in India: From Subaltern to Commander in Chief*, London, 1897, vol. 1, p. 219.
99. Metcalfe, *Two Native Narratives*, 'Narrative of Munshi Jiwan Lal', p. 209.
100. Ibid., p. 218.
101. Ibid. pp. 215–19. For replacing Zafar with Jawan Bakht, see OIOC, Montgomery Papers, Eur Mss D1019, no. 197, Delhee News, 31 August 1857.
102. NAI, Mutiny Papers, Collection 16, no. 20, 6 September 1857. See also Trial, p. 142.
103. Griffiths, *The Siege of Delhi*, p. 147.
104. Zahir Dehlavi, *Dastan i-Ghadr: An eyewitness account of the 1857 Uprising*, Lahore, 1955, p. 111.
105. OIOC, Eur Mss B 138, *Account of Said Mobarak Shah* for details of the *damdama*.
106. NAI, Mutiny Papers, Collection 73, No. 158, 8 September 1857.
107. Metcalfe, *Two Native Narratives*, 'Narrative of Munshi Jiwan Lal', p. 226. For the prominent role of the jihadis in attacking the construction parties, see *Memoirs of Hakim Ahsanullah Khan*, p. 31.
108. OIOC, Montgomery Papers, no. 198, 7 September 1857 (for the suicide *ghazis*) and NAI, Mutiny Papers, Collection 16, no. 27.

109. OIOC, Eur Mss B 138, *Account of Said Mobarak Shah*.
110. NAI, Mutiny Papers, Collection 65, no. 36, petition of Maulvi Sarfaraz Ali, 10 September 1857.
111. Greathed, *Letters*, p. 206.
112. OIOC, Eur Mss B 138, *Account of Said Mobarak Shah*.
113. NAI, Mutiny Papers, Collection 57, no. 461, 10 September 1857.
114. Barter, *The Siege of Delhi*, p. 45.
115. Griffiths, *The Siege of Delhi*, p. 147.
116. Barter, *The Siege of Delhi*, p. 45.
117. OIOC, Vibart Papers, Eur Mss F 135/19, Camp before Delhi, 12 September 1857.
118. Charles Ewart to his mother, cited in Hibbert, *The Great Mutiny*, p. 297.
119. Rotton, *The Chaplain's Narrative*, p. 260; also Hibbert, *The Great Mutiny*, p. 302.
120. NAI, Mutiny Papers, Collection 73, no. 167, 13 September 1857.
121. Metcalfe, *Two Native Narratives*, 'Narrative of Munshi Jiwan Lal', p. 229.
122. OIOC, Eur Mss B 138, *Account of Said Mobarak Shah*.
123. OIOC, Montgomery Papers, Eur Mss D1019, no. 184, 4 August 1857; no. 192, 24 August; no. 194, 23 August 1857; no. 196, 30 August. For the offer to blow up of the Bridge of Boats, see DCO Archive, Mutiny Papers, File No. 1, *Services performed by Mirza Elahee Bahksh by W. L. R. Hodson, 1 December 1857*.
124. Greathed, *Letters*, p. 217.
125. DCO Archive, Mutiny Papers, File no. 14, letter from Lt W. Hodson to C. B. Saunders on the terms of BSZ's surrender, 29 November 1857.
126. *Dihli Urdu Akbhar*, 13 September 1857.
127. Harriet Tytler, *An Englishwoman in India: The Memoirs of Harriet Tytler 1828–1858*, ed. Anthony Sattin, Oxford, 1986, p. 163.
128. Barter, *The Siege of Delhi*, p. 48.
129. South Asian Studies Library, Cambridge, Campbell Metcalfe Papers, Box 6, EC to GG (undated, but clearly the night of 13–14 September 1857).
130. Barter, *The Siege of Delhi*, p. 52.
131. Ibid., p. 52.

10: To Shoot Every Soul

1. Charles John Griffiths, *The Siege of Delhi*, London, 1910, pp. 156–7.
2. Letter signed 'Felix, to the Editor of the Lahore Chronicle', 30 September 1857.
3. Fred Roberts, *Letters Written during the Indian Mutiny*, London, 1924, p. 62.
4. Richard Barter, *The Siege of Delhi*, London, 1984, pp. 52–4.
5. Roberts, *Letters*, p. 62.
6. Letter signed 'Felix'. Also Roger Perkins, *The Kashmir Gate: Lieutenant Home and the Delhi VCs*, Chippenham, 1983, pp. 23–8.
7. National Army Museum (hereafter NAM), Coghill Letters, 6609-139, letter from Lt Coghill to his brother, datelined Delhi, 22 September 1857.

8. NAM, 6301/143, diaries of Col. E L. Ommaney, vol. A, pt 6, entry for 14 September.

9. Barter, *The Siege of Delhi*, London, 1984, p. 55.

10. Oriental and India Office Collections, British Library (hereafter OIOC), Eur Mss B 138, *Account of Said Mobarak Shah*.

11. John Edward Rotton, *The Chaplain's Narrative of the Siege of Delhi*, London, 1858, p. 275.

12. Roberts, *Letters*, p. 62.

13. OIOC, Photo Eur 31 1B, Hardcastle Papers, pp. 306, 333–5. See also the description of Zahir Dehlavi in *Dastan i-Ghadr: An eyewitness account of the 1857 Uprising*, Lahore, 1955, p. 113.

14. Charles Theophilus Metcalfe, *Two Native Narratives of the Mutiny in Delhi*, London, 1898, 'Narrative of Mainodin', p. 70.

15. OIOC, Eur Mss B 138, *Account of Said Mobarak Shah*.

16. Barter, *The Siege of Delhi*, p. 55.

17. Arthur Moffat Lang, *Lahore to Lucknow: The Indian Mutiny Journal of Arthur Moffat Lang*, London, 1992, pp. 90–92.

18. Ibid., p. 92; also Charles Allen, *Soldier Sahibs: The Men Who Made the North-West Frontier*, London, 2000, pp. 322–3.

19. Lord Roberts of Kandahar, *Forty One Years in India: From Subaltern to Commander in Chief*, London, 1897, vol. 1, p. 236.

20. Colonel George Bourchier, CB, *Eight Months Campaign against the Bengal Sepoy Army during the Mutiny of 1857*, London, 1858, p. 69.

21. Rotton, *The Chaplain's Narrative*, p. 295.

22. OIOC, Vibart Papers, Eur Mss F 135/19, Camp Delhi, 15 September 1857.

23. Roberts, *Letters*, pp. 63–5.

24. Major W. S. R. Hodson, *Twelve Years of a Soldier's Life in India*, London, 1859, p. 296.

25. Ibid., p. 294.

26. OIOC, Eur Mss B 138, *Account of Said Mobarak Shah*.

27. Barter, *The Siege of Delhi*, p. 58.

28. NAM, Coghill Letters, 6609-139, letter from Lt Coghill to his brother, datelined Delhi, 22 September 1857.

29. Lord Roberts of Kandahar, *Forty One Years in India*, vol. 1, p. 238.

30. OIOC, John Lawrence Collection, Eur Mss F 90, Folio 19b, NC to JL, datelined Skinner's House.

31. Lord Roberts of Kandahar, *Forty One Years in India*, vol. 1, pp. 238–9.

32. OIOC, John Lawrence Collection, Eur Mss F 90, Folio 19b, letter datelined Camp before Delhi, 17 December 1857.

33. Dehlavi, *Dastan i-Ghad*, pp. 111–12.

34. Ibid., p. 112.

35. Ibid., pp. 113–15.

36. Sarvar ul-Mulk, *My Life, Being the Autobiography of Nawab Server ul-Mulk Bahadur* trans. from the Urdu by his son, Nawab Jiwan Yar Jung Bahadur, London, 1903, p. 20.

37. Aslam Farrukhi, *Muhammad Husain Azad*, 2 vols, Karachi, 1965, vol. 1, p. 104.

38. Mirza Asadullah Khan Ghalib, *Dastanbuy*, trans. Khwaja Ahmad Faruqi, Delhi, 1970, p. 40.
39. Griffiths, *The Siege of Delhi*, pp. 97–9.
40. Rotton, *The Chaplain's Narrative*, p. 238.
41. South Asian Studies Library, Cambridge, Campbell Metcalfe Papers, Box 6, EC to GG, 25 September 1857.
42. Griffiths, *The Siege of Delhi*, p. 174.
43. Quoted in R. Montgomery Martin, *Indian Empire*, London, 1860, vol. II, p. 449.
44. Griffiths, *The Siege of Delhi*, p. 164.
45. William W. Ireland, *A History of the Siege of Delhi by an Officer who served there*, Edinburgh, 1861, p. 254.
46. NAM, Wilson Letters, AW to his wife, Delhi, 15 September 1857.
47. Griffiths, *The Siege of Delhi*, p. 178.
48. OIOC, Eur Mss B 138, *Account of Said Mobarak Shah*.
49. Ibid.
50. *Memoirs of Hakim Ahsanullah Khan*, ed. S. Moinul Haq, Pakistan Historial Society, Karachi, 1958, p. 32.
51. National Archives of India (hereafter NAI), Political Consultations, no. 12-27, 5 November, copies of telegrams arriving from Delhi at the Lahore telegraph office, received from Brig. General Neville Chamberlain, 17 September 1857.
52. *Memoirs of Hakim Ahsanullah Khan*, pp. 30–31.
53. OIOC, Eur Mss B 138, *Account of Said Mobarak Shah*.
54. NAM, Wilson Letters, AW to his wife, Delhi, 18 September 1857.
55. NAI, Political Consultations, no. 12-27, 5 November, copies of telegrams arriving from Delhi at the Lahore telegraph office, received from Brig. General Neville Chamberlain, 17 September 1857.
56. Ibid.
57. From interviews with Kulsum Zamani Begum's daughter, Zainab Zamani Begum, in Khwaja Hasan Nizami, *Begmat ke Aansu* (Tears of the Begums), Delhi, 1952.
58. Delhi Commissioner's office (hereafter DCO) Archive, Mutiny Papers, File no. 1, *Services performed by Mirza Elahee Bahksh for W. L. R. Hodson, 1 December 1857*.
59. *Memoirs of Hakim Ahsanullah Khan*, p. 32.
60. Munshi Faizuddin, *Bazm i-Akhir, Yani sehre e-Delhi ke do akhiri badshahon ka tareeq i-maashrat* (The Last Convivial Gathering – the Mode of Life of the Last Two Kings of Delhi), Lahore, 1965, p. 27.
61. Mehdi Hasan, 'Bahadur Shah, his relations with the British and the Mutiny: an objective study', *Islamic Culture*, Hyderabad, vol. 33, no. 2, 1959, pp. 95–111.
62. DCO Archive, Mutiny Papers, File no. 1, *Services performed by Mirza Elahee Bahksh*.
63. Ibid., File no. 14, letter from Lt W. Hodson to C. B. Saunders on the terms of BSZ's surrender, 29 November 1857. This crucial letter from Hodson is the earliest and most authentic account of the intrigues than preceded Zafar's surrender. It has never before been used by any historian.

64. Ibid.
65. Ibid.
66. *Memoirs of Hakim Ahsanullah Khan*, pp. 32–3.
67. Griffiths, *The Siege of Delhi*, p. 196.
68. Harriet Tytler, *An Englishwoman in India: The Memoirs of Harriet Tytler 1828–1888*, ed. Anthony Saltin, Oxford, 1986, pp. 163–4.
69. Dehlavi, *Dastan i-Ghadr*, pp. 117–18.
70. Farrukhi, *Muhammad Husain Azad*, vol. 1, p. 105.
71. Ibid., vol. 1, pp. 106–7.
72. Frances W. Pritchett, *Nets of Awareness: Urdu Poetry and Its Critics*, Berkeley and Los Angeles, 1994, pp. 25–6. Also Farrukhi, *Muhammad Husain Azad*, vol. 1, pp. 109–10.
73. NAI, Foreign, Foreign Dept Misc., *Precis of Palace Intelligence*, contains an entry that shows how much Zafar feared eclipses: in the entry for Thursday, 9 January 1851 it is written that 'Sookhamund Astrologer intimated that there would be an eclipse of the moon on Thursday night the 13th of Rubbee Ool Ouwal, and that HM should not appoint that day for his departure to the Kootub. Instructions were accordingly issued for HM's departure on the following day, Friday.'
74. Griffiths, *The Siege of Delhi*, pp. 183–4.
75. OIOC, Eur Mss B 138, *Account of Said Mobarak Shah*.
76. Khwaja Hasan Nizami, *Begmat ke Aansu*, Delhi, 1952.
77. Ireland, *A History of the Siege of Delhi*, p. 257.
78. NAM, 6309-26, Lt Gen. F. C. Maisey, 'The Capture of the Delhi Palace', pp. 4–7.
79. Ibid. pp. 7–11.
80. Ibid., p. 12.
81. NAI, Foreign Dept, Secret Consultations, 30 October 1857, pt 1, no. 83, to Chief Commr of the Punjab, 20 September 1857.
82. Allen, *Soldier Sahibs*, pp. 326–7.
83. Ibid., pp. 326–7.
84. NAI, Foreign Dept, Secret Consultations, 30 October 1857, pt 1, no. 86, from Mil. Secr. to Chief Commr of the Punjab, 23 September 1857.
85. OIOC, Vibart Papers, Eur Mss 135/19, Vibart to his Uncle Gordon, 22 September 1857.
86. Dehlavi, *Dastan i-Ghadr*, p. 128.
87. Rashid ul-Khairi, *Dilli Ki Akhiri Bahar*, ed. S. Zamir Hasan, Delhi, 1991, cited by C. M. Naim in his essay on Sahbai in Margrit Pernau (ed.), *Delhi College*, New Delhi, 2006.
88. Dehlavi, *Dastan i-Ghadr*, p. 127.
89. Ireland, *A History of the Siege of Delhi*, pp. 255–6.
90. Dehlavi, *Dastan i-Ghadr*, p. 128.
91. OIOC, Eur Mss B 138, *Account of Said Mobarak Shah*.
92. DCO Archive, Mutiny Papers, File no. 1, *Services performed by Mirza Elahee Bahksh*.
93. NAM, 6309-26, Lt Gen. F. C. Maisey, 'The Capture of the Delhi Palace', p. 13.

94. DCO Archive, Mutiny Papers, File no. 1, *Services performed by Mirza Elahee Bahksh*.
95. Hodson, *Twelve Years*, p. 300; for Mirza Ilahe Bakhsh, see DCO Archive, Mutiny Papers, File no. 14, letter from Lt W. Hodson to C. B. Saunders, 29 November 1857, para. 5.
96. Rotton, *The Chaplain's Narrative*, p. 318.
97. Ireland, *A History of the Siege of Delhi*, p. 274.
98. NAM, 6301-143, Col. E. L. Ommaney's diaries, entry for 21 September 1857.
99. DCO Archive, Mutiny Papers, File no. 14, letter from Lt W. Hodson to C. B. Saunders on the terms of BSZ's surrender, 29 November 1857.

11: The City of the Dead

1. Delhi Commissioner's Office (hereafter DCO) Archive, Mutiny Papers, File no. 14, letter from Lt W. Hodson to C. B. Saunders, 29 November 1857.
2. Ibid.
3. Ibid., File no. 10, letter no. 3, from Lt W. Hodson to C. B. Saunders, 28 November 1857, '*GUARANTEE THE LIFE OF THE KING FROM BE IZZAT AT THE HANDS OF THE GORA LOGUE*'.
4. Ibid., File no. 14, letter from Lt W. Hodson to C. B. Saunders, 29 November 1857.
5. William W. Ireland, *A History of the Siege of Delhi by an Officer who served there*, Edinburgh, 1861, p. 263. Ireland explicitly has the party entering the town through the Lahore Gate, though the Delhi Gate might be expected to be the obvious point of entry for a party coming from Humayun's Tomb.
6. James Wise, *The Diary of a Medical Officer during the Great Indian Mutiny of 1857*, Cork, 1894, pp. 114–15.
7. Major W. S. R. Hodson, *Twelve Years of a Soldier's Life in India*, London, 1859, p. 307.
8. National Army Museum (hereafter NAM), 6309-26, Lt Gen. F. C. Maisey, 'The Capture of the Delhi Palace', p. 13.
9. NAM, Coghill Letters, 6609-139, letter from Lt Coghill to his brother, datelined Delhi, 22 September 1857.
10. DCO Archive, Mutiny Papers, File no. 1, *Services performed by Mirza Elahee Bahksh for W. L. R. Hodson, 1 December 1857*.
11. Hodson, *Twelve Years*, pp. 310–12.
12. Ibid., p. 302.
13. NAM, 6309-26, Lt Gen. F. C. Maisey, 'The Capture of the Delhi Palace', p. 16.
14. Charles John Griffiths, *The Siege of Delhi*, London, 1910, pp. 204–5.
15. Sir George Campbell, *Memoirs of My Indian Career*, London, 1893, vol 1.
16. Oriental and India Office Collections, British Library (hereafter OIOC), Eur Mss Photo Eur 271, Letters of Hugh Chichester, letters to his father, Delhi, 24 September 1857.
17. Ireland, *A History of the Siege of Delhi*, pp. 307–8.

18. Griffiths, *The Siege of Delhi*, p. 202.
19. OIOC, Saunders Papers, Eur Mss E 187, correspondence pt IV, private letters 1857–60, K&J 716, 1–79, no. 44, Matilda Saunders to Eliza Saunders, Delhi Palace.
20. Ibid.
21. Cited by Christopher Hibbert, *The Great Mutiny: India 1857*, London, 1978, p. 317.
22. Frances W. Pritchett, *Nets of Awareness: Urdu Poetry and Its Critics*, Berkeley and Los Angeles, 1994, p. 27, quoting Hali's biographer Salihah Abid Hussain.
23. Mrs Muter, *My Recollections of the Sepoy Revolt*, London, 1911, p. 132.
24. NAM, 6301/143, Diaries of Col. E. L. Ommaney, vol. A, entry for 30 October 1857.
25. Ibid., entry for 23 December 1857.
26. Ibid., entry for 30 October 1857.
27. R. M. Coopland, *A Lady's Escape from Gwalior and Life in the Fort of Agra during the Mutinies of 1857*, London, 1859 pp. 268–9.
28. Michael Maclagan, *'Clemency' Canning*, London, 1962, p. 98.
29. Ibid., p. 140.
30. OIOC, Eur Mss Photo Eur 271, Letters of Hugh Chichester, letters to his father, Camp Delhi, 24 September 1857.
31. Ireland, *A History of the Siege of Delhi*, pp. 280–81.
32. DCO Archive, Mutiny Papers, Box 1, File no. 5, 2 October 1857, no. 279, C. B. Thornhill to G. I. Hansey.
33. *Delhi Gazette Extra*, 10 December 1857.
34. Ibid., 2 January 1858.
35. John Edward Rotton, *The Chaplain's Narrative of the Siege of Delhi*, London 1858, pp. 325–6.
36. Coopland, *A Lady's Escape*, p. 259.
37. Richard Barter, *The Siege of Delhi*, London, 1984, p. 76.
38. Lord Roberts of Kandahar, *Forty One Years in India: From Subaltern to Commander in Chief*, London, 1897, vol. 1, pp. 258–9.
39. NAM, 6301/143, Diaries of Col. E. L. Ommaney, vol. A, pt 6, entry for 1 November 1857. Ommaney's diary is the most important single source for the imprisonment of Zafar. As far as I am aware it has never been used before by any historian.
40. Ibid., entry for 24 November 1857.
41. Ibid., entry for 28 September 1857.
42. Coopland, *A Lady's Escape*, pp. 274–7.
43. Ireland, *A History of the Siege of Delhi*, pp. 280–81.
44. Coopland, *A Lady's Escape*, p. 276.
45. OIOC, Saunders Papers, Eur Mss E 186, correspondence pt III, official and demi-official letters, 1857–60, no. 128, Ommanney to Saunders, 1 October 1857 says that Zafar is asking for his barber 'to shave his once royal face'.
46. Ibid., no. 26, Lawrence to Saunders, 29 December 1857.
47. A cutting survives in Ommaney's diaries, entry for 6 November 1857: NAM, 6301/143, Diaries of Col. E. L. Ommaney, vol. A.

48. Ibid.

49. OIOC, Eur Mss Photo Eur 271, Letters of Hugh Chichester, letters to his father, Delhi, 24 September 1857.

50. Cited in Farhan Ahmad Nizami, *Madrasahs, Scholars and Saints: Muslim Response to the British Presence in Delhi and the Upper Doab 1803–1857*, unpublished PhD, Oxford, 1983, p. 219.

51. Coopland, *A Lady's Escape*, pp. 278–9.

52. Quoted in Charles Ball, *The History of the Indian Mutiny*, 1858–9, vol. 2, p. 179

53. NAM, 6301/143, Diaries of Col. E. L. Ommaney, vol. A, entries for 20 and 23 September 1857.

54. Ibid., entry for 15 October 1857.

55. Ibid., entry for 23 September 1857.

56. Ibid., entry for 19 November 1857.

57. Ibid., entry for 19 November 1857.

58. Ibid., entry for 13 November 1857.

59. Ibid., entry for 21 October 1857.

60. Ibid., entry for 19 November 1857.

61. These documents are now in the NAI and form the core of the Mutiny Papers collection.

62. NAM, 6301/143, Diaries of Col. E. L. Ommaney, vol. A, entry for 27 November 1857.

63. Griffiths, *The Siege of Delhi*, pp. 199–200.

64. Ibid., p. 234.

65. Mrs Muter, *My Recollections of the Sepoy Revolt*, London, 1911, pp. 137–8.

66. Griffiths, *The Siege of Delhi*, pp. 235–7.

67. *Records of the Intelligence Department of the Government of the North West Provinces of India during the Mutiny of 1857*, Edinburgh, 1902, vol. 2, pp. 298–9.

68. *A Short Account of the Life and Family of Rai Jawan Lal Bahadur, Late Honorary Magistrate of Delhi with extracts from his diary relating to the time of the Mutiny 1857 compiled by his son*, Delhi, 1902, p. 48.

69. DCO Archive, Mutiny Papers, File no. 1, *Services performed by Mirza Elahee Bahksh*.

70. NAI, Foreign Secret Consultations, no. 524, 29 January 1858, Ramchandra to Burn, 27 November 1857.

71. Mirza Asadullah Khan Ghalib, *Dastanbuy*, trans. Khwaja Ahmad Faruqi, Delhi, 1970, pp. 43–6.

72. Hali's account, from Ralph Russell, *The Oxford Ghalib: Life, Letters and Ghazals*, New Delhi, 2003, pp. 129–30.

73. Ghalib's own account, from ibid., p. 130.

74. Pritchett, *Nets of Awareness*, p. 20.

75. Cited in Pavan Varma, *Ghalib: The Man, The Times*, New Delhi, 1989, p. 153.

76. Cited in Gopi Chand Narang, 'Ghalib and the Rebellion of 1857', in Narang, *Urdu Language and Literature: Critical Perspectives*, New Delhi, 1991, pp. 2–3.

77. Ibid., p. 3.

78. Cited in 'The Sack of Delhi as Witnessed by Ghalib', *Bengal Past & Present*, no. 12, January–December 1955, p. 111n.

79. *Delhi Gazette*, 21 December 1857.

80. Russell, *The Oxford Ghalib*, p. 132.

81. Cited in Narayani Gupta, *Delhi between Empires*, New Delhi, 1991, p. 23. For the destruction of shanties, see 'The Sack of Delhi,' p. 112.

82. *Records of the Intelligence Department*, vol. 2, pp. 298–300.

83. Ireland, *A History of the Siege of Delhi*, pp. 279–80.

84. Sarvar ul-Mulk, *My Life, Being the Autobiography of Nawab Sarvar ul-Mulk Bahadur*, trans. from the Urdu by his son, Nawab Jiwan Yar Jung Bahadur, London, 1903, p. 21.

85. Ibid., p. 20.

86. Zahir Dehlavi, *Dastan i-Ghadr: An eyewitness account of the 1857 Uprising*, Lahore, 1955, p. 132.

87. Ibid., p. 135.

88. Ibid., pp. 140–42.

89. Ibid., pp. 163–7.

90. Ibid., p. 252.

91. NAM, 6301/143, Diaries of Col. E. L. Ommaney, vol. A, entries for 12 and 13 October 1857.

92. Ibid., entry for 13 October 1857. For the firing squad and their poor aim see Griffiths, *The Siege of Delhi*, p. 214.

93. Ireland, *A History of the Siege of Delhi*, p. 280.

94. Pritchett, *Nets of Awareness*, p. 18.

95. Arsh Taimuri, *Qila-i Mua 'lla ki Jhalkiyan*, ed. Aslam Parvez, Urdu Academy, Delhi, 1986.

96. The Mutiny Papers in the DCO seem to be almost completely unused by historians. As far as I can ascertain, only two historians – Narayani Gupta and Anisha Shekhar Mukherji – have to date published material from this astonishingly rich collection.

97. DCO, Mutiny Papers, Box no. 2, File no. 49, letter no. 110, Saunders to Sec. to the Gov. of the Punjab, 21 April 1859.

98. Ibid. See, for example, Box 2, File no. 73, Davies to Saunders, 13 June 1859, Davies to Beadon, 26 April 1859, and Davies to Beadon, 27 May 1859. For the lost prisoners and their eventual exile in Karachi, see Box 2, File no. 83, 29 June 1859; File 85, 1 July 1859; File 86, 2 July 1859; and File 87, 5 July 1859. For the absconding *salatin* from Karachi, see File no. 127, *Order passed by the Govt regarding the settlement of the Sulateens*, 10 October 1860.

99. Dehlavi, *Dastan i-Ghadr*, p. 151. There is a fine portrait of the Nawab in Stuart Cary Welch, *Room for Wonder: Indian Paintings during the British Period 1760–1880*, New York, 1978, pp. 120–21.

100. DCO, Mutiny Papers, File no. 10, letter no. 54, Saunders to Lawrence, 1 December 1857.

101. NAM, 6301/143, Diaries of Col. E. L. Ommaney, vol. A, entry for 9 November 1857.

102. Ibid., entry for 20 October 1857.

103. Ibid., entry for 23 December 1857.

104. Muter, *My Recollections*, pp. 145–6.

105. *Delhi Gazetteer*, 1883–4, p. 30.

106. NAM, 6301/143, Diaries of Col. E. L. Ommaney, vol. A, pt 6, entry for 5 November 1857.

107. Dehlavi, *Dastan i-Ghadr*, p. 151.

108. Coopland, *A Lady's Escape*, p. 212.

109. OIOC, Lawrence Papers, Eur Mss F 90, Camp near Goordaspur, 25 April 1858. Also C. B. Saunders Papers, Eur Mss E 187, correspondence pt IV, private letters 1857–60, K&J 716, 1–79, no. 24, Lawrence to Saunders (extract), Lahore, 15 December 1857; see also no. 24, Enclosure – William Muir to Lawrence, Agra, 12 December 1857.

110. OIOC, Lawrence Papers, Eur Mss F 90, JL to Saunders, Lahore, 6 October 1857; also JL to Saunders, letter datelined Camp Delhi, 2 March 1858.

111. South Asian Studies Library, Cambridge, Campbell Metcalfe Papers, Box 6, EC to GG, Delhie (undated but obviously September 1857).

112. Ibid., Box 10, EC to GG, Delhie, 30 September 1857.

113. Ibid.

114. This important point was well argued by F. W. Buckler (1891–1960) in his rightly celebrated essay 'The Political Theory of the Indian Mutiny', *Trans. of the Royal Historical Soc.*, 4(5), 1922, pp. 71–100 (also reprinted in *Legitimacy and Symbols: The South Asian writings of F. W. Buckler*, ed. M. N. Pearson, Center for South and Southeast Asian Studies, University of Michigan, Ann Arbor, c. 1985.

115. W. H. Russell, *My Diary in India*, London, 1860, vol. 2, pp. 58, 60–61.

116. Ibid., vol. 2, pp. 48–9.

117. Ibid., vol. 2, pp. 50–51.

118. NAM, 6301/143, Diaries of Col. E. L. Ommaney, vol. A, entry for 27 January 1858.

119. OIOC, Eur Mss E 186, Saunders Papers, Letters of Lt Edward Ommaney to Charles Saunders, no. 212, EO to CS, 27 January 1858.

120. NAM, 6301/143, Diaries of Col. E. L. Ommaney, vol. A, entry for 27 January. Also Harriet Tytler, *An Englishwoman in India: The Memoirs of Harriet Tytler 1828–1858*, ed. Anthony Sattin, Oxford, 1986, p. 167.

121. Edward Vibart, *The Sepoy Mutiny as Seen by a Subaltern from Delhi to Lucknow*, London, 1858, p. 148.

122. Charles Ball, *The History of the Indian Mutiny*, 2 vols, 1858–9, vol. 2, p. 171.

123. Ibid., p. 172.

124. NAM, 6301/143, Diaries of Col. E. L. Ommaney, vol. A, entry for 27 January. See also Ball, *History*, vol. 2, p. 172.

125. Ball, *History*, p. 177.

126. *Proceedings on the Trial of Muhammad Bahadur Shah, Titular King of Delhi, before a Military Commission, upon a charge of Rebellion, Treason and Murder, held at Delhi, on the 27th Day of January 1858, and following days London, 1859* (hereafter Trial), pp. 131–3.

127. Ibid., pp. 151–3.

128. Ibid., pp. 72, 151–2.

129. NAM, 6301/143, Diaries of Col. E. L. Ommaney, vol. A. entry for 27 March 1858.
130. Muter, *My Recollections*, pp. 149–151.
131. Ibid., p. 149.
132. Trial, p. 153.
133. Ibid., p. 153.
134. Ball, *History*, p. 178.
135. OIOC, Political Consultations, Range 203, 67, vol. 14, P/203/67, Fort William, 10 December 1858, no. 535A, Saunders to Ommaney, 4 October 1858.
136. OIOC, Saunders Papers, Eur Mss E 187, correspondence pt IV, private letters 1857–60, 1–79, no. 66, Matilda Saunders to her mother-in-law, Ludlow Castle, Dehlie, 13 October 1858.

12: The Last of the Great Mughals

1. Oriental and India Office Collections, British Library (hereafter OIOC), Eur Mss E 186, Saunders Papers, Letters of Lt Edward Ommaney to Charles Saunders, no. 278, EO to CS, 13 October 1858, Camp Soomha.
2. Delhi Commissioner's Office (hereafter DCO) Archive, Delhi, File 65A, 7 December 1858, *Report on the Character and Conduct of the Attendants of the ex royal King.*
3. *Delhi Gazette* (hereafter DG), 13 October 1858.
4. OIOC, Eur Mss E 186, Saunders Papers, Letters of Lt Edward Ommaney to Charles Saunders, no. 282, EO to CS, 5 November 1858.
5. Ibid., no. 280, EO to CS, 23 October 1858.
6. Ibid., no. 279, EO to CS, 19 October 1858 from Camp Etah.
7. DG, 13 October 1858.
8. OIOC, Eur Mss E 186, Saunders Papers, Letters of Lt Edward Ommaney to Charles Saunders, no. 230, EO to CS, 30 March 1858.
9. Ibid., no. 272, EO to CS, 1 October 1858.
10. OIOC, India Proceedings, Political Consultations, Range 203, vol. 14, Fort William, 10 December 1858, no. 77, From G. F. Edmonstone, Secr. to Govt of India, to C. Beadon, Off. Secr., Foreign Dept Calcutta, Allahabad, 16 November 1858. For Ommaney's meeting with Canning see OIOC, Eur Mss E 186, Saunders Papers, Letters of Lt Edward Ommaney to Charles Saunders, no. 283, EO to CS, 17 November 1858, Camp Wuhda Nugger.
11. OIOC, India Proceedings, Political Consultations, Range 203, vol. 14, Fort William, 10 December 1858, no. 66, *Proceedings of a committee of Medical Officers, assembled by the order of the Rt. Hon, the Governor General of India for the purpose of examining and reporting upon the physical condition of Mahomed Bahadoor Shah, lately King of Delhie. President, G. M. Hadaway, Dy. Inspector General of Queens Hospitals. Members: Superintending Surgeon Cawnpore Circle, Surgeon J. Leckie M.D., surgeon to the Governor-General.*
12. OIOC, India Proceedings, Political Consultations, Range 203, vol. 14, Fort

William, 10 December 1858, no. 4546, from Sec. to Gov. Gen. to Commissioner of Pegu, 13 November 1858.

13. OIOC, Eur Mss E 186, Saunders Papers, Letters of Lt Edward Ommaney to Charles Saunders, no. 284, EO to CS, 23 November 1858.

14. Ibid.

15. OIOC, Eur Mss E 186, Saunders Papers, Letters of Lt Edward Ommaney to Charles Saunders, no. 285, EO to CS, 14 December 1858.

16. Ibid.

17. Ibid.

18. *The Calcutta Englishman*, 1852, cited in Noel F. Singer, *Old Rangoon*, Gartmore, 1995, p. 69.

19. Ralph Russell, *The Oxford Ghalib: Life, Letters and Ghazals*, New Delhi, 2003, p. 182.

20. Cited by Eric Stokes, *The Peasant Armed: The Indian Revolt of 1857*, ed. C. A. Bayly, Oxford, 1986, p. 92, note 42.

21. OIOC, Lawrence Papers, Eur Mss F 90, Folio 12, Muree, June 1858.

22. Ibid., John Lawrence to Charles Trevelyan, Camp near Baree Doab Canal, 23 April 1858.

23. Cited in Gautam Chakravarty, *The Indian Mutiny and the British Imagination*, Cambridge, 2005, p. 41.

24. DCO Archive, Delhi, Foreign/General, January 1864, no. 16, *Copy of a Letter from the Commr Delhi Division, to the Sec, Govt of Punjab (no. 185 dated the 2nd Sept. 1863)*, points 3 and 10.

25. OIOC, Lawrence Papers, Eur Mss F 90, Folio 12, John Lawrence to Charles Trevelyan, Camp Multan Road, 16 December 1857.

26. NAI, Foreign Secret, 25 January 1858, 11-15, p. 51, Chief of Staff to Commanding Officer Meerut Division, 27 January 1858.

27. DCO Archive, Delhi, Foreign/General, January 1864, *Copy of a letter from the Offcg Commr, to the Commissioner Delhi Div. no. 256-209 dated 21st Aug. 1863*. Here the Dariba was said to have been saved 'by the strong representations of the Dep. Commr (Mr Philip Egerton) and Commr (Mr Brandreth)'.

28. Cited in in 'The Sack of Delhi as Witnessed by Ghalib', *Bengal Past & Present*, no. 12, January-December 1955, p. 110.

29. Ibid., p. 111.

30. Narayani Gupta, *Delhi between Empires*, New Delhi, 1991, p. 27.

31. Harriet Tytler, *An Englishwoman in India: The Memoirs of Harriet Tytler 1828-1858*, ed. Anthony Sattin, Oxford, 1986 p. 165.

32. James Fergusson, *History of Indian & Eastern Architecture*, London, 1876, p. 594.

33. Ibid., p. 311n.

34. Anisha Shekhar Mukherji, *The Red Fort of Shahjahanabad*, New Delhi, 2003, has much the best account of the destruction and Anglicisation of the Mughal palace – see pp. 203-7.

35. Mirza Asadullah Khan Ghalib, *Dastanbuy*, trans. Khwaja Ahmad Faruqi, Delhi, 1970, pp. 60-61.

36. Cited in Gupta, *Delhi between Empires*, p. 23. Gupta's remarkable book

is much the best souce for Delhi's transition from Mughal to colonial city.

37. NAI, Foreign Political Dept, Consultation 31, 31 December 1959, no. 2269, *Abstract Translation of a Petition from the Musulmans of Delhi trans. by I. B. Outram, asst sec. to Govt.*

38. *Mofussilite*, June 1860, cited in Gupta, *Delhi between Empires*, p. 25.

39. Gupta, *Delhi between Empires*, p. 24.

40. Ibid., p. 27.

41. Cited in ibid., p. 41.

42. C. F. Andrews, *Zakaullah of Delhi*, Cambridge, 1929, pp. 67, 75.

43. Russell, *The Oxford Ghalib*, p. 200.

44. For the Saunders inquiry into the rape of British women at the outbreak, see OIOC, Eur Mss E 185, Saunders Papers, no. 104, Muir to Saunders, Agra, 2 December 1857, and no. 111, Muir to Saunders, Agra, 14 December 1857. See also Muir's letter reproduced in S. M. Burke and Salim al-Din Quraishi, *Bahadur Shah: Last Mogul Emperor of India*, Lahore, 1995, pp. 178–9. For the mass rape of women of the royal house, see DCO Archive, Mutiny Papers, Box 2, File no. 109, 31 October 1859, *Report on the Surviving Members of the Taimur House who are assigned a maintenance*, no. 303 from Brandreth, Commr of Delhi to the Secr., Gov. of Punjab, dated 31 October 1859.

45. Russell, *The Oxford Ghalib*, p. 188.

46. Farhan Ahmad Nizami, *Madrasahs, Scholars and Saints: Muslim Response to the British Presence in Delhi and the Upper Doab 1803–1857*, unpublished DPhil, Oxford, 1983, p. 19.

47. Cited in Gupta, *Delhi between Empires*, p. 41.

48. Cited in Frances W. Pritchett, *Nets of Awareness: Urdu Poetry and Its Critics*, Berkeley and Los Angeles, 1994, p. 22. The great Urdu scholar S. R. Farooqi believes Ghalib may well have exaggerated the amount of poetry he lost in 1857.

49. Russell, *The Oxford Ghalib*, p. 187.

50. Ibid., p. 165.

51. Ibid., pp. 154, 157.

52. Ibid., p. 214.

53. Cited in Pritchett, *Nets of Awareness*, p. 29. There is a school of thought, championed by C. M. Naim, which argues that Zafar and the court had only a nominal influence on the Delhi renaissance, and that it flourished most successfully in centres of intellectual endeavour removed from the court, such as Delhi College and the madrasas. Yet the same elite – men like Sahbai, Fazl-i Haq and Azurda – moved between *mushairas*, madrasas, lecture halls and Zafar's durbar, and it seems – at least in the eyes of this writer – difficult to separate one from the other. Certainly with the fall of the city, all disappeared at the same time in the same cataclysm.

54. Myanmar National Archives (hereafter MNA), Series 1/1 (A), Acc. No. 983, File no. 85, 1859, *Confinement of Delhi state prisoners in Rangoon*; also OIOC, Foreign Political Proceedings, Z/P/203/50, Phayre to Beadon, 2 May 1859.

55. NAI, Foreign Consultations, 11 November 1859, pp. 124–5, from Capt. H. N. Davies in Charge of the State Prisoners, to C. Beadon, Secr. to Gov. of India, Foreign Dept, Fort William, dated Rangoon, 3 August 1859.

56. MNA, no. 5922, from Sec. to GG to Lt Col. Phayre, 27 September 1859.

57. Ibid., no. 5470 from Sec. to GG to Lt Col. Phayre, 6 September 1859.

58. Ibid., Series 1/1A, Acc. no. 555, 1860, File no. 58, 1860, Confinement of Delhi State Prisoners at Rangoon.

59. Ibid.

60. Ibid.

61. Ibid., Acc. no. 702, 1863, File no. 151, 1863.

62. Russell, *The Oxford Ghalib*, p. 207.

63. Mark Thornhill, *Personal Adventures and Experiences of a Magistrate, during the Rise, Progress and Suppression of the Indian Mutiny*, London, 1884, p. 7.

64. Cited in David Lelyveld, *Aligarh's First Generation: Muslim Solidarity in British India*, Princeton, NJ, 1978, p. 6.

65. Cited in Pritchett, *Nets of Awareness*, p. 30.

66. Ibid. This wonderful book is a beautifully written account of 'how the ghazal, for centuries the pride and joy of Indo-Muslim culture, was abruptly dethroned and devalued within its own milieu and by its own theorists'. It contains the best account yet written of the loss of Indo-Muslim cultural confidence following 1857, and has been a central influence on me in the course of writing this book.

67. Cited in ibid., p.xvi.

68. MNA, Series 1/1A, Acc. no.702, 1863, File no. 151, p. 59.

69. Ibid., Acc. no. 832, 1867, File no. 41, Delhi State Prisoners.

70. Ibid., Acc. no. 1434, 1872, File no.63, dated Rangoon, 29 August 1872.

71. Ibid.

72. Ibid.

73. Ibid., p. 33, letter from Secr. to Gov. of India, Foreign Dept, to CC British Burma, no. 28 C.P., dated on board *Outram*, 28 October 1872.

74. Burke and Quraishi, *Bahadur Shah*, p. 205.

75. MNA, Series 1/1A, Acc. no. 3656, 1905, File no. C, 4, Bahadur Shah (ex-King of Delhi) Preservation of Grave.

76. Ibid., Acc no. 3657, 1906–7, File no. 55/56, Bahadur Shah (ex-King of Delhi) Preservation of Grave.

77. Ibid.

78. Burke and Quraishi, *Bahadur Shah*, p. 205.

79. This information is contained in a map – Third Edition, 1944, HIND/SEA/1036, overprinted by Survey Dte Main HQ ALFSEA, April 1945 – apparently produced by British military intelligence during the Second World War, and showing Japanese positions in the town, including INA billets and 'The Jap officers' dance hall and brothel'. As the area was the former British cantonment it is unclear whether the placement was accidental or deliberate: it could have been either. I would like to thank the British ambassador, Vicky Bowman, for showing the map to me.

80. See, for example, Lelyveld, *Aligarh's First Generation*.

81. The Deobandis have received an excellent study in Barbara Metcalfe's magnum opus, *Islamic Revival in British India: Deoband 1860–1900*, Princeton, NJ, 1982. For more modern developments, see also Jamal Malik, *Colonisation of Islam: Dissolution of Traditional Institutions in Pakistan*, Manohar, 1988.

82. The provenance of this quotation is disputed: some attribute it to George Santayana.

BIBLIOGRAPHY

I. MANUSCRIPT SOURCES IN EUROPEAN LANGUAGES

Oriental and India Office Collections, British Library (formerly India Office Library), London (OIOC)

Edwardes Papers, Mss Eur E 211
Chichester Letters, Mss Eur Photo Eur 271
Hardcastle Papers, Mss Eur Photo Eur 31 1B
Johnson Diaries, Mss Eur A 101
John Lawrence Papers, Mss Eur F 90
Metcalfe Papers, Mss Eur D 610
Montgomery Papers, Mss Eur D 1019
Saunders Papers, Mss Eur E 185–187
Vibart Papers, Mss Eur F 135/19
The City of Delhi during 1857, translation of the account of Said Mobarak Shah, Eur Mss B 138
Home Miscellaneous, vol. 725, Kaye Mutiny Papers
Delhi Gazette
Delhi Gazette Extra
Lahore Chronicle
Bengal Wills 1780–1804 L/AG/34/29/4–16
Madras Inventories L/AG/34/29 185–210
Bengal Regimental Orders IOR/P/BEN/SEC
Bengal Political Consultations IOR/P/117/18

British Library

Wellesley Papers, Add Mss 13,582

South Asian Studies Centre Library, Cambridge

Campbell Metcalfe Papers

Bodleian Library, Oxford

Jennings Papers
Archives of the Society for the Propagation of the Gospel (SPG)

National Army Museum Library, London

Ewart Papers, 7310–48
Gambier Letters, 6211–67
Gardner Papers, 6305–56
Coghill Letters, 6609–139
Lt Gen. F. C. Maisey, 'The Capture of the Delhi Palace', 6309–26
Spy Letters, 6807–138
Col. E. L. Ommaney's Letters and Diaries, 6301–143
Wilson Correspondence, 5710–38, NAM

Nottingham University Library

Bentinck Papers, PW JF 1537–1556

National Archives of India, New Delhi

Precis of Palace Intelligence, Foreign, Foreign Dept Misc., vol. 361
Mutiny Papers
Dehli Urdu Akhbar
Siraj ul Akhbar
Ahsan ul Akhbar
Lahore Chronicle
Secret Consultations
Political Consultations
Foreign Consultations
Foreign Miscellaneous
Secret Letters to Court
Secret Letters from Court
Political Letters to Court
Political Letters from Court

Delhi Commissioners' Office Archive, New Delhi
Mutiny Papers
Mubarak Bagh Papers

Myanmar National Archives, Yangon

Records of the Delhi State Prisoners
Files on the Grave of the King of Delhi

Punjab Archives, Lahore

Delhi Residency Papers
Punjab Mutiny Papers

Private Archives

Fraser Papers, Inverness

2. UNPUBLISHED MANUSCRIPTS AND DISSERTATIONS

Ghosh, Durba, 'Colonial Companions: Bibis, Begums, and Concubines of the British in North India 1760–1830;' (unpublished PhD, Berkeley, 2000)

Hashmi, Shakila Tabassum Hashmi, 'The Trial of Bahadur Shah Zafar: Representation and Reality in Mughal-British Relations' (unpublished B.A. Honours thesis, Department of History, National University of Singapore 1, 1998/99)

Nizami, Farhan Ahmad, 'Madrasahs, Scholars and Saints: Muslim Responses to the British Presence in Delhi and the Upper Doab 1803–1857' (unpublished PhD, Oxford, 1983)

Shorto, Sylvia, 'Public Lives, Private Places, British Houses in Delhi 1803–57' (unpublished dissertation, New York University, 2004)

3. PERSIAN AND URDU SOURCES

A. Manuscripts

Oriental and India Office Collections, British Library (formerly India Office Library), London (OIOC)
The calligraphy of Zafar and Mirza Fakhru, OIOC: 3577 and 2972/42

Private family papers in the haveli of the late Mirza Farid Beg, Old Delhi

Bankipore Oriental Library, Patna
Farasu, *Zafar-uz Zafar* (also known as the *Fath Nama-I Angrezi*), Ms 129, Oriental Library, Bankipur

B. Published Texts

Ahmad, Naim, *Shahr ashob*, New Delhi, 1968
Ali, Ahmed, *The Golden Tradition: An Anthology of Urdu Poetry*, New York, 1973
Azad, Muhammed Husain (trans. and ed. Frances Pritchett and Shamsur

Rahman Faruqi), *Ab-e Hayat: Shaping the Canon of Urdu Poetry*, New Delhi, 2001

Dehlavi, Zahir, *Dastan i-Ghadr: Ya Taraze Zaheeri*, Lahore, 1955

Faizuddin, Munshi, *Bazm i-Akhir, Yani sehr e-Delhi ke do akhiri badshahon ka tareeq i-maashrat (The Last Convivial Gathering – The Mode of Life of the Last Two Kings of Delhi)*, Lahore, 1965

Farrukhi, Aslam, *Muhammad Husain Azad*, 2 vols, Karachi, 1965

Ghalib, Mirza Asadullah Khan, *Dastanbuy* (trans. Khwaja Ahmad Faruqi), New Delhi, 1970

Khairabadi, Allamah Fazl ul-Haqq, 'The Story of the War of Independence, 1857–8', in *Journal of the Pakistan Historical Society*, vol. 5, January 1957, part 1

Khan, Hakim Ahsanullah, 'Memoirs', in *Journal of the Pakistan Historical Society*, vol. 6, 1958

Khan, Dargah Quli, *The Muraqqa' e-Dehli* (trans. Chander Shekhar), New Delhi, 1989

Khan, Sir Sayyid Ahmad, *Asar us Sanadid*, New Delhi, 1990

Khan, Sir Sayyid Ahmad, *The Causes of the Indian Revolt, Translated into English by his Two English Friends*, Benares, 1873 (reprint edition introduced by Francis Robinson, Karachi, 2000)

Lal, Jeewan, *A Short Account of the Life and Family of Rai Jeewan Lal Bahadur, Late Honorary Magistrate of Delhi, with extracts from his diary relating to the time of the Mutiny 1857 compiled his son*, New Delhi, 1902

Latif, Abdul, *1857 Ka Tarikhi Roznamacha* (ed. Khaliq Ahmed Nizami), Nadwatul Musannifin Series (68), New Delhi, 1958

Nizami, Khwaja Hasan, *Begmat ke Aansu (Tears of the Begums)*, New Delhi, 1952

Parvez, Aslam, *Bahadur Shah Zafar: Anjuman Taraqqi-e Urdu Hind*, New Delhi, 1986

Qamber, Akhtar, *The Last Musha'irah of Delhi: A Translation of Farhatullah Baig's Modern Urdu Classic Dehli ki Akhri Shama*, New Delhi, 1979

Quraishi, Salim al-Din, *Cry for Freedom: Proclamations of Muslim Revolutionaries of 1857*, Lahore, 1997

Qureshi, Salim and Ashur Kazmi (trans. and ed.), *1857 ke Ghaddaron ke Khutut*, New Delhi, 2001

Rizvi, S. A. and M. L. Bhargava (eds.), *Freedom Struggle in Uttar Pradesh*, 6 vols, Lucknow, 1957

Russell, Ralph, *The Oxford Ghalib: Life, Letters and Ghazals*, New Delhi, 2003

Server ul-Mulk, *My Life, Being the Autobiography of Nawab Server ul Mulk Bahadur* (translated from the Urdu by his son, Nawab Jiwan Yar Jung Bahadur), London, 1903

Taimuri, Arsh, *Qila-i Mua'lla ki Jhalkiyan* (ed. Dr Aslam Parvez), New Delhi, 1986

Zafar, Bahadur Shah II, Emperor of Hindustan, *Kulliyat-I Zafar, or the complete poetical works of Abu Zafar Siraj al-Din Muhammad Bahadur Shah*, Lucknow, 1869–70
Zakaullah, *Tarikh-I-Uruj-e'Ahd -I Sultanat-I-Inglishiya*, New Delhi, 1904

4. CONTEMPORARY WORKS AND PERIODICAL ARTICLES IN

EUROPEAN LANGUAGES

Andrews, C. F., *Zakaullah of Delhi*, Cambridge, 1929
Anon. [probably Robert Bird], *Dacoitee in Excelsis, or the Spoilation of Oude by the East India Company*, London, 1857; Archer, Major, *Tours in Upper India*, London, 1833
Ball, Charles, *History of the Indian Mutiny*, 2 vols, London, 1858–9
Barter, Richard, *The Siege of Delhi*, London, 1984
Bas, C. T. Le, 'How we escaped from Delhi', *Fraser's* magazine, February 1858
Bayley, Emily, *The Golden Calm: An English Lady's Life in Moghul Delhi*, London, 1980
Beames, John, *Memoirs of a Bengal Civilian*, London, 1961
Bernier, François, *Travels in the Mogul Empire, 1656–68* (ed. Archibald Constable, trans. Irving Brock), Oxford, 1934
Blomfield, David (ed.), *Lucknow – The Indian Mutiny Journal of Arthur Moffat Laing*, London, 1992
Bourchier, Colonel George, CB, *Eight Months Campaign against the Bengal Sepoy Army During the Mutiny of 1857*, London, 1858
Campbell, Sir George, *Memoirs of My Indian Career*, London, 1893
Chick, N. A., *Annals of the Indian Rebellion 1857–8 and Life in the Fort of Agra During the Mutinies of 1857*, Calcutta, 1859 (reprinted London, 1972)
Coopland, Mrs R. M., *A Lady's Escape from Gwalior in 1857*, London, 1859
Dunlop, Robert Henry Wallace, *Service and Adventure with the Khakee Ressalah or Meerut Volunteer Horse During the Mutinees of 1857–8*, London, 1858
Eden, Eden, *Journals*, reprinted as *Tigers, Durbars and Kings*, London, 1988
Eden, Emily, *Up the Country: Letters from India*, London, 1930
Fergusson, James, *History of Indian & Eastern Architecture*, London, 1876
Greathed, H. H., *Letters Written During the Siege of Delhi*, London, 1858
Griffiths, Charles John, *The Siege of Delhi*, London, 1910
Haldane, Julia, *The Story of Our Escape from Delhi in 1857*, Agra, 1888
Heber, Reginald, *A Narrative of a Journey Through the Upper Provinces of India from Calcutta to Bombay, 1824–1825*, 3 vols, London, 1827
Hodson, Major W. S. R., *Twelve Years of a Soldier's Life in India*, London, 1859
Holmes, T. Rice, *A History of the Indian Mutiny and of the Disturbances which Accompanied it among the Civil Population*, London, 1898
Huxley, Aldous, *Jesting Pilate*, London, 1926

Imperial Records Department, *Press List of Mutiny Papers 1857, Being a Collection of the Correspondence of the Mutineers at Delhi, Reports of Spies to English Officials and other Miscellaneous Papers*, Calcutta, 1921

Ireland, William W., *A History of the Siege of Delhi by an Officer who served there*, Edinburgh, 1861

Jacob, E., *A Memoir of Professor Yesudas Ramchandra of Delhi*, vol. 1, Cawnpore, 1902

Jacquemont, Victor, *Letters From India (1829–32)*, 2 vols (trans. Catherine Phillips), London, 1936

Kaye, J. W., *A History of the Sepoy War in India 1857–8*, London, 1877

Khan, Sir Sayyid Ahmad, *The Causes of the Indian Revolt* (reprint edition introduced by Francis Robinson), Karachi, 2000

Lang, Arthur Moffat, *Lahore to Lucknow: The Indian Mutiny Journal of Arthur Moffat Lang*, London, 1992

Mackenzie, Col. A. R. D., *Mutiny Memoirs – being personal reminiscences of the Great Sepoy Revolt of 1857*, Allahabad, 1891

Maisey, Lt Gen. F. C., 'An Account by an eyewitness of the taking of the Delhi Palace', in *Royal United Services Institution Journal*, 1930

Majendie, Vivien Dering, *Up Among the Pandies or A Year's Service in India*, London, 1859

Maunsell, F. R., *The Siege of Delhi*, London, 1912

Metcalfe, Charles Theophilus, *Two Native Narratives of the Mutiny in Delhi*, London, 1898

Montgomery, Martin R., *The Indian Empire*, 6 vols, London, 1860

Muter, Mrs, *My Recollections of the Sepoy Revolt*, London, 1911

Norman, Sir Henry W. and Mrs Keith Young, *Delhi 1857*, London, 1902

Nugent, Lady Maria, *Journal of a Residence in India 1811–15*, 2 vols, London, 1839

Panday, Sitaram, *From Sepoy to Subedar: being the life and Adventures of Subedar Sita Ram, A Native Officer of the Bengal Army, Written and Related by Himself* (trans. Lt Col. J. T. Norgate), London, 1873

Parkes, Fanny, *Wanderings of a Pilgrim in Search of the Picturesque*, London, 1850

Peile, Mrs Fanny, *The Delhi Massacre: A Narrative by a Lady*, Calcutta, 1870

Polier, Antoine, *Shah Alam II and his Court*, Calcutta, 1947

Proceedings on the Trial of Muhammad Bahadur Shah, Titular King of Delhi, Before a Military Commission, upon a charge of Rebellion, Treason and Murder, held at Delhi, on the 27th Day of January 1858, and following days London 1859.

Records of the Intelligence Department of the Government of the North West Provinces of India During the Mutiny of 1857, Edinburgh, 1902

Reid, Major Charles, *Defence of the Main Piquet at Hindoo Rao's House as recorded by Major Reid Commanding the Sirmoor Battalion*, London, 1957

Lord Roberts of Kandahar (Fred Roberts), *Forty One Years in India*, London, 1897

Lord Roberts of Kandahar, *Letters Written During the Indian Mutiny*, London, 1924

Rotton, John Edward, *The Chaplain's Narrative of the Siege of Delhi*, London, 1858

Russell, W. H., *My Diary in India*, London, 1860

Sleeman, Major General Sir W. H., *Rambles and Recollections of an Indian Official*, Oxford, 1915

Thornhill, Mark, *Personal Adventures and Experiences of a Magistrate, during the Rise, Progress and Suppression of the Indian Mutiny*, London, 1884

Trotter Lionel J., *A Leader of Light Horse: A Life of Hodson's Horse*, Edinburgh, 1901

Trotter, Lionel J., *The Life of John Nicholson, Soldier and Administrator*, London, 1898

Turnbull, Lt Col, John, *Letters Written During the Siege of Delhi*, London, 1886

Tytler, Harriet, *An Englishwoman in India: The Memoirs of Harriet Tytler 1828–1858* (ed. Anthony Sattin), Oxford, 1986

Vibart, Edward, *The Sepoy Mutiny As Seen by a Subaltern from Delhi to Lucknow*, London, 1858

Wagentrieber, Florence, *The Story of Our Escape from Delhi in May 1857, from personal narrations by the late George Wagentrieber and Miss Haldane*, Delhi, 1894

White, Col. S. Dewe, *Indian Reminiscences*, London, 1880

Wilberforce, R. G., *An Unrecorded Chapter of the Indian Mutiny*, London, 1894

Wilkinson, Johnson and Osborn, *The Memoirs of the Gemini Generals*, London, 1896

Wise, James, *The Diary of a Medical Officer During the Great Indian Mutiny of 1857*, Cork, 1894

Young Mrs Keith, and Sir Henry Norman, *Delhi 1857*, London, 1902

5. SECONDARY WORKS AND PERIODICAL ARTICLES

Ahmed Aziz, *Studies in Islamic Culture in the Indian Environment*, Oxford, 1964

Alam, Muzaffar and Seema Alavi, *A European Experience of the Mughal Orient: The I'jaz-I Arslani (Persian Letters, 1773–1779) of Antoine-Louis Henri Polier*, New Delhi, 2001

Alavi, Seema, *The Sepoys and the Company: Tradition and Transition in Northern India 1770–1820*, New Delhi, 1995

Allen, Charles, *God's Terrorists: The Wahhabi Cult and the Hidden Roots of Modern Jihad*, London, 2006

Allen, Charles, *Soldier Sahibs: The Men Who Made the North-West Frontier*, London, 2000

Anderson, Olive, 'The Growth of Christian Militarism in Mid-Victorian Britain', in *English Historical Review*, Vol. 86, 1971

Archer, Mildred, *Company Drawings in the India Office Library*, London, 1972

Archer, Mildred and Toby Falk, *India Revealed: The Art and Adventures of James and William Fraser 1801–35*, London, 1989

Ashraf, K. M., 'Muslim Revivalists and the Revolt of 1857', in P. C. Joshi, *Rebellion 1857: A Symposium*, New Delhi, 1957

Bailey, Gauvin Alexander, 'Architectural Relics of the Catholic Missionary Era in Mughal India', in Rosemary Crill, Susan Stronge and Andrew Topsfield (eds.), *Arts of Mughal India: Studies in Honour of Robert Skelton*, Ahmedabad, 2004

Bailey, T. G., *History of Urdu Literature*, London, 1932

Banerji S. K., 'Bahadur Shah of Delhi and the Admin Ct of the Mutineers', in *Proceedings of the Indian Historical Records Commission*, vol 24, February 1948

Bayly, C. A., *Imperial Meridian: The British Empire and the World 1780–1830*, London, 1989

Bayly, C. A., *Empire & Information: Intelligence Gathering and Social Communication in India 1780–1870*, Cambridge, 1996

Beach, Milo Cleveland, and Ebba Koch, *King of the World: The Padshahnama, An Imperial Mughal Manuscript from the Royal Library, Windsor Castle*, London, 1997

Bhadra, Gautam, 'Four Rebels of 1857', in *Subaltern Studies*, IV (ed. R. Guha), New Delhi, 1985

Buckler F. W., 'The Political Theory of the Indian Mutiny', in Transactions of the Royal Historical Society, IV, series 5, 1922, 71–100 (also reprinted in *Legitimacy and Symbols: The South Asian Writings of F. W. Buckler*, ed. M. N. Pearson, Michigan, 1985)

Burke, S. M. and Salim al-Din Quraishi, *Bahadur Shah: Last Mogul Emperor of India*, Lahore, 1995

Burton, David, *The Raj at Table: A Culinary History of the British in India*, London, 1993

Butler, Iris, *The Elder Brother: The Marquess Wellesley 1760–1842*, London, 1973

Cadell, Sir Patrick, 'The Outbreak of the Indian Mutiny', in *Journal of the Society of Army Historical Research*, vol. 33, 1955

Chakravarty, Gautam, *The Indian Mutiny and the British Imagination*, Cambridge, 2005

Collingham, *Imperial Bodies: The Physical Experience of the Raj c.1800–1947*, London, 2001

Compton, Herbert (ed.), *The European Military Adventurers of Hindustan*, London, 1943

Crill, Rosemary, Susan Stronge and Andrew Topsfield (eds.), *Arts of Mughal India: Studies in Honour of Robert Skelton*, Ahmedabad, 2004

Dalrymple, William, *City of Djinns*, London, 1993

David, Saul, *The Indian Mutiny 1857*, London, 2002

David Saul, *Victoria's Wars: The Rise of Empire*, London, 2006

Davies, Philip, *Splendours of the Raj: British Architecture in India 1660–1947*, London, 1985

Ehlers, E. and Thomas Krafft, 'The Imperial Islamic City: 19th Century Shahejahanbad', in *Environmental Design – Proceedings of the 7th International Convention of the Islamic Environmental Design Research Centre in Rome*, July 1991

Ferguson, Niall, *Empire: How Britain Made the Modern World*, London, 2003

Fisher, Michael, *Counterflows to Colonialism*, New Delhi, 2005

Fisher, Michael H., 'An Initial Student of Delhi English College: Mohan Lal Kashmiri (1812–77)', in Margrit Pernau, *Delhi College* (forthcoming), New Delhi, 2006

Fisher, Michael H., 'Becoming and Making Family in Hindustan', in Indrani Chatterjee, *Unfamiliar Relations*, New Delhi, 2004

Forrest, G. W., *A History of the Indian Mutiny* (3 vols), London, 1904

Gilmour, David, *The Ruling Caste: Imperial Lives in the Victorian Raj*, London, 2005

Grey, C., and H. L. O. Garrett, *European Adventurers of Northern India 1785–1849*, Lahore, 1929

Guha, Ranajit, *Elementary Aspects of Peasant Insurgency in Colonial India*, New Delhi, 1983

Gupta, Narayani, *Delhi between Two Empires 1803–1931*, New Delhi, 1981

Gupta, Narayani, 'From Architecture to Archaeology: The "Monumentalising" of Delhi's History in the Nineteenth Century', in Jamal Malik (ed.), *Perspectives of Mutual Encounters in South Asian History, 1760–1860*, Leiden, 2000

Habib, Irfan, 'The Coming of 1857', in *Social Scientist*, vol. 26, no. 1, January–April 1998

Hardy, Peter, *The Muslims of British India*, Cambridge, 1972

Hasan, Mehdi, 'Bahadur Shah, his relations with the British and the Mutiny: An objective study', in *Islamic Culture*, 33 (2), 1959

Hawes, Christopher, *Poor Relations: The Making of the Eurasian Community in British India 1773–1833*, London, 1996

Hewitt, James, *Eyewitness to the Indian Mutiny*, Reading, 1972

Hibbert, Christopher, *The Great Mutiny: India 1857*, London, 1978

Hilliker, J. F., 'Charles Edward Trevelyan as an Educational Reformer', in *Canadian Journal of History*, 9, 1974

Hobhouse, Niall, *Indian Painting for the British 1780–1880*, London, 2001

Hughes, Derrick, *The Mutiny Chaplains*, Salisbury, 1991

Husain, Mahdi, *Bahdur Shah II and the War of 1857 in Delhi with its Unforgettable Scenes*, New Delhi, 1958

Hutchinson, Lester, *European Freebooters in Moghul India*, London, 1964

Ikram, S. M., *Muslim Rule in India and Pakistan*, Lahore, 1966

Jalal, Ayesha, *Self and Sovereignty: Individual and Community in South Asian Islam since 1850*, New Delhi, 2001

Kanda, K. C., *Masterpieces of Urdu Ghazal*, New Delhi, 1994

Khan, Nadar Ali, *A History of Urdu Journalism 1822–1857*, New Delhi, 1991

Lal, John, *Begam Samru: Fading Portrait in a Gilded Frame*, New Delhi, 1997

Lal, Krishan, 'The Sack of Delhi 1857–8', in *Bengal Past and Present*, July–December 1955

Leach, Linda York, *Mughal and other Paintings from the Chester Beatty Library*, 2 vols, London, 1995

Lee, Harold, *Brothers in the Raj: The Lives of John and Henry Lawrence*, Oxford, 2002

Lelyveld, David, *Aligarh's First Generation: Muslim Solidarity in British India*, Princeton, 1978

Liddle, Swapna, 'Mufti Sadruddin Azurda', in Margrit Pernau, *Delhi College* (forthcoming), New Delhi, 2006

Llewellyn-Jones, Rosie, *A Fatal Friendship: The Nawabs, the British and the City of Lucknow*, New Delhi, 1992

Majumdar J. K., *Rajah Rammohun Roy and the Last Moghals: A Selection of Official Records 1803–1859*, Calcutta, 1939

Majumdar, R. C., *Penal Settlements in Andamans*, New Delhi, 1975

Majumdar, R. C., *The Sepoy Mutiny*, Calcutta, 1957

Marshall, P. J. (ed.), *The British Discovery of Hinduism*, Cambridge, 1970

Masud, Muhammad Khalid, 'The World of Shah Abdul Aziz, 1746–1824', in Jamal Malik (ed.), *Perspectives of Mutual Encounters in South Asian History, 1760–1860*, Leiden, 2000

Metcalf, Barbara Daly, *Islamic Revival in British India, 1860–1900*, Princeton, 1982

Mukherjee, Rudrangshu, 'The Azimgarh Proclamation and some questions on the Revolt of 1857 in the North Western Provinces', in *Essays in Honour of S. C. Sarkar*, Delhi, 1976

Mukherjee, Rudrangshu, ' "Satan Let Loose upon Earth": The Kanpur massacres in India in the Revolt of 1857', in *Past and Present*, 128

Mukherjee, Rudrangshu, *Avadh in Revolt 1857–8: A Study of Popular Resistance*, New Delhi, 1984

Mukherjee, Rudrangshu, *Mangal Pandey: Brave Martyr or Accidental Hero?*, New Delhi, 2005

Mukherji, Anisha Shekhar, *The Red Fort of Shahjahanabad*, New Delhi, 2003

Mukhia, Harbans, 'The Celebration of Failure as Dissent in Urdu Ghazals', in *Modern Asian Studies*, 33, (4), 1999

Naim, C. M., *Urdu Texts and Contexts: The Collected Essays of C. M. Naim*, New Delhi, 2004

Narang, Gopi Chand, 'Ghalib and the Rebellion of 1857', in Narang, *Urdu Language and Literature: Critical Perspectives*, New Delhi, 1991

Nizami, Farhan, 'Islamization and Social Adjustment: The Muslim Religious Elite in British North India 1803–57', in *Ninth European Conference on Modern South Asian Studies, 9–12 July 1986, South Asian Institute of Heidelberg University*

Panikkar, K. N., 'The Appointment of Abu Zafar as Heir Apparent', in *Journal of Indian History*, 44, (2), 1966

Parel, A., 'A Letter from Bahadur Shah to Queen Victoria', in *Journal of Indian History*, 47, (2), 1969

Perkins, Roger, *The Kashmir Gate: Lieutenant Home and the Delhi VCs*, Chippenham, 1983

Peers, Douglas M., 'Imperial Vices: Sex, Drink and Health of British Troops', in David Killingray and David Omissi (eds.), *Guardians of the Empire*, Manchester, 1999

Pernau, Margrit, 'Middle Class and Secularisation: The Muslims of Delhi in the 19th century', in Imtiaz Ahmad and Helmut Reifeld (ed.), *Middle Class Values in India and Western Europe*, New Delhi, 2003

Margrit Pernau, 'The *Dihli Urdu Akbhar*: Between Persian Akhbarat and English newspapers', in *Annual of Urdu Studies*, vol. 8, 2003

Pernau, Margrit, 'Multiple Identities and Communities: Re-contextualizing Religion', in Jamal Malik and Helmut Reifeld, *Religious Pluralism in South Asia and Europe*, New Delhi, 2005

Powell, Avril Ann, *Muslims and Missionaries in Pre-Mutiny India*, London, 1993

Pritchett, Frances W. P, *Nets of Awareness: Urdu Poetry and its Critics*, Berkeley and Los Angeles, 1994

Quraishi, Salim al-Din, *Cry for Freedom: Proclamations of Muslim Revolutionaries of 1857*, Lahore, 1997

Qureshi, I. H., 'A Year in Pre-Mutiny Delhi', in *Islamic Culture*, 17, 1943, part 3

Ray, Rajat Kanta, *The Felt Community: Commonality and Mentality before the Emergence of Indian Nationalism*, New Delhi, 2003

Ray, Rajat Kanta, 'Race, Religion and Realm', in M. Hasan and N. Gupta, *India's Colonial Encounter*, New Delhi, 1993

Rizvi S. A. A. and M. L. Bhargava, *Freedom Struggle in Uttar Pradesh*, vols 1 and 2, Lucknow, 1957–60

Robinson, Francis, 'Religious Change and the Self in Muslim South Asia since 1800', in *South Asia*, vol. 22, 199

Robinson, Francis, 'Technology and Religious Change: Islam and the Impact of Print', in *Modern Asian Studies*, 27, (1), 1993

Roy, Dr Kaushik, 'Company Bahadur against the Pandies', in *Jadavpur University Journal of History*, vols 19–20, 2001

Roy, Tapti, *The Politics of a Popular Uprising: Bundelkhand in 1857*, Oxford, 1994)

Russell, Ralph (ed.), *Ghalib: The Poet and his Age*, London, 1975

Russell, Ralph, *Hidden in the Lute: An Anthology of Two Centuries of Urdu Literature*, New Delhi, 1995

Russell, Ralph and Khurshid Islam, *Ghalib: Life and Letters*, Oxford, 1969

Sachdeva, K. L., 'Delhi Diary of 1828', in *Proceedings of the Indian Historical Records Commission*, vol. 30, 1954, part 2

Sadiq, Muhammad, *A History of Urdu Literature*, Karachi, 1964

Sajunlal, K, 'Sadiq ul-Akhbar of Delhi', in *Proceedings of the Indian History Congress*, Seventeenth Session, 1954

Saksena, Ram Babu, *European & Indo-European Poets of Urdu & Persian*, Lucknow, 1941

Saroop, Narindar, *A Squire of Hindoostan*, New Delhi, 1983

Schimmel, Annemarie, *Islam in the Indian Subcontinent*, Leiden–Koln, 1980

Sen, S. N., 'A new account of the siege of Delhi', in *Bengal Past and Present*, 1957

Sen, Surendranath, *1857*, New Delhi, 1957

Shackleton, Robert, 'A soldier of Delhi', in *Harper's* magazine, October 1909

Shreeve, Nicholas, *Dark Legacy*, Arundel, 1996

Shreeve, Nicholas (ed.), *From Nawab to Nabob: The Diary of David Ochterlony Dyce Sombre*, Arundel, 2000

Shreeve, Nicholas, *The Indian Heir*, Arundel, 2001

Sikand, Yoginder, *Bastions of the Believers: Madrasas and Islamic Education in India*, New Delhi, 2005

Singer, Noel F., *Old Rangoon*, Gartmore, 1995

Smith, Vincent, *Oxford History of India*, Oxford, 1923

Spear, Percival, *The Twilight of the Moghuls*, Cambridge, 1951

Spear, Percival, *The Nabobs*, Cambridge, 1963

Spear, T. G. P., 'The Mogul Family and the Court in 19th Century Delhi', in *Journal of Indian History*, vol. 20, 1941

Stokes, Eric, *The Peasant and the Raj – Studies in Agrarian Society and Peasant Rebellion in Colonial India*, London, 1978

Taylor, P. J. O., *A Companion to 'The Indian Mutiny' of 1857*, Delhi, 1996

Taylor, P. J. O., *What Really Happened During the Mutiny: A Day-by-Day Account of the Major Events of 1857–1859 in India*, Delhi, 1997

Thompson, Edward, *The Life of Charles Lord Metcalfe*, London, 1937

Topsfield, Andrew (ed.), *In the Realm of Gods and Kings: Arts of India*, New York, 2004

Varma, Pavan K., *Ghalib: The Man, the Times*, New Delhi, 1989

Varma, Pavan K., *Mansions at Dusk: The Havelis of Old Delhi*, New Delhi, 1992

Ward, Andrew, *Our Bones are Scattered: The Cawnpore Massacres and the Indian Mutiny of 1857*, London, 1996

Welch, Stuart Cary, *Room for Wonder: Indian Painting during the British Period 1760–1880*, New York, 1978

Wilson, A. N., *The Victorians*, London, 2002

Yadav, K. C., *The Revolt of 1857 in Haryana*, Delhi, 1977

INDEX

Abbas, Ghulam, 172, 437
Abd ul-Haq, Maulvi, 35
Abdul Aziz, Shah, 33, 64, 69, 76, 83
Abdulla, Mirza, 216, 328; makes escape, 423–4
Abdurrahman, Hafiz, 12–13, 295
Abraham, 295
Abu Bakr, Mirza, 216, 218, 328; commands cavalry, 242–4; accused of embezzlement, 336; betrayed and killed, 396–8, 400–1, 414
Abyssinians, 98, 110
Act for the Better Government of India, 456
Ad Begum, 111
Adam, 375
Afghan Wars, 199, 284
Afghanistan, 88, 176, 322, 485
Afghans, 83, 199; allied with British, 381–2
Afridis, 202
Agra, 68, 125, 249, 320, 404, 436; Lieutenant Governor in, 54, 190, 221, 234, 467; British administrative centre, 98, 129; Uprising in, 196; refugees head for, 377; princes imprisoned, 425–6; statues, 478
Ain i-Akbari, 131
Ajmer, 145n, 439
Ajmeri Bazaar, 284
Ajmeri Gate, 111, 168, 230; ice factory, 210; parade, 287; firing from 312; Bakht Khan leads forces out, 329, 331; refugees leave by, 368, 372, 379; British capture, 385
Akbar Shah II, Emperor, 37, 39; and Mughal succession, 46, 47n
Akbar Shah, Emperor, 171, 432
Akbar, Emperor, 2, 96, 110, 130–1, 434, 479, 483
Akbarabadi Masjid, 457
Akhtar Mahal (Man Bai), 110
Aldwell, Mrs, 153
Alexander the Great, 89, 161
Ali, Farzand, 327
Ali, Imam, 82
Ali, Mansur, 140–1
Ali, Maulvi Nawazish, 337
Ali, Maulvi Rajab, 204, 249, 301, 342; and capture of Emperor, 392–4; and capture of princes, 396

Ali, Maulvi Sarfaraz, 285, 294, 296, 338, 365
Ali, Mir Akbar, 325
Ali, Mir Fateh, 144, 421
Ali, Mir Haidar, 388
Ali, Mir Niyaz, 387
Ali, Muhammad, 208
Ali, Qadir, 387
Ali, Turab, 319
Aligarh, 196, 477; Muslim University, 34n, 484
Alipore, 93, 241, 248–50, 278, 287, 455n
All India Radio, 473n
Allahabad, 47; princes imprisoned, 425–6; Emperor reaches, 447–50
al-Qaeda, 485
al-Wahhab, Ibn Abd, 76
Alwar, 360; Raja of, 210
Ambala, 83, 264, 277, 310; horse traders in, 107; British base, 188, 194–6, 203, 277, 344; unrest in, 139–40, 195; British forces concentrate in, 229, 241, 247, 304
Aminuddin, Hafiz, 261
Amritsar, 202
Anandi (woodseller), 261
Anarkali, tomb of, 15–16
Andaman Islands, 6, 425–6, 443–4, 458n
Andhra Pradesh, 17n
Anguri Bagh, 148
animals, 13, 79, 82, 134, 146, 267, 294–7, 339; elephants, 27–8, 30, 36, 49, 79, 103, 111, 195, 211, 334–5, 372; camels, 28, 30, 36, 79, 150, 169, 194, 234, 243, 249, 260, 279, 300, 419; horses, 30, 36–7, 79, 213, 389, 419; pigs, 69n, 134, 146, 267, 339; birds, 93–4; alligators, 102; bullocks, 195, 241, 243, 249, 344, 397, 419; ponies, 232, 310; flies, 278, 281, 409; snakes, 279; scorpions, 279; jackals, 279; dogs, 279; sheep, 310; tigers, 399n; antelopes, 399n
Anqa bird, 262
Anson, General George, 139, 203, 230, 234, 243; ineffectiveness, 194–5, 197, 200, 281, 306; death, 196, 281
Arabic, 64, 95, 100, 104; New Testament in, 64

Aravalli Hills, 249
Archaeological Survey of India, 8, 24
Archer, Major, 78
architecture, 2, 32–3, 53–4, 477–8
Aristotle, 95, 296
armaments: greased cartridges, 69n, 134–5, 139–40, 146, 172, 194, 248n; Enfield rifles, 133–4, 139, 188, 477; Brown Bess muskets, 134; ammunition, 194; percussion caps, 206, 322; sepoys' supplies run low, 322–3; explosives, 322–3
Armenian chapel, 89n
Arnot, Mr, 105n
Arya Samaj, 76n
Asadullah Khan, Mirza – 'Ghalib' (aka Mirza Nausha), 2, 35, 95, 422, 458n, 477; laments destruction of Delhi, 5–6, 454, 457; attitude to sepoys, 20; haveli destroyed, 24; feud with Zauq, 40–2; friendship with Fraser, 64–5; religion, 79–80, 82; arrested for gambling, 86; role as courtier, 103, 130; diet, 108–9; participates in mushairas, 111–12; decline in fortunes, 129–30; pessimism about India, 130–1; enthusiasm for electric telegraph, 131, 194; writes to Queen Victoria, 131–2; Loharu cousins, 141, 167; response to Uprising, 154–5, 190; praises Mirza Khizr Sultan, 215; life under siege, 259–60, 323; and assault on Delhi, 362; remains in Delhi, 416–20; brother killed, 417; interrogated, 417–18; changes name of Fort, 423; and position of Muslims in Delhi, 460, 462; and fate of royal women, 463; laments cultural decline in Delhi, 463–4; loss of ghazals, 463; learns of Emperor's death, 475; death, 479
astrologers, 96; Hindu, 76, 79, 81, 376
atrocities, 10, 14–15, 478; Meerut massacres, 140–2, 246; Nicholson's, 197–201; prisoners killed by sepoys, 224–5, 468; British, 244, 246–8, 289, 302–4, 314–16, 329, 362–4, 385–8, 455; Bibigarh massacre, 303; Kanpur massacre, 306, 313–14, 316; Nadir Shah's massacre, 391n; executions, 401–3, 426–9
Attock, 200
Auckland, Lord, 21, 39, 173
Aurangzeb, Emperor, 457
Avadh (Oudh), 10, 17, 135, 208, 290; Nawab of, 37, 126–7, 129, 450n; annexation of, 121, 126–9, 131, 137; Uprising in, 221, 291
Avadh Akhbar, 475
Avicenna, 95
Aylesbury, 409
Ayodhya, demolition of Baburi Masjid, 479
Azad (Muhammad Husain), 18, 33, 42, 99, 107, 111; and Urdu language, 34–5; describes Emperor as 'chessboard king', 37; assists with newspaper, 86; response to Uprising, 161, 190; leaves Delhi, 374–6; saves Zauq's ghazals, 374–6; daughter killed, 375; sees father hanged, 376; and decline of Mughal culture, 478
Azamgarh Proclamation, 220
Azim Beg, Mirza, 90
Azurda (Mufti Sadruddin), 92, 95, 111, 463; provides bridge with British, 75; organises police, 159; trial, 159n; madrasa, 285; signs fatwa, 294; mediates with mujahedin, 296; house sealed up, 302

Babur, Emperor, 123, 444
Babur, Mirza, 78, 379
Badakshan, 96
Badli ki Serai, battle of, 249–53, 334, 426
badmashes (ruffians), 145–6, 156–7, 381, 403, 411
Bagh Begum, 261
Baghpat, 183, 264
Bahadurgarh, 205; Nawab of, 457
Baig, Farhatullah, 111
Baiji, 96
Baird-Smith, Colonel Richard, 283, 335, 357
Bakhsh Bai, Rahim, 215
Bakhsh, Kadir, 82
Bakhsh, Khuda, 326
Bakhsh, Nabi, 44
Bakhsh, Pir, 326–7
Bakhsh, Qadir, 318
Bakhsh, Rahim, 155
Bakhsh, Shaikh Husain, 84, 96, 235
Bakhtawar Shah, Mirza, 216, 422–3
Balahiyya, 326
Balfour, Mrs, 106
Bali, Suraj, 326
Balish, Khwajah, 447
Ball, Charles, 437
Ballabgarh, Raja of, 426–7, 457
Ballimaran, 190, 358, 416
Bangladesh, 483
Baqar, Maulvi Muhammad, 59–60, 86–7; responses to Uprising, 18–19, 159–61, 190, 207, 209, 225–6, 228; urges attack on Meerut, 243; reports during siege, 261–3, 276, 295, 322, 324, 329; appeals to Hindus, 268–9; makes contact with British, 297, 301–2; recognises Uprising's failures, 317; publishes last issue of paper, 343; arrested, 362, 375–6; executed, 376; imambara of, 457
Bareilly brigade, 288, 320; arrives in Delhi, 284; leadership and independence, 284, 294; in attack on British rear, 329–30, 332; in defence of Delhi, 353, 356; flees Delhi, 368, 377

Bareilly, 264, 421
Barelvi, Sayyid Ahmad, 83
Barnard, General Sir Henry, 206, 245–6, 248; occupies Delhi Ridge, 253, 255; death, 281; ineffectiveness, 281, 306
Barrackpore, 20, 76n, 126; unrest in, 139, 248n
Barter, Richard, 195, 246, 250–2, 288, 294; and assault on Delhi, 344–7, 352; and march out of Delhi, 404–5
Baxter, Mrs, 133
Bazm i-Akhir, 108
Becher, Colonel, 194
Beg, Abdullah, 153
Beg, Ahmed, 471
Beg, Ashraf, 156
Begum Bagh, 457
Benares, 80, 135, 205, 425, 450
Bengal Army units: 34th Native Infantry, 62; 38th Native Infantry, 91, 138, 247; 5th Native Infantry, 97; Bengal Engineers, 119; 3rd Light Infantry, 140; Bengal Artillery, 147; 3rd Light Cavalry, 193; 54th Native Infantry, 193, 298; Haryana Regiment, 204, 329; 19th Native Infantry, 248n; 38th Native Infantry, 253; 60th Native Infantry, 271; 73rd Native Infantry, 284; 2nd Irregulars, 307; 59th Native Infantry, 451
Bengal Army, 3, 10, 135n, 264; regulations, 271; mutiny ends, 384
Bengal, 21, 70, 303; Hindu reformist movements, 76n; army unrest in, 126
Beresford family, 156, 160n, 164
Beresford, Mr, 96–7
Berhampore, 126
Berlin Wall, 9
Bernier, François, 36
bezoar, 78
bhatta (wartime allowance), 137
Bhikari, 326
Bibigarh, 303
bibis, 73, 89, 238, 290
Bible, 61–2, 198, 281; New Testament in Arabic, 64; classes, 74; Joseph, 215; Isaac, 295; justifies retribution, 315; 116th Psalm, 315; destruction of Nineveh, 341
Bihar, 17, 21n, 135, 208, 477
Bikaner, 234
Bird, Robert, 126–7
Birjis Qadir, 20
Bloody Gate, 397
Bombay Telegraph, 364
Bombay, 11, 322, 379; Uprising in, 191
Bose, Subhas Chandra, 478
Bourchier, Colonel George, 278, 284, 354
Brahma Yagya, 93
Brahmins, 135n, 159, 204–5, 266–7

Braj Basha, 2, 100
Brendish, Mr, 141, 193
Bridge of Boats, 206, 342; arrival of sepoys, 142, 144, 147, 193, 256, 309, 284; broken down, 244–5; under British guns, 377; Emperor leaves over, 445, 447
British Army units: Skinner's Horse, 28, 88, 90; Dragoon Guards, 62; 60th Rifles, 133; 75th Gordon Highlanders, 195, 246, 250–2; Hodson's Horse, 203, 206, 275; 9th Lancers, 246, 444, 446–7; Khaki Risalah, 246
British Army: religious fervour among, 62; uniforms, 288; 'Army of Retribution', 314–15; incorporates East India Company army, 456; see also Delhi Field Force
British Columbia, 458n
British Empire, 58–9, 61, 88, 439
British Residency: archives, 15–16; diary of court proceedings, 31; architecture, 33; mixed households, 66–7
British: expansionism and erosion of Mughal Empire, 2–3, 9, 15–16, 38–9, 121–4, 191–2; rudeness and arrogance, 3, 70–2, 124, 136; attitudes to Indians, 10; converts to Islam, 23, 64, 153; intellectual abilities, 33n; religiosity, 61–2; daily life in Delhi, 91–3, 97–8, 101, 104–6, 112; diet, 91–2, 104–5; officers, 136–7; flee Delhi, 183–90; previous acts of resistance to, 191–2; racial mix, 290–2
Budhana, 240
Bulandshahr, 125
Bulaqi Begum, 457
Bulubgarh, 205
Bundelkhand, 17
Burke, Edmund, 486
Burma, 96, 138, 425–6, 449, 464
Burn Bastion, 353, 365, 374, 377
Burn, Colonel, 414, 417
Burrowes, Captain, 140, 164
Burrowes, Miss, 177
Buxar, battle of, 450

Cadell, Lieutenant Thomas, 281
Cairo, 8
Calcutta Englishman, 453
Calcutta Gate, 144, 148, 176, 284, 457
Calcutta, 13, 20, 87, 198, 433, 476n; British administrative centre, 15, 54, 98, 307, 395, 402, 411, 444, 455, 472, 480, 482; bishop of, 32, 62; dress in, 73; Hindu reformists in, 76n; conditions in, 122–3; Government House, 122; science display, 131; Fort William, 133, 450n; Dumdum arsenal, 134; British forces in, 283; princes imprisoned, 426; Diamond Harbour, 450

Cambay, 66
Campbell, Georgina (GG; née Metcalfe), 55, 90, 106, 134, 274–6, 291, 429–31; courtship and marriage, 56–7, 114–16, 118; offers support to Theo, 132–3, 142, 147; reunited with husband, 248; racially mixed family, 290–1
Campbell, Sir Edward, 56, 106, 115, 118, 462; career flounders, 133; and discontent in army, 136; escapes Sialkot and joins Field Force, 248–9; assesses British position, 274–7; appointed Prize Agent, 340, 345, 384, 429–31; attends church service, 341; and assault on Delhi, 344, 380; and Delhi massacres, 363; housed in Red Fort, 415
Canada, 54
Canning, Lord, 121–4, 131, 134, 174, 479; rejects Emperor's overtures, 302; approval of Nicholson, 307; and capture of Emperor, 395; concern over executions, 402; and Emperor's trial, 431; and Emperor's exile, 449–50; and destruction of Delhi, 454, 456–7; and Metcalfe, 455; and amnesty, 455
Canova, Antonio, 52
Canton, 8
Cape Colony, 444, 449
Caravaggio, Father Angelo de, 67–8
Carnatic Wars, 17n
Catholicism, 239
Chamberlain, Neville, 357, 366, 384, 390
Chameli (maid), 258
Chand Bai, 44
Chand, Laxmi, 320
Chand, Ratan, 260
Chandan, 13, 327
Chandni Chowk, 96–7, 107, 109–10, 403; sepoys in, 18, 22, 260–1; wedding procession in, 27, 31; water seller, 35; canal, 87; Uprising reaches, 148, 153, 155, 157, 182; Begum Sumru's palace, 239; preachers in, 266–7; thanadar of, 319–20; shopkeepers threatened, 325; fighting around, 351–2, 358–9, 361, 364, 369, 374; Emperor returns down, 395; public executions, 401; dead bodies in, 404–5, 418; Jawan Bakht rides in, 407; demolition halted, 457
Chandru Chowk, 373
Chatta Chowk Bazaar, 29, 145, 210, 410
chaukidars (watchmen), 145n, 185, 295
Chauri Bazaar, 91, 110, 169, 359
Cheltenham, 87
Chhatarpur, 378
Chhedi, 327
Chhota Rang Mahal, 459
Chichester, Hugh, 399, 402, 408

China, 200
Chishti brotherhood, 77
chobdars (mace-bearers), 27, 44, 169–70
Chota Dariba, 208, 359
Christian Boys' Band, 176
Christianity, 9–10, 22–3, 74, 312, 443; Indian converts to, 23, 67–8, 74–5, 98, 153, 414–16; imposition in India, 58–70, 74–5; heterodox, 239
Christians: numbers in army, 135n; term used as taunt, 140; massacred in Meerut, 142; targeted in Uprising, 148, 153, 154n, 159–62, 185, 208–9, 213; saved by Emperor, 169–70, 190; and treatment of Indians, 409; remaining in Delhi, 414, 416
churches, 69, 104, 408; see also St James's Church
Clapham Sect, 76
Clark, William, 165–7
Clerk, Sir George, 204
Clifford, John, 362–3, 405–6
Clifford, Miss, 119, 151–2, 362
Clive, Robert, 384
Coghill, Lieutenant Kendal, 338n, 348, 356, 396
Cohen, John-Augustus Gottlieb, 239
coinage, 2, 20–1, 38–9, 220, 476n
Collins, Thomas, 160n
colonialism, 10, 13, 34
Colvin, Mr, 467
concubines, 3, 42–4, 81, 121; accompany Emperor into exile, 444, 447, 449; rape of, 463
Constantinople, 8, 439, 460
Coopland, Mrs, 404, 406–8, 410n, 428
Corps of Guides, 202, 309, 391
Court of Administration, 293–4, 319
courtesans, 12, 31, 35, 65n; sepoys and, 18–19; kothis, 31, 91, 110, 208; reputation and status, 99n, 110–11; caught in Uprising, 208, 327; royal, 463
Cowasjee and Co., 310, 410
Crimea, 88
Curl, Mr, 312
Curzon, Lord, 462n

Dacca, 138
Dagh, 111
dak (postal service), 186, 194, 259–60
Dalhousie, Lord, 39, 55, 122, 127–8; ignores army unrest, 136, 138
Daly, Henry, 309
Dar ul-Baqa, 285
Dara Bakht, Mirza, 46
Dara Shukoh, Emperor, 147, 479
Dariba, 31, 155, 457

Daryaganj, 32, 44, 150, 152, 407; set on fire, 146, 149; Bazaar Kashmir Katra, 165; Christians rescued, 170; dead camels in streets, 260

Das, Mahajan Narayan, 208

Das, Mahesh, 462

Das, Mathura, 158

Das, Ramji, 461, 463

Dastan i-Ghadr, 15

Davies, Captain Nelson, 1–2, 465–74, 480

Davies, Mrs, 467

Dawes, Colonel, 436

Dayal, Kishan, 318

Deccan, 191

Deccani language, 100

Dehlavi, Zahir, 15, 30, 94, 144, 428, 468; accounts of Uprising, 156–7, 170–1, 207, 213–14, 224, 250, 253–5, 258, 271; attempts to extinguish fires, 213; and Emperor's depression, 300–1; describes siege, 337; caught in assault on Delhi, 358–60; leaves Delhi, 372–5, 388–90, 421–2, 426; describes execution of poets, 387; family members killed, 388, 421

Dehlie Book, The, 53, 232

Dehra Dun, 245

Delhi: Mughal court, 2–3, 32; importance as centre of Uprising, 10–11, 17, 20–1, 196; newspapers, 14, 85–8, 95, 125; responses to Uprising, 18–20; importance of capture, 20, 22; modern, 24–5, 479; importance as centre of Mughal Empire, 32, 54; Mughal architecture and style, 32–3; Mughal traditionalism and *tahzib*, 33–5; paintings of, 53–4, 231–2, 458; revival of mujahedin network, 83–4; daily life, 91–112, 143; growing unrest, 124–6; impact of decline of Mughal court, 128–9; monuments photographed, 138; Uprising reaches, 3, 143–52; looting, 154, 156–8, 182–4, 192, 207, 214, 222, 225, 236, 242, 259–60, 287, 297, 374, 388, 390, 412–14; city magazine explodes, 174–5, 179, 236, 322; massacres, 4, 197, 246, 302–4, 362–4, 385–8, 391n; fires rage, 207, 213, 230; life under Uprising and siege, 207–14, 259–63, 316–29; growing concentration of jihadis, 23, 219, 229, 264–6, 268, 290, 297, 338; defences strengthened, 249–50, 337; sepoy reinforcements arrive, 256, 264, 270, 272, 309, 318, 337–8; rising prices in, 261, 454; growing communal tension, 294–7; city's wealth, 311; British assault on, 336–9, 345–92; residents flee, 368–9, 372, 377–8, 391, 411–12; sepoys flee, 377; executions in, 401–3, 426–9; conditions in environs, 419–20; destruction and redevelopment, 5–8, 14, 408, 454–60; loss of cultural reputation, 463–4

Delhi Amateur Dramatics, 106

Delhi Archaeological Society, 52

Delhi Bank, 31–2, 96–7, 160n; destroyed, 164, 275, 431; British capture building, 377, 380

Delhi College, 111, 240, 414, 464; looted, 18, 160; building and magazine, 33, 147; picture of tomb of Ghazi ud-din, 54; and madrasas, 71, 94; conversions and removal of children, 74–5; alumni, 86, 191; teaching of mathematics, 94; intellectual journals, 95; *mushairas*, 111; Ghalib loses post, 129–30; principal killed, 208; fighting around, 350–1, 364–5

Delhi Commissioner's Office Archive, 14, 19, 301, 424

Delhi Cricket Club, 87

Delhi Darwaza, 325

Delhi Derby, 87, 176

Delhi Field Force, 194, 196, 229; strength, 206, 263, 277, 283, 404; concentrates at Alipore, 241, 245–9; casualties, 245, 252–3, 279, 309, 350, 354, 365, 431; treasure chest, 247, 279, 344, 436; communications cut, 264; morale, 289, 306, 355, 364, 368; and Nicholson's arrival, 304–7; and Bakht Khan's attack, 331–4; preparations for assault, 335; assault on Delhi, 336–9, 345–92; indiscipline, 365

Delhi Gate, 222, 287, 360–1, 373; massacre, 385–6

Delhi Gazette Extra, 279, 303, 315, 402

Delhi Gazette, 55, 87–8, 204; reports wedding procession, 31, 49; criticism of Jennings, 59–60, 85; on White Mughals, 73–4; offices, 87, 93; prints farewell to White Mughals, 90; reports on British life, 104, 106; prints article on sepoys, 137–8; premises ransacked, 176; and Emperor's trial, 436; reports Emperor's exile, 447; records destruction of city, 459

Delhi Gazetteer, 428

Delhi Mission, 59

Delhi Race Course, 206

Delhi Resident, role and authority of, 37n, 54

Delhi Ridge, 4, 10–11, 19, 180; Flagstaff Tower, 176–8, 183, 185, 187, 193, 253–4, 279, 312, 345; sepoy defences, 249, 253–4; British occupy, 253–6, 258, 260, 263–5, 270–1, 287, 292–3, 297; weakness of British position, 256, 274–7, 292; sepoy attacks fail, 270–1; attacks on British rear, 273–4, 282, 316, 329–34, 365; conditions on, 277–81, 310–12; suppliers to British, 310, 410, 416; British defences strengthened, 281–2; British reinforcements arrive, 284, 304–5; presence of Indians, 289–90; British position

improves, 294, 302, 310–11; contacts with
Indians in Delhi, 297, 301–2, 316; and
Nicholson's arrival, 305, 307–8; field
hospital, 354, 357; Nicholson's death on,
384–5
Deoband, 485
Dharma Sobha, 76n
Dhobiwara, 457
Dhrupad, 109
Dihli Urdu Akbhar, 14, 78, 85–7; reports on
Uprising, 18–19, 159–61, 190, 209, 225, 228;
criticism of Jennings, 59–60, 85; attacks
corruption, 86; urges attack on Meerut,
243; reports during siege, 261–3, 322, 329;
last issue, 343
Dilkusha (Metcalfes' house), 53, 57, 274–5
Din Ali Shah, 96
disease: cholera, 195–6, 279, 281, 310, 354, 406;
dysentery, 235, 280; apoplexy, 277;
sunstroke, 277; among refugees, 420; in
Andaman Islands, 458n
Disraeli, Benjamin, 456
Diwali, 81, 239
Doab, 17, 93, 238, 311, 485
Doctrine of Lapse, 127
Douglas, Captain, 28, 35, 56, 59, 218n; learns
of Uprising, 144–5; caught in Uprising and
killed, 150–2, 170
Dunlop, Robert, 246
durbars, resumption of, 211–12, 215
Dussera, 81, 239

East India Company: early officials, 9; acts of
resistance to, 20–1; vassalage to Emperor,
21, 432; coinage, 21, 38–9, 432; and
imposition of Christianity, 22, 61–3, 68–9,
134–5, 137, 220; reduction of Emperor's
prestige, 47n, 119; and army, 62, 126–7, 134–
8, 192, 196, 264, 441, 456; charter, 62–3, 432;
Muslims in employ of, 64, 75; jails, 69;
recruitment, 73; racial discrimination, 89;
opium monopoly, 102; and annexation of
Avadh, 126–7, 137; Intelligence Department,
413; and Emperor's trial, 432, 434; great seal,
432; responsibilities pass to Crown, 456;
dissolved, 456n; efficiency of bureaucracy,
477
East Lothian, 281
eclipses, 376–7
Eden, Emily, 21, 173
Eden, Fanny, 89–90
Edmunds, Mr, 61
education, 94–5, 104; schools, 69n, 70;
Mughal, 99–100; female, 100; European,
469–71; English-language, 478; *see also*
madrasas

Edwardes, Herbert, 61, 197, 200
Egypt, 87
Ellenborough Tank, 208
Elliot, Sir Henry, 115–16, 118
Elveden, 471n
England, 47n, 240n, 427
English literature, 71
Etah, 196
Etawah, 196
Eton College, 311
Europeans, in Delhi, 33, 35
Evangelicals, 76, 83, 135, 484; imperial agenda,
9–10, 22, 61–2, 70; justifications of
atrocities, 304, 363; comparison with
modern politicians, 485

Faiz Bazaar, 32, 325
Fakhr ul-Masjid, 160
Fakhru, Mirza, 99, 112, 204, 216, 222, 396n;
and Mughal succession, 46–8, 113, 115;
death, 119, 121, 124, 128–9, 131; disgraced, 173,
215, 217
Farasu (Franz Gottlieb Cohen), 35, 238–41,
311, 325
Farooqi, Mahmoud, 11
Farrukhnagar, Nawab of, 426, 457
Fatehpur, 61
Fatehpuri Masjid, 93, 462
Fath e-Islam, 267
Fatima, Hand of, 28
fatwas, 83, 125, 294
Fazl i-Haq, 458n
Fergusson, James, 7, 459
Feridun, 34
Ferozepur, 196, 278, 284, 304, 310
Firangi Pura, 89n
Firdausi, 361
Firoz Shah, Mirza, 221
food and drink, 91–2, 94, 104–5, 108; wine, 33,
41, 69, 109; pork, 33, 65, 172, 315; beef, 65,
172, 295, 297, 315; banana leaves, 76;
breakfasts, 91–2, 94, 98, 100–1, 163, 312;
kedgeree, 92; mangoes, 94, 108–9, 262;
kebabs, 107–8, 143, 295; tiffin, 101; chapattis,
125, 167, 185; ghee, 135, 262; *sahri* (pre-fast
meal), 143; *iftar* (sunset meal), 182; ice, 210;
bhang, 214; *laddoo peras* (sweetmeats), 214;
nuqul (sweets), 251; shortages, 262, 316, 318,
323–4, 330, 366, 460, 476; British supplies,
277, 310; cow butchery episode, 294–7;
Emperor's allowance, 406–7; in Rangoon,
452, 465
Forrest, Annie, 91, 106, 164, 311–13, 348, 354
Forrest, Lieutenant, 179–81, 236–8, 241
Forrest, Misses, 180–2
France, 240n

Franklin, Lieutenant William, 8
Fraser, Revd Simon J., 120
Fraser, Simon, 119–23, 174, 312, 433; learns of Meerut uprising, 142; caught in Uprising and killed, 148, 150–2, 170, 428, 438
Fraser, William, 64–5, 72–3, 76, 119, 178n, 270
Freemasons' Lodge, 87
French, 9, 70
Furuksiyar, Emperor, 243

Gabbett, Lieutenant, 332
Galen, 34, 95
Gali Churiwallan, 323
Gali Qasim Jan, 227
Galloway, Arthur, 92, 147, 179, 312
Gambier, Lieutenant Harry, 91, 311–13, 354
games and pastimes: gambling, 86, 324–5; billiards, 101; chess, 101, 110, 136, 458n; kites, 102–3; swings, 102; nautches (dance displays), 136–7, 239; whist, 139
Gandhi, Mohandas Karamchand, 479, 482
Gandhi, Rajiv, 483
Ganges, river, 60, 80–1, 421, 450
Garden of Poetry, 100
gardens, 3, 52; Emperor's love of, 2, 94, 103, 213, 298; Palaces, 8; canals, 32; reflections of paradise, 103; tombs, 178n
Gardner, Captain, 175, 184, 186
Gardner, James, 66–7
Gardner, Mrs, 184, 186
Gardner, Susan, 67n
Gardner, William Linnaeus, 66–7, 72–3, 90
Garstin Bastion, 385
Garstin, Mrs, 428
gemstones, 96
General Service Enlistment Act, 137
Genghis Khan, 2
Ghalib see Asadullah Khan, Mirza (aka Mirza Nausha)
Ghantawallahs, sweet shop, 18, 107
Ghazi ud-Din, 54
Ghulam Ghaus, Mirza, 328
Ghulam Qadir, 37
Goa, 7
Gordon, Captain, 180
Gordon, Sergeant-Major, 153, 338
Grand Trunk Road, 94, 139, 186, 235; sepoys create defensive position, 249–50; sepoys advance along, 195, 256, 271; British move along, 196, 206, 246, 277, 304
Grant (interpreter), 251
Grant, Charles, 62, 119
Grant, Dr, 56
Grant, Mrs, 400
Graves, Brigadier, 176–7, 190
Great Mutiny, see sepoy uprising

Greathed, Hervey, 270, 282, 335, 338, 395, 399n; attitude to Metcalfe, 248; increasing optimism, 302, 310–11; ambivalent attitude to Nicholson, 307–8; and British retribution, 316; Zinat Mahal contacts, 342; death, 354
Greek, 95, 105
Griffiths, Lieutenant Charles, 278–9, 288, 305, 310–11, 335; and Bakht Khan's attack, 331–2; and assault on Delhi, 337, 339, 351–2, 364; and Delhi massacres, 362–4, 406; and evacuation of Delhi, 377, 411–12; approves Hodson's conduct, 398; guards Emperor, 399–400; and looting of Delhi, 412–13; and execution of princes, 423
Gujars, 12, 441; origins, 145n; attack Tytlers, 184; attack Wagentreibers, 187–8; terrorise Delhi hinterland, 209–10, 220, 225, 242, 261; seize Hali, 235; strip Vibart's party, 237–8; 311; seize munitions, 322; attack Indian refugees, 369–70, 372, 378–9
Gulab Singh, Rajah, 37
Gurgaon, 242, 264, 321, 327, 362, 426
Gurkhas, 136, 316; Sirmoor Regiment reinforces Wilson, 245; drive back sepoys, 254, 270; at Hindu Rao's House, 270, 307; kukhris, 254, 272; in assault on Delhi, 350, 377; firing squad, 423
Guru Arjan Dev, 207n
Guru Tegh Bahadur, 207n
Gurwala, Ramji Das, 321
Gwalior, 23, 377; brigade, 293, 309, 325

Hadiths, 33, 77
Hafiz, 81
Hajji (lapidary), 151–2
Hali, Altaf Husain, 95–6, 104, 235
Hamza (uncle of the Prophet), 107
Hansi, 66, 90, 196, 233–5, 264
Hanwa (concubine), 216
Haq, Hakim Mohammad Abdul, 426
Harchandpur, 240
Hare, Edward, 202
Harichandra, Pandit, 12, 266
Harriet, Mount, 458n
Harriott, Major J. F., 411, 422; prosecutes Emperor, 432, 436, 439–43
Haryana, 12, 21n, 107, 264, 318
Hasni (dancer), 12
Hastings, Warren, 10
Hauz Qazi, 208
Hawkins, Francis, 171
Hawthorne (bugler), 348
Hayat Bakhsh Bagh, 460
Hazrat Mahal, Begum, 69n
Hearsey, General, 76

Heatherly, Alex, 111
Heber, Bishop Reginald, 32, 62–3, 65, 100
Hejaz, 76
Henry VIII, King, 123
Herat, 124
Hewitt, General, 195, 197, 203, 306
Himalayas, 147
Hindan bridge, battle of, 244–5, 249, 426
Hindi, 61
Hindu Kush, 96
Hindu Rao's House, 274, 340, 350; defence of, 270, 275, 307, 312; counter-attack towards, 356–7; lookouts on, 368
Hinduism, 61, 326, 443; reform movement, 76n; Mughal attitude to, 80–1
Hindus, 21–3, 80; and Uprising, 12–13, 196, 220, 223–4, 228–9, 253, 264–9, 290, 303, 336, 339, 439–41, 475–6, 484; customs and diet, 24, 65, 68, 76–8, 81, 93–4, 127, 134, 146, 172, 295, 315; inclination for mathematics, 33n; poets, 35; and imposition of Christianity, 62, 68–9, 74–5; converts to Christianity, 74–5, 153; caste among, 134–5, 137–8; numbers in army, 135n; and cow butchery episode, 294–7, 301; and eclipses, 376; remaining in Delhi, 416; readmitted to Delhi, 420, 460; gain ascendancy, 461–2, 477
Hindustan: recognises and supports Emperor, 10–11, 20–1, 215, 297; extent of, 21n; under Marathas, 38, British conquest, 64, 69; land settlement, 69; British denigration of ruler, 123; right of sovereignty over, 434, 456
Hindustani, 21n, 61, 65–6, 90, 138, 436, 466
Hippocrates, 95
Hissar, 196, 235, 264
History of the Kings and Prophets, 99
HMS Magara, 451
Hodson, Captain William, 201–4, 249, 257, 271, 279, 305; cruelty, 4, 203–4, 207; intelligence network, 204, 206, 323; and assault on Delhi, 355–6, 368, 385; and capture of Emperor, 370–1, 383, 390, 392–5; contacts with Zinat Mahal, 301–2, 342–3, 371, 467; guarantee to Emperor, 393–5, 399, 431, 443; and capture of princes, 396–9; inquiries into conduct, 398–9; and escape of princes, 424
Holi, 81, 239, 254
Hudhud, Abd ur-Rahman, 40n
Humayun, Emperor, tomb of, 371, 390, 392–3, 396, 399, 406, 423
Hussaini, 326
Hutchinson, John Ross, 92, 148, 150–2, 167–8
Huxley, Aldous, 92n

Hyat ul-Nissa, Begum, 72
Hyderabad, 15, 30, 422

Ibrahim, Muhammad, 208
Ice House, 374–5, 388–9
'Id, 40, 67, 82, 243, 366; and cow butchery, 294–7
'Idgah, 12, 40, 96, 243, 326, 368
Ilahe Bakhsh, Mirza, 47, 204, 222, 321; and capture of Emperor, 370–1, 383, 392–4, 414; and capture of princes, 390, 396, 414; house looted, 414
Imamam, 327
India Museum, 460
India Office Library, 291
Indian Civil Service, 73, 455n
Indian Independence, 19, 478
Indian National Army, 482
Indian Partition, 484
intelligence: spies' reports, 14, 16, 19, 205–6, 226, 249, 266, 288, 298, 300, 319, 322–4; spy networks, 204–5; intelligence on mujahedin, 264; sepoys' lack of intelligence, 274, 292, 316; activities of spies, 329, 342; treatment of spies, 362, 413–14
interracial marriages, 9–10, 64, 66–7, 73, 77, 85
Inverness, 64
Iran, 439; Shah of, 124
Ireland, Major William, 388, 420, 423; and state of British troops, 289, 365; and British brutality, 390–1, 402
Irrawaddy Delta, 452
Isfahan, 460
Islam, 2, 159, 209; British converts to, 23, 64, 153; clergy, 64n; customs and sensitivities, 66; defence of, 70; reform movement and fundamentalism, 75–6, 83–4; kalima (profession of faith), 153; mercenaries convert to, 239; moderate, 485
Islam, Sheikh, 326
Istanbul, 8
Izalat al-awham (The Remover of Doubts), 70

Jacquemont, Victor, 65, 105
Jahanara, caravanserai, 457
Jahangir, Emperor, 2, 15
Jahangir, Mirza, 46, 47n, 78, 448n
Jains, 97, 158, 461
Jaipur, 33, 330; Maharaja of, 422
Jalandhar, 201, 264
Jama Masjid, 18, 32, 35, 93, 182, 285; daily crowds, 6, 464; khadims, 79; storytellers on steps, 107; flyer on wall, 124, 133; gong rings for Ramadan, 143; Uprising reaches, 155–6; standard of jihad raised, 23, 228;

bazaar, 262; jihadis set up camp in, 264; and cow butchery, 295; fighting around, 350–1, 359–60, 431; Sikhs occupy, 384, 453, 462n; destruction, 408, 457–8; returned to Muslims, 475

Jatmal, Lala, 325

Jats, 204, 225, 264, 379

Jawan Bakht, Mirza, 100, 128, 211, 217; wedding of, 27–32, 35–7, 40, 43, 49, 55, 58, 74, 83, 97, 146, 453, 480; and Mughal succession, 46–7, 49, 121, 215, 222, 336, 342, 400, 468n; and Uprising, 218n, 221; leaves Red Fort, 258; capture and guarantee of safety, 371, 394, 403; Ommaney and, 407, 410, 437, 448; and Emperor's trial, 436–7; accompanies Emperor into exile, 444n, 446, 448–9; squabbles with Zinat Mahal, 448; life in exile, 465, 469–71, 480–1; proposal for education, 469–72; death, 481

Jehangeer and Co., 310

Jennings, Annie, 119, 203, 362; caught in Uprising and killed, 151–2, 170, 176, 362, 406

Jennings, Revd Midgeley John, 63, 92, 104, 119, 141, 145; religious fervour, 58–61, 68–70, 72; criticised in newspapers, 59 60, 85; achieves conversions, 74–5, 83–4; caught in Uprising and killed, 151–3, 160n, 170

Jervis, Mary Anne, 240n

Jesus Christ, 18, 456

Jhajjar, 205, 421; Nawab of, 32, 150, 231–2, 299, 421, 426–7, 457

Jhansi, 11; annexation of, 127; Rani of, 478

Jheend, Raja of, 310

Jhelum, 197

jihad, 83, 159, 265, 285, 458n; declared in Jama Masjid, 23, 228; arguments for, 64, 75, 229; Emperor opposes, 228, 294

jihadis, 271–2, 337, 439–40, 484; growing concentration in Delhi, 23, 219, 229, 264–6, 268, 290, 297, 338; centres, 83, 462; tensions with sepoys, 264–6, 285; bravery, 269–70; women, 269–70; with Bakht Khan's force, 285, 289; in Nasirabad, 293; breach common front, 294–6; desertions, 319, 323; estimated numbers, 338; in defence of Delhi, 351, 356, 365–6; ambush Hodson, 393, 396; modern, 485

Jog Maya temple, 40, 82

Johari Bazaar, 254

Johnson, Allen, 97

Jones, Brigadier, 352

Jones, Sir John, 459

Jones, Sir William, 10

Jordain, Monsieur, 87–8

Julius Caesar, Father, 239

Kabul Gate, 93, 457; sepoys flee through, 252; firing from, 312; defence of, 341; fighting around, 350, 352–3, 356, 358

Kaghazi Gali, 156–7

Kairnawi, Maulana Rahmat Allah, 70

Kalka, 117

Kamran, Mirza, 43, 448

Kangra, 115–16

Kanhaiyya, 326

Kanpur, 10–11, 20, 163, 303, 316; religiosity gains ground, 61; massacre, 306, 313–14, 316, 441; British retribution, 329; princes imprisoned, 425–6; Emperor reaches, 447

Kapurthala, Raja of, 226

Karachi, 379, 425–6

Karen hill territories, 449

Karnal, 235, 243, 283, 365, 426; refugees head for, 183, 185, 187, 190, 372, 379; Anson's death in, 196, 281; British forces concentrate in, 203, 206, 230, 234

Kashmir, 36, 142, 146; Maharaja of, 356

Kashmiri Bastion, 339

Kashmiri Gate, 92, 141, 147, 178; *Delhi Gazette* offices, 87, 93, 176; bottleneck at, 104; counter-attack at, 149; bridgehead established, 163–5; escape from, 179–81; sepoys flee through, 252; firing from, 312; *damdama* constructed, 337; guns silenced, 339; assault on, 340, 347–50, 352, 380, 417, 476; fighting around, 352–3, 360, 373; refugees leave by, 372

Kashmiri, Mohan Lal, 71, 154n, 191

Katra Muhalla, 326

Katra Nil, 97, 319

Katra, 35

Kaus Shekoh, Mirza, 102

Khairum Bai, 216

Khan, Abd ur-Rahman, 299

Khan, Akbar, 322

Khan, Faiz, 327

Khan, General Bakht, 284–9, 302, 337, 370; British assessments of, 284–5; tactics, 287–8, 292; loses power, 292–4; leads attack on British rear, 329–32, 334, 342; returns in disgrace, 336; defence of Kabul Gate, 341; and defence of Delhi, 351, 353, 356–7, 365; troops abandon positions, 374; leaves for Lucknow, 390; pursued by British, 404; saves Dehlavi, 421–2

Khan, Ghulam Ali, 231–2

Khan, Hakim Ahsanullah, 81, 108, 342; and Metcalfe's death, 118; and Uprising, 144, 159n, 170–1, 173, 190, 213, 218, 221–2, 224, 267; contacts with British, 204, 301–2, 367, 390; and reception of Bakht Khan, 286; accused

of treason, 323; and Emperor's flight, 367, 372, 390; blamed by Emperor and wife, 468
Khan, Himmat, 109
Khan, Imdad Ali, 337
Khan, Imran, 473n
Khan, Jang Baz, 421
Khan, Mahbub Ali, 31, 45, 48, 82, 100; and Uprising, 171, 222, 250, 252; death, 259
Khan, Mazhar Ali, 53, 231–2
Khan, Meer, 381–2
Khan, Mehrab, 261
Khan, Moulvie Sadarud-Din, 159n
Khan, Muin ud-Din Husain, 167–70, 190, 245; appointed kotwal, 219, 223–4, 227; assists Metcalfe, 231; replaced as kotwal, 258; Mutiny Narratives translated, 291; and assault on Delhi, 362
Khan, Nawab Hamid Ali, 207, 242, 373–4, 389, 414, 426
Khan, Nawab Mohammad, 426
Khan, Nawab Muhammad Ali, 386
Khan, Nawab Ramzan Ali, 291
Khan, Nawab Zia ud-Din, 141–2, 167, 185
Khan, Rustam, 13, 208, 327
Khan, Shahzada Hamid, 300
Khan, Sir Sayyid Ahmad, 82, 96, 296; and Delhi intellectual life, 34, 52, 131, 285; founds Muslim University, 34n, 484; praises sitar player, 109–10; and Indian Muslims, 477, 484
Khan, Tanras, 109–10
Khan, Vilyat Ali, 178n
Khan, Walidad, 30, 32, 35–6
Khanam (singer), 110
Khanam Bazaar, 154n
Khanam, Ashuri, 90
Khanum ka Bazaar, 454
Khas Bazaar, 32, 454
Khasgunge, 66
Khizr Sultan, Mirza, 215–16, 218, 250, 252; accusations against, 293, 336; betrayed and killed, 396–8, 400–1
Khyber Pass, 11
Kilhih Bazaar, 359
Kishenganj, 89n, 209, 288, 350, 374
Kishor, Juga, 260
Knyvett, Colonel, 237–8, 311
Koh-i-noor diamond, 59
Kollesur, 37
Korali, 369
Koran, 33, 64n, 76–7, 79, 94, 96, 161, 295; Persian and Urdu translations, 77; engraved on shields, 272; Emperor consults, 341
Kucha Bulaqi Begum, 31, 155
Kucha Chelan, 4, 386

Kuliyat Khana, 151
Kulsum Zamani Begum, 369
Kumbh Mela, 60
Kussowlie, 344
Kutcherry building, 147, 160, 167, 179

Lahore Chronicle, 407–8, 454
Lahore Gate, 27, 59, 145, 148, 150–1, 223, 227; policeman attacked, 227; sepoys flee through, 252; sepoys attack through, 270, 331; firing from, 312; fighting around, 350–2, 356, 358, 369; British capture, 385, 459; Emperor returns through, 394–5; British march through, 405; refugees leave through, 412; Independence Day speeches, 479
Lahore, 282, 302, 342, 357, 429, 431; archives, 6, 15–16, 193; British administrative centre, 194, 366, 384; sepoys disarmed, 197; court of Ranjit Singh, 290; Wagentreiber re-establishes newspaper, 303, 315, 403; Azad reaches, 376
Lake, Lord, 39, 384
Lal Kuan, 258, 342–3, 371, 395, 428
Lal, Chunni, 150, 208, 222
Lal, Dr Chaman, 74, 83–4, 98; caught in Uprising and killed, 152–3, 160n, 414
Lal, Mohan, 208
Lal, Munshi Jiwan, 157–8, 159n, 223, 255, 287; and British intelligence, 204, 413; Mutiny Narratives translated, 291; arrested, 320–1; house looted, 414
Lang, Lieutenant Arthur Moffat, 352
Latif, Abdul, 154, 173
Latin, 95, 105
Lawrence, Sir Henry, 202, 204, 306
Lawrence, Sir John, 16, 54, 206; and Nicholson, 197–201, 309; and Wilson, 282–3, 309, 357–8; and Emperor, 302, 407; reinforces Delhi, 304; and princes' imprisonment, 425; and Metcalfe, 429, 455; moderates destruction of Delhi, 454–6, 458; recommends amnesty, 455–6
Layard, Henry, 409
Le Bas, Charles, 92, 148, 150, 176, 190
Lindsay, Lieutenant A. H., 430n
Locomotive Race, 87
Loharu, Nawabs of, 66, 141–2, 167, 231
London, 6, 298, 409
Lucknow, 11, 17, 20, 69n, 103n, 107, 313, 376; size, 32; Western architecture, 32–3; Uprising in, 221, 316; siege of, 291, 306, 404–5, 431; court of, 341, 476n; resistance continues, 390
Ludhianawi, Abd ur-Rahman, 159n
Ludlow Castle, 52, 97, 312, 350, 433

Macaulay, Thomas Babington, 71
MacDowell, Lieutenant, 396–7
Mackenzie, Colonel A. R. D., 315
Madhya Pradesh, 21n
Madras, 73, 376; fatwa posted, 125
Madrasa i-Rahimiyya, 77, 83–4, 94, 463, 485
madrasas, 23, 69, 81, 83, 94–6, 104; and Delhi
    College, 71, 94; closed down, 463–4;
    Deoband, 485
Mahabharat, 12, 267
Mahi Maraatib (Fish Standard), 30
Mahmoud Sultan, Mirza, 45
Mahtab Bagh, 171
Mainpuri, 196
Maisey, Fred, 380–4, 395, 398
Maisey, Kate, 384
Makhan (mace bearer), 150–2
Mal Jat, Shah, 264
Mal, Chhunna, 461–2
Mal, Lala Chunna, 97
Malagarh, 30
Mamdoh (bearer), 152
Mamnun, 463
Mandalay, 453
Manglo (courtesan), 13, 208, 327
Manifesto of the King of Delhi, *see*
    Azamgarh Proclamation
Marathas, 38, 64, 70, 89, 167, 190
Martello Towers, 339
Martineau, Captain E. M., 140
Marwaris, 97, 158
Masjid Kashmiri Katra, 93, 457
mathematics, 33n, 94, 100
Mathura, 22, 125, 320, 368, 475
Matia Mahal, 94, 156, 183
Meandoo, Mirza, 422–3
Mecca, 48, 66, 216, 228, 299–300, 379, 439
Medina, 76, 299
Meerut, 67n, 132, 178n, 245, 313, 326, 362;
    sepoys reach Delhi, 3, 144–5, 147, 149, 163,
    168, 170, 193, 475; rising and massacre, 16,
    20, 140–2, 172, 246, 301; Anglicised
    culture, 105; telegraph, 141, 144; jail, 145;
    British forces in, 149, 177, 182, 195, 230,
    241, 164, 306; sepoys sentenced in, 162,
    175; refugees head for, 183, 190, 193, 237,
    241, 372; Hodson's ride to, 203; plan to
    attack, 241–3; Indian refugees head for,
    369
mehfils (courtly entertainments), 98
Mehrauli, 47, 53, 171, 210, 215, 275, 421;
    summer palace, 14, 25, 40, 420, 446; Qutb
    Sahib shrine, 40, 82, 121, 370, 378, 439;
    Khwaja Saheb shrine, 228, 389; Khwaja
    Qutb shrine, 299, 372; taxation of, 321
Mehtab Bagh, 227, 385, 459

mendicants, 96, 143
mercenaries, 239, 290
Metcalfe House, 98, 101, 103, 114, 118, 163, 174;
    architecture and gardens, 52; closed up,
    132, 147; provides refuge, 181; attacked and
    burned, 182, 235–6, 274–5; base for attacks
    on Ridge, 273; gallows erected, 428; carved
    chairs, 430
Metcalfe, Charles, 291
Metcalfe, Charlie, 132–3, 142, 147
Metcalfe, Charlotte, 114, 116–17
Metcalfe, Emily, 49–51, 53, 56, 105–6, 231; and
    father's death, 114–16; daughter born, 115;
    and Uprising, 148; questions Lawrence
    about Theo, 455n
Metcalfe, Felicity, 50, 116
Metcalfe, Georgina, *see* Campbell, Georgina
Metcalfe, James, 290–1
Metcalfe, Sir Charles, 39, 54, 290, 432
Metcalfe, Sir Thomas, 167, 181, 198, 228, 274,
    290, 454; and Zafar, 37, 51, 54, 100; and
    salatin's petition, 45; and Mughal
    succession, 47–9, 51, 115–16; character and
    habits, 49–51, 55; fascination with Delhi, 51–
    2; houses, 52–3; commissions paintings, 53–
    4, 231–2; family relations, 54–7, 120, 234;
    dislike of Jennings, 59–60; uncovers
    mujahedin network, 83; daily life, 97–8,
    101, 104, 106; death, 113–19
Metcalfe, Theophilus (Theo), 55–5, 59, 90, 219;
    daily life, 92–3, 103, 106; and deaths of wife
    and father, 114, 116–18, 132; removes Jama
    Masjid flyer, 124–5, 133; suffers decline, 132–
    3; warned of Uprising, 142, 167; caught in
    Uprising and knocked unconscious, 146–
    50; makes escape, 168, 181, 190, 230–5, 274–5,
    299, 421; and revenge attacks, 234, 246;
    joins Field Force, 248–9; racially mixed
    family, 290–1; and Bakht Khan's attack,
    331; and assault on Delhi, 350–2, 359, 361,
    429; and executions, 403, 427–31; returns to
    England, 455
Mewati, Bhura Khan, 168, 230–1
Mewatis, 145n, 235; control Delhi hinterland,
    261; attack Indian refugees, 378
Minto Road, 147n
Mir Nawab, 242
Mir, 32, 40n, 111
Mirza Sahib, 41
Mirzapur, 450
Mofussilite, 461
Mogul Cup, 87
Mohalla, 208
Mohammed, Prophet, 18, 216, 370
Momin, 111, 422, 463
Mon, 454

moneylenders, 86, 109, 202; and Emperor's
    finances, 31; Marwari and Jain, 97, 158;
    plundered, 208, 260, 361; and finance for
    Uprising, 318–20; threaten poor, 325; long
    for return of British, 361; Prize Agent's
    treatment of, 429–30; Hindu, 461–3
monsoons, 279–81, 311, 379
Montgomery, Sir Robert, 342
Montrose, 89
Moradabad, 153n, 196
Mori Bastion, 312, 356, 372
Morley, James, 165–6, 183, 190
Moscow, 32
mosques, 69, 82, 89, 104, 264–5, 399, 408, 457;
    see also Fatehpuri Masjid; Jama Masjid;
    Masjid Kashmiri Katra; Zinat ul-Masjid
Moulmein, 426
Moveable Column, 197, 200–1, 304, 306–7, 331,
    405
Mubarak Bagh (Ochterlony Gardens), 178,
    253, 273
Mubarak Begum, 66, 111, 178n, 457
Mubarak un-Nissa, , 444n, 447
Mughal Empire: British undermining of, 2–3,
    15–16, 39, 121–4; Mughal elites, 13–14, 66–8,
    75, 77–8, 207; criticisms of court, 15, 86;
    revival of, 20, 191, 196, 297, 300, 475;
    mystique of Emperor, 20–2, 192, 475–6;
    insignia, 27–8, 30n; importance of
    processions, 36, 39–40; loss of authority,
    36–40, 48; and choice of succession, 46–9;
    hybrid culture of court, 66–8, 72, 83;
    imminent end, 128–9; increased importance
    of court, 214–15; factions emerge, 215–22;
    ancestral treasures, 369–70; royal family
    dispersed, 422–6; decline of cultural
    prestige, 464, 477–9, 485
Mughal, Mirza, 48, 211, 216–21, 226–7; defence
    of Delhi, 249–50, 253–5, 266, 272, 336–9, 341,
    351, 366; replaced as commander, 287, 292;
    heads administration, 293–4, 298–9, 319–22,
    477; betrayed and killed, 390, 396–8, 400–1;
    and Emperor's trial, 437–8
Muhalla Maliwara, 326
Muhammad, Habeeb Wali, 473n
Muharram, 82, 86, 457n
mujahedin, 83–4, 264; role in Uprising, 154,
    159, 229, 265; imam of, 285, 338; and cow
    butchery episode, 296–7
Mukherjee, Rudrangshu, 17
Mukhtar Begum, 66
Multan, 133, 305, 425
Mungalee, 331
Munir, Muhammad, 159n
Murphy, Mr, 414
Murshidabad, 32

musicians, 28, 109–10, 129
Muslims, 21–3, 33n, 80, 199; 'ulama, 64, 70, 75,
    76n, 77, 80, 82, 84, 86, 98, 285, 294–6; in
    British employ, 64, 75; customs and diet,
    64–8, 73–4, 82, 94, 13, 146, 172, 315;
    marriages with Christians, 66–7; and
    imposition of Christianity, 68–70, 74–5;
    rise of fundamentalism, 75–6, 83–4;
    syncretic practices, 76–8, 81; education, 95;
    numbers in army, 135n; converts to
    Christianity, 153; and Uprising, 196, 220,
    223, 228–9, 264–8, 290, 303, 336, 339, 439–43,
    475–6, 484; and cow butchery episode,
    294–7, 301; British retribution on, 329, 408;
    remain in Delhi, 416, 418, 460; excluded
    from Delhi, 420, 460–1; and Hindu
    ascendancy, 462; representations of, 477; in
    Rangoon, 481–2; radicalisation of, 486
Mussoorie, 56, 88, 241
Muter, Mrs, 413, 427, 441
Mutiny Papers, 11–14, 19, 22, 205, 209, 219,
    272, 293, 324–5, 483
Muzaffar ud-Daula, Nawab, 426
Muzaffarnagar, 17
Mysore, 70, 450n, 476n

Nadir Shah, 36, 391
Nagar Seth, 208
Nagpur, annexation of, 127
Nahur, 154n
Nainital, 122
Najafgarh, 24, 330–1, 336
Nana Sahib, 10
Nana, 441
Nanautawi, Maulana Muhammad Qasim, 485
Napier, Sir Charles, 56, 133, 136, 409
Napoleon Bonaparte, 52
Naqqar Khana Darwaza, 29, 382
Naqshandis, 264
Nasirabad, 196, 264, 273, 293; brigade, 331, 334,
    349–50
National Archives of India, 3, 11–12, 14, 205
nazrs (ceremonial gifts), 32, 37, 39, 81, 103n,
    211, 286, 338, 432
Nehru, Jawaharlal, 482
Neill, General, 314–15
Nicholson, Charles, 331
Nicholson, General John, 202–3, 206–7, 316;
    character and cruelty, 197–201, 306–7, 405;
    heads Moveable Column, 304–7; legendary
    status, 306–8; clashes with Wilson, 308–9;
    and Bakht Khan's attack, 331–3, 342; leads
    assault on Delhi, 340, 345, 350, 352–3; death,
    353–5, 357–8, 384–5
Nigambodh Ghat, 93
Nikal Seyn, 199

Nil ka Katra, 461
Nilgiri Hills, 376
Nili, Mirza, 406
Nimach brigade, 309, 318–19, 329–30, 332–4, 336, 356; flees Delhi, 368, 377
Nixon, Mr, 160, 187
Nixon, Mrs, 187
Nizami, Khwaja Hasan, 378, 380
Nizamuddin shrine, 81, 209, 369–71, 396, 420, 424
North Indian Coursing Club, 104
North West Frontier, 83, 193, 202, 306; Uprising on, 196; British recruitment in, 206, 290
North West Provinces, 129, 249, 449; Governor of, 45, 54, 68, 221, 467; Uprising in, 196
Nowshera, 196
Nugent, Lady Maria, 9
Nur Bai, 111
Nur Mahal, 383
Nur i-Maghrebi, 125

Ochterlony, Sir David, 75, 111, 178n, 253, 411, 458n; and Moghul culture, 49, 65–7, 72–3
Ommaney, Lieutenant Edward, 218n, 415n, 469; responses to brutality, 307, 391, 401, 405–6; serves as Emperor's jailer, 406, 409–10; and Jawan Bakht, 407, 410, 437; and execution of princes and nobles, 422–3, 427; and Emperor's trial, 436–7, 441; accompanies Emperor into exile, 444, 446, 448–52; returns to India, 464
opium, 102, 426, 481
Osborne House, 471n
Oude Blue Book, 126–7
Oudh, *see* Avadh
Ouvry, Henry, 401

Paharganj, 209, 230
painting, 53–4, 231–2, 478; Company School, 53, 231
Pakistan, 15, 483–5
Palam, 36–7; bridge, 330, 332, 334
Palmerston, Lord, 454
Pandey, Mangal, 20, 139, 248n
Pandey, Sitaram, 136
Panipat, 95, 190, 235, 421
Panja-kash, Miyan Amir, 387
Paris, 401
Parkes, Fanny, 61, 72
Parvez, Aslam, 15
Pathans, 202; horse traders, 107; allied with British, 200, 206, 290, 338n, 361, 377; Nicholson's servant, 308, 384
Patiala, Maharaja of, 416

Patna, 83
Patterson, Major, 163
Peake & Allen, 310
Pegu, 449; annexation of, 88
Pekin, summer palace, 8
Penny, General, 428
People of India, The, 477
Persia, 87–8, 200, 438–9, 443
Persian Army, 124–5, 322
Persian, 64–6, 74, 95, 100, 104, 268n, 284, 391, 414; poetry, 2, 81, 131, 238; historical sources, 15; translation of Ten Commandments, 61; abolished as language of government, 71; translation of Koran, 77; newspapers, 95
Persians, 438; sack Delhi, 215
Peshawar, 64, 83, 107, 194, 197, 306, 322; Commissioner of, 61
Phayre, Major, 449, 452
Philour, 196
Phulwalon ki Sair (Flowersellers' Fair), 6, 40, 82, 464
Pilkington, Mr, 141, 193
Piram Jan, 99
pirs, 3, 78–9, 441
Piya Bai, 43
Plassey, battle of, 432
Plato, 34, 95, 296
poetry, 35, 40–2, 100, 463; Zafar and, 2–3, 5, 25–6, 37–8, 42, 78–81, 98–9, 298, 300, 473; ghazals, 2–3, 79, 83, 86, 91, 108–9, 130, 161–2, 374–5, 478; *mushairas* (poetic symposia), 3, 86, 91, 98, 111–12, 478; Sufi, 78–81; Hindus and, 81; *marsiya* (mourning poems), 82; *tuzmin*, 98n; *Bismillah*, 112; *qasidas* (Persian odes), 131; English, 478
poets, 5, 17, 40–2, 91, 95–6, 111; dictionary of, 100, 439–40; patronage of, 131–2; Sardhana, 239; executed, 387; *see also* Azad; Azurda; Farasu; Ghalib; Momin; Zauq
Powell, Mr, 153n
Prasad, Sheo, 260
primogeniture, imposition of, 46
Pune, 66
Punjab, 54, 133, 193, 198, 200, 204, 471n; archives, 6, 15–16, 193; sepoys disarmed, 16; Commissioner of, 68, 197, 454–5; border with Sindh, 133; Uprising in, 196–7; British reinforcements from, 278, 282–3, 290, 304; supplies British forces, 310, 333n; ordnance factories, 334; spoils of Delhi reach, 388; government, 425, 455
Punjabi Katra, 457
Punjabi Muslims, 83–4, 154; allied with British, 290, 305, 335, 338n
Punjabi, 2, 100

Purana Qila, 369
purdah, abolition of, 69
pyjamas, 65, 73, 107, 170
pyrotechnics, 31, 230, 239

Qadam Sharif shrine, 86, 93, 272
Qadir, Birjis, 476n
Qadir, Ghulam, 171
Qudsia Bagh, 12, 340, 345–6, 348
Quli Khan, Mirza, 284, 336, 371
Qwaish, Mirza, 423–4

Radha, 326
Radio Ceylon, 473n
Rafi, Mohammed, 473n
Rahman, Abdul, 472
Raikes, Charles, 408
railways, 61, 447
Rajasthan, 65, 145n, 264, 309, 424
Rajghat Gate, 93, 146, 148, 152, 168, 387, 457
Rajputana, 196, 316, 360, 475
Rajputs, 77, 89, 135n, 158
Ram Lila, 81
Ram, Sahib, 457
Ramadan, 143
Ramayana, 268–9
Ramchandra, Master, 74–5, 83–4, 86; return
    to Delhi and appeal, 414–16
Ramji Ganj, 457
Rampur, 269, 418, 422
Ranghuirs, 158
Rangoon Times, 482
Rangoon, 6, 138, 444; Emperor's burial, 1–2;
    Shwe Dagon pagoda, 1, 452–3, 464;
    Emperor in exile, 5, 449, 452–4, 464–74;
    National Archives, 16; princes imprisoned,
    425; political situation, 453; waterfront, 454;
    Emperor's family in, 480; Muslims of, 481–
    2
Rangoon, river, 452
Rashid ul-Khairi, 387
Raushanara Bagh, 94, 121
Raushanara Begum, 36
Ravi, river, 306–7
Rawalpindi, 199
Red Fort: daily life, 3, 44, 98–100, 102–4, 108–
    10; importance to Delhi life, 6, 464;
    barracks, 7–8, 47; Mehtab Bagh, 32, 109n;
    stripped of treasures, 36; confines of
    emperor's authority, 37; British designs
    upon, 47, 51; promenade around walls, 49;
    challenged by Metcalfe House, 52; imperial
    zenana, 72, 151, 212, 258; Shah Burj tower,
    99, 258; prosperity and patronage, 128–9;
    cannon fires at dawn, 143; gates closed, 144,
    151, 358; sepoys enter and occupy, 169–74,
    207, 258; tasbih khana (private oratory), 169,
    190, 300, 369; Red Curtain (Lal Pardah),
    170–1, 258, 286, 383; Diwan i-Khas, 170–2, 211,
    286, 336, 383–4, 388, 404, 415, 436; Diwan i-
    Am, 212, 286, 382, 458, 460; Naqqar Khana
    (drum house), 223, 460; targeted by British,
    257–8; British attack, 350–1, 364, 377, 380–4;
    jihadis mass for counter-attack, 365–6;
    Emperor leaves, 369–70, 372–3; Emperor
    imprisoned, 395, 433; destruction and
    redevelopment, 5–7, 457–8, 460
Reed, General Sir Thomas, 281–2, 306
Reid, Colonel, 245
Reid, Major, 270, 307, 350, 356
Reinhardt, Walter ('Sombre'), 238–9
Rhai, 246
Ripley, Colonel, 163–4
Roberts, Fred, 195–6, 277, 335; racially mixed
    family, 291; and assault on Delhi, 346, 351,
    353, 355; and march out of Delhi, 405
Roberts, General Sir Abraham, 292
Roberts, John, 291–2
Rohilcund, 249
Rohillas, 38n, 284
Rohtak, 189, 242
Rome, 8, 67
Ross, Dr, 105, 118
Rotton, Felix, 291
Rotton, James, 291
Rotton, Revd John Edward, 256, 273–4;
    describes conditions on Ridge, 278–9;
    hospital duties, 281, 354; racially mixed
    family, 291; justifies British retribution, 315,
    363; conducts last service on Ridge, 341;
    thanksgiving service, 404
Roughhead, Robin, 106
Roy, Rajah Ram Mohan, 47n, 81
Roy, Tapti, 17
Royal Navy, 451
Royal Stud, 81
Russell, William Howard, 4–5, 272, 432–5, 473
Russia, 71
Russians, 125, 438

St James's Church, 92, 104, 140; winter cold,
    60; converts baptised, 74; construction, 89;
    choir, 119, 142; looted,160, 179; plaques to
    victims of Uprising, 160n; architecture,
    178n; fighting around, 349–50; British
    occupy, 384
Sa'adi's Gulistan, 100
Sabir (poet), 99n, 296
Sabzi Mandi, 89n, 93–4, 242, 254, 270, 273, 282
Sadat Khan ka Katra, 457
Sadiq ul-Akhabhar, 215
Safdarjung's tomb, 242

Saharanpur, 69
Sahbai, Maulvi Imam Bakhsh, 41, 95, 111, 387
Sakeld, Philip, 348
salatin, 44–5, 99, 102, 257, 366, 422; imprisoned, 425–6
Saligram, Lala, 97, 109, 158, 321
Salim, Mirza, 78
Salimgarh, 103, 144, 174, 249, 322
Saman Burj, 146, 148
Sanskrit, 71, 74, 205; chants, 93
Sardhana, 66–7, 238–9
Sarvar ul-Mulk, 155, 257, 265, 297; leaves Delhi, 360–1, 420–2
Satara, annexation of, 127
sati, 68, 220
Saunders, Charles, 395, 433, 456, 461; and Metcalfe, 234, 429; and Emperor's imprisonment, 399–400, 403, 406–7; reviews cases against princes, 425; and Emperor's trial, 436; and Emperor's exile, 444; Ommaney reports to, 448, 452; rape inquiry, 462–3; and Zinat Mahal, 467
Saunders, Matilda, 399–400, 436, 444, 460
Savarkar, V. D., 20
Sawai Bhuj, 145n
sawars, 164, 169, 185–6; arrive in Delhi, 144–5, 147–8, 150; hunt down Christians, 152–3; enter Red Fort, 170–1; rest in Ochterlony Gardens, 178; commit rape, 208; fight with infantry, 226; hunt Metcalfe, 233; under Mirza Abu Bakr's command, 242; target moneylenders, 260–1; flee British retribution, 314, 316
Sayf ur-Rahman, 159n
Sayyid dynasty, 36n
Sayyid, Maulvi Muhammad, 228
Sayyidani, Sharaf ul-Mahal, 216
Schoefft, August, 29, 217
science, 87, 95, 131
Scotland, 6–7
Second Anglo-Burmese War, 88, 138, 138
Second World War, 482
Selimgarh, 365, 377
sepoy Uprising: causes, 9–10, 22–3, 411; numbers involved, 10, 264, 277, 283, 293, 338; centred on Delhi, 10–11, 17, 20–1, 196; historical sources, 11–16; historiography of, 13–17, 219; terms used to describe, 19; as war of religion, 22–3, 153, 171n, 228, 268, 273, 290, 294, 336; begins in Meerut, 138–42; reaches Delhi, 143–52; and class, 154–9; mujahedin role in, 154, 159; potency of, 192; spreads across India, 196, 220, 306; lack of direction, 209; role of secular grievances, 220–1; divisions and problem of authority, 225–6, 228, 264–5, 284, 290, 294, 301, 329,

334, 336; tactics and strategy, 271, 273–4, 316; administrative and financial failure, 317–23, 476; and Emperor's trial, 439–43
sepoys: definition, 3n; disarmed, 16; attitudes to, 17–20; and courtesans, 18–19; and rumours of mass conversion, 76n, 134–5; and annexation of Avadh, 126–7; and caste, 134–5; unrest over pay and regulations, 135–8; breakdown by caste and religion, 135n; eschew violence, 196; disorder among, 226; engage British in open battle, 244–5; casualties, 254–5, 272; tensions with jihadis, 264–6, 285; religions, 268, 290; courage, 270–1, 310; desertions, 319, 323–4, 338
Seton, Archibald, 46, 47n
Shah Abbas, Mirza, 43, 444n; life in exile, 465, 469–71, 480–1; proposal for education, 469–72
Shah Alam II, Emperor, 37
Shah Alam, Emperor, 36, 38, 432, 450
Shah Jahan, Emperor, 2, 17n, 32, 47, 96, 457, 460
Shah Rukh, Mirza, 86, 158, 216, 328
Shah Zamani Begum, Nawab, 30, 451, 453, 469, 480–1
Shah, Sa'id Mubarak, 223, 244, 252; accounts of Uprising, 158, 206; and Emperor, 223, 341–2; appointed kotwal, 258–9, 296; and jihadis, 265, 269–70; and Bareilly force, 284; and Bakht Khan's attack, 330, 333–4; and Sergeant Gordon, 338; accounts of assault on Delhi, 350–1, 367–9
Shah, Wajd Ali, 126, 450n
Shahjahanabad, 17, 34–5, 94, 110, 284–5, 369
Shahjahanpur, 153, 338
Shahzadi Begum, 291
Shahzor, Mirza, 378–9
Shaikhs, 80, 82
Shalimar Bagh, 457
Shamli, 485
Shankar, Bhawani, 97, 358
Shankar, Gauri, 298, 322
sharia law, 33n, 64, 68
Shefta, 111
Shias, 86, 207, 242, 302, 373, 426, 439
Shiism, 82
shikastah (broken writing), 14
Shivaji, 478
Shorto, Sylvia, 147n
Showers, Brigadier, 436
Sialkot, 248, 306–7
Sikh States, 204
Sikh Wars, 136, 202, 207n, 471n
Sikhs, 70, 83; allied with British, 136, 203, 206–7, 290, 305, 307, 335, 338n, 377; commit torture, 315; general protects Azad, 375; occupy Jama Masjid, 384, 453, 462n;

plunder Delhi, 388, 414; allow princes to
    escape, 423–4; invade Rangoon, 453
Simla, 88, 116–17, 194–5, 243, 248–9, 274–5, 458n
Sindh, 133
Singh, Brigade Major Hira, 319, 331
Singh, General Sudhari, 319, 330–1
Singh, Lal, 271
Singh, Maharaja Dalip, 471
Singh, Major Kuray, 320
Singh, Ranjit, 290, 471n
Singh, Sirdar Man, 393
Singh, Thakur, 253
Siraj ud-Daula, 70
Siraj ul-Akabhar, 14, 125
Sita Ram Bazaar, 268
Skinner family, 66, 67n, 90, 104, 111
Skinner, Alec, 233–5
Skinner, Colonel James, 88–90, 142, 184, 189,
    225, 233; builds St James's church, 89;
    fighting around haveli, 349–50
Skinner, Elizabeth, *see* Wagentreiber,
    Elizabeth
Skinner, Frank, 67n
Skinner, Hercules, 89
Skinner, Joseph, 208
Skinner, Robert, 90
Skinner's House, 355, 365
Sleeman, Colonel William, 94
Smith, Sergeant, 348
Smith, Vincent, 12
Society for the Propagation of the Gospel,
    68, 74
Socrates, 95
Sohna, 261
Solomon, King, 34, 161
Sombre, David Ochterlony Dyce, 239, 240n
Somerset, 88
Sonepat, 375
Soz, Maulana, 387
sports: hunting, 3, 98, 137; horse racing, 87,
    139; fishing, 102–3, 310; coursing, 103–4; pig-
    sticking, 164; football, 310; cricket, 310;
    quoits, 310
Sprenger, Dr Alois, 105, 240
Sri Lanka, 33
steamships, 61, 131, 447, 450
Stokes, Eric, 17
storytelling, 107, 109
Subjee Mundi, 312
Sudbury, Suffolk, 240n
Sufi shrines, 8, 25, 40, 69, 78–9, 81–2, 86, 102, 107
Sufism, 2–3, 77–9, 82–3, 441
Sukul, Brigade Major Gauri Shankar, 204,
    235, 329
Sultan Bai, 44
Sumru, Begum, 31, 33, 66–7, 238–9

Suneheri Masjid, 32
Suniah, 447
Sunnis, 82, 86, 302, 439
Sussex, 88
Switzerland, 380

Tafta, Mirza, 463
Tagore, Debendrenath, 103n
Taimuri, Aish, 423
Taj Mahal Begum, 42–3, 336, 400;
    accompanies Emperor into exile, 447–9
Taj Mahal, 178n, 478
Taliban, 485
Tanras Khan, 43
Tansen, 110
Tartars, 71, 98
Taylor, Francis, 208
telegraph, electric, 61, 131, 141, 144, 194, 283
Telingana, 17n
Teliwara, 273
temples, 69, 89, 104, 376
Tennyson, Alfred, Lord, 478
Teresa, Mother, 7
Thomason, Lieutenant Charlie, 119, 176, 203
Thomason, Mr, 115–16, 118, 129
Thornhill, C. B., 122, 234
Thornhill, Mark, 22, 475
Thugs, 94
Tilangas, 17, 162; terrorise Delhi, 19, 158, 160,
    208, 210, 225–8, 262–3; show Emperor
    disrespect, 190; deserters, 324; impose
    order, 328
Times, 4, 272, 428, 432
Timur, Emperor, 2, 191; House of, 4, 39, 51,
    57, 72, 222, 299, 370, 411, 425, 442
Tipu Sultan, 70, 450n, 476n
Tis Hazari, 94, 289
Todd, Charles, 141, 193–4
Toll House, 144
Tombs, Major, 245
Tonk, 264, 266, 295, 424
Trevelyan, Charles, 71
Trimmu Ghat, 306
Trood and Co., Messrs, 87
Tucker, Robert, 61
Tughluq, Emperor, 157
Turkey, 443
Turkman Gate, 385
Turks, 98
Tytler, Captain Robert, 91, 141, 163, 174; and
    sepoys, 138–40, 162, 175–6; Flagstaff Tower
    episode, 176–9, 253; escapes Delhi, 183–4,
    186–7, 190; post with Field Force, 247, 279–
    80, 344, 436; saves camp follower, 247–8;
    and assault on Delhi, 344; governs
    Andaman Islands, 458n

Tytler, Frank, 176
Tytler, Harriet, 91, 118, 138–9, 162–3; Flagstaff Tower episode, 176–9; escapes Delhi, 183–4, 186–7, 190; attitudes to Indians, 247, 253; with Field Force, 279–80; son born, 280–1; and assault on Delhi, 344; expresses pity, 372; and Emperor's trial, 436; paints panorama, 458; subsequent life, 458n
Tytler, Stanley Delhi Force, 281

Udaipur, 424
Urdu, 52, 67n, 74, 100, 205, 391; poetry and literature, 2–3, 99n, 238–9, 291, 390, 473n; historical sources, 15, 21n, 23, 98n, 266, 368, 423; excellence in, 17, 34–5; translation of Ten Commandments, 61; translation of Koran, 77; newspapers, 95, 125, 242, 464; Emperor's written defence, 438; Ghalib laments decline, 464
Urdu Bazaar, 182, 454, 463
Utilitarians, 10
Uttar Pradesh, 17, 21n

Varma, Pavan, 24
Vedas, 93
Vellore, mutiny at, 191
Vibart, Edward, 4, 163–5, 178–82, 405; escape from Delhi, 190, 235–6, 240, 311, 313, 348; and massacres, 313–14, 385–6; and Bakht Khan's attack, 331, 333; and assault on Delhi, 339–40, 354–5; and Emperor's trial, 436
Victoria, Queen, 128, 131–2, 471n; toasts to, 384–5; informed of British vindictiveness, 402; amnesty proclaimed in her name, 456; Muslims petition, 461
Vishnu, 199

Wade, Captain J. M., 315
Wagentreiber (née Skinner), Elizabeth, 88, 91, 93, 111, 203; warned by Nawab of Loharu, 141–2, 167; at Flagstaff Tower, 176, 185; escapes Delhi, 184–90, 303; racially mixed family, 290; urges retribution, 303, 315
Wagentreiber, Florence, 177, 185, 203
Wagentreiber, George, 88, 90, 92–3, 203; warned by Nawab of Loharu, 141–2, 167; at Flagstaff Tower, 176, 185; escapes Delhi, 184–90; applauds executions, 403; describes conditions around Delhi, 419–20; and Emperor's trial, 436; and Emperor's exile, 447; and destruction of Delhi, 459
Wagentreiber, Julia, 185, 189, 203
Wahhabis, 76–7, 485; 'conspiracy', 84; role in Uprising, 229, 264–5; disdain for rulers, 285–6, 294

Waliullah, Shah, 76–8, 82–3, 296, 485
Wallace, 'Quaker', 315
Wallace, Captain, 163
Walsh, Colour Sergeant, 251
Wannell, Bruce, 11
Water Bastion, 339
Waterloo, battle of, 194
Wellesley, Lord, 38–9
Wheeler, Colonel Steven, 62
Wheeler, General, 11
White House, 175
White Mughals, 9, 72–3, 82–3, 88, 90, 111, 136, 238
Wilberforce, William, 76
Willock, Captain, 279
Willoughby, Lieutenant George, 147–8, 174
Wilson, General Archdale, 195, 203, 281, 316; ineffectiveness, 197, 200, 282; leaves Meerut and fights at Hindan Bridge, 241, 243–5; rendezvous with Field Force, 245–6, 248; assessments of British position, 277, 283–4; effective defensive strategy, 282, 309; writes to Lawrence, 282–3; recommends contact with Emperor, 302; clashes with Nicholson, 308–9; and Bakht Khan's attack, 330–1; and assault on Delhi, 340, 344–5, 350, 356–8, 365, 368, 374, 388; order to spare women and children, 364; victory toast, 384; and capture of Emperor and princes, 390, 395–6; treatment of spies, 413
Wilson, Lieutenant, 164
Windsor Castle, 433; Royal Library, 126n
women, 30n, 49; Mughal, 29; of Delhi, 34; special dialect, 35; white, 73; mendicants, 96; guards, 98; poets, 100; in Flagstaff Tower, 176–7; rape of, 246, 327, 362, 462–3; jihadis, 269–70; British massacre, 363–4; flee Delhi, 372–4; witness massacres, 385–7; seized by Sikhs, 388
Wordsworth, William, 478

Yal (wrestler), 111
Yamuna Bridge, 147, 168, 244–5; weekly walk, 6, 464; see also Bridge of Boats
Yamuna canal, 182, 236, 310; water quality, 277; bridges destroyed, 282, 330; flow cut off, 317; and Bakht Khan's attack, 330, 332
Yamuna, river, 52, 91, 275, 287, 369, 447; river front, 43, 258, 339; bathing in, 93, 100, 102; telegraph line under, 141; sepoys cross, 147–8; powder magazine, 163, 175, 213; executions, 387; waterfront, 459
Young, Colonel Keith, 194
Yusuf, 215
Yusufzais, 202

Zafar (Bahadur Shah II): birth, 2; succession, 2; and calligraphy, 2, 484; patronage of the arts, 2, 53–4; and gardens, 2, 94, 103, 213, 298; and architecture, 2; and poetry, 2–3, 5, 25–6, 37–8, 42, 78–81, 98–9, 130, 298, 300, 473, 484; languages and education, 2, 100; daily life, 3, 37, 42–5, 98–9, 102–3, 109–10; and hunting, 3, 98; role as leader of Uprising, 3, 10, 19–23, 192, 196, 212, 290; petitions to, 13, 19, 99, 209–12, 216, 263, 265–6, 268, 318, 324–7; portraits, 21, 29, 217, 220; and marriage of Jawan Bakht, 28–31, 36; finances, 31, 97, 171, 173; childhood, 37; restriction of authority, 37–40, 46; processions, 39–40, 207, 211; children, 43–4; and harem, 43–4, 56, 447; and *salatin*, 44–5, 99; and choice of successor, 46–9, 121–2; threatens to retire to Mecca, 48, 228, 299–300, 439; and Metcalfe, 51, 54; syncretic religion, 77–83, 376n; belief in charms, 78–9; gives protection to Hindus, 80–2, 229, 267, 295, 484; diet, 108, 406–7; title, 123; growing concern for family, 128; appoints Ghalib as court poet, 130; learns of Uprising, 144–6; protects Christians, 169–70, 190, 222; responses to Uprising, 172–4, 190–2, 221–2, 368; attempts to restore normality, 211–13; and massacre of prisoners, 223–5, 468; attempts to restrain Uprising, 226–9; urges attack on Meerut, 241–3; affected by shelling, 258–9; and Bakht Khan, 285–7, 292–4, 329–31, 336; and cow butchery episode, 295–7; contacts with British, 297, 301, 483; erratic behaviour and depression, 297–301, 323–4, 341; and assault on Delhi, 341–2; nerve fails, 365–8; leaves

Red Fort, 369–73; capture and guarantee of safety, 370–1, 383, 390, 392–5, 431, 443; held prisoner, 4–5, 399–400, 406–7, 409–10, 409, 433–5; age, 399, 473; learns of death of princes, 400; trial, 5, 299, 411, 431–43; ill health, 433–4, 436, 442; sentence, 443; departure from Delhi, 444–5; journey into exile, 446–54; life in exile, 464–73; death in exile, 5, 474–5; funeral, 1–2, 474; nostalgia for, 479; grave, 481–3
Zafar Mahal, 32, 53
Zafar Sultan, Mirza, 379–80
Zaka'ullah, Maulvi, 94, 266, 462
Zamir, 326
Zauq, 2, 24, 34–5, 86, 95, 99, 422, 463; feud with Ghalib, 40–2; participates in *mushairas*, 111–12; death, 130; Azad saves ghazals, 374–6
Zia ud-Daula, Nawab, 361
Zia ud-Din, Mirza, 369
Zinat Mahal, 29–31, 36, 113, 128, 284, 369; increasing influence, 42–3, 46, 48–9; squabbles with Taj Mahal, 42–3, 448; and Metcalfe's death, 115–16, 119; and Uprising, 190, 216–18, 221; contacts with British, 204, 301–2, 342–3, 371, 390, 438, 467; held prisoner, 218n, 409–10; leaves Red Fort, 258, 298; threat to depose, 336; capture and guarantee of safety, 371, 394; and death of princes, 400; treasure, 410–11; accompanies Emperor into exile, 446; squabbles with Jawan Bakht, 448; life in exile, 465, 467, 470, 480–1; death, 481; memorial stone, 482
Zinat ul-Masjid, 93, 264, 462; Gate, 148
Ziya, 326–7